OLATHE PUBLIC LIBRARY
OLATHE, KANSAS 66061

THE
Kansas Historical Quarterly

NYLE H. MILLER, Managing Editor
KIRKE MECHEM, Editor
JAMES C. MALIN, Associate Editor

Volume XXV
1959

(Kansas Historical Collections)
VOL. XLII

Published by
The Kansas State Historical Society
Topeka, Kansas

Contents of Volume XXV

Number 1—Spring, 1959

PAGE

SAMUEL HALLETT AND THE UNION PACIFIC RAILWAY COMPANY IN KANSAS,
Alan W. Farley, 1
   With Alexander Gardner photographs of bridge building across the Kaw, and office of the Union Pacific at Wyandotte, 1867, *frontispiece*, and portrait of Samuel Hallet, *facing* p. 1.

GATEWAYS TO THE PROMISED LAND: The Role Played by the Southern Kansas Towns in the Opening of the Cherokee Strip to Settlement,
Jean C. Lough, 17
   With photographs of campers near Arkansas City preparing to make the run, *between* pp. 16, 17.

TELEGRAPH BEGINNINGS IN KANSAS................*John E. Sunder*, 32

THE LETTERS OF THE REV. SAMUEL YOUNG LUM, PIONEER KANSAS MISSIONARY, 1854-1858: Part One, 1854-1855,
Edited by *Emory Lindquist*, 39

WILLIAM SUTTON WHITE, SWEDENBORGIAN PUBLICIST: Part Two, Kansas Exemplar of the Philosophy of Emanuel Swedenborg and Herbert Spencer..*James C. Malin*, 68

THE ANNUAL MEETING: Containing Reports of the Secretary, Treasurer, Executive and Nominating Committees; Election of Officers; List of Directors of the Society... 104

BYPATHS OF KANSAS HISTORY... 125

KANSAS HISTORY AS PUBLISHED IN THE PRESS................................. 126

KANSAS HISTORICAL NOTES... 127

Number 2—Summer, 1959

PAGE

U. S. ARMY AND AIR FORCE WINGS OVER KANSAS (In two installments, Part One):.. 129
   With photographs of scenes and activities at Pratt Army Air Base, Great Bend Army Air Field and Smoky Hill Army Air Force Base, Salina, *between* pp. 144, 145.

THE PIKE'S PEAK GOLD RUSH AND THE SMOKY HILL ROUTE, 1859-1860,
Calvin W. Gower, 158
   Reprint of a "Table of Distances" from Atchison to the Gold Mines, 1859, *between* pp. 160, 161.

THE LETTERS OF THE REV. SAMUEL YOUNG LUM, PIONEER KANSAS MISSIONARY, 1854-1858—*Concluded*......Edited by *Emory Lindquist*, 172

WILLIAM SUTTON WHITE, SWEDENBORGIAN PUBLICIST: Part Two, Kansas Exemplar of the Philosophy of Emanuel Swedenborg and Herbert Spencer—*Concluded*....................................*James C. Malin*, 197

RECENT ADDITIONS TO THE LIBRARY,
Compiled by *Alberta Pantle*, Librarian, 229

BYPATHS OF KANSAS HISTORY... 251

KANSAS HISTORY AS PUBLISHED IN THE PRESS................................. 252

KANSAS HISTORICAL NOTES... 255

Number 3—Autumn, 1959

	PAGE
IRONQUILL'S "THE WASHERWOMAN'S SONG"............*James C. Malin*,	257
With portrait of Eugene Fitch Ware, about 1881, *facing* p. 272.	
A CHRONOLOGY OF KANSAS POLITICAL AND MILITARY EVENTS, 1859-1865,	283
MARK W. DELAHAY: PERIPATETIC POLITICIAN; A Historical Case Study, *John G. Clark*,	301
With reproduction of painting of Mark W. Delahay, *facing* p. 304.	
RELIGION IN KANSAS DURING THE ERA OF THE CIVIL WAR (In two installments, Part One).............................*Emory Lindquist*,	313
With portraits of Lewis Bodwell, Pardee Butler, Richard Cordley, and Hugh Dunn Fisher, *facing* p. 320, and Charles H. Lovejoy, Samuel Young Lum, Peter McVicar, and Roswell Davenport Parker, *facing* p. 321.	
U. S. ARMY AND AIR FORCE WINGS OVER KANSAS—*Concluded*..........	334
With photographs of Boeing B-29 gunners at Smoky Hill Army Air Field, Salina, and Free French fliers at Dodge City Army Air Field, *facing* p. 336, and air force planes on Kansas fields, *facing* p. 337.	
BYPATHS OF KANSAS HISTORY..	361
KANSAS HISTORY AS PUBLISHED IN THE PRESS........................	363
KANSAS HISTORICAL NOTES	366

Number 4—Winter, 1959

	PAGE
THE PONY EXPRESS RIDES AGAIN.......................................	369
With photographs of altered Pony Express stations still standing in Seneca and Marysville, and map of the Kansas portion of the Pony Express route, *frontispiece*.	
CRITIQUE OF CARRUTH'S ARTICLES ON FOREIGN SETTLEMENTS IN KANSAS, *J. Neale Carman*,	386
THE FIRST KANSAS LEAD MINES..................*Walter H. Schoewe*,	391
With sketches and photographs of Linn county lead mine area, *between* pp. 400, 401.	
EUGENE WARE'S CONCERN ABOUT A WOMAN, A CHILD, AND GOD, *James C. Malin*,	402
RELIGION IN KANSAS DURING THE ERA OF THE CIVIL WAR—*Concluded* ....*Emory Lindquist*,	407
THE CENTENNIAL OF LINCOLN'S VISIT TO KANSAS.....................	438
BYPATHS OF KANSAS HISTORY..	444
KANSAS HISTORY AS PUBLISHED IN THE PRESS........................	445
KANSAS HISTORICAL NOTES..	450
ERRATA, VOLUME XXV	454
INDEX TO VOLUME XXV..	455

(iv)

THE
KANSAS HISTORICAL QUARTERLY

Spring 1959

Published by
Kansas State Historical Society

Topeka

NYLE H. MILLER KIRKE MECHEM JAMES C. MALIN
Managing Editor *Editor* *Associate Editor*

CONTENTS

PAGE

SAMUEL HALLETT AND THE UNION PACIFIC RAILWAY COMPANY IN KANSAS,
  Alan W. Farley, 1
  With Alexander Gardner photographs of bridge building across the Kaw, and office of the Union Pacific at Wyandotte, 1867, *frontispiece*, and portrait of Samuel Hallett, *facing* p. 1.

GATEWAYS TO THE PROMISED LAND: The Role Played by the Southern Kansas Towns in the Opening of the Cherokee Strip to Settlement,
  Jean C. Lough, 17
  With photographs of campers near Arkansas City preparing to make the run, *between* pp. 16, 17.

TELEGRAPH BEGINNINGS IN KANSAS................ *John E. Sunder*, 32

THE LETTERS OF THE REV. SAMUEL YOUNG LUM, PIONEER KANSAS MISSIONARY, 1854-1858: Part One, 1854-1855,
  Edited by *Emory Lindquist*, 39

WILLIAM SUTTON WHITE, SWEDENBORGIAN PUBLICIST: Part Two, Kansas Exemplar of the Philosophy of Emanuel Swedenborg and Herbert Spencer................................ *James C. Malin*, 68

THE ANNUAL MEETING: Containing Reports of the Secretary, Treasurer, Executive and Nominating Committees; Election of Officers; List of Directors of the Society................................ 104

BYPATHS OF KANSAS HISTORY................................ 125

KANSAS HISTORY AS PUBLISHED IN THE PRESS............... 126

KANSAS HISTORICAL NOTES................................ 127

The Kansas Historical Quarterly is published four times a year by the Kansas State Historical Society, 120 W. Tenth, Topeka, Kan., and is distributed free to members. Correspondence concerning contributions may be sent to the managing editor at the Historical Society. The Society assumes no responsibility for statements made by contributors.

Second-class postage has been paid at Topeka, Kan.

THE COVER

The Union Pacific railroad yard at Wyandotte in 1867, photo by Alexander Gardner. This and the two which follow are from a collection of 150 photographs which Gardner took along the line of the Kansas Union Pacific to its end of track, "20 miles west of Hays," in 1867.

OTHER GARDNER UNION PACIFIC PHOTOGRAPHS OF 1867

Upper: Building a bridge across the Kaw at Wyandotte.
Lower: Office, Union Pacific Railway Co., E. D., at Wyandotte.

Samuel Hallett
(1828?-1864)

Hallett energetically proceeded with the building of the Union Pacific from the Missouri-Kansas line in present Kansas City west through Kansas, until he was fatally shot by a disgruntled former employee in 1864. Had it not been for the early death of Hallett and subsequent delays in reorganization of the company, the Kansas Union Pacific might have been the line which met the Central Pacific in Utah in 1869, to form the first railroad link with the West Coast.

THE KANSAS HISTORICAL QUARTERLY

Volume XXV   Spring, 1959   Number 1

Samuel Hallett and the Union Pacific Railway Company in Kansas

ALAN W. FARLEY

(Copyright, 1958, by ALAN W. FARLEY)

THE honor of being first to suggest an overland railroad to the Pacific seems to belong to Robert Mills, engineer and architect, of Baltimore, who was later to design the Washington monument and several pre-Civil War buildings at the national capitol. Writing in 1820 with extraordinary clarity of vision and at least nine years before the first American railroad line on which a locomotive was used, Mills noted that the voyage around Cape Horn to the mouth of the Columbia river and return required about ten months and that a

> short direct and certain means of communication should be established *over* the continent to the Pacific ocean. . . . When the Yellow Stone expedition has accomplished the object of forming a settlement at or near the junction of this river with the Missouri, and an expedition is sent up the Columbia river to form a settlement for the protection of trade in that country, we shall no doubt find our government fully sensible of the importance of completing a good rail or turnpike road, between the two points. . . . To calculate on the aid of steamboats upon these waters, and upon an application of the same moving power to carriages upon railroads, across the mountains, we may estimate an average progress of eighty miles per day on this rout, which would enable us to accomplish the journey in little more than sixty five days from the City of Washington to the Pacific ocean.[1]

It wasn't until the 1850's that Mills' prophetic dream became a real possibility. The government then conducted surveys of several alternate transcontinental routes but sectional rivalry and bitterness in congress precluded the possibility of any compromise choice between several possible northern and southern roads.

ALAN W. FARLEY, president of the Kansas State Historical Society, 1957-1958, is an attorney of Kansas City. He is an outstanding authority on Western Americana, and has published several works on Kansas City and Western history. This article was Farley's presidential address before the annual meeting of the Kansas State Historical Society on October 21, 1958.

1. Robert Mills, *A Treatise on Inland Navigation* (Baltimore, 1820), pp. 53-59. The Carbondale and Honesdale railroad was the first railroad in America on which a locomotive was used. It opened in 1829. In 1832 an unknown writer in the *Emigrant*, a weekly newspaper of Ann Arbor, Mich., suggested a plan for a railroad from New York to Oregon by way of the Great Lakes and the Platte river valley.—Edwin L. Sabin, *Building the Pacific Railway* (Philadelphia, 1919), p. 14.

When the Civil War commenced, the two railroads extending the greatest distance west of the Mississippi were both in Missouri. The Hannibal and St. Joseph railroad joined those towns over a distance of 206 miles and the Pacific railroad of Missouri was slowly building west to connect St. Louis with Kansas City, helped by state aid. This latter road reached Sedalia in 1861 when military activity stopped railroad building. Both these routes were prime targets of guerrilla raids and service on them was often disrupted during the war.[2]

Of the more than eleven hundred railroads chartered by various Kansas legislatures, several were lines to run in and along the Kansas valley. The Kansas Central Railroad Company, one of the most important, had been surveyed and was designed to go west from Wyandotte, cross the river at Lawrence and through Lecompton and Topeka. Every town that hoped to grow and survive had to have one or more railroad lines—at least on paper. The Leavenworth, Pawnee and Western Railroad Company was chartered by the "bogus" Legislature of 1855 and had done some surveying on its route from Leavenworth to Fort Riley. But this was just another visionary railroad until it had acquired a fortune in Delaware Indian land. On May 30, 1860, through a treaty at Sarcoxieville on the Delaware reservation, the promoters of this road gained 223,966 acres of Kansas valley land for $1.25 an acre. The railroad had no money so by another treaty made on July 2, 1861, it was agreed that the company could give a mortgage to secure the entire purchase price. By selling this land in parcels to settlers and influential speculators, its railroad stock became valuable, and important support for congressional action in favor of the road was obtained.

When the Southern members of congress withdrew, several controversial measures that they had formerly successfully resisted were enacted into law. New states and territories were created, and the homestead law and the Pacific railroad law were enacted. This latter measure resulted from a compromise between the influences of St. Louis and Chicago, and was justified as a war measure to protect the Western coast. At the time it was stated that the passage of the Pacific railroad act was due to the efforts of California and Kansas. At any rate, on July 1, 1862, the Union Pacific and the Central Pacific railroads were created and the Leavenworth, Pawnee & Western Railroad Company was authorized to construct a railroad and telegraph line from the state line of Missouri at the mouth

---

2. Walter Williams and Floyd Shoemaker, *Missouri, Mother of the West* (Chicago. 1930), v. 1, p. 561 *et seq.*

of the Kansas river (there to connect with the Pacific railroad of Missouri on the south side of the Missouri river), thence westward to the 100th meridian of longitude, there to unite with several railroads from Missouri and Iowa. The route west of Fort Riley was to be subject to the approval of the President, and each company was required to complete 100 miles of road within two years after filing their assent to the conditions of the act.

In order to help finance construction, it was provided that government bonds in the amount of $16,000 per mile would be issued upon the completion of each 40-mile section of road after acceptance of the section by government commissioners; these bonds to be a first mortgage on all property of the railroad. A grant of alternate sections of land within the limit of ten miles on each side of the railroad was to be made upon the approval of each 40-mile section built.

The Leavenworth, Pawnee and Western Railroad Company, through its president, J. H. McDowell, accepted the provisions of the act on November 15, 1862, although O. B. Gunn and Colonel Medbury had commenced survey for the route several months earlier. The Union Pacific Railroad Company delayed until the following June to notify the government of its acceptance.[3] At the end of 1862 the press could report that only 30 men were employed on the railroad at Leavenworth.[4]

Previous to May 28, 1863, a controlling portion of the capital stock of the L. P. & W. was sold to Samuel Hallett and John C. Fremont.[5] In the business world of that day these were magic names. Hallett was a young investment banker with offices in New York City, who had acted as financial agent of the Atlantic & Great Western railway, one of the successful railroad enterprises in the East. He also had extensive connections with capitalists in this country and Europe. John C. Fremont had become wealthy through the sale of his Rancho de los Mariposas in California and was the darling of the radicals in Washington who opposed the Lincoln administration. He had been an authentic hero of Western exploration but his military failure in the Civil War presaged the decline of his fame.

A few days later the stockholders elected General Fremont president, and changed the name of the corporation to the Union Pacific Railway Company, Eastern Division. (In 1868 this name was again changed to the Kansas Pacific Railway Company.) Hallett became

---

3. James H. Simpson, *Report on the Union Pacific Railroad and Branches* (Washington, November, 1865), pp. 2-88.
4. Wyandotte *Commercial Gazette,* January 10, 1863.
5. *Ibid.,* June 13, 1863; *Points of Law and Argument for Complainant . . ., Stevens vs. Kansas Pacific Railway,* U. S. circuit court, district of Kansas (1874), p. 5.

general superintendent of the railroad and sole contractor for its construction.[6]

After making financial preparations and letting contracts for necessary rails and other iron for the first 50 miles of road, Hallett arrived at the offices of the company at Leavenworth on August 11, 1863. The following day he took possession of the railroad by the simple expedient of driving the employees of Ross, Steel & Company, contractors of Montreal, Canada, who had been employed by the L. P. & W., away from their job of grading the right-of-way. One account says that a company of cavalry from Fort Leavenworth was obtained to back up Hallett's party. The victims retaliated by resorting to sundry litigation but their suits were defeated in the United States circuit court at Keokuk.[7] At this time Hallett, who understood the uses of propaganda, published a long letter officially endorsing his project. John P. Usher, then Secretary of the Interior, with the approval of the President,[8] declared that the government favored the Kansas valley route for an overland railroad, an action which must have made the Union Pacific investors and residents of Iowa and Nebraska unhappy.

At the time Leavenworth had become the largest city of Kansas due to the many beneficial influences of the nearby fort and to the steamboat traffic of the Missouri river. Other cities, St. Joseph and Kansas City, coveted her trade and her metropolitan air as economic adjustments due to the Civil War boomed Leavenworth and slowed her rivals, notably Kansas City. But the location of the Union Pacific, E. D., and other railroads, helped to turn away all this wartime prosperity. Railroads were destined to supplant steamboats and the trade of Fort Leavenworth was to decline after the war, due to the economy of army activities.[9]

Warring political factions within the city of Leavenworth made concerted municipal action well-nigh impossible and were a horrid example of what can result from failure to exploit civic opportunity. The community assumed that it was indispensable to the railroad. The situation was clear to outsiders, for a Kansas City editor alluded to that attitude with some sarcasm:

The Leavenworth newspapers are perpetrating a huge joak [sic] about the Great Pacific Railroad. The entire editorial force of the city have turned out

---

6. *Ibid.*, pp. 5, 6.
7. *Western Journal of Commerce*, Kansas City, Mo., November 7, 1863; *The Daily Times*, Leavenworth, August 12, 13, 1863; John D. Cruise, "Early Days on the Union Pacific," *Kansas Historical Collections*, v. 11 (1909-1910), p. 535; C. A. Trowbridge to James F. Joy, September 26 and October 1, 1863, in "Burton Historical Collections," Detroit Public Library, Detroit, Mich.
8. Kansas City (Mo.) *Daily Journal of Commerce*, April 5, 1864; *The Daily Times*, Leavenworth, August 20, 1863.
9. The prosperity of Leavenworth was further retarded by high railroad rates which "broke" or dropped at Kansas City on shipments to the East.

with pick and shovel and gone to work on the road, and expect to have it completed through to California in a couple of weeks. They are going to have it run three times around Leavenworth, so as to be sure that it will stop there. But the great difficulty for them to determine is whether they will build most of it by telegraph, stage or newspaper puffs—probably the latter. They are going to commence it to-morrow or yesterday—and they are also discussing the propriety, after a few miles of it is built, of "breaking it off" and running it into the ground for fear it may go to some other town besides Leavenworth.[10]

Late in August, Hallett proposed to the mayor and council of Leavenworth that the city subscribe $100,000 for stock of the railroad.[11] The people of that metropolis were nobly trying to relieve the stricken inhabitants of Lawrence, who had been raided by the Quantrill gang just a week earlier. A conference with the city fathers about the subscription of stock was unsatisfactory, so Hallett retaliated by moving the principal offices of the company to Wyandotte.

It was then decided by the company that the main line would be built directly west to Fort Riley, instead of detouring through Leavenworth, then west from that place, as the Leavenworth investors desired. A branch line was designed to run from Lawrence to Leavenworth, there to connect with the Hannibal & St. Joseph railroad which had been extended south to Weston, Mo. To this day a resident of Leavenworth has to travel through Kansas City or St. Joseph going east by rail. The paved highways are similarly routed.

The *Congregational Record,* Lawrence, for October, 1862, carried a long account of Wyandotte and summarized its situation: "The [Indian] Reserve on one side, and Rebeldom on the other, have prevented Wyandot from reaching its early expectations. Loose clapboards, broken windows, and faded paint, indicate a place where early growth surpassed its subsequent importance." To this scene came Hallett & Co.

The railroad's eastern terminus was the Missouri line. It was to cross the Kansas river near Splitlog's mill two miles south of Wyandotte, and proceed up the north side of the Kansas valley. The company advertised for a thousand laborers and offered $1.50 per day, payable in cash every Saturday night.

On September 12, 1863, the Wyandotte *Gazette* recorded that

Last Monday at 10½ o'clock A. M. work on the Union Pacific R. Road was commenced. . . . Mr. Hallett . . . gave directions . . . to clear a space 50 feet on each side of the [state] line [for the eager spectators]. Mr. Silas Armstrong [a leader among the Wyandotte Indians], and A. B. Bartlett

10. *Daily Journal of Commerce,* January 6, 1863.
11. *The Daily Times,* August 29, 1863.

Esq., [attorney for the road], each claimed the privilege of cutting the first tree. Each held his ax, standing by trees of about the same size. Mr. Hallett gave the order to cut, and both trees fell about the same instant. A single cheer resounded through the woods. . . .

Within two days two miles of right-of-way had been cleared.

Hallett caused a great post to be set at this initial point at the state line; the side facing Missouri was inscribed "Slavery" and on the side facing west toward Kansas the symbol was "Freedom."

A week later the press exulted that the railroad had an excavating machine that does the work of a hundred men, and that a telegraph office was opened in Killin's building at Third and Minnesota. By September 26 nine miles of railroad had been located, half of that cleared, and more than a third graded. The following week the railroad office on Third street got an iron safe as large as a medium-sized store room, and five miles of road bed had been graded. One hundred Canadians arrived to work on the construction. The paper chronicled that they were at work on a deep cut a few miles beyond the Delaware Ferry on October 24 and were an honest and industrious lot of men.

All this activity boomed Wyandotte but the railroad right-of-way missed the town. Hallett's business acumen again came into play as he secured more working capital for the road. After some negotiation, the citizens by a margin of 286 to 3 voted that the county issue $100,000 in bonds to be traded to Hallett for paid stock in the railroad; and in return the railroad agreed to construct 1.77 miles of spur track to the Wyandotte levee, erect freight and passenger depots, and keep its turntables, machine shops, and engine houses there. That same month (November) the railroad was being graded at the rate of two miles a day, the graders reached the vicinity of Lawrence and the first section of 40 miles, most of the route through heavy timber, was ready for track. The city fathers were advised to fix "our magnificent spring on the bank of the Kaw" for the railroad spur had passed directly over it on a culvert.

In December ground was at last broken in Omaha for that "branch" of the Pacific railroad, while iron rails had been brought to Weston, Mo., by train, and shipped by steamer to Wyandotte. The same month the *Alexander Majors,* loaded with railroad iron got stuck on a bar 12 miles below Leavenworth and then became ice-bound and didn't get to the levee at Wyandotte until February 7, 1864. People were so elated they saluted the steamer by firing the local cannon. The following week more iron arrived and the first locomotive, *The Wyandotte,* was set on the tracks that had been quickly laid down on the spur at the levee. This locomotive had been used on the Platte Valley railroad during the bad weather until it could be brought here. V. J. Lane, who was at the Montana mines at the time, writing much later says that John Hallett managed to run the locomotive into the river, but the editor of the *Gazette* simply says that two wheels got off the track on one of its trips.

Much has been written about the route of the railroad at Lawrence and Topeka, for these cities were on the south side of the river. Originally it was designed that the railroad would pass both towns by several miles on the most direct westerly line. On December 7, 1863, the Department of Interior received a petition from Sen. James H. Lane and other citizens of Lawrence asking that Hallett & Co. be required to run the road to the north bank of the river opposite Lawrence and Topeka.[12] By January, 1864, the road was graded past Lawrence and the telegraph poles were set.[13]

Senator Lane is reputed to have used extraordinary pressure on the railroad officials in favor of the route to Lawrence, causing the abandonment of six miles of grading already completed, making the line two and one-half miles longer and causing the extension from Leavenworth which joined the road at that point to be two miles longer, all at costs estimated to be $315,000. All factions in the city joined in a resolution on January 6, 1864, that "the people of Lawrence are ready and willing to secure necessary depot grounds and *remunerate the U. P. R. R. for all accommodations extended to our city.*"[14]

During March a second locomotive, *The Delaware*, was delivered at the Wyandotte levee by the steamer *Emilie*; six miles of track had been laid, and the locomotive whistle resounded in the land. On April 6 the directors of the railroad took a trip about ten miles west on the new rails and afterward held a meeting in McAlpin's Hall in Wyandotte where they heard that the first section of 40 miles was ready for rails, and that 84 bridges along the line, including the bridge over the Kansas river, were all nearly completed. Later that month an excursion party of ladies and gentlemen from Wyandotte took a ride to Muncietown on the railroad and had a picnic dinner in the woods.

12. National Archives, "Journal of Letters Received—Lands and Railroads," December 7, 1863.
13. Hallett characteristically announced a celebration feast for the employees upon the completion of grading the first section of 40 miles. Among the delicacies to be consumed on the occasion were 500 tins of oysters.—*Western Journal of Commerce*, November 21, 1863.
14. *Daily Tribune*, Lawrence, August 28, 1864.

At the annual meeting of the stockholders at the office of the company in Leavenworth in April, John D. Perry, president of the Exchange Bank, of St. Louis, was elected president of the railroad in place of John C. Fremont, who was also dropped as a director. The same day another set of directors met at Leavenworth and elected its officers with General Fremont as president.

At the railroad meeting at McAlpin's Hall, Hallett discussed his difficulty with General Fremont who headed this rival organization of directors within the corporate structure. It seems that this crowd based its claim on the possession of certain stocks subscribed by J. C. Stone of Leavenworth, who was also a director of the Omaha group. The previous December the company had assessed a payment of ten percent on all stock and neither Stone nor the holders of this stock paid the assessment, and under the terms of the charter such delinquents had no right to vote. It was also disclosed that Hallett had since acquired the stock from Stone, had then paid the assessment, the company had ratified the transfer, and he had become the bona fide holder of the stock. Hallett said that the associates of Fremont had prevented an amicable settlement. By the purchase of Stone's interest, Hallet became the owner of most of the stock of the company.

The editor of the Kansas City (Mo.) *Journal of Commerce* was vitally interested in progress of the railroad. On April 5, 1864, he editorialized:

The inherent difficulties of the work itself are great. The country is denuded of labor, so that the workmen have had to be brought mainly from Canada. Wages are high; lumber, iron, locomotives, cars, etc., all cost more than ever before. The road is unconnected with any other completed railroad, and is at so great a distance from iron manufacturers that the transportation of rails is not only a tedious but a costly job. . . . But in addition to all this they [Hallett & Co.] have had the most vexatious and harassing opposition from outside parties to contend with. Suit after suit has been brought against them— their iron attached, their means locked up by injunctions, and every species of legal persecution practiced against them. We have now before us the printed briefs of a suit now pending in New York that reveal a species of opposition which, we venture to say, railroad enterprises in this country have very rarely encountered. So far, the parties prosecuting the work have triumphed over every difficulty.

He then quoted a letter from Secretary Usher and Postmaster General Blair, to show that Hallett & Co. had the complete confidence and support of the government.

Col. William C. McDowell also spoke at the railroad meeting, and the same editor summarized his remarks. As president of the old organization, the Leavenworth, Pawnee & Western railroad, he told of the failure of Ross, Steele & Co., the first contractors, to accomplish any results through lack of capital and initiative. McDowell then went to New York to try to interest capitalists there in the enterprise.

He met a number of them at Delmonicos, and laid the project before them, but none of them would touch it. Kansas was too far away. It was a time of war. The road was on the very border. There was too much risk in it. He found no encouragement until he met Mr. [Samuel] Hallett. That gentleman investigated the project, became satisfied of its feasibility, and at once embarked on it with all his might. He was the *only* man in New York who dared to risk his name and his money in the enterprise. It was due to his boldness and sagacity that we were indebted for the prospect now so fair of the successful carrying through of this great work.[15]

On July 1, 1864, Hallett sent letters with a beautiful engraved invitation to influential persons all over the country to attend the opening of the first section of 40 miles on the following August 18. Those who accepted were offered a free pass to Kansas and return, and would be met by a reception committee at Weston, Mo. It was evident that Hallett was intent on building on to meet the California section, then being constructed eastward from Sacramento. John Speer later remembered that Hallett had said, "I hope to live to ride on this road to the Pacific but if my life should be lost, my brothers will push the work as if I lived.[16]

The law under which the Pacific railroads were being built was amended by congress on July 2, 1864, to increase the land granted to 12,800 acres of land per each mile of right-of-way east of the Rocky Mountains, double the amount of land granted by the original act. The railroads were also allowed to issue first mortgage bonds in amounts equal to the government bonds, the latter to be a second lien on the railroad property. The act also required construction of the branch line from Lawrence to Leavenworth and directed that the right-of-way be built to the north bank of the river opposite Lawrence and Topeka, and in effect, the first railroad to reach the 100th degree of longitude was given the right of way to build westward to connect with the Central Pacific then building eastward from California. Hallett & Co. was influential in securing this legislation which made investment in the land-grant railroad much more attractive to investors and the future growth of the railroad seemed secure.

In Lawrence, where Hallett was advertising for more men to lay rails, the *Daily Tribune* announced a railroad meeting the following night to "give this Railroad King of the West a joyous greeting."

15. Kansas City *Journal of Commerce*, April 9, 1864.
16. *Kansas Daily Tribune*, Lawrence, July 28, 1864.

The following evening Hallett discussed the great celebration of August 18 and asked the city to furnish four committees to promote the occasion: (1) To locate the depot; (2) To procure workmen for the railroad; (3) To secure a large attendance from southern Kansas; (4) Ladies to provide for the large number of expected visitors. These plans were enthusiastically adopted, and a few days later 150 men were laying rails near Sarcoxie.[17] If this progress seems modest, it must be remembered that the Civil War made such material and labor hard to obtain.

At this point fate intervened. On July 27, Hallett was shot in the back by an embittered former employee, Orlando Talcott, near the company offices on Third street in Wyandotte. Talcott had been sent to Wyandotte as chief engineer by Fremont, and at the downfall of the general, had been replaced by Hallett & Co. It appears that Talcott retaliated by sending an unfavorable report of the manner of constructing the road-bed by the Halletts to the government, which was required to inspect and accept the road in 40-mile sections, before the railroad could draw the government bonds of $16,000 per mile allowed by law. All accounts agree that Samuel Hallett left instructions to kick Talcott out of the company office if he called there again. A few days later Thomas Hallett, a brother and a burly fellow, spanked Talcott and literally threw him out of the office, taking a pistol away from Talcott in the process.

Talcott brooded over his wrongs and planned to have revenge on Hallett.[18]

John D. Cruise, a prominent figure in early Wyandotte, was an eye witness to the murder, and pictures the tragic scene.

Samuel Hallett was sitting by me at the dinner table at the Garno House, remarking as he rose to go, "I will leave a telegram at your office; do not hurry your meal; it is not important." He crossed the street to write the message—it was a very warm day, and he recrossed to get his umbrella, and started north on Third Street toward the general offices, which were in what was known as the Brick Block. . . . He had gone half a block, spoke to persons sitting in front of Holcomb's drug store, Talcott among the rest, for he was a very affable, gentlemanly man. Talcott, after he had passed, raised the heavy repeating rifle which he carried and shot him in the back. Talcott had been in my office just before noon, and I had asked him to dine with me, but he refused. Jack Beaton, John M. Funk, the mayor, and myself had just finished our meal and saw the whole proceeding. We all ran to the scene, picked up Hallett, and carried him back to the Garno House, but he expired before we reached the hotel. The bullet cut the strap of his white duck trousers and lodged in his abdomen near the navel, but did not pass through. He exclaimed, "My God. My God!" Talcott instantly mounted his horse which he had

17. *Ibid.*, July 19, 20, 22, 1864.
18. Cruise, *loc. cit.*, p. 538; Wyandotte *Gazette*, July 30, 1864.

hitched conveniently, and rode off towards Quindaro, where he lived at the time. Because of the enmity towards Hallett by many of the people living at Quindaro, the hunt for Talcott was impeded and he was never apprehended. He stopped for a few moments at his home [at Quindaro] and rode on into oblivion, although a large reward had been offered for his arrest.[19]

Sabin quoted a government report which appraised Hallett as "a man of genius, of boundless energy and enthusiasm, fertile in expedients, bold and prompt in action. Had he lived he would have been a master spirit in the construction of the Union Pacific Railway, and probably one of the leading railroad men of the country."[20]

To follow the history of the U. P. E. D. after Hallett's death requires a look at the financing of the company so that the actions and motives of various parties may be understood. After coming into the railroad as financial agent of Fremont, Hallett had been employed on November 7, 1863, to construct the entire line of road by the board of directors.

Later he acquired 99,800 more shares of the capital stock of the Leavenworth, Pawnee and Western from James C. Stone and A. J. Isaacs. This made him virtually owner of the corporation, leaving only a few shares held by the other directors.[21] Besides the purchase of stock, he paid $625,000 into the railroad to create an operating fund.[22] In order to obtain more working capital, he went to John D. Perry, president of the Exchange Bank of St. Louis. By written agreements dated February 22, 1864, Perry agreed to loan $750,000, of which $250,000 was to be advanced for the construction of the first 40-mile section, this sum to be repaid when the government accepted the section, the government bonds then to be available to cover the debt. To secure this fund, Hallett was required to pledge one-third of all shares standing in his name (38,163 shares) and Perry was to get one-fourth of two-thirds of all the profits of Hallett's construction contract, but Perry was to have no control of the building of the road.[23]

At Perry's suggestion, Hallett had secured $150,000 more from John How, Adolphus Meier, and Giles F. Filley, three St. Louis merchants who were eager to get into the enterprise, but Hallett had to pledge 61,637 more shares of stock.[24] Hallett was also forced

---

19. "Criminal Appearance Docket," case No. 104, district court of Wyandotte county, Kansas.
20. Sabin, op. cit., pp. 88, 89.
21. Allegation in "Stevens vs. Kansas Pacific Railway," see Footnote 5.
22. Allegation in "Hallett's Heirs vs. Kansas Pacific Railway Company" in Supreme Court of United States, 1879.
23. Hallet-Perry contracts, in "John Byers Anderson Papers," manuscript division, Kansas State Historical Society.
24. Case No. 731, "Court Files," district court of Wyandotte county, Kansas.

to commission Thomas C. Durant, vice-president of the Union Pacific Railroad Company, as financial agent of the U. P. E. D., for which Durant was to take another one-fourth of two-thirds of Hallett's construction profits.[25]

Hallett was just 36 years old when he was slain, and his wife, Ann Eliza, with his children, were traveling in Europe.[26] The day after his death, John L. Hallett, a brother, told the press: "I shall push the work with as much vigor as ever. Shall pay on Saturday night." A few days later a delegation from Lawrence went out to the end of the road to confer with the surviving Hallett brothers, John L. and Thomas, about the approaching celebration. They had to go on to Wyandotte where after a consultation the festivity was postponed, due to the death of Samuel Hallett and the want of proper coaches.[27]

Perry's agents met Mrs. Hallett when she disembarked at New York and got her to renounce the right to finish her husband's construction contract and to surrender it to the railroad.[28] Thereupon Perry, as president of the company, discharged the Hallett brothers, who with the help of Durant, as a surviving partner, were trying to lay rails on the last four miles of the first section. Immediately the business of building the road ground to a halt. Workmen had to sue to collect their wages. So many small suits were filed that attorneys had their pleadings printed with a few blank spaces only needing to be filled in.

On August 21 Perry came out to Lawrence for another railroad meeting. He reminded the citizens of the resolution of January 6 and read a letter of Senator Lane to Hallett that ended with: "The City of Lawrence to pay the additional cost of that part of the grade you are compelled to vacate, and the additional expense of the grade per mile that the new route costs over and above the old route." The inevitable committee was appointed to deal with this matter.[29]

Perry wrote shortly afterward: "Mrs. Hallett will be here on Monday or Tuesday with Geo. McDowell. I know not what I can do with her. I have the road under my control, *all* the Hallett[s] left [of] it." [30]

---

25. Contract in National Archives, Railroad Package No. 80.
26. *Daily Tribune*, Lawrence, July 30, 1864; allegation in "Hallett's Heirs vs. Kansas Pacific," *supra*.
27. *Daily Tribune*, Lawrence, July 29, August 3, 1864.
28. Perry to Anderson, September 18, 1864, "Anderson Papers," *loc. cit.*; also allegation in "Hallett's Heirs vs. Kansas Pacific," *supra*.
29. *Daily Tribune*, August 21, 1864.
30. *See* Footnote 28.

Perry's agents brought Mrs. Hallett to Wyandotte and had her appointed administratrix of her husband's estate although neither of the Halletts were residents of Kansas. They provided an attorney, John K. Hale, who was a director of the railroad and a partner of Allison B. Bartlett, who represented Perry in the ensuing litigation. Mrs. Hallett was induced to appoint Hale as her attorney-in-fact and through him relinquished the valuable contract to construct the railroad and, being persuaded that Hallett was bankrupt, filed an inventory showing Hallett's estate to have assets of only $4,414.71, listing only tools and cheap equipment of no use to anyone but the railroad company.[31]

Perry sued Hallett's estate and Hale accepted service for Mrs. Hallett who was "temporarily out of the state." How, Meier, and Filley also sued under the same conditions. Perry got judgment for $264,250 which included interest, then had the 38,163 shares he held as security appraised for $290.85 and the shares were auctioned at sheriff's sale to the railroad for $287.73 which sum was duly credited in Hallett's estate against Perry's judgment. In the suit of John How, et. al., $462.28 was bid for 61,637 shares. Judgment was taken in both suits on April 11, 1865, and the sheriff's sale was held on August 14. So the railroad took all of Hallett's pledged stock for $740.01, or for about three-fourths of a cent per share. At the same time John Byers Anderson was buying stock from the railroad company and paying its full par value of $50.00 a share.[32]

This legal chicanery was perpetrated at the expense of all the urgency to build—to keep ahead of the Nebraska railroad so Perry and the investors at St. Louis could make a killing. It wasn't until April 25, 1865, that Perry could file an affidavit that the first section of 40 miles had been completed.[33] A few days later President Johnson appointed commissioners to examine the road, who made a favorable report on May 5, 1865, although they noted certain defects and that the railroad must count the 1.77 miles of the spur track to Wyandotte in order to have a whole section of 40 miles.[34]

Fate again intervened. John P. Usher, who had been quite friendly to the road and at one time expected to be its president, had resigned from the cabinet several months earlier and left the Department of the Interior on May 15. He was succeeded by Sen. James Harlan, of Iowa, who naturally favored the company about

31. "Estate of Samuel Hallett," deceased, probate court of Wyandotte county, Kansas.— See, also, Footnote 22.
32. Cases 731 and 732, "Court Files," district court of Wyandotte county, Kansas.
33. "Journal of Letters Received—Lands and Railroads," loc. cit.
34. Simpson, op. cit., p. 90.

to build the route through Nebraska,[35] where the first 20 miles of track was not reported laid until October 28, 1865. Perry and his friends had to conduct U. P. E. D. business with a government bureaucrat who had no desire to see them get ahead. Then, too, Usher became general solicitor for U. P. E. D. and Harlan disliked his cabinet predecessor intensely. So "red tape" in the current Washington fashion became a critical problem.[36]

Secretary Harlan after approving the report of the government commissioners reconsidered the matter and recommended that a re-examination be made by a new commission, to consist of a competent engineer to be selected by the Secretary of War, Harvey D. Scott of Terre Haute, and Governor Crawford, of Kansas. General McCallum, director and general manager of the military railroads, considered additional proofs concluding with a recommendation that the report of the former commissioners be accepted. This report was then certified to the treasury with a presidential endorsement.

In the meantime, the proponents of the Nebraska line were busy trying to delay approval by the government. Next the rival organization in the U. P. E. D., headed by Edward Learned and E. R. Meade, his attorney, addressed the secretary claiming that the group represented by John D. Perry and John P. Usher were spurious directors, and not entitled to the government subsidy. The secretary, taking heed of affairs in Kansas on September 7 asked that approval of the road be rescinded and new commissioners be appointed, due to the railroad bridge over the Kansas river near Wyandotte and certain portions of track having been swept away by recent storms. The President responded by appointing Lt. Col. James H. Simpson to serve with Harvey D. Scott and Governor Crawford.[37]

This board made a minute examination and an extended report unfavorable to the railroad, which was not signed by Governor Crawford, who addressed President Andrew Johnson by letter dated October 13, 1865. July, August, and September were

memorable for singular and disastrous succession of heavy rains, destructive storms and fearful tornadoes. On the 21st of August last, one of the most violent and destructive swept over an immense range. . . .

In the City of Leavenworth on one occasion many houses were swept into the Missouri river, carrying with them men, women and children, a number of whom were drowned.

---

35. Harlan as senator and member of a select committee had effectively promoted the interests of the main line through Iowa and Nebraska in the acts of 1862 and 1864.—See John P. Davis, *The Union Pacific Railway* (Chicago, 1894), pp. 102, 119.
36. Harlan to Perry, *ibid.*, p. 105.
37. *Ibid.*, p. 93.

In consequence . . . the Union Pacific Railroad suffered greatly. Portions of the track were temporarily damaged, bridges, ties and other property carried away and destroyed, all of which have been repaired except the bridge over the Kansas River near its mouth, and upon this work is going on and will be completed before the Missouri Pacific road is extended to the State line which is necessary to form the junction.[38]

About this time the *Daily Tribune* of Lawrence reported that there were good omens for the future of the railroad for it had purchased two passenger coaches and another engine and that there was a large shipment of rails at Weston. This may have helped satisfy one of the objections by the government.[39]

Perry was authorized by the board of directors to use the expected government subsidy to deal with the dissident directors led by Fremont and Learned.

On November 6 William J. Palmer, secretary and treasurer of the railroad, reported that he had assigned $200,000 in bonds to Fremont's agent, that he had disposed of Learned at Washington and that Durant's resistance had been ineffectual.[40] Perry felt that the settlement was a master-stroke, for the assignment of bonds when received by the company, would bind the Fremont group to support the future interests of the railroad.

Also, the company employed the Robert M. Shoemaker Company to build the rest of the road. This group agreed to build the branch line from Leavenworth to Lawrence for $600,000 in first mortgage bonds, plus $250,000 in Leavenworth county bonds, plus $22,000 per mile in full paid capital stock.[41]

At a conference with the President and Harlan in October, Perry and his associates consented to make whatever changes and improvements in the right-of-way and equipment required by the government. The first section was then finally accepted. An additional section of 20 miles was certified to be ready on November 11, 1865, and was officially approved a month later, but the delay of 16 months had allowed the Union Pacific in Nebraska to catch up, and the U. P. E. D. had lost the commanding lead over its rival, which had been secured by Hallett's enterprise.[42]

Mrs. Hallett delayed until 1873 to file suit against the Kansas Pacific railroad, successor of the U. P. E. D., in the circuit court of the United States at Leavenworth. By that time it was too late to

38. Crawford to Andrew Johnson, October 13, 1865, in National Archives, Railroad Package Nos. 345, 346. Also contains original report of Scott and Simpson.
39. *Daily Tribune,* October 29, 1864.
40. Palmer to Anderson, November 6, 1865, "Anderson Papers," *loc. cit.*
41. Union Pacific Railroad Co., E. D.—Robert M. Shoemaker, et al., agreement, July 1, 1865, *ibid.*
42. A. T. Andreas and W. G. Cutler, *History of the State of Kansas* (Chicago, 1883), p. 246.

complain of fraudulent actions that had been a matter of record nine years earlier. She itemized the value of her husband's estate to the aggregate of 15 million dollars, all of which the railroad had fraudulently taken from her. The allegations of the suit are quite interesting, but many details not mentioned herein are not susceptible to verification now. The Union Pacific Railroad Company simply does not now permit research in its archives and I do not know what careful inquiry there would disclose, if anything at all. Mrs. Hallett's suit was lost by demurrer at Leavenworth and the supreme court affirmed this judgment in 1879.

It is always great fun to speculate on what might have been—had Hallett survived. Of course, such a presumption is productive of nothing, but it certainly requires no great stretch of imagination to visualize Hallett, with his great energy and resources driving the road out to the one hundredth meridian before his rivals in Nebraska, and then forging on with friendly government help to join with the Central Pacific of California; for the Nebraska road did not reach the 100th meridian until more than two years after Hallett's death.

John J. Ingalls might well have had this Kansas railroad in mind when he wrote the immortal sonnet on lost "Opportunity."

PREPARING FOR "THE GREATEST RUN OF THE CENTURY" Registration area near Arkansas City, September 14, 1893. Photo courtesy Jessy Mae Coker.

Waiting for the opening of the Cherokee Strip (or Outlet) at a camp near Arkansas City, September, 1893. Photo courtesy Walter D. Hutchison.

Gateways to the Promised Land
THE ROLE PLAYED BY THE SOUTHERN KANSAS TOWNS IN THE OPENING OF THE CHEROKEE STRIP TO SETTLEMENT
JEAN C. LOUGH

FOR a brief while, in 1893, southern Kansas was the focus of attention throughout the United States. Thousands of people flocked to the area. Correspondents for the great Eastern newspapers were present, sending out dozens of dispatches daily. The cause of this tremendous interest was the opening of the Cherokee strip, Indian territory, to settlement.

Elsewhere in the United States lay millions of uninhabited acres, but the interest was in this strip of land—roughly 58 by 150 miles—where the very atmosphere was reputed to be "electric and full of life-giving properties." [1]

There were many reasons for this interest in the Cherokee outlet, or "strip," as it was called. Perhaps the greatest was that the land was forbidden. It had been supposed it would be the home of the Indian forever. Three railroads crossed it, but no settlement was permitted within it. The areas to the north and south were well populated. The homesteader wished to save the strip for civilization; he wished to break the power of the great cattlemen's combine, which, until 1890, had been using it. The railroads wished to see it settled, in order to increase their own profit.

The southern border towns of Kansas of course saw possibilities for great financial gain. They saw the strip as a vast new trade territory which would necessarily be dependent upon them for goods and services of all types. They also, expected the advent of many new residents—preferably "capitalists."

When the Indian appropriation bill of March 3, 1893, was finally approved by congress, it contained the legislation necessary to carry out the cession of the Cherokee outlet from the Cherokee nation to the federal government, to pay the Cherokee nation the sum agreed upon, $8,595,736.12 and to open the lands to public settlement. Specifically, the outlet was a strip of land directly south of and parallel to the southern Kansas border, bounded on

MRS. JEAN C. LOUGH, who received an M. A. degree in history at Colorado University, Boulder, in 1958, is a resident of Arkansas City.
1. W. S. Prettyman, *Indian Territory: A Frontier Photographic Record*, selected and edited by Robert E. Cunningham (Norman, University of Oklahoma Press, 1957), p. 120.

the east by the Arkansas river and on the west by Beaver county and Texas. To the south were the Cheyenne and Arapaho reservations, the Creek nation, and the territory of Oklahoma—or "old Oklahoma."

"Old Oklahoma" had been settled in 1889, ten years after the first boomers came to sit upon the Kansas border and gaze at Indian territory with longing eyes. David L. Payne, the boomer's most militant leader, had been fond of quoting—"The Lord commandeth unto Moses: Go forth and possess the Promised Land," and it became the watchword of the boomer campaign.[2] Naturally, the presence of an area of land in the middle of Indian territory, unassigned to any one tribe, had invited the greed of the land-hungry. Once this land was opened, most of the rest of the Indian's "permanent" home quickly went, piece by piece. Two years later the boomers were again camped on the Kansas border, looking southward, and the congress of the United States was in the process of negotiating for the cession of the Cherokee outlet.

The outlet was not actually occupied by Cherokee Indians. It had been Comanche and Kiowa territory,[3] which had been taken from them by the government and given to the Cherokees, in exchange for lands taken from the Cherokees in Georgia. The Cherokee nation resided upon a rectangular tract to the east of the outlet. The outlet gave them access to the hunting grounds to the west. For several years it had been leased by cattlemen for the grazing of their herds. These cattlemen, united in the Cherokee Strip Livestock Association, as well as the railroads, had tried unsuccessfully to buy the strip. The federal government had prohibited it.

Public opinion had become so strong, however, for the opening of the strip to settlement that the government eventually renounced its treaties with the Indians, and virtually forced them to sell. The official position was that the support which the Five Civilized Tribes (erstwhile owners of Negro slaves) had given the Confederate cause during the Civil War had automatically abrogated the treaties made with the tribes.

When the news reached Kansas that settlement had finally been arranged with the Indians for the cession of the outlet, the *Weekly Republican Traveler,* of Arkansas City, said:

2. *Ibid.,* p. 10
3. Marquis James, *The Cherokee Strip: A Tale of an Oklahoma Boyhood* (New York, Viking Press, 1945), p. 10.

For years a little band of faithful men in this city have worked in season and out of season for the consummation of the end which we are celebrating today. Money has been expended in large sums in a legitimate way and the rewards of these sacrificing men have too often been curses and misrepresentation. . . .[4]

Now there was hope of more substantial rewards.

The little town of Hunnewell was already receiving benefits. During the early 1890's, after the government had ordered all cattle removed from the strip, thousands of head of cattle were driven to the stockyards at Hunnewell for shipment to market or to other grazing grounds. There was a Santa Fe branch line terminus at Hunnewell, and the Frisco built an extension down from South Haven, three miles to the north.[5] The population of the town multiplied. It was a roaring cowtown in the tradition of the earlier shipping centers.

The nation of course expected an immediate Presidential proclamation setting the time of the opening of the strip, but it was slow in coming. Details needed to be taken care of, and an attempt was made to find a more satisfactory method of settlement than the "run" system used in the three previous openings.

While the government was studying, railroads and southern Kansas towns were acting. Promotion went into high gear. Boomer literature was printed and widely distributed. Businessmen's clubs and committees raised funds for advertising, and solicited names of people to whom they could send literature. Maps of the strip sold for 15 cents apiece. The homesteaders began arriving in increasing numbers.

Part of the influx was due to the Panic of 1893. Money was scarce. Banks were closing. Farm prices were dwindling steadily. The farmers of Kansas were in revolt, and were upsetting Kansas' political traditions by voting for Populist candidates instead of Republicans. The great boom of the 1880's had burst, and continued drought, small crops, and low prices, coupled with mortgage foreclosures, caused many to seek cheap land and a new start. The boomers were sometimes able to earn a little money by working for the farmers in the region, but more often they had to rely upon hunting and fishing to sustain them while they waited.

The Kansas towns which were closest to the border and the most likely to be the nucleus for would-be-settlers were Arkansas

---

4. *Weekly Republican Traveler*, Arkansas City, March 9, 1893.
5. Homer S. Chambers, *The Enduring Rock* (Blackwell, Okla., Blackwell Publications, Inc., 1954), p. 12.

City, Cale, Hunnewell, South Haven, Kiowa, Anthony, and Ashland. Of these, Arkansas City and Caldwell had by far the greatest attraction. The two main-line railroads which crossed the strip were the Santa Fe at Arkansas City, and the Rock Island at Caldwell. The best land was at the eastern end of the strip, priced at $2.50 an acre. West of the meridian of 97° 30′ it sold for $1.50 an acre, and west of 98° 30′ at $1.00 an acre—the latter figure 25 cents an acre less than the government paid the Indians for it.

Arkansas City had a population in 1893 of 9,264 people, an increase of almost 1,000 since 1892. Caldwell had 2,138 residents in 1893, an increase of around 140 persons. Doubtless these increases were attributable to the arrival of the earliest boomers, who found jobs and settled into the community, and the arrival of new businesses, preparing to take advantage of the great crowds expected and the anticipated business.

It was on August 19, 1893, that Cleveland finally issued the long-awaited Presidential proclamation. The strip was to be opened to settlement at 12 noon, September 16, 1893. The "run" system was to be used. At a given signal all participants would rush forward, and the first person to arrive at a location could drive a stake bearing his flag and lay claim to that homestead.

In an effort to prevent fraud, especially by people crossing the line sooner than the legal opening time, nine booths were to be erected—five on the Kansas border and four on the border of Old Oklahoma—where people were to register and receive certificates. These certificates were to be shown before legal entry could be made to the strip on opening day, and they must also be shown when filing claims. The booths were to open on September 11, remain open ten hours a day, and continue until closed by order of the secretary of the Department of the Interior. Three officers were to work in each booth.

In order to be eligible for a homestead, a person must be 21 years of age or the head of a family: this caused a few hasty marriages. He (or she) must be a citizen of the United States, or have declared his intention of becoming one, must not have exhausted his homestead right, and must not be a "sooner"— one who crossed the line too soon.[6] A married woman could not take her land if her husband did. No restrictions were put on registrants because of race.

---

6. James D. Richardson, *A Compilation of the Messages and Papers of the Presidents, 1789-1902* (Washington, Bureau of National Literature and Art, 1905), v. 9, p. 417.

Certain areas were withheld from the public settlement. A maximum of 70 allotments were open to members of the Cherokee nation—68 being finally approved. Land was set aside for the Camp Supply military reservation, for the Chilocco Indian Industrial School, for four government land offices, and for county courthouses, schools, parks, universities, agricultural colleges, and other public purposes.[7]

The area had already been divided into counties, given temporary alphabetical designations (K through Q), and county-seat locations had been established. A strip of land 100 feet wide around and immediately within the outer boundaries of the entire Cherokee strip was set apart for opening purposes, to allow the people to assemble without impediment just before the run.

Soldiers were patrolling the borders as well as the interior of the strip, looking for sooners. The railroads were also guarded, but the number of soldiers available was totally inadequate for the magnitude of the job at hand. Many, many sooners slipped through. Those who were caught were escorted out of the territory, sometimes held in custody until after the run, and they lost their right to homestead upon the strip. A few sooners were killed by the soldiers. Some of the soldiers could be bribed, however. One man paid a soldier $25 to hide him in a hole on a claim the Friday night before the opening. He emerged at 12 noon, Saturday, and found four other men had already staked on the claim.[8]

After the Presidential proclamation setting the date for the opening of the strip, migration increased tremendously. The New York *Times* carried an article from Topeka, on September 5, saying that the "movement toward the Cherokee Strip is increasing all the time. There has been a daily average of 100 teams passing through this city, with from two to six men to the team. This has lasted now two weeks, and it is yet nearly two weeks until the opening." It added that the first newspaper in the strip would be a daily at Perry, to be published by a John W. Jacks of Missouri, "who has his presses and materials already there." At least 60 newspaper plants in Kansas were reported to be boxed up and ready for shipment to the newly-settled territory. Twenty of these were said to be headed for Perry, which was believed by many to be "the coming city."

Along the border, stores were selling out their stocks and reordering almost daily. Prices were not higher in Kansas, but

---

7. *Ibid.*, pp. 409-411.
8. *Weekly Republican Traveler*, October 26, 1893.

Guthrie, Indian territory, reported shortages of supplies and prices rising.[9] Milk sold regularly for five cents a quart, bread for five cents a loaf, eggs for five or ten cents a dozen, and coffee from 25 to 30 cents a pound.[10]

The *Weekly Republican Traveler* of Arkansas City increased in size from four to eight pages. The Caldwell *News* said bluntly on September 7: "We are too full of strip business to pay much attention to politics till the gates swing open to the promised land."

The post office at Arkansas City had to put on three extra men to handle and distribute the mail.[11] Bakers at Wichita were working overtime to furnish bread to Caldwell, Kiowa, and Hunnewell, where the great number of boomers was causing a shortage.[12]

Warnings were issued to watch out for pickpockets and thugs of all kinds, as the towns were full of them. Many and bitter were the protests of having been taken at the old shell game.

Horses were put into training, and there were some complaints about racing through and near the towns. Harness was tested and strengthened, and wagons were gone over and repaired. An enterprising man from Wichita brought down a carload of horses to sell.[13]

Farmers received many requests from homesteaders wishing to camp upon their lands. One man built a temporary house with its door on the state line, so that he would be ready to go at a moment's notice.[14] The campers were so thick along the border, and the weather so dry, that the soil was eventually churned to dust. Water was soon very scarce; wells were pumped dry, and streams and water holes dried up. Washing was almost an impossibility. Water sold for a dime a cup.

Once the registration was begun, hardships multiplied. The booths opened only five days before the run was to be made. Thousands of people stood in line before each booth, day and night, awaiting their turns. The heat was intense, and numerous cases of heat prostration and sunstroke, with some deaths, were reported. Those who had families could rely on them to bring food and water, which was often shared with others in the line.

---

9. New York *Times*, September 14, 1893.
10. Chambers, *op. cit.*
11. *Arkansas Valley Democrat*, Arkansas City, September 1, 1893.
12. Jennie Small Owen, annalist, *The Annals of Kansas 1886-1925* (Topeka, Kansas State Historical Society, 1954), v. 1, p. 156.
13. Martha Jefferson Boyce, *History in the Making: A Story of the Cherokee Strip* (Beatrice, Neb., Franklin Press, 1948), p. 6.
14. *Weekly Republican Traveler*, March 16, 1893.

Women were usually ushered to the head of the line, the last piece of chivalry most of them were to see for some time.

In spite of all precautions, fraud was still possible at the booths. People joined the registrations lines, only to sell their places for from five to 25 dollars. Many certificates were sold or obtained in other illegal manners. Some of the soldiers guarding the booths were bribed to take registrants in the back door; booth officials sometimes obliged acquaintances by selling them certificates after hours, in the hotels. At Orlando, Oklahoma territory, the registration booths were robbed of certificates and the official stamp, and by the next morning thousands of forged certificates were on the market.[15]

The cattlemen had a meeting in Arkansas City on September 14, and sent a wire to President Cleveland protesting the booth system of registration as carried on at Booth No. 9, south of Arkansas City. The wire said, in part: "7,000 people are now in line and thousands more arrive on each train. A conflict between parties that are not registered and the troops is imminent unless the system is abandoned. . . . The conduct of the soldiers at Booth #9 is despicable. . . ."[16]

That same day between 4,000 and 5,000 persons were in line before the booth at Caldwell. Hunnewell reported being "overpressed," also. Orlando, Indian territory, had around 22,000 boomers, and the intense heat and bad water caused an epidemic of dysentery there.[17] Many people had shipped their horses, bedding, and camping equipment by railroad from Kansas, across the strip, in hopes of finding less crowded conditions and having a better chance in the run from there.

The Cherokees sent a telegram to Secretary of the Interior Hoke Smith requesting permission to put well diggers to work on the Indian allotments "that water may be in readiness for the crowds that will run into the new country on Saturday, and who will certainly suffer intensely from thirst."[18] The request was denied.

The appeal for help on the registration problem was heeded, however. Extra booths were opened and many new clerks were added, in a last minute attempt to alleviate the hardships of registration.

Among the hundreds of people arriving daily were several special

15. New York *Times*, September 17, 1893.
16. *Ibid.*, September 15, 1893.
17. *Ibid.*
18. *Ibid.*

groups with plans for establishing colonies of their own. One such group was comprised of 500 Presbyterians, reportedly on its way from Colorado.

Two hundred Scandinavians arrived in Arkansas City under the management of one Oscar Johnson of McPherson county. Their colony was chartered by the state of Kansas.[19]

Annette Daisy was also on hand. She had taken an active part in the three former openings. This time she organized a colony of single women, widows, and spinsters, dedicated to the purpose of building a community "across the sacred borders of which no man shall pass." [20] Thirty-four women had signed up by opening time.

In Guthrie, a colony of several hundred Negroes arrived. Each one of them had a printed certificate granting him a farm upon his arrival. These certificates had been bought in Louisiana for ten dollars apiece, and were obviously worthless.[21]

Other people had bought tickets entitling them to draw for the land, paying several dollars for that privilege—which was not to be granted.

Many of the people who traveled to the Kansas border before the opening day became disgusted with the crowds, the registration procedure, the dust and hot winds, and returned to their former homes. Their places were quickly filled by new arrivals. Fortunately, although the settlers had come from almost every part of the United States and from abroad, the great majority of them were from the Middle West, particularly Kansas, where climatic and drought conditions were not too different from those of the "promised land." These people were better able to endure the hardships prior to the opening.

On September 14, 1893, a Rock Island train crossing the strip was attacked, and despite desperate resistance from the trainmen, the Pullman cars were robbed of all their ice and water. The train crew was reported to bear the marks of fierce fighting.[22]

Thirsty sooners were not the only desperadoes loose in the strip. The Dalton and Starr gangs were making their headquarters there— as well as many less well-known train and bank robbers. Trains were frequently held up, and the gunmen appeared in Kansas boldly and apparently at will.

19. *Ibid.*, September 15, 1893.
20. *Ibid.*, September 17, 1893.
21. *Ibid.*, September 15, 1893.
22. *Ibid.*, September 15, 1893.

On the day before the run a scout appeared in Arkansas City, having just come from the Osage country, and notified all the banks that the remnants of the Dalton-Starr gang were camped about 30 miles south of the town. They were planning to rob the banks once the people had left town for the opening. A strong posse was organized to protect the banks, as almost the entire police force was going to make the run. The raid never actually took place.[23]

Hunnewell was having troubles of its own. A town of approximately 250 people, it was greatly overrun. Waiting lines were everywhere, at the hotels, restaurants, stores, post office. Feeling ran very high when it was discovered that four race horses had been killed and seven others had been hamstrung.[24] There was strong suspicion that someone planning to make the race afoot was responsible.

Violence and death were not unusual during these days. Men were killed for their money, or for their certificates. More often, they fought, and killed, over gambling, women, and even attempts to crash the waiting line at the registration booths. By far the vast majority of the boomers, however, were honest, hard-working people who behaved in an orderly manner—until the run started.

In Arkansas City the press seized its opportunity to extol the virtues of the town before a captive audience. Articles were printed enumerating the economic possibilities of the area, the water supply from two rivers, the three railroads, three newspapers, three mills, four banks, stockyards, streetcar lines, electric lights, and telephone exchange. The industries included a reclining chair factory, a canning factory, and makers of bricks, carriages, mattresses, and wind machines, as well as a wholesale grocery.[25]

As the *Canal City Dispatch,* of Arkansas City, said: "We have the location, the water power and everything else necessary to make a city. . . . people . . . will return . . . buy property. . . . Inside of the next year Arkansas City's population will be three times what it is at present. It will be the supply point for the south."[26] Fifty thousand people were in or near Arkansas City before the run was made.

At Caldwell the press was also busy promoting the town. There was one gloomy note. The Caldwell *Journal* kept printing a notice saying: "We have on our books the names of a great many who

---

23. *Ibid.,* September 16, 1893.
24. Caldwell *News,* September 14, 1893.
25. *Weekly Republican Traveler,* May 11, 1893.
26. *Canal City Dispatch,* Arkansas City, September 15, 1893.

owe us from one or two dollars on subscription. In all it reaches several hundred dollars. Many of these men will go into the strip without thinking of paying us. We can't afford to lose this money and ask all to call at once and settle." [27] The editor finally solved his problem by selling the paper and going into the strip himself to live.

For the last few days before the opening, prairie fires raged across the strip. Several sooners were believed to have burned to death. It was said that "If a crow attempted to fly the Cherokee Strip he'd have to take his own grub along." [28] A song was sung to the tune of "After the Ball Is Over":

> After the strip is opened,
> After the run is made,
> After the horses are buried
> After the debts are paid;
> Many a sucker'll be kicking,
> Many will have lost their grip,
> Many will wish they'd been hung,
> Ere going to the strip.[29]

At last the great day arrived. Well over 100,000 people were assembled on the northern and southern boundaries. For hours they waited; gambling, singing, praying—even preaching. Finally, at 12 noon (five minutes earlier on the Hennessey stretch of line) a shot rang out and was relayed along the line from soldier to soldier. The eager settlers, straining their eyes, could see the puff of smoke from the distant rifle before they could hear the sound of the shot. All along the line the horses leaped forward, and the great race was on. The horsemen and bicyclists were easily in the lead, followed by the heavier carriages and wagons. In the rear were those who were going in afoot. In one place, at the first steep ravine—an 18-foot embankment—the bicyclists were forced to quit. The horsemen, unwilling to lose time by looking for a more favorable spot to cross, in many cases leaped their horses down the embankment, often crippling them so that they had to be abandoned. Clouds of dust obscured the vision of the strippers, and one heavy wagon, loaded with six men, was accidentally driven over the same embankment. One man on the wagon suffered a broken leg.[30]

---

27. Caldwell *Journal*, August 24, 1893.
28. Chambers, *op. cit.*, p. 22.
29. *Ibid.*, p. 23.
30. New York *Times*, September 17, 1893.

There were many accidents. People fell off horses and were in danger of being trampled in the rush. A Mrs. Charles Barnes of El Dorado was killed under a falling horse.[31] Several other women, some of whom rode "clothes-pin fashion" were also injured. Broken arms, legs, and necks were not uncommon. Some who didn't fall from horses or wagons, or drive off cliffs, managed to fall off the overloaded trains which made the run, or be accidentally shot in the uproar. Sooners were shot by soldiers, and at least one soldier was shot by a sooner.[32]

As the horsemen established a good lead over the rest of the boomers, some of them dismounted and set fire to the prairie, so that those behind them could not advance. Other fires were set by claimants trying to burn off the grass and uncover their boundary markers. A number of people were burned to death, including a colored man named Tom Jameson[33] and a Mrs. Elizabeth Osborne of Newton, Mo.[34] Some of those burned to death could not be identified.

The fine race horses imported for the occasion did not hold up too well. They made good starts, but couldn't stand the distance or the terrain. Many dead horses littered the prairie the next day. One man had a most uncomfortable ride when his thoroughbred race horse became excited in all the turmoil and ran uncontrollably for 24 miles before dropping dead.[35]

The trains which made the run were jammed to the roof. At Caldwell, although very crowded, the business of loading the Rock Island trains proceeded in a fairly orderly manner.

As tickets were procured, the purchaser passed on from the east to the west side of the tracks, received successive numbers, were put into companies under captains, and placed in position along the track ready, each company to board a car when the train came along. The train was made up of Montgomery Palace Cattle cars—35 cars—and it was loaded with 5,200 persons who bought tickets and several hundred marshals and others, and officers of the road.[36]

In Arkansas City things did not go quite so well. The trains didn't pull out of the Santa Fe yards until long after 12 o'clock, and the jam then was terrible. "At least 15,000 people, including most of the population of Arkansas City, were there to board the trains. Special trains from Wichita, Winfield and other points came

---

31. *Weekly Republican Traveler*, September 21, 1893.
32. *New York Times*, September 17, 1893.
33. *Ibid.*
34. *Canal City Dispatch*, September 22, 1893.
35. *Weekly Republican Traveler*, September 21, 1893.
36. L. R. Elliott, as quoted in "The Greatest Race of the Century," *The Kansas Historical Quarterly*, v. 23 (Summer, 1957), p. 207.

in loaded with sightseers. . . . Engineers were instructed to run carefully, for it had been said attempts would be made to tamper with the trains." [37] Already spikes and straps had been removed from the rails and bridges, but were fortunately discovered before any accidents resulted. Trains also made the run from the south.

The trains had to stop at every station, and slow down or stop every five miles. They were forbidden to travel faster than 15 miles per hour. As a result, the men on horses arrived before the trains.

Many of those who made the run by train were town lot seekers, or investors in town lot companies, such as the Ponca Town Company and the Cherokee Town Site Trust Company.

At Orlando, Oklahoma territory, between 20,000 and 25,000 people were gathered for the race to the town site of Perry—a distance of ten miles. It took 45 minutes for the trains to get to Perry, and by that time there were approximately 1,000 horsemen there. By two in the afternoon there were 20,000 people in Perry, many of them without food or water.[38]

Some enterprising people made the run with improvised "water-wagons" and sold water for a dollar a bucket. Fortunately the weather was not as hot as earlier in the week.

Besides the difficulties of the run itself, there were the sooners and the claim jumpers to deal with. The leaders of the race frequently arrived, on sweaty horses, at a likely spot, only to find someone already there, with an unmarked horse, sometimes plowing a field near a partially-erected house. A whole town was reported stolen by sooners. Men made the run from the east side, contrary to instructions. Many cases were later taken to court, but it was difficult to prove a man a sooner. Nearly every sooner had two friends to swear that his claim was legitimate and his certificate legal.

In many cases men dropped out of the run and staked land unaware of the fact that someone else had already done so, or was doing so at that very moment. Some of these cases were settled on the spot, with a gun. Other claims were deliberately jumped.

Alexander Gillespie was staking a claim near Arkansas City when another boomer with a Winchester rode up and dismounted upon the same claim. "We will play a game of checkers for it," said he. "I've jumped and it's your move." When he raised his Winchester, Gillespie moved! [39]

37. *Denver Republican*, September 17, 1893.
38. New York *Times*, September 17, 1893.
39. *Canal City Dispatch*, September 22, 1893.

An estimated 30,000 people made the run from Arkansas City, and 10,000 from Caldwell, with a number going in from other Kansas border towns and the Oklahoma territory.[40] By nightfall many of them were on their way out again. Some merely went in to see the show. Others were too late to stake a claim.

While the excitement was going on in the Cherokee strip, the surrounding towns were practically deserted. The banks were closed and business was at a standstill. Everyone who possibly could had gone to see the run. However, within four hours of the start of the race, orders began to roll into Arkansas City for lumber and supplies. The eagerly awaited market had been opened.

One of the most successful profiteers from the opening of the Cherokee strip was a lawyer who went into the strip several hours before the opening, but without attempting to get land. Instead, he collected evidence against some 200 or more sooners and had no trouble in getting "an army of clients." [41]

The local press was shocked at the depopulation created by the opening of the Cherokee strip to settlement, but was pleased that it had "at last been wrested from the powerful cattle syndicate which for many years held dominion over it and would permit no home-seekers." [42]

Throughout the nation, though, criticism was rising over the manner in which the run had been conducted, and over the idea of having a horse race with the stakes a part of the public domain. The New York *Times* editorialized on September 17:

> The whole trouble has arisen from the fact that our homestead laws have been bequeathed to us from a period when the Government and the Nation were greatly interested in making sure that the public domain was occupied and utilized. That period is past. What there is left of the public domain is a national possession of great and increasing value that should be made to yield to the Public Treasury all that it is fairly worth.

A homestead of 160 acres of the best land, which sold for $2.50 an acre, would cost the settler around $516, including his fees and four percent interest for five years.[43]

The New York *Times* editorial expressed the current but curious view towards the Cherokee strip and public lands:

> The Cherokee Strip may be called the last remnant of the public domain. The United States of America do still own some land in various outlying

---

40. New York *Times*, September 17, 1893. These figures coincide with those given in the local papers at the time. Recent figures are much greater, giving Arkansas City 70,000 boomers.
41. *Canal City Dispatch*, September 22, 1893.
42. *Arkansas Valley Democrat*, September 22, 1893.
43. *Ibid*, September 8, 1893.

parts, but this is the last great tract that is thrown open to settlement. It is upon that count the more disgraceful and calamitous that the settlement of it should be attended by the outrageous scenes that have been witnessed during the last few days, and that are likely to be followed by scenes more disgraceful still.

To back up this prophecy, the *Times* carried a front page story on September 19, with numerous titles and subtitles as follows:

> Baptism of Blood and Fire.
> Flaming Passions and Prairies
> in Cherokee Strip.
>
> Homemakers Abandoning their Outfits and Fleeing for Their Lives— Thousands of Them Hastening Back from What a Few Days Ago Was the Promised Land— Tent Towns Demolished by a Fierce Gale— A Harvest of Corpses— Quarrels of Racers and "Sooners."

Conditions were bad, but it is doubtful if they were that bad! Many boomers did leave the strip very quickly. The weather, the burned-over earth, and the apparently endless winds encouraged the less resolute to leave. Some managed to sell their claims before filing, and turn a quick profit. Others were not so fortunate. Claims were advertised for sale in the local newspapers.

Perhaps the most frustrating experience was that of Jacob Lorenson. An article in the *Canal City Dispatch* on September 22 said:

> Jacob Lorenson is the name of the young man who cut his throat at Perry yesterday. He came here from Saginaw, Mich., and bought a lot for $500, which proved to be on the public square. He staked another lot for which he was offered $250 but refused the offer. It turned out that the lot was in the alley. Moneyless and discouraged, he cut his throat but was alive this morning, according to the report.

One group of unsuccessful homesteaders—a would-be colony from Illinois, which made the run on foot and secured nothing— had this to say: "We are glad to get back. . . . We honestly would not take a claim in the new country as a gift now, after what we saw of the country and its people." [44]

The trains running north out of the strip were overloaded. The railroads were doing exceedingly well, and continued to do so, for over their lines rolled the goods to build and stock not only stores but cities. Passenger trade was heavy, but as it slackened the freight trade increased.

Arkansas City was doing well economically. The orders rolled in, and Arkansas City boasted that it was supplying every city in the strip located on the Santa Fe line. In addition, an estimated $250,000 had been left there by the boomers. The city did suffer

---

44. Denver *Republican*, September 18, 1893.

a marked loss in population to the strip, but held firmly to the belief that the people would come back, and that others, becoming disenchanted with the strip, would settle there.

Caldwell did not fare as well as Arkansas City. It, too, was a supply center, but it was so seriously depopulated that it was necessary to hold a special election. The councilmen for the first, second, and third wards had left the state of Kansas.[45]

The population of Arkansas City fell from 9,264 in 1893 to 7,120 in 1894. Caldwell went from 2,138 to 1,386 in the same years. Kiowa fell from 1,358 people to 504. There were similar losses all along the border. These losses cannot be attributed entirely to the opening of the Cherokee strip, as the current depression undoubtedly contributed. It was estimated, however, that the opening of the Cherokee strip cost Kansas some 50,000 populist votes.

The opening of the Cherokee strip to settlement was an event for which the adjacent towns had long worked, propagandized, and invested. In return they expected substantial city growth and economic prosperity. Their goals were only partially attained. Temporary economic gains there were, but also the loss of residents. The losses were not quite as severe as they seemed, when it is realized that boomers were gathering for the expected opening as early as 1891, and those who got jobs locally were accepted and counted as part of the resident population, when in fact and intention they were not.

Those towns which were basically sound, with sufficient water, good railroad connections, and some local industry, survived the Cherokee strip opening and experienced a slow but steady recovery and growth. Others, which had had several rewarding years because of the strip boom, but which had no firm economic basis, never recovered. The hotel at Hunnewell has been torn down and most of the business houses have disappeared. On the site of Cale stands a lone grain elevator.

The people had exercised their traditional American prerogative, and moved on into the new frontier—looking, as always, for the "promised land" beyond.

45. Caldwell *News*, November 2, 1893.

Telegraph Beginnings in Kansas
JOHN E. SUNDER

KANSAS' great question—slavery—was settled. After five years of bloodshed, delegates to a new constitutional convention met July 5, 1859, at Wyandotte (now part of Kansas City), to draw up an antislavery document. Throughout the meeting a young man by the name of Philo H. Clarke sat at a telegraph key near convention hall, clicking stories to Eastern correspondents. His news brought fresh hope to the advocates of human freedom.[1]

Clarke's office was connected with the East by way of Missouri. His telegraph line also went through Quindaro, along the Missouri river to Leavenworth. And, during that summer of 1859, while the delegates threshed out their constitution, construction crews were stretching wires between Leavenworth and Atchison.

Telegraph lines, by 1859, already crisscrossed Missouri. For 12 years there had been a struggle for control of the state's expanding system. One casualty of the conflict was an early Missouri river line, completed in 1851. From St. Louis west its wires paralleled the south bank to Kansas City, then ran north along the east bank to St. Joseph. The line had fallen into disrepair, and when rebuilt in 1859 by Charles M. Stebbins, an independent operator, the link above Kansas City had been discarded.[2]

Western Union, in a series of corporate agreements, culminating in Missouri between 1857-1859, had won control of Stebbins' lines (and Stebbins' dreams of a transcontinental network) and encouraged its Western subsidiaries to expand into Kansas and Arkansas. Stebbins received $12,000 in cash from Western Union in return for a majority of stock in his Missouri river line, but theoretically he remained in control and was retained as general line-superintendent. He had no choice; the giant threatened to build a line, parallel to his, west from St. Louis to Kansas City. Capitulation, with the superintendency, was better than financial ruin.[3]

The plans for Kansas' first line were made by Stebbins and his agents before the Western Union victory. In 1855 the Kansas ter-

---

DR. JOHN E. SUNDER, native of St. Louis who received his doctor's degree from Washington University, is a member of the history department of the University of Texas, Austin.
1. Frank W. Blackmar, *Kansas* . . . (Chicago, 1912), v. 2, pp. 50, 51; Noble L. Prentis, *A History of Kansas* (Topeka, 1904), pp. 77-79; Topeka *Daily Capital*, January 16, 1955.
2. John E. Sunder, "The Early Telegraph in Rural Missouri, 1847-1859," *Missouri Historical Review*, Columbia, v. 51, No. 1 (October, 1956), pp. 42-53.
3. Charles M. Stebbins, *The New and True Religion* (New York, 1898), pp. 367, 368.

ritorial assembly incorporated two telegraph companies: the "Kaw River" and the "Occidental." Stebbins' "friends among the members (all Missourians)" sponsored the acts. He, his close friend Isaac M. Veitch, and several associates, were to construct the Kaw river line from a junction point on their Missouri river system near the mouth of the Kaw (Kansas) river "through such points on or near the Kansas river as the corporators may elect, thence westward to the western boundary of Kansas territory."[4] They were to build the Occidental from a similar junction point to Leavenworth and the northern boundary of the territory. Disruption within the Missouri system in the mid-1850's, however, prevented construction of the two lines, although Stebbins remained interested and optimistic.

While Stebbins was rebuilding the old Missouri river telegraph line, his agents were active in eastern Kansas. Though building plans beyond Kansas City were a bit indefinite, the *Kansas Weekly Herald* at Leavenworth was enthusiastic, and on February 6, 1858, called for an early public meeting to secure a link to Stebbins' line "for economic and military reasons." The response was heartening to agents S. A. Drake and Captain Scudder, and, by August, Leavenworth had subscribed $5,000. Russell, Majors & Waddell, together with Smoot, Russell & Company, put up better than one fourth of the total.[5]

In September the last poles on the new Missouri river line were going up on the prairies between Boonville and Lexington; Kansas City anticipated connection to the system by Christmas; and Drake was again on his way into eastern Kansas to rally more support for the line to and beyond Leavenworth. He passed through Kansas City in mid-October and reported that Stebbins was building at the rate of three miles per day. All outward signs pointed to success, including St. Joseph's demand to be part of the system.[6] The St. Joseph *Gazette* remarked: "This will always be our most important connection, for by it we will not only communicate with the Capitol . . . but with all the important points on the river . . ."[7]

The optimistic outlook, however, had to be qualified during the

---

4. *The Statutes of the Territory of Kansas; Passed at the First Session of the Legislative Assembly, One Thousand Eight Hundred and Fifty-Five* (Shawnee M. L. School, 1855), pp. 856-858.

5. *The Kansas Weekly Herald*, Leavenworth, February 6, August 21, 1858; *Western Journal of Commerce*, Kansas City, Mo., August 21, 1858.

6. Leavenworth *Times*, October 9, 1858; St. Joseph (Mo.) *Gazette*, September 28, 1858; St. Louis *Daily Morning Herald*, October 16, 1858; *Western Journal of Commerce*, September 4, October 16, 1858.

7. St. Joseph *Gazette*, September 28, 1858.

autumn. Stebbins was nearly out of funds by early October; incessant rain pelted the construction crews in western Missouri; and a few Leavenworth subscribers failed to meet their payments. Time was at a premium, since navigation during the winter would close on the lower Missouri, and telegraph equipment, especially instruments and batteries in sufficient quantity, had to be delivered in Kansas City before that time if any new stations were to be opened before the following spring. Stebbins believed he could overcome all obstacles, given some co-operation, but admitted that he had been behind schedule for weeks.[8]

Workmen had poles set into Kansas City by early December—but no wire. Stebbins explained the difficulty as a simple matter of supply and demand. The wire producers were slow in forwarding his orders, yet he intimated that even orders depended upon stock subscriptions and many in the Kansas City area had not met their pledges. Nevertheless, he was certain he could build the line cheaper than anyone else and remained confident that it would reach St. Joseph in a "very short time" and, perhaps, go on to Council Bluffs.[9]

Early in December, 1858, digging crews and hoisting-men reached the banks of the Kaw, crossed the stream near its junction with the Missouri, and commenced setting poles in Kansas territory through Wyandotte, Quindaro, and the Delaware Indian lands to Leavenworth. They followed the river bottoms, since the next best route was along Stranger creek five to ten miles inland across the bluffs; too far to serve as a direct route to the river towns. Stebbins' timetable, which called for wire in Kansas City by Christmas and to Leavenworth by the New Year, fell far behind schedule—partially due to the Delaware Indians who "had taken umbrage at the construction of a telegraph line through their domain, and threatened to impede or prevent its progress." Representatives of the telegraph line, and also, it seems, of the town of Leavenworth, met with a council of Delaware chiefs on December 10, and reached an agreement whereby Stebbins was authorized to obtain poles from the Indian lands upon his promise to respect the reservation's character.[10]

---

8. Letter, Charles M. Stebbins to Alfred Gray, September 18, 1858, "Alfred Gray Papers," in Mss. division, Kansas State Historical Society; Leavenworth *Times,* October 16, 23, November 6, 1858.

9. St. Louis *Daily Morning Herald,* December 8, 1858; Marshall (Mo.) *Democrat,* December 10, 1858; *Western Journal of Commerce,* November 20, 1858.

10. Leavenworth *Weekly Times,* December 11, 1858; Marshall *Democrat,* December 10, 1858; "Kansas Base Map (1921)," U. S. Department of the Interior Geological Survey; *World Geographic Atlas* (Chicago, 1953), pp. 136, 137.

At last, shortly before Christmas, Kansas City sent and received its first messages on the new line, and a temporary downtown office was opened. The wires were strung across the Kaw on tall supporting masts—later to be replaced by cables. An office was opened in Wyandotte, and the local *Weekly Western Argus* initiated a column of "Telegraphic Items." In Wyandotte and other localities Stebbins was accused of favoritism in the use of his line and had to exercise great tact to retain the support of both proslavery and antislavery factions. Another office was opened at Quindaro, although Stebbins at first considered by-passing the town. Between Quindaro and Leavenworth, however, it is unlikely that any office was opened at that time.[11]

Poles were up in Leavenworth before the wire was up in Kansas City, and on New Year's Day, 1859, it was announced that "in the course of a fortnight, the line will be completed." An office under the management of Agent Drake was located at the corner of Main and Delaware near the levee. The wire came through in January and on the 25th of the month was connected to the Leavenworth office.[12] A few days later, on the evening of Saturday, February 5, Drake sent his first long-distance message to New York City. The circuit was so constructed that the principal cities in between received the message simultaneously and joined in the celebration of Kansas' formal telegraphic birth.[13]

The military authorities at Ft. Leavenworth realized immediately the line's strategic value. The actual order issued by the commander of the Department of the West, permitting the line to be built north from Leavenworth proper across the reservation to Atchison, is missing, but it is known that the fort used the line to send and receive messages and that other similar utilities were in time allowed to enter the reservation. Lacking information to the contrary, we may conclude that Stebbins pushed his line through the fort along the riverbank right-of-way later used by the Leavenworth, Atchison & Northwestern and Missouri Pacific railroads.[14]

Between the northern edge of the fort and Atchison only Kicka-

11. Kansas City *Daily Western Journal of Commerce*, December 19, 21, 1858; *Weekly Western Argus*, Wyandotte, January 15, 1859; Stebbins to Gray, *loc. cit.*; Otis B. Gunn, *New Map and Hand-Book of Kansas & the Gold Mines* (Pittsburgh, 1859), p. 23.

12. Leavenworth *Weekly Times*, January 1, 1859; Martha B. Caldwell, compiler, *Annals of Shawnee Methodist Mission and Indian Manual Labor School* (Topeka, 1939), p. 105; W. M. Paxton, *Annals of Platte County, Missouri . . . to 1897* . . . (Kansas City, 1897), p. 274; Daniel W. Wilder, *The Annals of Kansas* (Topeka, 1875), p. 198.

13. *Daily Missouri Democrat*, St. Louis, February 10, 1859; Kansas City *Daily Western Journal of Commerce*, February 9, 1859; St. Louis *Daily Morning Herald*, February 8, 1859.

14. Elvid Hunt, *History of Fort Leavenworth 1827-1927* (Fort Leavenworth, 1926), pp. 130, 160, 252, 253; *U. S. Military Reservations, National Cemeteries and Military Parks* (Washington, D. C., 1916), p. 135.

poo was large enough to warrant a telegraph office, and it does not appear that the town either was offered or accepted one. The people of Atchison, however, heard directly from Stebbins. He wrote to John F. Tracy in April, 1859, requesting that Atchison subscribe $1,500 in stock to guarantee an office on the line. Stebbins estimated that he could complete the Atchison-Leavenworth connection in six weeks—the towns were only 21 miles apart—and stated that his line was already paying eight to ten per cent dividends. Robert C. Clowry, recently promoted to the Leavenworth superintendency, was to handle subscriptions.[15]

Subscribers in Atchison knew that the line through Leavenworth was a success and that Stebbins not only intended to build to St. Joseph, but contemplated sending a branch line from Leavenworth to Ft. Riley. They subscribed the $1,500 in stock requested and he pushed ahead with the line, so that by July 30 he had poles standing in the streets of Atchison. Tracy opened an office on the south side of Commercial street, between Levee and Second, and was ready for business by mid-August. The wire was connected on Monday August 8, and the first message, sent by the mayor to Leavenworth and St. Louis, went over the wires one week later. The editor of the Atchison *Union* telegraphed St. Louis: "We are indebted to the triple alliance of labor, capital and science for the final success of this great enterprise. We will now hand to you important news from Salt Lake one day earlier than heretofore, via Leavenworth." Atchison took pride in the fact it was then 14 miles farther west than any telegraph station east of the Rockies.[16]

North of Atchison there were two possible routes to St. Joseph. The line could cross the Missouri river to the east bank and proceed overland along the right-of-way of the Atchison-St. Joseph railroad, or it could be built along the west bank to Elwood opposite St. Joseph. Stebbins decided to follow the west bank through Doniphan to Elwood, and immediately set crews to work to complete the connection.[17]

15. *Daily Missouri Republican*, St. Louis, March 8, 1859; *Freedom's Champion*, Atchison, May 14, 1859.
16. *Daily Missouri Democrat*, February 10, 1859; *Freedom's Champion*, July 30, August 13, 20, 1859; Sutherland & McEvoy's *Atchison City Directory . . ., 1859-60* (St. Louis, n. d.), p. 77; A. T. Andreas and W. G. Cutler, *History of the State of Kansas* (Chicago, 1883), p. 377. Atchison, however, was not farther west than any other station east of the Rockies. In 1858 a telegraph line was completed between Houston and Galveston, Tex., and Houston is slightly west of Atchison.—See Frank W. Johnson, *A History of Texas and Texans* (Chicago and New York, 1914), v. 1. For the quote see *Daily Missouri Republican*, St. Louis, August 16, 1859.
17. *The Kansas Weekly Press*, Elwood, October 23, 1858; *The Weekly West*, St. Joseph, January 14, 21, 1860.

In St. Joseph, Edward Creighton, Stebbins' agent, and J. B. Jennings pushed the project; secured enough stock subscriptions to guarantee completion of the link; and arranged for an upstairs office on the corner of Jule and Second. The city council, at least two years earlier, had provided ordinance protection for telegraph poles and wires in St. Joseph. Everything was ready for the arrival of the wires, but how would they cross the Missouri at Elwood? By masts or by underwater cable? In 1858 soundings had been made in the river immediately below Elwood and a "telegraphic plateau" located suitable to an underwater cable. They decided, however, to use masts, at least temporarily, and the crossing was made by mid-March, 1860. The line had been built across 85 miles of countryside since leaving Kansas City, at a cost of about 65 dollars per mile.[18]

Meanwhile, St. Joseph was being connected by another telegraph line across northern Missouri to Hannibal and the extensive Illinois network. On July 4, 1859, that line, built along the right-of-way of the new Hannibal and St. Joseph railroad, was completed and congratulatory messages were exchanged between the two towns. An office was opened under C. H. Spillman in the St. Joseph railroad depot, from which, as one commentator remarked, "the giant young city of the border will be able to throw out Western Lightning and border ruffian news to the whole world." [19]

The major problem of a transcontinental line, however, was not entirely settled. The issue was confused by building projects, some of a fly-by-night nature, projecting a vast trans-Kansas telegraph network, especially into the newly opened Colorado gold country.[20] Nevertheless, out of the confusion—the babble of projects—two possibilities emerged: the line Stebbins was building in 1859 to Fort Smith, Ark., or the one he was building through eastern Kansas territory. Land surveys made by Edward Creighton predisposed Western Union to favor the Kansas route, and by early 1860 it was clear that the transcontinental line would be built by extend-

18. *The Revised Ordinances of the City of Saint Joseph Passed by the City Council, in the Years 1857-58* (St. Joseph, 1858), p. 154; Robert H. Thurston, ed., *Reports of the Commissioners of the United States to the International Exhibition Held at Vienna, 1873* (Washington, D. C., 1876), v. 2, p. 78; *Telegraph Age*, New York, May 16, 1907; Wilder, op. cit., p. 240.
19. *Daily Missouri Republican*, July 8, 1859; Hannibal (Mo.) *Messenger*, June 23, 1859; Liberty (Mo.) *Weekly Tribune*, July 15, 1859. For the quote see *The Central City Brunswicker*, Brunswick, Mo., July 20, 1859. See, also, Ben Hur Wilson, "From Coast to Coast," *The Palimpsest*, Iowa City, v. 7 (August, 1926), p. 235.
20. For examples of the acts of incorporation granted in Kansas see: *Private Laws of the Territory of Kansas, Passed at the Fifth Session of the Legislative Assembly . . . 1859 . . .* (Lawrence, 1859), pp. 77-80, and *Private Laws of the Territory of Kansas, Passed at the Special Session of the Legislative Assembly . . . 1860 . . .* (n. p., n. d.), pp. 428-432.

ing the Kansas City-St. Joseph section.[21] To further facilitate construction, Western Union, on January 7, 1860, secured from the Missouri legislature the incorporation of the Missouri and Western Telegraph Company—Stebbins was one incorporator—consolidating Western Union's control of the lower Missouri valley.[22]

Stebbins and Clowry extended their line from St. Joseph through Brownville and Nebraska City to Omaha. The connection was completed by September 5, 1860. The builders then pushed west, while, within Kansas, 42 operators kept the circuits open and the wires humming with news.[23] Messages to points east cost at least 60 cents from Leavenworth; at least one dollar from St. Joseph.[24] A few customers complained that the charges were exorbitant, and at times the lines were down from wind or ice, but the construction crews on the plains beyond Omaha were confident they could tie the nation together by a thin wire thread.

Another year, and enough thread would be unwound. Another year, 1861, and the transcontinental line would be finished.

21. John E. Sunder, "Arkansas' First 'Wonder Working Wire,'" *The Arkansas Historical Quarterly*, Van Buren, v. 16, No. 3 (Autumn, 1957), pp. 231-242.
22. J. Thomas Scharf, *History of Saint Louis City and County, From the Earliest Periods to the Present Day* . . . (Philadelphia, 1883), v. 2, p. 1429; *Laws of the State of Missouri* . . . *1859-1860* (Jefferson City, 1860), pp. 189, 190.
23. John W. Clampitt, *Echoes From the Rocky Mountains* . . . (Chicago, New York, San Francisco, 1889), p. 63; Henry M. Porter, *Pencilings of an Early Western Pioneer* (Denver, 1929), pp. 10-15; Joseph C. G. Kennedy, compiler, *Population of the United States in 1860* . . . (Washington, D. C., 1864), p. 187.
24. Tal. P. Shaffner, *The Telegraph Manual* . . . (New York, London, Berlin, Paris, 1859), p. 759; *Congressional Globe*, 36 Cong., 1 Sess. (1859-1860), pt. 3, p. 2252.

The Letters of the Rev. Samuel Young Lum, Pioneer Kansas Missionary, 1854-1858

Edited by EMORY LINDQUIST

I. INTRODUCTION

WHEN the Rev. Samuel Young Lum arrived in Kansas in September, 1854, he initiated a career of genuine dedication to his calling and the welfare of Kansas. He was born in New Providence, N. J., on May 6, 1821. In 1842 he entered the preparatory department of Oberlin College and was enrolled in the regular college course during the next two academic years, but did not complete the degree. He was a student at Union Theological Seminary, New York, 1845 to 1848. He went to California in 1849 and spent somewhat more than a year traveling in that area and in Mexico.

Upon returning from the Far West, Lum was ordained as pastor of the Congregational church in Middleton, N. Y., on November 19, 1851. He served that church until 1854. On April 21, 1852, he married Caroline Keep of Madison, N. J. In 1854 the 33-year-old clergyman was commissioned for service in Kansas by the American Home Missionary Society. The Lums arrived in Kansas about the same time as the second party which was sent out under the auspices of the New England Emigrant Aid Company. This group reached Kansas City, Mo., on September 6. Lum became closely identified with the party and was a member of the "Lawrence Association."

Lum conducted the first service in Lawrence on October 1, 1854. On October 15 the Plymouth Congregational Church of Lawrence was organized. The first services were held in the famous Pioneer Boarding House, or "hay tent," which was owned by the Emigrant Aid Company. He entered into his field of service with energy and enthusiasm. Lum preached his first sermon in Topeka in December, 1854; he was largely responsible for organizing the Free Congregational Church of Topeka in Constitution Hall in July, 1856.

In June, 1857, when the First Church of Christ in Wabaunsee was organized, Lum preached the sermon. He was active in the

DR. EMORY KEMPTON LINDQUIST, Rhodes scholar and former president of Bethany College, is dean of the faculties of the University of Wichita. He is author of *Smoky Valley People: A History of Lindsborg, Kansas* (1953), and numerous magazine articles relating to the history of this region.

(39)

organization of the General Association of Congregational Ministers and Churches of Kansas in April, 1857, although it is possible that an earlier meeting was held in his house in August, 1855. He resigned as pastor of the Plymouth Congregational Church of Lawrence in 1857 and was appointed the first Kansas superintendent of the American Home Missionary Society. He held this position until 1861, when he became pastor of the Congregational church at Rehobeth, Mass.

Lum returned to Kansas in 1869 as agent for the American Bible Society, a position he held until 1874, when he became pastor of a church at Mannsville, N. Y. He subsequently held pastorates in other places in New York and Connecticut. His last residence was at Rutherford, N. J., where he died on October 1, 1895, as a result of an accident at a railroad crossing near his home.[1]

Lum's letters in this collection were addressed, with but one exception, to the American Home Missionary Society, which was founded on May 10, 1826, in New York. The Congregationalists and the Presbyterians were the principal supporters of the society.[2] The Rev. Milton Badger was the senior secretary of the society. He was assisted by the Rev. David B. Coe and the Rev. Daniel P. Noyes. The offices of the society were at Bible House, Astor Place, New York City.

Lum was a keen observer of men and events in Kansas. Although he served principally at Lawrence, he traveled widely in Kansas, transmitting detailed letters and reports to the officials of the American Home Missionary Society.

II. THE LETTERS,[3] OCTOBER, 1854-DECEMBER, 1855

LAWRENCE, K. T.
October, 1854

To THE EDITORS, *The Home Missionary* [4]

When I arrived in Kansas, I found myself with little more than enough to support my family for a week, after all the expenses of getting here had been met. I knew not what to do. In this emergency, Mr. Pomeroy, Agent of the Emigrant Aid Company,

---

1. A sketch of the life of the Rev. S. Y. Lum by the Rev. Richard Cordley, Lum's successor as pastor of the Plymouth Congregational Church of Lawrence, is found in the *Minutes of the General Association of Congregational Ministers and Churches of Kansas*, Forty-Second Annual Session, Lawrence, Kansas, May 7-11, 1896, pp. 33, 34. Martha Oseniak, Union Theological Seminary, New York, and Donald M. Love, Oberlin College, Oberlin, Ohio, supplied helpful biographical information.

2. The United Domestic Missionary Society of New York, founded in May, 1822, merged with the American Home Missionary Society on May 10, 1826. The Presbyterian, Dutch Reformed, and Associate Reformed Churches were the leaders in the United Missionary Society.—Colin Brummitt Goodykoontz, *Home Missions on the American Frontier*

took me by the hand, as a true brother, and from his own pocket lent me the means of defraying expenses—in fact, did all for me that a man in his situation could do.⁵

As you supposed, I have been most busily engaged since my arrival in the Territory. There was no other course left me but with my own hands to prepare a place for my family before winter set in. Of course, none could be rented, for there was little else than the smooth prairie; and as most were engaged in building for themselves, I must do the same for myself.

At this place, which is, no doubt, as yet, the most important in the Territory, there are the most encouraging signs of progress in every direction. Many from the various companies that come on, either locate within the city limits, or secure farms in the immediate vicinity. Until now, within a circuit of five or ten miles there are not far from seven hundred persons, mostly heads of families, the representatives, in all, of little less than three thousand souls, most of whom will be here as early in the spring as possible. The site selected for a city, has many natural and local advantages. It is laid out on an extended scale, embracing about two miles square, and yet, from the rapidity with which lots are being taken for actual improvement, it will soon have few important lots unoccupied.⁶ Many are pledged by the terms on which they accept lots, to place improvements on them to the value of $2,000 to $3,000 each, within one year. If what is now promised be but partially

(Caldwell, Idaho, 1939), pp. 173-178. The late Professor Goodykoontz made a thorough and scholarly study of home missions with special reference to the American Home Missionary Society in the volume referred to above.

3. The original letters are in the splendid American Home Missionary Society collection of Hammond library, Chicago Theological Seminary, unless identified differently and are presented with the kind permission of Harvey Arnold, librarian. All the letters printed below are manuscript items except two which were printed in The Home Missionary, New York, in October, 1854, and December, 1855, and one published in The Independent, New York, December 7, 1854.

4. While this letter appeared in The Home Missionary for January, 1855, its contents indicate conclusively that it was written in October, 1854. A letter to The Independent, New York, under date of October 12, 1854, and published on October 26, 1854, contains much of the same information. The Lum family arrived in Kansas about the same time as the second party of the New England Emigrant Aid Company. This group reached Kansas City, Mo., on September 6, en route to the Wakarusa settlement.—Louise Barry, "The Emigrant Aid Company Parties in 1854," The Kansas Historical Quarterly, Topeka, v. 12 (May, 1943), pp. 129-131. Lum conducted the first service in Lawrence on October 1, 1854, according to a correspondent of the Puritan Recorder.—A. T. Andreas and W. G. Cutler, History of the State of Kansas (Chicago, 1883), p. 314. Lum's letter reproduced here was printed in The Home Missionary, New York, v. 27 (January, 1855), pp. 216-218.

5. S. C. Pomeroy, an agent of the New England Emigrant Aid Company and later a prominent Kansas figure, came to Kansas with Charles Robinson and the second party of emigrants sponsored by the company. See, supra, Footnote 4. The arrival of Pomeroy and his associates at Lawrence is described in Edgar Langsdorf, "S. C. Pomeroy and the New England Emigrant Aid Company, 1854-1858," The Kansas Historical Quarterly, Topeka, v. 7 (August, 1938), p. 231.

6. The organization of "The Lawrence Association" and general background factors dealing with this development are described in James C. Malin, "Emergency Housing in Lawrence, 1854," ibid., v. 21 (Spring, 1954), pp. 36-41.

fulfilled, we shall present city of as rapid growth as, I had almost said, any in California; and I can see no reason why it may not be so.

Of one thing we are certain, that the population, if what is already here be a fair criterion of the whole, will compare favorably with that of any State or Territory in the Union. For firmness of purpose, indomitable courage, and executive talent, they will equal the emigration to California; while in intelligence and moral worth, they will be surpassed by none. A holy purpose has called them to this western world, and they come with all the elements necessary, with God's blessing, for the accomplishment of that purpose. And yet this is at present no easy field for missionary labor. We have, however, succeeded in forming a church of about twenty members, and as soon as eastern certificates are received, it will number at least, thirty; and this again will be doubled, we hope, when all the families come on, since most of our present members are male heads of families.

Those who have as yet united in our church movement, are, for the most part, prominent members of New England churches, men who have been influenced to come here, not mainly from a desire for wealth, but to plant the standard of the cross in this fair land, and to secure all its attendant blessings. It is for this that they have left homes of comfort and posts of honor and usefulness in the East. They are not men of wealth, but they are such as can be relied upon in any emergency that requires wisdom in plan, or firmness of purpose in execution. They are not satisfied with the Sabbath worship simply, but engage with delight and eagerness in all the social duties of religion.

Our ordinary congregation numbers about one hundred. It has been over this at times, and were it not that we have no convenient place for public worship, our numbers, I think, would be considerably increased. For the present, we are compelled to meet in the general sleeping apartment of the Company, a room about 50 by 20 feet, made of poles and thatched with prairie grass.[7] Up to this time the weather has been so pleasant and mild as to render such a place comfortable, so far as temperature is concerned; yet, filled as it is with the baggage of the lodgers, it has little of the sacredness that attaches to the house dedicated especially to the worship of God. Those who come are led, we trust, by a

---

7. An interesting description of the "Pioneer Boarding House" is found in Richard Cordley, *Pioneer Days in Kansas* (New York, 1903), pp. 68, 69.

desire to worship God. In this place we have usually two services on the Sabbath; and, as there are already so many from other societies on the ground, I feel it but courteous to share the services with them. I speak thus, because the colony, in mass meeting, invited me to supply their pulpit for a year, and they feel as though I was "their minister."

In connection with our public worship, there has been a very interesting Bible class formed, of about twenty-five members, many of whom have been actively engaged in the Sabbath schools in the East. From these we expect the material for Sabbath school teachers; and we have taken steps for the organization of a Sabbath school as soon as a sufficient number of children can be collected. How the house we are using will do for worship when the weather becomes colder, we cannot as yet tell; but the proper authorities are making preparations for building a large house for school purposes. In this there will be a lecture room, 55 by 40 feet, which will be used as soon as opened, for church purposes. There will also be a smaller room for prayer and conference meetings.[8]

From this you will see that already a permanent commencement has been effected here; and I doubt not there are other places which, this fall or early in the spring, will afford equal facilities. The *great point* should be, to be on the ground at the *start*. And then, the minister, in all such movements, must be one of the people, capable and willing to bear his full share in all the toil, labor, and privation, necessary in first settlements. The estimation in which he is held with the settlers will vary, as he is thus one of them, or otherwise. I believe that there is more than one settlement now forming, where the right kind of a man would be able immediately to find all that his hands could do. Many parties are still to come; and if of sufficient size, they will form separate settlements and will desire a preacher sympathizing with your Society. Rev. C. E. Blood, of Illinois, is already here, and situated about sixty five miles above here, on the Big Blue.[9] I should be glad to see one or two men here, either this fall, or early in the spring.

Yours truly,
S. Y. LUM.

8. This building had dimensions 20 by 48 feet.—Malin, "Emergency Housing in Lawrence, 1854," *loc. cit.,* p. 42.

9. The Rev. Charles Blood settled at the Juniata crossing, four miles above the junction of the Blue and Kansas rivers in the autumn of 1854. In April, 1855, he preached the first sermon in what is now Manhattan.—Charles M. Correll, *A Century of Congregationalism in Kansas* (Topeka, 1953), pp. 20, 21.

LAWRENCE, K. T. Dec 6th. 1854

REV. MILTON BADGER D. D.

DEAR BROTHER

When last I wrote I promised another communication soon in reference to other positions in the Territory. Since then I have been some considerable distance further up than before & am thus better prepared to write from actual observation. From what I saw, I am disposed to think that there are perhaps two locations, now being made, that will soon prove worthy of the notice of your Society, in fact one of them may need a man immediately. This place is about 25 miles up the Kansas River from Lawrence, is just beginning to be settled by Eastern men.[10] A town is contemplated & soon to be laid out & judging from the manner in which Lawrence has progressed must as it is in similar hands, have just as rapid development. Before a man could be on the field if appointed immediately it will in all probability be in a more advanced state than this place when I came here & I have good reason to suppose I was none too early.

The truth is where eastern men take up a location & give evidence of will and ability to build a town, multitudes from all other sections of the country crowd rapidly on their footsteps, & in most cases, it is but a short time before the whole region, is set off into claims & cabins are rising on every side. From present appearances, the location of which I am now speaking is destined to be the second city in this part of [the Territory] for becoming this it has some decided advantages. I intend to visit there as soon as possible & if I can make the arrangements will preach there on next Sabbath. I am not yet certain that there is a building at all suitable for worship but no doubt one of the same kind as that which we occupy will be soon erected.

I think it highly important that such points as these should be early [entered on] by men from your society. Unless they are thus—they will not long remain unoccupied & perhaps & not always with those who hold the truth as it is in Jesus. I know that we have had various preachers here who have striven at all times

---

10. Lum refers here to the founding of Topeka. The Topeka Association was organized on December 5, 1854, with Cyrus K. Holliday as president. Holliday wrote a letter on December 3 from Lawrence in which he stated that he was "going about 40 miles up the Kansas River to assist in laying out a new town." On December 17 Holliday used Topeka, K. T., as the heading for a letter to his wife. Lum is often associated with the naming of Topeka.—Lela Barnes, ed., "Letters of Cyrus Kurtz Holliday, 1854-1859," *The Kansas Historical Quarterly*, Topeka, v. 6 (August, 1937), pp. 245-247; Fry W. Giles, *Thirty Years in Topeka* (Topeka, 1886), pp. 20-22. The relationship of Holliday to establishing Topeka is discussed in Wallace S. Baldinger, "The Amateur Plans a City," *The Kansas Historical Quarterly*, Topeka, v. 12 (February, 1943), pp. 3-13.

to force themselves upon the people & setting forth the wildest heresies as the truth of God. Unitarians, Christians, Swedenborgians, Universalists have not been idle; their men are already on the ground & openly declare that they will make it "too hot for the orthodoxy." From this it will be seen, that all who have the cardinal truth of the Cross should be most watchful & diligent.

About 55 miles still farther up the Kansas is another settlement, or rather a number of settlements, another town is laid out & there are quite a number of settlers within the area of a few miles & who have the services of Rev. Mr. Blood, from near Springfield, Illinois; he seems a man well adapted to pioneer life & a good man to do the work of a missionary. he told me he had corresponded with some one of the Secretaries. The field which he ocupies must be an important field though not perhaps, destined to as rapid growth as some others in the Territory. There are two or three other points on the river of some importance though not sufficient to merit particular attention as yet. They will be rather a outpost between the leading points. I did not reach Fort Riley but from reports, it is only a military post & it can be reached from the Big Blue where Mr. Blood resides.

From enquiries made in reference to the city of Leavenworth for as yet I have not been able to see it I should think it already quite an important place & not supplied with any one who cooperates with your society. They have occasional services by a Presbyterian Minister from Missouri & at other times by a Methodist local preacher but I cannot speak positively of its necessities.

On the South side of the Wakarusa, the settlers are rapidly filling up the country. At Ureka, the point selected by the New York Emigration [company] there will probably be little done this Winter;—but it would be well to watch the movement early in the Spring, as they intend large things. Still farther south, in the Osage country, many are coming in, & little communities are rising on every side. I shall endeavor to visit that part of the country early in the Spring if Providence permit.

In reference to the character of the emigration as a whole I hardly know what to think—many there are who come here with a noble purpose. They are willing to be martyrs in the cause of Religion & Liberty & yet I am compelled to think that the number of such is small in comparison to those who have some selfish or mercinary end to gain. I must confess that my mind has changed on this subject & I do not think so highly of the aggregate emigration as at first.[11] I find many, perhaps a majority, without any settled moral principles as a basis of action & when once outside the restraints of eastern society, they act out the native depravity of the human heart—profanity & Sabbath desecration are beginning to be fearfully rife & scarcely a Sabbath passes but our ears are compelled to hear the sound of the rifle & axe. . . .

In reference to our own "City" there has [been little change] since I wrote. Our public worship is much interrupted by the cold weather as we have no place much better than the open air. We find our thatch houses but poorly fitted for withstanding the piercing wind that sweeps over these boundless prairies. Our weather is not excessively cold, but the wind is so piercing & the coldest & most windy days of the season have been the Sabbaths. It is designed to construct a suitable building . . . as soon as possible but the first necessity is to provide for the suffering families. A weekly prayer meeting is sustained & considering the circumstances, well sustained. I give up my little room, a little more than 12 feet square for this purpose. There seems in a few at least, an earnest desire to enjoy the social prayer meeting & when we get together, though crowded into a small room & often interrupted by sickly children still we do enjoy the Savior's presence, & from this little circle I trust will go out an influence upon the surrounding elements. May it be as salt to save from moral putrification.

Perhaps you may feel an interest in knowing how many comforts we enjoy here. My own house, which is said to be as comfortable as any—is entirely without a floor or walls, nothing but bare "siding" & that so open as to give us views of the country, almost in any direction.[12] The winds of course take every occasion to visit. . . . One small room we store some things in another in which to perform all the duties attendant upon living & here too bed room, kitchen, sitting room & study etc all at hand. & even this is thought here as doing very well. In most countries the process of settlement has advanced further before the Missionary finds his way there, but here the development will be so rapid that it is necessary they should lead the van & in doing so they must be subjected to all the inconveniences attendant upon settlement.

You desired to know definitely the current expenses of a Mis-

---

11. In October, Lum had written with enthusiasm about the fine qualities of the settlers in Kansas. *Supra*, p. 42.

12. The first frame house erected in Lawrence was owned by Lum.—Malin, "Emergency Housing in Lawrence, 1854," *loc. cit.*, p. 43.

sionary here. These for the present must be rather large. There is but one article of food that is at all reasonable meat is certainly low, ranging from 5 to 10 cents per pound. Everything else is at exaggerated prices flour at 11 to $12 per barrel, corn-meal, $6.50 per barrel, potatoes $2.50 per bushel, apples, in the vicinity of $2.00 per bushel; butter, 35 cents per pound; molasses from 60 to 75 cents a gallon; all other things at this ratio. With almost a certainty of still further advances you can readily understand from this what must be the expenses if it is necessary for me to travel this will greatly increase the expense as at most stopping places, exhorbitant rates are demanded, often as high as at the St. Nicholas in New York, & then horse hire is set at $1.50 a day! When I first arrived in the Territory, I was *compelled* to pay at the rate of $25. a week for the board of my family. This was of short duration in my case, as I soon secured before one week had transpired a place at the Baptist Mission for about what it would have cost me to keep house myself.

I had intended to tell you something of the manner of putting up at night, when we found no stopping place,—how in travelling about the Territory we are often compelled to take the open air, the bare earth with nothing but the "broad blue" above, but I have not time at present. *Will you not send me all the back numbers of the Home Missionary from the date of my commission?* Written of necessity in *haste & confusion.*

Yours fraternally
S. Y. LUM

LAWRENCE, K. T.
Dec. 7th. 1854

TO THE EDITORS OF *The Independent:*[13]

I am sorry that the impression has been received (in various quarters) that you have a regular correspondent in Kanzas, because I begin to feel already the inconvenience of numerous letters of inquiry, questions to be answered through *The Independent,* etc., etc., all of which I could not possibly attend to, and still reserved time and energy for the arduous work that my connection with the Home Missionary Society lays upon me. Your valued correspondent from Iowa, I trust will continue his vigilant watch over this part of his former field. An occasional sheet at irregular intervals is all that can be expected from me.

13. This letter was printed in *The Independent,* New York, January 5, 1855.

Since I wrote, we have been surrounded by scenes of stirring interest.[14] Almost immediately, the sympathizers with slavery, made a bold push to dislodge us from our position here, and openly avowed their determination to drive us from the Territory. As the history of this affair has reached the public through other papers, it is needless to enter into details; sufficient to know that finding a sterness of purpose in Eastern men that they were unaccustomed to meet in such quiet people, they wisely concluded to let us take our time to withdraw—while they, in the meantime kept at a respectable distance. This decided course settled apparently all future contests of this nature, and I think the danger of violence is every day decreasing. Certainly we are on more intimate terms with the opposite party; they holding most of the wooded land, had refused to let the "Yankees" cut timber on any terms, but now they are glad of the privilege of bringing it to the mill *on any terms.* The advantages which they derive from a settlement of this character, begins to be apparent; and they no longer desire to rob themselves of these advantages.

After so long time, and in the face of so many discouragements, we have commenced to make lumber in good earnest. Day and night the music of the first steam engine ever set up in Kanzas Territory, is heard by willing ears, for upon its operations depend many of our comforts for the winter now upon us.[15] Lawrence and the country around it, will soon wear a new aspect, and comfortable dwellings will take the place of the cheerless hovels heretofore erected.

But this is not the only place about to assume importance in this part of the Territory; another location has been selected about twenty-five miles farther up the river, at a most beautiful point, possessing many natural advantages.[16] Eastern men are the projectors, and the country around is fast filling up with such. One object of the location at this particular point, is to check-mate the

14. Lum wrote to the editors of *The Independent* on October 12, 1854, and his letter was printed in the issue for October 26, 1854. Since this letter was of a general character and of only casual interest, it has not been included in this collection.

15. This sawmill was moved to Lawrence from Westport. The New England Emigrant Aid Company had purchased a sawmill at Rochester, N. Y., as early as September 1, 1854, but this project was abandoned as far as Lawrence was concerned because of a series of delays. The Rochester sawmill was operating in Topeka in May, 1855. The company sawmill was operating at Lawrence by about December 1, 1854.—Andreas-Cutler, *op. cit.,* p. 314; Giles, *op. cit.,* pp. 34, 35. The first pamphlet of the Emigrant Aid Company entitled "Organization, Objects and Plans of Operations . . .," stated that the company would provide a sawmill and other equipment.—Samuel A. Johnson, *The Battle Cry of Freedom; The New England Emigrant Aid Company in the Kansas Crusade* (Lawrence, 1954), p. 61. Prof. James C. Malin discusses housing, materials available, skills of mechanics, etc., in the interesting article "Housing Experiments in the Lawrence Community, 1854," *The Kansas Historical Quarterly,* v. 21 (Summer, 1954), pp. 95-121.

16. Lum refers to the founding of Topeka. See Footnote 10.

operations of a few Southerners, who are attempting to draw around them a community of propagandists, five miles lower down on the river; and the indications are that the Eastern men will be successful.[17]

The company from New York were rather late in their arrival to accomplish much this fall, though they hope for great things next year.[18] It is much to be regretted that a more substantial commencement could not have been effected this season—as the delay gives courage to those waiting and anxious to bring in their slaves. But I trust that New York capitalists will not be behind in furnishing what is necessary for the complete triumph of their undertaking. Certainly if the New England enterprise may be taken as a criterion, they need not fear in reference to the safety of the investment.

Since I have been in this country I have often wished that Eastern men could see the necessity of sacrificing (no, I don't mean sacrificing for it would be returned in large dividends, but lending) money as well as men in the great and momentous work of making Kansas a free State. In the North and East it is not looked upon as the test question in reference to slavery extension, or, if thus looked upon, it is not regarded as so soon to be decided. With all thinking men here, it is seen in a far different light.

All interested parties in Missouri look upon this struggle as the life or death struggle of their "peculiar institution." In accordance with this view, they are organizing secret societies to resist the dreaded issue; such societies, headed by men in high places, and reaching far into other Southern States, speak volumes in reference to the deep feeling that exists; they are pulses that tell of the feverish excitement within. True, it has often been said that the slaveholders of Missouri are but a small part of the aggregate number of inhabitants, and little to be feared; yet, generally, they are men of property and influence, and seem to be able to lead the poor and ignorant class directly in opposition to their own interests. It is astonishing what deep-seated hatred they have succeeded in infusing into the latter class, against all whom they can brand with the name "Yankee."

17. Tecumseh was located as a townsite during the spring and summer of 1854. When the first session of the territorial legislature met at Shawnee in July, 1855, Tecumseh was designated as a permanent county seat of Shawnee county. Tecumseh lost the territorial capitol to Lecompton.—Andreas-Cutler, op. cit., p. 533.
18. A party from New York under the auspices of the New York League arrived in Kansas City, Mo., on October 15, 1854, en route to Kansas. One group settled at Osawatomie.—Johnson, op. cit., p. 82; D. W. Wilder, The Annals of Kansas (Topeka, 1886), p. 50.

My mind has been led in this direction by the results of the recent election. Nothing has been more common in Eastern papers of *a certain class,* than the declaration that "Kanzas was safe, it was not adapted by soil, climate, etc., for slave-labor;" and others *who* have been earnest to secure the result, have allowed themselves to be deceived with the idea that it has already been attained. Many even of the most enthusiastic advocates of the recent movement from the North, begin to feel as though having fought *through* the battle, they might sit down and exult over the victory; but so do not we feel who are still in the midst of the struggle; and we think, when the fact that 2,200 Pro-slavery votes were polled against less than 600 for Freedom, comes to be generally known, it will go far to set the true state of things before the country.

It is true that Gen. Whitefield, representing the ultra South movement, has been elected to a seat at Washington, as delegate from Kansas. Whether he will retain that seat uncontested, is doubtful. There is evidence the most conclusive, that multitudes voting for him had no more right to vote than citizens now resident in New York had for his opponent, and there can be little doubt but that the election been confined to legal voters simply, the Free-Soil vote would have been the heaviest. But it could not be thus confined; the safeguards thrown around the ballot-box were not sufficient, and then force was at hand to control all efforts to sustain right.[19]

In a little settlement, about 7 miles from this place, where, it was a well-known fact, that there were only 60 *voters,* 260 *votes were cast.* In another, 700 illegal votes were known to be cast. They came upon the weakest points, in such numbers as to overbear all opposition. For days before the election they crowded by hundreds the roads leading to the various districts, always carrying with them a liberal supply of bad whiskey. Maddened by its influence, they were ready for any dishonorable or violent course. In the smaller districts, they could carry it all as they pleased, and they were even known to compel suspected persons to open their votes before casting them; and if not what they considered right, they were thrown out and the offerer threatened with violence. Acts similar to this, and even more atrocious, were the order of the day in most districts; and as might have been expected, two men were shot within a short distance from here. I do not think the annals of our country will furnish another instance of such high-minded mockery of the right of suffrage.

19. The first election for a delegate to congress from the Kansas territory was held on November 29, 1854. J. W. Whitfield, the Proslavery candidate, was elected, polling 2,258 votes out of a total of 2,833.—Wilder, *op. cit.,* pp. 52, 53.

One more fact has just at this moment come to hand; in one of the more important districts, a ring of armed men was formed around the ballot-box, and every man was compelled to pass their ordeal before voting. It would seem that when such things could be proved, it were sufficient evidence to warrant the order for a new election, but the Governor *thought differently.* . . .

But I would say a word of our church prospects. We have formed a church, now composed of about twenty male heads of families. When the families arrive they will add greatly to our numbers, so that we hope soon to have an efficient church. At least we greatly need the influence of such a church in holding in check the passions of men. The sooner we can surround ourselves with the safeguards that the youth among us have left behind, the sooner shall we present a society similar to that at the East. A few of our number spend an hour on Wednesday evening of each week, in a social prayer-meeting; and of all our meetings, this is the one most rich in blessing; we not only get nearer to our common Father, but we get nearer to each other's hearts, and feel an interest in each other that nothing else can awaken. After being deprived so long of this high privilege, it is deeply felt as the richest of all blessings.

Our public worship is somewhat interrupted by the cold weather; not that we have much severe cold; yet we have no way of defending ourselves from it. Our church, made of thatch, will do very well in mild weather, but when the winds sweep in from the prairies in all their violence, it is far different. On such occasions our audience is rather thin. . . .

In reference to reception-houses, we are not provided as well as an eastern city would be, yet all who are *reasonable* can be tolerably accomodated until they can supply themselves. The day of suffering is, we trust, mostly past.

Yours, etc.,

S. Y. LUM.

LAWRENCE, K. T. DEC. 23, 1854

SECRETARIES H. M. SOCIETY
DEAR BRETHREN

In making out the report of my first quarter's labor in this Territory, I feel that I have but little in addition to what I have already communicated. My time has of necessity been so much occupied with the preparation for the comfort of my family that I feel little *comparatively* has been accomplished; and yet, in the light of eternity—I trust, it will appear, that my first three months in the service of your Society, has not been altogether fruitless of good. Few of those who are not on the ground can appreciate the disadvantages in the midst of which we have been compelled to labor. In most respects it is hardly likely that any which follow will be like the past.

It is but a little more than four months since the first wave of emigration began to swell along the border of this then unknown Territory. Since then, wave has followed wave, with increasing rapidity & volume, until the desolate has become inhabited, & the unknown has become pretty thoroughly discovered. Late as was the season when the majority reached here, & actually destitute, as we then were of anything like protection from the approaching winter, there was apparently but one thought prevalent in all minds & all our energies were taxed in giving a physical form to that one thought—. We must have buildings or perish & buildings have arisen one after another until at this one point they number over eighty & accomodate a population of about 500.[20] Scarcely another example of such rapid growth can be found, even in California—. & though here it is undoubtedly the most rapid, yet all over the Territory is to be found abundant proofs of the interest which is taken in the settlement of Kansas.

In the midst of the excitement which such a state of things naturally produces, it is not wonderful that the majority should feel little interest in spiritual things, time & thought were wholly absorbed in what appeared an immediate & absolute necessity.— Considering these circumstances, I have been most pleased to find so large a number actuated by unwavering principles, so many ready to cooperate in every work likely to advance the interests of truth & righteousness. Yet that number is not yet by far so large as I at first supposed. The large majority of all who come to the Territory, so far as I have the means of judging, are actuated solely by selfish or mercenary motives. Many such are the open enemies of the dearest doctrines of the Cross, & declare themselves determined to wage war against the introduction of "Orthodox sentiments."

In my intercourse with this community, I have been pained to find not a few who have been professors of religion in Eastern Churches, openly avow themselves the enemies of the truths they

---

20. A contemporary, John Doy, wrote on December 1, 1854, that on that date 33 houses had been built in Lawrence.—Malin, "Emergency Housing in Lawrence, 1854," *loc. cit.*, p. 45. The *Herald of Freedom,* as cited by Professor Malin, reported on January 13, 1855, that "three months ago there were no residences here other than tents; now there are over ninety in the city limits, and new ones added daily."—Malin, "Housing Experiments in the Lawrence Community, 1855," *loc. cit.*, p. 107.

once espoused, trampling on the Sabbath, & ridiculing sacred things. On the other hand, I find a goodly number of true spirits, who have joyfully sacrificed the comforts of eastern homes, & the communion of eastern Christians, for the rescue & salvation of Kansas & here they maintain a character such as might be expected from such principles. They are truly sources of encouragement to which the missionary can go when depressed in view of temporal difficulty, or discouraged at the manyfold trials his field present. The weekly prayer meetings & we have two are made doubly precious from the presence & earnest prayers of such spirits. It is in these praying circles, & the *dear Savior* whom we are sure to meet there, that we place our hope in reference to a favorable issue in the times of conflict that now surround us.

As I stated in a former letter there is already a liberal supply of missionaries from the various societies at this point, but two that I know of have gone to another part of the Territory— one of these a Baptist Missionary & the other Rev. Mr. Blood, while no less than five Missionaries besides myself remain at this point. These are from the Baptist Home M. So. (they have two in the Territory) the American M. Ass.— the United Brethren M. Ass. & the Methodist Episcopal— beside these, though not *openly* "missionaries" there are two from the Christian denomination, one from the Swedenborgian, & one or two more of the Methodist etc. While this is so, yet I do not feel called to give up this important point & seek another. I was first on the ground & was unanimously chosen to supply the place for a year. Some of these whom I have noticed are excellent brethren & such as I would feel confidence in as fellow laborers; yet I think the Committee would justify me in not yielding the field, however much it might be desired by others especially as my people desire I should stay.

This is one reason why I have as yet devoted nearly all my time to this point. As it becomes necessary from the urgency of certain parties, that something should be done, & as I desired an opportunity to enter another very important opening, about 25 miles above here, I have given up to the others, every alternate Sabbath, —that is for the present.[21] I find in my new field a few professing Christians, mostly connected with the New England Cong. Chs. If the place has the rapid growth that is expected in the Spring it will not be many months ere it will be expedient to form another

---

21. Lum makes reference here to his ministry at Topeka. *See* his letter of December 6, 1854, *supra*, p. 44. Lum conducted services ferquently in Topeka. On December 31, 1854, Cyrus K. Holliday described a visit by Lum.—Barnes, *loc. cit.,* pp. 249, 250.

church at that point; but these points are so far distant from each other that it will be a difficult matter for one man fully to attend to the duties thus devolving upon him; especially will this be true when the tide of emigration opens next season. This point will alone demand the entire energies of one and I have some hope that it will be able to do something for the support of a Mission— though much cannot be expected, until we begin to be producers instead of consumers.

I preached at this new point last Sabbath to about 25 as attentive listeners as I ever addressed, & was happy in being the first to declare the truth as it was in Jesus, upon a spot where thousands will yet congregate in the worship of God. . . . Our sanctuary was a small log house of Indian construction, formerly used for a dance house, but now as a store room. It is entirely without windows or means of light except the crevices left when building. Yet even here, in a room scarcely tententable by our poorer families, East, & in almost total darkness, we had a most delightful season of communion with each other, & with our Heavenly Father; & I had the satisfaction of feeling that a good impression had been made upon some careless minds. I find that external circumstances have little to do with our real enjoyment. If the heart only be right, it is possible to put up with privations & that without feeling discomfort which would be thought in our former homes. . . .

It is my opinion that there are few countries more healthy than this. Compared with the exposure there is little sickness but this is admitted on all hands to be a very favorable season. Were it not so, there must be much suffering. . . .

Yours fraternally,
SAMUEL Y. LUM.

LAWRENCE, KANSAS TERRITORY Feby 28th 1855
REV. DAVID B. COE
DEAR BROTHER

Not being acquainted with the usual form of filling out a report such as is expected from me at the present time, I have adopted the following:

1. The Church is called the Plymouth Congregational Church of Lawrence, K. T.[22] We are not yet divided into counties.

2. During that part of the year, over which my commission extends, I have had but two regular preaching places, one at Law-

---

22. The Plymouth Congregational Church of Lawrence was organized on October 15, 1854, under the leadership of Lum.—Richard Cordley, *A History of Lawrence, Kansas* (Lawrence, 1895), p. 17.

rence & the other at Topeka, 25 miles further up the river. The last has been a regular point for a little less than three months. I have preached at one other place, but only occasionally.

3. The Church is composed of 14 members, 9 male and 5 female. Besides these there is an equal number whom we confidently expect, at as early a day as possible, as soon, as they can get their letters from the East. Communication with the East is so much interrupted, from some cause, that letters of all kinds are often detained for more than a month on passage. Some are waiting for their friends to bring on their letters in the Spring.

4. The attendance during the past winter has been very much under the control of the weather. Our house of worship has not been such as to protect us from the inclemency of the weather, when the cold was most severe; & from this cause at times we have been compelled, to suspend public worship, & meet in smaller circles in private rooms. This has been a serious drawback upon our little Society. When the weather has been at all fitting, there has been an average attendance of about 60 at Lawrence, though it has often doubled that number. At Topeka we have had an average of 20 in attendance, with a continual increase, and prospects of a rapid increase in the Spring. As these stations are so far a part & as there is every prospect of a rapid growth, it seems mighty important that another man should be on the ground as early as possible in the Spring. Either one of these [posts] must require the full energies of a missionary and unless thus occupied, there is reason to fear that they will be taken up by those whose object is to destroy the truth as it is in Jesus. In view of these facts the inhabitants are very anxious that the right kind of a man should be sent out by your society.

5. As yet, it is not my privilege to report any cases of conversion. The mind of the community has been kept in a continual state of intense excitement on subjects connected with land claims, the election, & slavery, that there seemed little room for subjects not so immediately connected with these temporal interests. At times, I have almost thought that the church was about to be engulfed in the wild vortex of excitement. It has proved a severe test of Christian Character. In the midst of such circumstances I have been pleased to find so many, not included in the church, who were thoughtful in reference to a future state. Never have I, in the East, preached to congregations more deeply interested, so far as appearances are an indication. I have found also, in my

private intercourse with the people, a feeling of inquiry, & a tenderness in reference to the subject of heartfelt religion, that has led me to hope that the truth is having its purifying effect.

6. We have had no additions by Profession.

7. The number who have handed in their letters, is 15; of this number, one has already left us, to join, as we confidently hope, the "Church triumphant." Mr. Lewis L. Litchfield, after a protracted and painful illness, which he bore with true Christian resignation, died two weeks since, triumphing in God. . . . To die battling for the truth in Kansas, seemed a short way to the crown; & as we reviewed the scene, we felt new courage for the conflict before us, wishing only to fall in complete armor.

8. Our Sabbath school numbers 32, & the Bible Class 25. The former includes nearly all the children of the proper age in the vicinity. . . .

9. But one church has as yet been organized, that is the one at this place. Another will soon be demanded at Topeka, where there are a number of families who sympathize with evangelical truth, & much desire a church & a preacher. . . . I have also received an invitation from persons at Osawattomie, a town at the junction of the Osage and Potawatomie rivers, to come & organize them into a church. There are 12 families all of whom desire a Cong. Chh. formed among them. This is about 50 miles south of this point.

10. Our contributions have, of course, been small. Most of our members are of the poorer class, & find all they can do to meet current expenses. Yet they intend commencing in the spring to do what they are able for my support. The amount depends entirely upon the character of the Spring emigration—I hope it will be conciderable. At the Monthly Concert which was instituted at as early a day as possible the contributions have amount to $2.53— so small that no disposition has as yet been made of it. The sum would have been much larger were it not that most of our prominent men have been absent during the Winter. Some of them have returned to the states for their families, others have been absent on business. Thus the responsibility has devolved upon the young men of the Church & in many ways have I found them of valuable service.

During most of the Winter we have not been at all protected in our Public Worship but about 2 weeks since a hall 20 by 30 feet was completed, & placed at our disposal. This though rough in appearance is so much in advance of what we had occupied up to that time, that we feel quite satisfied for the present though it will barely hold all who sometimes turn out. We hope that something will be done soon at the East to aid us in the erection of a church edifice. No doubt this would aid materially in attracting here the right kind of persons & thus the more surely & speedily build up a self-sustaining & efficient church.

I find that when I wrote last I had not become fully acquainted with all classes of men I had to come in contact with out here & the more of experience [?] I have on this subject, the more am I led to believe that, in many respects, there are few fields of labor more difficult of cultivation than this. All kinds of radical ideas are pretty fully represented here, and I have almost thought, at times, that all this class of persons from the entire Union, are flowing in, in hopes of realizing their wildest schemes. Time after time, they have made their boast that they would crowd orthodoxy out of Kansas. Yet I trust, in this they will be disappointed; there is no kind of misrepresentation or misstatement, to which they have not already resorted, to shake, if possible, the confidence of the community in those who adhere to the truth. Their influence with candid men is constantly decreasing.

I trust that there will be soon large numbers of true men join us who will help to stay the flood of iniquity & infidelity that is threatening. Especially is it important that the churches, who feel any interest in the development of the truth in Kansas, should manifest that interest in nobly sustaining those Societies that are to be the instruments, under God, of making this new & beautiful territory all that our hearts could desire. I do most sincerely hope that the church, North and East, will speedily furnish your Society with the means of sending a large reinforcement to this field at the earliest possible moment. Would that they could see, as we on the ground see, the important issues that are pending & so soon to be settled for the truth or otherwise. If the advocates of a free Gospel, do not occupy the position *it will not therefore, be left unoccupied,* as is already clearly indicated. . . .

Respectfully yours
S. Y. LUM

LAWRENCE KANSAS TERRITORY
April, 1855

DEAR BROTHER COE

My report for the quarter ending March 23 is as you see, some days behind its proper time. circumstances beyond my control have delayed my writing until the present time & until within the last few days but little has occurred to give interest to my correspondence. All has been excitement with reference to our coming election.[23] This one subject seemed to assume in most minds more importance than all others. In this district, we were particularly interested, from the fact that we were expecting a large delegation from Mo. to assist us in choosing a legislature.

The excitement pervaded all minds, & could be seen nowhere more clearly than in the lessened number at our religious meetings. Almost every thought was concentrated on the issue just before us & every effort put forth to meet that issue. If such times of trial lead the church *to God* as their only resource, they will tend to a rapid Christian growth; but if, as was too much the case here, they seek aid from human wisdom alone, they are the most disastrous occurrences that can befall any Christian community. Thus I do not feel that the few weeks past have secured much in a right direction.

The election has passed & passed in such a manner as to render it almost certain that it will be declared void, & another one ordered, which will in all probability, be more exciting & violent than the last. It has been estimated from the best information that can be gathered, that there was not less than 5000 persons, from Missouri & other Southern States in the Territory on the day of election & here for the sole purpose of *voting* after which they would return to their homes, until another similar case should call them here. The polls at Lawrence were surrounded at an early hour by about 700 of these visitors, prepared to carry every thing before them for the legal voters in the district do not amount to 400. in other districts near, the proportion of transient voters was even much greater; & there is no kind of abuse or violence which they are not ready to offer to all promiscuously, who come from the North or East.

---

23. The election, which resulted in the "Bogus" legislature, was held on March 30, 1855. The election returns by districts are listed in Wilder, *op. cit.*, pp. 59-61. Prof. James C. Malin points out that "according to the census taken preceding the election, settlers of slave state origin were present in a clear majority. Although the facts are not available to provide proof one way or another, the reasonable presumption is that the so-called Proslavery party could have carried the election decisively. Upon that basis, the action of Missourians in invading Kansas and voting illegally, was an inexcusable blunder."—James C. Malin, "Judge Lecompte and the 'Sack of Lawrence,' May 21, 1856," *The Kansas Historical Quarterly*, Topeka, v. 20 (August, 1953), p. 466.

What is to be the result of these things if they continue, is more than human eye can foresee. One thing is certain, they check very much the progress of true Christianity. Should the emigration of the present season be large, it will do much to controll these things; especially, will it be so, if it be exactly the right kind. Oh that the churches East, would send us hosts of their tried & faithful men, men who would stand firm trusting in the Lord of hosts even amid the wildest waves of excitement. Such are the men for Kansas! those whom neither fear nor a bribe can move from their steadfastness! There is sterling work to be done, not the least of which is to controll the outbreaking passions of men, on both sides of the great question that so deeply agitates us. But there are other dangers that await the comers to this new Territory, than those which grow out of the political agitation. Every month's residence here develops this fact more fully.

The circumstances under which mind is thrown in this wild frontier life, for it can be called nothing else as yet, engenders a recklessness, & freedom from restraint, that too often, prove fatal to the principles, as well as the practices of a home society & it is not too much to say, that we have the material, for either the worst, or the best, state of society in our country. There are surely enough influences at work, unless counteracted by the Infinite One through the efforts of His church to overthrow any society.

The first waves of eastern emigration begin to be felt here, & they bear to us some choice spirits.[24] From present appearances, I think we may hope for a higher state of character in some respects, than that which came last Fall. A greater proportion seem earnest Christians & from the interest, with which they enter into our social gatherings for prayer, they encourage the hope of eminent usefulness in our midst. As the families move in the Sabbath school is rapidly increasing, & the Bible Class receives new accessions & awakens a deeper interest.

But the emigration brings with it some disadvantages. We have been compelled to give up our comfortable place of worship to be fitted up as a boarding house & we are again driven to the thatch house, which will soon also be filled with the coming. Would that some liberal hands might be opened to give us a permanent place of worship! Nothing could do more to aid the missionary in his work for while thus driven from place to place it is very difficult to secure a permanent audience. S. Y. LUM.

24. Three parties left for Kansas during March, 1855, under the auspices of the New England Emigrant Aid Company.—Louise Barry, "The New England Emigrant Aid Company Parties of 1855," *ibid.*, v. 12 (August, 1943), pp. 227-248.

LAWRENCE, K. T. JUNE 23rd/55

DEAR BRO. COE.

During the quarter that has just passed, I had intended to have written another communication but we have been thrown into such circumstances as to render it impossible. My labors have never been more excessive & burdensome than for a few months past, while at the same time I have not had the same amount of physical energy as heretofore to bring to the issue.

We have been realizing some of the effects of the exposure to which most of us were subjected last Winter: & considering the circumstances, it would have been wonderful had there been no more than an ordinary amount of disease. Exposure & bad diet had prepared the way for disease & death; & yet they have not been as prevalent as would have been expected, in any ordinary climate.

My own family have not been exempt from suffering. Early in the spring, we were called to part with one of our dear children. The anxiety & watching necessary, added to the causes already noticed, prostrated nearly every member of my family. I began to fear I should be left alone & we began to fear that there was little romance in pioneer life, as we were experiencing it. It required not a little faith to toil on, under such circumstances, with bad health & in many ways destitute of the common comforts of life. Yet it was a position of usefulness & promise, & trusting in God, we were determined to go forward, leaving health, & life even, in his hands.

God has been better to us than our fears, & in love has kept us while in the midst of sickness & danger. But not a few have died around us, & I have been called to attend from 3 to 4 funerals a week. Almost all of this kind of work devolved upon me, adding quite materially to my other labors, & often preventing me from fulfilling my regular appointments.

Thus it is true that during the past three months my station at Topeka has been left almost entirely to other hands. I had hoped, that before I was compelled to give it up, a man would have been designated for that field by your Soc, but as most of my time is demanded here, & as there are several places where congregations could be collected near at hand & where they are very desirous to have preaching, I have thought best to withdraw from that field, & I have done so with not a little reluctance. Could I have spent my whole time there, or could some one from your Society have gone in early Spring, there might now have been a strong organization—strong for this Territory. I hope yet someone may arrive in time to gather the scattering elements, before they are all absorbed by denominations teaching few if any of the essential doctrines of the Cross.[25] A strong effort has been made there, as well as here, to produce an union of all denominations upon a basis having no creed & no discipline. By such means, those who ignore Christ's divinity, the need of regeneration, &c. &c., hoped to get a controling influence. But thus far the plan has not succeeded. The true children of God stand aloof from such schemes, & are anxious to have the lines between the church & the world distinctly drawn & the character of Christianity elevated rather than lowered.

Since my last report 3 more Sabbath schools have been formed in connection with the society with which I labor. In these schools, there are about 80 children regularly collected to learn the way of life. Nothing gives more hope in reference to the future of Kansas, than the fact that many of the children are learning the truths of God's Word in the Sabbath school. Many of these children too are from parts of the Western states where they never heard of the Sabbath School & were in darkness almost heathenish.

The spring emigration has brought with it some valuable accessions to our little society, & we feel that we have a steady though not as rapid a growth as we expected.[26] There is also a deeper interest manifested among those who have been here during the Winter, & who have scarcely attended divine worship so that on every hand there is ground for encouragement.

There is nothing we want next to the blessing of God more than a place of worship that we can have the control of & call our own. The hall where we meet is not uncomfortable, but it is subject to the direction of others for much of the time. There will probably be two churches erected during the present season, one by the Methodist Soc. & the other by the Unitarian Soc. Rev. Mr. Nute has brought on $5000, so it is understood, for the purpose of erecting a Unitarian church though there is no Society formed here as yet.[27]

The very fact of having a comfortable church edifice will give to any Soc. or preacher an influence under the circumstances in

25. The organization of the "Free Congregational Church of Topeka" was completed at Constitution Hall on July 14, 1856. The Rev. Lewis Bodwell, well-known frontier minister, preached his initial sermon in Topeka as the first regularly appointed pastor on October 26, 1856.—Russell K. Hickman, "Lewis Bodwell, Frontier Preacher; The Early Years," *ibid.*, v. 12 (August, 1943), pp. 271, 279.

26. Nine parties had arrived in Kansas under the auspices of the New England Emigrant Aid Company by the time that Lum wrote this letter.—Louise Barry, "The New England Emigrant Aid Company Parties of 1855," *loc. cit.*, pp. 227-268.

27. On May 27, 1855, Mrs. Sara Robinson described the arrival in Lawrence of the Rev. Ephraim Nute, a clergyman sent to Kansas by the Unitarian Association, as follows: "We are glad he has come among us with his genial sympathies, his heart warmth, his earnest ways, his outspoken words for truth, and his abiding love for freedom and right."— Sara T. L. Robinson, *Kansas; Its Interior and Exterior Life* (Boston, 1857), pp. 59, 60.

which we are placed that will be important. In no way could the work be more advanced than by the churches of the East, who are looking with such interest to Kansas, than by sending the means for such a building in every important town. We feel that this is an important matter. We are willing to do all in our power, but we are too weak to accomplish what is necessary.

Would that I could reach the ears of the Church at the East! I would say There is no way in which you can accomplish what you desire for Kansas, no way in which you can secure the institutions which you desire to establish there, so certainly, as by furnishing her with faithful heralds of the Cross, & then by giving them the means of accomplishing the work which a man might almost as well not enter a field, as to be left, when there, unfurnished for his work. There is much responsibility resting upon the churches of our land, in reference to the Home Missionary work. They have, as yet, only begun to see it in its true light.

The quarter closes June 23rd. The amount due me from the Society is $125 as I have received nothing from any quarter during the past 3 months.

Yours truly,
S. Y. Lum.

Lawrence K. T. Aug 6th 1855

Dear Bro. Coe

Your letter accompanying a draft for $125. arrived a few days since. You say it completes my salary for the year, & wonder that I "insinuated" otherwise. I thought I had good reason to suppose that the first remittance was a donation— at least Mr. S. C. Pomeroy stated that he had received a letter in answer to one he had written in which it was declared thus to be but not feeling sure from the language of the letter which contained it I wrote once & again specifically to know, whether it were thus or not, whether I should consider it a part of my stipulated sum. To those enquiries I received no direct answer— but in the note from the clerk, accompanying the draft of Apr 21st it was stated that the enclosed was for the quarter ending March 25th. Of course that is the way I supposed my account stood for the books, & was not a little surprised to find it otherwise.

As the misunderstanding has caused some little embarrassment I hope there will be no cause for it in the future. I have been endeavoring to make arrangements for a more comfortable house for the coming winter but have concluded to suspend in part my preparations. The year has been one of very high prices in nearly every direction— flour has been until very recently as high as $14.50 a barrel, corn meal $8.—molasses from 75 cents to $1 a gall cheese 20 to 25 cts a lb. This is of course very destructive to a persons funds, (& all that has kept us along, is the means secured by Mrs. Lum's keeping boarders.)

When I came to Lawrence I did hope that long ere this my people would feel able to contribute something toward my support & have endeavored to bring their mind to this point but as yet no one from any of the Missionary associations have been assisted by the people here & then under the expenses of the *high* living & starting anew in every direction feel at liberty to hold back in this direction thinking that the East should supply their spiritual wants. I do intend that it shall be materially otherwise at the commencement of a new year & shall do all in my power to make it so. . . .

There have been times during the month or two past when I have thought it impossible to remain here with my family— We have been called to part with one of our dear little ones & Mrs. Lum by constant labor, above her strength & the excessive excitement that surrounds us has for weeks been laid upon a bed of sickness which we feared would prove fatal. She was taken with Nervous Typhoid fever in the midst of the hot weather but by the blessing of a kind Providence she is slowly recovering. Church matters are in about the same condition they were when I wrote last but not so encouraging as we could desire.

Yours truly

S. Y. LUM.

P. S. *If any part of this are made public please withhold that enclosed in brackets.*

LAWRENCE, K. T. Sept 23rd 1855

DEAR BROTHER COE

Another quarter of my missionary labor has passed & this completes the first year of my connection with the A. H. M. Soc. Though in some respects my hopes have not been realized, yet there has been steady & encouraging progress made— so much so that the time has come when the erection of some kind of a comfortable house of worship is a necessity. Where, but one year ago I found but little over a hundred persons—just arrived in this unknown country, without shelter from sun or storm, I now find near 1000 inhabitants with first class buildings of stone in every direction, either erected, or in process of erection. Business men— with all the caution that characterizes that class in reference to new settlements have invested largely in what they feel, is to be the 1st. or one of the 1st cities of Kansas, & already, 6 large stores are in successful operation, some of them in buildings that would be no discredit to Eastern business places.

This seems also to be the center of religious influence in the Territory— at least all denominations deem it highly important to have a foothold here. 4 churches have been formed & another is in immediate prospect— these are,—the Congregational, Methodist, Baptist, United Brethren & Unitarian. These divisions of evangelical Christians seems most unfortunate, where the whole united are so weak, & will remove, much further off the time, when the gospel can be sustained independent of foreign help, but it was impossible to avoid it. Two of the churches named above intend to erect suitable houses of worship this fall or rather I should say, commence them this fall. the others—would they keep pace with the rapid movement around us, must not hold back in this respect.

During the three months just closed I have found the interest in our prayer meetings constantly increasing & this too in the midst of the excitement, which the doings of our *Missouri* legislature, have produced.[28] God's children have felt that in Him was their only resource from legislative tyranny, & appealing to Him for wisdom & guidance, they are resolved to follow the path of right & duty at whatever hazzard. But we do not anticipate any violent enforcement of those iniquitous acts, the authors know too well, that the result would be anything but healthful to themselves, or advantageous to their cause. Infinite Wisdom will turn the wrath of man to the furtherance of its own purposes. . . .

It should be borne in mind by those who contribute to the support of missions in Kansas, that our circumstances are peculiar, unlike those of any other Territory, no emigration had preceded us, & we had—(the first year) no means of support within ourselves— it has been one continual drain upon our pockets, which in most cases has taxed all our energies to supply. prices of the commonest necessities of life have been what our neighbours of Mo have

---

28. The "Bogus" legislature elected on March 30, 1855, assembled at Pawnee, near Fort Riley, on July 2, 1855, and adjourned on July 6, to meet at Shawnee on July 16. The legislature passed many laws which are found in the volume of 1,058 pages entitled *The Statutes of the Territory of Kansas*. Included was a strong statement of the Proslavery position in an "Act to punish offenses against slave property."—Wilder, *op. cit.*, pp. 73, 74.

seen fit to ask—in most cases very exorbitant. The coming year in this respect will be very different as we now begin to have a supply of many things within ourselves. . . .

Yours truly,
S. Y. LUM

LAWRENCE, K. T. December, 1855

EDITOR, *The Home Missionary* [29]

In some respects, our prospects as a church were never brighter than at present. We have frequent accessions, and of a character that will be permanent and valuable; and we certainly *need* all of the right stamp that can be induced to come here, for we have much work for Christians to do. Sin and error of every kind grow with vigorous and rapid strides in a soil such as is afforded in a new and forming community like this; and while the church has advanced slowly, evil, in some directions has made fearful headway.

A few months since, public sentiment was such, that not a drop of liquor could be publicly obtained in the vicinity; and it was necessary to secure the certificate of a physician, before it could be obtained for medicinal purposes. Now, there are grog-shops on every hand, and the majority of young men are frequenters of such places.[30] This is naturally attendant upon the wild excitements in which we are compelled to live. For months past, our young men have been in constant drill for *war*; and such associations stir up the worst passions of our nature. We hope that the worst excitement has passed; but we have thought so before, and have been disappointed; and it may be thus in the present case.

There never has been such danger of actual hostilities—a *civil war*—as that which we have just passed through, and which you no doubt, have received full reports ere this. But as reports are

---

29. The contents of this letter indicate conclusively that it was written in December, 1855. The letter was printed in *The Home Missionary*, New York, v. 28 (March, 1856), pp. 364, 365. *The Herald of Freedom*, December 29, 1855, reported that the thermometer had reached 22 degrees below zero during the week, in keeping with Lum's description in the last paragraph. The issue of the paper could not be printed on schedule because it was impossible to thaw out the paper stock.

30. The response to grog shops in Lawrence in January, 1857, has been described as follows: "Action was forthcoming on Saturday, January 24, 1857, [when] at half past ten in the morning about forty women of Lawrence, who had carefully worked out their plans at previous meetings, set out on a tour of inspection of reputed groggeries. Instead of two they found no less than seven in full operation. This was a discouraging situation in a town of a thousand inhabitants, which prided itself on being a temperance community, but the women were equal to the task they had set for themselves. With true frontier simplicity they resorted to the one remedy that they had effective and with little waste of time they went from liquor shop to liquor shop and in each case speedily wrought the destruction of all the intoxicants that could be located. No determined resistance was offered by the liquor dealers, probably because of a strong body of men who had come prepared to protect the women against molestation."—Otto F. Frederickson, "The Liquor Question in Kansas Before Constitutional Prohibition" (Ph. D. thesis, University of Kansas, 1931), pp. 159, 160.

very conflicting, it may be satisfactory to hear the facts from a known source.[31] Early in November, a peaceable and unoffending citizen, a Free-State man, was brutally murdered in cold blood by a Pro-Slavery man, a few miles from Lawrence. The settlers in the vicinity, having no hope from the mock-law of the Territory, which was not made for *such* men, designed administering justice in defiance of law. The culprit, shielded by Pro-Slavery men, escaped into Missouri; and, as he left, set fire to his own house, and also to one or two others of his associates, thus giving the impression that the Free-State men had commenced the work of exterminating their opposers. This report flew on the wings of lightning through all parts of Missouri; and the Governor, to give it countenance (without investigation), issued his proclamation.

In these ways, in the course of two weeks, there were collected near Lawrence, at three points, somewhere near two thousand armed men, who openly avowed their intention of burning the town, and entirely exterminating the whole Free-State party; and I have but little doubt that they fully intended to put in execution their fell purpose. Matters began truly to assume a warlike attitude. The Free-State men came pouring in from all quarters, in order that they might repulse the enemy at the first attack, and thus prevent a general devastation. Mud forts were thrown up in several parts of the town, sentinels were constantly on duty, and scouting parties, day and night, were watching the movements of the enemy. All the public buildings were turned into barracks—the preaching hall with the rest; and nothing was thought of but the best means of defense.

The members of my little church, though deprived of their place for public worship, met in the private circle for prayer, and with deep earnestness and holy confidence in God, sought wisdom as well as strength from on high. They felt much like the fathers

---

31. Lum describes the events associated with the Wakarusa War. Franklin Coleman, a Proslavery settler, killed C. W. Dow, a Free-State man, at Hickory Point, 12 miles south of Lawrence. The cabins of some Proslavery settlers in the community were burned by Free-State sympathizers. Jacob Branson, a friend of Dow, was arrested by Sheriff Samuel J. Jones on November 27, 1855. The prisoner was rescued by a Free-State party under the leadership of S. N. Wood. The events developed as described by Lum. Wilson Shannon was the governor. The spokesman for the Free-State group at Lawrence was Dr. Charles Robinson. The agreement signed at Lawrence on December 9 by Shannon, Robinson, and Lane is often referred to as the "Treaty of Lawrence." It is in this period that John Brown became active in Kansas developments.
Lum's statement in this letter that the cabins of Proslavery settlers were set on fire by Coleman as a ruse to blame the Free-State men is not in accord with the version generally cited.—Johnson, *op. cit.*, pp. 138-144; Wilder, *op. cit.*, p. 90. However, *The Herald of Freedom*, December 29, 1855, stated: "It is the opinion of every person well-informed on the subject in Kansas, that the Coleman and Buckley houses at Hickory Point were burned by pro-slavery persons, for the purpose of stimulating outrages upon the Free-State men." A contemporary account of these developments is found in Sara Robinson, *op. cit.*, p. 128-159. The agreement between Shannon, Robinson, and Lane is found in *The Herald of Freedom*, January 12, 1856.

of the Revolution, determined to die; if necessary, in the cause of God and the right. After two weeks of such excitement, a deputation from the enemy's camp came into town, in company with the governor, to see if anything could be done to prevent a general slaughter. They began to wish for some honorable way out of their bad position. The settlers were too well prepared for defense, to permit them to hope for an easy victory; and they did not like to look at the certain death which would undoubtedly have been the fate of most of their number in case of an attack. So they concluded to try diplomacy. The delegation were treated respectfully, were told our position, and our determination either to live or die by them.

The consultation was continued for two days; when the Governor professed himself satisfied, and gave orders to the army of invasion to beat a retreat, which they were not slow to do. As has been since said by those interested on their side, they did not expect such stern resistance; and though they brought several batteries of canon, yet they were only for use in case there was no fighting on our side!

We are now experiencing most severe weather; the thermometer has been within a week as low as 24° below zero; and it is about impossible to keep warm enough to write.

S. Y. LUM

(*The Concluding Installment, Containing the Lum Letters of 1856-1858, Will Appear in the Summer, 1959, Issue.*)

William Sutton White, Swedenborgian Publicist

JAMES C. MALIN

PART TWO—KANSAS EXEMPLAR OF THE PHILOSOPHY OF EMANUEL SWEDENBORG AND HERBERT SPENCER

I. INTRODUCTION

THE question of the influence of ideas is often beset with difficulties, but in the case of William Sutton White, editor of the Wichita *Beacon*, 1876-1887, the major influences upon his thought are clear; the principal one, Emanuel Swedenborg (1688-1772), and less explicitly, Herbert Spencer (1820-1903), Swede and Englishman respectively. For present purposes only the briefest indication of their systems of thought can be given, and of White's use of them. Any really adequate presentation of White's dozen years as publicist would require a full-length book.

II. EMANUEL SWEDENBORG

BIOGRAPHICAL SKETCH

Emanuel Swedenborg (1688-1772) was a scientist, technologist, philosopher, and theologian; unquestionably one of the significant savants of the 18th century; the second son of Jesper Swedberg, bishop of Skara, and earlier a professor at the University of Uppsala, where in 1709, ES completed his formal university training. In 1719 the family was ennobled by Queen Ulrica Eleanora, the name then changing to Swedenborg. ES's first tour of foreign study began in 1710; two and one half years in London and Oxford, where his principal interests were mathematics and astronomy. He continued his studies on the continent, in the Netherlands, and in Paris, 1713-1715, returning to Sweden to devote himself to natural science, engineering, and invention, interrupted only by successive extended periods of foreign travel and study. In 1716 King Charles XII appointed him extraordinary assessor of mines. Swedenborg distinguished himself in the several major branches of science: anatomy, astronomy, chemistry, geology, mathematics, mineralogy, physics, physiology, and psychology.

Until 1734 Swedenborg's career is usually viewed as strictly

DR. JAMES C. MALIN, associate editor of *The Kansas Historical Quarterly* and author of several books relating to Kansas and the West, is professor of history at the University of Kansas, Lawrence.

that of scholar, scientist, and engineer; an investigator of nature, especially in its physical aspects. The second period of his life, 1734-1745, focused upon biology, in which he is said to have made important scientific contributions to anatomy, physiology, and psychology. In the interpretative sense, this second period has been designated as the search for the soul in nature. His third period, 1745-1772, was devoted to theological studies, or to "The Kingdom of God," subsequent to his "Illumination," when he insisted that he had been admitted to the world of spirits and thereafter considered himself as merely the instrument of the Lord to explain the internal meaning of the "Word," the Scriptures. Although some anticipation of this new departure appeared earlier, the transition period proper extended over the years 1743-1747, when, in 1747, he resigned from the board of mines to devote his entire time to this new mission.[1]

THE SWEDENBORG THEOLOGY

The Swedenborg theology as summarized for present purposes is treated under four heads: Jehovah Creator, The Word (Scriptures), the succession of churches, and the Lord as Redeemer and Divine Activity. Jehovah God is infinite and eternal. The universe and man are created, therefore, finite and exist in space and time as emanations from the Eternal. As all this is beyond the comprehension of finite man, by analogy the Sun metaphor is used as the nearest, although inadequate mode of conveying the meaning. The Sun as the center of the solar system radiates light and heat into outer darkness.

Matter is that which is more remote from the central source of force and motion; the material and the immaterial both being force and motion, only differently organized. Swedenborg conceived of the universe as being formed by an evolutionary process, a spiral

---

1. The best single biography of Swedenborg, is Cyriel Odhner Sigstedt, *The Swedenborg Epic; The Life and Works of Emanuel Swedenborg* (New York; The Book Associates, 1952). See, also, George Trowbridge, *Swedenborg: Life and Teaching*, fourth edition of 1934 (New York; The Swedenborg Foundation, 1955); Signe Toksvig, *Emanuel Swedenborg: Scientist and Mystic* (New Haven; Yale University Press, 1948). All of these biographical studies are from the Swedenborg point of view. No competent independent biography has appeared.
Brief biographical sketches of Swedenborg appear in the encyclopedias, the more significant being L. B. DeBeaumont, *Encyclopedia of Religion and Ethics*, edited by James Hastings, 12 volumes (New York; Charles Scribner's Sons, 1951), v. 12, pp. 129-132; Alexander James Grieve, *Encyclopedia Britannica*, eleventh edition (1910), v. 26, pp. 221-223; *ibid.*, 1957 edition, abbreviated and revised by "X," v. 21, pp. 653-654; Frank Sewall, *The New Schaff-Hertzog Encyclopedia of Religion*, edited by Samuel Macauley Jackson (New York; Funk and Wagnalls Co., 1911), v. 11, pp. 183-189; N. A. Weber, *The Catholic Encyclopedia*, edited by Charles H. Hebermann, 15 volumes (New York; Robert Appleton Company, 1912).
On the New Church, or the Church of the New Jerusalem, the best, and almost the only work, except encyclopedia articles, is Marguerite Beck Black (1889-), *The New Church in the New World* (New York, Henry Holt, 1932).
In American perspective, a particularly interesting book is Helen Keller, *My Religion* (New York; The Swedenborg Foundation, Inc., 1956 edition).

nebular hypothesis. The smallest unit in his conception of physics is a mathematical point, which, if extended traces a line, a line extended becomes a plane, and a plane extended encloses a solid; thus space is accounted for by means of mathematical physics. Matter is organized in space into vortical atoms; particles at the core with other particles rotating around them. Each atom sets up a magnetic field. Solar systems are formed out of atoms; the galaxies are composed of solar systems; and the whole universe is a system of galaxies, with its magnetic field of force. Here, in his mathematical-physical system by which Swedenborg accounted for creation according to his version of the nebular hypothesis, he set up his model of a macrocosm-microcosm relationship which prevailed as between each order of magnitude from the smallest atom to the whole universe. By analogy, God had a similar relationship, so far as infinite and finite could be compared.

Man is created in the image of God. The individuation of man was accounted for by conceiving of his material body as a temporary receptacle for the soul, and the soul in turn received life by influx from God. As God is order, all creation is according to order. In other words, all created things are governed by Divine law, without exceptions—not even God can suspend Divine law as the expression of Divine wisdom. This point must never be lost sight of if Swedenborg's concept of evil, of salvation, and of regeneration are to be understood. Man is created with complete freedom of will, and out of love of self and of the world, is free to choose evil, and by doing so sins against God and withdraws himself from the love of God. Thus by his free choices, man is good or evil, and creates his own heaven or hell, which are not places, but states of being.

The Word of God is recorded in the Scriptures allegorically in three degrees of correspondences; the literal, the spiritual, and the celestial, and is understood according to the capacities of men. By being admitted to the world of spirits, Swedenborg was convinced he became the servant of the Lord to reveal the highest form of truth as it was clothed in allegorical form in the Scriptures.

Just as men created their own heaven or hell, so each man became a church: "The church is within man and not outside of him; and that every man is a church in whom the Lord is present in the good of love and of faith." In another context, the exposition asserted that "the right understanding" of the Word, "constituted the church." Prior to the Lord's First Advent, the churches were representative. This requires some explanation because Swedenborg held that there had been four churches or dispensations prior to the Second Coming of the Lord in 1757 which ushered in the New Church, or the Church of the New Jerusalem. The four were the Adamic, the Noahtic, the Israelitish (or Jewish), and the Christian.

At the beginning of the Adamic or Most Ancient Church (Adam was an era, not a man), men conversed with Angels, knew truth from falsehood intuitively, and thus received the doctrine in a spiritual sense. But man being free to choose, closed his mind to the Lord and the heavenly love with its truth. Step by step the Adamic mind withdrew further until the Lord intervened to restore equilibrium, and conditions requisite for the exercise of a true freedom of choice. The second, the Noahtic, or Ancient Church, appeared after the flood—not of water, but of evils and falsities—by which a new start was made by some people called Noah, whose nature underwent a change whereby they survived, were given a faculty called conscience or reason, to replace intuition, and they developed writing by the use of symbols; the records of Moses were in symbolic language, and not meant to be historical. True historical writing began with Abraham. This church degenerated and was succeeded by the third, the Israelitish, which in turn degenerated, and was replaced by the Christian church. The advent of the Lord through His Divine Humanity was to battle against accumulated evil and to redeem mankind. Thus Jehovah God, Creator, became also Redeemer, and Divine Activity—the Trinity of Person with which the Christian dispensation opened.

In this capacity of God, as Creator, Redeemer, and Divine Activity, Swedenborg differed from the orthodox Christian interpretation of the Trinity—the Nicene creed, endorsed by the Council of Nicaea in A. D. 325, which, according to his interpretation, introduced a polytheism in the Trinity of Persons. In the Swedenborgian theology, Father, Son, and Holy Spirit, were three manifestations of one and the same Being.

Swedenborg repudiated also that version of the traditional plan of salvation which represented God as angry, whose Son was crucified to propitiate Him, and to cancel "the sentence of damnation, yet only in behalf of those for whom the Son should intercede, and that so He becomes a Mediator in the presence of the Father forever." Swedenborg could not accept any representation of God except in terms of Divine love, who could not logically operate upon any plan involving anger, vengeance, or punishment from the Lord. Man brought upon himself by his free choice the punishments of sin. According to order, the consequences of sin could not be remitted. By the Passion on the Cross, the Lord, in his Divine humanity underwent temptation as man, but in overcoming temptation restored the equilibrium in the spiritual world under which the free choice of man between good and evil was effective.

Correcting further what Swedenborg considered the prevailing errors of the orthodox church, he emphasized that, as effects from cause, the penalties of sin were not remitted, removed or shifted. By being saved from sin was meant, saved from sinning that he might undergo regeneration, the regeneration being effected through the Holy Spirit, the Divine Activity, the third aspect of the Trinity of Person. The process of regeneration begins in this world by the free choice of man in accepting the plan of reconciliation with the Lord, and is continued in the next world to eternity—the man chooses good instead of evil, hates evil as a sin, and does good to the neighbor according to the Divine order; not as a reward—it is his life.

For the Swedenborgian, death of the natural body is viewed as a continuation of life of the soul in a substantial spiritual body. The soul is eternal. In Heaven every man's life passes in review from his memories, and upon this inescapable record, he is his own prosecuting attorney, witness, and judge. He seals his own fate for eternity; he is not judged by law and sentenced or sent to heaven or hell. Whatever his life was on earth, in the natural body, his change of state is only a continuation of that life to eternity. His choice of a good life and the regeneration begun in the natural body continues to eternity.

To the question, who can be saved? Swedenborg replied: "the Lord's church is universal, and is with all who acknowledge the Divine and live in Charity" (*Heaven and Hell*, n. 308). He warned: "Everyone knows that the heathen as well as Christians live a moral life, and many of them a better life than Christians . . . and a moral life that is lived out of regard to the Divine is a spiritual life." For Swedenborg, the universality of the church extended to the inhabitants of other worlds in the universe. And to a Christian world which was not clear on infant damnation, ES comforted: "every child, wherever he is born . . . is received when he dies by the Lord and trained up in heaven. . . ."

Every man is born with three universal loves, the love of heaven, of the world, and of self. The first is necessarily spiritual; the other two are natural, but man may through them make his own heaven and hell: "What a man loves supremely is the main end and object of his life. . . . it is the motive power of his life. . . . A man's entire character is that of his ruling love. . . . It cannot be changed after death, because it is the man himself." Necessarily, the natural loves, in particular, are related to the doctrine of uses. Led by the Lord, the three loves may be co-ordinated and make man perfect. Riches and honors of public service, subordinated to spiritual love, are not to be condemned, but public service should be rewarded commensurately.

As a biologist who had specialized in human anatomy, physiology, and psychology, Swedenborg looked with wonder upon the body as an organism. He rejected the widely held Christian attitude toward the flesh as necessarily associated with evil, and something of which to be ashamed:

Every man ought to have a sound mind in a sound body; he must therefore provide the proper food and clothing for his body; and also the intellectual and critical matters which are the proper food of the mind; he will then be in a condition to serve his fellow-citizens, his country, the church, and the Lord. He who does this provides for himself to eternity.

To each individual in society, ES assigned a responsibility or duty:

Charity is to act justly and faithfully in one's office, business, or employment, because everything so done is of use to society, and use is good, and abstract good is the neighbor. . . . For example: Some kings. . . . A [faithful] clergyman. . . . A just judge. . . . An honest merchant. . . . The same is true of every workman, sailor, farmer, servant, indeed, of everybody who does his work honestly and faithfully.

This is charity, because charity may be defined as daily and continuously doing good to the neighbor, individually and collectively. This means doing good work in one's daily employment; and even when a man is not engaged in good work; it may be the frequent subject of his thought and intention. He who thus practices charity, becomes more and more an embodiment of charity; for justice and fidelity form his mind, and their exercise form his body; so that in process of time, from the form thus acquired, he intends and thinks nothing but what is charitable. Of such men it is said in the Word, that they have the law inscribed on their hearts. They attach no merit to their works, for they never think of merit but only of duty, which is a good citizen is bound to perform. . . .

At another place, Swedenborg emphasized that admission to heaven is not to be looked upon as a reward or as a merit for works: "The joy of doing good to the neighbor is their reward, and this is the joy of the angels in heaven; for it is spiritual and eternal, and infinitely surpasses every natural delight."

Swedenborg warned against charity in the sense of indiscriminate giving of alms or relief to the poor—"this must be done prudently" or "these benefactors are ultimately the cause of mischief to the good." Charity includes public, domestic, and private duties; compulsory public duties like paying of rates and taxes; domestic duties like the reciprocal relations of husband and wife, parents and children, and master and servants; and private duties like payment of wages and interest, fulfillment of contracts whether based upon statute, civil, or moral law—"Those who have charity perform them justly and faithfully; for the law of charity requires that a man should act justly and faithfully in all his dealings. . . ." ES covered also under the rule of charity, recreational activities, whether of the church, or strictly social intercourse.

Swedenborg carried the doctrine of uses to an extreme: "everything good is good in the measure of its use. . . ." The knowledge which men acquired through the exercise of intellectual powers was viewed by Swedenborg as an instrument, and as a trust from the Lord, which man in his freedom might use for good or evil. In this context he stated his motives in undertaking to explain the internal sense of the Word:

Now because it has been granted me to be in the spiritual world and in the natural world at the same time, and thus to see each world and each sun, I am obliged by my conscience to manifest these things; for what is the use of knowing, unless what is known to one be also known to others? Without this, what is knowing but collecting and storing up riches in a casket, and only looking at them occasionally and counting them over, without any thought of use from them? Spiritual avarice is nothing else. . . .

This insistence upon use of knowledge in contrast with hoarding was according to order and correspondence with other things, like wealth and power, entrusted by the Lord to the free choices of men for good or evil.

Living in an age of monarchy, Swedenborg emphasized that superiority in government, according to his standards of divine justice, was to be found where the principle of popular responsibility prevailed. Although not rated as a social reformer in the fashion of the highly publicized philosophers and philosophies in 18th century France, who were his contemporaries, the social implications of his theological system were highly explosive socially in their potentialities.

Had Swedenborg been a crusader, who stopped at nothing to impose his system of social revolution upon his generation, or had he established a sect comparable to those of Luther and Calvin, or had he undertaken a political career comparable to Cromwell or Napoleon, the consequences might have been portentous. Instead, his methods were essentially passive; man must not in any manner be coerced into doing good, not even by the Lord, or by His servant, Swedenborg. Such restraint is rare indeed among men possessed of a sense of mission. His faith that right, as he saw the right, would prevail eventually, seemed to be without limit. He would not organize a church as an institution to propagate his doctrines; the church is in the hearts of men and would prevail. In an age in which natural rationalism, materialism, and cynicism were so strongly emphasized, both his spiritual interpretation of history and his manner of implementing it were not of his 18th century, when the most conspicuous characteristic was the intolerance manifested by the advocates of tolerance.

Antecedents of ES Ideas

A perspective upon Swedenborg is impossible to attain except at an inordinate expenditure of time and effort. The scholarly world which prides itself in being "enlightened" and "scientific" has been inclined to ignore, or to ridicule the Great Swede because of his claim of "Illumination." The orthodox religious groups tend to dismiss him as a heretic. Swedenborgians generally refuse to accept as valid any discussion of him that does not recognize the "Illumination" and all of its implications as the point of departure, thus dissociating him from the main stream of the history of thought —his theological ideas are derived from the Lord, not from the historical ancestry of all modern human thought.

The uncommitted historian is not obliged to pass judgment upon matters of theological faith, as such, but is deeply concerned about any body of thought that has impact upon men, and thus upon the course of human history. The influence of a body of thought so comprehensive as that under consideration extended far beyond the confines of what is conventionally accepted as the province of religion. A decision on the question of originality of Swedenborg's work is not necessary for present purposes, but essential to any real understanding of his place in history is the determination in general terms of the sources or antecedents of the ideas found in his works. This means that investigation is necessary of his technological, scientific, philosophical, and theological works in their entirety, both for themselves and in their setting of the mid-18th century.[2] And furthermore, the independent historian is interested in the manner in which, and the extent to which, Swedenborg's thought was integrated into later history as a culture-forming factor. Whether or not original or valid, Swedenborgian thought dominated the Wichita *Beacon* during the period 1876-1887. The

---

2. Note on the Emanuel Swedenborg *Theological Works,* the editions used and the method of citation. The individual books bear long titles but are usually known by short titles. For citation purposes abbreviations are used. Quotations are from the Standard edition published by the Swedenborg Foundation, New York (English translation from the original Latin), for the most part, and references are not to page numbers unless so indicated, but are to numbered articles in the respective works, as these are common to all editions.
Arcana Coelestia: The Heavenly Arcana Contained in the Holy Scriptures or Word of the Lord Unfolded, Beginning With the Book of Genesis, Together With the Wonderful Things Seen in the World of Spirits and in the Heaven of Angels (12 volumes), translated by the Rev. John Faulkner Potts (New York, 1949-1951), (short title, *Arcana*); *Heaven and Its Wonders, and Hell; from Things Heard and Seen,* (short title, *Heaven and Hell*); *Angelic Wisdom Concerning the Divine Providence* (short title, *The Divine Providence*); *The Four Doctrines,* four short treatises originally published separately; I. The Doctrine of the New Jerusalem Concerning the Lord; II. The Doctrine of the New Jerusalem Concerning the Holy Scripture; III. The Doctrine of Life for the New Jerusalem from the Ten Commandments; IV. The Doctrine of the New Jerusalem Concerning Faith; *The True Christian Religion* (Everyman's Library edition, No. 893); *Angelic Wisdom Concerning the Divine Love and the Divine Wisdom* (short title, *Divine Love and Wisdom*); *The Apocalypse Revealed, Wherein Are Disclosed the Arcana There Foretold Which Have Heretofore Remained Concealed* (2 volumes), (short title, *Apocalypse*); *Miscellaneous Theological Works.* (Of the eight short treatises in this collection, two are used: "The Intercourse Between the Soul and the Body"; and "The Earths in the Universe.") *Posthumous Theological Works* (2 volumes).
Of importance for an orientation on the chronology of Swedenborg's works, the times of their actual composition, and of their first publication, is "A Brief Bibliography of Swedenborg's Works" included at the end of volume 2. Among Swedenborg's miscellaneous writings are some autobiographical letters and extracts from other correspondence, and *The Coronis,* an appendix to *The True Christian Religion* which is published with the latter book in some editions.
Note on Swedenborg's *Scientific Works.* No standard edition, in English translation, of the scientific works of Swedenborg is available. Some of the volumes that have been published are now "out of print." For present purposes the works examined are listed here in chronological order of composition:
Some Specimens of a Work on the Principles of Chemistry, With Other Treatises, translated from the Latin by Charles Edward Strutt [with an "Introduction" by the translator] (London and Boston, 1847). *The Principles of Chemistry* (these parts only had been printed) had been published in 1721, and some of the other treatises reprinted in 1847 were of the same date. *The Principia or the First Principles of Natural Things to Which Are Added the Minor Principia and Summary of the Principia,* translated from the Latin by James R. Rendell and Isaiah Tansley, with an "Introduction by Isaiah Tansley . . .," 2 volumes (London, The Swedenborg Society, 1912). *The Principia,* as printed here with the additional materials, 1,214 pages, was part one of a three-part work *Opera Philosophica et Mineralia,* published in 1734.
The Infinite and the Final Cause of Creation, Also the Intercourse Between the Soul and the Body: Outlines of a Philosophical Argument, translated from the Latin by James John Garth Wilkinson, with a new introduction by Lewis Field Hite (London, The Swedenborg Society, 1902, reprinted 1915). Wilkinson's original translation was in fact published first in 1847. *The Economy of the Animal Kingdom, Considered Anatomically, Physically, and Philosophically,* translated from the Latin by the Rev. Augustus Clissold, 2 volumes (Bryn Athyn, Penn., The Swedenborg Scientific Association, 1955 reprint). Published originally in 1740, 1741, and part three posthumously published.
The Medullary Fibre of the Brain . . . and Diseases of the Fibre; Rational Psychology, translated from the Latin by Norbert H. Rogers and Alfred Acton (Bryn Athyn, Penn., The Swedenborg Scientific Association, 1950). This work was written in 1742. *The Animal Kingdom,* three parts were published by ES in 1744-1745. Other parts have been posthumously published in Latin and in translation. Only the "Prologue" in a reprint form, has been used for the present study.
Ontology; or The Signification of Philosophical Terms, translated from the Latin by Alfred Acton (Boston, Massachusetts New-church Union, 1901). This short treatise, never completed, was composed in 1742. *The Worship and Love of God,* translated from the Latin by Alfred H. Stroh and Frank Sewall (Boston, Massachusetts New-church Union, 1856). Parts one and two were published by Swedenborg in 1745, but part three was published for the first time in this book. This work is an allegory of creation, not a scientific work, and represents conspicuously the transition into Swedenborg's theological period, but nevertheless his science affords the background.
The Letters and Memorials of Emanuel Swedenborg, translated and edited by Alfred Acton, 2 volumes (Bryn Athyn, Penn., The Swedenborg Scientific Association, [1948] 1955). *Psychological Transactions,* translated and edited by Alfred Acton (Bryn Athyn, Penn., The Swedenborg Scientific Association [1920], 1955). The several short works included in this volume were written at various times and none were published by Swedenborg. Some are published in this book for the first time.

writing of local history is not a simple operation. That fact should not require further elaboration.

Ignoring the controversies that have so largely controlled the writing about ES, the contention of the present study is that, so far as history of thought is concerned, continuity in Swedenborg's intellectual development is the conspicuous fact. There is no more reason to fragment his thought at the shift, 1843-1845, of the center of his interest from biological science to theology, than at the shift in 1834 from physical science to biological science. The same philosophical tradition was employed from the beginning in organizing and interpreting, in sequence, physical science, then biology, then theology and ethics.

Such difference as is apparent is only such as might be expected with maturity, depth and scope of knowledge, along with the successive shifts in subject matter. Necessarily the shift in subject-matter of investigation from the theoretical bases of mathematical physics and chemistry to the subject-matter of life in organisms meant the acquisition of assumptions not formerly applicable. Again, in the shift from biological material to spiritual subject-matter further assumptions were required. These successive additions did not mean necessarily the abandonment or repudiation of what was valid and usable from the prior stage in the development of the later stages.

When men fail to find satisfactory answers to ultimate questions in the so-called material world, physical and biological, through reason applied to evidence of the fine senses, they appeal to the supranatural, to the mystical in some form; that is to reasoning beyond the tangible evidence.[3] One extreme version of appeal beyond the evidence of the five senses is absolute scepticism—nothing is certain, not even uncertainty or existence, a materialistic paradox of negative mysticism.

The alternate extreme, and the one that Swedenborg adopted eventually was a theological mysticism, a conviction of union with the infinite. Some of his highly publicized 18th century contemporaries, especially in France, Voltaire, etc., made a show, at least, of taking positions near the materialistic extreme; according to conventional classifications, enlightened liberals. Measured by such classifications, because of theological commitments, Swedenborg was a conservative or even a reactionary. But compared with orthodox Catholics, Lutherans, and Calvinists, Swedenborg was

---

3. For want of a precise word, the term mystical is used there in spite of the multiple meanings it has already acquired.

a heretic, or radical. Under inspection, the conventional classifications became nonsense. Each individual emerges with unique properties in his own right, which give his life significance and meaning as a living, unclassifiable personality.

One of the first characteristics to be recognized in Swedenborg's philosophy, which provided the theoretical framework for the organization and interpretation of his science, is the eclecticism under which he exercised the widest freedom of choice in the selection of features from the several sytems available. From the Greeks, for example, among others, he drew from Empedocles, Leucippus, Pythagoras, Democritus, Plato, Aristotle, and the Stoics. Several Romans were used. From the writers of the early Christian era—Hebrews, Arabians, and non-Christian Neoplatonists—Philo, Plotinus, Avicenna (Ibn Sina), and even Iamblichus are represented. The last named was a later Neoplatonist whom late 19th century scholarship considered an exponent of the decayed period of that movement, although in the 20th century his standing seems to have improved.

In his first major biological works, Swedenborg cited the early church fathers, especially those prior to A. D. 325, the Council of Nicaea which adopted the Nicene creed, or "Trinity of Persons" as ES called it.[4] This was the period prior to the establishment of orthodoxy, when conflicting versions of Christian doctrine, drawn from several sources, were competing for recognition. Furthermore, the long tradition of Christian Mysticism was in evidence in the writings of Swedenborg's scientific period as early as 1719.[5] All this should be clear from his explicit citations of authority. To the student of the history of philosophy and theology, the evidence is inescapable that the origins of Swedenborg's thought have much deeper roots than superficially these citations would seem to indicate.

In Swedenborg's theological works, as differentiated from his scientific works, with only slight exception, he cited nothing but the Bible. That fact of citation did not change, however, his basic thinking. All the main outlines of his philosophy had been well established prior to 1745 when the theological phase of his life supposedly began. In fact, some of his theology was a matter of record prior

---

4. See the lists compiled in *The Economy of the Animal Kingdom*, v. 2, pp. 41, 349.
5. Letter, ES to his brother-in-law, November 25, 1719, *The Letters and Memorials of Emanuel Swedenborg*, 2 volumes, translated and edited by Alfred Acton, (Bryn Athyn, Pa., The Swedenborg Scientific Association, 1948), v. 1, pp. 220-221. ". . . God nas his seat in the Sun. . . ." Also: "That the most eminent light and glory is in the sun, while far away therefrom is darkness. . . ." This was further developed in Neoplatonic metaphor in *The Economy of the Animal Kingdom* (1740-1741), article 251.

to that date. To be sure, the shift in the center of gravity in subject-matter from science to theology and ethics resulted in a development of a theological system, as in his prior period he had formulated a biological system, and still earlier a mathematical-physical system. Furthermore, the fact should not be overlooked that in his theological system the scientific subject-matter of physics and biology was integrated into the theological subject-matter and argument. One Swedenborgian interpreter has admitted categorically that unless the claim of "Illumination" is insisted upon no obstacles stand in the way of interpreting the thought of ES as representing historical continuity.[6]

A survey of Greek thought and of its contacts with other systems usually called Eastern, and the intermingling with the Judaeo-Christian-Islamic tradition would be revealing, but space does not permit.

A survey of the history of Christian mysticism and of Neoplatonism makes clear the extent to which Swedenborg partakes of that tradition.[7] Typologically, religions may be divided into two groups on the basis of their treatment of the relation between God and man. One group emphasized the *difference* between God and man, God's transcendence: Zoroastrianism, Judaism, Christianity, and Islam. The other group emphasized the identity of God and man and the *immanence* of God; and the desire on the part of the soul as an emanation from God to be purified and to return to the One. Christian Mysticism undertook, with varying degrees of success, to combine these quite different points of view, and so did Swedenborg.

The speculative Christian Mysticism emphasized the unity, or wholeness, of life, which meant devotion to the business of the world as well as to that of the spirit. Thus John Tauler (ca. 1300-1361) declared "One can spin, another can make shoes; and all these are gifts of the Holy Ghost. I tell you, if I were not a priest, I should esteem it a great gift that I was able to make shoes, and would try to make them so well as to be a pattern to all." Jacob Boehme (1575-1624) was a shoemaker who became also a mystic. Aristotle had said that everything has a function; the good is to per-

---

6. The Rev. Lewis Field Hite, "Introduction" to ES, *The Infinite and the Final Cause of Creation.* . . . (1915), pp. xx-xxi. Hite's claim, in this introduction, that Swedenborg pioneered in the explicit analysis of the infinite and the finite, cannot be accepted. That distinction belonged clearly to Nicolaus Cusanus (1401-1464). See Wilhelm Windelband, *A History of Philosophy* . . ., translated by James H. Tufts (New York, 1895), pp. 344, 345. This book is available in paperback, Harper Torchbooks, TB 38/39.

7. William Ralph Inge, *Christian Mysticism* [1899]. Paperback reprint (New York, Meridian Books, 1956), Living Age Books, LA 3; Evelyn Underhill, *Mysticism* [1910], paperback reprint (New York, Meridian Books, 1956), MG 1.

form that function well; the highest good is to perform it in the highest and most complete manner; a harpist plays a harp, but a good harpist plays the harp well. In this respect, speculative Christian Mysticism was also in the tradition of Aristotle. Plotinus emphasized the beautiful things of this world, and that this world is not evil because it is the image of the Divine Mind: "What more beautiful image of the Divine could there be than this world, except the world yonder?" This macrocosm-microcosm metaphor of Greek philosophy was conspicuous also in Christian Mysticism in the view that man is made in the image of God. But the distinction made by Origen (ca. 185-254) was generally accepted; that the likeness exists in man only potentially, subject to development.

The role of mysticism in the history of human culture has had varied verdicts. Inge said: "Asiatic Mysticism is the natural refuge of men who have lost their faith in civilization, but will not give up faith in God" (p. 115). Also, it is a revival of spirituality in the midst of opposites: formalism, which is emptiness; and scepticism, cynicism, and relativism, in which there is no certainty— Mysticism is an adventure into the unknown. An unregenerated historian may add that this is a good definition also of science—an adventure into the unknown.

Returning again to the main line of philosophical development, the modern beginnings that lead to Swedenborg are seen in Nicolaus Cusanus (1401-1464) who undertook the first systematic analysis of the infinite and the finite, developing the macrocosm-microcosm metaphor, and with the aid of the atomic concept of Democritus (460-360 B. C.), and the mathematics of the Greek Pythagoreans concluded that in individuation each thing is different and that place and motion are relative. The philosophical succession from this beginning down to Liebniz and Christian Wolff in the 18th century worked out the main lines of thought from which Swedenborg made his choices.

Critical, however, to such promise of originality as was in evidence in Swedenborg's earlier scientific work was his assumption of the role of reformer and his growing obsession with functionalism, a trait which he shared with other social reformers—the Locke tradition in England, the "Enlighteners" in France, and Christian Wolff and his disciples in Germany. In ES functionalism was expressed in the exaggerated doctrine of use, and the doing of good to the neighbor as of the Lord as the ultimate measure of the value of all things. The partial, but not a sufficient saving feature for Swedenborg, however, was his even more stubborn insistence upon free will—no act performed under coercion of any sort has moral value, not even an acceptance of Swedenborg's own system of thought. This was evidenced also in his objection to the institutionalization of his "Church"—that is, forming a cult. But nevertheless, functionalism is always fatal to content, to substance, and cumulatively to creative thought. This was Swedenborg's tragedy.

III. HERBERT SPENCER

Herbert Spencer (1820-1903), English philosopher and pioneer in sociology, came from a family rooted for seven centuries in Darbyshire, England. His father, a Quaker, and an uncle, who were most influential in his education, were both committed to educational careers. Herbert received little formal training, terminating what little he did have by the age of 17. The major ideas which were to characterize his career took shape early. In 1842 he formulated his theory of the functions of the state; maintenance of order and protection of life and property—that and no more. In 1851 came his first book, *Social Statics,* in which he elaborated upon the general statements of 1842. The following year he published an article which expounded "the development hypothesis"; a generalized statement of the concept of evolution, physical as well as biological. This was six years prior to Charles Darwin's first public formulation of organic evolution under the name "natural selection."

In 1855 Spencer's book *The Principles of Psychology,* for the first time, applied the development idea to that subject. By 1858 he formulated a plan for his major life work, *The System of Synthetic Philosophy,* to be issued in parts on subscription, an enterprise that was not completed until 1896. His book on *Education* came in 1860. *The First Principles* of his philosophical system in 1862, *The Principles of Biology* in 1864 and 1867, *The Principles of Sociology,* volume I, in 1877, *Data of Ethics* in 1879, *The Man Against the State* in 1884, and *Justice* in 1892. These titles, some of them not being a part of his formal series, were the ones available to W. S. White, except the last named. As D. Appleton and Company, of New York, became Spencer's publisher in the United States, the American editions of his books, especially the *Social Statics,* are pertinent for the present study.[8]

---

8. The data are not available to determine which of these books White used, or when he made his acquaintance with Spencer. One historical evaluation of Spencer's philosophy as a whole, stated that "the metaphysical top-dressing with which Spencer decorated his system is in all essentials lifted from [Sir William] Hamilton." Another writer stated that Spencer is due for a revival: "If his own age overrated him, ours has underrated his merits." —Anthony Quinton, "The Neglect of Victorian Philosophy," *Victorian Studies,* v. 1 (March, 1958), p. 253.

Spencer denied the existence of God in any orthodox religious sense, thinking of himself as a scientist, he sought to eliminate the supernatural, or the supranatural, from his system. In his *Social Statics,* he used the term "Divine Idea," but in his book *The First Principles,* this gave way to "The Unknowable." In any case "creative purpose" was recognized, and the supernatural was admitted into his universe in spite of himself, depriving him of any true claim to the designation of materialist. His Christian critics, however, were not usually disposed to accept such differentiations.

Spencer believed that man's guide to action lay in absolute principles that could be discovered by scientific investigation. Such principles were valid, he admitted only in a perfect world for perfect men. His term Social Statics referred to this ideal, under which men exercised full self-control, which was a badge of their freedom, and government was unnecessary. Under these conditions the greatest happiness to all would be achieved through the "exercise of all the faculties." Spencer's first principle of freedom was, therefore, that: "Every man has the freedom to do all that he wills, provided he infringes not the equal freedom of any other man." Under this freedom, he was entitled "to get drunk or to commit suicide." Evil, in Spencer's system, meant non-adaptation of society and individual men to the perfect law of existence.

As society is the product of development, government is a growth and a necessary evil in the process by which savage men become civilized on their way to an eventual perfection when government should atrophy. Thus expansion of the functions of government and coercion was an evidence of moving in the wrong direction. In an imperfect world among imperfect men, choices of alternatives of conduct are relative; one finds himself in a position where no course of good action is offered, only choices of the least wrong from several possibilities, all of which are wrong. This is what makes an understanding of absolute principles so important as standards of measurement. As government can rightfully do nothing more than protect life and property, Spencer opposed state control of church and education. These were the responsibility of the family and the individual, even to the extent of the right to be ignorant. Most anything is preferable to compulsory indoctrination (education) at the hands of the state. No action can posess moral quality if it is performed under coercion. The reformer's demand for legislation to coerce men to be good, only created worse evils and demand for further legislation to enforce the former laws. According to the principles of development, man had come a long way already on the road toward civilization, but had a long way yet to travel. In the meantime, Spencer insisted, the best mode of facilitating the achievement of the final goal was patience, and the relatively best choices of modes of conduct—which necessarily excluded all laws extending the powers of the state.

IV. WHITE'S SOCIAL PHILOSOPHY

SYNTHESIS OF SWEDENBORG AND SPENCER

The foregoing review of the thought of Swedenborg and Spencer reveals so clearly some of the similarities and contrasts as to make any extended comparison unnecessary. At no time did White hold up Spencer as his model social philosopher. Quite the contrary. The first explicit reference to him by name was in February, 1880, when Spencer's materialism was emphatically condemned.[9] In White's synthesis of systems, the fact that Spencer had no positive formulation about God meant that, unopposed, the Swedenborg version of the Neoplatonic theology occupied the central position. As in all cases where Spencer's lack of religious sanctions was involved in the fusion, the positive character of the Swedenborgian system was unopposed. The effects of this fact might suggest that, instead of fusion of the thought of Swedenborg and Spencer, White's philosophy might be described more accurately as essentially Swedenborgian, influenced by Spencer, or with an admixture of Spencer. Like so many people of the late 19th century, much of White's debt to Spencer was by way of reaction against certain of his teachings. But there were areas of agreement, most strikingly in social policy. Although a century later, and by a different line of reasoning, on so many things Spencer had arrived at much the same conclusions as Swedenborg. The coincidences are so striking that they cannot be casually dismissed.

THE "NEW CHURCH" ACTIVITIES IN WICHITA

The "New Church" was represented in Kansas as early as territorial days, but did not achieve a self-sustaining status. During the latter half of the 1870's, the Rev. Adams Peabody was missionary to Kansas, visiting Wichita on the average of once a year from 1876 to 1882 inclusive.[10] Others appeared later. One attempt

9. Wichita *Weekly Beacon*, February 18, 1880, report on the Paige lectures.
10. *Ibid.*, February 9, 1876; March 21, 1877; September 11, 25, 1878; December 3, 1879; March 3, 1880; May 11, August 10, 1881; January 11, 1882.

at organization of a local society at Wichita has been recorded.[11] In 1877 the convention of the Missouri-Kansas association of the New Church met at Osage City, Editor White attending. In 1881 the Kansas Association met in Wichita. The Wichita Library Association received a gift from the Swedenborg Foundation, in January, 1878, of 20 volumes of Swedenborg's *Theological Works,* and in November, 1886, 20 volumes of collateral works.[12]

By his editorial policy, White kept the Swedenborg philosophy before the readers of the *Beacon* in several forms, much of it not identified by name. White's devotion to Swedenborg was unqualified: "The greatest, most rational and philosophical theologian of his, or any other age." [13] A characterization of White was inspired by the completion of the new *Beacon* building in 1885, when a former associate wrote that he had always entertained a

"kinder hankerin feelin" towards the sheet ever since we were devil in that office, years ago, when its present editor used to hoof it in from his claim, clad in an army overcoat, and Swedenborgen ideas, to stick type, when the grasshopper was in the land, and the typos played "devil among the tailors" for the beer.[14]

"Clad in an army overcoat, and Swedenborgen ideas," indeed! Symbols of a profound philosophy of clothes—expressed succintly and picturesquely! Regardless of sharp differences among soldiers of the American Civil War about its issues and consequences, there was agreement in an uncompromising patriotism. The old army overcoat was a visible symbol. But White possessed what many others lacked, an implicit faith in an invisible symbol, one that he applied rationally and systematically to life.

In a long commentary on Swedenborg, upon the occasion of the first gift of his books to the library, among other things White wrote:

They are the ripe thought of the grandest man of all the centuries . . .; whose vast, varied and comprehensive learning in all the domains of thought is the wonder of the world and whose moral and spiritual excellence and emanations fix him as the central human figure of all the ages. . . . His theology is the philosophy of being and existence, and yet to the earnest student and disciple his figure dwarfs out of the range of the intellectual organs of vision and his personality is swallowed up in the depths of the truths he declared. He bases his science of religion on the Bible, the mother of all science and the inexhaustible reservoir of truth and life. . . .

    11. *Ibid.,* August 10, 1881.
    12. *Ibid.,* January 23, 1878; Wichita *Daily Beacon,* December 1, 1886.
    13. *Weekly Beacon,* November 14, 1877.
    14. *Daily Beacon,* October 27, 1885.

White's meaning here is to be explained by the allegorical interpretation of the Word:

His profundity is so simple, that the little child may comprehend its essentials and his simplicity so profound that the succeeding ages will not exhaust the particulars of it. It is the philosophy of life. . . .

On matters other than theology, White emphasized that:

he is not to be measured by whole colleges of ordinary scholars. No one man is able to judge of the merits of his works on so many subjects. He anticipated much of the science of the 19th century—in astronomy, in magnetism, in anatomy, in chemistry, and first demonstrated the office of the lungs. His literary value has never been rightly estimated.

White closed with citations of appreciation by other writers of Swedenborg's importance.[15]

Misunderstanding and misinterpretation of Swedenborg appeared in several forms, one of which was confusion with modern or scientific Spiritualism. Taking advantage of a discourse in Chicago by the Rev. L. P. Mercer, on the subject of Spiritualism, White reprinted the full text and wrote an approving editorial. Mercer pointed out that orthodox Christian churches and materialists both repudiate Spiritualism, but for different reasons. The more "scientific" the world became the more insistent the demand for evidence of immortality at the materialistic level of the senses with which science deals—a contradiction of concepts. The New Church is the only system of faith resting upon Divine revelation that "admits of the possibility" of spirits returning, and offers an explanation. For that reason it is confused with Spiritualism. In fact, the New Church denounced Spiritualism or more properly "Spiritism"; "intercourse with the departed is possible in two ways, one orderly and the other disorderly." Although possible to invite the spirit to invade the consciousness, it is "expressly forbidden, always dangerous, and at the best, only negative in its results." Swedenborg recognized this and warned against it. The spiritual and the material are not opposites, but different by discrete degrees. For the spiritual to invade the natural consciousness was to degrade it. The orderly mode of intercourse occurs only to those in a state to receive "the opening of the spiritual senses of man." This means "the seer's temporary elevation from this world to that."[16] The knowledge derived during such states of elevation, was what Swedenborg had written into his *Theological Works*—this was the New Church view and was in no sense comparable with modern spiritism.

15. *Weekly Beacon*, January 23, 1878.
16. *Ibid.*, September 17, 1879.

White's Understanding of New Church Doctrine Applied to Life

White's understanding of New Church doctrine as applied to the late 19th century world was stated in numerous forms as called forth by specific events. Some of these are much more generalized and comprehensive than others, but none of them singly or in series approached a systematic treatise on religion and life. Possibly such an undertaking is what White had in mind when he retired from the editorship of the *Beacon*. His views on the "continuation of life" have been presented at sufficient length already. Among the doctrinal problems that agitated the minds of his generation, disturbed as they were by the challenge of science and by the "higher criticism" a few may be summarized from three quite substantial editorial articles.

The religious significance of Christmas and Easter observances occasioned many expositions of the Christian plan of salvation. The ascension of Jesus on the 40th day after the resurrection, celebrated by the ritualistic churches, was the occasion for an article: "A Spiritual Ascension." The Biblical text is: "And when he had spoken these things, while they beheld, he was taken up; and a cloud received him out of their sight." (Acts, 1:9.)[17] In White's exposition he reminded his readers that space and "place cannot be predicated of heaven"; "By going up it is not meant that He went up through space, but up in quality, up beyond the intellectual eyesight of the Apostles." The language, he asserted, was allegorical: "The Scriptures are not the word of God or truth, but only its manifestations. They are the ultimate and lowest expression of the truth or word, as literally understood, but as ultimates they contain as a vessel, the fullness of God." The revelation to man depended, therefore, upon man: "The Lord comes to all men in all ages through His divine truth and his manifestations depend at all times, upon the state or condition of man's spiritual nature." The conclusion about the Twelve was that: "If the Apostles could have followed him, in thought and affection, He never would have disappeared from their sight, but would have been a constant presence to them." In this sense the literal ascension "symbolized the perfect unition of the humanity with the divinity within it. . . . It completes the cycle or plan of salvation: "The incarnation or the material manifestation of the truth in the person of Christ . . . was rendered necessary by . . . the perverted state of the

---

17. The Douay (confraternity) edition reads: "And when he had said this, he was lifted up before their eyes, and a cloud took him out of their sight."

human understanding, and will be forever unnecessary again." Thus the second coming of the Lord was not a material manifestation. Such a view "brings God down to our level, instead of raising us towards Him." "The Lord never ascends nor descends. As to the disciples at the Ascension, so with us, it is an appearance dependent upon our changing spiritual states. . . ."[18]

Integral with this was the theological meaning of the crucifixion of Jesus, discussed under the title: "Substitution—Sacrifice." According to the doctrine of the atonement attributed to the orthodox Christian churches, Christ became a vicarious sacrifice to save man from the penalty of his sins. The penalty for sin was eternal punishment in hell. Under this theory Christ as the substitute for man assumed these punishments, which logically could mean only one thing; that instead of being at the right hand of God, he would be spending eternity in hell suffering the penalties of the sins of the world. Furthermore, White argued, if Christ was an infinite substitute, and there was so much as one soul in hell, then the devine plan was a partial failure, and if partial an infinite failure. White's conclusion was that:

The church, as surely as it lives, will ultimately sooner or later, utterly reject the awful dogma of the *vicarious* atonement, or the sacrifice of the second person of its trinity, to appease the wrath of the first person, and it will accept the true at-one-ment, or the reconciliation of man to God, and will worship one God, in the sole person of the Lord Jesus Christ. . . .

The sacrifice aspect, in contrast with the substitution aspect, was then analyzed to clarify the nature of sacrifice as a religious rite, and then to apply it to the crucifixion of the Lord:

To sacrifice does not mean to kill, much less to kill with vindictiveness. It means in its high and primary significance, to make holy, to consecrate.

The rite of sacrifice was preceded by purification by the priests, by consecration, and was performed with reverence in order that the offering might be acceptable to God. Then, referring to the crucifixion, White declared:

We cannot understand how an infamous act can be a holy sacrifice—a propitiatory offering. . . . If there is any parallel between the murder of the just Man, on Calvary, by a howling, cursing mob of sectarians permitted and assisted by the indifferent and scoffing Roman soldiers . . . and the holy sacrifices of the tribes of Israel . . . we fail altogether to recognize it.

And then referring to the pending Methodist church heresy trial, he concluded: "No wonder that the Rev. Doctor H. W. Thomas,

18. *Weekly Beacon*, May 28, 1879.

quoting another eminent divine, denounced the vicarious theory, as the 'Butcher Theory'." [19]

In a third article, "A change of Base Necessary," White drew a comparison between Copernicus and Swedenborg, the latter doing for the spiritual and moral what the former had done for the planetary system. Physically, Copernicus showed how the earth revolved around the sun, instead of the reverse, and had made astronomy the most exact of the sciences. Instead of the body being the central part of man, "the soul was the man" and "the body was the mere clothing of the soul of the real man." The result is "a rational theology that is scientific and philosophical. A true theology is the most comprehensive of all sciences. . . ." But that was only a part of White's argument. The concentration upon the body had produced only a false theology and metaphysics, but he insisted that it had resulted in "a perverted system of law and an empirical medical practice." Thus Swedenborg "made the most momentous discovery of all the ages," in demonstrating the truth about the relation of the soul and body of man.

The consequences of this change of base were then described as applied to man and government: "the nations begin to realize that the law is a yoke and a curse, as was the laws of the Jews. . . . The law has taken society as the unit to measure the man, instead of taking the man ["the soul was the man"] as the unit to measure society."

The Government is everything, the individual nothing—only so far as he adds to the power and strength of the government; while the truth is that the individual is everything, and the government nothing, only so far as it secures the welfare of the man. The man is not made for the government, but the government was made for the man, to add to his freedom, to secure him in the possession of every right God has conferred upon him. Man is the master, the government is the servant; man is internal, the government is external, and must be auxilliary and subordinate to the highest welfare of the individual. Man lives forever; governments change, and rise and fall upon the ebb and flow of the passions and the thoughts of men. Both church and state must change their base of operation.[20]

---

19. *Ibid.*, December 14, 1881. The second part of this two part editorial was mostly a reprint, without reference, from the *Beacon* of March 13, 1878.

20. *Ibid.*, August 31, 1881. Not all Swedenborgians viewed the *laissez faire* role of government as White did. Without going into detail, the Rev. W. M. Goodner, minister of the New Church at Larned, wrote, July 14, 1881, making general reservations about White's editorial position on "politics, temperance, and other questions," and by inference on public education. Goodner was greatly agitated about the shooting of President Garfield and "the vast number of foreigners," but more important, as he saw the general social crises, were the great monied corporations, "the general war upon the interests of the laboring masses," and professional politicians. He thought the schools should aid in the matter.—*Ibid.*, July 27, 1881.

ROLE OF THEOLOGICAL CRITIC TO WICHITA MINISTERS

Introduction and Personnel

The failure on the part of the Swedenborgians to organize a congregation of the New Church in Wichita, left White free on Sundays. Whether or not from a sense of editorial obligation or from a conviction of religious need, White was a remarkably regular attendant upon church services, both morning and evening, even of services during the week, especially during religious revival meetings. Either he carried his reportorial pencil with him, or he had cultivated a remarkable facility to reproduce from memory the substance of the sermons, and to differentiate the salient points of doctrine and their application.

During the 1870's the leading churches were the Methodist, Baptist, and Presbyterian. About 1880 the Protestant Episcopal and Christian churches supported regular pastors of ability, and by 1885 the Congregational organization was represented.[21] Other ministers were the subject of White's searching criticism from time to time, depending primarily upon whether or not they had something to say that seemed significant. The word criticism is used here in its strict sense, as analysis and evaluation, which might be favorable or adverse or both. As White put it himself: "The *Beacon* representative in his notices from time to time of sermons from our city ministers, trusts he has been as far from flattering as he has endeavored to be from irreverence or carping criticism."[22] A partiality for ministers was one of the charges sometimes leveled against White. Heartily, he pleaded guilty: "Jesus went about doing good, and verily he has some followers in this town."[23]

On the whole the ministers accepted White's criticisms with good grace. Sometimes they corrected him from the pulpit or replied through the *Beacon's* columns. On a few occasions they quarreled openly and violently, but usually that was not about theology proper, but about moral issues in politics. In January, 1880, a substitute editor pretended (possibly he was serious) to find himself in an embarrassing dilemma:

Capt. White is absent on a short tour, and as it is usual to comment on Sunday sermons, we are at a loss to know just how to fill this part of the bill. We are informed by reliable outside parties that several of the Ministers have taken advantage of Capt. White's absence to preach on the absolute

---

21. The Catholic church activities were seldom the subject of White's commentary, usually being handled strictly as news items. A lecture series was reported in the *Beacon*, February 25, March 10, 1880.
22. *Daily Beacon*, February 8, 1886.
23. *Ibid.*, January 13, 1886.

certainty of a personal devil. We know that this does not accord with his views, but we don't know just why, nor where, we simply enter protest by stating very frankly that, it won't do! it won't do!—vide Capt. White's return.[24]

Contemporaries had their fun about White and 24 volumes of Swedenborg versus the preachers. The *Leader* evaluated the relative sophistication and religious status of the four Wichita newspapers as of 1882:

> The Wichita editors are all bad men. Marsh Murdock is as guileless as a child when the preachers are around, but at other times he is a backslider, as it were, and seems to have no respect for divine truth; the old sinners who conduct the *Times* need no comment; [R. E. Field] the editor of the *Leader* don't believe in certain little sundries which constitute a good share of the orthodox faith, and he will probably be lost. Then there's Capt. White. Ge whillikins! What a terror he is. Every little while some unsophisticated gospel pedler winks at the burly old fellow, just for fun, and then this border ruffian sallies out of his den with the Bible and twenty-four volumes of Swedenborg under his arm and proceeds to wipe up the floor with the preacher. Jerusalem! how the preacher does pant to get away, but White is like a magnetic battery; when you take hold of him you can't let go. And when he has made an end of terrifying the preacher, he pulls his head into his shell and waits for his next victim. Golly! We's an awful wicked crowd![25]

During his first year as editor of the *Beacon*, White was kept busy apparently just in orienting himself in his new profession and in producing a Democratic county newspaper that would compare favorably with Murdock's Republican *Eagle*. Not until he had been at his post for about a year did he strike out aggressively on the several new lines which were to make his *Beacon* the distinctive and unique factor of Kansas journalism. So far as his positive approach applied to religious exposition, his editorial course must have kept the Wichita ministers on the alert. Every minister knew from experience that White's presence in his congregation meant that some critical comment, favorable or otherwise, would appear in the next issue of the *Beacon*. Not one of them was immune to his adverse criticism if White thought it deserving, and every one received his frank commendation for a logically constructed sermon even though the editor disagreed with his premises. Frequently White gave scant attention to the discourse as a whole, but used some point made by the preacher, either in approval or disagreement, as a text for his own sermon for the day. Thus Swedenborgian doctrine reached more people numerically and directed attention to a wider range of thought than if the New

---

24. *Weekly Beacon*, January 28, 1880.
25. *Ibid.*, January 4, 1882.

Church as an institution had existed in the community. Each denomination found its own distinctive doctrines, as voiced by its minister, analyzed and inspected publicly in cold print. Like Murdock of the *Eagle* in the field of journalism, the ministers needed the "old self-abnegator" as a challenge and a stimulus, and apparently some of them appreciated his independent criticism. Certainly the church-going and the newspaper-reading public benefited regardless of whether or not as individuals they agreed with either of the participants in these good tempered but earnest intellectual exchanges.[26]

Pulpit and Secular Press

The minister's concern about the everyday life of his church members was commended in the case of the Rev. J. T. Hanna, Methodist. White was of the opinion that: "The public common sense will sustain any preacher who fulfills the duties of his office fearlessly, honestly and kindly." [27] The same view was expressed a year later with reference to the Rev. John Kirby's (Hanna's successor) discourse on the relations of church and state: "The true end of religious teaching is to teach us how to live here, that we may live hereafter." [28]

The following week, Kirby discussed the dangers threatening the church. Possibly with White's comment in mind he emphasized "that safety lay in increased devotion to the church, to her prayer meetings, and her love feasts." White may have worded his comment in such a manner as to give Kirby's remarks a Swedenborgian slant that went beyond the minister's intent. If so, the emphasis this time would tend to redress the balance in his own favor. White also maneuvered for position and on his own part also avoiding overt disagreement echoed yes, "to an extent": "But we believe

---

26. The ministers most conspicuous during the decade of White's tenure as theological critic in Wichita are listed, together with their terms of tenure. For the First Presbyterian church, the Rev. J. P. Harsen served from December, 1871, to April, 1879. His successor was the Rev. J. D. Hewitt (sometimes spelled Hewett), June, 1879, through the remainder of White's editorship. At the First Methodist church the rotation system operated to permit each man during this period, with one exception, to serve three years: the Revs. J. T. Hanna, 1874-1877; John Kirby, 1877-1880; R. H. Sparks, 1880-1881; Barney Kelly (Kelley), 1881-1884; T. S. Hodgson, 1884-1887. The Baptist tenure was not continuous: the Revs. J. C. Post, 1873-1875; I. F. Davis, August, 1877-1878; A. L. Vail, January, 1879-March, 1881; and W. F. Harper, April, 1882-____. At St. John's Protestant Episcopal church, three of the succession of rectors figured largely in Wichita life: the Rev. Dr. L. DeLew, July, 1880, to September, 1881; the Revs. E. H. Edson, 1885, to March, 1886; Charles J. Adams, June, 1886-____. At the Christian church, the first tryout proved unfortunate. The Rev. T. J. Shelton arrived in June, 1880, dissension followed, the congregation split, and Shelton attempted to establish an independent congregation. Eventually becoming involved in several controversies, he turned to prohibition journalism, editing the *Republican Times*, June, 1881, to November, 1881 when the paper changed hands and editors. Later ministers at the Christian church only occasionally received attention in the *Beacon*.

27. *Weekly Beacon*, June 14, 1876. The minister's name was sometimes spelled Hannah.

28. *Ibid.*, July 11, 1877.

the true strength of a church lies in the daily business. . . . We judge of a man, not from his life in but out of the church. . . ." At the close White added that he had expected Kirby to include this: "it would have been characteristic of the man." [29]

The Presbyterian minister (1871-1879) J. P. Harsen made a practice of devoting his sermon on the first Sunday of each year to a discussion of the practical duties of life. He asserted that more was expected of Christians than of others because, among other things, the Lord did more for them. To this White objected, insisting that: "He does all He can for every creature of His born into the world. . . . [any difference lies in] the subject's willingness to receive. . . ." [30] Thus Harsen's faulty logic was corrected by consistent New Church doctrine.

In a private conversation a minister told White that the secular press had "no right to criticize the church or discuss its doctrines or dogmas," and that by so doing the "people would stop their subscriptions. . . ." White admitted that he had forgotten to ask if the minister had ever advised such a procedure. According to his code: "No province of ethics is exempt from honest discussion in the secular press, which is the avenue used by the leading divines all over the world to reach the masses." Nearly six weeks later, the young Baptist minister, I. F. Davis, advised the temperance people to transfer their patronage from the *Beacon* and the *Eagle* to the *Herald*. Later he denied it. At issue was the liquor question, not theology.[31]

The district conference of the Methodist church met at Wichita, May 15, 1878, where 15 essays on various subjects were read. White was distressed by the procedure. All debate on substance was cut off, he charged, discussion being limited to "criticism of style, grammar and diction, after the fashion of the school boy literary club. . . ." White suggested that next time, the limitation be placed upon the number of topics to allow time "for a good discussion of the subject." He passed up the opportunity to elaborate upon what he evidently had in mind—the sterility of a society so dominated by a false sense of sophistication as to subordinate substance to mere technicalities of form. Or to put it in the converse, original and vital societies place the focus upon substance, form being only incidental.

29. *Ibid.*, July 18, 1877.
30. *Ibid.*, January 9, 1878.
31. *Ibid.*, February 6, March 20, 27, April 3, 1878. Although trying to conciliate, Harsen appears to have admitted the substantial truth of the *Beacon* story. Also, Robbins, editor of the *Herald* confirmed the charges.

In 1880 the *Beacon,* January 21, commended the Rev. John Kirby, Methodist, for carrying his precepts into the market place, but more particularly the sermon of October 31 by the Rev. A. L. Vail, Baptist, and the Rev. J. D. Hewitt, Presbyterian, elicited extended comment under the heading: "Politics in the Pulpit":

The sooner the pulpit comes to recognize the great and awful truth that the church is primarily . . . responsible for the moral condition of the people in every relation of life—further, that the church is the spiritual mother of every social evil cursing humanity to-day, the sooner the pulpit will preach a religion that has relation to life in politics, in trade, in society, in the family as much as in the church and around the sanctuary. The church should preach the politics of the people, and not the politics of a party.[32]

Likewise the *Beacon* commended the sermon of the Rev. Barney Kelly, Kirby's successor: "He had no mercy on our corns." While not agreeing with him in all particulars: "We believe a preacher has a right to discuss any question under the sun that is of practical importance to the people. The pulpit is the place to utter the truth as God gives the power to see it. . . ." But, "A preacher has no business to be a policeman. The church has no business to appeal to the penal compelative law to enforce morals. The churches should unite in demanding the repeal of the prohibitory law"; also all laws against Sabbath desecration, blasphemy, and all penal laws that invade man's moral freedom to do right or do wrong. "All appeals to the penal power, by the churches, is blasphemy against God, and is an open confession of spiritual impotency."

The differentiation made by White in the foregoing declaration of rights was peculiarly appropriate to a complex, explosive situation that was developing. One aspect of it was a series of meetings to support the enforcement of the liquor prohibitory law, including a visit by Gov. John P. St. John, July 21, who spoke at the Presbyterian church in the afternoon, and at the Methodist church in the evening. At an earlier meeting, on Sunday, July 10, after Hewitt had spoken, Kelly demanded a show of hands to test enforcement sentiment. White had protested, and called this procedure cowardly and bulldozing.

At one or both of the meetings of July 21, a standing vote was proposed, but before it was taken, Kelly demanded that White leave the meeting. The *Beacon* for July 27 was largely devoted to the several aspects of the episode in which White denounced in bitter personalities the ministers involved. No one realized more

32. *Weekly Beacon,* November 3, 1880.

keenly than the editor of the *Beacon* the betrayal by all parties of basic principles of moral conduct. He differed from his opponents, however, in admitting wherein he had failed, his editorial apology being headed: "If We Were a Christian." The opening sentence was confession: "Nothing could show more conclusively that we are a sinner, than this issue of the BEACON. It is full of derision, scorn and contempt, of hatred and all uncharitableness. We are not proud of the issue. . . ." The manner of the presentation he admitted, would "prevent its reception by those who need it the most. . . . You can't make a man receive the truth by striking him with a club." The second paragraph opened: "If we had been a christian we would not have published this issue. When smitten, we would have 'turned the other cheek. . . .'" And the closing sentence read: "If we *were* a Christian, we would be awful lonesome."

The following week, a long editorial, "The Church Is Responsible," dealing with the Atonement, was introduced by a sequel in which White insisted that he had never intentionally misrepresented any man:—"A man's honest opinions are as dear to him as his reputation and character. . . . Since our connection . . . with the BEACON, our relationship with the ministry has always been cordial. . . ." A differentiation was then made between a man's private and his public status. The former was not a proper subject of public commentary, but the latter, being of concern to society, must submit to public scrutiny:

> Until last week we have never uttered a word or written a line that would reflect upon the private character or professional integrity of any minister. Last week we reflected upon the public action and methods of public men. . . .

In the public category also were public institutions: "The creeds —the doctrines of the churches, are proper subjects for fair and free criticisms. We propose freely to exercise our right. . . . We court criticism. We do not deprecate the condemnation of our opinions or principles."[33] He then proceeded to discuss the doctrine of the Atonement in blunt Swedenborgian terms, concluding that the doctrine of the "vicarious Atonement is . . . the prime cause of social evils and disorders of the world. It amounts to a license to sin. . . . The only danger he runs is sudden death, giving him no time to utter the cabalistic words— 'Open Sesame.'"

33. *Ibid.*, June 22, 29, July 13, 20, 27, August 3, 1881.

Relations between White and Kelly did not improve. In December, 1881, Kelly, with the aid of a visiting minister, was holding his annual winter revival. Under the title "False Doctrines, the Cause of Evil," White disagreed with the preacher's presentation of the plan of salvation, including again the doctrine of the vicarious Atonement:

Our readers may ask: "What right has the BEACON, a secular, political newspaper, to discuss theological questions?" We answer: Just because the BEACON is a secular and political newspaper. All truth has relation to life, and secular and political matters include about the most of our life's affections, thoughts and actions.

In other words, the secular and the political reflected the "character and quality of the theology of the day. There is no possible hope of a radical regeneration in politics and in society until there is a radical revolution in our theological ethics. The *Beacon* deals in practical questions of every day life, for they make and form the man."[34]

On the evening of the day the *Beacon* appeared with the above editorial, "after the *religious* exercises were over," Kelly

gave the press a swinger, applying his remarks especially to the Wichita papers. We were present, and enjoyed it. We know of no institution among men, save, perhaps, the church, that is more open to and needs more honest and unsparing criticism than the press. There is no institution save the church, that can be more productive of good than the press. We do not say that Brother Kelly's criticisms were judicious, or were given in the right spirit, but we hope he will keep giving them, for peradventure he may sound the key note of true reform in the press.

The liberty of the press is worth all protection. The license of the press should be boldly condemned and even punished. The press has the right to its opinions. It has the right to express in proper phrase, its opinion of any man's opinion, whether he be a preacher or a proletariat. Brother Kelly, we think, is as free with his criticism and censure of men and things, as the press can possibly be. We don't object, we glory in his freedom of speech. To prevent him we would not close his mouth, nor his pulpit. There is nothing on earth too sacred for the freedom of thought. Brother Kelly sets himself up as a censor of the press, and if his censorship is not duly respected, he threatens to break down the business of the papers. We believe in the censorship of public opinion, and when the press violates the decencies of life, deals in slander, is obscene and filthy, public opinion should voice itself, and the court should lay its hands upon the offender, but it won't do for public opinion, the courts or the preachers to attempt to obstruct nor throttle the freedom of opinion or its expression properly couched. Ecclesiastical organizations are human institutions, preachers are human teachers, and are not always inspired, and never infallible, and we shall always freely, and will try to decently, ex-

34. *Ibid.*, December 7, 1881.

press our opinion of the so-called church and its preachers. We say this with all due respect for our Brother.

In 1882 a new Baptist minister, the Rev. W. F. Harper, began his pastorate in Wichita. He preached his first regular sermon April 9, and his second, "Relation Between Pastor and People," April 16, in which "he advanced, on the whole, very sound and practical views. He thinks . . . a pastor . . . should not cease to be a citizen. . . . We think this is sound." But, the *Beacon* insisted upon differentiation between the priest and the citizen. When acting in the latter capacity "he should leave his gown and cassock in the pulpit. The church and its priests have no official business outside of the spiritual and moral sphere." For example, the priest must differentiate between the moral and police phases of temperance;

the church, as a church, has no right to demand the passage of a penal law. . . . The church should be a leader, a teacher, an example and a life, but it seems to be ambitious to be only a driver, and we do not want to see him [Harper] become a driver. The measure of the immorality and degradation of a people is the number of its courts, its prohibitive, restrictive, directive penal statutes. Every increase of power in Topeka or in Washington City is an incontrovertible proof of the intellectual and moral deterioration of the people, an evidence of lawlessness and crime. If the church were virile, Washington would annually become more insignificant; the center of the nation would not be a geographical location but it would be in the heart and soul of every man. . . . The church is primarily and in the highest degree responsible for the present moral condition of the people, and it must acknowledge this responsibility.[35]

During the campaign of 1882, Governor St. John ran for re-election to a third term using prohibition as his principal issue. A large part of the evangelical church membership was mobilized in his support, resulting in one of the most vicious and vindictive of Kansas political experiences. Pressure was put on Harper, and during midsummer he appeared to be committed, but late in August he declared "the emancipation of his church from all connection with politics and police law. The church was a teacher and preacher of the Man Christ Jesus. It deals with the spirit and conscience of man, and not with rituals and laws. . . ." The *Beacon* appealed to the public to "Hold Up His Hands."[36]

During such a political campaign the *Beacon* also felt the pressure and abuse of the self-styled reform element:

The pulpit is continually whacking us over the head, because it asserts we want to limit its functions. It does this in the face of the fact that lately, and

35. *Ibid.*, April 19, 1882.
36. *Ibid.*, August 30, 1882.

many times in the past, we have asserted the fullest right, liberty and duty of the pulpit to discuss every question that affects the moral, social and political welfare of the people. We republished an article, written nearly two years ago, to show that we have not been backward in demanding for the pulpit the fullest liberty to *teach*. We believe the church is a great teacher. We believe that all the blessings of God come through the church. The form of the church is divine truth; . . . the sects—so-called churches—are instrumentalities of the church of God, and they are members of the church so far as they teach what is true and do what is good. All the good and truth in those sects comes from God; all the evil and falsity have been injected by man.

And White was insistent upon this last point—evil in the church —and pointed to church history, Jewish, Catholic, and Protestant. He objected to ministerial brag and bluster about what good had been done for the world; and ministers reminded him of the unprofitable servant. The ministers wanted to convert the non-Christian peoples first, the heathen—"but don't! Go among the Christian nations, beginning with this one"; then England and Europe. As for the non-Christian peoples:

Don't call on the heathen until you have gone through your own households, visited your relatives and dwelt among your wife's relations, and after you have got all through, stand up in your pulpits and brag, if you dare; but you won't brag if you have any sense left. The churches will say, Lord, we have been unprofitable servants. . . .[37]

Inter and Intra-cultural Relations: Incompatibility, Rivalry, and Conflict

To an uncommon degree, White was able to view his own time and culture as though he was an outsider. Whatever the origin of his manner of viewing cultural relations, this trait was encouraged by familiarity with Swedenborg's example in having the inhabitants of the several planets describe their own customs and contrast them, especially with those of the earth, to the latter's disadvantage or advantage, as the case might be. Problems agitating White's generation were presented by conflicts within the culture of the United States in relations with the American Indian "savages," and with "immoral" polygamous Mormons; and outside the United States with the so-called Christian nations in Europe, and in Asia, Africa, and elsewhere with the allegedly "heathen" people. What, indeed, were the distinguishing characteristics that were assigned to the people that labeled them as savage, immoral, Christian, or heathen? In the Swedenborgian sense, that true religion had relation to the

---

37. *Ibid.*, June 21, 1882. The article referred to, "Politics and the Pulpit," and reprinted in this issue, had been published first in the *Beacon*, November 3, 1880, instead of September, 1880, the reference given by the editor.

life people led, were not all these terms no more than exhibitions of prejudices damaging only to the user by revealing his own sin of self-love? White thought so, and said so in terms so blunt and uncompromising as sometimes to infuriate even his friends.

The Sioux Indians were described by Joe Haskins, a mixed-blood member of the Indian police, as controlled by their religion; they respected the rights of both person and property within the tribe, reverenced the Great Spirit, had no belief in an evil one (White interjected, "unhappy wretches, with no devil"), had no profanity comparable to that of white men, their respect for the marriage relation was noteworthy, although wives were bought. "Here is a great field for missionary labor," jeered White,

> We are in doubt whether to send them a delegation from the churches, of the class connected with the Indian bureau; or a corps of scientific evolutionists, athiests, and materialists. A people who act upon principle of right as they see it, and not from rapacity, greed, lust of power and dominion; who know nothing of the political doctrine of a "Scientific Frontier;" who are not skilled in the "art diplomatic," which is the high art of lying and deception, are a dangerous people to have hanging on our frontiers. Their example is corrupting.

White suggested probable explanations of the condition of these Indians: "their degraded religious principles," lack of "a civilized political system," and of "a free educational system." "How destitute they must be," he explained, "—no houses of prostitution, no assignation houses, no Dago dens, no foundling hospitals, no Magdalen hospitals, no adultery, no rapes and seductions, no divorce courts. . . . In the name of God had we better not don the breech clout and the blanket? . . ." In connection with a press report of an annual Baptist convention in New York, White concluded that "They [the Indians] do not yet know that the grandest result of all church work is a law and a penitentiary. . . . We very much doubt that if the savages had a clear and an intelligent understanding of these things, they would not run to escape our culture." [38]

Using as a text ex-Vice-President Colfax's proposal to suppress Mormonism by law, White pointed out that "Mormonism really seems to thrive the more the effort is made to suppress it. It is a great evil, but the law is powerless to eradicate it." He then proceeded to differentiate between what he called social and non-social evils. The element of collusion was the key to his classification. A social evil involved collusion; polygamy, adultery, prosti-

---

38. *Ibid.*, March 16, 1881; *Daily Beacon*, November 19, 1885.

tution, liquor traffic, were named. Nonsocial evils did not involve collusion; slavery "lacked the element of agreement or assent," likewise, murder, theft, embezzlement, arson; and because of the absence of this collusive or social element, "society is easily arrayed against them, and all the moral and intellectual forces aid the police element,"—also, the police element can punish when a crime is committed by one person against another, but all prohibition by law is useless in a matter of collusion between parties. In order to drive home his point about the extent of evil, the variety of its forms and the large proportion of the population who are themselves guilty of some variety of sin, and the confusion involved in groups of sinners joining forces against other particular groups of sinners, White resorted to what might be termed the shock technique to jar his readers loose from the smugness of their conventional modes of thinking, or more properly feeling, about the sins of others, especially those geographically remote whom they never met face to face:

Polygamy is a hard nut to crack; so is adultery; so is prostitution. Suppose all the prostitutes, male and female, and all the adulterers, in this Christian land whose holy horror is excited against polygamy, were gathered into one community; does anyone doubt that they would be numerous enough to go out and lick the Mormons any day in the week before breakfast. Now, this fact makes the nut a great deal harder to crack. On account of the irritating beams in our own eyes, we can't hit hard nor straight. It strikes us as a little funny, that people as full of the devil as we are should get so outrageously mad with a people as full of the devil as the Mormons are.

Next, in order to prepare his sequence of argument, White returned to the policeman:

He can abate a nuisance, when that nuisance affects directly society or an individual. He can arrest a man when he is drunk; not for getting drunk, for the law has no business with what a man does. A man has an immoral right—if that is not too great a paradox—to get drunk, and it's none of the policeman's business. The law has only the right to abate him as a public nuisance; and so with every other social evil.

Open adultery is a nuisance, and the policeman ought to abate it. He has no right to punish the parties for the evil of adultery, nor for the sin of the act. . . . His right attaches only when and only because it becomes a public nuisance and infringes upon the public decency and peace. And so with polygamy. It's none of the government's—the policeman's—business whether polygamy is moral or immoral. . . . The government has a right to attack Mormonism, on the ground that it is a nuisance, destructive of the safety, peace and good order of society.

Having made these distinctions in order to focus his main point, White resorted once more to his shock example:

Our plan would be, if we were the policeman, to declare polygamous Mormonism a nuisance and then arm our adulterers and prostitutes and send them out to suppress this nuisance. The greater would absorb the lesser evil. The attacking forces could be walled in and left to devour each other.

White recognized that this procedure would have momentous consequences, but would accomplish one objective so much desired by the reform forces:

This would, no doubt, largely diminish our population and belittle our greatness, for this is measured by the vastness of our population, by overshadowing monopolies, by the number and magnificence of our police palaces—state capitols, penitentiaries and lunatic asylums.

"Selfishness is a moral evil and disease," the editor insisted,

infinitely worse than polygamy, adultery or murder. But what moral, rational right would the government—the police element—have to suppress, limit, restrict or prohibit selfishness? It has only the right to take cognizance of the ultimate effects of selfishness so far as they directly and injuriously affect some factor or community of factors. Its action must not be based upon the immorality of the act, but upon its outward and injurious effects upon the individual safety and property.

This essay on the basic principles of jurisprudence stirred up *Beacon* readers, and made further explanations necessary. The difficulty in mobilizing the punitive forces, White insisted, could be met by declaring the Mormons outlaws, their property confiscated, and by granting to the members of the expedition a fee simple title to all property they could lay hands on. Mormonism would be cleaned out of Utah, but would not be suppressed—only driven elsewhere. White accused Switzerland of solving its criminal pauperism problem, not by overcoming criminal pauperism, but by shifting its geographical location to the United States.[39]

The Mormon question persisted and somewhat later, in referring to the symbolic personality of the United States as Old Samuel, White alluded derisively to his activities in the field of morals:

Polygamy is a great moral evil, and if Samuel is anything he is a moral reformer and his great mission is to conserve, preserve and pickle morals, so they will keep. Why do not Mormons drop polygamy and adopt pollywogamy, prostitution, and free (love) divorce, and become decent and self-esteemed people?[40]

At the Baptist convention previously mentioned, among the diversities of opinion expressed on American Indian and Mormon cultural patterns, one MacKinney struck what White approved as a true note on the Mormon question: "The Mormons support many

39. *Weekly Beacon*, December 28, 1881, January 4, 1882.
40. *Daily Beacon*, May 6, 1885.

wives at once, but how many Americans support a number of wives one after another?"[41]

In editorializing on enforcement of the Edmunds anti-polygamy law, White related a news story datelined Bridgeport, Ill., reporting the abuse and egging of Mormon converts at that place. This was an example, he pointed out, of how Illinois was willing to supplement the Edmunds act by mob violence, and thus the problem was solved. Or was it—

There is nothing like a bill for a social evil. Salvation by faith alone in a bill is becoming universal faith, taught in all our churches and formulated in codes and statutory creeds. It used to be a general faith that the Son of God came to save the world, but that was before the birth of Edmunds. The coming was an unnecessary work.[42]

The non-Christian heathen became the subject of a number of *Beacon* articles in which inter-cultural relations received equally candid treatment. The first occasion was the visit of a woman missionary who had been active in India in a campaign to elevate the status of women and to terminate infanticide, especially of girl babies. White raised the question of hypocrisy in the United States—contraception and foeticide compared with infanticide. Do American women kill their infant daughters?—

Oh, no, no, God forbid! We are a free, enlightened Jesus loving, God fearing nation. . . . this is wrong—we don't wait till they are born. We kill them—both male and female, before they are born. We have numerous medical schools, where eminently scientific men are educated to teach us how to destroy life. . . .

We would like to know a crime of heathendom, that we can't discount. We said last week that we were a nation of infernal pharisees and hypocrites. . . . The heathen might justly say to all propagandists, "We don't see difference enough to warrant us in making a change."

Foeticide is a thousand times worse than intemperance.[43]

Shortly afterward, White drew another type of paradoxical parallel:

The Christian nations under the divine ministrations of the Churches, are beacon lights to the rest of the world. . . . The heathen are sending their brightest youths to study the art of war in our military and naval academies.

Referring specifically to England and the United States, the *Beacon* declared: "Both nations occasionally bombard their seaports to compel them to receive their goods and their gospel."[44]

41. *Ibid.,* November 19, 1885.
42. *Ibid.,* October 17, 1885.
43. *Weekly Beacon,* March 9, 1881.
44. *Ibid.,* July 13, 1881.

In another instance a lecturer on Japan told about "the cleanliness, orderliness, industry, ingenuity, skill, and above all, their wonderful honesty" (with concrete examples as illustrations). White made his point clear by the headline given to report: "Heathendom, Where Is It?" [45]

But the more usual report on conditions among the "heathen" were those typical of returned missionaries: "It is the invariable rule among christian nations to hold the church in China and all other so-called benighted heathen lands altogether and wholly responsible for all kinds of evils." The mode of procedure on the part of Christian nations for putting an end to the evils of which they disapprove is to attack religion—to change their religion is to change their way of life. The *Beacon* agreed that this reasoning was logical. But the same formula is equally applicable to the religion and evils in the United States. But here the unanimous explanation of evil is not the religion, but "the Devil." To this White replied, of course, according to his "New Church" doctrine, that denied the existence of the Devil; each man is his own devil:

It seems to us that the missionary who goes abroad to save the souls of the heathen with his creeds and rituals, has a cheek of brass and an impudence that would shame his devil.[46]

Taking as a text the address, in the old stereotype, of a woman missionary returned from Siam, White protested as unjust the reflection upon the Christian God implied in assuming that he had done nothing to save these heathen people. Swedenborg had insisted upon the universality of the true religion, comprehending within the love of God, not only the so-called Christian nations, but the so-called heathen of this earth, and of all possible earths in the universe:

It seems not to have occurred to the benighted missionaries that God was as much with the Siamese, overshadowing them with his love and solicitude, all these centuries, as he has been with the so-called Christians; that he gave them all the light and life they could receive, and that they were saved just so far as they were obedient to the light received. It is horrible to think that these untold millions are and have been trooping to hell simply because they have not known what Calvin thought of God.

White insisted that if the missionaries would but list all the crimes of Christian civilization, they would not dare tell them to any intelligent heathen as evidence that missionaries had anything to offer them: "What we need is missionaries . . . to . . . save

45. *Ibid.*, March 12, 1884.
46. *Daily Beacon*, April 9, 1885.

us from a so-called civilization that makes us frauds, dead beats, robbers, and oppressors on the earth. . . ."[47]

White commended President Arthur's veto of the Chinese exclusion bill in 1882. Later he denounced the policy adopted in the territory of Washington which paraphrased Gen. Phil Sheridan's Indian maxim: "The good Chinaman is a dead Chinaman." Later, he praised President Cleveland for stopping the massacre and robbery of the Chinese in the Far West. And at home, *mirabile dictu*, the Wichita local of the Knights of Labor published in the *Beacon*, December 26, 1885, in a peculiar perversion of Christmas spirit, an appeal to the citizens of the city and county to boycott Chinese laundries and "to prevent Chinese labor in any shape whatever from gaining a foothold in our fair city."[48] White did not protest! And neither did Murdock! What an opportunity to make political capital out of the democratic paper's inconsistency! But the Bird in his aerie on Douglas avenue tucked his head under his wing and did not see.

47. *Ibid.*, May 20, 1885.
48. *Weekly Beacon*, April 12, 1882; *Daily Beacon*, November 12, 13, December 26, 1885.

(To Be Concluded in the Summer, 1959, Issue.)

The Annual Meeting

THE 83d annual meeting of the Kansas State Historical Society and board of directors was held in Topeka on October 21, 1958. Subject for the special public meeting in the G. A. R. auditorium at 10 A. M. was "Techniques for the Small Historical Museum." Edgar Langsdorf, assistant secretary of the State Historical Society, presided. Feature of the program was a slide talk by Stanley Sohl, the Society's museum director.

The meeting of the Society's board of directors was held concurrently in the newspaper reading room. Called to order by President Alan W. Farley, the first business was the annual report by the secretary:

SECRETARY'S REPORT, YEAR ENDING OCTOBER 21, 1958

At the conclusion of last year's meeting the newly elected president, Alan W. Farley, reappointed Charles M. Correll and Frank Haucke to the executive committee. Members holding over were Will T. Beck, John S. Dawson, and T. M. Lillard.

Four members of the Society's board of directors have died since the last report. R. F. Brock of Goodland, banker and stockman, and member of the Society since 1918, died November 11, 1957. History was Mr. Brock's hobby; he was a collector of firearms, maps, documents, and rare coins and currency. He served on the Society's board of directors from 1938 and was president in 1948-1949. Mr. Brock's interest was genuine and unfailing through the years, and he was a friend who was always ready to give of himself and his means.

Mrs. Lalla Maloy Brigham, a member since 1931, died December 26, 1957, at the age of 90. Mrs. Brigham was known as the unofficial historian of Council Grove, having lived there almost all her life. She was the author of a book, *The Story of Council Grove on the Santa Fe Trail*, in addition to many historical articles. She also took a leading part in the promotion of centennial celebrations in 1921 and 1925, the first to commemorate William Becknell's successful pack trip over what came to be the Santa Fe trail and the second to commemorate the birth of the trail.

Lynn R. Brodrick, for many years publisher of the Marysville *Advocate-Democrat* and widely known as a leader of the Democratic party in Kansas, died January 29, 1958. Mr. Brodrick had served from 1942 to 1955 as the U. S. internal revenue director for Kansas and at the time of his death was state highway director. Earlier he had been a member of the bipartisan committee that drafted the first Kansas highway law during the administration of Governor Paulen, and he had served as a member of the Highway Commission under Governors Woodring and Landon.

Frank Motz, founder and editor of the Hays *Daily News*, died August 15, 1958. The son of pioneer residents of Hays, he spent his life in the newspaper field. After graduation from the University of Kansas school of

(104)

journalism he worked as a reporter on the Kansas City (Mo.) *Star* and then on various Kansas newspapers until 1929, when he established the *Daily News*. The loss of these friends is noted with sincere regret.

Appropriations and Budget Requests

The Society this year was fortunate in receiving legislative appropriations for several important projects which had been rejected in previous sessions. Funds were allocated for laying an asphalt tile floor in the museum, for replacement of the exterior doors and installation of steel shelving in the basement vault, and for several other long-needed improvements. Appropriations for normal operating expenses were approved. Requests for air-conditioning, and steel flooring for the main stack area, however, were again denied.

Budget requests for the fiscal year ending June 30, 1960, were filed with the state budget director in September. Appropriations requested for salaries and operating expenses are about the same as for the current year. New capital improvement requests include sand-blasting to clean up the exterior of the building and construction of a suspended ceiling on the fourth floor to conceal the unsightly steel beams which detract from what is otherwise one of the finest and most attractive museums in the Middle West. A new elevator, to be installed in an existing but unused shaft, has also been requested.

By far the largest single request in the budget is for remodeling of the G. A. R. hall on the second and third floors. The 1958 legislature provided $7,500 for architect's fees, and planning has progressed to the point where realistic cost estimates have been made. These requests are aimed at making the building as attractive and functional as possible for the approaching centennial in 1961. An auditorium of proper size, with good acoustics is essential to take care of school and other groups which visit the Society, and where meetings—including our own—can be held. More museum space, both for displays and storage, and a larger microfilm reading room are also needed. All these are provided for in the proposed remodeling.

Appropriations for the various historical properties out of Topeka remain at about the same level as before. The only capital improvement requests approved for the current year were $150 for trimming trees at the Kaw Mission and the Funston Home. Requests for next year generally are limited to the same improvements which have been budgeted unsuccessfully for the past several years.

Publications and Special Projects

Featured in the four issues of *The Kansas Historical Quarterly* for 1958 are the letters of Daniel R. Anthony, edited by Edgar Langsdorf and R. W. Richmond. Colonel Anthony was an early resident of Leavenworth, founder of the Anthony dynasty now in its fourth generation as publishers of the Leavenworth *Times*, and a vigorous and colorful personality who played a significant role in Kansas history. A new series by Dr. James C. Malin on early Kansas philosophers began in the Summer issue. Other articles scheduled for publication this year include letters written by members of the First U. S. cavalry while in the Indian country in 1859-1861, edited by Louise Barry, and a story of the Mudge ranch near Jetmore by Margaret Evans Caldwell.

Increased printing appropriations have made it possible to enlarge the *Quarterly* to 128 pages, 16 more than formerly. Many articles of substantial worth have been submitted to the editorial board and readers may look forward to entertaining and meaty fare in the issues just ahead.

The *Mirror,* sent every two months to members to give them current news of the Society's work, has been well received since its inception four years ago. It has proved especially helpful in calling attention to materials needed in the museum, and many valuable items have been donated as a direct result of requests made in its columns.

Items from the Kansas press of 100 years ago continue to be sent to Kansas editors in the form of monthly news releases. This program was begun over four years ago as part of the territorial centennial observance, and has proved so popular that it has been continued.

The work of indexing the 17 volumes of the *Kansas Historical Collections,* the *Biennial Reports* for 1877-1930, and the three small volumes of special publications has been completed and the index entries are now being alphabetized and assembled. The 1958 legislature appropriated $5,000 for publication of this index, which it is hoped will be finished by the fall of 1959. Upon its completion work will begin on a general index of the *Quarterly,* to be published as a companion volume.

Texts for two more historical markers were written and sent to the State Highway department. One marker, located at Baldwin, tells something of the early history of that community, and the other, at Beeler, reviews the career of George Washington Carver, who homesteaded in Ness county in 1886.

Within a month the Society will publish a new list of Kansas imprints prior to 1877. Alan W. Farley, the Society's president, and Lorene Anderson Hawley of the library staff have been working on this compilation for several years. Titled *Kansas Imprints, 1854-1876,* the new publication will be issued as a supplement to the original *Check List of Kansas Imprints, 1854-1876,* which was published in 1939 by the American Imprints Inventory of the Historical Records Survey. The new book, containing 405 entries and eight pages of illustrations, is now on the press. Considering the nature of the work, the printing has been limited, and the volume will be offered for sale.

The Kansas Centennial Commission and its committees have held several meetings during the year. Preliminary arrangements were made for the designing and issuance of a commemorative stamp in 1961 by the Post Office Department and numerous ideas and suggestions have been received. An appropriation of $25,000 was made by the 1958 legislature for the work of the commission during the fiscal year ending June 30, 1959, the fund to be administered through the Historical Society.

ARCHIVES DIVISION

Public records from the following state departments have been transferred during the year to the archives division:

Source	Title	Dates	Quantity
Agriculture, Board of...	Statistical Rolls of Counties,	1951	1,727 vols.
Auditor's Office	Plats and Surveys: Surveyor General for Kansas and Nebraska	1854-1875	9 portfolio vols.
Engineering Examiners, Board of	Engineer License Application Folders	1951-1956	17 reels microfilm

Source	Title	Dates	Quantity
Insurance Department	Annual Statements	1949-1951	1,792 vols.
Workmen's Compensation Commissioner	Awards and Orders in Docketed cases, Nos. 14,000-18,279	1945-1949	8 boxes

Annual reports were received from the Director of Alcoholic Beverage Control, Registration and Examining Board of Architects, Auditor of State and Department of Post-Audit, Crippled Children Commission, Larned State Hospital, State Library, Board of Medical Registration and Examination, Board of Podiatry Examiners, Real Estate Commission, School for the Blind, Soldiers' Home and Mother Bickerdyke Annex, Traveling Libraries Commission, State Treasurer, Veterans' Commission, Water Resources Board and Workmen's Compensation Commissioner for the fiscal year ending June 30, 1957, and from the Anti-Discrimination Commission for the fiscal year ending June 30, 1958.

The original enrolled laws of Kansas territory, 1855-1860, contained in nine large volumes, have been microfilmed. Most of the volumes were of a size difficult to shelve and they were also so badly deteriorated that they were virtually unusable in their original form. However, the three volumes for 1855, the famous "Bogus Laws," were reasonably well preserved and even though they are now on film, the originals will be kept permanently on file in the archives.

LIBRARY

The number of library patrons increased substantially again this year. The total was 4,602, of whom 1,905 were interested in Kansas subjects, 1,741 in genealogy, and 956 in general subjects. The largest percentage of increase has been in requests for Kansas material. Many researchers have indicated that the Kansas section is one of the finest local history collections in this country. The completeness of the Kansas material is due largely to the foresight of the first administrators in obtaining early books and pamphlets while they were yet available, and to the generosity of individuals and organizations in donating their own publications and other items which pertain to Kansas. Locally printed books are often difficult to collect because the supply is so soon exhausted. Thanks are due to many patrons and friends who send in copies or furnish information on these local items.

During the year letters were sent to all county superintendents of schools requesting copies of county school directories which are issued each year in compliance with a law passed by the 1955 legislature. As a result directories have been received from 80 counties and, in some cases, files for previous years as well. These directories, if received regularly, should be of immense value for reference through the years.

In addition to the seven daily newspapers read regularly by the clipping department, 13 other dailies and ten weeklies, plus a number of miscellaneous papers—a total of 7,276 separate issues—were searched for local items. Special editions of 11 newspapers were also read and clipped. The department mounted 5,474 new clippings and remounted 1,325 older ones. In addition, the difficult and painstaking task of remounting the "Webb Scrapbooks" is nearly completed. This 17-volume collection of clippings from Eastern newspapers for the period 1854-1860 has been used by hundreds of students since it was acquired by the Society in 1877.

New material on microfilm added during the year included: "A Descriptive Roll of Kansas Volunteers, 1861-1865," loaned by the Adjutant General of Kansas; general, special and court-martial orders and circulars, with indexes covering the period, 1868-1875, issued by the Department of the Missouri, U. S. Army; and minutes of various Baptist association meetings in Kansas from 1858 to 1876. Two theses, "Corporation Farming in Kansas," by Emy K. Miller, and "Dr. John R. Brinkley, Candidate for Governor," by Francis W. Schruben, were lent for microfilming. Seven volumes of Perrin's histories of Kentucky counties were purchased on microfilm. These histories, published between 1884 and 1888, are long out-of-print and cannot now be purchased in book form.

A number of Kansas and genealogical books were donated by their authors, and collections of older books were given by Mary Smith of New York City, Mrs. Alice Gordon Wilson of Topeka, and Mrs. Clif Stratton of Topeka. An unusual gift, a scrapbook of theater programs largely from Topeka theaters, was received from Mrs. Roy Crawford, Topeka. Typed copies of the following theses were donated by the authors: "A Study of the Use of Editorial Expression in the Weekly Newspapers of Kansas for the Years 1925, 1940, and 1955," by Maurice C. Lungren; "The Revolt of Little Wolf's Northern Cheyennes," by William D. Mather; "The Lecompton Conspiracy: the History of the Lecompton Constitution Movement in Kansas and the Nation, 1857 and 1858," by Clifford Wayne Trow; and " 'I'm Not Selling Anything'—Some Folklore From Kansas," by P. J. Wyatt.

Typed records, printed books and pamphlets were given by the Kansas Societies of the Daughters of the American Revolution and the Daughters of American Colonists. The National Society of Colonial Dames in the State of Kansas, the Wichita Town Committee of the same organization, and the Elizabeth Knapp chapter, Daughters of American Colonists, Manhattan, made gifts of money for the purchase of local histories and the 1850 federal census on microfilm.

Very little Kansas history has appeared in book or pamphlet form this year. Centennial booklets were published at Eudora, Gardner, and Salina, and Alfred B. Bradshaw of Turon wrote a book of reminiscences entitled *When the Prairies Were New.* Homer E. Socolofsky, of Kansas State College, edited *A Bibliography of Theses and Dissertations Pertaining to Kansas History*, a project of the Kansas Association of Teachers of History.

Library accessions, October 1, 1957-September 30, 1958, were:

```
Bound volumes
   Books
      Kansas ..........................  183
      General .........................  618
      Genealogy and local history......  135
      Indians and the West.............   58
      Kansas state publications........   58
         Total ........................        1,052
   Clippings ..........................           17
   Periodicals ........................          236
                                               -----
         Total, bound volumes..........        1,305
   Microfilm (reels) ..................           18
```

Pamphlets
  Kansas 1,103
  General 468
  Genealogy and local history 48
  Indians and the West 17
  Kansas state publications 224
    Total .... ——— 1,860

MANUSCRIPT DIVISION

The papers of Alfred M. Landon, received during the year, constitute a large and important addition to the holdings of the Society. Besides more than 90 file drawers of correspondence, the collection includes photographs and scrapbooks, and should prove a rich source of information for researchers in the field of political history. Much of the material pertains to the presidential campaign of 1936. The collection has not been cataloged and at this time may be used only with the permission of Mr. Landon.

A large body of papers was received from the estate of the late Cora Dolbee, for many years a member of the faculty of the University of Kansas. There are more than 800 letters in the collection, which was originally held by the family of the Rev. John S. Brown, a pioneer Unitarian minister of Lawrence. It was lent to Miss Dolbee for research purposes with the understanding that it would be deposited in the Society. The letters fall within the period 1818-1906 and were written by friends and members of the Brown family in Kansas and the East. Included are 15 letters by Charles A. Dana, 1842-1861. The manuscripts were accompanied by an extensive collection of anti-slavery poems taken from newspapers and magazines, 1854-1861. These have been placed in the library.

Seventeen pages from the day book of the Western Bakery, Lawrence, dated 1861, were received from Mrs. Thomas T. Parker, Phoenix, Ariz. Mrs. Parker is the granddaughter of Louis A. Wise, operator of the bakery, which was burned during the Quantrill raid. The pages were found in the ruins. Among the patrons were John Speer, Lyman Eldridge, Dr. S. B. Prentiss, A. D. Searl, S. W. Eldridge, the Home Guards, and the Eldridge House.

Mrs. Homer Wark, Topeka, gave three diaries kept by her husband, the Rev. Homer Wark, 1917-1919. Dr. Wark was a chaplain in the A. E. F. and served with the 137th U. S. infantry from May until September, 1918, when he was assigned to the base hospital at Rimaucourt, France.

Two ledgers from the grocery firm of C. W. Myers & Co., Topeka, 1903, 1904-1908, were given by Fritz Leuenberger, Jr., Topeka.

Mrs. Harry Dobson, Wichita, gave a diary kept by her father, John Hannibal Trautwine, September 3-December 23, 1873, in which he gives an account of a buffalo hunt.

Three somewhat unusual letters by John James Ingalls, written in 1855, 1859 and 1862, were received from the estate of the late Ann Downs Ingalls of Shokan, N. Y.

A small group of papers of H. C. Harrison, Brandon, Vt., 1880-1892, were received from his daughter, Mrs. George C. Cobb, Rutland, Vt. They relate mainly to the Barton County Bank, Great Bend, of which Harrison was president although he never maintained residence in Kansas.

Papers of Dr. Franklin Loomis Crane and members of his family were received from a great granddaughter, Mrs. Carl F. Trace, Topeka. Included are 192 manuscripts, mainly family and Civil War letters, and two manuscript volumes: a record of the Topeka Town Association's account with F. L. Crane; and a diary with scattered entries from 1853 to 1869. Dr. Crane first came to Kansas in 1854 and settled permanently in Topeka the following year. He was one of the builders of the city. A portion of his diary for 1856-1857, was received from Caroline K. Wallbridge, Topeka.

An unpublished book length manuscript, "Citizenship and Essential Liberties and Rights," by the late Parley Paul Womer, was given by his wife. Dr. Womer was a leader in the development of Washburn University. He served as president for 16 years, 1915-1931, and later as professor of American citizenship and public affairs.

A typescript of portions of the diary of Anne Jones Davies was given by her daughter, Priscilla Davies, Denver, Colo. Both Mrs. Davies and her husband, John Davies, came to America from Wales and after their marriage in the 1870's settled in Arvonia township, Osage county. John Davies was a stone mason, and during his absences on construction work Anne managed their farm. The years of the diary are 1882-1884, 1886-1888.

Correspondence relating to floods in Kansas, their prevention and control, was received from the estate of Snowden Dwight Flora, author and government meteorologist at Topeka. There are 81 items.

Microfilm copies of the following have been acquired:

Twelve reels of letters and reports from Congregational missionaries and church groups in Kansas to the American Home Missionary Society, New York, 1854-1877, 1892, and 1893. The letters are not limited to church matters and contain many references to conditions in Kansas. The film was obtained from the University of Chicago; originals are held by the Chicago Theological Seminary.

Reminiscences of the early West and experiences of the Bowlby family. Original manuscript lent by Mrs. E. B. Brown, Denison.

The original records of the Manhattan Town association, seven manuscript volumes covering the period 1855-1877. Included are the constitution and bylaws of the association, lists of town lots, town shares, and stockholders. The first volume contains records of the Boston association. The originals are in the possession of Sam C. Charlson, Manhattan, who lent them for copying.

Papers of Elizabeth Ann Berryman Eddy, Topeka, consisting of miscellaneous documents, talks and letters. Originals were lent by her grandson, Leo B. Dixon of Hanston.

Letters, 1862-1864, and diary, 1861-1862, of Alva Curtis Trueblood. Trueblood served with the 13th regiment Indiana Volunteers and his letters were written from the field. In 1880 he came to Atchison where he engaged in business and served as city clerk. The papers were lent by Mr. and Mrs. R. A. Goodhue, San Gabriel, Calif.

Records of the Secretary of the Interior: Journals and field books relating to the Eastern and Central division of the Fort Kearny, South Pass and Honey Lake wagon road, 1857-1859. Included are rough notes of travel of the advance party under W. H. Wagner, chief engineer, from Belmont, Kansas territory, to Oronville, Calif., 1859.

Other donors were: Mrs. C. T. Barker, Liberal; E. A. Benson, Kansas City; Edward E. Bill, Garden City; Mrs. Henry Blake, Sr., Topeka; Mrs. Frank W. Boyd, Mankato; Berlin B. Chapman, Stillwater, Okla.; Charles Darnell, Wamego; Mrs. Lavilla Eastham, McPherson; Mrs. Ella Funston Eckdall, Emporia; Mary and A. Blanche Edwards, Abilene; Alan W. Farley, Kansas City; Mrs. Philip Fox, Evanston, Ill.; Mrs. Edna P. Gilpin, Phoenix; the Haise family, Russell; Mrs. Ralph W. Heflin, Pearland, Tex.; Henry Gaffney, Jr., Irvington, N. J.; Mrs. Meta Howard Geary, Wichita; Walter A. Huxman, Topeka; H. R. Landes, Topeka; Mrs. O. H. Landrith, Enid, Okla.; Laura Loughmiller, Topeka; Pearl Maus, Topeka; Henry A. Meyer, Evansville, Ind.; Ottawa County Historical Society; Jennie Small Owen, Topeka; Lyle Owen, Tulsa, Okla.; Elmo Richardson, Lawrence; Joseph G. Rosa, Ruislip, Middlesex, England; Mrs. William E. Stanley, Wichita; Mrs. E. E. Swanzey, Abilene; Ailine Thomas, Merriam; Mrs. J. R. Throckmorton, Hays; Mrs. W. V. Turner and sons, Las Vegas, Nev.; Mrs. Charles H. Watson, Evanston, Ill.; Mrs. Alice Wilson, Topeka; Mrs. Blodwen Williams Zeitler, Ft. Madison, Iowa.

MICROFILM DIVISION

As of September 30, 1958, the microfilm division has made 4,896,000 photographs since it began operation in 1946, 349,000 of them in the past 12 months. Nearly 278,000 were of newspapers, 64,000 of archival records, 4,000 of library materials, and 1,500 of manuscripts. The balance were negatives produced for private purchasers.

The largest newspaper project of the year was the filming of the Topeka *State Journal* for January 1, 1943-June 29, 1946, and April 6, 1949-December 31, 1957. The Wichita *Eagle*, both morning and evening editions, was filmed for the period September 1, 1953-February 28, 1957; the Kinsley *Mercury* for August 18, 1899-December 27, 1956; the Cheney *Sentinel* for March 1, 1894-December 26, 1940; the Osage City *Free Press* for July 10, 1875-December 28, 1916; and the *Johnson County Herald*, Overland Park, for January 1, 1942-December 27, 1956. Other newspapers microfilmed included the Topeka *Commonwealth*, May 20, 1869-November 1, 1888; the Kansas City *Labor Bulletin*, February 23, 1940-December 27, 1957; *Lucifer, the Light-Bearer*, Chicago, Ill., January 6, 1897-June 6, 1907; Marion *Record*, July 23, 1875-December 28, 1900; Oskaloosa *Independent*, August 27, 1870-December 28, 1900; and 18 other newspapers and periodicals requiring less than two rolls of film each.

Microfilming of archives was concentrated primarily on the state census of 1895. Approximately half has been completed and work is continuing on this project.

MUSEUM

The museum has completed another highly successful year. The number of visitors was 58,494, breaking last year's all-time record by more than 6,000. The total was swelled by 375 school and scout groups which took advantage of the guided tours conducted as part of the museum's educational program, and a new monthly record of 9,564 was established in May.

Twenty new display cases were received and exhibits installed in them during the year. This completes, for the time being, the case displays planned for the fourth floor. Replicas of a doctor's office, a dentist's office, and an old-time general store, all of which were mentioned in last year's report, were completed in the east gallery, and have attracted much favorable comment. The appearance of the museum has also been greatly improved by the installation of an asphalt tile floor.

The Society appeared in a new field last month by setting up a display at the Kansas Free Fair at Topeka. Space was made available through the courtesy of Maurice E. Fager, manager of the fair, and 11,695 persons visited the exhibit during the week. Many learned for the first time about the Society and its work, and the display was so well received that a request has already been made for the use of the same space next year.

During the spring and summer the assistant museum director, Roscoe Wilmeth, conducted an archaeological survey in the Pomona and Melvern reservoir areas in Osage county. The work was done under an agreement with the National Park Service. The 1958 legislature appropriated funds for the purchase of basic archaeological field equipment, including instruments for surveying and mapping. Plans are being made to conduct a survey of the John Redmond reservoir area and to send a field party to make excavations in the Pomona reservoir area next summer under new contracts with the National Park Service.

There were 227 accessions comprising 897 objects during the year. Donations included clothing and accessories from Mrs. Roy Crawford and her grandson, Berry, of Topeka; Spanish-American War souvenirs from Adna G. Clarke, Jr., of Honolulu, Hawaii; items for the general store from Mr. and Mrs. Charles Darnell of Wamego, Mrs. Fred W. Gauch of Kansas City, and Mrs. Duane McQueen Ward of Peabody. Wayne Herneison of Wamego donated a blacksmith forge and many tools; other blacksmith equipment was received from E. W. Jaeger of Hope.

Oil portraits of Mr. and Mrs. Franklin L. Crane, Topeka pioneers, were given by Mr. and Mrs. Erwin Keller, Topeka. Dental equipment for the 1900 dental office period room was donated by Dr. William McInerney of Abilene, and clothing and accessories belonging to Mrs. Eliza Abbott Root were received from Mrs. Louise S. Woodward of Eskridge.

Other donors included: Atchison, Topeka & Santa Fe railroad; Wallace Baker, Protection; Mrs. Ethel Ballinger, Ozawkie; Mrs. Olive Bell, Topeka; Roderick Bentley, Shields; Mrs. Henry Blake, Sr., Topeka; Mrs. Eugene L. Bowers, Topeka; Mrs. Claude Brey, Ozawkie; Mrs. D. J. Brown, Rochester, N. Y.; Mrs. Maclure Butcher, Neodesha; W. C. Byington, Winchester; Mrs. Minnie Campbell, Topeka; E. C. Cannon, Phillipsburg; estate of Arthur Capper, Topeka; Mr. and Mrs. Eldon W. Cessna, El Segundo, Calif.; Mrs. Charles F. Chrisman, Jackson Heights, N. Y.; Dr. Orville R. Clark, Topeka; Mrs. Martina Clarkson, Harper; Mrs. W. B. Collinson, Topeka; Mrs. Gerald J. Courtney, Topeka; Mrs. Warren M. Crosby, Jr., Topeka; Mrs. Edwin W. Davis, Topeka; Mrs. Flora E. Davison, Kansas City, Mo.; Mrs. Lyndon Day, Topeka; Esther Delker, Chapman; Vern Donge and sons, Larry and Ronnie, Soldier; Lupe Duran, Teseque Pueblo, N. M.; Arrold R. Earhart, Topeka; Dr. E. W. Eustace, Lebanon; D. S. Farman, Manhattan; Mrs. Earl Ferguson, Valley Falls; Mrs. Phillip Fox, Evanston, Ill.; Barbara Funston, Mill Valley, Calif.; Mrs. Meta Howard Geary, Wichita; Mrs. Edna Piazzek Gilpin, Phoenix, Ariz.; Governor's office, Topeka; Harold C. Grinnell, Cedar Point; Mrs. Asa Hagans, Melvern;

Harold L. Hale, Topeka; Dale W. Hall, Topeka; Mrs. R. C. Harding, Wamego; Mrs. Frank Haucke, Council Grove; Grace Haven, Council Grove; Mrs. Ralph W. Heflin, Pearland, Tex.; Chester Heizer, Caldwell; Mrs. Bessie Hereford, Topeka; Wesley R. Hurt, Vermillion, S. D.; Mrs. Minnie Jacobs, Council Grove; A. M. Jarboe, Topeka; Mrs. Virginia A. Johnson, Gardner; Mrs. Carl Jones, Topeka; Dean L. Jordan, Sr., Abilene; Kansas State Printing Plant, Topeka; Mrs. B. Gage Kenny, Lincoln; Mr. and Mrs. R. L. Kingman, Topeka; W. A. Kingman, Springfield, Mo.; C. L. Kinley, Augusta; Mrs. Lucy M. Large, Lecompton; Mrs. Laura Loughmiller, Topeka; Mrs. P. A. Lovewell, Topeka; Mrs. V. E. McArthur, Hutchinson; Florence McCall, Salina; Dr. Duncan C. McKeever, Houston, Tex.; Mrs. F. M. Manshardt, Topeka; Marquart Music Co., Topeka; Lakin Meade, Topeka; Roy Mendez, Topeka; Mrs. Grace Menninger, Topeka; B. F. Messick, Topeka; Mrs. Esther Pennock Miller, Topeka; Mr. and Mrs. Henry W. Miller, Delavan; Carl Mullendore, Howard; Mrs. Pearl Nellans, Portland, Ore.; Mrs. Myra Perrings, Topeka; Mrs. A. G. Pickett, Topeka; estate of Mrs. George W. Porter, Topeka; Ray B. Ramsey, Topeka; estate of Cora E. Ream, Kansas City, Mo.; Mrs. C. H. Reser, Hamilton; Charles R. Richards, Detroit, Mich.; Ned Richardson, Topeka; John Ripley, Topeka; Mrs. J. C. Ruppenthal, Russell; Mrs. R. A. Schwegler, Lawrence; Sears Roebuck & Co., Topeka; Mary Alice Smith, Abilene; Mr. and Mrs. W. V. Snyder, Berryton; Stanley Sohl, Topeka; Mr. and Mrs. Albert Speer, Topeka; Mrs. W. E. Stanley, Wichita; Mrs. Fred Straley, Topeka; Annie B. Sweet, Topeka; Capt. Dorr Thomson, Hutchinson; Mrs. Elsa M. Tindell, Burlingame; Mr. and Mrs. Chester Trower, Topeka; Jim Wahwasseck, Topeka; Louis Walddy, Americus; Washburn University, Topeka; Mr. and Mrs. J. D. Weidman, Topeka; Walter W. Wendell, Topeka; Mr. and Mrs. Ben E. White, Bonner Springs; R. D. Wiley, Melvern; Mary Willbrandt, Washington; Mrs. Alice Wilson, Topeka; Mr. and Mrs. William J. Zeidler, Topeka; and Mrs. J. F. Zimmerman, Valley Falls.

NEWSPAPER AND CENSUS DIVISION

Over 4,800 patrons were served in person by the newspaper and census division, and more than that number were given assistance by mail.

Use of the Society's newspapers increased considerably this year. Single issues used totaled 6,911, bound volumes 7,898, and microfilm reels 2,498.

This was the first full year during which a charge of $1.00 each was made for certified copies of the Society's records. The result has been a substantial decrease in the number of census and newspaper certifications requested. A total of 4,876 certificates were furnished, less than 40 percent of last year's figure. However, the number of census volumes searched was 23,164, as compared with 36,134 reported a year ago.

Nearly all Kansas publishers continue to contribute their newspapers to the Society for filing. Fifty-four dailies, 12 semiweeklies, and 291 regular community weeklies are now being received. Also, 143 newspapers published by Kansas schools, labor unions, churches and other institutions are donated by their publishers for the Society's files. Nine out-of-state newspapers are received.

During the year the Society added 438 reels to its collection of newspapers on microfilm. Thirteen Kansas publishers donate microfilm copies of their current issues to the Society.

Older Kansas newspapers added to the files included: *Nemaha Courier,* Seneca, 20 issues scattered from November 28, 1863, to November 16, 1865, donated by the New York State Historical Society; *Southern Kansan,* Lawrence, May 1, 1886, donated by the Illinois State Historical Library; *Howard County Ledger,* Longton, February 23, 1871, donated by Mrs. Richard W. Leach, Evanston, Ill.; and *Once A Week,* Lawrence, July 14, 1883, donated by Gorton V. Carruth, Pleasantville, N. Y.

Other donors of newspapers were: Mrs. Henry Blake, Sr., Topeka; Mrs. Dale Brown, Delphos; Mrs. Maurene Buckmaster, Topeka; Adna G. Clarke, Jr., Honolulu, Hawaii; Bob Ellis, Topeka; Mrs. C. H. Engle, Topeka; Alan W. Farley, Kansas City, Kan.; Mrs. Ralph W. Heflin, Pearland, Tex.; Mrs. Charles McGill, Paola; B. F. Messick, Topeka; Norman Niccum, Tecumseh; Lena M. Smith, Princeton, Ind.; Mary Smith, New York City; Etta Templeton, Topeka; Mrs. Carl F. Trace, Topeka; Mrs. Alice Wilson, Topeka; and B. W. Zeitler, Ft. Madison, Iowa.

PHOTOGRAPHS AND MAPS

During the year 1,994 photographs have been added to the Society's collection. Of these, 1,135 were gifts, 482 were lent for copying and 301 were taken by the Society staff. Seventy-six color slides have been accessioned.

Several large groups of photographs were given to the Society. Among the more important were over 400 glass negatives of Russell county scenes, obtained through J. C. Ruppenthal of Russell and Elmo Mahoney of Dorrance; 23 views of Osborne and vicinity in the 1890's from Mrs. Nellie Baldwin, Osborne; 13 Ottawa county scenes from Don D. Ballou, Kansas City; 56 glass negatives of Lawrence and Topeka views from J. Leland Benson, Topeka; 59 pictures of the 20th Kansas regiment in the Philippines from Adna G. Clarke, Jr., Honolulu, Hawaii; 22 post card views of Kansas at the turn of the century from Dr. Duncan C. McKeever, Houston, Tex.; and 67 pictures of Fort Riley hospitals and officers, from Maj. George Omer, Jr., Fort Riley.

Excellent collections of early Kansas pictures were lent for copying by C. M. Correll, Manhattan; Jess Denious, Jr., Dodge City; the Dickinson County Historical Museum, Abilene; the Eisenhower Museum, Abilene; the College of Emporia; St. Benedict's College, Atchison; George Eastman House, Rochester, N. Y.; Paul Gibler, Claflin; Mrs. Frank Motz, Hays; the Riley County Historical Society, Manhattan; Mrs. Paul Shahan, Marion; the *Smith County Pioneer,* Smith Center; Homer Socolofsky, Manhattan; Floyd Souders, Cheney; C. C. Tinkham, Topeka; and Mr. and Mrs. J. I. Ziebolz, Ness City.

The Society has furnished photographs during the year to such publications as *Holiday, American Heritage* and *Life,* to several of the nation's leading book publishers, and to the National Broadcasting Company. In addition, many authors, newspapers and other historical institutions have obtained prints from the Society's collection. The current interest in the old West has brought requests for photographs of cowtowns and peace officers from all parts of the United States and from Holland, England and Italy.

Ninety new maps have been accessioned this year, 45 of which are recent issues of the United States Geological Survey. Photostats of 25 maps of Kansas military posts were obtained from the National Park Service, Omaha. Other recently received maps include a plat of Pleasant Hill, 1855, and a map of the Missouri river, 1878-1881, from the State Auditor's office; a plat of Colby, 1887, from August Lauterbach, Colby; an ownership map of Miami county, 1958, from Harry Hemphill, Paola; Woodson county, about 1910, from H. R. Landes, Topeka; and Riley county pioneer roads and trails from Morris Werner, Manhattan.

G. L. Chadborn of Kansas City, through Alan Farley of Kansas City, presented the Society with a photographic copy of an 1869 lithograph of the town of Wyandotte.

SUBJECTS FOR RESEARCH

Subjects for extended research during the year included: Protestant missionaries to the Indians; early transportation in Kansas; '89ers; Kansas songs, Civil War songs; Otoe Indians; overland journals; early mail systems in Kansas; farmers' diaries; Sharps rifles; Cherokee Strip and Kansas border towns; the town of Rolla; motion picture censorship in Kansas; public utilities; the Kansas Power and Light Co.; Emporia *Gazette*; German language publications; western Kansas cattle trails; mental hospitals; Kansas Turnvereins; history of Fort Scott, 1842-1872; Fort Scott Baptist Association; Kansas, 1930-1935; Kansas governors' wives; sunflowers; Indian medicine; John R. Brinkley; Luke Short; James B. Hickok; Wyatt Earp; William Barclay Masterson; Vernon L. Parrington; James A. McGonigle; "Doc" Holliday; Albert H. Horton; Elam Bartholomew; Edmund G. Ross, Arthur Capper, and Alfred M. Landon.

SOCIETY HOLDINGS, SEPTEMBER 30, 1958

Bound Volumes
  Books
    Kansas 9,969
    General 56,937
    Genealogy and local history 10,099
    Indians and the West 1,523
    Kansas state publications 3,201
      Total 81,729
  Clippings 1,284
  Periodicals 17,294

      Total, bound volumes 100,307
Manuscripts (archives and private papers,
  cubic feet) 5,750
Maps and atlases 5,366
Microfilm (reels)
  Books and other library materials 244
  Public archives and private papers 1,392
  Newspapers 7,089
    Total 8,725
Newspapers (bound volumes)
  Kansas 57,551
  Out-of-state 11,983
    Total 69,534
Paintings and drawings 421

Pamphlets
Kansas	92,830
General	38,464
Genealogy and local history	3,762
Indians and the West	1,071
Kansas state publications	5,732
Total	141,859
Photographs	33,037

THE FIRST CAPITOL

Registration of visitors at the First Territorial Capitol, on the Fort Riley reservation, totaled 6,906, an increase of 324 over last year. Although it was expected that the by-passing of the fort by the new U. S. 40 highway would result in fewer visitors, the contrary, so far at least, has proved to be the case. The efforts of the Junction City Chamber of Commerce in promoting tours to Fort Riley and the old Capitol, and the new directional markers which were placed on U. S. 40 at the request of John Montgomery, second district highway commissioner, have resulted in substantial increases during the past two years.

Visitors registered from all states except Nevada. Alaska, the District of Columbia, Puerto Rico, and Hawaii were also represented as were the Philippine Islands, Canada, Panama and 14 other foreign countries.

THE FUNSTON HOME

This property, located in a less heavily traveled area than the Society's other historic sites, was visited by 955 people, about 50 less than last year. Twenty states were represented in addition to Kansas, but "home folks" provided most of the visitors, 820.

The Funston home has continued to develop as an interesting attraction. Barbara Funston of Mill Valley, Calif., a daughter of Gen. Frederick Funston, presented articles belonging to her father, including a pair of snowshoes and two Eskimo fishing spears from his Alaskan trip, a plumed military dress hat, and a pair of shoes which he wore during the Aguinaldo expedition. Also, through the courtesy of Maj. Gen. Joe Nickell, the adjutant general, the Society received from the Department of Defense replicas of four medals awarded to General Funston, among them the Medal of Honor.

THE KAW MISSION

Kaw Mission, at Council Grove, enjoyed another successful year. Attendance totaled 5,732, about 200 more than last year. Visitors came from 43 states in addition to Kansas, and from two territories and 17 foreign countries.

The Council Grove *Republican* continued its weekly publication of a "Museum Scoreboard" and the information booth operated by the Junior Chamber of Commerce directed many tourists to the Mission. Two more rose bushes were presented by the Nautilus Club.

A number of interesting accessions were received for the museum. Donors included Frank Allen, Mrs. Norma Comer Bates, Mrs. Floyd Bramick, Mrs. Eugene Chase, V. S. Coltrane, Russell Dodderidge, the Dwight Library, Ivy Foster, Mrs. Minnie Jacobs, Oscar Larson, Clarence Reveal, Leslie Ruttledge, Ocie Shemwell, and Neil L. Tweedman.

Old Shawnee Mission

Registration at Old Shawnee Mission was 6,182, of whom 1,301 lived outside of Kansas. Visitors came from 39 states, the District of Columbia, and 14 foreign countries.

They included Edna Williams, related to Charles Bluejacket, a Shawnee Indian chief; Robert Russell, Joe Russell, and Jerome Berryman, II, great grandsons of the Rev. Jerome C. Berryman who was superintendent of the mission at the time the North building was built; and Fred Chouteau, grandson of Cyprian Chouteau.

Several rooms in the East building were painted, the floors of three were sanded and varnished, and the exterior of the building was waterproofed. An asphalt parking strip also has been constructed for the convenience of visitors.

The Society is indebted to the Daughters of the American Revolution, the Daughters of 1812, the Daughters of American Colonists, the Colonial Dames, and the Shawnee Mission Indian Historical Society for their continued assistance at the mission.

The Staff of the Society

Acknowledgement is due the Society's staff for the accomplishments noted in this report. They have worked faithfully and conscientiously to make the Society truly a service institution. It is not possible to mention here all the individuals whose efforts have contributed to the total result, but each has my sincere thanks. Special attention should be called to the work of Edgar Langsdorf, assistant secretary, and the department heads: Mrs. Lela Barnes of the manuscript division, who is also treasurer of the Society; Robert W. Richmond, archivist; Alberta Pantle, librarian; Stanley D. Sohl, museum director; and Forrest R. Blackburn of the newspaper division.

Appreciation is also due the custodians of the historic sites administered by the Society: Mr. and Mrs. Harry A. Hardy at Shawnee Mission, Mr. and Mrs. Elwood Jones at Kaw Mission, Mr. and Mrs. V. E. Berglund at the Funston Memorial Home, and Mr. and Mrs. J. L. Brownback at the First Territorial Capitol.

Respectfully submitted,
NYLE H. MILLER, *Secretary.*

At the conclusion of the reading of the secretary's report, Robert Aitchison moved that it be accepted. Motion was seconded by Kirke Mechem and the report was adopted.

President Farley then called for the report of the treasurer, Mrs. Lela Barnes:

TREASURER'S REPORT

Based on the post-audit by the State Division of Auditing and Accounting for the period August 9, 1957, to August 4, 1958.

Membership Fee Fund

Balance, August 9, 1957:
Cash	$3,479.24	
U. S. bonds, Series K	5,000.00	
		$8,479.24

Receipts:
Membership fees	$1,129.94	
Gifts	136.60	
Interest on bonds	138.00	
Interest, Bowlus gift	27.60	
Interest, savings	28.12	
		1,460.26
		$9,939.50
Disbursements		$1,067.72

Balance, August 4, 1958:
Cash	$3,871.78	
U. S. bonds, Series K	5,000.00	
		8,871.78
		$9,939.50

JONATHAN PECKER BEQUEST

Balance, August 9, 1957:
Cash	$50.64	
U. S. bonds, Series K	1,000.00	
		$1,050.64

Receipts:
Interest on bond	$27.60	
Interest on savings account	3.34	
		30.94
		$1,081.58

Balance, August 4, 1958:
Cash	$81.58	
U. S. bond, Series K	1,000.00	
		$1,081.58

JOHN BOOTH BEQUEST

Balance, August 9, 1957:
Cash	$132.13	
U. S. bond, Series K	500.00	
		$632.13

Receipts:
Interest on bond	$13.80	
Interest on savings account	1.69	
		15.49
		$647.62

Balance, August 4, 1958:
Cash	$147.62	
U. S. bond, Series K	500.00	
		$647.62

Thomas H. Bowlus Donation

This donation is substantiated by a U. S. bond, Series K, in the amount of $1,000. The interest is credited to the membership fee fund.

Elizabeth Reader Bequest

Balance, August 9, 1957:		
Cash (deposited in membership fee fund)	$595.19	
U. S. bonds, Series K	5,500.00	
		$6,095.19
Receipts:		
Bond interest (deposited in membership fee fund)		151.80
		$6,246.99
Disbursements: books, prints, mss.		$284.35
Balance, August 4, 1958:		
Cash (deposited in membership fee fund)	$462.64	
U. S. bonds, Series K	5,500.00	
		$5,962.64
		$6,246.99

State Appropriations

This report covers only the membership fee fund and other custodial funds. Appropriations made to the Historical Society by the legislature are disbursed through the State Department of Administration. For the year ending June 30, 1958, these appropriations were: Kansas State Historical Society, including the Memorial building, $240,593.61; First Capitol of Kansas, $6,432; Kaw Mission, $4,198; Funston Home $3,780; Old Shawnee Mission, $16,131.

Respectfuly submitted,

Mrs. Lela Barnes, *Treasurer.*

Kirke Mechem moved that the report be adopted. Frank Haucke seconded the motion and the report was accepted.

In the absence of Will T. Beck, chairman, T. M. Lillard presented the report of the executive committee on the post-audit of the Society's funds by the State Division of Auditing and Accounting:

REPORT OF THE EXECUTIVE COMMITTEE

October 17, 1958.

To the Board of Directors, Kansas State Historical Society:

The executive committee being directed under the bylaws to check the accounts of the treasurer, states that the State Department of Post-Audit has audited the funds of the State Historical Society, the Old Shawnee Mission, the First Capitol of Kansas, the Old Kaw Mission, the Funston Home, and Pike's Pawnee Village, for the period August 9, 1957, to August 4, 1958, and that they are hereby approved.

Will T. Beck, *Chairman,*
Charles M. Correll,
Frank Haucke,
T. M. Lillard.

On a motion by James E. Taylor, seconded by E. A. Thomas, the report was accepted.

President Farley then presented a recommendation by the executive committee that the election of officers be regularly scheduled for the morning meeting of the board instead of for a meeting following the afternoon session. It was felt by the committee that under the proposed plan more appropriate recognition could be given the President-elect, also that it was desirable to omit the late afternoon board meeting. There was no objection and the report of the nominating committee was presented by T. M. Lillard:

NOMINATING COMMITTEE'S REPORT

October 17, 1958.

To the Board of Directors, Kansas State Historical Society:

Your committee on nominations submits the following report for officers of the Kansas State Historical Society:

For a one-year term: Richard M. Long, Wichita, president; E. R. Sloan, Topeka, first vice-president; and Jerome C. Berryman, Ashland, second vice-president.

For a two-year term: Mrs. Lela Barnes, Topeka, treasurer.

Respectfully submitted,
WILL T. BECK, *Chairman*,
CHARLES M. CORRELL,
FRANK HAUCKE,
T. M. LILLARD.

James E. Taylor moved that the secretary cast a unanimous ballot for the officers named in the report. E. A. Thomas seconded the motion and the officers were declared elected.

Following the election of officers, the secretary outlined plans for the proposed remodeling of the G. A. R. hall area. He stated that the legislature of 1958, in response to a resolution in 1957 by the Society's board of directors, had appropriated $7,500 for architects' fees; that plans provided for a small auditorium, badly needed display and storage space and another reading room; and that the entire cost might be as much as $280,000. Several expressed the hope that the 1959 legislature would appropriate the required amount and that the work could be completed by early 1961 when centennial celebrations of both statehood and the Civil war will commence.

There being no further business, the meeting adjourned.

Annual Meeting of the Society

The annual meeting of the Kansas State Historical Society opened with a luncheon at noon in the roof garden of the Jayhawk hotel. About 175 members and guests attended.

The invocation was given by William E. Berger, head of the history department of the College of Emporia.

Following the luncheon President Farley introduced guests at the speakers' table. These included Governor and Mrs. Docking and officers of the Society and their wives. President Farley delivered his address, "Samuel Hallett and the Union Pacific Railway Company in Kansas," which appears elsewhere in this issue.

Following the address, President Farley presented a small plaque to each of the following past presidents of the Society and to Kirke Mechem, former secretary, all of whom had received a special invitation to attend the meeting: Thomas M. Lillard, James C. Malin, Fred W. Brinkerhoff, Robert T. Aitchison, Charles M. Correll, Frank Haucke, F. D. Farrell, Wilford Riegle, and Rolla Clymer. Three past presidents were unable to attend: John S. Dawson, Will T. Beck, and Angelo Scott. Mr. Farley was given a plaque by the newly elected president, Richard M. Long.

John Ripley, Topeka, was introduced and spoke briefly of his work in collecting old lantern slides. He then presented his talk, "Take Me Out for a Joy Ride," which was illustrated with slides of many early views of Topeka.

The following memorial to the late R. F. Brock of Goodland, former president, was read by the secretary who was instructed to send a copy to Mrs. Brock:

> The death of Roland F. Brock on November 11, 1957, meant the loss of an old and cherished friend. Mr. Brock was a banker and stockman by vocation, a historian and collector by avocation. He was born in Kentucky in 1887, came to Kansas in 1910, and from that time until his retirement on January 1, 1957, was a prominent business man of western Kansas.
>
> His banking career took him from Yoder, Kan., to Hutchinson, McCracken, Greensburg, Sharon Springs, and finally to Goodland. For four years in the early 1920's he served as a national bank examiner, and after that for another five years he was a farmer and rancher before turning again to banking. He served on the loan committee of the Reconstruction Finance Corporation and as a member and secretary of the Kansas Livestock Commission.
>
> Mr. Brock's fondness for history was sincere and of long standing. His hobbies included the collecting of rare coins and currency, Indian relics, firearms, documents, maps, and newspapers. His study of the Civil War led him to visit many battlefields, his last trip being made during the spring of 1957.

He contributed scores of articles to museums at Wallace, Goodland, Fort Hays State College, and the State Historical Society. One of his last projects was the erection and dedication of a monument to the memory of members of the German family, who were massacred by Indians in present Logan county.

Mr. Brock joined the State Historical Society in 1918, and took an active and continued interest in its work. He served on the board of directors for nearly 20 years, from 1938 until his death, and was president in 1948-1949. His warm spirit and friendly understanding will be missed by his many friends.

Mention was made by the secretary of the attendance at the meeting of Donald F. Martin of Los Angeles. Mr. Martin is a grandson of George W. Martin, secretary of the Society from 1899 to 1914.

The report of the committee on nominations for directors was called for and read by Charles M. Correll:

REPORT OF COMMITTEE ON NOMINATIONS FOR DIRECTORS

October 17, 1958.

To the Kansas State Historical Society:

Your committee on nominations submits the following report and recommendations for directors of the Society for the term of three years ending in October, 1961:

Barr, Frank, Wichita.
Berryman, Jerome C., Ashland.
Charlson, Sam C., Manhattan.
Correll, Charles M., Manhattan.
Davis, W. W., Lawrence.
Denious, Jess C., Jr., Dodge City.
Hall, Standish, Wichita.
Hegler, Ben F., Wichita.
Jones, Horace, Lyons.
Kampschroeder, Mrs. Jean Norris, Garden City.
Kaul, Robert H., Wamego.
Lauterbach, August W., Colby.
Lillard, T. M., Topeka.
Lindquist, Emory K., Wichita.
Maranville, Lea, Ness City.
Means, Hugh, Lawrence.

Montgomery, John D., Junction City.
Owen, Arthur K., Topeka.
Owen, Mrs. E. M., Lawrence.
Payne, Mrs. L. F., Manhattan.
Reser, Mrs. C. H., Hamilton.
Richards, Walter M., Emporia.
Riegle, Wilford, Emporia.
Robbins, Richard W., Pratt.
Rupp, Mrs. Jane C., Lincolnville.
Scott, Angelo, Iola.
Sloan, E. R., Topeka.
Smelser, Mary M., Lawrence.
Stewart, Mrs. James G., Topeka.
Taylor, James E., Sharon Springs.
Van De Mark, M. V. B., Concordia.
Wark, George H., Caney.
Williams, Charles A., Bentley.

Respectfully submitted,

WILL T. BECK, *Chairman,*
CHARLES M. CORRELL,
FRANK HAUCKE,
T. M. LILLARD.

Mr. Correll moved that the report be accepted. Fred W. Brinkerhoff seconded the motion and directors for the term ending in October, 1961, were elected.

Reports of local societies were called for and given as follows: Mrs. H. M. Trowbridge for the Wyandotte County Historical Society; Mrs. Eugene Kotterman for the Shawnee Mission Indian Historical Society; and William E. Koch for the Riley County Historical Society. Reports from several other societies were also received in writing. President Farley introduced a group from the Kansas City Posse of the Westerners.

There being no further business, the meeting was adjourned. All members and guests were invited to attend an open house at the Memorial building where special displays had been arranged.

DIRECTORS OF THE KANSAS STATE HISTORICAL SOCIETY AS OF OCTOBER, 1958

DIRECTORS FOR THE YEAR ENDING OCTOBER, 1959

Aitchison, R. T., Wichita.
Anderson, George L., Lawrence.
Anthony, D. R., Leavenworth.
Baugher, Charles A., Ellis.
Beck, Will T., Holton.
Chambers, Lloyd, Clearwater.
Chandler, C. J., Wichita.
Clymer, Rolla, El Dorado.
Cochran, Elizabeth, Pittsburg.
Cotton, Corlett J., Lawrence.
Dawson, John S., Topeka.
Eckdall, Frank F., Emporia.
Euwer, Elmer E., Goodland.
Farley, Alan W., Kansas City.
Gard, Spencer A., Iola.
Knapp, Dallas W., Coffeyville.
Lilleston, W. F., Wichita.

Lose, Harry F., Topeka.
Malin, James C., Lawrence.
Mayhew, Mrs. Patricia Solander, Wichita.
Menninger, Karl, Topeka.
Miller, Karl, Dodge City.
Moore, Russell, Wichita.
Rankin, Charles C., Lawrence.
Raynesford, H. C., Ellis.
Reed, Clyde M., Jr., Parsons.
Rodkey, Clyde K., Manhattan.
Shaw, Joseph C., Topeka.
Somers, John G., Newton.
Stewart, Donald, Independence.
Thomas, E. A., Topeka.
von der Heiden, Mrs. W. H., Newton.
Walker, Mrs. Ida M., Norton.

DIRECTORS FOR THE YEAR ENDING OCTOBER, 1960

Bailey, Roy F., Salina.
Baughman, Robert W., Liberal.
Beezley, George F., Girard.
Beougher, Edward M., Grinnell.
Bowlus, Thomas H., Iola.
Brinkerhoff, Fred W., Pittsburg.
Cron, F. H., El Dorado.
Docking, George, Lawrence.
Ebright, Homer K., Baldwin.
Farrell, F. D., Manhattan.
Hall, Fred, Topeka.
Hamilton, R. L., Beloit.
Harper, Mrs. Jesse C., Ashland.
Harvey, Mrs. A. M., Topeka.
Haucke, Frank, Council Grove.
Hodges, Frank, Olathe.
Lingenfelser, Angelus, Atchison.

Long, Richard M., Wichita.
McArthur, Mrs. Vernon E., Hutchinson.
McCain, James A., Manhattan.
McFarland, Helen M., Topeka.
McGrew, Mrs. Wm. E., Kansas City.
Malone, James, Gem.
Mechem, Kirke, Lindsborg.
Mueller, Harrie S., Wichita.
Murphy, Franklin D., Lawrence.
Rogler, Wayne, Matfield Green.
Ruppenthal, J. C., Russell.
Simons, Dolph, Lawrence.
Slagg, Mrs. C. M., Manhattan.
Templar, George, Arkansas City.
Townsley, Will, Great Bend.
Woodring, Harry H., Topeka.

DIRECTORS FOR THE YEAR ENDING OCTOBER, 1961

Barr, Frank, Wichita.
Berryman, Jerome C., Ashland.
Charlson, Sam C., Manhattan.
Correll, Charles M., Manhattan.
Davis, W. W., Lawrence.
Denious, Jess C., Jr., Dodge City.
Hall, Standish, Wichita.
Hegler, Ben F., Wichita.
Jones, Horace, Lyons.
Kampschroeder, Mrs. Jean Norris, Garden City.
Kaul, Robert H., Wamego.
Lauterbach, August W., Colby.
Lillard, T. M., Topeka.
Lindquist, Emory K., Wichita.
Maranville, Lea, Ness City.
Means, Hugh, Lawrence.
Montgomery, John D., Junction City.
Owen, Arthur K., Topeka.
Owen, Mrs. E. M., Lawrence.
Payne, Mrs. L. F., Manhattan.
Reser, Mrs. C. H., Hamilton.
Richards, Walter M., Emporia.
Riegle, Wilford, Emporia.
Robbins, Richard W., Pratt.
Rupp, Mrs. Jane C., Lincolnville.
Scott, Angelo, Iola.
Sloan, E. R., Topeka.
Smelser, Mary M., Lawrence.
Stewart, Mrs. James G., Topeka.
Taylor, James E., Sharon Springs.
Van De Mark, M. V. B., Concordia.
Wark, George H., Caney.
Williams, Charles A., Bentley.

Bypaths of Kansas History

THE ICE WOMAN GOETH

From the Marysville *Locomotive*, July 16, 1870.

The Otoe Injuns have lately had some pay from the Government, and they are now visiting our town in large numbers, purchasing a supply of fine combs, soap and scrubbing brushes, preparatory to taking an annual clean-up. An injun with two dollars and a half is the happiest mortal in existence. They squander it vigorously for any and everything that the eye may feast on until it is all gone. One squaw was induced to buy a piece of our clear, sparkling Big Blue river ice, and, having wrapped it in a greasy piece of calico, deposited it in her bosom and started for her wigwam. A few moments after she was seen tearing down the street, strewing her garments as she went, and giving vent to the most unearthly gibberings, among which were audible only the words, "Ugh, d—n white man; wetem squaw all over. Ugh!"

WHEN EARLY-DAY DODGE CITY HAD A SNIFF AT "CULTURE"

From the Dodge City *Times*, November 24, 1877.

A ROW AMONG THE BELL RINGERS.—The Alleghanian bell ringers were here last Thursday, and aside from a few other catch-penny hum bugs they were the snidest outfit we ever saw. The performance opened with a row between the manager, who had managed to get outside of about a barrel of Dodge City whiskey, and the ticket seller; and the only reason we blame the ticket seller is because he did not put a head on the manager. The passage way to the floor was crowded with people trying to get in, and the old drunken manager got on his ear and refused to let them come in, and kept them standing there while he and the ticket seller quarreled and made donkeys of themselves. Finally some of the other members of the troupe got them quieted, and after waiting an hour and a half the performance commenced inside.

There was nothing good in the whole performance except when some one in the audience made a remark, which was not in itself very lucid, but at which one of the exquisitely charming performers laughed, exhibiting forty or fifty clay teeth, and a pair of ruby lips at sight of which pumpkin pies would shudder. The brightest star in the constellation, Madame Nani Bach was clad in a garment cut low necked in the back, and when she sang the very timbers of the building cracked. A young light haired professor with a long nose would run out on the stage occasionally and toot on a tin instrument for about two minutes and three quarters, then smile like a pile of grave stones and trot back. Another fellow beat on a lot of beer glasses with a wire, the sight and sound of which caused groans. The performance closed by the ringing of cow bells, and the tooting of fog horns.

Kansas History as Published in the Press

Publication of Orville W. Mosher's column, "Museum Notes," in the Emporia *Gazette* has continued in recent months. Mosher is president of the Lyon County Historical Society and curator of the society's museum in Emporia. The column largely features Emporia and Lyon county history.

"Early-Day Events in Shaping an Empire," Simon E. Matson's series on the history of the St. Francis area, first printed June 14, 1956, continues regularly in the St. Francis *Herald*.

St. Boniface Catholic church at Scipio reached its 100th year in 1958. A history of the church was published in the *Anderson Countian*, Garnett, August 28, 1958.

Historical articles on the Trinity Lutheran church, Great Bend, were published in the Great Bend *Tribune*, September 2, 1958, and the Great Bend *Herald-Press*, September 6. The church was organized August 30, 1908.

An article by Ruby Basye on Old Fort Hays and the Fort Hays museum was published in the Hutchinson *News*, September 3, 1958.

Biographical information on Boston Corbett, who shot John Wilkes Booth, Lincoln's assassin, appeared in the Concordia *Kansan*, September 4, 1958, and in the Concordia *Blade-Empire*, October 23. Corbett homesteaded in Cloud county in 1878. A marker was recently placed at the homestead site.

Among recent articles in the *Ellis County Farmer*, Hays, were: "History of Catholic Church in Hays Shows Catholics First to Erect Building," September 11, 1958, and "Pioneer Moore Family of Ellis County Endured the Direst of Hardships Here," by Mrs. Mabel Moore Raupp, November 13.

Barbara and John Adam Warneke settled near present White City in 1857. An account of their descendants appeared in the Herington *Advertiser-Times*, September 11, 1958.

A history of the Santa Fe trail, printed in a recent issue of the *Panhandle Lines*, publication of the Panhandle Eastern Pipe Line Co., was reprinted in the *Southwest Daily Times*, Liberal, September 16, 1958.

Kansas Historical Notes

Current officers of the Riley County Historical Society include: William E. Koch, president; John Holmstrom, vice-president; Homer Socolofsky, recording secretary; Mrs. C. M. Correll, membership secretary; Sen. Sam C. Charlson, treasurer; and Joe D. Haines, Bruce Wilson, Mrs. C. B. Knox, James C. Carey, Ward C. Griffing, Mrs. Paul G. Brown, George A. Filinger, Earl Ray, and Holmstrom, directors.

Kingman observed its 75th anniversary with a four-day celebration October 3-6, 1958. A historical production called "Prairidrama" was presented each evening. The final day was old settlers' day.

Dr. J. E. Turner was elected president of the Border Queen Museum Association at a meeting of the organization in Caldwell, November 28, 1958. Other officers chosen were: Doyle Stiles, first vice-president; Walker Young, second vice-president; Frederick Thompson, Jr., secretary; and Harry Jenista, treasurer. Young was the retiring president.

Members of the Shawnee County Historical Society gathered in Topeka for their annual dinner December 4, 1958. The program featured the histories of Auburn, Dover, and Wakarusa. Bessie Moore, of Auburn, was the principal speaker. Re-elected to the board of directors for three-year terms were: Annie B. Sweet, Mrs. Wilber Galloway, Robert H. Kingman, Louis R. Smith, Otis Allen, Euphemia Page, Nyle Miller, R. C. Obrecht, Milton Tabor, and Erwin Keller.

Plans for publication of a Kearny county history were recently announced by the Kearny County Historical Society. Committees have been appointed to compile material for the project. C. A. Loucks is president of the society.

Nyle Miller, secretary of the Kansas State Historical Society, was the principal speaker at a December 11, 1958, gathering of the Ottawa County Historical Society in Minneapolis. The January 10, 1959, meeting of the society, in Minneapolis, featured the histories of the Hall and Lamar churches, given by Mrs. Jessie Adee Dayhoff.

Officers of the Augusta Historical Society for 1959 are: Stella B. Haines, president; Mrs. Ralph Ralston, vice-president; Florence Hudson, secretary; and Mrs. Ethel Shriver, treasurer.

Harry E. Hanson was elected president of the Wyandotte County Historical Society at the society's annual meeting, January 8, 1959, in Kansas City. Ralph Clark was elected vice-president; Hazel Zeller, secretary; Raymond Lees, treasurer; Mrs. Harry Trowbridge, historian; and Harry Trowbridge, curator. New trustees are Alan Farley and Mrs. Clyde Glandon. Mrs. Trowbridge was the retiring president.

Rolla A. Clymer was named president of the Butler County Historical Society at a meeting of the trustees in El Dorado, January 19, 1959. Charles E. Heilmann was chosen vice-president; Joy Wigginton, secretary; and Clifford W. Stone, treasurer.

Wayne Randall, Osage City, was elected president of the Native Sons, and Evelyn Ford, Topeka, president of the Native Daughters, at the annual meeting of the Native Sons and Daughters of Kansas in Topeka, January 28, 1959. Other officers chosen by the Native Sons include: Dean Yingling, Topeka, vice-president; Floyd Souders, Cheney, secretary; and Emory Fager, Overbrook, treasurer. The Native Daughters elected Mrs. J. C. Tillotson, Norton, vice-president; Mrs. Chester Dunn, Oxford, secretary; and Lela Hough, Topeka, treasurer. Roy Bulkley, Topeka, and Mrs. Hobart Hoyt, Lyons, were the retiring presidents. Mrs. Bea Johnson, Kansas City, Kan., was the principal speaker. "Kansan of the Year" award went to Mrs. Frank W. Boyd, Mankato.

"First Ladies of Kansas" was the theme of the annual meeting of the Woman's Kansas Day Club in Topeka, January 29, 1959. Dolls representing the first ladies, dressed in replicas of the inaugural gowns, decorated the luncheon tables. Brief biographies of the first ladies were given as part of the program. At the close of the meeting the dolls were donated to the Kansas State Historical Society. The president, Mrs. Lucile Rust, Manhattan, presided at the meeting. Mrs. Harry Chaffee, Topeka, was chosen president for the coming year. Other officers elected include: Mrs. McDill Boyd, Phillipsburg, first vice-president; Mrs. Marion Beatty, Topeka, second vice-president; Mrs. Claude R. Stutzman, Kansas City, recording secretary; Mrs. Roy Gibson, Chanute, treasurer; Mrs. Frank Huffman, Topeka, historian; Mrs. Larry E. Vin Zant, Wichita, auditor; Mrs. R. T. Unruh, Kinsley, registrar. The following district directors were elected: Mrs. James V. Blue, Topeka; Mrs. George Widder, Kansas City; Mrs. Harold Medill, Independence; Mrs. J. P. Fallin, Wichita; Mrs. J. O. Carter, Garden City; and Mrs. Lillie Washabaugh, Natoma.

THE
KANSAS HISTORICAL
QUARTERLY

Summer 1959

Published by

Kansas State Historical Society

Topeka

NYLE H. MILLER KIRKE MECHEM JAMES C. MALIN
Managing Editor *Editor* *Associate Editor*

CONTENTS

PAGE

U. S. ARMY AND AIR FORCE WINGS OVER KANSAS (In two installments, Part One): 129
    With photographs of scenes and activities at Pratt Army Air Base, Great Bend Army Air Field and Smoky Hill Army Air Force Base, Salina, *between* pp. 144, 145.

THE PIKE'S PEAK GOLD RUSH AND THE SMOKY HILL ROUTE, 1859-1860 .... *Calvin W. Gower,* 158
    Reprint of a "Table of Distances" from Atchison to the Gold Mines, 1859, *between* pp. 160, 161.

THE LETTERS OF THE REV. SAMUEL YOUNG LUM, PIONEER KANSAS MISSIONARY, 1854-1858—*Concluded* .... Edited by *Emory Lindquist,* 172

WILLIAM SUTTON WHITE, SWEDENBORGIAN PUBLICIST: Part Two, Kansas Exemplar of the Philosophy of Emanuel Swedenborg and Herbert Spencer—*Concluded* .... *James C. Malin,* 197

RECENT ADDITIONS TO THE LIBRARY,
                      Compiled by *Alberta Pantle,* Librarian, 229

BYPATHS OF KANSAS HISTORY 251

KANSAS HISTORY AS PUBLISHED IN THE PRESS 252

KANSAS HISTORICAL NOTES 255

The Kansas Historical Quarterly is published four times a year by the Kansas State Historical Society, 120 W. Tenth, Topeka, Kan., and is distributed free to members. Annual membership dues are $3; annual sustaining, $10; life membership, $20. Membership applications and dues should be addressed to Mrs. Lela Barnes, treasurer.

Correspondence concerning articles for the *Quarterly* should be sent to the managing editor. The Society assumes no responsibility for statements made by contributors.

Second-class postage has been paid at Topeka, Kan.

THE COVER

    B-29 Super Fortresses at the Smoky Hill Army Air Force Base, Salina. *Official photo U. S. Army Air Forces.*

THE KANSAS HISTORICAL QUARTERLY

Volume XXV   *Summer, 1959*   Number 2

U. S. Army and Air Force Wings Over Kansas

INTRODUCTION

MONTGOMERY county, Kansas, was named for Maj. Gen. Richard Montgomery, of Revolutionary War fame.

That historical fact at the moment seems to have no connection with this story on air force wings over Kansas. Yet it was most important, for quite likely this article would never have materialized had the county been named for Joe Doakes—or perhaps for anyone else. It came about as follows:

The secretary of the Kansas State Historical Society attended a luncheon and dedication ceremony sponsored by the Esther Lowrey chapter of the Kansas D. A. R. in Independence June 14, 1957, at which a plaque honoring the Revolutionary War general was placed in the county courthouse.

Important among the guests was Maj. Gen. Richard M. Montgomery, deputy commander of the Second Air Force, Barksdale Air Force Base, Louisiana. This General Montgomery, native of Pennsylvania and no relation to the Revolutionary War general, had come to Montgomery county as a lieutenant colonel in 1942 to activate the Independence Army Air Field. He immediately gained the respect and co-operation of the local community, and the feeling quickly became mutual. Thus it seemed appropriate to plan the dedication of the plaque to the Revolutionary War General Montgomery at a time when the Air Force General Montgomery could be the honored guest.

During the luncheon the Historical Society secretary mentioned to General Montgomery the Society's interest in obtaining historical sketches and pictures of some of the activity at the several air force bases in Kansas during World War II. It was explained that the Society had been trying over a period of years to obtain these records without success. Many of these bases had been built, had been used with spectacular success, and had been abandoned, but the Historical Society had been able to obtain only scraps of information about them.

General Montgomery listened attentively, and replied that he would see if anything could be done—and it was! So, the State Historical Society now finds itself happily indebted to Mrs. R. R. Bittmann, the arranger of the D. A. R. meeting in Independence, to Gen. Richard M. Montgomery, presently of Guam, and, finally, to the chief of the historical division of the United States Air Force at Barksdale Air Force Base, Joseph P. McGinley, and his associates at Barksdale and Maxwell bases, who prepared the following factual—but interesting—sketches of 16 army and air force bases in Kansas. Except for minor changes, and the addition of several footnotes, the histories are published here as written.

Unfortunately, even with air force help, only a few photographs of these bases have been located. The State Historical Society will appreciate receiving copies of others, or information as to where such photographs can be obtained. Understandably, unofficial picture taking in bases during war time was prohibited. However, photographs may have been snapped, and the Society would like to know their whereabouts—whether official or unofficial—before they are lost to the Kansas archives.

When air power began its development, with stove pipes the nearest thing to bombsights, as at Fort Riley about 1912, the army's air activities were conducted by the signal corps. By July 10, 1941, the army air arm had become sufficiently important to be designated the Army Air Forces. Finally, under the Armed Services Unification Act of July 26, 1947, the Army Air Forces became the United States Air Force when the new Department of Defense became operative the following September 18. The air force now operates as one of the Defense Department's three main divisions— air, army, and navy. Although practically all army air activity has been transferred to the air force, Kansas' two forts, Leavenworth and Riley, continue to maintain army air fields. But their use is limited to the immediate servicing of regular post activities.

COFFEYVILLE ARMY AIR FIELD
(1942-1946)

COFFEYVILLE Army Air Field was located seven miles northeast of Coffeyville, on a 1,456-acre tract of land which had been purchased by the United States government. Construction, which was accomplished by contract under the supervision of the U. S.

District Engineers, Tulsa, Okla., commenced on 1 June 1942, and continued over a period of eight months. Actually, however, the field was activated on 17 June 1942, with Col. Carlisle I. Ferris as the commanding officer. Construction work was sufficiently advanced by 16 September following to accommodate the headquarters staff which had been located temporarily in the city of Coffeyville. Meanwhile, on 3 August the Army Air Forces Gulf Coast Training Center had assumed jurisdiction over the installation.

Despite the generally level nature of the site selected for the Coffeyville Army Air Field some grading was necessary. Other construction work of a general nature included a water storage and distribution system; a sewage system and disposal plant; electric transmission and distribution lines; a railway spur line; access roads to nearby highways; paved streets on the site; and gasoline and oil storage systems.

The remaining major installations and structures at the field may be noted conveniently under the following headings: airfield; cantonment; training; recreation and welfare; and hospital. Unless otherwise indicated, all the buildings listed were the theater-of-operation type structures.

Airfield.
- a) 4 runways, 4,100, 5,700, 5,871, and 5,872 feet long, and each 150 feet wide.
- b) 5 taxiways, 400, 400, 1,200, 1,800, and 2,400 feet long, and each 50 feet wide.
- c) 3 hangars (semipermanent construction).
- d) parking apron, 5,200 feet long and 450 feet wide.
- e) control tower.

Cantonment.
- a) 67 enlisted men's barracks.
- b) 25 cadet barracks.
- c) 3 WACs' barracks.
- d) 18 officers' quarters.
- e) 8 mess halls.
- f) 1 guard house.
- g) 1 commissary.
- h) 13 warehouses.
- i) 11 administration buildings.
- j) 12 supply rooms.
- k) 1 post headquarters building.
- l) 1 finance building.
- m) 1 post engineer building.
- n) 6 operations buildings.

o) 1 fire station.
p) 1 telephone building.
q) 1 signal office building (semipermanent construction).

Training.
a) 1 ground school building (semipermanent construction).
b) 2 miscellaneous buildings.
c) 6 link trainer buildings (semipermanent construction).
d) 1 chemical warfare building.

Recreation and Welfare.
a) 17 general recreation buildings.
b) 1 chapel (semipermanent construction).
c) 1 theater (semipermanent construction).
d) 1 post office.
e) 1 post exchange.

Hospital.
a) 1 administration building (semipermanent construction).
b) 5 wards (semipermanent construction).
c) infirmary (semipermanent construction).
d) 1 dental clinic (semipermanent construction).
e) 1 nurses' quarters.
f) 1 nurses' recreation building.

Coffeyville Army Air Field had four auxiliary airfields. Indicated by numerals, their size and location with reference to the base field may be indicated as follows: No. 1, comprising 206 acres, approximately 6.2 air miles to the southeast; No. 2, with 241 acres, about 14.25 air miles almost due east; No. 3, with 633 acres, 12.5 air miles to the northeast; and No. 4, comprising 241 acres, just over nine miles slightly east of north. Auxiliary No. 3 was the only one with a regular concrete runway system.

During July 1942 detachments of the following units were organized at Coffeyville: the 908th Quartermaster Company, Aviation (Service); the 852d Ordnance Company, Aviation (Service); the 778th Chemical Service Company (Aviation); and a Finance Department. Early in September following detachments of two other units, the 1038th Guard Squadron and the 857th Signal Service Company, Aviation, were organized. These were followed before the end of the year by medical and veterinary detachments and by the 23d Airways Communications Squadron.

Coming for the most part from Enid Army Air Field, Enid, Okla., the bulk of the original military personnel arrived at Coffeyville during October and November 1942. They included troops of the 366th Base Headquarters and Air Base Squadron, the 317th Army Air Forces Band, and the 820th, 821st, 822d, and 823d School

Squadrons. From a total of 63 officers and 190 enlisted men on 1 October 1942 the permanent party strength increased to 283 officers and 2,369 enlisted men by 1 February 1943.

The mission originally assigned to the Coffeyville Army Air Field was the basic, or second-stage, training of aviation cadets. Hence the designation, Army Air Forces Basic Flying School, when it was activated on 17 June 1942. As of 1 January 1943 it was redesignated the Coffeyville Army Air Field, although the mission was unchanged. From 6 August 1943 until 31 May 1944 the flying training unit at the field was known as Army Air Forces Pilot School (Basic). On 1 June the Coffeyville installation was transferred from the Army Air Forces Central Flying Training Command (successor to the Army Air Forces Gulf Coast Training Center) to the Third Air Force. Thereafter basic flying training was no longer conducted there.

The training of cadets at Coffeyville actually began on 14 November 1942 with Class 43-C. Of the 137 in that group, 116 graduated at the end of the course on 13 January 1943. Meanwhile, the second class, 43-D, with 156 cadets had begun training on December 1942. It completed the course, with 129 individuals graduating on 15 February 1943. From beginning to end, approximately 4,840 cadets and aviation students began the basic flying course, in 16 separate classes, at Coffeyville. Incompletions, however, because of physical and flying deficiencies, serious accidents, and resignations were fairly numerous. As a result, only 3,881 successfully completed the course.

Col. Carlisle I. Ferris remained as commanding officer at Coffeyville Army Air Field from its activation until 3 June 1943. He was replaced by Lt. Col. Charles B. Harvin who served in that capacity until the end of April 1944. Then Col. Nicholas T. Perkins assumed command.

When it took over the field on 1 June 1944, the Third Air Force organized there the Coffeyville Replacement Training Unit (Photo Reconnaissance) which was assigned to Headquarters Reconnaissance Training Wing (Provisional). Colonel Perkins remained as commanding officer of the field, while Lt. Col. Frank E. Dunn was named commanding officer of the training unit. The primary mission of the latter was to train pilots for combat photo reconnaissance. Three months later the unit was redesignated the Coffeyville Combat Crew Training Station (Photo Reconnaissance), with some emphasis being placed upon the preparation of photo reconnaissance pilots for overseas movement. In mid-September it was assigned to the III Tactical Air Command. On 1 October 1944 this training unit and the base administrative unit were integrated under the command of Colonel Perkins.

The first group of photo reconnaissance pilots reported to Coffeyville for training on 12 June 1944. Other groups followed in rapid succession. Operating at first on a 10-weeks' schedule, the students divided their time, roughly in the ratio of one to four, between ground school studies and flying training. In the beginning there were some B-25 pilots, but during the latter part of the period the aircraft used generally for this part of the work was the P-38. Commencing in January 1945 the students were required to complete four weeks of special instrument training before taking up their photo reconnaissance work. Because of limited facilities during the summer of 1945, some classes which had completed the instrument training course at Coffeyville were shipped to Will Rogers Army Air Field, Oklahoma City, Okla., for the photo reconnaissance work. During the latter part of July, however, the instrument training program was transferred from Coffeyville to Will Rogers Army Air Field, while the photo reconnaissance section at Will Rogers was transferred to Coffeyville Army Air Field.

During the 12-months' period ending on 4 June 1945 over 460 photo reconnaissance pilots completed all their training requirements at Coffeyville, and were shipped to staging areas for processing and assignment to overseas shipments. In addition, more than 200 pilots received their instrument flying training at Coffeyville, and were shipped to Will Rogers for training as photo reconnaissance pilots. There was no diminution in this indicated rate of training during the few remaining weeks of World War II.

Colonel Perkins continued to serve as commanding officer of Coffeyville Army Air Field until 9 November 1944. His successor was Lt. Col. Paul A. Zartman who remained in that post until just a few days before the surrender of the Japanese the following August. The next commanding officer was Col. James M. Smelley.

Early in the post-war period Coffeyville Army Air Field was earmarked for eventual inactivation. In a temporary inactive status it was transferred to the Tactical Air Command on 21 March 1946. As soon thereafter as the necessary arrangements could be effected the Tactical Air Command transferred it to the U. S. District Engineers, Omaha, Neb., who assumed jurisdiction over the field on 26 August 1946.

Dodge City Army Air Field
(1942-1945)

THE Chamber of Commerce, through its president, Jess C. Denious, was active during early 1942 in encouraging the government to locate an airfield in Dodge City. Mr. Denious, editor of the Dodge City *Daily Globe*, and lieutenant governor of Kansas, 1943-1947, made several trips to Washington to interview the appropriate authorities. In order to demonstrate the advantages of the locality, Denious had compiled considerable information on such things as weather, terrain, and utilities.

The first public announcement of the government's intention to construct an airfield at Dodge City was made on 10 June 1942 by Capt. R. E. DeBolt of the Division Engineers Office, Albuquerque, N. M. The purpose of the field, as stated at the time, was to provide bomber training for the Royal Air Force. However, nothing further was heard of this, and the base was scheduled to be an advanced flying school, so that its original designation was "Army Air Forces Advanced Flying School." This remained the field's intended function until February 1943, when, three or four months before operations would begin, the mission was changed to B-26 transition training.

Although the United States Engineers had surveyed the land desired for the field, bids for construction were let before the land was acquired. When the bids were opened it was discovered that only one bid had been submitted. A group of contractors, known as the Liston-Clarke, San-Ore, D. H. Hardman group, had joined to make the bid. The contract was awarded this group and the first truck load of building materials was unloaded on 6 August 1942.

Pending final settlement of the purchase, possession was obtained by Rights of Entry granted by the owners. On 15 August 1942 the Office of Chief of Army Engineers issued a directive authorizing the acquisition of approximately 2,520 acres at an estimated cost of $191,353.

Since the Division Engineers Real Estate Branch was unable to come to an agreement with the eight landowners involved, it was necessary to proceed by condemnation. A Declaration of Taking was consequently filed in the District Court of the United States at Topeka. This action of course vested title in the United States. At the same time the sum estimated by the War Department to be fair compensation was deposited with the District

Court. During the summer of 1943 final settlements were made between the government and the owners. Additional land was acquired during 1943. In January 1943 authorization was issued for purchase of over 16 acres for the construction of a railroad spur. Part of this property was obtained by direct purchase, and part by condemnation. In this same general period, that is from November 1942 to April 1943, an additional 1,180 acres, for the construction of an auxiliary airfield, were purchased at a total cost of $45,610. The only other land acquired was the lease of something over 11 acres as a site for a radio beam station. Total expenditures for the purchase of land came to approximately $116,135.

Located close to Dodge City, a city of about 14,000 population in 1942, the main establishment of Dodge City Army Air Field was contained within the following boundaries, beginning at the

north quarter corner of Section 11, Township 26 South, Range 26 West, thence south 2 miles to the south quarter corner of Section 14, Township 26 South, Range 26 West, thence east 2 miles to the south quarter corner of Section 18, Township 26 South, Range 25 West, thence north 2 miles to the north quarter of Section 7, Township 26 South, Range 25 West, thence west 2 miles to the point of beginning.

The principal construction job consisted of building a cantonment, airdrome, roads, and facilities. The arrangement was standard rectangular, with building exteriors consisting of wood sheeting covered with 15-pound felt and asbestos-siding shingles. Housing was prepared for close to 4,000 men, while the hospital had a capacity of 177 beds. Warehousing was built to provide 71,186 square feet of space, and the airdrome could accommodate 165 aircraft. Four runways (150 feet wide and 6,500 feet in length) were constructed, while six 75-foot taxiways connected the parking apron (600 x 5,300 feet) with the runway system.

Work on the main construction job, begun on 5 August 1942, was completed by 31 December. Three or four days prior to completion of the main job, work was begun on the second most important project (principally concerned with completion of the runway system), which was finished by 31 March 1943. Total construction expenditures (as of 1 March 1944) were $7,409,551, thus exceeding the original total allocation by $347,370.

The first soldiers assigned to the base consisted of a detachment of 27 enlisted men of the Quartermaster Corps, under Capt. J. M. Cooper, who arrived on 1 November 1942. Somewhat over a month later, on 11 December, the base was formally activated with the official designation "Army Air Forces Advanced Flying School, Dodge City, Kansas." As a result of a change of mission for the base, it was redesignated, 27 May 1943, "Army Air Forces Pilot School (Specialized 2-Engine), Dodge City Army Air Field, Dodge City, Kansas." Lt. Col. Charles B. Root assumed command on 11 December 1942 and served as commanding officer until 17 February 1943, when he was succeeded by Col. Charles B. Oldfield. Colonel Oldfield remained commanding officer until 27 January 1944, when Colonel Root reassumed command. After official activation of the base there was a rapid build-up of personnel strength, so much so that the local paper could observe on 2 February 1943: "Enlisted men are pouring into the new field by the hundreds."

Training at the base was under the immediate supervision of the director of training. The training function was broken up under the director into flying training under a director of flying, and ground school instruction under a director of technical training. The first planes to be used for instruction, a dozen B-26's, were delivered to Dodge City Army Air Field on 26 April 1943. On the same day, the first group of officer students, 36 in all, reported for B-26 transition training. No time was lost, for on 28 April the first training flights began. In addition to the regular category of officer students in training, several of the classes included French nationals, as well as contingents of Women's Air Force Service Pilots (WASP's). The women pilots compared favorably with the men in all phases of the training, which was the same for both sexes. During the active training period at the base, that is from 28 April 1943 to June 1945, an estimated 2,215 student officers, French nationals, and WASP's received B-26 transition training.

The school made a genuine contribution to the war effort in its training program. The B-26 "Marauder" was looked on askance by Air Force personnel and by the general public as a dangerous and unstable aircraft. It was the task of the school, while teaching proficiency in operation of the aircraft, to break through the negative "mystique" which had been built up around the B-26, and to instill in the students a confidence in the aircraft as an efficient fighting instrument. This was achieved to a remarkable degree, with earned recognition coming from Maj. Gen. G. C. Brant of the Central Flying Training Command in the form of a letter to Colonel Root:

It is noted that the B-26 has finally come into its own and is recognized by the public at large as being a most valuable implement of effective warfare against our enemy.—In my mind, it is a much belated acknowledgment that is made possible only by the thousands of successful hours which you, your staff and your mechanics have been able to secure on this airplane at an operational rate which compares favorably with all other aircraft of our Command. It is my pleasure therefore to express to you and the members of your field my pleasure and satisfaction at seeing your successful efforts recognized by your fellow countrymen and I wish to add my personal congratulations to each of you on the spirit and enterprise which brought about this transformed thinking on the part of the American public. You and your men undertook this task when everyone said it could not be done and in so doing, you brought credit to yourself and the service.

The relations between the base and Dodge City were uniformly good. The limited size of the town created problems of housing for married officers and enlisted men, but this was the universal and normal wartime condition. The people of Dodge City showed themselves most co-operative in welcoming a large number of troops into their community. For example, during February 1943, various civic organizations co-operated in furnishing day rooms for the squadrons on the base. In March, the local Rotary, Kiwanis, and Lions Clubs presented a minstrel show which netted about $1,200 to aid in furnishing the day rooms. Friendly co-operation was by no means a one-way street. During the Boot Hill Fair and Rodeo in September 1943, the Technical Training Department exhibited various types of equipment and instructional aids in a booth on the fair grounds. Outstanding for its co-operation was the Dodge City *Daily Globe,* which was consistently generous with publicity releases.

As the war in Europe ground to a halt the need for B-26 transition training was sharply curtailed. Consequently, all training activities ceased with the class which graduated on 28 June 1945. Two days later the official inactivation announcement was made, whereupon the officer in charge began the inactivation process. By 9 July all property had been turned in. Inactivation was officially completed on 12 July 1945 and all personnel had been transferred as of that date. Whereupon, Dodge City Army Air Field was placed on the inactive list.

FAIRFAX FIELD
(1942-1950)

PRIOR to World War II Fairfax Field, located about three miles north of the center of Kansas City, Kan., was a municipal airport, apparently without military installations. It acquired importance to the Air Corps as the site of a factory set up on the edge of the field by the North American Aviation Company to manufacture the B-25, Mitchell, medium bomber. A modification center for B-25's was established there later. Production began at the factory in December 1941, and planes began moving through the modification center in May 1942. Primarily for the testing and flying of these planes the four rather short runways at Fairfax were expanded to 150 feet in width and respectively to 6,500, 6,100, 5,800, and 4,500 feet in length, all of stout concrete, and 185,000 square yards of parking apron was laid out.

At first pilots were brought in from elsewhere to fly out the B-25's, but, as production increased, the Ferrying Division of Air Transport Command concluded that it should have a unit at Fairfax to do the job. Accordingly, on 15 April 1943 the Second Ferrying Squadron of the 5th Ferrying Group was moved from Love Field at Dallas, Tex., to Fairfax. The squadron set promptly to work and ferried out 157 B-25's during May.

Maj. William J. Fry was squadron commander from before the move until 12 October 1943 when he was succeeded by Maj. Harry E. Watson. To expedite its administration the squadron was made independent of the 5th Group on 1 January 1944, and on 1 April, in recognition of its growing size and importance, it became the 33d Ferrying Group. Major Watson continued as commander until 4 September 1944 when he gave way to Maj. Charles E. Hanst, an Air Service pilot in World War I, and a past president of the American Association of Airline Executives. A detachment of Women's Air Force Service Pilots (WASP's) was organized at Fairfax on 1 May 1944 to assist in the ferrying and did excellent service before being disbanded in September. Its head, Miss Helen Richie, held the woman's record for endurance flying, was the only woman to have served as co-pilot on a commercial airline, and had been in charge of a detachment of American women transport pilots in England.

The 33d Group continued to grow until at the end of 1944 it had 393 officers and 578 enlisted men. However, early in 1945 North American reduced its B-25 output, so the Ferrying Division in an effort to consolidate its activities arranged to close out Fairfax as a ferrying base and have pilots from Rosecrans Field at St. Joseph, Mo., do what ferrying still had to be done at Kansas City. The 33d Group was discontinued, and on 15 April 1945 Fairfax, losing its status as a base, became merely an operating location of Rosecrans.

While based at Fairfax the 33d Group delivered 6,202 aircraft to destinations within the United States and 251 abroad. Of 1,881 deliveries in 1943 by the Ground Ferrying Squadron all but 129 were B-25's, but at the end of that year pilots from Fairfax began ferrying B-26's from a modification center at Omaha and B-24's from a center at St. Paul. Thereafter activities expanded until early in 1945 the 33d Group controlled ten operating locations and was flying a wide variety of planes, including as many as 60 B-29's a month. Capt. Robert V. Barlow of the group was given the Air Medal in November 1944 for piloting the first P-38 flight over ATC's South Pacific route. Another remarkable flight or pair of flights was Capt. Robert P. Pendleton's delivery of a B-29 to Twentieth Air Force in the Marianas Islands and return of a war-weary B-29 to the United States within a period of 140 hours in December 1944. On 9 November 1944 the 33d Group furnished plane and crew to fly Sen. Harry S. Truman from Fairfax to Washington for ceremonies following his election as Vice-President.

On 22 September 1944 the 33d Group began daily scheduled Military Air Transport flights to Minneapolis and Omaha to move military cargo and passengers. These flights proved so useful that two more were soon added. When the ferrying group at Fairfax was eliminated the Ferrying Division contemplated making that airfield the mid-continental focus of its MAT operations. With this in mind it moved to Fairfax on 2 March 1945 to an air freight terminal which had previously been in Kansas City, Mo. In June Fairfax with 362 personnel, commanded by Maj. Alfred Oberg, was much the largest operating location in the division. During July, 1,044 military transports used the field. Among the passengers who landed there that summer was President Truman, who was en route to his home in Independence, Mo. However, in August plans to concentrate operations at Fairfax were shelved, and by November Topeka had been chosen instead. As of 6 December 1945 the operating location at Fairfax was discontinued. Moved from there to Topeka were personnel and equipment including nine C-47's and 80 pilots and co-pilots. Henceforth the regular and special MAT flights which had been used Fairfax would take off or land at Topeka.

Between February and October 1943 two technical training detachments operated at Fairfax. One, activated on 4 February and designated on 5 October as the 76th AAF Technical Training Detachment, administered a six-weeks' course to train AAF mechanics under the direction of the Aircraft Accessories Corporation in the repair and maintenance of hydraulic systems. About 300 students were admitted before the school was prematurely closed in October. It had done a good job but had duplicated a course given at Chanute and, perhaps for that reason, classes had been too small to pay the contractor or justify the use of skilled men as instructors. The other training unit, activated on 22 February and designated, effective 30 August, as the 81st AAF Technical Training Detachment, was treated to supervise apprentice crew chiefs at the North American B-25 Modification Center. An AAF policy adopted in January provided that mechanics selected to be crew chiefs be each assigned an aircraft as it left the factory, follow it through the modification center to see what was done to it, then go with it to be its crew chief in an operating unit. For a couple of months after the program began modification of B-25's took only a week, and the future crew chiefs did little but stand and watch. Then on introduction of the B-25G, modification time lengthened to two or three months. The detachment used the additional time for refresher training in mechanics and instruction in the duties of crew chiefs. It also tactfully won permission for the men to participate in aircraft maintenance and even in some modification and to gain flying experience by going on test hops. Peak enrollment came on 27 June when 296 mechanics were present. Abandonment of the apprenticeship program led to inactivation of the detachment on 31 October 1943.

After December 1945 the Air Force used Fairfax almost exclusively for reserve training. The 4101st AAF Base Unit (Res Tng) was activated there on 12 July 1946 to handle training responsibilities, and on 6 January 1947 a reserve unit, the 564th Bombardment Squadron, was activated there. This unit was vigorous enough to send 127 pilots to summer camp in 1948. In October that year Fairfax had 37 planes in which the reservists flew 1,844 hours. The 4401st Unit was redesignated, effective 28 August 1948, as the 2472d AF Reserve Training Center. A general shift of the reserve program from combat to troop carrier units in 1949 caused the replacement of the 564th Bombardment Squadron at Fairfax by the 442d Troop Carrier Wing, which was activated there on 27 June.

The reserve center at Fairfax was badly cramped for lack of space and facilities. This could have been remedied by taking all or part of the old modification center when a lease that Trans-World Airlines had on it expired in 1950. However, public reaction to the idea of moving the TWA shops from Kansas City was so unfavorable that it was decided to move the reserve center instead. Thus on 22 May 1950 the 2472d Center and the 442d Wing were moved to the Olathe Naval Air Station, about 25 miles from Kansas City.

Forbes Air Force Base
(1942-1954+)

THE history of Forbes Air Force Base begins in the early days of World War II, when work was started on an Army Air Field at Topeka. The installation was assigned to the Second Air Force in June and was accepted by the Army Air Forces on 15 August 1942. When the first troops began arriving that month, housing facilities had not been completed; consequently, the personnel were quartered temporarily in the Agriculture building at the Topeka Fair Grounds. But construction progressed rapidly, and by September 1942 Topeka Army Air Field was in use for heavy bombardment training.

From 24 August 1942 until February 1943 the 333d Bombardment Group was stationed at Topeka to give heavy bombardment crews 30 days of final training prior to their movement overseas. Those crews were trained in both B-17's and B-24's. In February 1943 the 333d Bombardment Group was replaced by the 2d Heavy Bombardment Processing Headquarters. At that time the base came under the jurisdiction of the 21st Bombardment Wing, which established its headquarters at Topeka in June 1943. Instead of training, the main function of the base became that of processing and equipping heavy bombardment crews for shipment overseas and preparing B-17's and B-24's for combat. Early in 1945 the base began processing B-29's and B-29 crews, and by March 1945 fighter pilots and tow target personnel also were being processed. Among the B-29 crews which passed through Topeka was one headed by Col. Paul W. Tibbets, Jr., who later piloted the B-29 that dropped the first atomic bomb on Japan.

In August 1945 command of the base shifted from the 21st Bombardment Wing to the 1st Staging Command. No change of personnel was involved, and the base continued to stage and process heavy bombardment crews and aircraft. By October 1945, however, emphasis was placed on shipping ground personnel overseas, and approximately 2,000 men were sent to the base to be staged for duty as overseas replacements. This project was completed in February 1946 by the Air Transport Command (ATC), which assumed jurisdiction of the base on 28 November 1945.

The Air Transport Command used the field at Topeka in performing its regular missions of transporting cargo and personnel. Later the base housed an operational training unit for pilots newly assigned to the command. In December 1945 the base became the only mid-continent stop for ATC's "Statesman," a daily transcontinental flight carrying key military and diplomatic travelers between Washington, D. C., and Hamilton Field, California. During December the base also became a stop for the "Globester," which provided daily shuttle service between Washington, D. C., and San Francisco. And in May 1946 the base took over operation of the daily "Alamo" flight between San Antonio, Tex., and Washington, D. C. Thus the field at Topeka became a major air terminal.

At various times the field acquired additional functions and projects. In January 1946, for example, it became a refueling point for jet aircraft. The following June ferrying operations were added to its mission. The base figured largely in a program of ferrying 1,300 aircraft to 40 fields in the United States and in a project for delivering 2,600 planes to reserve units throughout the country. In addition, pilots from Topeka and four other stations ferried surplus training planes and combat fighters from depots in the United States to various countries in South America. To add to the ever-increasing activity at Topeka, the Northwestern Sector, which supervised and coordinated ATC's operations at 14 stations, established its headquarters at the base in August 1946.

Because of a cut in Congressional appropriations, a drastic curtailment of activities at the base went into effect after 1 October 1946. Both military and civilian strength were greatly reduced. The field still served as an air terminal and as an operating base of the Air Transport Command, but the majority of the transport crews were transferred to other stations and several flights were discontinued. Only two flights were scheduled to come into the base daily. The "Statesman" flight was cut to every other day. The base, however, was involved in a number of special projects. During October 1946 the Air Transport Command began transferring excess C-54's to Topeka Army Air Field to be placed in storage. One month later the base was designated a separation center for officers and enlisted men. In November 1946 air reserve training was started at the base, but that activity was discontinued in March 1947. During December 1946 the base participated in "Operation Santa Claus," a project in which hundreds of amputees and litter cases were evacuated from Army hospitals to their homes for Christmas. From December 1946 to February 1947 the base trained 26 members of the Portuguese Air Force in air-sea rescue operations in B-17's and C-54's.

Removal of the Northwestern Sector Headquarters during March 1947 left the base with no regular mission other than servicing transient aircraft and maintaining the surplus aircraft in storage on the field. Those activities continued until the base was inactivated on 31 October 1947.

Topeka Army Air Field was reactivated on 1 July 1948 as an installation of the Strategic Air Command. It housed the 311th Air Division, Reconnaissance and the 55th Strategic Reconnaissance Wing until 14 October 1949, when the base was inactivated again. During that time it had been redesignated Forbes Air Force Base in honor of Maj. Daniel H. Forbes, Jr., a native of the Topeka area, who was killed while testing the XB-49 "Flying Wing." [1]

On 1 February 1951, during the Korean conflict, Forbes Air Force Base was reopened and assigned to the Strategic Air Command. The 21st Air Division was activated there on 16 February 1951, and the Division's 90th Bombardment Wing moved to the base during February and March 1951.

Forbes developed into a highly important training station as the 90th Wing trained newly activated units, the 376th, 308th, and 310th Bombardment Wings, of the Strategic Air Command. From June 1951 to August 1953 the 90th Wing also trained B-29 replacement crews for combat. About ten crews were trained each month until August 1952, when the bombardment wing training program was discontinued and the number of crews was increased to twenty per month.

On 16 June 1952 the 90th Bombardment Wing was redesignated 90th Strategic Reconnaissance Wing, Medium, and in November the wing commenced training reconnaissance crews as replacements for the Far East Air Forces.

The 90th Wing terminated its training mission in August 1953, but prior to that date it had begun to develop its own capability for reconnaissance operations. During the remainder of 1953 the Wing trained its crews in refueling operations required for strategic reconnaissance. The 55th Strategic Reconnaissance Wing, which

---

1. Maj. Daniel H. Forbes, Jr., was killed June 5, 1948, near Muroc, Calif., on the seventh anniversary of his entry into service. He was not yet 28 years old. His career included service with Elliott Roosevelt's photographic squadron in Tunisia, Algiers, India, and Egypt during World War II. He also took the first U. S. aerial reconnaissance photos of Japan. After the war he was assistant operations officer at the Bikini atomic bomb tests and his films of those tests were the first to be shown to officials at Washington. —Topeka *Daily Capital*, June 6, 1948; Topeka *State Journal*, June 10, July 13, 1949.

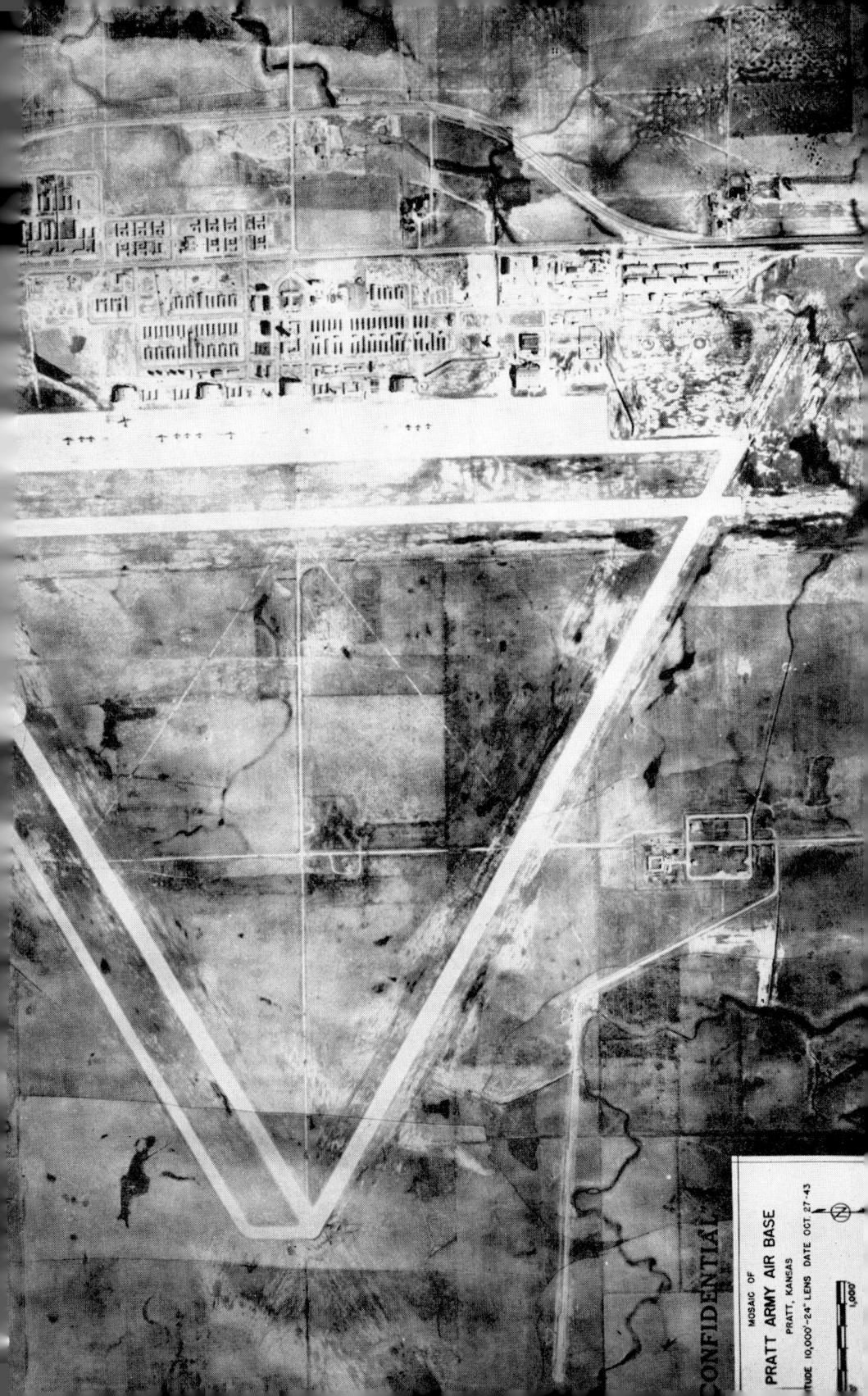

MOSAIC OF
PRATT ARMY AIR BASE
PRATT, KANSAS
ALTITUDE 10,000' – 24" LENS DATE OCT 27-43

Processing at Pratt Army Air Base.

Operations tower, Smoky Hill Army Air Force Base, Salina.
Official photo U. S. Army Air Forces.

GREAT BEND ARMY AIR FIELD
Upper: Part of the 8,000-foot ramp as seen from the west. This photograph was taken on January 1, 1945, when all aircraft were either on flight or in the hangars.
Center: Bomb Group area, May 28, 1943.
Lower: Crash station on the air field.
Official photos U. S. Army Air Corps.

Armory, Smoky Hill Army Air Force Base, Salina.
Courtesy Norbert Skelley.

Radio training, Pratt Army Air Base.

had moved to Forbes in October 1952, continued its program of photography, photomapping, and electronic reconnaissance.

During February 1954 action was taken to procure an additional 528 acres of land for Forbes. At the same time the United States Congress approved the construction of a 12,000 foot runway to accommodate RB-47's. The 90th Wing began converting to RB-47's in March 1954 and the 55th Wing in June 1954. Thereafter, both Wings trained at Forbes to attain combat readiness in RB-47's. After the Wings were declared combat ready they began temporary duty tours at overseas stations, but they returned to Forbes and continued training in order to maintain their effectiveness as combat units.

GARDEN CITY ARMY AIR FIELD
(1942-1947)

THE Garden City Chamber of Commerce, under the leadership of Ben Grimsley, did most effective work in getting an air field established in this area. At first all energies were concentrated on acquiring one of the British training fields which were to be established in the United States during 1941-1942. R. H. Rhoads, Kansas Industrial Development Commission representative in Washington, having obtained the RAF requirements, which included a large bombing range, began to push western Kansas as a logical area. In June 1941, Grimsley sent an elaborate booklet to Rhoads, setting forth the advantages of locating a flying school in Finney county, buttressed by photographs of the area, and containing information on water and natural gas resources, and weather conditions.

Perhaps the major obstacle to locating a training base in Kansas was the decision of the AAF Gulf Coast Training Center not to locate primary or basic training bases north of the Kansas-Oklahoma border because of poor flying weather compared to Oklahoma and Texas. To combat this decision, the Kansas delegation prepared detailed weather statistics which showed that the south portion of Kansas has as many clear and partly cloudy days as San Antonio, Tex. Over a period of 18 months a great amount of data was filed with the War Department. The cumulative effect of this information, plus the later government surveys which were largely in agreement, was in large part responsible for a reversal by the War Department of the decision of the Gulf Coast Training Command.

The first knowledge of a firm intention to construct a base in the Garden City area came to the local civic leaders by telegram, 8 April

1942, from Washington announcing the imminent arrival of a board of officers to choose a site for the base. Three days later the board of officers arrived and, under the guidance of the aviation committee of the Garden City Chamber of Commerce, a site was chosen 12½ miles east of Garden City on US Highway 50 South. On 16 June 1942 surveying crews began work at the site outlining runways and staking buildings.

When the crews arrived, the area of the projected base was a ripe wheat field. Consequently, the first days were a sort of combined operation, which began by the farmers threshing a strip down the proposed runways to enable surveyors to start. Farming and surveying proceeded simultaneously.

The construction program at Garden City was cut off before it really got under way by the orders of Headquarters, Army Air Forces, in June 1942, stopping work on nine of the 14 proposed British Operational Training Units. This change wiped out the entire western Kansas project of British bases, including Garden City, Dodge City, Pratt, and Liberal. From the middle of June until the latter part of July 1942 the Garden City officials did not know what kind of installation would be located in their community, if any at all. But by 27 July it was definitely understood that Garden City was to have a basic flying training school.

By the middle of July the Division Engineers had received a set of plans for the construction of the new type of base. The engineers were forced to remove every stake that had been driven for the former project and start anew. Contracts were let for construction before all the new stakes had been set out.

The Garden City *Daily Telegram*, of 6 August 1942, announced the start of actual construction the following day. It reported that holders of the contract for runways, roads and drainage will "begin clearing the site and start moving dirt. Wheat stubble which remained on the air base site east of Garden City after the crop was removed, will be burned to make way for grading operations."

The main base of the Garden City Army Air Field consisted of 1,584.66 acres, lying in Sections 27, 28, 29, 33, and 34, Township 24 South, Range 31 West, approximately 489 acres of which was reserved for the building area. The base was located on an irregular plot of high ground adjacent to the Arkansas river. The field extended one and one-half miles north and south and one and eight-tenths miles east and west along US Highway 50 South in Finney county, about 11 miles southeast of Garden City and 42 miles southwest of Dodge City. The land was acquired by judgments of Declaration of Taking in the Kansas District Court of the United States, Second Division.

Some 66 barracks, with a total capacity of 2,224 persons, were built for enlisted personnel, while 520 cadets could be accommodated in 26 barracks. Officers' quarters consisted of 17 buildings, with a total capacity of 272. Two buildings were provided for nurses' living quarters and mess hall. Total housing capacity for all personnel was 3,219. The base hospital was constructed with five wards, with 151 beds.

Five runways were built, four with a dimension of 150 x 6500 feet, and one 150 x 4,960 feet, with a gross load capacity of 74,000 pounds, wheel load of 37,000 pounds. Runways and apron (500 x 4,750 feet) were constructed with a ten-inch gravel base placed in layers on a six-inch compacted earth subbase, and surfaced with one and one-half-inch asphalt cement; the service strip (80 feet wide) was a six-inch concrete slab, thickened to nine inches at the expansion and construction joints. Five taxiways, 50 feet wide, completed the runway system. Fronting on the field, three squadron hangars, 120 by 80 feet, were built.

Four auxiliary fields were planned, but only three were constructed. Runways on Auxiliary Field No. 1 were of concrete, while those of Nos. 2 and 4 were of the bituminous mat type. The runway area was the same on all three auxiliary fields—4,950 square feet. None of the auxiliary fields were completed when training began, and, as a result, the Garden City Municipal Airport served as an auxiliary field in the interim.

Construction was officially completed on 25 May 1943 when the Project Completion Report was signed by the Area Engineer. As of 23 March 1943, funds apportioned for construction reached a total of $9,224,432.16.

But long before actual completion of construction the base was in operation. The field was officially activated on 21 December 1942, with Col. Jergan B. Olson assuming command at that time. Colonel Olson remained as commanding officer until succeeded on 26 August 1944 by Col. John W. Egan, who retained command of the base and school until the inactivation of the latter. Official designation of the school at the time of activation was Army Air Forces Basic Flying School, Garden City Army Air Field. On 30 April 1944, this school organization was replaced, without transfer of personnel, by the 2521st AAF Base Unit (Pilot School, Basic).

The assigned mission of Garden City Army Air Field was pilot training for basic students. As originally planned, the first class was to arrive on 15 March 1943, but this schedule was moved up to 15 January 1943. The class began training on 16 January. From then on the base was the scene of feverish and effective training activity. Until September 1943 BT-13 aircraft was used exclusively for flying training, but after that date twin-engine training was introduced. For a time during 1944 a few Women's Air Force Service Pilots (WASP's) were stationed at the field, serving as engineering test flight pilots.

The field did not go without official recognition of its contribution to the AAF training program, as witnessed by a letter, dated 9 September 1943, from Brig. Gen. A. Hornsby, Commanding General of the 32d Flying Training Wing (Basic), Perrin Field, Texas, to Colonel Olson:

> The excellent appearance of your post, and the morale and loyalty of those under you as well as the training results achieved, reflect the superior manner in which you have exercised your command. It is a pleasure to write this commendation to you and make it a matter of record.

Much in the same vein was the indorsement of the basic letter, dated 13 September 1943, from Headquarters, AAF Central Flying Training Command:

> The Commanding General, AAFCFTC, desires to add his personal commendation and appreciation for your superior performance of duty. This communication has been made a part of your official record. It is further desired that this communication be called to the attention of all members of your command.

The need for basic flying training schools having considerably lessened by the latter part of 1944, the basic flying school at Garden City Army Air Field was discontinued by Headquarters, Central Flying Training Command, effective 23 November 1944. Since training was somewhat ahead of schedule, 18 November became the final training date. Immediately thereafter both instructors and students were transferred. The upper class of cadets were transferred to advanced training, while students of the lower class were dispersed among other schools in order to complete the basic course.

Garden City Army Air Field was transferred to the jurisdiction of the Oklahoma City Air Technical Service Command on 15 December 1944 and placed on a standby status. On 27 February 1945 authority was granted to place the base on an active status as a storage depot for strategic aircraft of Class I. The 4132d AAF Base Unit (Air Base) was organized on 16 December 1944 to man what was now an aircraft storage depot. The peak of the storage mission was reached by July 1945, when 1,456 aircraft were stored on the base. After July 1945 the primary mission was reversed—that is, the major activity became the preparation of aircraft to be flown away from the base. By autumn of 1946 this phase of the mission was completed. On 29 October 1946, in anticipation of deactivation of Garden City Army Air Field, the base was declared excess to the Army Air Force, and on 15 March 1947, the 4132d AAF Base Unit was discontinued. The physical plant was officially transferred to the jurisdiction of the Corps of Engineers on 18 May 1947.

Great Bend Army Air Field
(1942-1945)

THE first public announcement of intentions to build an airfield at Great Bend, on the Arkansas river in Barton county, came in the form of a telegram from Sen. Arthur Capper of Kansas to the secretary of the Great Bend Chamber of Commerce on 30 September 1942. But, of course, by then all the preliminary work had been done. In July of that year the site at Great Bend had been chosen. Nor was all the initiative left to the Army. A committee of leading citizens from Great Bend and Hoisington had made the original proposal. Originally, plans called for the Civil Aeronautics Administration to supply the funds, and, with war's end, Barton county and Great Bend would acquire ownership. However, this tentative arrangement was subsequently changed so that the field was built under the auspices of the Air Force.

Originally intended to serve merely as a satellite base of Smoky Hill Army Air Field at Salina, the physical plant at Great Bend was initially decidedly limited in its functional utility and in size. Most of the construction work was done by Patti-McDonald Construction Company of Kansas City, but the concrete work on runways and taxiways was undertaken by the W. L. Johnson Construction Company. Essentials were completed first. These were followed in time by facilities for recreation and services. During the summer and fall of 1943 a service club, theater, and bowling alley were completed.

Capt. Theodore C. Reid, post engineer, was the first officer to report for duty on the base. He arrived on 18 January 1943. The first enlisted men to arrive, detachments of the 501st Base Headquarters and Air Base Squadron, the 1159th Guard Squadron, and the 902d Quartermaster Company, were necessarily housed in

Great Bend for a time, there being no facilities on the base. On 13 February 1943 the 501st was transferred to Great Bend to become the headquarters squadron of the new field. Capping the inchoate organizational structure, Lt. Col. Glenn M. Pike assumed command of the field on 26 February. The first recorded Morning Report, dated 5 March 1943, lists 13 officers and 182 enlisted men. From these modest beginnings, which was, of course, a skeleton force even for the limited role the field was originally designed to play, Great Bend was to grow impressively, both as to mission and physical plant. By 31 January 1945 a total of 6,409 personnel would be stationed there.

In keeping with its scheduled function of processing heavy bombardment groups, Great Bend Army Air Field was assigned to the 21st Bombardment Wing on 16 January 1943. It was the function of the 21st to operate processing bases, but, besides processing it did some training also. For instance, it provided certain types of navigational flights in those instances in which these had not been accomplished in third-phase training of the group. In addition, the wing provided training in "Prisoner of War Behavior and Escape."

As early as March 1943 it was known that the Second Air Force was to be charged with the responsibility of training personnel for the new B-29 very heavy bomber. And the first tangible step toward executing this mission was the activation of the 58th Bombardment Operational Training Wing at Smoky Hill Army Air Field at Salina, on 1 May 1943. But before much in the way of implementation could be done, the 58th was withdrawn from Second Air Force jurisdiction on 8 June 1943.

Knowing this delay to be purely a temporary one, on 1 July 1943 Second Air Force chose as the instrument to achieve this objective the 5th Heavy Bombardment Processing Unit, stationed at Salina. Since Great Bend Army Air Field had been designated as one of the bases to participate in the B-29 program, it was transferred to the 5th Heavy Bombardment Processing Unit on the same day.

If Great Bend was to assume a different and greatly enlarged mission, physical expansion of necessity became the order of the day. Original plans were altered, providing for considerable additions to the runway and taxiway systems. Additional troop housing was built, and new hangars were constructed especially designed to accommodate the B-29.

To bring its nomenclature more into harmony with its function, the 5th Heavy Bombardment Processing Unit was redesignated the 73d Bombardment Operational Training Wing on 17 August 1943. But the new organization endured for scarcely four months before it was disbanded on 22 October 1943, subsequent to the reassignment of the 58th Bombardment Operational Training Wing to the Second Air Force on 15 October. Both the personnel and the several bases of the 73d, among which figured Great Bend Army Air Field, were relinquished to the 58th.

Fortunately, despite the somewhat impermanent organizational picture at higher levels, the B-29 training program did get under way at the bases which were assigned the task. Great Bend received the 444th Bombardment Group (VH) and by April 1944, its training completed, the 444th departed for overseas service. During the remainder of its career, Great Bend was destined to train three more very heavy bombardment groups, the 498th, the 19th, and the 333d, and in addition, it retrained the ground echelon of the 489th back from Europe for redeployment to the Pacific. The extreme dearth of B-29 aircraft, however, hampered the training efforts for some time. Consequently, for several months the group in training at Great Bend perforce used B-17's and B-26's for the most part, with a sprinkling of B-29's to leaven the loaf.

Great Bend Army Air Field was fortunate in the calibre of cooperation received from surrounding communities. The neighboring municipalities, such as Great Bend and Hoisington, were particularly active in promoting recreational opportunities for the troops.

On 25 March 1944 the units permanently assigned to Great Bend Army Air Field were reorganized in the 243d AAF Base Unit (OTU) (VH). Thereafter, Great Bend was organized under the standard plan for OTU (Operational Training Unit) bases. This plan consisted of three major sections: administrative and services section, supply and maintenance section, and the training section. In addition, the air inspector and the hospital were referred to as sections. The office of the director of training was set up in April 1944, with the responsibility of providing flying and ground school training to all flying personnel of the very heavy bombardment groups successively stationed at Great Bend. In addition, the directorate was charged with the training of ground crew personnel. However, since the new directorate was not prepared immediately to take up its burden, the group in training at that time, the 498th, continued to train itself as the 444th had done before it. Consequently, it was only with the 19th Bombardment Group (VH), which began training in September 1944, that the training directorate took over the training responsibilities. Thereafter, the tactical units stationed at Great Bend were trained by the base directorate of training, although they maintained their individual organizations and operated independently of the base unit insofar as administration was concerned.

It came to be common procedure for the maintenance echelon of a group to move to Great Bend while another group was being trained there. This was done in order that these men could receive "on-the-job" training which would enable them to maintain the aircraft of their own group when it arrived. For instance, an advanced detachment of the 19th Bombardment Group (VH) were given jobs alongside the men of the 498th.

Beginning with the winter of 1945, part of the flying training was conducted at Borinquen Army Air Field, Puerto Rico. The primary purpose of this program, termed the "Gypsy Task Force," was to take advantage of the good flying weather in Puerto Rico during the winter months, enabling the crews to complete their training much quicker than would otherwise have been the case. With this phase of training over, the crews would return to Great Bend to prepare for departure to a staging area. The program was discontinued in April 1945, after only one season.

If the operations of the base were not crippled, they were certainly impeded by the critical manpower shortage resulting primarily from heavy transfers to the Army Ground Forces during the autumn and winter of 1944-1945.[2] By 31 January 1945, Great Bend had furnished the Army Ground Forces with 244 enlisted men. The reciprocal arrangement with the Ground Forces did not solve the problem, since by 31 January 1945, the field had received only 90 enlisted men replacements from the Ground Forces.

With the arrival of the ground echelon of the 489th Bombardment Group in February 1945 from the European theater, Great Bend became one of the first redeployment installations in the country. At that time the 333d Bombardment Group (VH) was receiving its regular training, but the ground echelon of the 489th was trained on B-29 maintenance alongside the men of the 333d. After a relatively short transition course in the B-29 (they were already experienced maintenance men) the 489th left in March to join the

---

2. These transfers were occasioned by the all out Allied ground push in Europe in which the Battle of the Bulge was a factor. Obviously, the transfers were part of an attempt to get every immediately available man on the line.

air echelon of the group, which had received transition training at several different bases.

Victory over Japan had a direct effect on the mission and activity of the base. The 333d Bombardment Group (VH), having completed its training, left Great Bend during July and August 1945. No other groups were assigned for a full schedule of training, but the 44th Bombardment Group (VH) and the 405th Service Group used Great Bend as an assembly point. Indeed, in this period the primary mission of the base became that of discharging qualified men—or rather of transferring them to separation centers.

On 25 October 1945 the base was officially informed by Second Air Force that the installation would be put on a standby basis on 31 December 1945. Following this announcement, activities on the base (except that of shipping men to separation centers) slowed up considerably. During December the 44th Bombardment Group (VH) and the 405th Air Service Group were transferred to Salina. Second Air Force had placed Great Bend in the category of those fields whose retention was desirable for standby, with a possibility of being reopened on 30 days' notice. Consequently, one of the principal activities of December consisted of inactivating buildings.

Sources are lacking by which to trace the subsequent steps leading to complete inactivation and transfer to the District Engineers. As late as March 1946 Great Bend was still in the category of temporarily inactive or standby under the Second Air Force. However, the field was never subsequently activated. For a short time, during 1950 (and possibly 1949), the field was host to an Air Force reserve unit. However, by March 1951 no unit was stationed there, nor has the Air Force made use of the field since.

HERINGTON ARMY AIR FIELD
(1942-1947)

HERINGTON Army Air Field was located eight miles from Herington, on a 1,700-acre tract of land which had been purchased by the United States government. It was planned as a satellite of Topeka Army Air Field, a Second Air Force installation which was situated some 70 miles to the northeast and which served as the headquarters for the 21st Bombardment Wing. Construction of Herington Army Air Field, accomplished by contract under supervision of the Air Service Command, commenced in September 1942, and continued over a period of 14 months. On 1 November 1942, however, Maj. Harold Painter, who was slated to become the first commanding officer, arrived to take over the field.

Construction work of a general nature relative to the site chosen for the army air field near Herington, included a water storage and distribution system; a sewage collection and disposal plant; an electric distribution system; two gasoline storage and distribution systems; 128,000 square yards of paved roads and streets; 14,000 square yards of paved walks; and a swimming pool.

The remaining major installations and structures at Herington Army Air Field may be listed conveniently under the following headings: airfield; temporary cantonment type buildings; temporary theater of operations type buildings; and auxiliaries.

Airfield.
- a) 3 concrete runways, 6,884, 6,793, and 6,780 feet long and each 150 feet wide.
- b) 4 taxiways, 4,431, 5,919, 1,208, and 425 feet long and each 100 feet wide.
- c) 3 small hangars.
- d) control tower.
- e) 1 concrete apron 3,384 feet long and 400 feet wide, with access aprons to the hangars.
- f) 4 hardstandings, three 100 feet in diameter and the other one 50 feet.

Temporary Cantonment Type Buildings.
- a) 1 mess hall.
- b) 15 storage houses.
- c) 4 administration buildings.
- d) 3 quarters.
- e) 1 barracks.
- f) 9 technical maintenance shops.
- g) 7 hospital buildings.
- h) 19 miscellaneous structures.

Temporary Theater of Operations Type Buildings.
- a) 6 mess halls.
- b) 45 storage houses.
- c) 25 administration buildings.
- d) 17 quarters.
- e) 56 barracks and dormitories.
- f) 8 technical maintenance shops.
- g) 97 miscellaneous structures.

Auxiliaries (off base).
- a) gasoline and oil storage area.
- b) radio homing station.
- c) rifle and pistol range.
- d) asphalt storage area.

On 26 January 1943 Major Painter formally assumed command of Herington Army Air Field and appointed an adjutant, a provost marshal, a post engineer, a quartermaster, and a medical officer.

On the same day also the following units were activated: the 503d Base Headquarters and Air Base Squadron; the 1161st Guard Squadron; and the 399th Army Air Forces Band. In the ensuing weeks a Base Signal Office was created, a Base Operations Section organized, a Finance Department set up, and a Base Chemical Service inaugurated. Commencing with only one officer on 1 November 1942, the number of military personnel on the field grew to 12 officers and 145 enlisted men by 1 March 1943 and to 103 officers and 1,768 enlisted men at the end of the following June. The first contingent of WAC's, consisting of one officer and ten enlisted women, arrived one year later. The peak in the strength of the permanent party military personnel was reached in August 1944, with totals of 113 officers and 2,123 enlisted men and women. Major Painter served as commanding officer of the field until 6 November 1943 when he was succeeded by Lt. Col. Charles B. Stead.

The 21st Bombardment Wing was charged with the responsibility of the final processing of heavy bombardment crews and equipment just prior to their leaving for overseas assignments. To carry out that program the wing utilized Topeka Army Air Field, and three satellite fields (Herington, Bruning, and Fairmont) in Kansas and Nebraska. This processing of heavy bombardment crews and equipment, sometimes called staging and also preparation for overseas movements, proved to be the principal function of Herington Army Air Field. A preliminary step leading to the development of the program there was the assignment on 25 January 1943 of the 47th, the 48th, the 49th, and the 50th Airdrome Squadrons. On 17 February following the 6th Heavy Bombardment Processing Headquarters was activated at Herington. The dominant role played by the processing function is indicated by the fact that in January 1944 the commanding officer of the 6th Heavy Bombardment Processing Headquarters, in the person of Lt. Col. Henry Dittman, assumed command over the entire field. That move in effect consolidated three units which existed there: the Processing Headquarters itself; the 503d Base Headquarters and Air Base Squadron; and the 406th Sub-Depot, jurisdiction over which the Second Air Force but recently had taken over from the Air Service Command. Two months later, incidentally, the whole was organized as the 274th Army Air Forces Base Unit.

The first combat crews and aircraft arrived at Herington for processing during the latter part of June 1943; and the program immediately got under way. Spread out over a period of approximately five days, the schedule involved the performance of the following functions on all such crews and aircraft which were temporarily assigned to the field: 1) auditing and processing of personnel records, orders, and allied papers of each person, and bringing payments up to date; 2) a physical fitness examination; 3) a clothing and equipment inspection; 4) the issue of certain critical items of equipment; 5) the assignment of the final type aircraft, and the conduct of specified vital inspection tests thereon; 6) a prisoner of war lecture; 7) communications instructions; 8) the assignment of crews and aircraft to scheduled overseas projects; 9) briefings on routes to be traveled; and, finally, 10) arranging the schedule for departure to the port of embarkation.

For the first 11 months of the active program Herington was primarily a B-24 staging field, with a few B-17 crews and aircraft being assigned there for processing. During the months of June, July, and August 1944, however, it was converted into a B-29 staging field. That meant, of course, the processing of very heavy bombardment crews and aircraft just prior to their departure for overseas assignments. Personnel who were routed to Herington for processing, incidentally, included such well-known officers as Maj. Gen. Curtis LeMay of the XX Bomber Command; Brig. Gen. Emmett O'Donnell of the 73d Bombardment Wing; and Brig. Gen. Roger M. Handy of the XXI Bomber Command.

By working around the clock during rush periods the 274th AAF Base Unit at Herington was able to process an average of nine combat crews a day. Normally, however, the rate of processing was much more moderate. Figures for the year ending 30 June 1944 may be regarded as typical. They reveal that during that interval an average of just over 86 crews and 76 aircraft were processed each month. With some slight diminution this rate was maintained until the end of World War II. On the whole most of the crews involved left Herington with their own aircraft. Some of the others traveled by train to the ports of embarkation. The remainder, along with some few aircraft, were transported to ports of embarkation by the Air Transport Command.

In May 1945 the Continental Air Forces assumed jurisdiction over the Second Air Force. On 18 July following Herington Army Air Field and the entire 21st Bombardment Wing were placed under the direct supervision of Headquarters, Continental Air Forces. In September 1945 Herington became an installation of the I Staging Command, with the change in the name of the 21st Wing to that designation. Soon thereafter Headquarters I Staging Command was moved from Topeka Army Air Field to Merced Army Air Field in California. There was no further change in the status of Herington, however, until its inactivation on 14 November 1945.

Col. Henry Dittman remained as commanding officer of Herington Army Air Field from 25 January 1944 until after the close of the war. Lt. Col. Maurice Horgas was serving in that capacity at the time the field was inactivated. Thereafter jurisdiction over it formally passed from the Continental Air Forces to the Oklahoma City Air Service Technical Command. The installation then was placed on an inactive status, and a declaration of surplus was prepared. On 18 October 1946 the War Department listed the field as surplus to its needs. After disposal had been made of all remaining property and a final audit had been made, jurisdiction over Herington Army Air Field was transferred to the Division Engineers, Kansas City, Mo., on 19 March 1947.

(To Be Concluded in the Autumn, 1959, Issue.)

The Pike's Peak Gold Rush and the Smoky Hill Route, 1859-1860

CALVIN W. GOWER

KANSAS territory, 1854-1861, extended from the western border of Missouri to the crest of the Rocky Mountains and included much of present-day eastern Colorado. When hordes of gold seekers participated in the Pike's Peak gold rush in 1859 and 1860, they not only passed through eastern Kansas territory in many instances, but they also did most of their prospecting in far western Kansas.

Eastern Kansas towns seemed to be in an ideal position to benefit from the rush. Undoubtedly many people went overland through Iowa and Nebraska, but the easiest approach was to go up the Missouri river to one of the Kansas, Missouri, or Nebraska river towns. By the early part of 1859 those who could afford it were crossing Missouri via the Hannibal and St. Joseph railroad. Kansas City and St. Joseph in Missouri and Omaha in Nebraska were good outfitting points, but the Kansas river towns claimed certain advantages. Kansas City and St. Joseph were said to be on the wrong side of the river, and the Nebraska town was too far up and too small.

Which route gold seekers might select was of much importance to river towns. Three main routes were used in 1859 and 1860. The southern followed the old Santa Fe trail for a large part of the way. Much of this traffic eventually started from Kansas City, Mo. None of the larger Kansas towns were on this trail. It attracted quite a few emigrants in 1859, not as many in 1860. The northern route followed the old Oregon trail in part, via the Platte river. Some extreme northeastern Kansas towns benefited, but few others. Atchison, Kan., and St. Joseph, Mo., were the chief starting points, with the latter gaining much of the trade. Several "central" routes supposedly existed, but by the early spring of 1859 the most popular was the Smoky Hill. This was by way of the Kansas river and its southern fork, the Smoky Hill, with Leavenworth as its principal starting point.

Of all the routes, the Smoky Hill was the most direct.[1] As early as September, 1858, Kansas newspapers were printing statements to

---

DR. CALVIN W. GOWER, Colorado born, recently received his Ph. D. from the University of Kansas, Lawrence. He is currently an instructor in history at St. Cloud State College, St. Cloud, Minn.

1. See William Crane Johnston, Jr., "The Smoky Hill Trail" (master's thesis, University of Denver, 1927). This work is incomplete, but it gives an outline of the history of the trail. The events covered in this article are not touched on to any great extent by Johnston.

this effect. One account asserted that the distance from Wyandotte by the Smoky might be only 500 miles.[2] Another newspaper estimated that the air line distance from Leavenworth was only 555 miles and said there were settlements to within 250 miles of the mines.[3]

Citizens of Wyandotte held a meeting in September, 1858, to push it as an outfitting point. It was argued "that the true route is directly up the Kansas river and Smoky Hill fork."[4] The Lawrence *Republican* noted on October 7, 1858, that Leavenworth and Kansas City were in contention, with Leavenworth defending the Smoky and Kansas City the Santa Fe. The *Republican* claimed that the Smoky passed through settled areas farther. A letter to the Junction City *Sentinel* stated that a man who had returned by way of the Smoky said the distance was shorter, the roads better, the wood, water, and game plentiful, and the settlements farther out.[5]

Besides these newspaper stories, three guide books published early in 1859 stressed the advantages of the Smoky Hill route. The author of one said it was the shortest but cautioned that until it was definitely opened up emigrants should take one of the better established routes. But he stated, "A central route will be opened the coming season," undoubtedly the Smoky Hill route.[6] A second guide book recommended the Smoky, stating that it followed the banks of streams except for about 130 miles. It advised striking south to meet the Arkansas river in the extreme western portion of the route.[7] A third guide book supported the Smoky for the same reasons.[8]

Praise of the Smoky continued into 1859. The Leavenworth *Weekly Times* reported on February 12 that the Junction City *Sentinel* advised emigrants to travel via Leavenworth. This fact was significant, said the *Times*, because Junction City was in the western portion of the settled part of Kansas and had no interests to serve but the good of the emigrant. What it neglected to mention was that these travelers were also expected to pass through

---

2. Leavenworth *Ledger* and Wyandotte *Commercial Gazette*, quoted in the *Herald of Freedom*, Lawrence, September 18, 1858.
3. White Cloud *Kansas Chief*, September 23, 1858.
4. *Western Weekly Argus*, Wyandotte, September 30, 1858.
5. James S. Graham to the editor of the *Sentinel*, no date.—Junction City *Sentinel*, quoted in the Lawrence *Republican*, October 7, 1858.
6. O. B. Gunn, *New Map and Hand-Book of Kansas & the Gold Mines* . . . (Pittsburgh, 1859), pp. 40, 42.
7. William B. Parsons, *The New Gold Mines of Western Kansas* . . . (Cincinnati, 1859), pp. 40, 42.
8. *The Illustrated Miners' Hand-Book and Guide to Pike's Peak* . . . (St. Louis, 1859), p. 66.

Junction City. In March a letter in the *Times* from William Larimer, a correspondent in Denver, stated that four men had recently arrived by way of the Smoky. He reported that they had been very well satisfied with the route.[9] One account noted that in 1843 John C. Fremont had explored the country between the Missouri river and the Rocky Mountains and in his narrative had recommended the Smoky route to the area. "Subsequent explorations have corroborated the view taken by the Great Explorer, and the bulk of the spring emigration will, undoubtedly, select this as their main road." [10]

In Lawrence the *Republican* printed a letter March 24, 1859, advising emigrants to go directly up the Smoky Hill to its head and then west.[11] The *Herald of Freedom* agreed, and said Lawrence was the best outfitting point.[12] A letter from the gold fields to the Wyandotte *Commercial Gazette* stated that several parties had come through by the Smoky Hill. "They report a good supply of wood, water and grass." [13] The Junction City *Sentinel* even became poetic, "Let Hercules do what he may, The Smoky Hill Route MUST have its day." [14]

Within months it was clear that the ideas expressed by these newspapers were incorrect in most instances. As one historian pointed out, in 1858 and 1859 "there was no discernable trail at all after one left Fort Riley. . . . Added to this lack of knowledge of the route to be taken, those who recommended the Smoky Hill trail had little knowledge of distance." [15] Another writer has commented, "Although it was the most direct, the Smoky was, due to scarcity of water, the hardest and most dangerous of the three great prairie roads from the Big Muddy to the Pike's Peak Gold Region." [16]

The Kansas City (Mo.) *Western Journal of Commerce* stated on April 9, 1859, that it had heard that suffering was occurring on the Smoky Hill route. Said the *Journal*, "How often will it be necessary to tell the public that *there is no road up the Smoky Hill.*" The *Cherry Creek Pioneer*, which appeared only once and then dis-

---
9. William Larimer, Jr., to the editor of the *Times*, February 2, 1859.—Leavenworth *Weekly Times*, March 5, 1859.
10. *Ibid.*, March 19, 1859.
11. A. Cutler to the editors of the *Republican*, March 10, 1859.—Lawrence *Republican*, March 24, 1859.
12. *Herald of Freedom*, Lawrence, March 26, 1859.
13. D. C. Collier to the editor of the Wyandotte *Commercial Gazette*, February 12, 1859, quoted in the Lawrence *Republican*, April 14, 1859.
14. Junction City *Sentinel*, quoted in the *Freedom's Champion*, Atchison, March 26, 1859.
15. Johnston, *op. cit.*, p. 14.
16. Margaret Long, *The Smoky Hill Trail, Following the Old Historic Pioneer Trails on the Modern Highways* (Denver, 1953), p. 20.

TABLE OF DISTANCES
FROM
Atchison to the Gold Mines,
VIA THE

First Standard Parallel Route to the Republican Fork of the Kansas River, thence following the trail of Col. Fremont on his explorations in 1843, to Cherry Creek and the Mines.

Compiled from Col. Fremont's Surveys, and the most reliable information derived from the traders across the Great Plains.

FROM ATCHISON TO	MILES	TOTAL	REMARKS
Lancaster,	9		Settlement, provisions and grass.
Muscotah, on Grasshopper,	11	20	Settlement, provisions and grass,
Eureka	11	31	Settlement, provisions and grass.
Ontario, on Elk Creek,	10	41	Settlement, provisions and grass.
America, on Soldiers Creek,	9	50	Settlement, provisions and grass.
Vermillion City,	25	75	Settlement, entertainment and provisions.
Crossing of Big Blue,	3	78	Heavy timber and grass.
Little Blue Creek,	17	95	Timber and grass.
Head of do do	23	118	Wood, water and grass.
Republican Fork,	12	130	Col. Fremont describes this section as "affording
do do Crossing,	2	132	an excellent road, it being generally over high and
Branch of Solomon's Fork,	38	170	level prairies, with numerous streams, which are well
Leaves do do do	75	245	timbered with ash, elm, and very heavy oak, and
Branch of Republican Fork,	15	260	abounding in herds of buffalo, elk and antelope."
Following up Rep. to its head,	190	450	Heavy timber and grass along the course
Beaver Creek,	23	473	Wood, grass and buffalo.
Bijou Creek,	22	495	Wood, grass and buffalo.
Kioway Creek,	15	510	The route from this point to the mines runs thro'
Cherry Creek and the Mines,	25	535	a country well timbered and watered, with luxurient grass and plenty of wild game.

ROUTE FROM ATCHISON,
VIA

The Great Military Road to Salt Lake, and Col. Fremont's Route in 1841.

FROM ATCHISON TO	MILES	TOTAL	REMARKS
Mormon Grove,	3½		Junction of the Great Military road,
Lancaster,	5½	9	Provisions and grass.
Huron, (crossing Grasshopper,)	4	13	Provisions and grass.
Kennekuk, do main do.	10	23	First Salt Lake Mail Station.
Capioma, (Walnut Creek,)	17	40	Provisions, timber and grass.
Richmond, (head of Nemaha,)	15	55	Provisions, timber and grass.
Marysville,	40	95	Salt Lake Mail Station and provisions.
Small Creek on Prairie,	10	105	Water and grass.
do do.	10	115	Luxurient grass.
do do.	7	122	Water and grass.
Wyth Creek,	7	129	Wood and grass.
Big Sandy Creek,	13	142	Wood and grass.
Dry Sandy Creek,	17	159	Wood and luxuriest grass.
Little Blue River,	12	171	Heavy timber.
Road leaves Little Blue,	44	215	Wood and grass.
Small Creek,	7	222	Wood and grass.
Platte River,	17	239	Wood, grass and buffalo.
Ft. Kearney,	10	249	Salt Lake Mail Station and provisions.
17 Mile Point,	17	266	Wood, water and grass.
Plum Creek,	18	284	Wood and grass.
Cottonwood Spring,	40	324	Wood and grass.
Fremont's Springs,	40	364	Luxurient grass.
O'Fallon's Bluffs,	5	369	Wood, water and grass.
Crossing South Platte,	40	409	Wood, water and grass.
Ft. St. Vrain,	200	609	Provisions, and from this to the mines the route is
Cherry Creek,	40	649	well timbered and watered.

ROUTE FROM ATCHISON,
VIA THE
SMOKY HILL FORK ROUTE

FROM ATCHISON TO	MILES.	TOTAL.	REMARKS.
Mormon Grove,	3¼		Junction of the Great Military Road.
Monrovia,	8½	12	Provisions, entertainment and grass.
Mouth of Pill's Creek,	13	25	On the Grasshopper. Wood and grass.
Ter. Road from Nebraska,	15	40	Wood, water and grass.
Soldier Creek,	10	50	Wood and grass.
Lost Creek,	15	65	Wood and grass.
Louisville,	10	75	Water and grass,
Manhattan City,	12	87	Water, wood and grass.
Ft. Riley,	15	102	Water, wood and grass.
Salina,	52	154	Wood, water and grass.
Pawnee Trail—Smoky Hill,	130	284	Grass and buffalo chips,
Pawnee Fork.	35	319	Grass and buffalo chips.
Arkansas Crossing,	35	354	Wood, water and grass.
Bent's Fort,	150	504	Wood, water and grass.
Bent's Old Fort,	40	544	Water and grass.
Huerfano,	40	584	Water and grass.
Fontaine qui Bouille,	15	599	Wood, water and grass.
Crossing of same,	18	617	Wood, water and grass.
Jim's Camp,	15	632	Water and grass.
Bush Corral,	12	644	Wood, water and grass.
Head of Cherry Creek,	26	670	Wood, water and grass.
Crossing of same,	35	705	From this point to the mines there is heavy timber,
Mines,	6	711	and grass and water in abundance.

A SAMPLE OF TRAVEL INFORMATION AVAILABLE IN KANSAS 100 YEARS AGO

Kansas towns vied for "tourist" traffic in 1859 as now. These travel directions, covering three main routes west from Atchison, contain several place names familiar to today's travelers. The tables were published in 1859 issues of an Atchison newspaper, *Freedom's Champion*.

Since the return of the buffalo (on scattered reservations, of course) today's traveler might even be able to locate buffalo chips for fuel if he looks closely enough. But beware of the buffalo.

continued operation, reported from Denver on April 23 that several men who had recently arrived via the Smoky Hill route had become lost because of the absence of markers on it. Stated the *Pioneer*, "Any other route is better than the smoky Hill road." [17] A man from Council Grove brought a report to Kansas City of a company of 100 men who had come down from the Smoky Hill route, lost and without provisions. He said they robbed the trading post at Cottonwood crossing, beat up the keeper, took 80 to 100 sacks of corn and all the flour, provisions, and groceries on hand, and headed for the mines.[18] The *Rocky Mountain News* asserted, "Every day we meet men arriving from the States by the above route—most of them in an almost famishing condition." This newspaper reported that three men had died from starvation. Other stories of deaths and disappearance appeared. One emigrant related a tale of 17 men who had died or disappeared, and another claimed the remains of one hundred men could be seen along the trail. The *News* bitterly condemned the people who had induced emigrants to start over the route with a short supply of provisions expecting to find a good road with good camps; a road 250 miles shorter than any other route. Instead, said the *News*, the emigrants found no road at all, very little wood or water, and a distance to travel of 800 instead of 600 miles.[19]

These stories of suffering on the Smoky Hill route continued until the most dreadful of all appeared. It was related in a published pamphlet by one of the survivors.

Daniel Blue, his two brothers, Alexander and Charles, and two other men left their homes in Illinois in February, 1859, to seek gold in the Pike's Peak gold region. They proceeded to Lawrence, purchased a pony, put their luggage on the animal, and started walking to the mining area. In Topeka they bought 200 pounds of flour. At Manhattan they joined a party of nine other Pike's Peakers and proceeded on to Fort Riley. By the time they reached that place the party had swelled to 16. The group decided to take the Smoky Hill route on the recommendation of one of their number who claimed to have traveled that trail before. Nine of the men stopped to hunt buffalo, but the rest pushed ahead. These seven became lost west of Fort Riley, their pony wandered away, and they were left with practically no provisions.

17. *Cherry Creek Pioneer*, Denver, April 23, 1859.
18. *Western Journal of Commerce*, Kansas City, Mo., May 7, 1859.
19. *Rocky Mountain News*, Denver, May 7, 1859.

About March 17 they reached the head of the Smoky Hill fork and believed themselves to be only about 55 miles from Denver. Actually, said Daniel Blue, they were about 170 miles away. They had no course to follow and used the sun for a guide. They were lost and had virtually no food left. To add to their troubles a severe snowstorm occurred. Soon the party of seven split up, three of the men pushing ahead, leaving behind a group of four, the three Blue brothers and a man named Soley. Before long two of them were too weak to walk. The four ran out of provisions and subsisted upon boiled roots, grass, and snow for eight days.

In their desperate situation, realizing that they faced death from starvation, the men determined to resort to cannibalism. They agreed that if one of them died the others should eat his flesh in an attempt to regain their strength and permit them to push on to some settlement. Soley died, and after lying beside him for three days the Blue brothers ate his flesh. Then Alexander Blue expired and the other brothers partook of his flesh. Finally, Charles Blue perished and Daniel Blue devoured some of his flesh. A short time later some Arapaho Indians found Daniel and saved him. They contacted the express company which took Daniel to Denver where he arrived on May 11. He found that only five of the 16 who had left Fort Riley had reached the gold fields.[20]

These tales of suffering brought forth bitter attacks on Leavenworth by the Kansas City *Western Journal of Commerce*. Said the *Journal*, "We are informed that they have a couple of bottles, filled with brass filings at a banking house in Leavenworth, which they place in the window, labeled 'Pike's Peak Gold.' It is this sort of stuff, together with 'painted wagons,' 'ten days Expresses,' that never run at all, that has killed so many on the Smoky Hill." [21] The Leavenworth *Weekly Herald* replied that in carping Kansas City all the bottles were filled with "instanter whiskey" and that was the way the people wanted them to continue.[22]

A short time later two journalists explained why suffering had occurred on the Smoky Hill. One of them stated, "That route will doubtless turn out as good in the end as either the Northern or Southern. But at the time of the beginning of the Pike's Peak emi-

20. Daniel Blue, *Thrilling Narrative of the Adventures, Sufferings and Starvation of Pike's Peak Gold Seekers* . . . (Chicago, 1860), pp. 6-8, 10-17. See, also, Henry Villard, "To the Pike's Peak Country in 1859 and Cannibalism on the Smoky Hill Route," *The Colorado Magazine*, Denver, v. 8 (November, 1931), pp. 225-236.
21. *Western Journal of Commerce*, May 28, 1859. Somehow the impression was gained in some quarters that the Jones and Russell express was using the Smoky Hill route. This was not true, but the express company was blamed for some of the emphasis which was placed on the Smoky Hill route.
22. *Weekly* Leavenworth *Herald*, June 4, 1859.

gration it was but partially explored. . . ."[23] The other asserted, "Thousands took an unexplored route, up the Smoky Hill river, where grass and water proved woefully scarce and fearful suffering prevailed."[24]

The unfortunate results of the 1859 spring emigration struck a deathblow to the Smoky Hill route. Very few items appeared in the papers concerning it during the summer and fall of 1859. However, in late September a meeting was held in Manhattan to consider the possibility of surveying and constructing a road from Leavenworth to Denver via Manhattan, Fort Riley, and the Solomon fork. The group appointed a committee to talk to the people of Leavenworth and other towns along the route.[25] This movement never developed further but a similar one concerning the Smoky Hill route did.

In the early part of 1860 discussion of the Smoky Hill route occurred in the Kansas legislature and in some newspapers. Two bills were introduced in the territorial council to establish roads up the Smoky Hill river to some point at the base of the Rocky Mountains.[26] In February the *Rocky Mountain News* printed a letter from someone in Denver who said the Platte route was the best, but that most of the people from the South and Southwest would select the Arkansas (the Santa Fe) route. Only the "fool-hardy and insane" would come up the Smoky Hill, this writer declared.[27] The *Kansas Press* of Council Grove, located on the Santa Fe route, said of the Smoky Hill route in late February, "we trust no one will be so foolish as to attempt to travel it."[28]

In spite of this attitude and in spite of the failures of the preceding year, Leavenworth still contained supporters of the Smoky Hill route in the spring of 1860. One of these sent a letter to the editor of the *Times* of that town late in February. Leavenworth must do something, this correspondent wrote, to offset the advantage obtained by St. Joseph through the establishment of the Hannibal and St. Joseph railroad. He suggested "that a Committee of arrangements . . . organize and equip as soon as possible, a

23. Henry Villard, *The Past and Present of the Pike's Peak Gold Regions*, reprinted from the edition of 1860, with introduction and notes by LeRoy R. Hafen (Princeton, 1932), p. 25.

24. Albert D. Richardson, *Beyond the Mississippi* . . . (Hartford, Conn., 1875), pp. 157, 158.

25. Manhattan *Express*, October 1, 1859.

26. *Council Journal of the Legislative Assembly of Kansas Territory* . . . 1860, pp. 34, 67.

27. "D." to the editor of the *News*, January 27, 1860.—*Rocky Mountain News*, February 1, 1860.

28. *The Kansas Press*, Council Grove, February 20, 1860.

party, who are to proceed and examine the region between Fort Riley and the Gold Region of Western Kansas—the route to follow the Smoky Hill fork to its source. . . ." This party should consist of not less than 18 well-equipped men, under the direction of an engineer, and should make a thorough survey of the route and construct good crossings over all the streams. The motive of the letter writer appeared in his last sentence: "By thus securing a short, commodious and direct route to the mines, Leavenworth can yet secure this season, the greatest part of the trade and travel to and from the Gold region, as their nearest river route." [29] The Smoky Hill route boom which subsequently developed in Leavenworth was clearly linked to efforts to secure more outfitting trade for that town and to combat the efforts of St. Joseph and other rivals.

Another letter writer shortly thereafter asserted, "At present, the great struggle is for the Lion's share of the Pike's Peak trade." Leavenworth could secure this by obtaining machinery for the quartz interests to purchase and by establishing a central route to the gold fields up the Smoky Hill fork. This correspondent suggested that the people in the towns from Leavenworth to Junction City collect funds toward constructing the road. He maintained that "every town, and every farmer on the route is interested, and can be induced to contribute in some way to the result." [30]

The *Times* supported this movement. It maintained that the best and shortest route to the gold fields lay from Leavenworth, but that the people interested in the route must improve it. Thirty to thirty-five thousand dollars would suffice to cover the expense of the necessary improvements, the newspaper declared. This sum would permit the employment of 100 to 150 men on the road who could complete the work in a short time. Adherents must act upon the plan quickly though, the *Times* concluded.[31]

As a result of this publicity, some Leavenworth residents held several road meetings in March. Those attending decided the principal stumbling block for road planners was financial. How much money would road construction require, and where would this money come from? The number of people at these meetings was not large. A committee was appointed at one meeting to collect subscriptions and information on the subject and to report at a later meeting.[32]

29. "Wide Awake" to the editor of the *Times*, February 29, 1860.—Leavenworth *Daily Times*, March 1, 1860.
30. "Progress" to the editor of the *Times*, no date.—*Ibid.*, March 2, 1860.
31. *Ibid.*, March 12, 1860.
32. *Ibid.*, March 15, 17, 1860; *Weekly* Leavenworth *Herald*, March 24, 1860.

Other towns supported this move. The Lawrence *Republican* defended the Smoky Hill route with the explanation:

Some parties who started out on that route last season took an insufficiency of provisions, and therefore incurred great suffering. But that was no fault of the route. Large numbers of persons returned from the mines by that route last season, and all spoke of it as the shortest and best.[33]

Later this paper reported,

The citizens of Leavenworth are moving in the matter of a road to the gold mines, up the Smoky Hill river. This is a sensible movement, and should have been made long ago. It will not be possible for Leavenworth long to retain the Pike's Peak trade, if the present northern route is maintained. The people of our own locality are also interested in this route, and will gladly second the efforts of our Leavenworth neighbors.[34]

The *State Record* of Topeka stated that the Smoky Hill route was doubtless the shortest and best.[35]

The *Rocky Mountain News,* on the other hand, protested against attempts to build up the Smoky Hill route again as a fine usable route. Inducing emigrants to use the route "for the benefit of speculators and lot owners, in prospective towns along the line of travel, has been tried once over this fated *Smoky Hell* route with only too lamentable success, and its instigators stand to-day, in the sight of Heaven, guilty of manslaughter, to say the least." The *News* suggested that the promoters of the Smoky Hill route try it themselves and "if they get through without eating each other up, some adventurous individuals may be induced to follow." [36]

Such an attitude did not deter Leavenworth promoters. The general meetings did not seem to be making much progress, so the Leavenworth city council accepted the proposition of an experienced mountaineer to open up the route. This move prompted the first of the two Leavenworth-sponsored expeditions sent to locate a road over the Smoky Hill in 1860.

Late in March Green Russell, one of the pioneer prospectors in the Pike's Peak region, appeared in Leavenworth on his way to the gold fields. He went before the city council and offered to locate a road over the Smoky Hill route for $3,500. He promised to provide a guide for this road giving the distances between camping grounds and information on the supply of wood, grass, and water, and he agreed to send a report of his findings to the mayor and the council of Leavenworth. If he passed over the route in 40 days,

33. Lawrence *Republican,* March 8, 1860.
34. *Ibid.,* March 29, 1860.
35. *State Record,* Topeka, March 31, 1860.
36. *Rocky Mountain News,* March 21, 1860.

he promised to deduct one third of the sum charged. The council unanimously accepted the proposition. Commented the *Times* concerning the report Russell would send back, "If favorable, that report will influence one half the return travel in the fall, and control a large portion of the outgoing emigration in the summer." [37]

Other towns in Kansas approved the Green Russell expedition. A Lawrence paper asserted,

> The citizens of Leavenworth are at last awaking to the necessity of opening a road from that city direct to the mines, via the Smoky Hill Fork. It is the only method by which Leavenworth can hope to retain her Pike's Peak trade, or maintain her position as the outfitting emporium for the gold regions. For the northern route, Atchison and St. Joseph are two powerful competitors.

The newspaper added that if the Smoky Hill route were not opened, the Pacific railroad would go by the Platte route.[38] The Topeka *State Record* commented, "The entire Kansas Valley is deeply interested in this project, and should co-operate with Leavenworth to the extent of their ability in securing the opening of the route." [39] An editor in Manhattan declared, "This is a sensible movement, and should have been made long ago. . . . The people of our own locality are also interested in this route, and will gladly second the efforts of our Leavenworth neighbors." [40] A letter to a Leavenworth paper from a man in Junction City stated that Junction City favored Leavenworth's attentions to the Smoky Hill route.[41] Even the *Rocky Mountain News* approved the plan to send Green Russell out to explore and to mark the route. However, the editor of the gold fields paper did not think anyone could construct a good road via the Smoky Hill, and, therefore, he declared he would not recommend any travel over that route until the road had been definitely established.[42]

In early May Green Russell's party arrived in the gold fields.[43] On May 15 the mayor of Leavenworth received Russell's report. The *Times* reported that this account was very favorable. Now, counseled the *Times*, Leavenworth should immediately call a convention of representatives from all the cities and towns interested in the route and should ask the national government to send over the route a survey team of 60 men or so accompanied by an engineer.[44]

37. Leavenworth *Daily Times*, March 30, 1860.
38. Lawrence *Republican*, April 5, 1860.
39. *State Record*, April 7, 1860.
40. Manhattan *Express*, April 7, 1860.
41. "Keystone" to the editor of the *Herald*, April 14, 1860.—*Weekly* Leavenworth *Herald*, April 21, 1860.
42. *Rocky Mountain News*, April 25, 1860.
43. *Rocky Mountain Herald*, Denver, May 5, 1860.
44. Leavenworth *Daily Times*, May 16, 1860.

Even before Green Russell had completed his journey and sent back his report, the Leavenworth *Weekly Herald* had opined that the towns along the Kansas river and Leavenworth must set up a fund of $30,000 to $50,000 for a complete exploration of the Smoky Hill route and the opening up of a government wagon road over the route. For, even if Green Russell did a good surveying job, "neither his say so, nor any other private person's say so will secure popular faith in a route which once proved so disastrous to those who tried it." Also, the editor of the *Herald* believed that Russell's party was too small to do a thorough job of exploring. He suggested a convention of representatives from Leavenworth, Atchison, Kansas City, and all Kansas river towns to set up a comprehensive plan of survey, because the Smoky Hill route was important to the economy of all these towns.[45]

Thus, although the Green Russell expedition evoked an abundance of enthusiasm when it began and even later when its report came back, some observers had seen at an early date that it would have only limited value. Earlier complaints that the expedition was almost worthless seemed to be confirmed by subsequent events. Just a few weeks after the completion of Russell's trip another exploration was on its way to open up the Smoky Hill route.

When Russell's report arrived in Leavenworth, interested citizens of that town held a public meeting to consider their next step.[46] The *Times* declared, "No citizen having any interest in Leavenworth should forget or overlook the meeting to-night at the City Hall."[47] A report which appeared in the *Rocky Mountain News* late in May explained the urgency of this meeting. This report came from an anonymous Eastern correspondent of the *News* who wrote from St. Louis May 6. He stated that many emigrants were going to the Rocky Mountains at this time:

St. Joseph particularly furnishes ample evidence of the numerical strength of this spring's emigration. . . . The emigration from Atchison, Leavenworth and Kansas City, is not very heavy this spring. More freight trains, it is true, are started from these three towns than from those farther north, but the bulk of the emigration itself seems to avoid them. Leavenworth, especially, appears to be much less attractive as an outfitting point than last year.[48]

At the meeting held to consider Russell's report in mid-May in Leavenworth the assembly set up a committee to devise a plan

---

45. *Weekly* Leavenworth *Herald*, April 21, 1860.
46. Leavenworth *Daily Times*, May 19, 1860.
47. *Ibid.*, May 18, 1860.
48. Letter to the editor of the *News*, May 6, 1860.—*Rocky Mountain News*, May 23, 1860.

concerning the Smoky Hill road. The committee suggested the following program: "First, to raise means in the city. Second, to secure, forthwith, the co-operation of cities and counties along the line. Third, to start a party, headed by practical and thorough men, upon the road, to build and establish it." [49] A few days earlier the city council of Leavenworth had appointed the mayor and two other citizens to constitute a committee to correspond with other towns interested in opening a wagon road from Leavenworth to Denver over the Smoky Hill.[50]

Conferences between the interested towns occupied the next few days. Newspapers in the Kansas river towns responded favorably to Leavenworth's overtures. The Manhattan *Express* urged both Manhattan and Junction City to foster the movement.[51] The Topeka *State Record* stated, "Measures should now be taken immediately for opening this route, and turning to practical account the important facts developed." [52]

The *Times* noted on May 23 that "delegates have been sent to Lawrence, Topeka, Manhattan and Junction [City], and ere a fortnight passes a company will be out to build the road." [53] Leavenworth's plan was to send out a construction train to make bridges, fix crossings, and dig wells. The train should consist of 35 men and a competent superintendent sent out to work for 65 days. The estimated cost of this operation was $7,500, and Leavenworth reportedly had already raised $2,000. The town would raise most of the remainder of the sum, but it expected the Kansas valley towns who were interested to contribute something also. Lawrence planned a meeting to decide what its participation in the activity would be, and a local paper urged the importance of the movement upon the merchants of that town.[54] Topeka residents held a public meeting May 23 to confer with the Leavenworth Smoky Hill route committee to discuss plans.[55] Manhattan citizens held a conference about the same time and discussed various means to finance the endeavor.[56]

Money was scarce in Kansas at this time, but Topeka offered to furnish five yoke of cattle and whatever amount of money it could

---

49. Leavenworth *Daily Times*, May 21, 1860.
50. *Ibid.*, May 19, 1860.
51. Manhattan *Express*, May 19, 1860.
52. *State Record*, May 19, 1860.
53. Leavenworth *Daily Times*, May 23, 1860.
54. Lawrence *Republican*, May 24, 1860.
55. *State Record*, May 26, 1860.
56. Manhattan *Express*, May 26, 1860.

raise, probably between three and five hundred dollars.[57] Junction City appropriated $500 in bonds and declared it would double that amount if necessary. Ogden offered a yoke of oxen, and Manhattan promised $500 in bonds. Vermillion offered a mare, Auburn promised three yoke of cattle, and Lawrence raised $155 in cash. The total cash value of subscriptions from the Kansas valley towns by June 2 was $2,165. The Leavenworth city council authorized the issuance of $3,000 in bonds.[58]

The financial arrangements were thus fairly well underway by the time authorities in Leavenworth completed the organization of the expedition. Superintendent of the party was Henry T. Green, a 34-year-old attorney from Virginia, who had lived in Leavenworth since 1854.[59] Green, who was not an experienced prairie traveler, led a party which included a guide, an engineer, and a practical surveyor.[60] The expedition consisted of about 40 other persons, five wagons, 60 days' provisions, and plenty of firearms and ammunition. The group left Leavenworth about June 18.[61]

The Green expedition reached Topeka on June 22 and Manhattan four days later. Green visited the office of the Manhattan *Express* and told some of his plans. He intended to halt at the extreme headwaters of the Smoky Hill and make a thorough investigation of the country between that point and Cherry Creek. Also, the expedition planned to bridge all streams which travelers had difficulties crossing, smooth out abrupt declivities, fill all steep hollows, remove bad rocks, try to make as direct a route as possible, and set up suitable guideboards and other markers. The *Express* stressed the long-range importance of the expedition by emphasizing that the road which the expedition opened would be the forerunner of a railroad "which will soon be demanded by the importance which the Gold Mines on our Western border are beginning to assume."[62]

Green and his men were in Salina on July 4 and that town prepared a Fourth of July picnic for them.[63] A Leavenworth paper reported July 23,

The last heard from the Smoky Hill Expedition, was when at a point fifty miles beyond Salina. As far as the work had progressed, the route was excellent, and no difficulty of any kind had been experienced. The road was

57. Leavenworth *Daily Times*, May 29, 1860.
58. *Ibid.*, June 2, 1860.
59. "United States Census, 1860," v. 10, p. 222.—Archives division, Kansas State Historical Society, Topeka; A. T. Andreas and W. G. Cutler, *History of the State of Kansas* (Chicago, 1883), p. 444.
60. Leavenworth *Daily Times*, June 6, 1860.
61. *Ibid.*, June 16, 1860.
62. Topeka *Tribune*, June 23, 1860; Manhattan *Express*, June 30, 1860.
63. "J. R. F." to the editor of the *Times*, July 4, 1860.—Leavenworth *Daily Times*, July 11, 1860.

marked by mounds, about a mile apart, so that there could be no trouble in finding it hereafter.[64]

About a month later the *Times* received a letter from its special correspondent who was traveling with the expedition. He announced that the party had reached the gold fields after 57 days on the trail; the expedition, he wrote, had made a good road to both Denver and Colorado City. The *Times* greeted this announcement with the statement, "Leavenworth City will soon recover her former vitality. . . ."[65]

Green sent a letter from Denver shortly after his party reached that place. He wrote that wood was scarce on the Smoky Hill route in many places but plenty of buffalo chips were available. Up to Big Grove an abundance of water existed, and beyond Big Grove the longest stretch without water was only 22 miles. "All through the route we have mounds and sign boards so that no man can lose it." Green intended to start back to Leavenworth soon and promised that upon his arrival he would "furnish a report of our financial condition, which is quite low, also a diary of our travel, water, grass, wood, buffalo chips, and the face of the country."[66]

Green and others arrived back in Leavenworth on October 6. Several Leavenworth citizens visited him on his first evening in town, organizing into a meeting to decide what steps should be taken to present Green's report to the people of Leavenworth. They decided to have Green and other officers of the expedition report to the city council on October 9 and then later relate their experiences at a meeting of all the citizens of Leavenworth. The *Times* commented that the opening of the route was of great significance to Leavenworth. Expectations were that a large emigration would roll to the gold fields in 1861.[67]

Green reported before a general meeting of the people of Leavenworth on October 16.[68] Three days before this meeting, authorities auctioned off all of the equipment used by the Green expedition and a large crowd collected to bid on the various items.[69] In March, 1861, the report was distributed in pamphlet form.[70] This pamphlet also contained an explanatory preface by the publishing committee of the Leavenworth city council and a table of dis-

---
64. *Ibid.*, July 23, 1860.
65. James Brown to the editor of the *Times*, August 16, 1860.—*Ibid.*, August 28, 1860.
66. H. T. Green to the editor of the *Times*, August 29, 1860.—*Ibid.*, September 10, 1860.
67. *Ibid.*, October 8, 1860.
68. *Ibid.*, October 17, 1860.
69. *Ibid.*, October 15, 1860.
70. *Ibid.*, March 23, 1861.

tances between Leavenworth and Denver.[71] With this publication the Green expedition completed its activities.

Some Kansas newspapers greeted the work of the Green expedition with enthusiasm. The Lawrence *Republican* stated, "We shall soon have the immense trade and travel of the entire gold regions directed through our city. . . ."[72] The Topeka *State Record* commented that the Smoky Hill route had innumerable advantages, and the Manhattan *Express* asserted that the Smoky Hill would "positively be the great thoroughfare to the gold regions."[73]

People from the gold fields who traveled back over that route sustained the enthusiasm for the Smoky Hill road. A man who had recently returned over the route declared in October, 1860, that he believed it was shorter and better than the Platte or Arkansas.[74] Four men who came over the route to Leavenworth from Denver asserted that it was the best road from the mines, over one hundred miles shorter than any other.[75] Another returned Pike's Peaker praised the road, but noted one drawback. His complaint was: ". . . the landmarks erected by the surveying expedition, are being demolished by the herds of buffalo on the plains, and . . . unless measures are speedily taken to restore them, an entire new survey, much of the distance, will have to be made."[76]

Actually the destruction of the landmarks made little difference in the history of the route. The desperate endeavor by Leavenworth and the Kansas river towns to construct a route which would gain a place beside the Platte route came two years too late. The peak of the rush to the gold fields had occurred in 1859. The traffic in 1860 was still of sizeable proportions, but the Smoky Hill road was constructed too late in that year to benefit from it. In 1861 the rush was over. The improved route did not help the Kansas valley towns gain much of the gold seekers' trade, but it did serve a useful purpose later as the road for the Butterfield stage line and even later for the Kansas Pacific railroad.[77] The route proved its usefulness, but only at a later date and under different circumstances than those which prevailed in 1859 and 1860.

71. H. T. Green and O. M. Tennison, *Report and Map of the Superintendent and Engineer of the Smoky Hill Expedition* . . . (Leavenworth, 1861).
72. Lawrence *Republican*, August 30, 1860.
73. *State Record*, October 13, 1860; Manhattan *Express*, September 29, 1860.
74. S. J. Willes to the editor of the *Republican*, October 8, 1860.—Lawrence *Republican*, October 11, 1860.
75. Leavenworth *Daily Times*, October 30, 1860.
76. *State Record*, November 17, 1860.
77. Johnston, op. cit., pp. 49, 62, 66.

The Letters of the Rev. Samuel Young Lum, Pioneer Kansas Missionary, 1854-1858—*Concluded*

Edited by EMORY LINDQUIST

III. THE LETTERS, MARCH, 1856—MARCH, 1858

Lawrence, K. T. March 10th, 1856.

REV. MILTON BADGER, D. D.
DEAR BROTHER

My report for the year is necessarily detained chiefly on account of ill health & at present I do not feel competent to the task of a lengthened report but shall endeavor to supply what is now deficient in the next quarterly, which will follow this in little over a week.

I cannot report the realization of what we so earnestly hoped at the commencement of the year. Circumstances new & trying in the extreme, have arisen to retard the progress of truth; & there have been times when a full confidence in the overruling hand of an all wise Father has been all that could keep our little band of praying ones, from utter despair, so far as our prospects here were concerned.

All has for a great part of the time been wild excitement.[32] Our place of worship has been taken for soldiers barracks, & our meetings, when we could have any, were held in *little* private rooms, where but very few could be assembled. In such a state of things all has looked dark. A few of the brethren & sisters have been drawn nearer to God, & have felt their entire & absolute dependence upon him in every trial, but the great majority even of the church have been influenced in a contrary direction. Excitement seemed to dissipate serious reflection, & the mind lost its delight in the worship & service of God. I hardly think it possible for the interests of truth to be advanced, even with ordinary rapidity, under such cir-

---

DR. EMORY KEMPTON LINDQUIST, Rhodes scholar and former president of Bethany College, is dean of the faculties of the University of Wichita. He is author of *Smoky Valley People: A History of Lindsborg, Kansas* (1953), and numerous magazine articles relating to the history of this region.

32. There was much agitation and conflict in Kansas associated with the Topeka constitutional movement. Officials were elected under the constitution on January 15, 1856. On February 11 President Franklin Pierce issued a proclamation commanding "all persons engaged in unlawful combinations against the constituted authority of the Territory of Kansas, or of the United States, to disperse, and retire peaceably to their respective abodes."—Daniel W. Wilder, *Annals of Kansas* (1886), pp. 106, 109. The text of the Topeka constitution is found in *ibid.*, pp. 91-106. Various factors in the Topeka movement are described in an interesting manner by James C. Malin, "The Topeka Statehood Movement Reconsidered: Origins," in *Territorial Kansas; Studies Commemorating the Centennial* (Lawrence, 1954), pp. 33-69.

(172)

cumstances; & for this reason mainly I shall have but little progress to report. We think that a permanent peace has at last been secured; not but that we shall have excitement still, but I do not think they will be of the bloody character they have heretofore been; & I trust will in their influence be less hostile to truth.

The name of our Church is Plymouth Cong. Chh. of Lawrence, Kanzas. During most of the year I have had 2 stations 25 miles apart. Since Sept. I have entirely withdrawn from Topeka, & have taken a station within the bounds of my Lawrence congregation. Thus I have still 2 & soon as practicable expect to take another.

The church is composed of ten male & eight female members. Beside these, three have left us for the church triumphant, & one has taken his letter to another church.

It is difficult to state what is the average attendance. When we have the hall, which we resumed last Sabbath, there are about 100 in attendance, & probably, if our circumstances were at all favorable, the average attendance would be twice that number.

It is not yet my pleasure to report any hopeful conversions though there are a few who manifest much interest in their future welfare. No additions by profession. There have been (8) eight additions by letter though it is probable that some of these may be noticed in my last report. Some of our most promising, prospective members have been induced, from one cause & another, to either return East, or to seek some other location, not so exactly in the focus of danger.

The Sabbath school has been much interrupted as also the Bible class; & there is a less attendance than one year ago. The neighborhood schools have been omitted during the vigor of the winter; & the school in Lawrence numbers but about 30 with about 20 in the Bible class.

The contributions at the monthly concert amount to $20.00 most (if not all of which) will be for Home Missions.

The steps taken last fall for the erection of a church edifice, are likely to be crowned with success. We hope before the close of the year to see our hopes in this direction fully realized; steps have been taken for the formation of Bible & Tract Societies.[33]

Yours in the Gospel
S. Y. LUM.

---

33. The church building was started in the autumn of 1855. While the church was used before it was fully completed, it was not dedicated until November 16, 1862.—Richard Cordley, *Pioneer Days in Kansas* (1903), pp. 82, 83.

LAWRENCE, March 22, 1856.

REV. MILTON BADGER, D. D.
DEAR BROTHER

When I wrote my yearly report, I promised to be more full in my next quarterly report & intended to make my promise good, but I fear I shall be compelled to be a delinquent as I am now writing under anything but favorable circumstances, watching day after day, & I may say, night after night at the bed of sickness & death. I find but little time, and feel but little disposition, to perform mental labor. One of the members of my church, a young man & full of promise, both for the church & the world, lies by my side, just on the verge of eternity. . . . I feel that I am ministering to my dear Savior, in the person of his loved disciple, & it is a pleasure, though a wearisome one to the flesh. . . .

We begin to hope that the hostile demonstrations of our Missouri neighbors are over. This is desirable not only for the *temporal* advancement of the Territory, but more especially for its growth in spiritual things. Those who have not seen, cannot feel as we do, what an awful influence the wild excitements of the past year have had on the morals & virtue of this community. All the effects of the Missionary are more than overbalanced by the agencies for evil; & the character of the place, as a whole, has been sinking instead of rising. It is with pain that we are compelled to admit such a state of things; yet we do not give up our hope in reference to the future. Should the peaceful state of things which now exist, continue, the mind of men will be better prepared to receive the truth, & much more likely to give thought to the subject of Eternity, salvation.

The legislature that met under the Constitution for the "State of Kanzas," has just adjourned, & without any difficulties.[34] Gov. Shannon threatened to arrest them, but they proceded with such caution, & yet with so much firmness, that he seemed to think it wisest not to interfere. Whether their doings will amount to anything depends upon the action of our National Government, of which there is but little hope.

I have written this in the sick room in the midst of constant interruptions, the natural result of which appear throughout it.

Please send the amount for the past quarter as heretofore ($100) one hundred dollars.

Yours respectfully,
S. Y. LUM.

---

34. The Topeka legislature adjourned on March 8, 1856, to reassemble on July 4, 1856.—Wilder, *op. cit.*, p. 114.

LAWRENCE, KANSAS,
June/1856
REV. MILTON BADGER, D. D.
DEAR BROTHER
Another year of my labor in this field has expired; & in looking over it I find little to report, calculated to gladden the hearts of those who feel an interest in the religious development of Kansas. The whole time of my labor has been filled with excitements & commotion, of such a character as to retard, if not entirely destroy the influence of truth; but the past three months more than any other time, seems *worse* than lost, in a moral point of view.

My ministrations have been regular, & at times well attended— our little hall being frequently so thronged as to compel many to leave,— & while there, the audiences have appeared attentive & serious, but at the threshold, as they left the house of prayer, the ever present subject would meet the mind in some new form, & crowd out all serious thought of the future. It has seemed as though the Sabbath was selected as the day for special excitements; & not infrequently have the members of my congregation & even members of my church, left the morning service to be called upon to go to the rescue of their brethren attacked by the banditti who surround us. Without a knowledge derived from seeing & feeling, one cannot estimate the fearful influence that such a state of things has upon the character of even the professed children of God.

Those who love God here earnestly pray, for a season of rest & quiet, a time when the soul can hold communion with itself, & discover its true position & prospects. We hope too that we shall not be forgotten by our Eastern brethren. While they pray for our temporal relief, let them not forget that we are in even greater danger as a community of spiritual death than temporal. . . .

Since writing my last, I have been compelled to confine myself almost entirely to this immediate vicinity. One cannot feel safe, no matter what his position or what his business, in going in any direction through the territory. Bands of armed men have been, & are still arresting travellers, all about us, taking whatever they find upon them of value. . . . Every day accounts are brought of persons robbed & murdered & for no offense except, of holding opinions not corresponding with those of the ruling powers. We are truly experiencing a reign of terror. A few sabbaths since, when going to an evening prayer meeting about a mile & a half distant, I was twice pursued by two suspicious persons on horses, but failing to overtake me they turned back. Thus you see that it is not safe to travel at all.

You doubtless have received full accounts of the destruction of property and of the robberies that have taken place. These will be seriously felt by our church, some having lost nearly their all, & all being sufferers to a greater or less extent. The salary which was pledged here will be almost entirely lost. The brethren had hoped that the Spring would enable them to make up for the deficiency of last Fall; but now they are much worse off than then. They are placed in a position where they cannot redeem their pledges.

I have myself been a sufferer to the amount of not less than three hundred dollars. When I first came to the Territory, I had a valuable horse given to me by a member of my church, one deeply interested in the cause of the truth here. Last Winter he became temporarily disabled; & I procured another—also a gift. They were both taken the same day with the burning of the hotel, & I have not seen them since.[35]

On the morning after the destruction of Lawrence, I visited the camp of the Marshal's posse, & made an effort to recover my property; but succeeded only so far as to get thoroughly abused. They threatened to hang me; & I barely escaped with my life. Kanzas is now passing through the furnace. Her character is being formed under a welding heat. What type it will assume depends much upon what material the churches of our land shall throw into the crucible. We hope it may emerge from the fire bearing the same impress that New England received from her early trials.

As to the issue between Freedom & Slavery, it cannot be decided wrong if the Free States do what they now seem determined upon. This is however, the darkest hour that Freedom has ever seen in Kanzas; the entire force of the Government is brought to bear against it, & there is no indignity, no outrage which is not practiced upon the Free-State settlers. The scenes that followed the *"coup de tat"* of Louis Napoleon are reenacted here under our free gov-

---

35. Lum describes the "sack of Lawrence." On May 21, 1856, the posse assembled by United States Marshal Israel B. Donalson, when disbanded, was used by Sheriff Samuel J. Jones of Douglas county, contending that it was needed to make some arrests and to abolish some nuisances as ordered by the grand jury. Earlier, on April 23, 1856, when Jones came to Lawrence to make some arrests, he was shot in a leg while asleep in a tent. On May 21, 1856, the group under Jones destroyed the presses and equipment of the Lawrence *Herald of Freedom* and the *Kansas Free Press.* The New England Emigrant Company hotel, the home of Charles Robinson were burned and other property was destroyed.—Richard Cordley, *A History of Lawrence, Kansas* (1895), pp. 87-89; 99-103. The grand jury indictment which Sheriff Jones carried with him is printed in Frank W. Blackmar, *The Life of Charles Robinson* (Topeka, 1902), pp. 196, 197. Prof. James C. Malin describes the background factors in the interesting article "Judge Lecompte and the 'Sack of Lawrence,' May 21, 1856," *The Kansas Historical Quarterly,* Topeka, v. 20 (August, 1953), pp. 553-597.

ernment with additional violence.[36] Men are arrested *without legal process*, & when arrested are driven off before the pretended officers like cattle. I can but feel that these things are developing clearly the true nature of our national foe & preparing the true men in all parts of the country to resist successfully its grasping demands.

We are all ready to commence the work of church building; & were it not for the peculiar state of things, the work would have been in quite an advanced state. As it is, it is difficult to get anyone to run the risk of so large a contract, as it may be arrested at any moment. We shall commence, however, as soon as possible. Our desire will not be to secure the most costly edifice. One is now building that will cost not less than twelve thousand dollars. We shall be confined to the neighborhood of $5,000. For this, we can get a comfortable though not large a building. We fear we shall have to dispense with the tower & bell; though to us they seem almost essential.

I have just returned from a visit to the camp where the prisoners of State are held; but was not permitted to see them.[37] No one but their counsel are at present allowed even to speak to the prisoners. Every thing is rendered as uncomfortable as possible. They were cheerfull & confident of the final success of the cause for which they suffer; so we learned from the Governor's wife, Mrs. Robinson.

You will please remit the quarter's salary as heretofore & I much fear I shall be compelled to ask for a further remittance [because] every thing has gone contrary to our expectations. I should be [by] this [time] have preached a sermon in behalf of the A.H.M.S. but circumstances have prevented. The pecuniary result would be inconsiderable yet its influence on the future might be important could I find a time when thought could be secured to the object. I have not received the Home Missionary for the past year. Will you not have it sent with the past numbers from April last?

Yours truly
S. Y. Lum.

36. On December 2, 1851, Louis Napoleon gained complete mastery of France as a result of a *coup d'etat* planned largely by his half brother, the Duc de Morny.

37. Charles Robinson, who had been elected governor of Kansas in January, 1856, under the Topeka constitution, was one of several Free-State prisoners at Lecompton. They were held on an indictment for treason on the basis of the action by the grand jury of Douglas county.—Cordley, *A History of Lawrence, Kansas*, pp. 88-92; Blackmar, *op. cit.*, pp. 190-205.

LAWRENCE, K. T. Dec 24th 1856

SECRETARIES A. H. M. SOC.
DEAR BRETHREN.

It is just one month since my return to my field of labor yet I have been back long enough to see,—or at least to think I see,— brightening prospects for Kansas.[38] We are enjoying, & with fair prospects of continuance, a state of peace & quiet unlike anything I have witnessed, during the two years of my residence here. We do not even hear the distant role of the thunder that has heretofore preceded the storm. This may result from an entire confidence— on the part of the enemies of Freedom—that the powers that be will more perfectly accomplish the work they desire than they can do by pursuing their former course of action.

Some think they have given up the field. I cannot believe that they have done anything more than change their tactics, while the purpose remains the same. Important changes in this respect have taken place; firstly withdrawing from the field their most unscrupulous & daring leader—Col. Titus with his band of outlaws; next by superseding the most pliant tools of the slave power in office.[39] There is also a manifest desire on the part of the southern faction to cultivate feelings of friendship, where before every effort was made to stir up the bitterest feelings of depraved nature. From whatever cause this state of things may proceed, I can but rejoice in it, as it opens a prospect for the advancement of that pure & peaceable Gospel upon which the institutions of Liberty must rest as a permanent base. Long & earnest must the disciples of Jesus labor, before they can hope to see the difficulties which strife & war have engendered removed. Yet it is no small ground of encouragement, that the causes of evil are not as actively at work as formerly.

I am now enabled to hold regular public worship, & I have two prayer meetings during the week. The attendance on each of these occasions is somewhat increased; yet nothing is more apparent than that *habits* of inattention & carelessness, in reference to the Sabbath & sacred worship, have taken deep hold of—I might almost say— the entire community. I suppose in reference to no other part of the Territory is this state of things so prevalent as here. We feel

---

38. Lum had returned East with his family. He cited as the reason "the health of my family seemed to render it necessary that they should have a release from the excitements and exposures of our unhappy Territory during the coming Winter."—*The Home Missionary,* New York, v. 29 (December, 1856), p. 192.

39. Charles B. Lines, writing from Lawrence on August 24, 1856, described Col. Henry T. Titus as follows: "This, Titus, by the way, is one of the most blood thirsty men in the whole country. He has been a fillibuster and sort of land pirate during much of his life, and is now the terror of all peaceable citizens in the territory. We know him well."— Alberta Pantle, ed., "The Connecticut Kansas Colony; Letters of Charles B. Lines to the New Haven (Conn.) *Daily Palladium,*" *The Kansas Historical Quarterly,* Topeka, v. 22 (Summer, 1956), p. 176.

deeply the need of the presence & power of the Divine Spirit in our midst to break up this fatal carelessness; & we must earnestly crave to this end, the prayers of all who sympathize with us in these matters.

The churches have a responsibility beyond that of praying for the success of the truth in Kansas— from present indications there is to be a large addition to the hosts of Freedom in the Territory early in the Spring. There should—there must be at least, an equal increase among the soldiers of the Cross. It is not enough that Kansas should be made free from the curse of Slavery; it must be rescued from the curse of sin; & there are weighty reasons why this is not an ordinary case in this respect. Never in the history of this country, has a Territory been settled in the midst of so many influences calculated to counteract the spread of truth, & to foster the growth of sin; & unless the tendency of these influences be arrested, we have no reason to expect that they will fail to work out their legitimate results. Those who have young friends in Kansas should weigh well these facts.

I have subscribed for a number of the "Herald of Freedom" which will doubtless reach you with this. I have not yet written to Bro. Noyes in reference to the wants of the settlers as I have had more than I could do—my health not being very good. There will be constant need of assistance in the shape of money, as nothing else could reach us, navigation being closed. I could mention cases where I have been compelled to give away some of my own children's clothing—they being now at the East—to the little sufferers about me.

Since I arrived from the East I have received 2 boxes & 1 barrel of clothing—from those who sympathize with the cause of Christ & the suffering children— one box from Dedham, Mass. valued at near 200 dolls., another from Bro. Jones society—Worcester, Mass., a valuable box— also in connection with this a barrel from the Ladies of Boylston, Mass., for general distribution. A large part of these I have distributed to the actually suffering. The box from Dedham contained several vols of very valuable works, just what my scanty library needed.

We are having very variable climate this Winter thus far— 2 days ago the mercury stood at sun-rise at 8° below zero— today the air is balmy as the breath of Spring— for the sake of the exposed & they are legion, it would seem desirable that it might continue so but "He doeth *all things* well." Yours truly,

S. Y. LUM

LAWRENCE, KANSAS Jan 15th 1857

REV. DR. BADGER
DEAR BROTHER

Your letter containing a draft for Forty Six (46) dollars arrived a few days since & would have been acknowledged before this were it not that I have been in such a state of health as scarcely to be able to attend to my duties at all. The disease—which I left the East to escape, & which I began to hope had entirely disappeared, is returning upon me. I am often seriously afflicted with vertigo.[40] Excitement & application which I have attempted somewhat this winter, produce the same results here as at the East, & I fear will bring me to the same condition in which I was, one year before accepting your commission. What is to be the result, a few months will determine. This field demands the energies of a *whole* man. With the present prospect of Kansas, & the position in it that Lawrence occupies, it would be difficult to find a more important field. Oh, how I dread, in one view, what I fear. Yet God will provide for his church here.

Every day, I feel more & more the baneful effects of Unitarianism here. This is its central, & at present, only point; but here it has already secured an influence, more potent than of any other society & the condition of our community is such, that it is likely to continue & increase that influence. A reckless & daring spirit, created by the scenes of the past two years, predisposes the mind to doubt those truths that would hold it in check. Excitements 1st of war, & now of speculation, bear the mind irresistably away from the peaceful & quiet influences of the Gospel. Where no doctrines taught, but those of the truth as it is in Jesus, there would be strong hope then of overcoming these influences— but when the truth—as it is called —is so presented as to fall in with all the natural inclinations of the sinful heart, it fortifies the way against that which is distasteful. Thus I find, that Unitarianism is more in the way of the progress of *saving truth,* than any or *all other influences combined.*

It has also an advantage in having its church nearly completed, with funds to finish it.[41] Our building is far advanced; but the funds are expended, & how we are to go on with it in the Spring, is yet unknown. It cannot be done among ourselves. *We are compelled*

---

40. Vertigo is characterized by "dizziness, giddiness, a sensation of irregular or whirling motion, either of oneself or of external objects."—Norman Burke Taylor, ed., *Stedman's Medical Dictionary* (Baltimore, 1953), p. 1493.

41. The construction of the Unitarian church at Lawrence started in the spring of 1856 under the leadership of the Rev. Ephraim Nute. Although it was occupied in the spring and summer of 1857, it was not completed until the autumn of that year.—A. T. Andreas and W. G. Cutler, *History of the State of Kansas* (Chicago, 1883), p. 327.

to look somewhere else, for from one to two thousand dollars. I do trust that with all the sympathy that is felt for Kansas at the East, this work will be completed there for us.

You will doubtless have heard ere this of the purchase of a town site near the mouth of the Kansas river, on the Mo. I have not been there but from what I can learn, from reliable sources, it bids fair to be the entrepot of the Territory. It is wholly "Free State;" & has large amount of capital interested in its increase.[42] Should it grow, as is desirable, & as is expected, they will need a Missionary there quite early in the Spring. Yet that cannot be decided upon at this early date.

Since I have been writing this, I have had two calls from distressed families for relief. The cold is vigorous; & must be to the destitute a cause of great suffering. Both of these families were sick; one of them, nearly every member— sickness induced by exposure. It afforded me the pleasure, the more so from the fact that they were followers of Jesus, to be able through your remittance to be able to furnish them their immediate necessities. I have constant calls on such business; & esteem it a privilege thus to recommend the truth to those who might thus be led to receive it but there are numerous cases that the small amount at my disposal will not reach; & some cases of destitute families, whose modesty & diffidence will not permit them to make application to *public* distributors. . . .

Yours truly
S. Y. LUM.

LAWRENCE KANSAS Mar. 24th/57

REV. DR. BADGER.
DEAR BROTHER.

Another quarter of my labor in the service of the Soc. has expired & at its close I am compelled to resign my position as a home missionary not I trust from a want of love for the work, but from an entire inability to perform it, from what I said in a former letter it cannot be unexpected by the Soc. though perhaps it may have been sooner than was anticipated. I had hoped to be able to continue until my successor could have been procured but from recent violent attacks of vertigo I am compelled to avoid all severe mental labor. On last Sabbath I was obliged to dismiss the congregation when

---

42. Lum refers here to the founding of Quindaro. It was surveyed as a townsite in December, 1856, by O. A. Bassett. Building was started January 1, 1857, two weeks prior to Lum's letter.—Alan W. Farley, "Annals of Quindaro: A Kansas Ghost Town," *The Kansas Historical Quarterly*, Topeka, v. 22 (Winter, 1856), pp. 306, 307. Congregational work was started at Quindaro by the Rev. Sylvester D. Storrs, a member of the famous Andover Band, in 1857.—Charles M. Correll, *A Century of Congregationalism in Kansas* (1953), p. 25.

half through the services. My physician advises me not to attempt again as it is a disease whose attack is so sudden as to give but little warning of its approach.

Our prospects are continually brightening as a church & Soc. & should the Lord in his goodness send us just such a man as we need —our temporal affairs would advance rapidly. I trust we shall not long be left long destitute— it is important that we should not be at all so.

As I intimated in my last [letter] we have to secure the money (by loan) with which to complete our edifice & we hope it will be open for worship before the Spring is past. How we shall be able to pay the loan is the question. We think there are some friends in the East for us yet. The matter of raising our future preachers salary is more doubtful— we ought to have a first class-man & we may not be able to support him.

I do not know what is the rule in such cases. Could we look to the A. H. M. S. for any part? say something like the amount we have been receiving during the past? This I ask by the desire of the Com.

I should have been glad to have written a lengthy report as it is the last, but my head is not in a condition to allow it.

I have received in Home Missionary money during the half year Six dollars & seventy cts. ($6.70) which is to be deducted from my quarters salary leaving One hundred forty three 30/100 (143.30) which you may send as heretofore by draft.

Yours truly,
S. Y. Lum.

Lawrence Kansas June 10th/57

Milton Badger D. D.
Dear Brother.

Your letter of May 23 reached me a few days ago, & finds me still engaged in the labor of my position here. When I prepared my last quarterly report I thought it an *absolute necessity* that I should stop & that immediately, all close mental application, & wrote accordingly, but how to avoid labor was the question. My people felt as well as myself that at all events our regular worship should be kept up & this was particularly so as Mr. Nute the Unitarian minister was making special efforts to draw off the young to their eternal destruction. I have thus felt myself compelled to keep right on & as long as I could get to the church or until my successor arrived.

When Mr. Woodford came I felt more at liberty, & hoped he might be the man. He has preached three times, & preaches again next Sabbath which will I fear will be the last with us as he is quite desirous to be permanently located & our people think he is not the man for them.[43] We have just gone into our own building, though it is simply enclosed & now feel *at home*.[44] Oh that I had a head fit to labor, but I must rest for a while perhaps forever, just as soon as possible.

I have no idea that we will be able to support our own minister as soon as I thought we should when I last wrote. We have been compelled to do so much in raising funds for completing our church. Several of the prominent men have given as high as $500, a piece for this project & feel it is all they can do at present.

But in reference to the business of which you spoke. I have visited several places in the immediate neighborhood that is within 12 or 15 miles. One of these is Lecompton which I think would afford labor enough for one man if he was of the judicious kind. It is the present capitol & rather proslavery though there is quite a large minority of good free state men. There is at present no preaching there & some of the leading men ride 12 miles to attend church at Lawrence. Near Lecompton are several out posts that could be collected. These if filled at all are filled by very illiterate Methodist preachers part of the time.

I propose to start tomorrow to visit as soon as possible all the principal points in the Territory & shall report as soon & as fully as possible. From what I know of the wants of the Territory I feel that we shall surely need at least the "half dozen" you speak of but I shall feel more competent to speak confidently after I have been over the field again for this special object. . . .

Truly your brother,
S. Y. Lum.

43. The Rev. O. L. Woodford settled in Grasshopper Falls (now Valley Falls) in 1857.—*Ibid.*, 202.

44. The construction of Plymouth Congregational Church at Lawrence was started in the spring of 1856. It was partially completed and services were held in it at the time of Lum's letter, June 10, 1857. The building was dedicated on November 16, 1862. It was built of limestone with dimensions 40 x 65 feet.—Cordley, *Pioneer Days in Kansas*, pp. 82, 83; Andreas-Cutler, *op. cit.*, p. 327.

LAWRENCE KANSAS
June 24th 1857

MILTON BADGER D. D.
DEAR BROTHER.

Since writing two weeks since I have visited that part of the Territory bordering on the Mo. river; most of this ground was new to me. As you know, it was the stronghold of the Border Ruffianism, & could not be visited during times of excitement,—without peculiar danger to a "marked man" & as my duty never led me in that direction—I have been satisfied without seeking more stirring adventure than could be found near home. Now however there is little danger to a traveller in Kansas whatever may be his opinions touching "peculiar institutions"—as in any new country. In this respect the change is wonderful to those who have had experience in the past here, & those just entering Kansas are naturally inclined from present quiet to believe but a small part of what is true of the past.— We begin to confidently hope, that so far as sanguinary conflicts are concerned they "are among the things that were," that what remains to be done is to avoid the dangers of political trickery, on the one hand, & the quicksands of speculation on the other.

This state of things, though perhaps not less dangerous to the morals of a community, does not so completely interfere with the efforts of the Christian ministry, & therefore Kansas presents today, one of the most important—perhaps one of the most promising fields for missionary labor, & to a great extent it is unoccupied— not one of the river towns have a preacher connected in any way with the churches that sustain the A. H. M. Soc.—This is true of the most important towns on the river— even Leavenworth is now destitute— with a population of over four thousand—mostly free state men,—it has but one educated preacher, & he is so connected with the South & its peculiar institution as to be not very acceptable to the mass about him—so I hear, I am not acquainted with him. Leavenworth needs a good man, & right away, but whoever comes there must expect to find a community not in the habit of sympathizing with truth & its claims— it will be a difficult but *very* important field— no man with ordinary prudence need fear from violence as all parties desire peace.

Below Leavenworth about 8 to 10 miles is Delaware, a point until the present season wholly under proslavery influences it is now changing hands & would be a good spot for an out post from Leavenworth. It has about 500 inhabitants. Below this near 30 miles is Quindaro a town started entirely under free state influences during the past Winter, it contains several hundred inhabitants has a Cong. Soc organized & contemplate securing a preacher as soon as one is found as they think just adapted. They hope from the start to be free from the necessity of foreign help in this I think they will be disappointed. Wyandot is just below at the confluence of the Mo. & Kansas rivers started about the same time as the last & a rival to it, with about the same number of inhabitants.— should either become a large place, it would eventually absorb the other.

From Leavenworth going up the river the first place of sufficient importance to require the attention of the Soc. is Atchison— named after the *great* Senator; it was started as an ultra pro slavery town, & has been the most rabid & dangerous town in Kansas, it is the home of one of the Stringfellows & has been notorious as the place where the "Squatter Sovereign" is published & where Rev. Pardee Butler was tarred & feathered then tied to a log, & sent down the Mo. river.[45]

Now, it is earning for itself quite a different character. Gen. Pomeroy & others, thinking it was one of the best points on the river have bought out a large part of the property, set up a good hotel, put a first rate free state editor at the head of the "Sovereign" & are introducing the best class of eastern emigrants who are quite anxious to have someone sent from your Soc. to "open to them the Scriptures."[46] About 5 miles above this is another town just emerging from its bondage to slavery.—Gen Lane is at the head of affairs here & has associated with him quite a number of the "old free settlers" from other points.[47]

The land office is located here which with its enterprising citizens renders it quite a formidable rival to Atchison. These two points need at once a missionary. The people are anxious, & there would be no opposition from any quarter, together with the neighborhoods in the vicinity several thousand settlers could be reached in some way by a faithful missionary, & part of his support could be secured. Rev. Mr. Woodford is thinking of this field & probably

---

45. David Rice Atchison served as a United States senator from Missouri from 1843 to 1855. The principal phases of his career are described in the *Dictionary of American Biography* (New York), v. 1, pp. 402, 403. John H. Stringfellow and Robert S. Kelley started the *Squatter Sovereign* at Atchison on February 3, 1855.—Wilder, op. cit., p 56. The trying experience of Butler is described in *Personal Reminiscences of Pardee Butler* (Cincinnati, 1889), pp. 106-109.

46. The executive committee of the New England Emigrant Aid Company authorized S. C. Pomeroy on March 9, 1857, to develop a town on the Missouri river. Pomeroy believed that the Proslavery town of Atchison would be most desirable. In arrangements worked out with Robert McBratney, the agent of the Cincinnati emigration society, and others, Pomeroy secured the controlling interest in the town and ownership of the *Squatter Sovereign*.—Edgar Langsdorf, "S. C. Pomeroy and the New England Emigrant Aid Company, 1854-1858," *The Kansas Historical Quarterly*, v. 7 (November, 1938), pp. 394, 395.

47. The reference here is to Doniphan. Lane became a part owner of the *Crusader of Freedom*, founded by James Redpath, which was as strong for the Free-State cause as the Doniphan *Constitutionalist* had been for the Proslavery cause.—Andreas-Cutler, op. cit., p. 475.

would have visited there, were it not that he has been sick for a few days.

Above these points, there is none quite so promising,— there are however,—about 50 or 60 miles above Doniphan, 2 points near together named Iowa Point & White Cloud where the labors of a man could be profitably employed— though not destined to be large places yet the country about them is full of actual settlers & in four or five different localities not 10 miles apart a congregation of about 50 could be collected.

I was surprised to find the settlers, in the north eastern portion of Kansas, such as they are, they are mostly from the north intelligent, thrifty, enterprising men & they possess a country that will richly reward their energies, & from the indications, everywhere we must now have a population of more than 100,000, & nearly the entire number are unsupplied with ministers sympathizing with your Soc.—

I hope to start tomorrow for the western part of the Territory, & from the enormous expense of travelling etc. I shall get over the ground as soon as possible.

Yours truly
S. Y. Lum.

LAWRENCE KANSAS July 10, 1857

REV. MILTON BADGER D. D.
DEAR BROTHER.

A longer time has elapsed since writing my last than I intended but circumstances have been such as to render the delay necessary. My last trip was one of great fatigue, owing to the extreme heat & drouth, which now prevail through the Territory— We have had no rain of any importance since early spring, & every thing is parching up— the thermometer too is standing daily in the shade from 90° to 98°.—Thus you can imagine the circumstances of one travelling on horse-back, or in an open conveyance over these shadeless prairies. Were it not that I feel the work imperatively important I should remain in the most quiet & cool situation attainable. Last week I started to visit the Kansas valley, westward.

The first town west of this is Lecompton, 12 miles distant. I should rather say the 1st town of any importance for there are 3 projected towns, which we pass through on the valley road. I mentioned Lecompton, on a previous occasion, though as a pro-slavery town at first, it is now mostly occupied by Free State men to the number of some 500. They are without preaching (almost entirely,) but the place would not be an enviable one in any point of view though perhaps it is none the less important to be filled— About 4 miles south, there is already organized a Congl. Chh under the care of a Missionary from the American Miss. Association.[48]

About 5 miles west, & about an equal distance from the river, is Big Spring not much of a town, but filled with settlers,—all the "claims" having families upon them. This is one of the points at which Rev. Mr. Shepperd, your missionary, is preaching.[49] From this point it is 5 miles to Tecumseh on the Kansas River. This is getting to be quite a town; & as the river is now being bridged at that point, so that trade & travell will be attracted to it, it will furnish a good field for the labor of Mr. Shepperd.

Five miles further west is Topeka, the "Free State Capitol"— where Mr. Bodwell is located. His people are anxiously looking for his return, to minister both, to their spiritual & *temporal* wants.[50] From present appearances, this is the most promising church in the Territory, though not in as important a position as the one at Lawrence.— West of Topeka for 30 miles is the Reserve of the Pottawatomie & of course unsettled by white men. 2½ miles about this Reserve, we come to Wabaunsa, settled by the colony from Conn. Here I spent the last Sabbath of June & assisted in the organization of a Congl. Chh.[51]

They have no house in which to worship, but are preparing a temporary one, & the trustees of the church have in their hands a sufficient fund to secure the erection of a good substantial edifice— The church was formed in a grove, near what now constitutes the village, & to all present it seemed an occasion of the deepest interest. The church, at its formation numbers near 30, & contains more men of education than any other in the Territory. At present they are supplied by a Missionary of the A. M. Assn. who preaches also at another little church at Queendale 5 or 6 miles distant. . . .

48. The American Missionary Association was organized on "Bible principles" in New York City in 1846 by individuals who felt that the American Home Missionary Society was not taking a strong enough stand on the antislavery question. The association was nonsectarian although the support came primarily from Congregationalists.—Colin Brummitt Goodykoontz, *Home Missions on the American Frontier* (Caldwell, Idaho, 1939), pp. 292-294.

49. The Rev. Paul Shepherd started his work in Kansas in 1856.—Correll, *op. cit.,* p. 199.

50. The Rev. Lewis Bodwell preached his first sermon in Topeka as the regularly appointed minister of the Congregational church on October 26, 1856. The career of Bodwell, based on correspondence with the American Home Missionary Society, is described in detail in Russell K. Hickman, "Lewis Bodwell, Frontier Preacher; the Early Years," *The Kansas Historical Quarterly,* v. 12 (August, November, 1943), pp. 269-299; 349-365.

51. The Connecticut Kansas Colony, known as the "Beecher Bible and Rifle Colony," was established at "Waubonsa" in April, 1856, according to a letter of Charles B. Lines to the New Haven (Conn.) *Daily Palladium.* Lum preached the sermon on that occasion. Interesting letters from Lines are found in Pantle, *loc. cit.,* pp. 1-50; 138-188.

Some 8 miles further up the river is the settlement of Ashland, first settled by Free State men from Ky. It is mostly under the influence of the Campbelites.[52] Bro. Blood of Manhattan has a station here, & preaches once in 3 weeks.

Still west of this there are no villages of sufficient importance to call for a stated ministry. There are a number of small communities up the Smoky Hill & Republican forks, where a man, not confined by family to any one locality might travel & preach as occasion offered. One of these stations, on Republican fork about 20 miles from Manhattan, is occupied by Bro. Blood of Manhattan once in three weeks.

Descending the river, on the North side, from Fort Riley—which is only a Military station & supplied by a chaplain—we first find the town of Ogden, just out side of the Military reserve. Here is located the land office for the Western division of the Territory. . . . Rev. Mr. Parsons formerly of Cape Cod, Mass is preaching at this place, though not any connection with any Miss Society.[53] Twelve miles below this is Manhattan, where Rev. Mr. Blood resides with his family. . . .

Thus you will perceive that I have visited all the important points of the Kansas valley, & north of it. Next week I intend starting for the south of the Territory; & from what I learn I shall find more destitution than I have in the north— I have felt compelled to lay by for a week, the heat has been so excessive.

Yours truly,
S. Y. LUM

LAWRENCE KANSAS
July 25, 1857

REV. MILTON BADGER, D. D.

When I wrote you a little more than a week ago I expected to be (at this time) in the South part of the Territory, & I did start, as I contemplated, but was unable to travel but two days, the reason is the excessive heat we are now experiencing,— for about 10 days past our weather, has been the most oppressive I ever knew, the heat soon after sun rise indicating 90° & upwards—& during the day, rising as high as 102° to 107° & continuing up to 96 & 98 until near sun down. I travelled 2 such days laying up during the middle of

---

52. The Campbellites are known as the Disciples of Christ or members of the Christian Church. They trace their origin to Thomas and Alexander Campbell. The first congregation was established at Brush Creek, Penn., in 1811.—William Warren Sweet, *The Story of Religions in America* (New York, 1930), pp. 340-344.

53. The Rev. J. U. Parsons came to Ogden in 1855.—Correll, *op. cit.*, p. 197.

the day, & I found it producing such an effect on my head as to render it extremely unsafe to continue. I have therefore felt it my duty to suspend my investigations until I can travel more safely, & if it be the wish of the Soc. I shall commence against just as soon as possible.

During the 2 days I mentioned, I visited 2 places about 20 miles south of Lawrence, the one Prairies City is almost entirely in the hands of the Methodists,— they have established a College there, & will bring it mostly under their influence—[54] at the other, Centropolis I found a few Congregational brethren, who were anxious to have a man from your Soc. The town itself is but small, but the country around is filled with settlers, there being but few claims untaken, & they will need a business centre.

From what I learn—from *reliable* sources, I am led to believe that there is need of more men in the south part of the Territory than in the North, but I shall know more definitely when I visit there as it is,—according to my judgment the following places need preachers immediately: Leavenworth, Doniphan, Quindaro if they have made no arrangements for themselves & Centropolis.

Grasshopper Falls is already supplied by Bro. Woodford.[55] I think I shall not fail to find an equal number in the South— At Indianola & Kansapolis, if Bro. Bodwell finds his hands full on the south side of the river. There must also be a man;—Indianola is growing rapidly. And perhaps a man could be found who could make his mark upon Lecompton. it would be a difficult work, & a hard field & I would not advise its occupancy while other important points are destitute. Unless we succeed in getting a man adapted for this field,—Lawrence—before the arrival of your Missionaries I do hope there will be one of their number, just the man. We are suffering not a little already shall suffer in important respects unless we are supplied before long, & we are not able as we hoped to support him ourselves. Some of the Soc. are anxious to know whether it would be possible to receive help from the A. H. M. Soc. in giving more than your accustomed salary. I cannot answer them.

Yours truly,
S. Y. LUM

54. A charter was granted by the territorial legislature to the Kansas Educational Association of the Methodist Episcopal Church on February 3, 1858, for establishing an institution of learning which is known as Baker University, Baldwin City.—Andreas-Cutler, *op. cit.*, p. 355. The background factors in the founding of Baker University are described in Homer Kingsley Ebright, *The History of Baker University* (Baldwin, 1951), pp. 37-54.

55. See Footnote 43.

LAWRENCE, KANSAS. Oct 5th 1857

REV. MILTON BADGER, D. D.
DEAR BROTHER.

I have just completed a tour of exploration, through the South part of the Territory; & I find it everywhere filling up with the enterprising & intelligent free state settler[s]. I was hardly prepared to find so many centers, where should be immediately set up the standard of the Cross. Two thirds of the entire territory lies south of the Kansas river & yet—except at Lawrence & Topeka—upon that river—there has never been a missionary in connection with your Soc. permanently located. It is now assuming an importance that demands attention—

In a former letter I spoke of Centropolis, & in passing through it again, I found several families that greatly desire the labors of a missionary— they have only occasional preaching—from a Methodist brother but as I found afterward other places of more importance—this must give place to them for the present. In a south east direction—about 25 miles distant is Ohio City, a thriving town, of but few months growth, giving promise of a prosperous future The country about it is all settled up so that it is the center of a population of several hundreds, & from present appearances the village population will rapidly increase. . . .

From this point it is about 30 miles S.E. to Moneka—on Sugar Creek—about 12 miles from the Mo. line— but little has been done on the town site, & yet amoung the first things, they have commenced the erection of a building 25 by 40 feet for school purposes, the 2nd story to be used for a preaching hall. I was told that at any time a congregation could be secured, of at least 100, some of the leading men are desirous to be supplied from your Soc. though in the vecinity there are quite a number of "spiritualists" who of course would not look with favor upon such a movement. They intend starting a "manual labor school" It seems important that truth should enter the field, at the very onset if it would contend successfully with such dangerous error. Moneka derives some prospective importance—from the fact that as the Pacific R. R. looks for a passage away from the Mo River & less expensive— Southern Kansas presents itself fertile & fast filling with a dense population— & it is upon the most direct rout. This matter has been already under discussion by the director[s] of P. R. R.

But a short distance from Moneka there are several points that would occupy part of the time of a Missionary.—Paris 6 miles distant & Mapleton 15.— Nearly west, 30 miles distant, on the head waters of the Pottowatomie I found Hyatville, but little developed as yet, & perhaps sufficiently supplied, as I learned they have frequent, if not regular preaching, orthodox in its character.

Travelling S.W. for 25 miles I reached the Neosho river, it is next in size to the Kansas, & it is dotted with little towns all struggling for the supremacy. I intended to strike the river at Neosho City, but as I was travelling without guide, compass or trail, over an entirely new country, I fell below about 8 miles at LeRoy much larger than Neosho, though of but little importance. (Should the enthusiastic proprietors of these numerous towns become acquainted with my appreciation of their "important locations" they would pay but little honor to my judgment I fear, as each seem to think that just upon their spot is concentrated all the peculiar advantages of the entire region.)

The entire Neosho valley is settled, where any timber can be secured, & often, all that is in the vicinity of timber. As we travel up it, we are continually passing improvements that remind us of the older States. The first town that seems to demand immediate attention from the Soc. is Burlington—on the south side of the river—opposite Hampden— this last mentioned place you will remember as the place where the colony from Mass with Rev. Mr. Knight located more than 2 years ago,— in building a town they have done nothing as yet, though they begin to give signs of life, in this vicinity.[56] There are ten individuals desirous of forming themselves into a church to be under the care of your Soc.

At Burlington there is already quite a town with as I think a good prospect. Between the two a missionary could be most profitably employed while within 15 miles there are 3 other little centers. Rev. Rodney Payne has gone down there but whether he will locate or not I cannot tell.[57] I had thought of sending one of the four to this field. But if Mr. Payne is the man, there will be room enough left.

Up the valley of the Neosho, there are several smaller towns. N. W. of Hampden & 30 miles distant between the Neosho & Cottonwood is Emporia, this seems a natural point & has already a numerous population depending upon it, several towns (as is usually the case at a good point) have been laid out near by— but

---

56. The Rev. Richard Knight organized the Congregational church at Hampden in 1856.—Correll, op. cit., p. 195.
57. The Rev. Rodney Paine settled as a Congregational missionary at Burlington in 1857.—Ibid., p. 197.

this, seems to lead in the race, & must be supplied this fall.[58] One fact renders this more important. There is an effort to establish a Unitarian Soc. there, which perhaps would not be attempted should there be a preacher of Jesus on the field. South of this on the Verdigris crowds of settlers are pushing in & taking possession of the best locations—Here will soon be new fields for operations. On the return from Emporia I passed over the high prairie, called the divide between the Kansas & the Neosho, it is beautiful & fertile, but will not be settled until the timbered land is all taken.

From this survey I have become fully impressed with the absolute need that there should be more laborers in the field—The country is rapidly filling up with men who need, more than ordinary emigrants, the restraining influences of the Gospel. Kansas is developing as no new state—except perhaps California—has done, & developing with all the elements of permanence. The question of its being free, is settled; though the will of the people may be defeated for a little while longer, the end is certain, humanly speaking. Your Soc. in company with kindred societies, has done much to secure this result. The temporal as well as spiritual interests of the people, are advanced most under an efficient ministry. Those towns give most evidence of permanent prosperity, where the earnest faithful preacher, was on the ground at the *very beginning* & in view of this I hope that the Society will feel it within the limits of their ability, to send *2 or 3 more here this fall*. They can be employed to good advantage. Mr. Morse has just arrived; & starts, if it is pleasant, tomorrow, for the Southern part of the Territory— He was ordained previous to starting.

The long talked of election has passed—so far as we have heard— without excitement. In this Co. the entire free state ticket is elected; & we can be free of local Border-ruffian rules. I very much fear, the general result will be against us; as in some districts heard from, large numbers of imported votes were poled.[59] If we are defeated, it will be with much caution that we take the next step. . . .

Yours etc.
S. Y. Lum.

---

58. The Rev. Grosvernor Morse, a member of the Andover band, began his work at Emporia shortly after Lum's visit there. A description of Morse's career is found in Cordley, *Pioneer Days in Kansas*, pp. 14-18.

59. Lum was mistaken as to the results of this election because the Free-State party controlled both the council and the house. An analysis of the election is found in Wilder, *op. cit.*, pp. 192-194.

LAWRENCE KANSAS, Nov. 16th 1857

REV. MILTON BADGER D. D.

DEAR BROTHER.

I suppose that my labor for the Soc. is (for the present) accomplished. Three of the brethren from Andover have arrived & entered their fields of labor.[60] Of the two first Mr. Stors & Morse I hear encouraging reports & the prospect is that they are just the men, for the places to which they are assigned. Mr. Parker has just entered his field at Leavenworth, the most important & perhaps the most difficult missionary field in the Territory, he has not been on the field sufficiently long, to know what can be accomplished. . . . Bro Cordley has not appeared yet on the ground ill health detained him in Michigan. We are now looking for him every day, & expect him to take up his possition at Lawrence. . . .[61]

The members of churches East are not the only individuals, who should feel deeply interested in sending the right kind of missionaries to Kansas— true the work of saving men is their first work & the influence of the truth they preach will be mainly to free from the slavery to sin,— but apart from this they are doing another work of no small value. They are exerting an influence more mighty than any other, to overthrow that great American Curse, slavery. In my exploration of the Territory I have found—that those places more than any others—where a pure gospel was preached—have been centers of a mighty influence for Freedom. Such communities are always more reliable in any emergency.

All your Missionaries in Kansas are men of this stamp, & the lovers of Freedom—even though not lovers of God—have a deep interest in sustaining an agency that sends forth such an influence. I trust that until Kansas is free from all kinds of slavery, it will not be compelled to abate one iota of all that it desires to do for God & Humanity.

The Constitutional Convention that has been sitting at Lecompton, has accomplished its work & adjourned, a constitution is framed not to be submitted to the people, though one of its provisions is to be voted upon, a provisional government is appointed to go in operation previous to the sitting of the Territorial Legislature to prevent that body from doing anything to inturrupt the

---

60. Lum refers to the famous Andover band, Richard Cordley, Roswell D. Parker, Sylvester D. Storrs, and Grosvernor C. Morse. Cordley settled at Lawrence, Parker at Leavenworth, Storrs at Quindaro, and Morse at Emporia. The Andover band is described in Cordley, *Pioneer Days in Kansas*, pp. 7-30.

61. Cordley arrived in Lawrence on December 2, 1857. He presents an interesting description of his trip to Kansas.—*Ibid.*, pp. 31-54.

operation of the plan marked out by the Convention.[62] Thus our Free State triumph is a nullity— a Pro Slavery Constitution is to be fastened upon us "nolentes volentes" & even before it has been passed upon by Congress. *Perhaps such a course will succede; We shall see.* It looks as though there might be some spice ahead, though we are getting pretty well used to that sort of thing. While such despots plan & rave, it is a pleasant peaceful thought to the Christian that "The Lord reigneth." . . .

Your brother
S. Y. LUM.

LAWRENCE Dec. 30th 1857

REV. D. P. NOYES
DEAR BROTHER.

Your letter came to hand by last mail, & I shall try to take an early opportunity to comply with your request To day I write on business. My last letter containing the statement of expenses incurred for the Soc. last Summer may not have reached you as I have not heard from it though I have been waiting several weeks in expectation.

As it may be some fault of the mails I send it herewith. I am truly sorry to learn of the state of the Soc. finances for I am satisfied that to Kansas it will be most unwelcome news. Your Missionaries here are all of them in a situation where they must suffer absolutely without their accustomed remittance. The hard times falls most heavily upon them because in addition to the absence of money, every thing is at enormously high prices. Think of $13.—thirteen dollars a barrel for flour 6 to 8 for corn meal— molasses from $1.15 to $1.50 per gallon potatoes $1.25 bush. *& every thing in proportion.* With a prospect of much higher rates before Spring, & you can imagine our situation. I know of some of your Missionaries who are without a dollar & some who are even worse than that. A family cannot live with comfort on $600, (for to begin with, the rent of two rooms will cost near ½ of it). What can they do if the supply is withheld.

One of your Missionaries (Rev. Mr. Morse) in order to avoid the expense of rent, hired money to put up a little home, for which

---

62. The delegates to the Lecompton constitutional convention assembled on September 7, 1857. The convention adjourned on September 11, to meet on October 19. It finally adjourned on November 3. The one provision to be voted upon, as described by Lum, is found in section 7 of the "Schedule," namely, the "Constitution with slavery" or the "Constitution with no slavery." The Lecompton constitution is printed in Wilder, *op. cit.,* pp. 177-191. An interesting study of the background of the delegates is found in Robert W. Johannsen, "The Lecompton Constitutional Convention: An Analysis of Its Membership," *The Kansas Historical Quarterly,* Topeka, v. 23 (Autumn, 1957), pp. 225-243.

agreeing to pay an enormous rate of interest (which was better than to pay rent) confidentally expecting the next quarters remittance would give him the ability to meet his engagements. (I signed on the note) & in a few days it must be paid.—but how. I fear by sacrificing his home or by my sacrificing for him. I do not think that the churches have a right to permit their servants to be thrown into such positions of distress. Let them think of our possition,— first—in a new country like this, money is of necessity much more scarce than in an older one. Next all the necessities of life, are three or four times as high in price, with no resource to which we can turn for relief.

I do not write this to urge that I be treated better than my companions in arms, but through fear that the account,—or the remittance might have miscarried. It is true, I am in more straightened circumstances than I have ever been before. In making the tour of the Territory I left my crops upon which I was depending for the support of my family—much to my pecuniary disadvantage & am by that cause several hundred dollars behind, but if any good has been done I am satisfied. . . .

Yours truly
S. Y. Lum.

Lawrence Kansas March 8th, 1858

Rev Milton Badger D. D.
Dear Bro.

Your letter making a call upon me for a March report has remained for a few days unattended to while I have been busily engaged, watching with a sick wife. Now I feel it cannot be put off longer & attend to it, though not as fully as I could wish. Would that you & the churches & the "young ministers" of the East could get a view of this most important field such as only a residence with us could give. Its demands would then be more promptly met, & the numbers of laborers sustained by your Soc. would be greatly increased. In no respect is Kansas an ordinary field, & it cannot be made to conform to ordinary rules, it must be furnished with the living preachers in numbers to keep pace with the influx of population, & that tide rolls in upon us by thousands. In little over three years, the wild unbroken prairie is teeming with life crowded with busy intelligent farmers, & the towns are springing up as if by magic are crowded by thousands of earnest business men & mechanics.

Today we have a population sufficient to claim admittance as one of the "sovreign" states of the Union. The A. H. M. Soc. has done for these communities what it could, during the past year six have been sent out & are now all of them I think wielding a mighty influence for good in large & rapidly growing communities. this swells the number—under the direction of the Soc—to (10) ten, ministering to over twenty congregations. Dividing the population equally amoung them each man would have the care of 10,000 souls, scattered over a country of some 50 miles square & embracing several centers of influence. . . .

The importance of placing the communities, that are springing up all over the Territory, under the influence of Gospel institutions cannot be over estimated no one who has not had an experience formed on the ground can appreciate the strength of the current, setting against truth & duty, nothing but the presence of the man of God, nothing but the force of truth, as it flows from his lips & life & shines in his life, can oppose even a partial barrier to its impetuous tide, as it bears the great majority on to ruin. It is heart rendering to witness the defection of many who were concidered lights in the churches from which they came. All former associations are broken up, all former barriers removed. the narrow way in which it seemed easy to walk, while it was walled on either side, now that those walls are broken down, becomes less & less defined, until it is well nigh lost amoung the thousand bye paths that digress from it. Many a professed child of God gets bewildered & lost in one or another of these digressions.

For these reasons it seems that the work in which the A. H. M. Soc. is engaged is of all others the most important. Churches at the East would suffer less by the absence of the ministry, for they have more colateral influences to confine & control the passions of men. They are surrounded by temptations less in number & influence.

The work is a promising one. The fruit of his labor, may not be always so immediately apparent numbers may not be seen flocking into the Kingdom of God under his efforts. Yet the preparation that will ultimate in such results is being secured, the ground is being broken, the tough roots of a rank vegetation, are thrown up to the action of light & heat, & a rich, mellow, & fruitful field will ere long be the consequence. God grant that many laborers may speedily enter this great garden of the West. . . .

Yours truly.
S. Y. LUM.

William Sutton White, Swedenborgian Publicist

JAMES C. MALIN

PART TWO—KANSAS EXEMPLAR OF THE PHILOSOPHY OF
EMANUEL SWEDENBORG AND HERBERT SPENCER
—*Concluded*

Theology and Science

IF broadly interpreted, the factor most disturbing to the theology of the decade of the 1870's, was the scientific mode of verification of everything that had been held to be knowledge. Such a statement of the question is so comprehensive as to cover more than the formal sciences. To do justice to the situation and all points of view, nothing less will meet the requirements of fair and equitable intellectual operations. More rigidly rational methods were being employed by many within the traditional scope of theology. At some points a substantial recognition was in evidence of social responsibilities of religion implicit in the rapid mechanization and urbanization of society. In that context, the emergence of more systematic, if not altogether scientific, methods for organizing and interpreting social data exerted important influences even among those who were not yet self-conscious about Comte, Spencer, Marx, and Darwin. The controversies about the interpretation of the statistical data of the federal census of 1870 and the deficiencies of its method and execution, and the near-revolutionary methods employed in the enumeration of 1880 left their mark. Among the formal sciences, the impact of geology and its allied disciplines had exerted a longer-term influence than the biological theories associated with Darwin. But the new impetus given to linguistic study and the criticism of written documents, supplemented by archeological discoveries in the eastern Mediterranean area, associated with the history of Judaeo-Christian religion, and the crude beginnings of the anthropology all entered sooner or later into most any extended consideration of theology.

Wichita was no exception. During the latter part of 1877, Harsen, the Presbyterian minister since 1871, reviewed from a liberal point of view the doctrines of the "Westminster Confession of Faith," the seventh and last of his series of sermons dealing with

DR. JAMES C. MALIN, associate editor of *The Kansas Historical Quarterly* and author of several books relating to Kansas and the West, is professor of history at the University of Kansas, Lawrence.

the creation. Incidentally, this is the series that opened the rift between him and the more literally orthodox members of his congregation, and led to his resignation in April, 1879. In his discourse on the "Creation" he dismissed the literal interpretation of the Biblical account because it was intenable in the light of geology. At the same time he examined the scientific theories and dismissed them also. Other theories that made allowances for greater duration of time than "six days"—six revolutions of the earth around the sun—while not completely satisfying, he tentatively accepted them because there were no better ones.

Editor White, after reporting the substance of Harsen's survey, pointed out that the best authorities rejected the theories that the minister thought the more tenable, citing his authorities by author and title. Among other scientific procedures, he cited philology, the linguistic approach, as one form of authoritative evidence.[1] White was unhappy about one aspect of Harsen's performance. Although he had reason to believe that the speaker was acquainted with "an interpretation which is rational, scientific, and scriptural," he made no reference to it. By this White meant Swedenborg's account of creation, but the name was not specified and the matter was not pushed. Indeed, the course of a minister was not easy. A few weeks later, Bishop Bowman, of the Methodist church, delivered a similar sermon, apparently taking comparable ground on the so-called "long day" theory. Again White disagreed. But one point more is worthy of mention as evidence about how seriously this generation took the subject. For two hours the bishop "riveted the attention of the entire audience"—except a heavy weight of the Wichita bar "who slept the sleep of the innocent" during the whole time.[2]

The Methodist church sponsored a lecture series during three winters, the early months of 1879, 1880, and 1881. Conspicuous among the speakers were men who, at the time, were making science and religion a lecture specialty. George E. Wendling, scheduled for January, 1879, cancelled his engagement on account of illness but appeared in 1880 to deliver his reply to Ingersoll. Paige appeared for three lectures, February 9-11, 1880; "The Origin and Growth of the Worlds," "The Evolution of Life," and "Life." White

---

1. The books specifically cited were Eleazar Lord, *The Epoch of Creation*, Edward Hitchcock, *Religion of Geology*, John Anderson, *The Course of Creation*. He referred also to the Rev. Dr. Dickinson's introduction to Lord's book, and referred to the work of Dr. Chalmers, of Scotland, without citing the title.—Wichita *Weekly Beacon*, November 21, 1877.

2. *Ibid.*, January 30, 1878.

was convinced only that the speaker was a materialist, who betrayed religion in his own house. If White's reports were accurate, Paige's information and logic were both quite faulty.[3] The Wendling lecture of 1880 drew the fire of the Rev. A. L. Vail, Baptist minister, who pointed out, among other things, how in one form or another William Paley's old argument was only given a new dress. Vail insisted the finite mind could not prove God, the infinite: "The Bible does not prove God, it announces him." White added that Wendling's lecture contributed nothing new; that he was merely an elocutionist.[4] It was when Wendling came in 1881 that White branded him as a Sartor Resartus—a mere mender of old clothes.[5]

Vail presented his own views on "Creation" during the summer of 1880, and in announcing the presentation White defined the situation in his characteristic fashion:

A subject of great interest to the scientific and theological mind. From his stand point, that of literal record and not a divine allegory, Mr. Vail will handle it with ability, and he will interest his hearers even though they differ from him.

Possibly it is not necessary to record White's view, that of divine allegory according to Swedenborg, and that the minds of both Vail and White were each equally firmly fixed.[6]

White's views on science and religion were manifested in several ways, but some of them are appropriately entered into the record here. Darwinism had not reached the point of extensive controversy in this area and thus was given only brief attention. White pointed out that—"Free determination was not a factor in Darwin's doctrine of the 'Survival of the Fittest.'" Again "it cannot apply to individuals who are supposed to live forever." Starting with man, freedom of choice is basic fact, a man's future is "not settled by an immutable law of the survival of the fittest." If it were, there would be no alternative to the "Presbyterian doctrine of predestination and foreordination."[7] "A true science is the essential basis of a true religion. . . ." was one of White's assumptions, and "man must reach God by the inductive process and must come back to himself by the deductive process." Not by external force nor by acts of legislation, does a man grow, only "by orderly development from within. All development is according to use."

---

3. *Ibid.*, January 15, 22, February 5, 1879; January 14, 21, February 11, 18, March 3, 1880.
4. *Ibid.*, March 24, 1880.
5. *Ibid.*, March 23, 1881. A Hatfield lecture was scheduled in 1881, *ibid.*, April 6, 1881, but was not adequately reported.
6. *Ibid.*, July 7, 1880.
7. *Ibid.*, May 10, 1882.

White was convinced that "every mistake is an incentive and a basis for correction," and that eventually:

He [man] will see clearly the effect in the cause, rather than, as now, the cause in the effect. . . . Knowing causes he will have much more patience in working out effects. . . . He will know that the evil is in the cause, and not in the effect. . . . He will see that causes are essentially internal and spiritual, and cannot be reached by any external remedy.

For White, "God is the causative cause, . . . the central life of all life." [8]

At a session of the Allen Drug Store symposium, the principals were two physicians, one of the soul, and one of the body, and the subject was their respective public responsibilities. The physician of the body argued that his private and his public life were separate, his public responsibility attaching only to his professional character, while his opponent was bound equally in both aspects of life. But the physician of the soul concluded that "After all you are bound to be as good a man as I am," and after the laugh, added, "As good as I am, bound to be." The editor's verdict, when appealed to by the soul doctor, was that every man was obliged to be right as far as he had the light—but the external social effects were different as among men. Significantly, the article was captioned: "Being and Seeming." [9]

During 1885 Henry Ward Beecher was delivering in New York a series of eight sermons on *Evolution and Religion*, later to be published in book form. The sixth of these was on "The Bible and Evolution," the purpose being a reconciliation of the two. White thought that Beecher and many others were assuming that evolution was the standard of truth by which the Bible was to be measured, and according to that standard the fate of the Bible as true or false was to be determined. In other words, the Bible was true only to the extent that it agreed with and anticipated modern revelation by science. White stated his own position: "As a scientific theory it [evolution] relates to what we call nature, and to man as an animal, while the bible . . . is a revelation of man's spiritual birth and regeneration." Under the circumstances White did not expect Beecher to remove any of the difficulties: "evolution is yet a mere theory, and in fact will always remain a hypothesis, more or less strongly buttressed by phenomena." [10]

During the same year a group of young men organized the Wichita Secular Union, or Liberal League and brought to the city a

8. *Ibid.*, September 20, 1882.
9. *Ibid.*, November 8, 1882.
10. Wichita *Daily Beacon*, July 2, 1885.

so-called liberal, A. O. Phelps, for a series of lectures. Exercising the prerogative of youth, who considered themselves intellectually emancipated and quite sophisticated, they framed the announcement of their enterprise in the following provocative language: "These are liberal lectures—the kind that the 'truly good' call 'infidel.' All are invited. Lectures free. . . ."[11]

After the first lecture, White reported that "in many respects Mr. Phelps impresses us very favorably," but "Mr. Phelps is as extravagant in his claims for Infidelity as the preachers are for so-called Christianity, as to what each has done for civilization." He was given to exaggeration, to slovenly expression of thought, and as an advocate, was lop-sided, but for perspective, White turned to some general observations:

The world has moved forward or backward by two great systems—forward by truths, backward by falsities. Freedom of thought has been the prime mover in both, for there is freedom to think falsely as well as to think truly. The man of the church has been as much in freedom of thought as the man not in the church. Science has been as dogmatic as religion has been; and the man of the church of to-day is as fully in the freedom of thought as the so-called scientific thinker. The leaders of both find many servile followers.

Hahnemann and Harvey were persecuted as bitterly by the scientifics of the past as the dissenters of the church were in their day. Gallileo, Bruno, Copernicus, Tycho Brhae were sneered at, persecuted and maligned by the scientists of their day fully as much as they were by the church. In fact, it is true that the [scientific] fraternity largely instigated the church to persecute them. In later days we sneered at Fulton, heaped ridicule on Morse, and called Darwin a fool. Free thought in the church, as in the scientific school has eliminated many errors. Truth in its entirety is the property of no man nor of any school.

With these preliminaries disposed of, White took up some of Phelps' main points. First, the problem of infinite and finite. The lecturer had challenged Christianity on the ground that finite man can not comprehend any part of an infinite God such as the system presumed. In spite of this indictment of religious thought, the Phelps school of materialists posited eternal matter and infinite force. White pointed out the paradox, and spelled out the conclusion that if finite man could not comprehend an infinite God neither could he comprehend an infinite force: "Mr. Phelps said he was talking philosophically. Well, a good many philosophers have talked nonsensically and irrationally. We insist on holding Mr. Phelps down to the full application of his doctrine of the unknowableness by the finite mind of the infinite subject." Although Herbert Spencer was not named, the terminology of matter, force, and the unknowable suggest that Phelps was a disciple.

11. *Ibid.*, September 28, 1885.

"Mr. Phelps said that religion was a matter of geography and brain boundary."—that is an environmental determinist. White took the opposite extreme of heredity as a determinist, or at this point appeared to do so. But in the following paragraph he reasserted his usual contention. To Phelps' contention that if religion was true, it should produce the same results in Mexico as in Massachusetts, White countered that science should do likewise. But White insisted that in both cases: "Each receives according to his genius, according to his heredity, and variously according to his receptivity."

Prayer was an object of Phelps' ridicule and White reminded him: "That was not scientific. A careful teacher will distinguish between form and essence—between use and abuse. Prayer, in its essence, is the innermost desire of the soul, and all men not only receive but act from this principle." Although objecting to the illustration of the mother-child relationship used, the old bachelor "self-abnegator," at any rate, revealed himself in the correction offered: "Every act of the mother is in answer to the prayer of the child. The child is a bundle of prayer appealing to the mother." It might reach for a flame or for the moon. So man might "ask for the impossible or the hurtful." Apparently the statement had been made that, although there was no proof of God, yet, should there be one, Phelps could trust him without knowing anything about him and need not pray to him. White interjected: "Nothing could be more unscientific." The editor's view was that trust is in relation to knowledge. He suggested that Phelps "resurrected some old dogmas and then reburied them." Phelps claimed "that if a [theological] dogma was true four or five centuries ago, it ought to be true now." If so, White insisted that the same principle would apply to scientific dogmas. He reminded Phelps that "a dogma is not the truth, but our apprehension of the truth . . ." and was subject to reappraisal.[12]

In White's remarks introductory to his report on the next lecture, he conceded that from Phelps' standpoint the lecture was an able presentation: "But we object to his standpoint. We do not think it a central one." Two themes received attention in the report: a further comparative discussion of theological and scientific hypotheses, and a refutation of Phelps' evaluation of doubt.

On the first of these subjects White stated his own view:

Theology, so far as it is hypothetical, is scientific just as much as evolution is. Both are erected upon the experiences and observations of men, and science may be rational or irrational. The Ptolemaic system was scientific, but it was irra-

12. *Ibid.,* September 29, 1885.

tional. Scientific theology has its free thinkers as well as Scientific Evolution, Conservation of Energy, the molecular or the atomic theories of scientists.

Theology has its hypotheses and science so-called, has, if anything, more. Even the most exact sciences must start from axiomatic, self-evident truths, which the mind accepts, almost intuitively. Theology has its enlightened doubters who have faith in better things, and more rational theories and systems of truth. It is in the loud-mouthed whoopers-up on the outskirts of thought who hold to the irrational dogmas so well, so soundly and so effectively denounced by Mr. Phelps.

Two points may be placed in sharper focus at this stage of the presentation: first, systems of thought are frequently brought into a disrepute by irresponsible controversalists who confuse the essential issues by injecting elements that are not central, secondly, negative and destructive criticism is easy, offers opportunity for notoriety, but is not necessarily an evidence of any capacity for constructive or original thought.

Phelps had opened his second lecture with a glorification of doubt; all advancement was "ascribed to doubt and the doubters." White condemned this extreme position as unphilosophical and unscientific; "It was a one-sided statement of the case, and that the unconsequential side—the negative side. The truth is that doubt never accomplished anything." Possibly he had forgotten the second and third of his own "Sartor Resartus" contributions to the *Beacon* of February and March, 1875, when he had taken the same extreme application of the Descartian principle of doubt. At any rate, a decade had intervened and now he replied to Phelps that: "It is the affirmative state of the mind that enables it to perform every act which is its own act. . . . The thinker constructs his philosophy not on doubt, but on faith. The doubting architect would never build a magnificent temple. The man who denies does not doubt or he would not deny. He denies because he sees intellectually and rationally, and then he constructs by rational faith." In other words, denial is not rationally possible except the denier has faith, positive conviction about constructive thought. But lest he had been too negative in his criticisms, White concluded his remarks by asserting: "We like any man who can stir the people to think." [13]

Phelps delivered four lectures in his series, the first three, September 28-30, financed by the Secular Union, the fourth, October 1, was a test of local interest, which was negative, the voluntary collection yielded only four dollars. This final lecture had ridiculed

---

13. *Ibid.*, September 30, 1885.

the Christian plan of salvation. Whether or not he approved the method of argument is not clear, but White made his position unequivocally clear that no literalist could answer Phelps or Ingersoll.[14]

The Secular Union's lecture series had focused attention upon two points of view; those of the materialist, Phelps, and the Swedenborgian theologian—Editor White. So far as the orthodox Christian ministry was concerned both were heretics. The champion of orthodoxy who entered the lists was the Rev. E. H. Edson, the rector of St. Johns Protestant Episcopal Church, a relative newcomer to Wichita. A young man himself, he issued an invitation directed "especially to the young men of the city," the formal published "card" being headlined: "To the Liberal League," and dated October 23, 1885. On successive Sunday evenings, a series of three lectures would be given on the general theme, "Evidences of Christianity." Evidently Edson intended to be tactful and correct in his approach, explaining carefully that:

> These lectures are not intended to be an answer to any man, nor a challenge to any. I respect the individual rights of all men, and no individual or class of individuals will be assailed. . . . From the title of your society and its work in the past I infer that you desire to receive light upon the subject of my lectures. . . .

In response to the first lecture "One of the Liberals," or so he signed himself, reported "What they think of it,"—"dogmatic and pedagogical," and

> Mr. Edson quite mistakes the character, intelligence and experience of the members of the Secular Union, if he expects to effect any change of their views by the stale sylogistic sophisms and theological dogmas. The story of the watch found in the desert, etc.
>
> Every portion of matter exhibits phenomena, but no one can hence reason that these phenomena are the result of intelligent design. They are the product of the properties of matter.

Of course, the young liberal was too immature philosophically to realize that he had given no answer to the question; he had only restated it in a different form which required him to explain how matter had acquired the identifiable properties which he assigned to it.

"Another Liberal" criticized adversely Edson's title "The Evidences of Christianity" and demanded definitions of God, of Christianity, proof of the existence of God, or of the Christian conception of God. He insisted there are many Gods. He asked whether the

---

14. *Ibid.,* October 5, 1885.

Edson God meant "an aggregate of natural forces," or "a person of parts and passions, a material substance, a something separate and apart from nature, or natural forces." Edson said that no one had proved there was no God, but the "Liberal" countered that Edson not only assumed a God, but requires "us to believe or be damned," and excluded all other Gods. In general terms the "Liberal" insisted that all people believed in Gods, and used the same argument Edson used; even Thomas Paine would have accepted it. Furthermore "Liberal" pointed out that evidence of general truths did not prove that they were the exclusive property of Christianity. Also, even if the idea of God was accepted, that did not prove that the earth was made in six days, and "that he made man, and did such a bad job of it that it was necessary to murder a part of himself to correct the blunder, and that even this is only a partial correction." In closing, the "Liberal" reminded Edson that he had promised information: "We hope he will define his terms and get down to business. . . . We want evidence, if he has it. Nothing but facts will do us. Let Mr. Edson try again." [15]

The second Edson lecture afforded no more satisfaction to the young men of the Secular Union than the first. The liberal who commented in a letter to the *Beacon* explained that he had not considered it "advisable to offer any criticisms on the stale absurdities advanced . . ." and then continued sententiously:

for it did not appear that those who had listened to such dogmas for many years, and who still hold allegiance to them, would patiently consider anything presented in opposition to them; and unprejudiced investigators in search of naked truth readily discovered that the lecture was but a series of postulates—empty shells, pericarps of a past age, shed from an old theological tree that grew from the soil of ignorance in an atmosphere of superstition and dread.

With reluctance, however, this "Liberal" yielded to the insistence of his associates. He conceded, in a qualified form, Edson's proposition that things are believed that are not known—yes, tentatively, when not contrary to known facts. He rejected Edson's comparison of the morals of heathendom and Christianity by contrasting ancient Rome with modern England and America, challenging as a matter of method, the contrast of civilizations from different time periods. Lastly, "Liberal" rejected Edson's definition of God—according to Edson, God "amounted to a nothing-something," and a miracle was a war against nature by this "nothing-something" in which nature is defeated for a time.[16] Without Edson's own lan-

15. *Ibid.*, October 24, 28, 30, 1885.
16. *Ibid.*, November 7, 1885.

guage, or a more objective summary of it as a guide, it is impossible to conclude with certainty what Edson had said. The wording reported implies that Edson's definition of God was in the tradition of mystical Christianity under the influence of Neoplatonism. The miracle reference implies that "Liberal" was thinking in the mechanistic tradition of Greek philosophy which posited the principle that every effect must have a cause. The Swedenborg theology had followed the Neoplatonic version that made no exception even in the case of "miracles."

The *Beacon* did not print any criticism of the third of Edson's lectures, from the liberal point of view, but White himself took over the task of summing up. The situation had become most complex and reflected much more than what appeared on the surface. The evidence is not available from which to make a satisfying analysis, but some of the more obvious elements may be specified. Edson's tenure as rector had been brief, but the attendance had grown beyond the capacity of the church; the building was remodeled and enlarged, being completed in September, and officially recognized in the visit of Bishop Vail in mid-October. At that time Bishop Vail had been most tactful in complimenting the congregation and the rector, including a rather insistent admonition urged upon all, "the duty of . . . tolerance in their dealings with one another. . . . The motto of the Church is 'Unity in essentials, liberty in non-essentials and charity in all things.'" As already noted, in another context, Edson preached his farewell sermon in March, 1886, explaining how he had been compelled to resign because of the issue of freedom of opinion. The Secular Union lectures had come immediately after Bishop Vail's visit. Here is a case where there was more fire than visible smoke.

As commentator on the lectures, White was speaking as an outsider as respects both the church and the union. Speaking of Edson's series: "The effort was certainly deserving of a larger hearing . . . his style and matter indicate maturity of intellect." White made no attempt to summarize the doctrinal arguments, pointing out that as was necessary in order to convince others, Edson had first convinced himself of their validity: "He has disciplined his intellect to implicit belief; after all, probably the most enviable state of mind." In conclusion White insisted that: "In these lectures, Mr. Edson has acquitted himself with much credit. They have been scholarly, earnest and eloquent and would make a good showing in printed form." One victory on White's part should not be passed over without recognition. By heroic effort he had refrained from disagreeing with anything said by either Edson or the liberal letter writers, or from using their remarks as a peg upon which to hang a Swedenborgian lecture. He had a more immediate and delicate office to perform.

Edson did not get off unscathed. White wrote in much the same spirit which he had noted about four weeks earlier in reporting Vail's visit: "The venerable Bishop Vail preached an affectionate discourse . . . in which the advice of a father was mingled with the dignity of the sage." This is all the more noteworthy for White because Edson had taken exception to one of White's extended editorial essays on the theory of government and had persisted in having his say through several sharp exchanges. But returning to the Secular Union lectures question, White commented:

Mr. Edson is yet a young man. . . . Of course, as a young champion, he feels it incumbent on himself to make formal battle with the foes of Christianity, still the reporter doubts the efficacy of any set argument on this subject. If at this day Christianity is not a proved and substantiated fact, it can never be made so by discussion.

The next step in the task of orienting the unfortunate controversy in the perspective of history demonstrated White's role as sage:

It has been fifteen centuries now since Celsus [c. 180] made his celebrated argument against the religion of Christ. This covered every objection that has ever been urged, and is the quiver from which Voltaire, Payne, and Ingersoll and the whole crowd of infidels have drawn their keenest shafts. At the time this argument of Celsus was made Christianity was yet struggling for existence, and every point he made met with instant and hearty approval in both the literary and scientific circles of the [Roman] empire. The claims of Christianity were certainly effectually answered and refuted, so far as human reason could do it. But strange as it may seem, the Christians not only survived this tremendous shock, but it seemed to inspire them. . . . [soon] pagan Rome bowed to the supremacy of the cross.[17]

Revivalist Methods

Well established in the traditions of many of the Protestant religious denominations was the annual revival meeting, or protracted meeting. Because services were held at least once a day over a period of some weeks, the regular pastor was assisted by other ministers of the community in some form of joint or co-operative effort, or a preacher and/or a singer was brought in—often people who were more or less professional exhorters. When the Methodist revival was scheduled for February, 1877, Editor White agreed

17. *Ibid.*, November 9, 1885. The account of Vail's visit is in *ibid.*, October 19, 1885.

that "a revival of true religion is one of the great needs of the day." He objected however to emotionalism and excitement of fear as the basis of decision:

> Let us have a new departure in the methods and aims of this revival. Arouse and convince the rational faculties rather than appeal to the fear of punishment or the hope of reward, both of which are based upon pure selfishness which is the essence of hell.

Again, placing the negative and the positive in contrast, and implying the term conversion as distinct from regeneration, he admonished: "Tell us that regeneration is not the operation of a moment, nor of the duration of a revival . . . ; that it is the work of a lifetime, however lengthened. . . . Religion teaches men, not how to die, but how to live here, in order to live hereafter." Furthermore, in emphasizing that conversion actuated by fear of punishment or hope of reward was "pure selfishness," self-love, the source of evil and "the essence of hell," he emphasized in the positive sense that "true religion" includes not only the individual, but society, government, justice, equity, "that it is the very breath of the physical, moral and spiritual life of every man." All this was "New Church" doctrine, but without the label, and White was urging this doctrine in true Swedenborgian tradition; not as that of a competing denomination or sect, but as a religion of life adapted into the existing churches, until unity of doctrine would ultimate in unity in one church: "Orderly, gradual and continuous growth is the law of the spiritual as well as the physical man." [18]

The following year White challenged the sermon of the Rev. J. P. Harsen, Presbyterian minister, on the conversion of Zacheus, insisting that it cannot be synonymous with regeneration. By conversion, White insisted, a man "has simply ceased to *do* evil; and then he must *learn*, gradually, to do well. He can, and will have to, learn while life lasts." Furthermore, he can never attain "the humanly possible state of regeneration." White persisted in urging the practical importance of the distinction by arguing that the doctrine of instantaneous conversion and regeneration was not only untrue, but hurtful—there were innumerable causes that have led up to a conversion. Harsen replied to the Beacon, defining his view of conversion and of sanctification, equating the latter term with White's term regeneration, not warranted by the Bible. In Harsen's language, regeneration is an act, not a process: "Regeneration is the work of God; conversion is the work of man." Evidently, the two

18. *Weekly Beacon*, February 14, 1877.

men were not using the same language, although they were using the same English words.[19]

Only a few selected examples can be used here, chosen to illustrate so wide a variety of implications of revival practice as they stimulated White into action. One of these instances occurred in November-December, 1881, when the Rev. John Kelly was being assisted by a Mr. Gibler. The latter organized his sermon on redemption under three heads: Who came? for what? and the scope of His work? The answer to the first question was that Christ came as the "representative man." The second question was answered: "He came, only and solely, to die! ! ! That is so-called orthodoxy boiled down." White argued that if Christ came as a representative, a vicarious Savior, to assume the penalty for the sins of the world and expiate them on the Cross—that and nothing else—then he was totally distinct from God. That was inconsistent with his Godhead.

Conventionally, the Cross was associated with death; but White insisted there is no death, not even of the natural body which never lived, only transformations of the material into successive receptacles of life in innumerable forms since Adam. In this context, Christ's material body did not die. In such a universe the only kind of death is of the soul, and this is not annihilation—the soul is eternal —but also mere change of form. The death from which Christ came to save men was the substantial death of the soul—the kind of death that came into the world with the fall of Adam. God did not create death, "He is life. . . ." Spiritual death for man in this sense is suffering the torments of hell to eternity. If Christ was a substitute, a representative man, according to this reasoning he would be suffering the torments of hell to eternity. Actually, Christ's so-called death on the Cross was not redemption, it was a crime, murder, not a holy sacrifice, but incidental to redemption: "The real sacrifice He made, was in the consecration of His assumed humanity to the work of redemption. He came . . . to point out the path of life and to remove . . . the hellish obstacles that prevented man's from walking there in." The death of Christ on the Cross, at the hands of the Jews, White insisted, represented the consummation of the Jewish church, done by the will and acts of depraved men. Christ came to re-establish the Kingdom of God on earth and in heaven—the Christian church to replace the Israelitish church.

19. *Ibid.*, February 20, 27, 1878.

White was certain that the preacher was equally in error about the scope of Christ's works: "The Lord came, and comes continually, not to save men from the penalty of their sins," but "to give us the truth, that *it* might persuade . . . us" and thus "save us from" further sinning. According to Swedenborg's rationalism, every sin had its penalty; for sins already committed the penalties followed as cause and effect, and according to order no penalty could be remitted or transferred—not even the Lord could intervene contrary to order.[20]

At the revival meetings one type of religious doctrine was being expounded and the success of the effort in terms of conversions depended upon the ability of the exhorters to convince their hearers of the exclusive truth of their plan of salvation. On the other hand, White's unrelenting attack was devastating; his adverse criticisms of the validity of their doctrine, and his presentation of his own, argued with incisive logic, was directed to appeal to the rational faculty in contrast with emotion and fear. In addition to the issue of validity of religious doctrine in itself, he was repeatedly going further and was declaring unequivocally that the revivalist doctrines were not only false, but they were positively vicious, sinful, and that these "false doctrines" were "the cause of evil." That was his headline, and a few months earlier, he had declared with brutal directness that the doctrine of the "vicarious Atonement is . . . the prime cause of social evils and disorders of the world. It amounts to a license to sin . . .," and under the delusion of escaping the penalties by a last minute "conversion." The plain implication was that this doctrine upon which the revival was based was a fraud perpetrated by the church upon a gullible public—that the "license to sin" had no efficacy.[21] In addition, the questions of religion and the liquor traffic, in its prohibition phase, had become entangled and the revivalists tended to make liquor and its associations the chief source of evil in Kansas. The fury of Kelly's blasts at the Wichita press and especially at the *Beacon* are thus easily understandable.[22]

Revival efforts continued through January, 1882, attention being focused for most of the month upon the efforts of a woman evangelist, a Mrs. Rogers. Evidently, White was much impressed by her personality and ability. At the close of her series of meetings he conceded the great interest she had aroused, but only time would

---

20. *Ibid.*, December 7, 1881.
21. *Ibid.*, August 3, 1881.
22. *Ibid.*, December 7, 14, 1881. This one, and later conflicts, have been presented in the section on "The Pulpit and the Press."

tell, he warned, about the lasting results. Any failure, he reminded his readers, was not her fault, but her honesty, warmth of heart, and other qualities could prevent the evil results of false principles and irrational methods:

A falsity in the church (a spiritual sphere) flows down with a demoralizing and degrading effect into all the so-called practical spheres. We term them "so-called practical" spheres for we profoundly believe that the spiritual sphere of all spheres is the most practical, for in that sphere is built up and culminates all the activities of life on all planes of thought and action. The spiritual sphere, represented by the church, is the character sphere, and character is the only treasure that any man can lay up against the day of wrath—the only treasure that moth and rust will not corrupt. Every rational man must hope that her labors were full of substantial meat and drink which will strengthen and vitalize the moral tone of this city.[23]

On Sunday morning, January 29, the Rev. J. D. Hewitt, Presbyterian, asked the general question why the world had not been converted, and answered: "Because their deeds are evil, therefore they love darkness rather than light." White reported this much of the preacher's idea with qualified approval resorting to his characteristic "but" technique: "That is the truth, but it is not all of the truth. May not the quality of the light be some to blame? Evidently the Lord thought so, for He came to bring light to the world. Is it not possible that the light He brought has been obscured or falsified?" The editor reminded his readers that Protestants accused the Catholics of having obscured the light: "Let the [Protestant] church examine the quality of the light it calls divine light."

Regardless of Hewitt's possible response to this admonition, White pretended to do some examining on his own account. The Rev. John Kelly was the recipient of the honor of the *Beacon's* presence at the evening service of the same Sunday where the minister proposed to follow up the revival series by Wednesday evening cottage prayer meetings. The city was divided for this purpose into four sections, and the homes of as many members of the congregation were designated as meeting places, a general service to follow at the church on Thursday evening. Kelly announced that these exercises were to be continued until Wichita was saved. White pointed out that this procedure was not in the Apostolic tradition: "they were sent out to teach the truth" and the people convinced rationally of the truth accepted it and were saved by His loving mercy. On the contrary, "the tenor of Brother Kelly's prayer, Sunday night, was an appeal to God to have mercy and

23. *Ibid.*, January 25, 1882.

save the people. That was a waste of breath." It was worse: "every appeal for mercy is a charge that He is not a merciful and saving God. . . . Praying won't save the people. The idea that God will save men because of somebody else's prayer, is a monstrous heresy." White admonished them: "If these prayer meetings are to bring a pressure on God to save Wichita, they will be a failure. God will come to Wichita as fast as Wichita will receive Him, and if Wichita won't receive Him, He can't come. The people are not to be converted by this beseiging throne of grace." White had referred them to the Apostolic method, the teaching of the truth to the people; the decision to accept it was theirs not God's: "He has mercy, infinite mercy, all the time" if only man will receive—"Wichita is to be saved [if she is saved] by a knowledge of God's truth, and an obedience to His commands. . . ." [24]

In the same issue of the *Beacon* and in the same context, White wrote another editorial, not captioned, but later referred to as "Prayer and the Mercy of God." The inspiration for the article reached back by a chain of circumstances to the German philosopher-scientist and poet, Goethe. As attributed to him, at second hand, he had admitted "that he never read of a murder or any other horrid crime that he did not fear that under certain conditions he might be capable of perpetrating the same." A distinguished American minister had confessed that the identical sentiment, applied to himself, but drew his own conclusion: "Brethern, if we are not murderers, burglars and incendiaries, it is due to the mercy of God which has prevented us from the commission of these crimes." This rationalization infuriated White—a selective mercy of God! Such "mercy" is not mercy, and such a God who could but would not prevent murder and thus save both murderer and victim

"is no God worthy of the name. . . . The spirit of murder leads to the act, and there is no power in Heaven or on Earth to prevent a man having the spirit or cultivating the spirit of murder, save the man himself, and man can prevent himself only so far as he receives into his mind and heart those principles of mercy, of love to God and the neighbor, which our Father is continually offering to each of us."

In White's opinion the key to the whole problem was self-love: "The love of self has in it the possibility of every crime. The suppression of this love of self is man's duty and not God's. Man must have the desire to suppress it, or God can give him no power to do it."

In undertaking to answer one minister, White succeeded only in

24. *Ibid.*, February 1, 1882.

arousing another. Elder Poole, of the Christian church read the above editorial in the pulpit and commented upon it the following Sunday, branding it "poor logic and poor theology. . . . God never comes to any man. Man must go to God." White repeated substantially his previous central points. Although not so prevalent as formerly, he pointed out that the opinion still prevailed "to an alarming extent, that the will and purposes of God are to be changed by prayer. . . . that God is not always merciful, but is made merciful by the prayer . . ." of man. "If a man knew what he was doing it would be blasphemous." In his closing sentence, White stated his own doctrine by a definition: "Prayer is an outward expression of an inward desire, and it works a change in the suppliant and not in God." [25]

When a minister provided an opportunity White praised him, although, as in the case of Hewitt, on occasion he had disagreed with him on doctrine, and waged open warfare on him on account of his participation in prohibition politics. Hewitt's sermon of April 2, 1882, was reported under the caption, "The Dawn" when White pronounced the message as "correct doctrine." In this Hewitt had controverted the common idea of conversion, and compared the spiritual growth to the natural growth of the animal and vegetable kingdoms. "Conversion was just the beginning of the new life. . . . All truth . . . must be received by the individual in freedom. No force or compulsion must be used to compel him to receive it in his understanding and affections. . . ." [26]

Three years later a review of the revival issue called attention to two in progress in Wichita proper, and one in West Wichita, all crowded. According to the conventional language on such occasions, many souls were being saved, but—that ubiquitous but—"If these revivals are of any spiritual value to the man and to the community, we will see the effects in our social and business life." Since the revivals had been in progress two suicides and two attempts at murder had occurred. Although there was no necessary connection, self-love drove to crime and to the mourners' bench. The fear upon which the revival thrived was the same as the fear of the penitentiary. And then White inquired whether schools and colleges could teach their subject by emotion and fear?—"Next to the character

25. *Ibid.*, February 8, 1882. Men had become so accustomed to pressure, organized to persuade; propaganda had become so prevalent in man's thought; and principle of right and wrong so hazy, that the assumption was tacitly made that all that was ever necessary, even at the spiritual level, was to organize and apply pressure to God, and he would yield as group conditioned men yield under the "group struggle" principle of operations.

26. *Ibid.*, April 5, 1882.

of the truths taught, comes, in importance, the methods of teaching." Nearly two years later, and shortly before leaving his editorial chair, White was still teaching his own doctrine, and was objecting to teaching religion by emotion: "Religion is not something for a man to get. It is something for the man to be. It is a life, and not a mere faith or belief. . . ."[27]

SCIENCE AND TECHNOLOGY; MAN, FREEDOM, AND USE

The effect upon society of science and technology through mechanical powered machines had been a matter of increasing concern with the passing of the 19th century. Particularly disturbed were those who were anxious about the fate of human freedom. Central to White's philosophy was freedom—not "Liberty, Equality, and Fraternity." Two very different philosophies. In watching railroad consolidation, the growth of other industrial monopolies, the concentration of capital in corporations, the arbitrary conduct of organized labor, White asserted that:

Every new invention, ever[y] fresh discovery of science seems to increase the wealth in the hands of the few. . . .

Machinery in the hands of selfish capital, is not only not emancipating, but enslaving, the masses, and by the division, subdivision and unlimited specialization of skilled labor, the class of artisans is becoming degraded into mere factory hands, hardly one of whom can make a shoe, a coat, a piano or an engine. The number is constantly decreasing, of those who can take their kit of tools and start out to do for themselves. In the first place they are not educated as artisans, but are skilled only in the manufacture of parts, and in the second place they cannot compete against capital. They are as much tied down to the factories of their masters as the serfs of Russia were to the soil. Every incorporated company for any purpose, is a blow at the individual independence of the man.[28]

White was most accurate in analysis of what was taking place; the passing of the skilled artisan and the deprivation of the worker of even the opportunity to feel pride in the thing he made and the skill with which he wrought a completed product. With this loss of pride in his trade and in himself as an artisan, the worker was without incentive. White was himself an artisan, a printer by the apprentice route. The artisan's trade was a way of life as well as employment by which to earn a living. Although White's primary concern in this editorial was the artisan, small business and the farmer were involved. The corporation was the nemesis of small business. The farmer, under the impact of the horse-power

27. *Daily Beacon*, January 31, 1885; November 15, 1886.
28. *Weekly Beacon*, June 29, 1881.

revolution in agriculture and the mechanization of other segments of society, was experiencing a different but a comparable displacement. White had been a farmer and still owned a farm, and was a partner in a newspaper plant faced with the hazards of bigness. As individual enterprises, owners of farms and small businesses had had pride in their personal independence and accomplishment. But all three, artisan, farmer, and small business man, found themselves threatened or deprived of their traditional position and function in this flux induced by mechanization of society and had not succeeded in a new orientation and adjustment. As were some others, White was analyzing with keen perception what was taking place, but without finding in positive terms the means of adjustment to the new conditions of life that would afford incentive to effort, pride in work, and safeguards to freedom. The old had slipped away without the new being created, and the result was frustration and blind revolt. And the end was not yet. Was a reconciliation possible, not of freedom to mechanization, but of mechanization to freedom?

The subject could be discussed at length in this strictly presentist context, but something would still be wanting. Man's primitive past arises yet to haunt him. Through the process by which he is said to have been civilized from a state of savagery, he learned the ideal of combining his contriving brain and his skillful hand in conceiving an idea and actualizing it out of raw or unformed material. Aristotle called this entelechy — potentiality actualized. God is pure Act. Man, the microcosm, expresses his innermost self and comes nearest to his realization of God in exercising this freedom to convert his potentiality into Act. Being finite, not infinite, he falls short of pure Act, but his ideal is not satisfied unless he has done the best his talents and circumstances permit.

Aristotle defined virtue in these terms, "if everything is successfully performed when it it performed in accordance with its proper excellence, it follows that the good of man is an activity of soul in accordance with virtue. . . ." The Christian mystics had emphasized this practical aspect as integral also with the complete life. John Tauler, the German mystic, has expressed this ideal—to make shoes so as "to be a pattern to all." Dr. Carl Jung, psychiatrist, insists that mankind has acquired a "collective unconscious," but whether or not this is valid, human culture has developed an archetype of cultural behavior that is more deeply embedded in his individuality than man is aware—as economics, as ethics, as aesthetics, as unity of personality, and as unity in God. Mechanization had made the worker "skilled only in the manufacture of parts"—neither his life nor the thing made was an expression of completion, self-realization.

Referring some months later to the game of shinny, White titled an editorial: "Every Fellow Shinnies On His Own Side"—his goal is victory for himself: "Self-love is the deadly virus in religion, in politics, in society, in the family and in the individual," and breeds war, not peace. He then paraphrased Swedenborg: "self-love and love of the world are the ruling loves of the hells; they make hell. . . . the love of God and the neighbor are the ruling loves of the heavens—they make heaven." Likewise, following Swedenborg, knowledge in and for itself is not virtue. Its instruments are subject to use for either good or for evil:

Every discovery of science, every victory over the silent and imponderable agencies of nature only place new instruments of torture and death in the hands of self-love. Every school, college and seminary of learning, every advance and development of the intellect of the age, is but increasing the power of evil. Society is engaged in a desperate struggle against the evils that infest it, and the warfare is in vain, because society manufactures them faster than it eradicates. . . .

White saw the fatal error inherent in this system, motivated by the evil of self-love, embodied in the penal or police state as the exponent of a blind faith in regeneration of man by the enactment of a law and coercion in its enforcement. His argument was that the intervention of the police state deprived man of freedom of choice, thus also of the personal responsibility for his acts that is essential to ethical conduct. Incidentally, the statement of this basic ethical principle occurred at least as far back in time as Aristotle. The faith in the efficacy of a law in the hands of the police state was a major delusion of the late 19th century:

The ingenuity of the evil forces of society surpass the ingenuity of the law makers, and no law can be made that self-love cannot drive through it with a coach and four. And yet the moral and religious elements of society have become so depraved and impotent that, for every form of evil, internal and external, they seek an external application of force.

But basic to White's contention was the insistence that the origin of evil is internal, whether corruption in office, the ruthless exactions of monopolies, the abuses of labor unions, the liquor traffic, murder, sex crimes, or theft. "Penal statutes and policemen" applied externally to the outward manifestations of evil are worse than futile. They aggravate the evil by requiring more statutes and policemen, an endless cumulative spiral. Evil, being internal, requires an internal remedy, "The Golden Rule of God," and, "The remedy will have to be worked out through the slow procession of the centuries. . . . In the meantime there will be revolution in the religious, civil and social ethics of to-day." [29]

The ice and snow storm of February 21, 1882, snapped off telephone poles, snarled the wires, and disrupted communications. Telephone service was quite new, but already it was a necessity. The storm was more than local, paralyzing New York City's communications and causing losses or even disaster over a large part of the world already dependent upon machines:

> This slight interruption showed us how convenient and necessary this latest scientific appliance has become. Science is ameliorating the condition of the people, facilitating exchanges, increasing the supplies, multiplying our productive facilities, and in many ways, revolutionizing the industries and thought of the world, and while we seem to be growing more independent, richer and more prosperous, yet we are becoming more dependent upon these external mechanical appliances. If they work well it is all right. If they work badly, it's all wrong. . . .

White questioned whether the individual was "deriving substantial benefit" from the machinery and labor saving devices. Although "in the aggregate we seem to be growing stronger, it is a growing at the expense of the individual and the growth is only seeming. If all . . . labor . . . could be performed by machinery, would the world be strong or weak?" There would be production, but no one with the means to buy. If supply doubles and wants increase at the same ratio is a man any richer? If a machine makes possible the discharge of 75 percent of the workers and no one else is in a position to employ them, "has it added anything to the sum of human happiness?" Labor saving machines require long readjustment periods:

> In every new discovery and application of mechanical energy, there is loss and destruction to some vested interest, and adaptation to the changed condition is accomplished with loss, distress and sore suffering. Substitution of one thing requires the death of the other thing, and what is one man's gain is another man's loss. The human family seems to be preying on itself, as well as on all below it. Is this its normal condition? . . . If the genius of one man discovers a new and useful application of the forces of nature, he has to seek the protection of the law against those who would rob him of the reward and the profits of his discovery, and he in turn becomes a robber in levying an excessive royalty on all the public.

---

29. *Ibid.*, December 7, 1881, supplementing especially the preceding citation. The major arguments about the interrelations among the three types of institutions, church, school, and state—are too numerous to make any complete citation practicable.

In every invention of machines, there is a surrender of individual power and independence to the machine. If a man owns a horse, he surrenders a part of his vitality to the horse, and finally the horse becomes a necessity. . . . The question is how long can we stand the surrender of vital force to machinery? Isn't our servant, science, becoming our master?

The world rides to-day, whereas yesterday it walked, and its "calves" are dwindling in size and strength, and if tomorrow it was deprived of its vehicles it couldn't walk because it has no "calves."

There is a quick adaptation to the luxury of scientific supports, to mechanical aids and whatever strength the machine gets the body loses. The man and the machine are strong combined, but divide them by natural or artificial causes and both are impotent.[30]

In all this apparently pessimistic analysis of science, invention, and machines, White wrote in Swedenborgian perspective. Conspicuously applicable to the problem in hand was the doctrine of uses. Knowledges, sciences, learning, skills,—by whatever name they were instruments which man in freedom might use for good or for evil. Pointedly, and with a certain partisan zest, sharpened by many encounters, White took the Topeka *Commonwealth* to task on the subject of science in the schools—"Tell us, 'What For'?" The *Commonwealth* had said that: "it cannot be considered true that the world was made for man, but it is certainly true that if there exists a science that cannot be shown to be useful to man, that science is unworthy of human study." White asked two questions. First, if the world was not made for man, "what was it made for?" Second, what is use? The second proposition:

strikes us as supremely nonsensical. "Science" is a comprehensive term. It means, to know. Knowledge is the fundamental basis or foundation for all the rational, moral and spiritual faculties, without which the latter could not cohere or even exist, not even in the divine mind. All that a man knows relates to himself; all that he is capable of knowing, and we know of no limit to his capacity, relates to him. The very knowledge of himself depends upon his knowledge of his environments, and the conception of the existence of a science that has no use is impossible or unthinkable. Even though such a science existed and man were conscious of the fact, the knowledge of the fact would broaden the man's intellectual vision and therefore the nonuseful science would have its use. The writer evidently has a narrow and sensuous conception of the "useful"—it, to him, means bread and butter.[31]

The theme of "Cure *vs* Quackery" afforded White the opportunity to castigate comparatively some "sacred cows"; the medical profession, the church, and the law. His contention was that a remedy always aggravates the disease:

30. *Ibid.*, February 22, 1882.
31. *Ibid.*, February 6, 1884. Among other articles touching on the general theme was one in the *Daily Beacon*, May 5, 1885, commenting that instead of swords being beaten into plowshares, the reverse was taking place on a grand scale. Another discussed the Mason cotton picker, which was to be placed on the market.—*Ibid.*, June 26, 1885.

The remedy is not a cure, it is the effect of the disease. If there were no disease there would be no remedy. . . . The quacks of the physical sphere are called doctors: the quacks of the social sphere are called lawyers and statesmen.

The so-called church is the prolific mother of quackery. Its *scheme* of salvation—the vicarious atonement, and all the correlatives, and the consequential dogmatics flowing from it, is a scheme of quackery. . . . It is to save a man from the penalties of his sins. Just as the purgative and the emetic are used to save a man from the penalties of his violation of physical laws. . . . Some medical and legal doses are taken to relieve a pain, others are taken to prevent pain, but neither relate to the causes, nor remove them. The spiritual quack dose is not to remove the cause in character, but to cheat the cause of its effects.

One example of attacking the cause rather than providing remedies was cited in the case of New Orleans. Doctors had sought specifics for cholera and yellow fever, but without effect. Ben Butler solved the problem by installing sanitary facilities. Also, if a specific was found for dyspepsia, a new remedy would immediately become necessary to save the victim from the effects of gluttony. Again, if a specific for syphilis were found, "the remedy would add intensity to lust. . . ."

White insisted upon giving attention to cause, rather than to effect:

If it were not for the discovery and obedience to the laws of health our multiplying remedies would depopulate the earth. The laws of hygiene are waging a war with diseases and their specifics. The enlightened members of the medical profession, those who love their neighbor better than they do their fees, are beginning to see the truth. . . .

Likewise, White declared: "The penal law system of remedies is unmitigated quackery," and instead the statesmen should discover the principles of "political and social hygiene." And then, bringing all three types of quacks into one generalization:

We close by repeating that the church, of all quacks, is the most dangerous and deadly. Its very gods are quacks, that provide such a miserable and God-condemned scheme of patent medicine salvation. The drench bottle in medicine, law and gospels is filled with a deadlier poison than ever chemist discovered.[32]

A year and a half later, and from his theological premises, White again challenged the medical doctors on the ground that they misconceived the nature of their profession: they should approach it as the science of health, not the science of medicine; they mistook causes and effects, and consequently, remedies. In 1885 he

32. *Weekly Beacon,* December 26, 1883.

was irritated by Louisa Alcott's article in the *Woman's Journal*, in which she declared that mind cure was a failure:

As the genesis of all diseases is in the spiritual (the moral and mental) world, it seems to us a significant, if not hopeful, sign to see any effort, however empirical and tentative, directed in what we think is surely the right direction. Getting down to first principles, and viewing the subject philosophically, we do not hesitate to think and say that the body has no disease of its own. All diseases are primarily and essentially, in their generative or first principles, mental or moral, or mental and moral, and the body is only the sphere of their manifestations and ultimations. . . .

Of necessity, he reasoned, causes must "be found in the sphere of causes—the soul—the mind—rather than in the body, the sphere of effects. The soul is the sphere of the active principle, the body of the reactive." To answer objections that his views did not account for hereditary diseases, or predisposition to disease, he conceded that point "if the principle was confined to the life of one man. . . . But 'heredity is not a material law; it is a law of life—a spiritual law, belonging primarily to the soul and made manifest in the body."

The mode of thought to which White was committed was so different to that which prevailed that he found explanations necessary that made his arguments appear more involved than they might otherwise have been. Thus, at this point, in discussing his theory of hereditary disease, he was diverted into an explanation of natural law: "In fact, there is no such thing as a natural law. Nature has no laws. Nature is a subject and not a law maker. Law has nature for its sphere of manifestation and operation, and law creates nature."

In this context, then, the cause of nature is spiritual law, and the cause of disease is spiritual. The cure of disease, therefore, is spiritual. On the negative side: "The world, physically, is never to be saved by medicine." Historically, drugs administered to cure disease, have done great harm in doing the opposite. "The doctor, as a mere patcher up of broken constitutions, as the stimulator and galvanizer of decrepit frames, is of no permanent value to the world." The man with a cure-all remedy is a quack.

On the positive side, White pointed out that:

So far as medical science sets itself to the discovery of the laws which control health, so far has it been, and so far will it become, a useful science, and as it discovers true law the drug and the patent medicine will disappear. . . .

and renaming it the science of health, it

is still in the beginning of the inductive period. It has very closely explored the body. If it stops there it stops almost at the beginning. Above, within, and anterior to the body, is the real man, where the productive cause, the spiritual germs, are to be found; and the permanent cure is to be reached in the mind, and thence in the body. . . .

The divine physician did not administer a pill. He gave truth, and it was by the truth he gave that he promised to save the world morally, mentally, physically. . . .[33]

RESTATEMENT OF WHITE'S THOUGHT AS A SOCIAL PHILOSOPHER

Thus far White's philosophical and theological views have been discussed in the setting in which he stated them, and as applications to particular issues. If the readers of the *Beacon* articulated them into a system, each one must do it for himself. The readers of this study have some advantage perhaps over the *Beacon's* subscribers in so far as a certain selection and classification has been applied for purposes of a more orderly presentation and continuity. White wrote several extended theological editorials, but none of them singly or together undertook a formulation of systematic theology. Although hazardous, a brief exposition of his philosophy and theology and its implications for the immediate social scene seems now to be in order. Because White was a newspaper editor, and supposedly the major spokesman for the Democratic party in southwestern Kansas, and the time was the late 19th century, his Swedenborgian inheritance necessarily had undergone a substantial modification. Certainly, it became more realistic when applied to southwestern Kansas than the original, however insistent Swedenborg had been in identifying religion and life.

Although the starting point of White's theology must necessarily be God as creator, he was more intimately concerned with man, the created. The Wichita of 1870-1887 was in need of such concern.[34] There was more truth than exaggeration in his confession after the quarrel with Preacher Kelly, "If we *were* a Christian, we would be awful lonesome." Yet, he still insisted, as the central fact of theology, that man was created in freedom—freedom to choose good or evil. Events do not happen by mere chance, but are effects of causes, yet a man can be held ethically responsible for his conduct only on the assumption of freedom of the will. Aristotle had stated the principle, but had not solved the conflict of cause-effect order and freedom of choice. Philosophers and

33. *Daily Beacon*, May 1, 1885.
34. The subject of White's political philosophy; the role of government separated from church and education, both in theory and in practice in Kansas, 1876-1887, requires a fuller treatment than is possible here. This section, with but few specific citations, undertakes only to restate briefly what has already been written, and to survey in very general terms, as one whole, an outline of what must yet be done.

theologians had failed to solve the dilemma conclusively, and St. Augustine and John Calvin in particular, had added new confusion by the doctrine of predestination.

The Swedenborg-White doctrine of the origin of evil did not recognize that God could be held responsible as creator, and repudiated a personal devil. The origin of evil was self-love; to do evil is sin. In freedom, man had the right to choose evil, but in doing so he alienated himself from God. The emphasis is upon the word himself; he alone is responsible for his condition—God did not punish; God is love.

In view of the fact that man has withdrawn himself from the love of the Lord, can be he convinced of his error, return, and be reconciled? The plan of salvation offered that opportunity by the Atonement, "At-one-ment," to all who would repent and become willing to return to the love of God and of the neighbor by loving and doing good. The path of regeneration was not a sudden endowment of perfection as a free gift, but is a way of life through self-discipline, by the help and love of the Lord. Self-discipline grows through the exercise of the will and understanding by uses. Thus man is saved from sin—from sinning, or committing sin—not from the penalties therefor, but only if he continues through free choice to pursue his life of regeneration. Any form of compulsion operates against the will and freedom of choice and cannot effect regeneration. The doctrine of salvation by faith, or by grace, or merits of others, in a different manner, but as effectively, would deprive the man of his freedom of choice, self-responsibility, through which alone lies the path of regeneration. To do evil is sin, and under the cause-effect principle, sin has consequences, penalties. He is the cause of his own punishment. According to order, effects, penalties, cannot be escaped, shifted, or remitted.

White emphasized monotheism for much the same reason that ES did, but with White the peculiar late 19th century emphasis on the Trinity lent it a special coloring that was not present in the 18th century. The "higher criticism" and the challenge of evolutionary science placed the orthodox version derived from the Council of Nicaea under added strain, even within the ranks of orthodox denominationalism. The Thomas heresy trial was only an indicator that ideas similar to the New Church interpretation had permeated the Trinitarian churches. As White lost no opportunity to point out, the abandonment of the Trinity of Persons doctrine would change the whole theology of the Christian plan of salvation.

Monotheism held other significances which were more conspicuous in White's writing as local editor than in Swedenborg's books. The macrocosm-microcosm analogy was emphasized in man as the image of God; complete within the concepts of the finite as He was complete. Life is religion and religion is life, was not a mere aphorism to be repeated on convenient occasions just for effect. The monotheism of God, by analogy, meant the wholeness of man in his daily life at Wichita. Monogamy and the paternal unity of the family as microcosm were, for him, derivatives of monotheism. The family is the minimum social unit in the divine plan. Philosophic love—a disinterested love, without self interest—is the ruling principle in the universe; love of God for man, parent for child, man for the neighbor. In living according to this principle of disinterested love, man exercises self-restraint—he is self-governing.

The state, whatever its form, is an artificial instrument formed by men. The occasion for the state is man's sinfulness. Out of self-love he encroaches upon his neighbor and his neighbor's property. If only man would return voluntarily to the love of the Lord all occasion for the state would disappear. But a man cannot be compelled; no act committed under duress, or from an appeal to self-love (advantage or reward) can be a moral act. The state is to be tolerated only to the extent to which it is necessary. But what is the nature of the necessity? Only such functions are necessary or to be tolerated as protect or extend man's freedom of individual decision and action, and thereby strengthen his exercise of self-responsibility and self-discipline, and self-government. Although not stated in the form of the Swedenborgian doctrine of equilibrium, the role of government appeared to serve only as the instrument by which social equilibrium might be maintained, that man might be free to exercise his true freedom and responsible choice of action.

Any free gift, regardless of source is a detriment to the man, what White branded as the pauper principle, whether applied to salvation in what is conventionally called theology, excessive parental solicitude for the child, or at the hands of government, poor relief, free medicine, free public schools, free libraries, free passes on railroads for clergy, editors, politicians, or public officials—even free Swedenborgian lectures, as in 1877; "The lecture being free a large number felt under no obligations to attend, and so the audience was small."[35] Such applications of the doctrine of free gifts (without price) may appear, under superficial examination as frustrating, even ridiculous. But, at any rate, they call attention to the logical inconsistencies in

35. *Weekly Beacon*, March 21, 1877.

prevailing human institutions, which is embarrassing, even irritating, because they expose the contradictory rationalizations by which existing institutions and practices are justified. They give a certain point to the cynical doctrine, conspicuously held in modern society, that virtue lies in the action itself, and justification of the accomplished fact is only incidental.

Within the overall framework of this Swedenborgian-White philosophy and theology, the role of government is to protect persons and property but not to educate or reform the man. When the government intervenes to protect, it does so solely for the maintenance of public order and peace, not on the grounds of morals—morals are not a concern of police power. The punishment inflicted is for breech of peace, not to reform the offender's morals. Whenever government goes beyond its legitimate police powers, it makes a political issue of any and all questions that come up for action by the legislature. Thereby they become a part of the policy of the state. Nevertheless, White denied that popular demand for such action legitimized the extension of the penal power into such areas. Man cannot dispossess himself of a natural right. When the liquor question came up in form of the prohibitory amendment and subsequent enforcement legislation, White opposed such assumption of state power on the basis of principle. Mistakenly, the political opponents of liquor restriction and other sumptuary legislation, who acted upon traditional grounds, hailed him as a hero. They were due for a shock. As a Democratic party editor, he was expected to justify, from the traditional point of view, the party stand against prohibition.

The logical and consistent application of White's theory of government, however, did not limit his opposition to governmental intervention to that one area. As government had no jurisdiction over morals, he opposed that aspect of Indian and Morman policy, and foreign policy, corrupt practices acts, public schools, public libraries, public parks, regulation of railroads, monopolies, banking practices, and labor legislation. He denounced the railroad regulation act passed by the legislature in 1883, insisting that it would fail and its failure to reform men would lead to a demand, and the legislature would yield to the demand, for amendatory laws, and that cycle would go on indefinitely just as had occurred in connection with prohibition of the liquor traffic by passing a law.

As an individualist, White was a firm believer in popular government, even though he astonished his community by certain aspects of his theory. The individual possesses absolute rights derived from his spiritual origin. Society being an artificial body is entitled only to relative rights. Participation in the government of society, therefore, is not a right—society can not confer rights, something that it does not itself possess. Society confers duties upon individuals. Not only is office holding a duty, but in the same sense, voting is a duty conferable only upon the individual, not upon classes, races, or sexes as such. Voting is neither a right nor a privilege. White's inability to become a partisan was revealed conspicuously and disconcertingly by his insistence that permanent political parties should not be permitted to exist. "After every election electors should resolve themselves into parties of one man, who should think and act for himself." After each election—and he was writing about political parties, plural, not about the Republican party—their "corrupt machinery should go into the hands of a receiver, and . . . [those] who fatten on party corruption should be driven out into the wilderness to work or starve." [36]

In view of his political theory, the events of his generation were peculiarly distressing as they had to do with government. The first responsibility of the individual was for self-government; to overcome his self-love; to love the neighbor and the Lord, and do good. The first failure of government was with the man himself. All other failures in government followed in sequence, because if each man could succeed in governing himself, no other government was needed. Even the minimum protective functions of government resulted from failure at this initial point—the man. Consequently, all reforms must begin at this point—moral regeneration of the man.

But the trend toward the expansion of the scope of political power, and toward centralization was conspicuous and growing under late 19th century conditions. Man's failure at personal self-government had been used as an excuse for expansion of the scope of political government; local government failing called upon county government, and county government called upon state government, and state called upon the national government—centralization by chain reaction. As mechanization of society encouraged centralization of economic power, so the cumulative effect of failure of each man to govern himself as an individual, and of failure of govern-

36. *Ibid.*, July 13, 1881.

ment at the lower levels geographically, tended to centralize all power at Washington. In consequence, the more remote the seat of governmental power from its theoretical source, the individual man, the less power the man possessed to control it, and the more irresponsible and arbitrary the exercise of that power.

In 1887, when White abandoned the editorial chair in the *Beacon* office, the climax of this phase of the process was being completed in the enactment of the Interstate Commerce Act. Prior to about 1887 the question had been, will the federal government enter the broad field of economic, social, and moral regulation? That question was answered in the affirmative by the Interstate Commerce Act and assorted legislation; big business, food and drugs, immigration restriction on the ground of morals and dangerous political theories, contagious and infectious diseases, polygamy, obscene literature, etc.

The role of the church is to teach spiritual and moral truth. The extent of the demand, therefore, for the government to act in the moral department was an index of the failure of the spiritual and educational forces to function effectively. When ministers and churches entered politics by asking a legislature to enact legislation on public morals, or to enforce such legislation when passed, to that extent there was no longer a separation of church and state.

The role of the schools also was to teach knowledge and morals. The church taught all the people, the schools traditionally taught the children. Education was a responsibility of parents—the family—not of the public generally. White found himself in deeper trouble over his opposition to the free public schools than most any other of his unpopular policies. One ground for his opposition to the pauper free public schools was the argument that the government had no right to tax the property of one man for the benefit of another. Recipients of free education were taught that they had a right to something for nothing, both free without price and a freedom without responsibility. If free education was justified, then he extended the principle logically to the bitter end; why not free clothes, food; or even why not freedom from work? White insisted that the individual, not property, should be held responsible. Freedom meant the right to be ignorant, just as it meant the right to get drunk. So long as a man did not disturb the public peace and order, this theory denied the right of government to intervene.

Among White's arguments against the public schools was their failure at moral education—this charge was leveled at both major educative forces in society, the church and the schools. He insisted that the Kansas penitentiary population has "a higher average of wit, shrewdness, cleverness, sharpness and intelligence . . . than can be found in any other section of the state, if you gather up a crowd promiscuously." Without moral responsibility, White warned that the educated were the state's most dangerous classes.[37]

White vigorously warned against the "itching for more power" by the state teachers' association, their lobbying for appropriation of other people's money, and for a situation where the parents had less power over their own children's education than over the election of the President: "The parents—the community—are now nearly powerless in the clutches of this police system."[38] The Massachusetts and the New England free public school system had been held up as models for the other states, yet, as White pointed out, those states led the country in divorces and courts for punishment of law breakers.[39] Edmunds, the author of the Anti-Polygamy act of 1882, was from New England, where polygamy was practiced in the form of multiple wives in succession, rather than simultaneously, and without safeguarding the children of the divorce type of polygamy.

Libraries as well as schools and churches, White insisted, should be supported by private associations of their patrons. Wichita Library Association operated from February, 1876- late 1885, before it was taken over by the city—"pauperized." The same principle, private association, applied to music, literature, and art. White played the violin—according to his own testimony, very badly. Furthermore, White advocated fighting the saloon, gambling institutions, etc., by providing, on principles similar to support of churches, schools, and libraries, places of entertainment and recreation—something positive, not negative. Freedom of the mind and of the soul (religion) White insisted, could not be a reality without complete separation of the educative forces, all of them, from the state. White made no concessions—to admit the right of the state in any area of religion, morals, or education, meant to place in the power of the state the dictation of what constitutes religion, morals, or education, and the manner in which they are taught; self-perpetuation being the core of motive: "The true church is the still,

37. *Ibid.*, March 12, November 26, 1884.
38. *Daily Beacon*, January 4, 1886.
39. *Weekly Beacon*, March 12, 1884.

small, pleading voice, that awaits the invitation to enter. The police state is the devil that will enter in at all hazards." [40]

In conclusion, regardless of the validity of his theology, there was no question about the fact that White's religion did have relation to life, and his life was a virile expression of his religion. To review his journalistic career is to be compelled to re-examine the whole of society, its ideals and procedures, in fresh perspectives.

40. A selection from extended editorials illustrative of the major propositions in the final summary section: *Weekly Beacon*, July 6, August 10, 1881; May 3, August 9, November 8, 29, 1882; *Daily Beacon*, December 18, 1884; October 16, 1885.

Recent Additions to the Library

Compiled by ALBERTA PANTLE, Librarian

IN ORDER that members of the Kansas State Historical Society and others interested in historical study may know the class of books the Society's library is receiving, a list is printed annually of the books accessioned in its specialized fields.

These books come from three sources, purchase, gift, and exchange, and fall into the following classes: Books by Kansans and about Kansas; books on American Indians and the West, including explorations, overland journeys and personal narratives; genealogy and local history; and books on United States history, biography and allied subjects which are classified as general. The out-of-state city directories received by the Historical Society are not included in this compilation.

The library also receives regularly the publications of many historical societies by exchange, and subscribes to other historical and genealogical publications which are needed in reference work.

The following is a partial list of books which were received from October 1, 1957, through September 30, 1958. Federal and state official publications and some books of a general nature are not included. The total number of books accessioned appears in the report of the Society's secretary printed in the Spring, 1959, issue of *The Kansas Historical Quarterly.*

KANSAS

ADRIAN, ARTHUR A., *Georgina Hogarth and the Dickens Circle.* London, Oxford University Press, 1957. 320p.

ALLIS, MARGUERITE, *Free Soil.* New York, G. P. Putnam's Sons [c1958]. 288p.

APPELL, GEORGE C., *The Man Who Shot Quantrill.* Garden City, N. Y., Doubleday & Company, 1957. 189p.

BEELER, MAXWELL N., *The Garden of Babies, an Answer to Children's Queries About Their Origin.* New York, Exposition Press [c1958]. 122p.

BESSEY, AMOS J., *Diary; Copied From Notes Made During Service in the Civil War* . . . No impr. Typed. Unpaged.

BLAIR, WILLIAM NEWTON, *Gold in Korea.* Topeka, H. M. Ives & Sons, 1957. 140p.

BRADSHAW, ALFRED B., *When the Prairies Were New.* Turon, Kan., Arthur J. Allen, 1957. 96p.

BURGESS, JACKSON, *Pillar of Cloud.* New York, G. P. Putnam's Sons [c1957]. 254p.

BURTON, THOMAS E., and GRACE D. BURTON, *Chamade.* [Topeka] Privately Printed, 1954. 68p.

CAMPBELL, VIRGINIA, *Unexpected Verdict.* New York, Dodd, Mead & Company, 1958. 210p.

CAREZ, HENRY SUMNER, *Poems.* No impr. 27p.

CARTER, E. RUSSELL, *The Gift Is Rich.* New York, Friendship Press [c1955]. 117p.

CASEMENT, DAN DILLON, *Random Recollections; the Life and Times—and Something of the Personal Philosophy—of a 20th Century Cowman.* Kansas City, Mo., Walker Publications, 1955. 111p.

CHILDS, MARQUIS, *Eisenhower: Captive Hero . . .* New York, Harcourt, Brace and Company [c1958]. 310p.

CLAFLIN *Clarion, City Directory, Claflin, Kansas, Sept. 1, 1958.* Claflin, Claflin *Clarion,* 1958. [28]p.

CROOKS, RUTH (WILLIAMS), *The Signature of God.* Kansas City, Mo., Beacon Hill Press [c1957]. 64p.

Cross Reference Directory, Topeka, September, 1957. Independence, Kan., City Publishing Company, c1957. Unpaged.

[DANNER, SCIOTO (IMHOFF)], *Mrs. Danner's Fourth Quilt Book.* [El Dorado] n. p. [c1958]. 23p.

————, *Mrs. Danner's Third Quilt Book.* [El Dorado] Privately Printed [c1954]. 26p.

DAUGHTERS OF THE AMERICAN REVOLUTION, COFACHIQUE CHAPTER, IOLA, *Lineages and Bible Records [Copied by Kate B. Shields].* No impr. Typed. [45]p.

————, EUNICE STERLING CHAPTER, WICHITA, *William & Mary Parke of Hunterdon County, New Jersey, With Descendants & In-Laws . . . [Copied by Mrs. Hal M. Black].* Wichita, n. p., 1957. Typed. 170p.

————, FLORES DEL SOL CHAPTER, WICHITA, *Tombstone Inscriptions From Afton Cemetery in Afton Township, Located One Mile South and Two Miles West of Goddard, Sedgwick County, Kansas . . . 1874-1956.* Wichita n. p., 1958. Typed. 15p.

————, ISABELLA WELDIN CHAPTER, AUGUSTA, *Tombstone Inscriptions of Sutton Cemetery, Northeast of Augusta, Kansas. Dates From 1798 to 1945.* No impr. Typed. 10p.

————, KANSAS SOCIETY, *The Kansas Centennial of Statehood, 1861-1961.* No impr. Folder.

————, KANSAS SOCIETY, *Proceedings of the Sixtieth Annual State Conference, March 13, 14, 15, 1958, Topeka, Kansas.* No impr. 235p.

DAVIS, CLYDE L., *A Kansan at Large.* Forest Hills, N. Y., Bernice Carter Davis, 1924. 143p.

DELAWARE SQUATTER ASSOCIATION, *Constitution of the Delaware Squatter Association Embracing All the Laws Passed by the Different Squatter Meetings From June 10, to Dec. 2, 1854.* Leavenworth, K. T., Eastin & Adams, 1855. Photostat Copy. 8p.

DERBY, FLORENCE, *Rocks and Roses.* Grand Rapids, Mich., William B. Eerdmans Publishing Company [c1957]. 187p.

DE VRIES, PETER, *The Mackerel Plaza.* Boston, Little, Brown and Company [c1958]. 260p.

DOBBS, MARY E., *Kansas Voters' Manual, Third Edition, Revised July, 1920.* [Wichita, Author, c1920.] 83p.

EATON, QUAINTANCE, *Opera Caravan, Adventures of the Metropolitan on Tour, 1883-1956.* New York, Farrar, Straus and Cudahy, 1957. 400p.

EHRLICH, ELIZABETH, *All Things Lovely, and Other Verses.* Berkeley, Cal., Privately Printed, 1957. 18p.

ENGLISH, E. LOIS, *Of Course I've Faith; Verses of Affirmation.* New York, Exposition Press [c1958]. 119p.

———, *On Wings of Faith, Stories of Kansas Pioneers and Other Tales.* New York, Exposition Press [c1956]. 166p.

EUDORA, LION's CLUB, *Eudora Centennial Magazine, 1957.* N. p., 1957. 52p.

FELTON, RALPH A., *Hope Rises From the Land.* New York, Friendship Press [c1955]. 135p.

FITZGERALD, EARL ARCHIBALD, *Heart's Desire.* N. p., 1956. Unpaged.

———, *Voices in the Night.* Bellingham, Wash., Pioneer Printing Company [c1948]. 203p.

FLEMING, ROSCOE, *The Man Who Reached the Moon, and Other Poems, Including "Kansas"* . . . [Denver, Golden Bell Press, c1957.] 125p.

FLORIAN, SISTER MARY, *Chamber Music.* New York, Pageant Press [c1957]. 142p.

FLOYD, WILLIAM H., 3rd, *Phantom Riders of the Pony Express.* Philadelphia, Dorrance & Company [c1958]. 142p.

Fort Riley, Its Historic Past, 1853-1953. [Fort Riley, U. S. Army] n. d. Unpaged.

FORT SCOTT, FIRST PRESBYTERIAN CHURCH, *History of the First Presbyterian Church of Fort Scott, Kansas* . . . Fort Scott, *Monitor* Binding and Printing Company, 1909. 79p.

FRANCIS, MRS. HELEN D., *Double Reverse.* New York, Doubleday & Company, 1958. 214p.

FRANKLIN, FRIEDA K., *None but the Brave.* New York, Crown Publishers [c1958]. 278p.

FRANKLIN, MIRIAM, *Rehearsal, the Principles and Practice for the Stage.* Englewood Cliffs, N. J., Prentice-Hall [c1950]. 327p.

FRIENDS, SOCIETY OF, *Seventy-Fifth Anniversary Argonia Friends Meeting, Sept. 29, 1957.* N. p. [1957]. Unpaged.

GARD, ROBERT E., *Run to Kansas.* New York, Duell, Sloan and Pearce [c1958]. 143p.

GIBSON, WILLIAM, *The Miracle Worker.* New York, Alfred A. Knopf, 1957. 131p.

GILBAUGH, JOHN W., *The Bull With the Golden Horns.* San Jose, Cal., Modern Education Publishers [c1958]. 246p.

Golden Anniversary of the Ordination of The Reverend Timothy J. O'Sullivan, Pastor of the Church of the Blessed Sacrament, June 12, 1955, Wichita, Kansas. Wichita, n. p., 1955. Unpaged.

HADLEY, JOHN M., *Clinical and Counseling Psychology.* New York, Alfred A. Knopf, 1958. [702]p.

HARLAN, HARRY V., *One Man's Life With Barley* . . . New York, Exposition Press [c1957]. 223p.

HARRINGTON, HORACIO J., and ARMANDO F. LEANZA, *Ordovician Trilobites of Argentina*, Lawrence, University of Kansas Press, 1957. 276p.

HENRY, IONA, with FRANK S. MEAD, *Triumph Over Tragedy.* [Westwood, N. J.] Fleming H. Revell Company [c1957]. 125p.

HEWITT, ALBA ASHBY, *Riding the Rockies.* New York, Vantage Press [c1957]. 231p.
History of the Original Company "A" 110th Engineers, 35th Division, A. E. F., From June 21, 1917 to May 3, 1919. No impr. Unpaged.
HOLLISTER, OVANDO J., *Boldly They Rode, a History of the First Colorado Regiment of Volunteers.* Lakewood, Colo., Golden Press, 1949. 190p.
HORTON, SCOTT, *Even the Leaves.* Dallas, Triangle Publishing Company [c1957]. 60p.
HUBER, FLORENCE M., *In a Village Garden.* Columbus, Trowbridge Printing Company, c1956. 14p.
HUNT, ELSIE DENEAN, *The Ship of Peace.* New York, Pageant Press [c1957]. 178p.
INGE, WILLIAM, *The Dark at the Top of the Stairs.* New York, Random House [c1958]. 108p.
ISELY, FLORA KUNIGUNDE (DUNCAN), *Lincoln's Teacher.* Great Barrington, Mass., Advance Publishing Company [c1958]. 177p.
JACKSON, MARY VIOLET, *Spiritual Truths, Spiritual Law.* New York, Vantage Press [c1956]. 176p.
JAMES, JESSE, JR., *The Facsimile Edition of Jesse James, My Father, the First and Only True Story of His Adventures Ever Written.* New York, Frederick Fell, Publishers [c1957]. 198p.
JOHNS, GLOVER S., JR., *The Clay Pigeons of St. Lo.* Harrisburg, Pa., Military Service Publishing Company [c1958]. 257p.
JOHNSON, VIRGINIA ARMSTRONG, *Gardner, Where the Trails Divide.* Gardner, Gardner Centennial Committee, 1957. 73p.
JONAS, CARL, *Our Revels Now Are Ended.* New York, W. W. Norton & Company [c1957]. 343p.
JONES, SCHUYLER, *Under the African Sun.* London, Hurst & Blackett [1956]. 256p.
KANSAS AUTHORS CLUB, *1958 Yearbook.* No impr. 109p.
————, *1957 Yearbook.* No impr. 96p.
KANSAS CITY, FIRST PILGRIM CONGREGATIONAL CHURCH, *Pilgrim Heritage, 1858-1958* [by Don D. Ballou], N. p. [1958?]. Unpaged.
KARSON, MARC, *American Labor Unions and Politics.* Carbondale, Southern Illinois University Press, 1958. 358p.
KEITH, HAROLD, *Rifles for Watie.* New York, Thomas Y. Crowell [c1957]. 332p.
KELLER, ALLAN, *Thunder at Harper's Ferry.* Englewood Cliffs, N. J., Prentice-Hall [c1958]. 282p.
KERSEY, RALPH T., *Buffalo Jones (a True Biography).* [Garden City, Elliott Printers, c1958.] 184p.
KICK, LENI PELLEGRINI, *The House on Walnut Grove, the Gibbons Children in Winter.* New York, Vantage Press [c1958]. 139p.
KIRKS, M. M., *He Called and I Answered.* No impr. 84p.
KIRTLAND, ELIZABETH, *Buttons in the Back.* New York, Vanguard Press [c1958]. [160]p.
KLINK, THOMAS W., *Clergyman's Guide to Recognizing Serious Mental Illness.* New York, National Association for Mental Health, n. d. [12]p.
LEACH, GABRIELLE (HINMAN), *Congregationalism and Fairmount Church.* Wichita, Fairmount Community Church, Congregational, 1958. Unpaged.

LEAVENWORTH, PILGRIM UNITED CHURCH OF CHRIST, *A Short Historical Sketch of Pilgrim Church (United Church of Christ), Leavenworth, Kansas* . . . N. p., 1958. Unpaged.

————, SALEM CHURCH, *Salem Church (Evangelical and Reformed), 1887-1937* . . . *Fiftieth Anniversary Memento*. St. Louis, Eden Publishing House, n. d. 25p.

LEWIS, GEORGE, and JOAN LEWIS, *Rolling in the Isles*. Lawrence, Allen Press [c1957]. 135p.

LOVEWELL DAM DEDICATION COMMITTEE, *Lovewell Dam Dedication Brochure*. Belleville, *Telescope* Publishing Company [1958?]. Unpaged.

LUNGREN, MAURICE C., *A Study of the Use of Editorial Expression in the Weekly Newspapers of Kansas for the Years 1925, 1940, and 1955*. A Thesis Submitted to the William Allen White School of Journalism and Public Information and the Faculty of the Graduate School of the University of Kansas in Partial Fulfillment of the Requirements for the Degree of Master of Science. N. p., 1957. Typed. 88p.

[LYMAN, EUNICE], *In Memoriam of Professor Linnaeus A. Thomas, Born October 8, 1845, Died November 11, 1881*. [Topeka, Kansas State Teachers Association, 1882.] [7]p.

[MCCLOUD, MRS. MARGARET], *Collection of Original Poems Used on "God's Half Hour."* No impr. Unpaged.

MCCRACKEN, HAROLD, *The Charles M. Russell Book, the Life and Work of the Cowboy Artist*. Garden City, N. Y., Doubleday & Company, 1957. 236p.

MALLORY, AILEEN, *Paying Projects for Clubs*. Minneapolis, T. S. Denison & Company [c1957]. 186p.

MATHER, WILLIAM D., *The Revolt of Little Wolf's Northern Cheyennes*. A Thesis Submitted to the Graduate School in Partial Fulfillment of the Requirements for the Degree of Master of Arts, Department of History, the University of Wichita. Wichita, University of Wichita, 1958. Typed. 127p.

MENNINGER, WILLIAM C., *How You Grow Up*. New York, Sterling Publishing Company [c1957]. 187p.

————, and HARRY LEVINSON, *Human Understanding in Industry, a Guide for Supervisors*. Chicago, Science Research Associates, c1956. 104p.

MIDDLETON, HARRY, and WARREN KIEFER, *Pax*. New York, Random House [c1958]. [280]p.

MILTONVALE, FIRST PRESBYTERIAN CHURCH, *Seventy-Fifth Anniversary of First Presbyterian Church, Miltonvale, Kansas, 1882-1957* [by Fannie Palmer]. No impr. Unpaged.

MONTGOMERY, SAPHRONIA G., *The Christian Woman, a Religious Miscellany*. New York, Exposition Press [c1954]. 58p.

NEMER, ALYCE E., *Cooks and Capitols, a Book of Foods and Facts for Folk*. Wichita, n. p., c1958. 56p.

NORTON, IMMANUEL LUTHERAN CHURCH, *Fiftieth Anniversary* . . . *1908-1958*. N. p. [1958?]. 15p.

[OMER, GEORGE E., JR.], *An Army Hospital From Horses to Helicopters*. [Fort Riley, U. S. Army] n. d. [106]p.

OSAWATOMIE, CHAMBER OF COMMERCE, *John Brown Memorial State Park and Other Historic Spots in and Around Osawatomie*. No impr. Folder.

PAXTON, JUNE LEMERT, *My Life on the Mojave*. New York, Vantage Press [c1957]. 168p.

PERRINGS, MYRA, *The Circle Is Forever.* Dallas, Triangle Publishing Company [c1957]. 40p.

PETERSON, ELLEN (WELANDER), *A Kansan's Enterprise (the Story of Enterprise, Kansas).* Enterprise, Enterprise Baptist Church [c1957]. 260p.

PHILLIPS, EULA MARK, *Chuco, the Boy With the Good Name.* Chicago, Follett Publishing Company [c1957]. 141p.

Polk's Topeka (Shawnee County, Kansas) City Directory, 1958, Including Shawnee County Taxpayers . . . Kansas City, Mo., R. L. Polk and Company, c1958. [1604]p.

ROBINSON, ALICE M., *The Unbelonging.* New York, Macmillan Company, 1958. 165p.

RULEY, A. N., comp., *Ruley's Directory, Hiawatha City, the Business Man's Guide, July, 1915* . . . [Hiawatha] Compiler, 1915. Unpaged.

RUSSELL, ETHEL GREEN, *Deep Bayou.* Lowell, Mass., Alentour House, 1941. 63p.

————, *Land of Evangeline.* Cincinnati, Talaria, 1950. 78p.

SCHADT, RODNEY MARVIN, *The Independent Rural High School District in Kansas.* A Dissertation Submitted to the Graduate School [of] Northwestern University in Partial Fulfillment of the Requirements for the Degree Doctor of Education. N. p., c1957. Typed. 326p. Microfilm. 1 Vol. on 1 Reel.

SCHAEFERS, WILLIAM, *Catholic Highlights of Europe (Kansans Abroad).* Boston, Christopher Publishing House [c1956]. 205p.

SCHUMACHER, ALVIN J., *What Will I Be?* Milwaukee, Bruce Publishing Company [c1957]. Unpaged.

SEIFERT, WILLIAM E., JR., *Tempest Tossed.* New York, Vantage Press [c1958]. 113p.

SHARP, W. A. SEWARD, *History of Kansas Baptists.* [Kansas City, Kan., Kansas City Seminary Press] 1939. 259p.

SHIRLEY, GLENN, *Pawnee Bill, a Biography of Major Gordon W. Lillie.* Albuquerque, University of New Mexico, 1958. 256p.

SHOEMAKER, RALPH J., *The Presidents Words, an Index. Vol. 3, Eisenhower, 1956. Vol. 4, Eisenhower, 1957.* Louisville [Elsie DeGraff Shoemaker and Ralph J. Shoemaker, c1957, 1958.] 2 Vols.

SOCOLOFSKY, HOMER E., ed., *Bibliography of Theses and Dissertations Pertaining to Kansas History* . . . Manhattan, Kansas State College, 1958. 74p.

SPENCER, CHARLES, ed., *Atchison's Storm Disaster, Friday, July 11 and Wednesday, July 30, 1958, Photographed by Jess Torbett.* Revised Edition. Atchison, Sutherland Printing Company [1958?]. Unpaged.

STATE CONVENTION OF THE COLORED PEOPLE OF KANSAS, *Proceedings of a Convention of Colored Citizens, Held in the City of Lawrence, October 17, 1866.* Leavenworth, Evening *Bulletin* Steam Power Printing House, 1866. Photostat Copy. 8p.

STOUT, RUTH, *Company Coming, Six Decades of Hospitality, Do-It-Yourself and Otherwise.* New York, Exposition Press [c1958]. 155p.

STRONKS, JAMES B., *William Dean Howells, Ed Howe, and The Story of a Country Town.* (Reprinted from *American Literature,* Vol. 29, No. 4, January, 1958.) [6]p.

STUMBO, CHARLES WILLIAM, *Clouds Over Destiny.* New York, Vantage Press [c1957]. 241p.

THOLEN, HERMAN J., *History of St. Joseph's Council No. 1325, Hays, Kansas, Knights of Columbus, Commemorating the Golden Jubilee of Its Founding, May 17, 1908.* N. p. [1958?]. 35p.

TOPEKA, HIGH SCHOOL, *Topeka High School, 1955-1956, General Information and Curriculum Handbook.* [Topeka] n. p., n. d. Mimeographed. [200]p.

———, ORDINANCES, 1957, *The Topeka Code of Revised Ordinances, 1957 . . . Prepared by the League of Kansas Municipalities Under the Supervision of the City Attorney . . .* Topeka, Hall Lithographing Company, n. d. Unpaged.

TROW, CLIFFORD WAYNE, *The Lecompton Conspiracy; a History of the Lecompton Constitution Movement in Kansas and the Nation, 1857 and 1858.* A Thesis Submitted to the Faculty of the Graduate School of the University of Colorado in Partial Fulfillment of the Requirements for the Degree Master of Arts. N. p., 1958. Typed. 181p.

TUCKER, SAMUEL, *Price Raid Through Linn County, Kansas, October 24-25, 1864.* N. p. [c1958]. 17p.

Union Cemetery, Winfield, Kansas. No impr. Typed. [3]p.

VAIL, JANE, *Becky's Little World.* New York, Exposition Press [c1957]. 48p.

VAIL, THOMAS HUBBARD, *Annual Address . . . Before the Diocesan Convention at Fort Scott, May 10, 1871.* Lawrence, Journal Book and Job Printing House, 1871. 21p.

VAN NES, MARY F., *Into the Wind.* Philadelphia, J. B. Lippincott Company [c1957]. 224p.

WALTON, WILLIAM M., *Life and Adventures of Ben Thompson, the Famous Texan . . .* Houston, Frontier Press of Texas, 1954. 232p.

WARK, HOMER E., *The Religion of a Soldier.* No impr. 23p.

WELLMAN, MANLY WADE, *Fastest on the River, the Great Race Between the "Natchez" and the "Robert E. Lee."* New York, Henry Holt and Company [c1957]. 234p.

WELLMAN, PAUL ISELIN, *Ride the Red Earth.* Garden City, N. Y., Doubleday and Company, 1958. 448p.

WOOLF, MAURICE D., and JEANNE A. WOOLF, *Remedial Reading, Teaching and Treatment.* New York, McGraw-Hill Book Company, 1957. 424p.

WYATT, P. J., *"I'm Not Selling Anything"—Some Folklore From Kansas.* A Thesis Submitted to the Graduate School in Partial Fulfillment of the Requirements for the Degree of Master of Arts. Bloomington, Indiana University, 1956. Typed. 178p.

AMERICAN INDIANS AND THE WEST

ADAMS, RAMON F., comp. and ed., *The Best of the American Cowboy.* Norman, University of Oklahoma Press [c1957]. 289p.

ALEXANDER, LLOYD, *Border Hawk, August Bondi.* N. p., Farrar, Straus and Cudahy [c1958]. 182p.

BARTHOLOMEW, ED., *Biographical Album of Western Gunfighters . . .* Houston, Frontier Press of Texas, 1958. Unpaged.

BLASINGAME, IKE, *Dakota Cowboy, My Life in the Old Days.* New York, G. P. Putnam's Sons [c1958]. 317p.

BROWN, DEE, *The Gentle Tamers, Women of the Old Wild West.* New York, G. P. Putnam's Sons [c1958]. 317p.

CARPENTER, WILL TOM, *Lucky 7, a Cowman's Autobiography,* Edited . . . by Elton Miles. Austin, University of Texas Press [c1957]. 119p.

CARTER, KATE B., *Riders of the Pony Express,* Special Edition. N. p., Pony Express Mid-Century Memorial Commission of Utah [1952]. 54p.

CROGHAN, GEORGE, *Army Life on the Western Frontier, Selections From the Official Reports Made Between 1826 and 1845,* Edited by Francis Paul Prucha. Norman, University of Oklahoma Press [c1958]. 187p.

CROY, HOMER, *Trigger Marshal, the Story of Chris Madsen.* New York, Duell, Sloan and Pearce [c1958]. 267p.

DAVIS, BURKE, *Jeb Stuart, the Last Cavalier.* New York, Rinehart & Company [c1957]. 462p.

DEBARTHE, JOE, *Life and Adventures of Frank Grouard.* Norman, University of Oklahoma Press [c1958]. 268p.

EWERS, JOHN C., *The Blackfeet, Raiders on the Northwestern Plains.* Norman, University of Oklahoma Press [c1958]. 348p.

FIELD, MATTHEW C., *Prairie and Mountain Sketches,* Collected by Clyde and Mae Reed Porter . . . Norman, University of Oklahoma Press [c1957]. 239p.

GARNSEY, MORRIS E., *America's New Frontier, the Mountain West.* New York, Alfred A. Knopf, 1950. [323]p.

GOTTFREDSON, PETER, comp. and ed., *History of Indian Depredations in Utah.* [Salt Lake City, Skelton Publishing Company, c1919.] [369]p.

HAFEN, LEROY R., and ANN W. HAFEN, eds., *The Utah Expedition, 1857-1858; a Documentary Account of the United States Military Movement Under Colonel Albert Sidney Johnston* . . . Glendale, Cal., Arthur H. Clark Company, 1958. 375p. (*The Far West and the Rockies Historical Series, 1820-1875,* Vol. 8.)

HAGAN, WILLIAM T., *The Sac and Fox Indians.* Norman, University of Oklahoma Press [c1958]. 287p.

HANSEN, MARCUS L., *Old Fort Snelling, 1819-1858.* Minneapolis, Ross & Haines, 1958. 270p.

HARDIN, JOHN WESLEY, *The Life of John Wesley Hardin, From the Original Manuscript as Written by Himself.* Seguin, Tex., Smith & Moore, 1896. 144p.

HARPENDING, ASBURY, *The Great Diamond Hoax and Other Stirring Incidents* . . . Edited by James H. Wilkins. Norman, University of Oklahoma Press [c1958]. 211p.

HEAP, GWINN HARRIS, *Central Route to the Pacific* . . . Edited by LeRoy R. Hafen and Ann W. Hafen. Glendale, Cal., Arthur H. Clark Company, 1957. 346p.

HOIG, STAN, *The Humor of the American Cowboy.* Caldwell, Idaho, Caxton Printers, 1958. 193p.

HOWARD, ROBERT WEST, ed., *This is the West.* New York, Rand McNally & Company [c1957]. 248p.

HUNT, AURORA, *Major General James Henry Carleton, 1814-1873, Western Frontier Dragoon.* Glendale, Cal., Arthur H. Clark Company, 1958. 390p.

HUNTER, JOHN D., *Manners and Customs of Several Indian Tribes Located West of the Mississippi* . . . Minneapolis, Ross & Haines, 1957. 402p.

JACKSON, WILLIAM HENRY, *Pageant of Pioneers . . . by Clarence S. Jackson.* Minden, Neb., The Harold Warp Pioneer Village [c1958]. 89p.
JAHNS, PAT, *The Frontier World of Doc Holliday, Faro Dealer, From Dallas to Deadwood.* New York, Hastings House [c1957]. 305p.
KEITH, ELMER, *Sixguns by Keith, the Standard Reference Work.* Harrisburg, Pa., Stackpole Company [c1955]. 308p.
KUHLMAN, CHARLES, *Did Custer Disobey Orders at the Battle of the Little Big Horn?* Harrisburg, Pa., Stackpole Company [c1957]. 56p.
LEE, NELSON, *Three Years Among the Comanches, the Narrative of Nelson Lee, the Texas Ranger.* Norman, University of Oklahoma Press [c1957]. 179p.
MCREYNOLDS, EDWIN C., *The Seminoles.* Norman, University of Oklahoma Press [c1957]. 397p.
MALONE, HENRY THOMPSON, *Cherokees of the Old South, a People in Transition.* Athens, University of Georgia Press [c1956]. 238p.
MARQUIS, THOMAS BAILEY, *Rain-in-the-Face and Curly, the Crow.* N. p., c1934. [8]p.
———, *She Watched Custer's Last Battle . . .* N. p., c1933. [8]p.
———, *Sitting Bull and Gall, the Warrior.* N. p., c1934. [8]p.
———, *Sketch Story of the Custer Battle . . .* N. p., c1933. [8]p.
———, *Two Days After the Custer Battle . . .* N. p., c1935. [8]p.
———, *Which Indian Killed Custer? Custer Soldiers Not Buried.* N. p., c1933. 10p.
MARRIOTT, ALICE, *María: the Potter on San Ildefonso.* Norman, University of Oklahoma Press [c1948]. 294p.
MASTERSON, WILLIAM BARCLAY, *Famous Gunfighters of the Western Frontier . . .* Houston, Frontier Press of Texas, 1957. 112p.
MILLER, DAVID HUMPHREYS, *Custer's Fall, the Indian Side of the Story.* New York, Duell, Sloan and Pearce [c1957]. 271p.
MOORHEAD, MAX L., *New Mexico's Royal Road, Trade and Travel on the Chihuahua Trail.* Norman, University of Oklahoma Press [c1958]. 234p.
MUMEY, NOLIE, *James Pierson Beckwourth, 1856-1866 . . . a History of the Latter Years of His Life.* Denver, Old West Publishing Company, 1957. 188p.
———, *March of the First Dragoons to the Rocky Mountains in 1835, the Diaries and Maps of Lemuel Ford . . .* Denver, Eames Brothers Press, 1957. [116]p.
MURRAY, JOHN J., *The Heritage of the Middle West.* Norman, University of Oklahoma Press [c1958]. 303p.
NEIDER, CHARLES, ed., *The Great West.* New York, Coward-McCann [c1958]. 457p.
PEYTON, JOHN ROWZÉE, *3 Letters From St. Louis.* Denver, Libros Escogidos, 1958. 45p.
POWELL, LAWRENCE CLARK, *Books, West Southwest; Essays on Writers, Their Books and Their Land.* Los Angeles, Ward Ritchie Press [c1957]. 157p.
———, *A Southwestern Century, a Bibliography of One Hundred Books of Non Fiction About the Southwest . . .* Van Nuys, Cal., J. E. Reynolds [c1958]. 29p.
PRATT, FLETCHER, *Civil War on Western Waters.* New York, Henry Holt and Company [c1956]. 255p.

PRETTYMAN, W. S., *Indian Territory, a Frontier Photographic Record, Selected and Edited by Robert E. Cunningham.* Norman, University of Oklahoma Press [c1957]. 174p.

PREUSS, CHARLES, *Exploring With Frémont . . . Translated and Edited by Erwin G. and Elizabeth K. Gudde.* Norman, University of Oklahoma Press [c1958]. 162p.

REMINGTON, FREDERIC, *'Buckskins,' Portraits of the Old West; the Original Folio of Eight Color Prints Superbly Reproduced.* [New York, Penn Prints, c1956.] 8 Broadsides.

REYNOLDS, J. E., *History of the Westerners.* [Los Angeles] Los Angeles Corral of the Westerners [1957]. Unpaged.

RICKEY, DON, *War in the West—the Indian Campaigns.* Crow Agency, Mont., Custer Battlefield Historical Museum Association [c1956]. 37p.

RISTER, CARL COKE, *Comanche Bondage; Dr. John Charles Beale's Settlement . . . in Southern Texas of the 1830's With an Annotated Reprint of Sarah Ann Horn's Narrative . . .* Glendale, Cal., Arthur H. Clark Company, 1955. 210p.

SANDOZ, MARI, *The Cattlemen, From the Rio Grande Across the Far Marias.* New York, Hastings House [c1958]. 527p.

SHIRLEY, GLENN, *Buckskin and Spurs, a Gallery of Frontier Rogues and Heroes.* New York, Hastings House [c1958]. 191p.

SOLLID, ROBERTA BEED, *Calamity Jane, a Study in Historical Criticism.* [Helena, Mont.] Western Press, c1958. 147p.

TANNER, CLARA LEE, *Southwest Indian Painting.* Tucson, University of Arizona Press [c1957]. 157p.

TAYLOR, Ross McLAURY, *We Were There on the Chisholm Trail. Historical Consultant, Stanley Vestal.* New York, Grosset & Dunlap [1957]. 176p.

TEMPLE, WAYNE C., *Indian Villages of the Illinois Country; Historic Tribes.* Springfield, Printed by Authority of the State of Illinois, 1958. 218p.

THORP, RAYMOND W., and ROBERT BUNKER, *Crow Killer, the Saga of Liver-Eating Johnson.* [Bloomington] Indiana University Press [c1958]. 190p.

WALTON, WILLIAM M., *Life and Adventures of Ben Thompson, the Famous Texan.* Houston, Frontier Press of Texas, 1954. 232p.

WATERS, FRANK, *Masked Gods, Navaho and Pueblo Ceremonialism.* [Albuquerque] University of New Mexico Press [c1950]. 438p.

WEBB, WILLIAM S., and RAYMOND S. BABY, *The Adena People, No. 2.* N. p., Ohio Historical Society [c1957]. 123p.

WESTERMEIER, CLIFFORD P., *Who Rush to Glory, the Cowboy Volunteers of 1898 . . .* Caldwell, Idaho, Caxton Printers, 1958. 272p.

WESTERNERS, DENVER, *1956 Brand Book of the Denver Westerners.* Denver, The Westerners, 1957. 383p.

———, LOS ANGELES, *Brand Book, Book Number 7.* [Los Angeles, The Los Angeles Westerners, c1957.] 293p.

WHEAT, CARL I., *Mapping the Transmississippi West, 1540-1861, Vol. 1, Spanish Entrada to the Louisiana Purchase, 1540-1804.* San Francisco, Institute of Historical Cartography, 1957. 264p.

WISTER, OWEN, *Owen Wister Out West; His Journals and Letters, Edited by Fanny Wister.* [Chicago] University of Chicago Press [c1958]. 269p.

GENEALOGY AND LOCAL HISTORY

ALVORD, SAMUEL MORGAN, *A Genealogy of the Descendants of Alexander Alvord* . . . Webster, N. Y., A. D. Andrew, 1908. 823p.

BEIRNE, FRANCIS F., *Baltimore, a Picture Story, 1858-1958* . . . Compiled Under the Auspices of the Maryland Historical Society . . . New York, Hastings House [c1957]. 153p.

BELL, RAYMOND MARTIN, *Heads of Families in Mifflin County, Pa., 1790 (Including Present Mifflin, Juniata, and Part of Centre County)* . . . Lewistown, Pa., n. p., 1958. Mimeographed. 30p.

―――, *Supplement to the Baskins-Baskin Family* . . . Washington, Pa., n. p., 1958. 102p.

BOWEN, RICHARD LEBARON, *Massachusetts Records, a Handbook for Genealogists, Historians, Lawyers, and Other Researchers.* Rehoboth, Privately Printed, 1957. 66p.

BRAND, DONALD D., *History of Scotts Bluffs, Nebraska.* Berkeley, Cal., Department of the Interior, National Park Service, Field Division of Education, 1934. 83p.

BRIMLOW, GEORGE FRANCIS, *Harney County, Oregon, and Its Range Land.* Portland, Binfords & Mort [c1951]. 316p.

BRINK, BENJAMIN MYER, *The Early History of Saugerties, 1660-1825.* Kingston, N. Y., R. W. Anderson & Son, 1902. 365p.

BROWER, BLANCHE FRENCH, comp., *French Geneology, 1798-1957.* [Scott City, Kan., *News Chronicle* Printing Company] 1957. 20p.

BROWN, MARGUERITE, and VERNON BROWN, *Ewing—McCulloch—Buchanan Genealogy.* Dallas, Royal Publishing Company [c1957]. 110p.

BUNCE, JULIA LOCKE FRAME, *Some of the Descendants of David Frame-Fraim and His Wife, Catherine Miller.* [Ann Arbor, Mich., Edwards Brothers, c1953.] 238p.

CARR, NANON LUCILE, comp., *Marriage Records of Clay County, Missouri, 1822-1852.* N. p., Compiler, c1957. Mimeographed. 78p.

―――, comp., *Marriage Records of Clinton County, Missouri, 1833-1870.* N. p., Compiler, c1955. Mimeographed. 89p.

―――, comp., *Wills and Administrations of Clinton County, Missouri, 1833-1870.* N. p., Compiler, c 1954. Mimeographed. 54p.

CHARLESTON, FREE LIBRARY, *Index to Wills of Charleston County, South Carolina, 1671-1868.* Charleston, Charleston Free Library, 1950. 324p.

CHILDS, JAMES RIVES, *Reliques of the Rives (Ryves)* . . . Lynchburg, Va., J. P. Bell Company, 1929. 750p.

CLIFT, G. GLENN, *The "Corn Stalk" Militia of Kentucky, 1792-1811* . . . Frankfort, Kentucky Historical Society, 1957. 265p.

Cody Family in America, 1698; Descendants of Philip and Martha, Massachusetts. N. p., Lydia S. Cody, 1954. 257p.

Commemorative Biographical Record of Northeastern Pennsylvania Including Counties of Susquehanna, Wayne, Pike and Monroe . . . Chicago, J. H. Beers & Company, 1900. 1852p.

COMSTOCK, JOHN MOORE, *Chelsea, the Origin of Chelsea, Vermont, and a Record of Its Institutions and Individuals.* N. p., 1944. 62p.

CONDIT, JOTHAM H., and EBEN CONDIT, *Genealogical Record of the Condit Family, Descendants of John Cunditt* . . . N. p., Privately Printed, n. d. 470p.

COPE, GILBERT, comp., *Genealogy of the Smedley Family, Descended From George and Sarah Smedley, Settlers in Chester County, Pennsylvania* . . . Lancaster, Pa., Wickersham Printing Company, 1901. 1000p.

COPPER, WALTER G., *Official History of Fulton County [Georgia].* N. p., History Commission, c1934. 912p.

COX, STANLEY M., comp., *Joseph Cox, Ancestors and Descendants.* N. p., 1955. 144p.

CRIDER, MRS. GUSSIE WAYMIRE, and EDWARD C. CRIDER, eds., *Four Generations of the Family of Strangeman Hutchins and His Wife Elizabeth Cox, as Known January 10, 1935* . . . [Kokomo, Ind.] Privately Printed, n. d. 20p.

DARDEN, NEWTON JASPER, comp., *Darden Family History With Notes on Ancestry of Allied Families* . . . No impr. 190p.

DARTER, OSCAR H., *Colonial Fredericksburg and Neighborhood in Perspective.* New York, Twayne Publishers [c1957]. 333p.

DAUGHTERS OF THE AMERICAN REVOLUTION, ILLINOIS SOCIETY, *Illinois State Directory of Members and Ancestors* . . . N. p., Society, 1957. 556p.

DAVIS, BAILEY FULTON, *Index to Sixth Edition of History of Kentucky, by Perrin, Battle, and Kniffin, Published in 1887* . . . N. p., c1956. Mimeographed. 67p.

DAVIS, EARL H., comp., *Hobson, Descendants of George and Elizabeth Hobson* . . . Long Beach, Cal., n. p., 1957. 323p.

DAYTON, ALTA ALLDREDGE, *Record of the Posterity of Samuel Harrison Smith and Caroline Mooney Smith and Mary Ellen Batman Smith* . . . N. p., 1957. [193]p.

Descendants of Nicholas Perkins of Virginia. [Ann Arbor, Mich., Edwards Brothers, c1957.] 700p.

DE WOLFE, EDITH, ed., *History of Putney, Vermont, 1753-1953.* Putney, The Fortnightly Club, 1953. 221p.

DILLS, R. S., *History of Greene County . . . and the State of Ohio* . . . Dayton, Odell & Mayer, 1881. 1018p.

DORMAN, JOHN FREDERICK, *Orange County, Virginia, Will Book 1, 1735-1743.* Washington, D. C., n. p., 1958. Mimeographed. 72p.

DOUGHTIE, BEATRICE MACKEY, *The Mackeys (Variously Spelled) and Allied Families.* N. p., Privately Printed [c1957]. 1002p.

DUTCH SETTLERS SOCIETY OF ALBANY, *Yearbook, Vols. 32 and 33, 1956-1958.* Albany, N. Y., [Society, 1958]. 57p.

DUTCHESS COUNTY [NEW YORK] HISTORICAL SOCIETY, *Year Book, Vol. 41, 1956.* N. p. [c1958]. 73p.

EAST TENNESSEE HISTORICAL SOCIETY, *Publications, No. 29, 1957.* Knoxville, Society, 1957. 202p.

EISENHART, WILLIS W., *Abbott-Adlum-Green Families.* N. p., 1957. 78p.

———, *Ancestry of the John Franklin Eisenhart Family.* Abbottstown, Pa., n. p., 1951. 150p.

ELLIOTT, LOUISE GERVAISE, and MAREE STARKEY (CUSHING) DURAN, *Genealogy of Alexander Elliott & Delayede Belisle & Mose Gervaise & Marie Vegiard-Labonte* . . . N. p., 1958. 63p.

Encyclopedia of Pennsylvania Biography, Vol. 30. New York, Lewis Historical Publishing Company, 1957. 297p.

ESSEX INSTITUTE, *The Essex Institute Historical Collections Name, Place and Subject Index of Volumes 23 to 43, 1886 to 1907.* N. p., Printed for the Essex Institute, 1958. 624p.

EVANS, MABLE E. ADAMS, *Kimble and Elvina (Smith)Adams.* Manhattan, Kan., Author, 1859. [17]p.

EVERTON, GEORGE B., and GUNNAR RASMUSON, *Handy Book for Genealogists, Third Edition* . . . Logan, Utah, Everton Publishers [c1957]. 205p.

FLETCHER, ROBERT HOWE, JR., comp., *Genealogical Sketch of Certain of the American Descendants of Mathew Talbot, Gentleman.* N. p., Privately Printed, 1956. 70p.

FORTSON, JOHN, *Pott Country and What Has Become of It, a History of Pottawatomie County [Oklahoma].* N. p., Pottawatomie County Historical Society, 1936. 90p.

GAINES, B. O., *History of Scott County [Kentucky].* Georgetown, Ky., Frye Printing Company, 1957. 120p.

GENEALOGICAL FORUM OF PORTLAND, OREGON, *Genealogical Material in Oregon Donation Land Claims, Vol. 1.* Portland, Genealogical Forum, 1957. 152p.

GERBERICH, ALBERT H., *The Brenneman History.* Scottdale, Pa., Mennonite Publishing House, 1938. 1217p.

GREGG, JACOB RAY, *Pioneer Days in Malheur County [Oregon]* . . . Los Angeles, Privately Printed, 1950. 442p.

GROVES, JOSEPH A., *Alstons and Allstons of North and South Carolina* . . . Atlanta, Ga., Franklin Printing and Publishing Company, 1901. 367p.

HAMILTON, JAMES MCCLELLAN, *From Wilderness to Statehood, a History of Montana, 1805-1900.* Portland, Ore., Binfords & Mort [c1957]. 620p.

History of Marion County, Iowa . . . Des Moines, Union Historical Company, 1881. 807p.

History of Marion County, Ohio. Chicago, Leggett, Conway & Company, 1883. 1031p.

History of Mercer County, Pennsylvania . . . *Also a Condensed History of Pennsylvania.* Chicago, Brown, Runk & Company, 1888. 1210p.

History of Schuylkill County, Pennsylvania, With Illustrations and Biographical Sketches . . . New York, W. W. Munsell & Company, 1881. [450]p.

History of Southern Oregon, Comprising Jackson, Josephine, Douglas, Curry and Coos Counties . . . Portland, A. G. Walling, 1884. 545p.

History of Steele and Waseca Counties, Minnesota . . . Chicago, Union Publishing Company, 1887. 756p.

HODGES, FRANCES BEAL SMITH, *Gordons of Spotsylvania County, Virginia, With Notes on Gordons of Scotland.* Wichita Falls, Tex., Wichita Multigraphing Company, c1934. 35p.

HOOK, JAMES W., comp., *George Michael Eller and His Descendants in America* . . . New Haven, Conn., Compiler [1957?]. 485p.

[HOWELL, MRS. CLARENCE S.], *The Howell Genealogy.* No impr. Typed. 7p.

————, *The Pettibone Genealogy.* No impr. Typed. 11p.

————, *The Roe Genealogy.* No impr. Typed. 5p.

HUGUENOT SOCIETY OF SOUTH CAROLINA, *Transactions, No. 62.* Charleston, Society, 1957. 52p.

[HYNES, LEE POWERS], *Our Heritage; a Record of Information About the Hynes, Wait, Powers, Chenault, Maxey, Brewster, Starr and McIntosh Families* . . . [Haddonfield, N. J.] n. p. [1957]. 90p.

KENNEDY, ROBERT P., *Historical Review of Logan County, Ohio, Together With Biographical Sketches.* Chicago, S. J. Clarke Publishing Company, 1903. 823p.

KENTUCKY, ADJUTANT GENERAL, . . . *Soldiers of the War of 1812.* Frankfort, Printed by Authority of the Legislature of Kentucky, 1891. 370p.

KINSEY, FRANK STEWART, comp., *Stewarts, Dressers, Tafts, Cones.* Los Angeles, American Offset Printers, 1956. 388p.

KNORR, CATHERINE LINDSAY, comp., *Marriage Bonds and Ministers' Returns of Brunswick County, Virginia, 1750-1810.* N. p., Compiler, 1953. Mimeographed. 138p.

————, comp., *Marriage Bonds and Ministers' Returns of Halifax County, Virginia, 1753-1800.* N. p., Compiler [c1957]. Mimeographed. 134p.

————, comp., *Marriage Bonds and Ministers' Returns of Pittsylvania County, Virginia, 1767-1805.* N. p., Compiler, 1956. Mimeographed. 127p.

————, comp., *Marriage Bonds and Ministers' Returns of Powhatan County, Virginia, 1777-1830.* N. p., Compiler, 1957. Mimeographed. 101p.

————, comp., *Marriages of Culpeper County, Virginia, 1781-1815.* N. p., Compiler, 1954. Mimeographed. 127p.

KOZEE, WILLIAM C., *Pioneer Families of Eastern and Southeastern Kentucky.* Huntington, W. Va., Standard Printing and Publishing Company [c1957]. 272p.

LAMBETH, MARY WEEKS, *Memories and Records of Eastern North Carolina.* N. p., Privately Printed [c1957]. 252p.

LATTA, F. F., *The Lord's Vineyard, Including the Life of E. C. Latta, 1831-1909.* Shafter, Cal., Author, 1940. 91p.

[LEDLEY, W. VAN D.], *Index to the First Book of Records of the Dutch Reformed Church of Brooklyn, New York.* [New York] n. p. [1957]. Typed. 45p.

LONDON, HOYT H., *A Genealogical History of One Branch of the London Family in America* . . . Columbia, University of Missouri, 1957. 52p.

LOOMIS, NOEL M., *The Texan-Santa Fe Pioneers.* Norman, University of Oklahoma [c1958]. 329p.

MCCULLOUGH, ROSE CHAMBERS GOODE, *Yesterday When It Is Past.* Richmond, Va., William Byrd Press, 1957. 403p.

MACLYSAGHT, EDWARD, *Irish Families, Their Names, Arms and Origins.* Dublin, Hodges Figgis & Company, 1957. 366p.

MACMILLAN, SOMERLED, *Emigration of Lochaber MacMillans to Canada in 1802.* [Ipswich, Mass., Privately Printed] c1958. [15]p.

MCPHERSON, LEWIN DWINELL, comp., *Calhoun, Hamilton, Baskin and Related Families.* N. p. [c1957]. 447p.

McReynolds, Edwin C., *Oklahoma, a History of the Sooner State.* Norman, University of Oklahoma Press [c1954]. 461p.

Marshall, Harry A., *Our Children, 1818-1954.* N. p., 1954. Chart.

Massachusetts Historical Society, *Proceedings, Vol. 70, October, 1950—May, 1953.* Boston, Society, 1957. 418p.

Metcalf, John G., comp., *Annals of the Town of Mendon [Massachusetts] From 1659 to 1880.* Providence, R. I., E. L. Freeman & Company, 1880. 723p.

Mississippi Genealogical Society, *Cemetery and Bible Records.* Jackson, Miss., Society, 1957. 233p.

————, comp., *Survey of Records in Mississippi Court Houses.* Jackson, Miss., Society, 1957. 180p.

National Society of Daughters of Founders and Patriots of America, *Lineage Book, Vol. 31.* N. p., 1958. 432p.

National Society of the Daughters of the American Colonists, *Lineage Book, Book 2, Supplementals, 1945-1949.* N. p., 1957. [159]p.

————, *Lineage Book, Vol. 11, 10001-11000, 1957.* Annandale, Va., Society, 1957. [420]p.

Nye, Mary Green, *Early History of Berlin, Vermont, 1763-1820.* N. p., Norbert J. Towne and H. J. Dodge [c1954]. 98p.

Our Quaker Friends of Ye Olden Time . . . Hanover County and . . . Campbell County, Va. Lynchburg, Va., J. P. Bell Company, 1905. 287p.

Panhandle-Plains Historical Review, Vol. 30. Canyon, Tex., Panhandle-Plains Historical Society, 1957. 132p.

Past and Present of Eaton County, Michigan . . . With Biographical Sketches . . . Lansing, Michigan Historical Publishing Association, n. d. 663p.

Past and Present of Kane County, Illinois . . . Chicago, William Le Baron, Jr., & Company, 1878. [826]p.

Pennypacker, Samuel Whitaker, *Annals of Phoenixville [Pennsylvania] and Its Vicinity: From the Settlement to the Year 1871 . . .* Philadelphia, Bavis & Pennypacker, 1872. 295p.

Perrin, William Henry, ed., *[Kentucky History.]* [Chicago, F. A. Battey, 1884-1888.] Microfilm. 7 Vols. on 3 Reels.

Peterson, Emil R., and Alfred Powers, *A Century of Coos and Curry; History of Southwest Oregon.* Coquille, Coos-Curry Pioneer and Historical Association, 1952. 599p.

Phillips, Harry A., *History of Glover and Runaway Pond, a Poem in Two Cantos.* [Lyndonville, Vt., Northeastern Vermont Development Association] n. d. 50p.

Pollard, Annie M., *History of the Town of Baltimore, Vermont.* Montpelier, Vermont Historical Society [c1954]. 208p.

Powell, William S., *North Carolina Histories, a Bibliography.* Chapel Hill, University of North Carolina Library, 1958. 27p. (University of North Carolina *Library Studies,* No. 1.)

Preston, Richard A., trans., and Leopold Lamontagne, ed., *Royal Fort Frontenac.* Toronto, Champlain Society, 1958. 503p. (*Publications* of the Champlain Society, Ontario Series, Vol. 2.)

PRITCHARD, RUTH MITCHELL, comp., *The Genealogical Record of the Ancestors and Descendants of Perley and Phebe (Lewis) Mitchell of Parke County, Indiana.* N. p., 1958. Mimeographed. 28p.

PUGH, JESSE FORBES, *Three Hundred Years Along the Pasquotank, a Biographical History of Camden County.* Old Trapp, N. C., n. p. [c1957]. 249p.

PUTNEY, VT., FORTNIGHTLY CLUB, comp., *People of Putney, 1753-1953.* [Putney, Fortnightly Club] 1953. 86p.

RANDOLPH, WASSELL, *Pedigree of the Descendants of Henry Randolph I (1623-1673) of Henrico County, Virginia.* Memphis, n. p., 1957. 277p.

REYNOLDS, ELON G., ed., *Compendium of History and Biography of Hillsdale County, Michigan.* Chicago, A. W. Bowen & Company [1903]. 460p.

RICKS, JOEL E., and EVERETT L. COOLEY, eds., *The History of a Valley, Cache Valley, Utah-Idaho.* Logan, Utah, Cache Valley Centennial Commission, 1956. 504p.

ROYSE, MINTIE ALLEN, *The Bennet Family.* Indianapolis, Indiana Historical Society, 1958. 98p. (*Indiana Historical Society Publications,* Vol. 20, No. 1.)

SAN JOAQUIN GENEALOGICAL SOCIETY, comp., *Gold Rush Days; Vital Statistics Copied From Early Newspapers of Stockton, California, 1850-1855.* Stockton, Society, 1958. Mimeographed. 103p.

SCARBOROUGH, JEWEL DAVIS, *Southern Kith and Kin. Volume 3, Major James Scarborough, His Ancestors and Descendants.* Abilene, Tex., Abilene Printing Company [c1957]. 218p.

SHEEHAN, BEATRICE LINSKILL, comp., *Descendants of William Lain and Keziah Mather With Her Lineage From Reverend Richard Mather.* Brooklyn, N. Y., Theo. Gaus' Sons, 1957. 310p.

SHIELDS, JOHN A., *The Bennett Book, a Family History* . . . [Seymour, Ind., Author, 1956.] Mimeographed. 112p.

SIMS, EDGAR B., *Making a State; Formation of West Virginia* . . . N. p., State of West Virginia [c1956]. 213p.

————, *Sims Index to Land Grants in West Virginia.* N. p. [State of West Virginia, c1952]. 866p.

SMITH, CHARLES A., *The Family of William Collins.* N. p., 1951? Chart.

SMITH, FRANK, *Genealogical History of Dover, Massachusetts* . . . Dover, Historical and Natural History Society, 1917. 268p.

SMITH, MELLCENE (THURMAN), *Kin of Mellcene Thurman Smith* . . . No impr. [1035]p.

SOCIETY OF INDIANA PIONEERS, *Year Book, 1957.* Published by Order of the Board of Governors, 1957. 137p.

SOCIETY OF MAYFLOWER DESCENDANTS, *Meetings, Officers and Members Arranged in State Societies, Ancestors and Their Descendants.* N. p., General Congress, 1901. 447p.

SONS OF THE AMERICAN REVOLUTION, OHIO, CINCINNATI CHAPTER, *1958 Lineage Book, Compiled by Charles Hughes Hamlin.* [Cincinnati] Cincinnati Chapter, Ohio Society Sons of the American Revolution, c1958. 540p.

SOUTH DAKOTA HISTORICAL SOCIETY, *Collections and Report, Vol. 27, 1954.* Pierre, South Dakota Historical Society, c1954. 582p.

————, *Report and Historical Collections, Vol. 28, 1956.* Pierre, South Dakota Historical Society, c1957. 573p.

SPENCER, RICHARD HENRY, *Genealogical and Memorial Encyclopedia of the State of Maryland* . . . New York, American Historical Society, 1919. 2 Vols.

STARK, JAMES H., *Loyalists of Massachusetts and the Other Side of the American Revolution*. Boston, James H. Stark, 1910. 509p.

STILES, JESSIE VERNAN, *The Family of Jonathan Stiles of Guernsey County, Ohio* . . . N. p., Privately Printed, 1957. 398p.

STUCKER, ESSIE, comp., *Michael Stucker of 1759 and His Kinsmen* . . . N. p. [c1957]. 218p.

SZARKOWSKI, JOHN, *The Face of Minnesota*. Minneapolis, University of Minnesota Press [c1958]. 302p.

TERRILL, HELEN ELIZA, and SARA ROBERTSON DIXON, *History of Stewart County, Georgia* . . . Columbus, Ga., Columbus Office Supply Company, 1958. 804p.

THURSTON, GEORGE H., *Allegheny County's Hundred Years*. Pittsburgh, A. A. Anderson & Son, 1888. 312p.

TOPPING, CHARLES E., comp., *Topping*. N. p., 1958. Typed. 50p.

TOTTEN, JOHN R., *Thacher-Thatcher Genealogy*. N. p., New York Genealogical and Biographical Society, 1910-1915. 842p.

TREAT, JOHN HARVEY, *The Treat Family, a Genealogy of Trott, Tratt, and Treat* . . . Salem, Mass., Salem Press Publishing & Printing Company, 1893. 637p.

WAHL, DORIS (SEYMOUR), and CYNTHIA WALKER RUMMEL, comps., *The Skinner Kinsmen. Volume 1, The Descendants of Richard Skinner of North Carolina*. N. p., 1958. 78p.

WAYLAND, JOHN W., *Twenty-Five Chapters on the Shenandoah Valley to Which is Appended a Concise History of the Civil War in the Valley*. Strasburg, Va., Shenandoah Publishing House, 1957. 434p.

WEANER, ARTHUR, and WILLIAM F. SHULL, SR., *History and Genealogy of the German Emigrant Johan Christian Kirschenmann, Anglicized Cashman . . . Volume 1*. [Gettysburg, Pa., Privately Printed] 1957. Various paging.

WEIS, FREDERICK LEWIS, *Colonial Churches and the Colonial Clergy of the Middle and Southern Colonies, 1607-1776*. Lancaster, Mass., Society of the Descendants of the Colonial Clergy, 1938. 140p.

————, *Colonial Clergy of Maryland, Delaware and Georgia*. Lancaster, Mass., Society of the Descendants of the Colonial Clergy, 1950. 104p.

————, *Colonial Clergy of Virginia, North Carolina and South Carolina*. Boston, Society of the Descendants of Colonial Clergy, 1955. 100p.

WHEELER, LOIS, *History of Cavendish, Vermont*. Proctorsville, Vt., Author, 1952. 70p.

WILEY, SAMUEL T., *Biographical and Portrait Cyclopedia of the Nineteenth Congressional District, Pennsylvania* . . . Philadelphia, C. A. Ruoff Company, 1897. 578p.

WISE, JENNINGS CROPPER, *Col. John Wise of England and Virginia (1617-1695)* . . . [Richmond, Bell Book and Stationery Company, c1918.] 352p.

WOMER, LESLYE HARDMAN, *Willford-Hardman Ancestorlore.* N. p. [1957]. [52]p.

WRIGHT, ESTHER CLARK, *Loyalists of New Brunswick.* Fredericton, New Brunswick, Privately Printed [c1955]. 365p.

GENERAL

ALDEN, JOHN RICHARD, *The South in the Revolution, 1763-1789.* [Baton Rouge] Louisiana State University Press, 1957. 442p. (*History of the South,* Vol. 3.)

AMERICAN ANTHROPOLOGICAL ASSOCIATION, *Memoirs, Nos. 86-87.* [Menasha, Wis.] Association, 1958. 2 Vols.

AMERICAN ANTIQUARIAN SOCIETY, *Proceedings at the Annual Meeting Held in Worcester, October 16, 1957.* Worcester, Mass., Society, 1958. [215]p.

―――, *Proceedings at the Semi-Annual Meeting Held in Boston, April 17, 1957.* Worcester, Mass., Society, 1957. 76p.

AUMANN, FRANCIS R., *The Changing American Legal System: Some Selected Phases.* Columbus [Ohio State University] 1940. 281p. (*Contributions in History and Political Science,* No. 16.)

―――, *Instrumentalities of Justice: Their Forms, Functions, and Limitations.* Columbus, Ohio State University Press, 1956. 137p. (*Contributions in History and Political Science,* No. 18.)

AYER, N. W., and SON'S, *Directory of Newspapers and Periodicals, 1958.* Philadelphia, N. W. Ayer & Son [c1958]. 1554p.

BARRET, RICHARD CARTER, *Bennington Pottery and Porcelain, a Guide to Identification.* New York, Crown Publishers [c1958]. [348]p.

BEEBE, LUCIUS, and CHARLES CLEGG, *The Age of Steam, a Classic Album of American Railroading.* New York, Rinehart & Company [1957?]. Unpaged.

BEERS, HENRY PUTNEY, *French in North America, a Bibliographical Guide to French Archives, Reproductions, and Research Missions.* Baton Rouge, Louisiana State University Press [c1957]. 413p.

BLIVEN, BRUCE, JR., *The Wonderful Writing Machine.* New York, Random House [c1954]. 236p.

BLOYD, LEVI, *Campbell Brothers Great Consolidated Shows . . . the Story of the Second Largest Circus in the World.* [Fairbury, Neb., Holloway Publishing Company, c1957.] Unpaged.

BRISTOL, LEE HASTINGS, JR., *Seed for a Song.* Boston, Little, Brown and Company [c1958]. 244p.

BROWN, TRUESDELL S., *Timaeus of Tauromenium.* Berkeley, University of California Press, 1958. 165p. (*University of California Publications in History,* Vol. 55.)

CLARK, IRA G., *Then Came the Railroads, the Century From Steam to Diesel in the Southwest.* Norman, University of Oklahoma Press [c1958]. 336p.

COHN, DAVID L., *The Good Old Days; a History of American Morals and Manners as Seen Through the Sears, Roebuck Catalogs, 1905 to the Present.* New York, Simon and Schuster, 1940. 597p.

COLONY, HORATIO, *Young Malatesta.* Rindge, N. H., Richard R. Smith Publisher, 1957. 55p.

THE CONNOISSEUR, *Concise Encyclopedia of Antiques, Vol. 2.* New York, Hawthorn Books, n. d. 279p.

CRISWELL, GROVER C., and CLARENCE L. CRISWELL, *Criswell's Currency Series.* Pass-A-Grille Beach, Fla. [Criswell's Publications], 1957. 277p.

―――, *Price List and Supplement to Volume 1 of Criswell's Currency Series.* [Pass-A-Grille, Fla.] Criswell's Publications, 1957. 16p.

CUNLIFFE, MARCUS, *George Washington, Man and Monument.* Boston, Little, Brown and Company [c1958]. 234p.

CUNNINGHAM, H. H., *Doctors in Gray, the Confederate Medical Service.* Baton Rouge, Louisiana State University Press [c1958]. [339]r

DENISON, CAROL, *Animal Stories.* New York, Simon and Schuster [c1957]. 127p.

Dictionary of American Biography, Vol. 22, Supplement Two (to December 31, 1940). New York, Charles Scribner's Sons, 1958. 745p.

DI PESO, CHARLES C., *The Reeve Ruin and Southeastern Arizona . . .* Dragoon, Ariz., Amerind Foundation, 1958. 189p.

DRAPER, THEODORE, *Roots of American Communism.* New York, Viking Press, 1957. 498p.

DUFFY, JOHN ED., *Parson Clapp of the Stranger's Church of New Orleans.* Baton Rouge, Louisiana State University Press [c1957]. 191p. (*Louisiana State University Studies. Social Science Series, No. 7.*)

DURANT, JOHN, and ALICE DURANT, *Pictorial History of the American Circus.* New York, A. S. Barnes and Company [c1957]. 328p.

Encyclopedia of American Biography. New Series, Vol. 27. New York, American Historical Company, 1957. 460p.

ERDMAN, LOULA GRACE, *The Short Summer.* New York, Dodd, Mead & Company [c1958]. 304p.

FRANCHERE, RUTH, *Willa.* New York, Thomas Y. Crowell [c1958]. 169p.

FULLER, J. F. C., *Grant & Lee, a Study in Personality and Generalship.* Bloomington, Indiana University Press, 1957. 323p.

GEIGER, LOUIS G., *University of the Northern Plains, a History of the University of North Dakota, 1883-1958.* Grand Forks, University of North Dakota Press, 1958. 491p.

GIBSON, JOHN M., *Soldier in White, the Life of General George Miller Sternberg.* Durham, N. C., Duke University Press, 1958. 277p.

GIMBUTAS, MARIJA, *Ancient Symbolism in Lithuanian Folk Art.* Philadelphia, American Folklore Society, 1958. 148p. (*Memoirs of the American Folklore Society, Vol. 49.*)

GORDON, B. LEROY, *Human Geography and Ecology in the Sinú Country of Colombia.* Berkeley, University of California Press, 1957. 117p. (*Ibero-Americana: 39.*)

HARPER, HOWARD V., *Days and Customs of All Faiths.* New York, Fleet Publishing Corporation [c1957]. 399p.

HARRISON, HARRY P., *Culture Under Canvas, the Story of Tent Chautauqua . . . as Told to Karl Detzer.* New York, Hastings House [c1958]. 287p.

HARWELL, RICHARD B., ed., *The Confederate Reader.* New York, Longmans, Green and Company, 1957. 389p.

HELD, ROBERT, *The Age of Firearms, a Pictorial History.* New York, Harper & Brothers [c1957]. 192p.

HESSELTINE, WILLIAM B., and DONALD R. MCNEIL, eds., *In Support of Clio; Essays in Memory of Herbert A. Kellar.* Madison, State Historical Society of Wisconsin, 1958. 214p.

HIGBEE, EDWARD, *The American Oasis, the Land and Its Uses.* New York, Alfred A. Knopf, 1957. [266]p.

HILL, FOREST G., *Roads, Rails & Waterways; the Army Engineers and Early Transportation.* Norman, University of Oklahoma Press [c1957]. 248p.

HODGES, FLETCHER, JR., *Swanee Ribber and a Biographical Sketch of Stephen Collins Foster.* White Springs, Fla., Stephen Foster Memorial Association, c1958. Unpaged.

HOLBROOK, STEWART H., *Dreamers of the American Dream.* Garden City, N. Y., Doubleday & Company, 1957. 369p.

HOOVER, J. EDGAR, *Masters of Deceit, the Story of Communism in America and How To Fight It.* New York, Henry Holt and Company [c1958]. 374p.

HOTCHKISS SCHOOL, LAKEVILLE, CONNECTICUT, CLASS OF 1910. *The Mischianza.* Lakeville, Hotchkiss School, 1910. [179]p.

JEFFERSON, THOMAS, *Papers. Vol. 14, 8 October 1788 to 26 March 1789.* Princeton, Princeton University Press, 1958. 708p.

JOHNSON, WILLIAM, *Papers of Sir William Johnson, Vol. 12.* Albany, University of the State of New York, 1957. 1124p.

KELLAR, JAMES H., *An Archaeological Survey of Perry County.* Indianapolis, Indiana Historical Bureau, 1958. 40p.

KELLEY, STANLEY, *Professional Public Relations and Political Power.* Baltimore, Johns Hopkins Press, 1956. 247p.

KENT, WILLIAM WINTHROP, *Rare Hooked Rugs . . .* Springfield, Mass., Pond-Ekberg Company [c1941]. 223p.

KEY, WILLIAM, *The Battle of Atlanta and the Georgia Campaign.* New York, Twayne Publishers [c1958]. 92p.

KIMMEL, STANLEY, *Mr. Lincoln's Washington.* New York, Coward-McCann [c1957]. 224p.

KOVEL, RALPH M., and TERRY H. KOVEL, *Dictionary of Marks—Pottery and Porcelain.* New York, Crown Publishers [c1953]. 278p.

LAWSON, EVALD BENJAMIN, *Two Primary Sources for a Study of the Life of Jonas Swensson.* Rock Island, Ill., Augustana Historical Society, 1957. 39p. (*Augustana Historical Society Publications,* Vol. 17.)

LEE, ROBERT E., *Dispatches; Unpublished Letters of General Robert E. Lee, C. S. A., to Jefferson Davis and the War Department of the Confederate States of America, 1862-65 . . . Edited by Douglas Southall Freeman.* New York, G. P. Putnam's Sons [c1957]. 416p.

LIFE MAGAZINE, *America's Arts and Skills.* New York, E. P. Dutton & Company [c1957]. 172p.

LORANT, STEFAN, *Lincoln, a Picture Story of His Life. Revised and Enlarged Edition.* New York, Harper & Brothers [c1957]. 304p.

MCKEARIN, HELEN, and GEORGE S. MCKEARIN, *Two Hundred Years of American Blown Glass.* New York, Crown Publishers [c1950]. 382p.

MANKOWITZ, WOLF, and REGINALD G. HAGGAR, *Concise Encyclopedia of English Pottery and Porcelain.* New York, Hawthorn Books [1957?]. 312p.

MARCOSSON, ISAAC, *Anaconda.* New York, Dodd, Mead & Company [c1957]. 370p.

MASON, J. ALDEN, *George G. Heye, 1874-1957.* New York, Museum of the American Indian Heye Foundation, 1958. 31p.

Mennonite Encyclopedia, a Comprehensive Reference Work on the Anabaptist-Mennonite Movement, Vols. *1-3, A-N.* Scottdale, Pa., Mennonite Publishing House, 1955. 3 Vols.

MULDER, WILLIAM, and A. RUSSELL MORTENSEN, eds., *Among the Mormons, Historic Accounts by Contemporary Observers.* New York, Alfred A. Knopf, 1958. [496]p.

National Cyclopaedia of American Biography, Vol. 41. New York, James T. White & Company, 1956. 611p.

NATIONAL HISTORICAL PUBLICATIONS COMMISSION, *Writings on American History, 1952, James R. Masterson, Editor.* [Washington, D. C., U. S. Government Printing Office, 1958.] 573p.

NEW YORK HISTORICAL SOCIETY, *Dictionary of Artists in America, 1564-1860, by George C. Groce and David H. Wallace.* New Haven, Yale University Press, 1957. 759p.

[NEWHALL, JOHN B.], *A Glimpse of Iowa in 1846.* Iowa City, State Historical Society of Iowa, 1957. 106p.

ORNDUFF, DONALD R., *The Hereford in America, a Compilation of Historic Facts About the Breed's Background and Bloodlines.* Kansas City, Mo., Privately Printed [c1957]. 500p.

OSTRANDER, GILMAN M., *The Prohibition Movement in California, 1848-1933.* Berkeley, University of California Press, 1957. 241p. (*University of California Publications in History, Vol. 57.*)

PARSONS, JOHN E., *Smith & Wesson Revolvers, the Pioneer Single Action Models.* New York, William Morrow & Company, 1957. 242p.

PEARSON, LESTER B., *The Free Press, a Reflection of Democracy, an Address . . . May 15, 1958.* Williamsburg, Va., Colonial Williamsburg [1958?]. 16p.

PERRY, JOHN, *American Ferryboats.* New York, Wilfred Funk [c1957]. 175p.

PETERSON, THEODORE, *Magazines in the Twentieth Century.* Urbana, University of Illinois Press, 1956. 457p.

Philadelphia Bibliographical Center and Union Library Catalogue, Union List of Microfilms, Revised, Enlarged and Cumulative Edition, Supplement, 1952-1955. Ann Arbor, Mich., J. W. Edwards, 1957. 1019p.

PHILLIPS, JOSEPH D., *Little Business in the American Economy.* Urbana, University of Illinois Press, 1958. 135p. (*Illinois Studies in the Social Sciences, Vol. 42.*)

[PHILLIPS PETROLEUM COMPANY], *Pasture and Range Plants, Vols. 1-4.* N. p. [Phillips Petroleum Company, 1955-1957]. 4 Vols.

PIUS II, POPE, *Commentaries, Books 10-13, Translation by Florence Alden Gragg.* Northampton, Mass., Department of History of Smith College, 1957. [300]p.

POSEY, WALTER BROWNLOW, *The Baptist Church in the Lower Mississippi Valley, 1776-1845.* [Lexington] University of Kentucky Press [c1957]. 166p.

PUTNAM, CARLETON, *Theodore Roosevelt, Vol. 1, The Formative Years.* New York, Charles Scribner's Sons [c1958]. 626p.

RADDOCK, MAXWELL C., *Portrait of an American Labor Leader, William L. Hutcheson.* New York, American Institute of Social Science [c1955]. 43p.

REDDING, SAUNDERS, *The Lonesome Road, the Story of the Negro's Part in America.* New York, Doubleday & Company, 1958. 355p.

RESOURCES FOR THE FUTURE, *The Federal Lands, Their Use and Management, by Marion Clawson.* Baltimore, Published for Resources for the Future by Johns Hopkins Press [c1957]. 501p.

RIDDLE, DONALD W., *Congressman Abraham Lincoln.* Urbana, University of Illinois Press, 1957. 280p.

Riggs, Robert E., *Politics in the United Nations, a Study of United States Influence in the General Assembly.* Urbana, University of Illinois Press, 1958. 208p. (*Illinois Studies in the Social Sciences*, Vol. 41.)

Rightmire, George W., *Federal Aid and Regulation of Agriculture and Private Industrial Enterprise in the United States, a Survey.* Columbus, Ohio State University Press, 1943. 126p. (*Contributions in History and Political Science*, No. 17.)

Robert, Joseph C., *The Story of Tobacco in America.* New York, Alfred A. Knopf, 1952. [320]p.

Roseboom, Eugene H., *A History of Presidential Elections.* New York, Macmillan Company, 1957. 568p.

Scamehorn, Howard L., *Balloons to Jets.* Chicago, Henry Regnery Company, 1957. 271p.

Simonhoff, Harry, *Jewish Notables in America, 1776-1865, Links of an Endless Chain.* New York, Greenberg Publisher [c1956]. 402p.

South Carolina (Colony), Assembly, *Journal of the Commons House of Assembly, September 10, 1745—June 17, 1746, Edited by J. H. Easterby.* Columbia, South Carolina Archives Department, 1956. 291p.

Story of the Midwest Synod, U. L. C. A., 1890-1950. No impr. [392]p.

Thornbrough, Emma Lou, *The Negro in Indiana, a Study of a Minority.* N. p., Indiana Historical Bureau, 1957. 412p. (*Indiana Historical Collections*, Vol. 37.)

Thornbrough, Gayle, ed., *Outpost on the Wabash, 1787-1791.* Indianapolis, Indiana Historical Society, 1957. 305p. (*Indiana Historical Society Publications*, Vol. 19.)

Tilden, Freeman, *Interpreting Our Heritage, Principles and Practices for Visitor Services in Parks, Museums and Historic Places.* Chapel Hill, University of North Carolina Press [c1957]. 110p.

Vandiver, Frank E., *Mighty Stonewall.* New York, McGraw-Hill Book Company [c1957]. 547p.

Vincent, John H., *The Chautauqua Movement.* Boston, Chautauqua Press, 1886. 308p.

West, Richard S., *Mr. Lincoln's Navy.* New York, Longmans, Green and Company, 1957. 328p.

West, Robert C., *Pacific Lowlands of Colombia, a Negroid Area of the American Tropics.* Baton Rouge, Louisiana State University Press [c1957]. 278p. (*Louisiana State University Studies. Social Science Series*, No. 8.)

White, Patrick C. T., *Lord Selkirk's Diary, 1803-1804; a Journal of His Travels in British North America* . . . Toronto, Champlain Society, 1958. 359p. (*Publications* of the Champlain Society, Vol. 35.)

Who's Who in America, Vol. 30, 1958-1959. Chicago, Marquis—Who's Who [c1958]. 3388p.

Williamson, Harold F., and Orange A. Smalley, *Northwestern Mutual Life, a Century of Trusteeship.* Evanston, Ill., Northwestern University Press, 1957. 368p.

Wilson, Robert A., *Genesis of the Meiji Government in Japan, 1868-1871.* Berkeley, University of California Press, 1957. 149p. (*University of California Publications in History*, Vol. 56.)

Writers' Program, Utah, *Utah, a Guide to the State.* New York, Hastings House, 1945. 595p.

Bypaths of Kansas History

GAME FOR ALL TASTES AT WELLINGTON

From *The Sumner County Press*, Wellington, November 20, 1873.

Game is abundant in this market. At the City hotel, last Sunday, the boarders were treated to bear meat. Buffalo and venison, Euchre, antelope, seven-up, prairie chicken, Poker, Jack rabbits, California Jack, and other game abound.

FIGHTING IT OUT ON THE DODGE CITY FRONT

From the *Ford County Globe*, Dodge City, January 21, 1879.

"SCARLET SLUGGERS."—A desperate fight occurred at the boarding house of Mrs. W., on "Tin Pot Alley," last Tuesday evening, between two of the most fascinating doves of the roost. When we heard the noise and looked out the front window, which commanded a view of the situation, it was a magnificent sight to see. Tufts of hair, calico, snuff and gravel flew like fur in a cat fight, and before we could distinguish how the battle waned a chunk of dislocated leg grazed our ear and a cheer from the small boys announced that a battle was lost and won. The crowd separated as the vanquished virgin was carried to her parlors by two "soups." A disjointed nose, two or three internal bruises, a chawed ear and a missing eye were the only scars we could see.

YOU'VE HEARD IT!—"THE SHORT GRASS VOICE"

From the Sabetha *Herald*, June 25, 1908.

Did you ever hear the short grass voice? If you have ever been within forty rods of it, you have undoubtedly heard it. Away out in western Kansas the wind is always blowing. It roars through the corn fields, it screeches in the windmills, it moans in the eaves of the houses, it thrums on the barbed wire fences, and it hisses through the cottonwoods, and as it swings past it hammers and bangs at everything that is lose or can be worked loose. Once in awhile out there in western Kansas, when the sun sinks out of sight in the west, the wind will drop to a whisper, but far in the night perhaps it will suddenly awaken and lash itself into a fury, and roar past again.

People who live out there, and become accustomed to talking in the wind, acquire the short grass voice. And in passing we might say that in time a short grass character goes with the voice. For the past fifteen or sixteen years we have known William Wells, formerly of Hamlin, east of Sabetha. Wells now lives near Hill City, out in western Kansas. Before he went to Hill City his voice was notable for its quiet, retiring disposition. But when he visited us a year or so ago, his voice came in the fortissimo of the western Kansas wind; it was no longer the tame, docile creature it had been in the former environment.

Kansas History as Published in the Press

"What's the Matter With Kansas?"—today, was the subject of a Wichita *Beacon* editorial by Ralph S. Hinman, Jr., published June 4, 1958. Mr. Hinman concluded: "There's nothing the matter with Kansas—nothing a healthy dose of pride and affection in the hearts and minds of her people wouldn't cure—fast!" On March 1, 1959, the *Beacon* published an article by Hinman entitled "Buffalo Bill Legend Grows Out of [Cowley County] Kansas Ranch Home."

A profusely-illustrated series of articles on the history of Maple Hill began appearing in the Alma *Signal-Enterprise*, September 18, 1958.

On September 24, 1958, the Dodge City *Daily Globe* published an eight-page "Back to Santa Fe Trail" section. Featured were excerpts from *Four Centuries in Kansas*, by Bliss Isely and W. M. Richards, relative to the trail and cowboy days in Kansas.

"Historic Johnson County," Elizabeth Barnes' column in the *Johnson County Herald*, Overland Park, has continued to appear regularly. Among recent features were: a history of the Shawnee State Savings Bank, September 25, 1958; reminiscences of Herman J. Voigts, 82-year-old Mission township resident, November 6; a history of the Linwood church and cemetery in northeast Johnson county, January 15, 1959; a history of the *Johnson County Herald* by Mrs. Elizabeth Barr Arthur, a former publisher of the *Herald*, January 22; and the story of the Shawnee lodge of the Ancient Free and Accepted Masons, January 29.

The Barnes *Chief*, September 25, 1958, published a history of St. Peter Lutheran church, near Barnes, in observance of the church's 75th anniversary.

A history of the Mariadahl Lutheran church, near Cleburne, by Ruby Johnson, appeared in the Clay Center *Dispatch*, September 29, 1958. Said to be the oldest Augustana Lutheran church west of the Missouri river, the Mariadahl congregation observed its 95th anniversary in October. The church is not expected to reach its centennial due to the building of the Tuttle creek dam.

The Lawrence P. T. A. Council sponsored a series of articles on the activities, personalities, and history of the Lawrence public schools, beginning in the Lawrence *Journal-World,* September 30, 1958.

A history of the Evangelical Mission Covenant church at Savonburg appeared in the Chanute *Tribune,* October 8, 1958, and in the Humboldt *Union,* October 9. Although formally organized in 1898, the history of the church goes back to 1883 when meetings were first held.

The Herington *Advertiser-Times* printed a history of the St. Paul Lutheran church, Herington, in the issue of October 16, 1958. Organization of the church was in 1908 under the guidance of the Rev. Martin Senne.

Lily B. Rozar is the author of a sketch of the Shawnee Methodist Mission in Johnson county, printed in the Independence *Reporter,* October 19, 1958. The mission was established in 1830.

In 1885 the James K. Pugh family settled in Lane county. The story of the family's early years in the county was told by a daughter, Mrs. Myrtle Bradstreet, in the Dighton *Herald,* October 22, 1958.

St. Rose of Lima Catholic church, Council Grove, is the subject of an article in the Council Grove *Republican,* October 24, 1958. The history of the church is traced from 1883.

In 1858 G. W. Hutchinson started the Centropolis Christian church, according to a brief history by Lloyd Ballhagen in the Ottawa *Herald,* October 24, 1958. The church was reorganized in 1881 and chartered in 1883.

On November 6, 1958, the *News Chronicle,* Scott City, printed a full-page history of the last major Indian battle in Kansas. A group of Cheyenne Indians, escaping north from Indian territory, was attacked in present Scott county by federal troops, September 27, 1878. The site was recently acquired by Scott county and is now a county park operated by the Scott County Historical Society.

Histories of the Haven Congregational church were printed in the Haven *Journal,* November 13, 1958, and in the Hutchinson *News,* November 15. The church was organized in November, 1883.

The first Presbyterian church of Natoma was organized June 11, 1898. Historical sketches were published in the Natoma-Luray *Independent,* November 13, 1958, and the *Osborne County Farmer,* Osborne, November 20.

A brief history of the Immaculate Conception Catholic church, Danville, was printed in the Harper *Advocate*, November 13, 1958. The church was started in 1883 under the direction of Father Gregory Kelly.

On November 13, 1958, the Russell *Record* published a history of Fairport, a Russell county community, by Laura Knight Napper. Mrs. Napper's father, William Knight, built a mill on the townsite and was one of the town's founders. The mill began operating in 1880. On November 27 the *Record* printed a letter from Royal S. Kellogg, recalling more history of Fairport and Russell county.

A biographical sketch of Emma Grant, 1872-1958, by J. S. Jent, was published in the Cedar Vale *Messenger*, November 20 and 27, 1958. Miss Grant was a native and long-time resident of the Cedar Vale community.

Burchfiel Methodist church, near Anthony, now beginning its 76th year, was the subject of a history by Mrs. Myrtle Moore, published in the Anthony *Republican*, December 4, 1958. The Rev. J. R. Burchfiel served as the first pastor.

Broughton, Clay county, has had four names: Rosevale, Morena, Springfield, and Broughton, according to an article on the town's history by L. F. Valentine, printed in the Clay Center *Dispatch*, December 6, 1958.

Damar, Rooks county, is the subject of a history by Theresa and Armond Benoit, published in the Hays *Daily News*, December 7, 1958, and the *Rooks County Record*, Stockton, December 18. The community was settled by French Canadians of Catholic faith.

Alfaretta Courtright is the author of an article on the Indian raid of 1878, printed in the Atwood *Citizen-Patriot*, December 18, 1958.

A history of the John McBee family, by Mrs. Lillian McBee Myers, a granddaughter, was printed in the Howard *Courier-Citizen*, December 18, 1958. The McBees left Alabama in 1867, settling near present Howard in 1868.

"Yuletide Was Quiet Here 100 Years Ago for Frank Marshalls, Others," was the title of an article by Frances R. Williams, in the Marysville *Advocate*, December 25, 1958.

Kansas Historical Notes

Martin Van De Mark, Concordia, was elected president of the newly-organized Cloud County Historical Society at a meeting in Concordia, January 30, 1959. Robert H. Hanson, Jamestown, was elected vice-president; Mrs. Raymond A. Hanson, Jamestown, recording secretary; Mrs. Sidney Knapp, Concordia, membership secretary; Ernest Swanson, treasurer; and Fred Ansdell, Jamestown, Leo Paulsen, Concordia, Dr. Leo Haughey, Concordia, Robert B. Wilson, Concordia, Mrs. George Palmer, Miltonvale, and Clark Christian, Clyde, directors. Nyle Miller, secretary of the State Historical Society, spoke to the group.

The Smith County Historical Society met January 30, 1959, in Smith Center, and was addressed by Nyle Miller, secretary of the State Historical Society. Membership in the new Smith county organization was reported to be around 450.

All officers of the Lyon County Historical Society were re-elected at the annual meeting, January 30, 1959, in Emporia. They include: Dr. O. W. Mosher, president; Dr. Thomas P. Butcher, first vice-president; John G. Atherton, second vice-president; Myrtle Buck, secretary; Warren Morris, treasurer; and Mrs. F. L. Gilson, Mabel Edwards, and Lucina Jones, historians. The Cottrell flat-bed printing press purchased by William Allen White in 1895 and used for printing the Emporia *Gazette* until 1906 has been donated to the society by the William Allen White Foundation. In more recent years the press was used for printing the Hope *Dispatch*.

Dr. Leroy Hood, superintendent of schools at Garden City, was the principal speaker at the annual meeting of the Finney County Historical Society in Garden City, February 10, 1959. R. G. Brown, Mrs. Frank Crase, William Fant, Arthur Stone, J. E. Greathouse, and Amy Gillespie were re-elected directors of the society. New directors chosen include: Mrs. Merle Evans, Damon Cobb, Mrs. Claude Owens, Taylor Jones, and Mrs. Claudine Lindner.

New officers of the Shawnee County Historical Society, elected February 11, 1959, are: John Ripley, president; Leland Schenck, vice-president; Grace Menninger, secretary; Mrs. Frank Kambach, treasurer; and Mrs. Harold Cone, editor of the *Bulletin*.

Indian raids in Mitchell county in the summer of 1868 were reviewed by Alan B. Houghton in a 17-page booklet entitled *The Frontier Aflame*, published by the Beloit *Daily Call* in 1958.

A 32-page pamphlet, reviewing the history and summarizing the activities of the Sisters of Charity of Leavenworth, was recently published in observance of the Sisters' centennial.

Organizing a Local Historical Society, by Clement M. Silvestro, was recently issued as a special *Bulletin* of the American Association for State and Local History. Copies are available at 75 cents each to nonmembers at the American Association for State and Local History, 816 State Street, Madison 6, Wis.

Dr. B. M. Dobbin is the author of a recently published, 15-page pamphlet on the history of the Synod of the Plains of the United Presbyterian Church of North America. The synod was created in 1869 as Kansas Synod. It was merged with synods of the Presbyterian Church, U. S. A., in 1958.

Kansas medical history and the role of the Kansas doctor during the past 100 years as practitioner, specialist, teacher, and health officer are reviewed by Thomas Neville Bonner in his new 334-page book, *The Kansas Doctor—a Century of Pioneering*, published by the University of Kansas Press.

Noble Women of the North is the title of a 419-page volume containing excerpts from diaries, letters, memoirs, and journals of women who served as volunteer nurses with the Union forces during the Civil War, compiled and edited by Sylvia G. L. Dannett, and published recently by Thomas Yoseloff, New York. Among the women was Sarah Emma Edmunds, who, disguised as a man, served as a soldier and spy, and who later lived in Kansas.

□

THE
KANSAS HISTORICAL
QUARTERLY

Autumn 1959

Published by

Kansas State Historical Society

Topeka

NYLE H. MILLER   KIRKE MECHEM   JAMES C. MALIN
Managing Editor   *Editor*   *Associate Editor*

CONTENTS

                                                                                 PAGE

IRONQUILL'S "THE WASHERWOMAN'S SONG"............*James C. Malin,* 257
    With portrait of Eugene Fitch Ware, about 1881, *facing* p. 272.

A CHRONOLOGY OF KANSAS POLITICAL AND MILITARY EVENTS, 1859-1865, 283

MARK W. DELAHAY: PERIPATETIC POLITICIAN; A Historical Case Study
                                                                           John G. Clark, 301
    With reproduction of painting of Mark W. Delahay, *facing* p. 304.

RELIGION IN KANSAS DURING THE ERA OF THE CIVIL WAR (In two installments, Part One)..............................*Emory Lindquist,* 313
    With portraits of Lewis Bodwell, Pardee Butler, Richard Cordley, and Hugh Dunn Fisher, *facing* p. 320, and Charles H. Lovejoy, Samuel Young Lum, Peter McVicar, and Roswell Davenport Parker, *facing* p. 321.

U. S. ARMY AND AIR FORCE WINGS OVER KANSAS—*Concluded*.......... 334
    With photographs of Boeing B-29 gunners at Smoky Hill Army Air Field, Salina, and Free French fliers at Dodge City Army Air Field, *facing* p. 336, and air force planes on Kansas fields, *facing* p. 337.

BYPATHS OF KANSAS HISTORY.. 361

KANSAS HISTORY AS PUBLISHED IN THE PRESS........................ 363

KANSAS HISTORICAL NOTES 366

    The *Kansas Historical Quarterly* is published four times a year by the Kansas State Historical Society, 120 W. Tenth, Topeka, Kan., and is distributed free to members. Annual membership dues are $3; annual sustaining, $10; life membership, $20. Membership applications and dues should be addressed to Mrs. Lela Barnes, treasurer.

    Correspondence concerning articles for the *Quarterly* should be sent to the managing editor. The Society assumes no responsibility for statements made by contributors.

    Second-class postage has been paid at Topeka, Kan.

THE COVER

    Clean-shaven Abraham Lincoln as he appeared about the time of his visit to Kansas 100 years ago. Mr. Lincoln arrived in Elwood on November 30, 1859, speaking there that evening, at Troy and Doniphan on December 1, at Atchison December 2, and at Leavenworth December 3 and 5. (*See* pp. 285, 308.)

    A caravan to cover Lincoln's Kansas itinerary of 1859 is being planned for early December, 1959. Further details will be published in the newspapers.

THE KANSAS HISTORICAL QUARTERLY

Volume XXV   *Autumn, 1959*   Number 3

Ironquill's "The Washerwoman's Song"

JAMES C. MALIN

THE WASHERWOMAN'S SONG

In a very humble cot,
In a rather quiet spot,
    In the suds and in the soap,
    Worked a woman full of hope;
Working, singing, all alone,
In a sort of under tone:
    "With a Savior for a friend,
    He will keep me to the end."

Sometimes happening along,
I had heard the semi-song,
    And I often used to smile,
    More in sympathy than guile;
But I never said a word
In regard to what I heard,
    As she sang about her friend
    Who would keep her to the end.

Not in sorrow nor in glee
Working all day long was she,
    As her children, three or four;
    Played around her on the floor;
But in monotones the song
She was humming all day long:
    "With a Savior for a friend,
    He will keep me to the end."

It's a song I do not sing,
For I scarce believe a thing
    Of the stories that are told
    Of the miracles of old;
But I know that her belief
Is the anodyne of grief,
    And will always be a friend
    That will keep her to the end.

DR. JAMES C. MALIN, associate editor of *The Kansas Historical Quarterly* and author of several books relating to Kansas and the West, is professor of history at the University of Kansas, Lawrence.

Just a trifle lonesome she,
Just as poor as poor could be;
   But her spirits always rose,
   Like the bubbles in the clothes,
And, though widowed and alone,
Cheered her with the monotone,
   Of a Savior and a friend
   Who would keep her to the end.

I have seen her rub and rub,[1]
On the washboard in the tub,
   While the baby, sopped in suds,
   Rolled and tumbled in the duds;
Or was paddling in the pools,
With old scissors stuck in spools;
   She still humming of her friend
   Who would keep her to the end.

Human hopes and human creeds
Have their roots in human needs;
   And I should not wish to strip
   From that washerwoman's lip
Any song that she can sing,
Any hope that songs can bring;
   For the woman has a friend
   That will keep her to the end.

THE PUBLICATION OF THE POEM AND THE RESPONSE

ON Sunday morning, January 9, 1876, the Fort Scott *Daily Monitor* printed, without any explanation, Eugene F. Ware's poem, "The Washerwoman's Song," in the form given above.[2] The printing of poetry in the *Monitor* was not unusual, some being reprints of well known and obscure poets identified by name, some unidentified and on occasion unquestionably local, and some signed pieces by local aspirants to literary recognition identified by name, by initials, or by a pen name. Ware's poem was designated as written for the *Monitor* and was signed by his pen name "Ironquill," which was already known in a modest way in Kansas. If the editors were impressed by this poem as being any different from their customary poetic contributions, no hint was given, not even a distinctive position or typographical display. The reading public, both local and state, allowed no room for doubt, however, register-

---

1. The wording used here is essentially that of the original printing in the Fort Scott *Daily Monitor,* January 9, 1876, but the punctuation follows that of the third edition of the *Rhymes of Ironquill,* 1892.
2. The date given by D. W. Wilder, *Annals of Kansas* (1886), p. 698, is an error. He printed it in the original wording.

ing immediately and with enthusiasm a hearty approval, even when disagreeing in part with some of the ideas expressed.

At Leavenworth, the *Times* and the *Commercial,* January 12, the Anthony morning and evening papers at the moment, commented in identical editorials: "The Fort Scott *Monitor* has an original poem by 'Ironquill,' entitled 'The Washerwoman's Song,' which possesses much more than ordinary merit, and deserves to take rank with Hood's 'Song of the Shirt.'" [3] The poem was printed in both papers a few days later, with the comment that it was "a beautiful little poem by Eugene Ware." [4]

The Topeka *Daily Commonwealth,* January 16, 1876, the Sunday issue, admonished its readers: "Don't fail to read the poetry on the third page, written by Eugene Ware of Fort Scott. It is worth any sermon you will hear today." Two days later, in calling attention to the approval given the poem by the Leavenworth *Times,* the *Commonwealth* added its bit of praise: "Eugene never wrote anything better."

Whatever the *Monitor's* private views may have been on Sunday morning, January 9, when "The Washerwoman's Song" was first printed, the editors purred in the reflected sunlight of such praise like kittens who had just licked up a saucer of cream. On January 14 they acknowledged Anthony's approval and added their own first recorded verdict: "It is one of the best poems Mr. Ware has ever written." To be sure, that was a guarded commitment—"one of the best." Four days later, the *Monitor* reported the printing of the poem in the *Times* and the *Commonwealth* on Sunday, January 16, and the comments. But, in the locals column appeared the following wry verdict — bluntly practical and materialistic — "The Washerwoman's Friend — The person who pays his wash-bill promptly." In another two days, the exchanges received led the *Monitor* to another self-satisfied acknowledgment: "Eugene Ware's last poem, 'The Washerwoman's Friend,' is going the rounds of the press. Most of our exchanges have published it, and many of them highly complimented it." [5] Again, February 2, the *Monitor* noticed that it was "going the rounds" having been reprinted in the Leavenworth *Times,* the Topeka *Commonwealth,* the Sedalia *Bazoo,* the Girard *Press,* and the Columbus *Courier,* the Humboldt *Union,* and the Manhattan *Industrialist*—"It is one of the most popular of Mr. Ware's productions."

3. At this particular time most of the first column of the editorial page was identical in both papers, and was printed from the same type. Later in the year the *Commercial* was discontinued.
4. *Daily Times,* January 16; *Daily Commercial,* January 17, 1876.
5. Is it unkind to call attention to the newspaper's error in the title of the poem?

"The Washerwoman's Song" was indeed printed widely in Kansas by the weekly press, and the news service that printed "Patent Outsides" and "Insides" thought well enough of it to print it and promptly.[6] The Paola *Spirit* was among those that commented, not only on the poem, but upon Ironquill's stature as a literary man:

> Mr. Ware makes no pretention to poetical genius, yet he has already achieved an enviable reputation in the literary circles of the West as a writer of brilliance, not only on the poetical line, but in prose, and the field of wit. The Spirit is only too glad to be able to "pick up" anything written by the gifted and talented gentleman, Eugene Ware—"Ironquill." He will make his mark.

This was reprinted by the Parsons *Sun*, February 19, 1876, along with the news that Ware had accepted an invitation to read a poem at the Parsons pioneer celebration, March 8.[7]

The Nichol Poetry Episode

On home ground the reception of Ware's poem was remarkable and significant. Among the items recorded, the first in the sequence was the publication, in the *Daily Monitor,* January 18, or nine days after the historic Sunday of January 9, of a "poem" signed "Leon Love" (Thomas M. Nichol):

> THE WASHERWOMAN'S FRIEND
>
> "With a Savior for a friend
> He will keep me to the end."
> Thus the washerwoman sings
> And bright hope within her springs,
> That the words are truth, she knows
> And she rubs and rubs the clothes,
> Trusting in her Savior friend
> Who will keep her to the end.
>
> As she washes all day long,
> And keeps humming at her song,
> It is not the song she sings
> To her bosom hope that brings;
> But she rather sings the song,
> Knowing well 'twill not be long
> Till her Savior friend will come
> And will take her to her home.
>
> It is not the mere belief
> That's the "anodyne of grief;"
> Her Savior friend is real—
> He's not a mere ideal.

---

6. Parsons *Sun*, January 22; Oswego *Independent*, February 5, 1876, both "patent outsides."

7. Later Ware found it necessary to cancel this engagement. Parsons *Sun*, March 4, 1876; *Daily Monitor*, February 19, March 7, 1876.

Though He's all unknown to you
He's a person, real, true,
And he *is* the woman's friend;
He *will* keep her to the end.

You may smile at what she sings,
And may scorn the hope that springs
From "the stories that are told
Of the miracles of old."
But the woman at her tubs,
As each day she rubs and rubs
Still will trust her Savior friend
Who will keep her to the end.

It might well be worth your while
Never more at her to smile,
In your sympathy or guile,
Till you've thought more of the things,
Of the song the woman sings.
You may be assured of this,
There's a world of purest bliss
Comes from knowing that dear friend
Who will keep her to the end.

And although for all her hope
She would scarcely give the soap
That she rubs upon the clothes
Yet, in all her wants and woes,
She is certain at the last
When all her wants and woes are past
That her Savior friend will come
And will take her to her home.

This is why the woman sings—
It's to tell herself the things—
The only things—that cheer her,
And keep her Savior near her,
And *he'll keep her*—thought sublime!—
To the *end of endless time*—
For he is her only friend
Who will keep her to the end.[8]

Nichol had been on the *Monitor* staff for a time, having resigned in December,[9] and was devoting himself to the promotion of the Kansas Clipper sulky and gang plows which he had invented. These plows had been awarded the first premium at the Kansas State Fair at Leavenworth, which opened September 7, 1874. The Kansas State Grange had been contracted with the Fort Scott Foundry to manufacture them, and this arrangement had brought Nichol from

---

8. In the sixth line of stanzas one and four, the words "rubs and rubs" were a reflection of Ware's original version of "The Washerwoman's Song," which used them in the sixth stanza, line one, instead of "rubs and scrubs," used in the book printings.

9. *Daily Monitor*, December 23, 1875.

Humboldt to Fort Scott. He was born in Ohio, came to Kansas from Illinois, and in 1876 was 29 years of age.[10]

Anthony's papers, the Leavenworth *Times* and the *Commercial*, for January 20, ridiculed Nichol's effort at versification. "The fledglings are already attempting to ape Ware's song of the washerwoman. *Leon Love's* [Nichol's] doggerel in Tuesday's *Monitor* is the first. You will have to make stronger 'suds' than that, Love, if you expect your clothes to be 'fit to be seen.' " In printing this blunt verdict by Anthony, the *Monitor* attempted, the next day, to draw somewhat the sting with the comment: "Rather rough on 'Leon Love.' " Then, on January 23 (Sunday), by request, the *Monitor* reprinted both poems, along with the admonition: "They are good Sunday reading."

The Fort Scott *Pioneer*, January 27, the Democratic weekly rival of the *Monitor*, edited by U. F. Sargent, could not pass up such an opportunity to deride the opposition. His barbed jibe, inspired by Anthony's ridicule, was: "Poor Nichol! His wishy-washy parody on Ware's 'Washerwoman's Song' finds but little favor." And in the same issue Sargent wrote a two-paragraph introduction to an anonymous "poem." Of course, it might have been his own brain child, whose paternity he did not have the courage to acknowledge.

THE WASHERWOMAN'S SONG
By a matter-of-fact-man

I've read the short haired poet's song
Of the woman all forlorn,
    Who took in washing by the day,
    And never asked about her pay.

But continued working right along,
Singing a mythical sort of song,
    All the long and weary day
    While the children about her play.

Long and earnestly I have looked
Through our new directory book,
    Hoping, trusting, I might find
    One with confidence so sublime.

For the washer that I have had
Has kept me feeling very, very sad,
    Whenever we have chanced to meet,
    In the church or on the street,

---

10. Kansas state census, 1875 (Ms.), v. 5, Bourbon county, City of Fort Scott, p. 55; his name appeared a second time, p. 91, with an age of 30, in 1875; State Board of Agriculture, *The Third Annual Report* . . ., 1874, p. 75; *Daily Monitor*, August 28, December 3, 9, 1874, February 26, March 6, 1875. He was later to have a remarkable career elsewhere.

By asking in a weary way
If I ever intend to pay;
   If I don't she will put me through,
   Then I beg her not to sue.

And then she tells it on the street
That I am a high-toned beat,
   And if she had a friend,
   Who would keep her to the end,

She would quickly find a way
Whereby I would promptly pay,
   Or the end would quickly be
   A case of assault and battery.

We met in the bank yesterday,
And she said, "Now you will pay,
   For I have waited very long,
   And I'm a widow all forlorn."

I asked her not to speak so loud,
For she was drawing quite a crowd;
   But she didn't seem to care a cent,
   And on mischief seemed intent.

So I gave her all I had,
Still she seemed exceeding mad;
   And departing, wildly said,
   "Oh! I wish that I was dead."

Had she the faith it would be
Better for her and for me,
   Could she feel she had a friend
   Who would pay her in the end.

This had been preceded in the *Pioneer*, January 20, by an article in which Sargent had noticed unfavorably the structure of Nichol's versification. Nichol defended himself at length. Though the *Pioneer* article is missing from the files, he quoted much of it.[11] In printing it the *Monitor* editor warned his readers in a local: "'Leon Love' criticizes a critic this morning at great length. In a contest between giants the fur must fly." Also, at the top of the reply, the *Monitor* accommodated with the headline: "What a Critic! A Few Words About Poetry, Criticism, Ignorance, Stupidity and Meanness."[12]

Nichol began by quoting from the *Pioneer* editorial of January 20 entitled "What a Poet," which had ridiculed his rhyme and had characterized his effort as a "wishy-washy parody on Ware's *Washer-*

---

11. *Monitor*, January 30 (Sunday), 1876.
12. The authorship of the headline is not clear; if the origin was Nichol, at least, the editor accommodated by not "killing" it.

woman's Song. . . ." In defense Nichol showed a familiarity with a wide range of literature, but he took the ground that principle, not his own verses, was his concern. He condemned the tendency to greet new writers "with words not of welcome and encouragement, but of derision and ridicule."

The partisan verdict of the *Monitor* editor was that: "The worst used-up critic we ever saw, is the universal expression in regard to 'Leon Love' vs. Sargent." [13] Immediately, the *Monitor* printed another of Nichol's "poems," "The Sentry Boy" which indulged also in unusual "poetic forms," and later, one called "Seed Time and Harvest." [14] As he had asserted in his criticism of the critic, he was not easily crushed by ridicule.

As the recipient of such forthright castigation, Sargent would have had his readers believe that he was convinced of his error and was contrite, so he printed "Our Apology" in the *Pioneer*, February 3, which closed: "Then it follows that what we pronounced 'wishy washy,' 'doggerel' is in fact, poetry descended from the gods. Poet grant us pardon."

On February 17, while editor Sargent was absent, the *Pioneer* printed another "poem," inspired by, if not a "parody" of "The Washerwoman's Song." The author was not indicated but the title asserted: "I Do Not Like to Hear Him Pray." [15]

> I do not like to hear him pray
>   "Let blessings on the widow be!"
> Who never seeks her home to say
>   "If want o'er take you, come to me."
> I hate the prayer so loud and long,
>   That's offered for the orphan's weal,
> By him who sees him crushed by wrong,
>   And does not for his suffering feel.
> I do not like to hear her pray
>   With jeweled ear and silken dress,
> Whose washerwoman toils all day
>   And then is asked to "work for less."
> Such pious shavers I despise;
>   With folded hands and face demure.
> They lift to heaven their "angel eyes,"
>   And steal the earnings of the poor.

Who came off victor in this literary exchange is probably immaterial, but this "contest between giants" made an impression, at least temporarily, upon the community.

---

13. *Daily Monitor*, February 1, 1876.
14. *Ibid.*, February 3, 15, 1876.
15. The *Mirror and Newsletter*, Olathe, February 24, 1876; the Arkansas City *Traveler*, March 29, 1876, were among those printing this "poem."

The Poem Outside Fort Scott—Perspective

Lest the reader conclude that all this has been taken too seriously, the following, in lighter vein, by some unknown "Goosequill" appeared in the Topeka *Daily Commonwealth,* April 2 (not All Fools day), 1876:

The Baby's Song

She pushed a baby wagon,
    As she passed along the street—
    While her curly head was hatless,
    And no shoes were on her feet—
    Yet she sang a childish song,
    As she gaily tripped along,
    And the baby crowed in concert
    On the seat—

She smiled a cordial greeting,
    As I bid her kind good-day—
    While the baby's blue eyes twinkled,
    And she lisped in childish way—
    "I wuz zing, too, iz I could,
    For I zink ze world iz good,
    "Cause my sister takes me ridin
    Evvy day!"

An Anchorite, while dreaming
Of the buffetings of time—
    Caught an echo of the child song,
    And both wrought it into rhyme—
    Homely though the picture be
    'Twas a pleasing one to see—

. . . .

"I would sing, too, if I could,
For I think the world is good—"

. . . .

And the child caught up the strain
With a blithesome, glad refrain
Like the blended rhythm of bell notes
    In a chime—

An Eastern reader did take "The Washerwoman's Song" too seriously, however, and sent a ten dollar bill to Mr. Manlove, editor of the *Monitor,* accompanied by a note:

Tell me, Mr. Manlove, do you know "Ironquill?" If so, was that tender, touching little song the simple image of the mind, or does the subject of his song actually live and toil in the by-ways of your city. If so hand "Ironquill" the enclosed ten dollars that when he wanders that lonely way he may leave it at the "humble cot" with my hope that an hundred hearts may beat in unison, with his, and cheer with solid sympathy the widow's bleeding heart. A lay so limpid and so soft could only flow from a pure and benevolent fountain.

This letter elicited from Ware the only contemporary hint found thus far about the origin of "The Washerwoman's Song." To be sure it was negative, but that in itself eliminated a whole class of conjectural origins. Under the date February 29, 1876, Ware wrote:

> I regret that I cannot apply your friend's $10 bill to any one as indicated in the letter.
> The washerwoman is a myth and the character and scene wholly ideal.[16]

There is a positive side to this negative assertion, and it issues a challenge to the historian to discover, if possible, the circumstances out of which such an "ideal" might have emerged.

In the 1890's David Leahy ran a story in the Wichita *Eagle*[17] about "How Ware wrote it." Without specific dating, Leahy's story was that in reply to a direct question Ware related the details. In Leahy's words: "One dull day Mr. Ware was in his office and his thoughts were turned to religion by hearing a church bell ring. The following two lines flashed across his brain":

> "Human hopes and human creeds
> Have their root in human needs."

Using this as a focus, supposedly the poem was written backwards. In December, Leahy says, when Ware and the postmaster, a man of literary interests, sat on the steps of the Catholic church, Ware read the poem. His friend was silent. Ware was discouraged and stuck the poem into a pigeonhole in his desk where it rested until some time later a *Monitor* reporter wanted something for his column and Ware dug it out. Leahy's account included the story of the ten dollars, but with the wrong name attached and some improbable glosses. With modifications and without the more exaggerated details, a similar story was told in the *Tribune-Monitor* obituary notice about Ware, July 3, 1911. A kernel of truth may be involved in these tales, which serve as human-interest stories, but they do not explain anything.

THE REAL

On January 8, 1876, the day before the unheralded publication of "The Washerwoman's Song," the locals editor of the *Daily Monitor*, under the title "The Last Resort" explained apologetically to his readers:

16. Fort Scott *Daily Monitor*, March 1, 1876.
17. Reprinted in the Topeka *State Journal*, January 10, 1898.

Local news is so scarce that probably a few items like the following will have to be written up occasionally: "We are very sorry indeed to be called on at this juncture to announce that Mr. So-and-So's little pussy, in an attempt to get into the safe [cupboard] and try a piece of chicken, fell with a thud upon the floor and hurt its little back. . . .

Suffice it to say no such drastic measures were necessary. Besides the argument over poetry stirred up by Nichol's efforts at versification, the fundamental issues involved in "The Washerwoman's Song" were discussed in lectures and sermons, and were the subject of public debates immediately after the publication of the poem.

Two traveling lecturers appeared in Fort Scott, advertised to discuss Spiritualism. One called himself Prof. S. S. Baldwin, "Exposer of Spiritualism," and the other, W. F. Jamieson, Spiritualist. The latter attacked Christianity in the name of science and challenged any clergyman to engage in public debate. No minister accommodated Jamieson in his publicity stunt. Apparently, however, there was some demand that Christianity be defended, and that a dull winter be enlivened. Although some difference of opinion developed about how it happened, Thomas M. Nichol found himself nominated to make the sacrifice. Nichol had delivered one of the "home talent" lectures in the series arranged the preceding winter. His subject had been theological, but as a Universalist, he insisted that in the current instance he was not qualified to speak in the name of orthodox Christianity. Altogether, the debate ran through three nights, with partisans of each side claiming victory. It turned out to be good "entertainment," but there was a serious side, and unless the press reports were quite misleading, that aspect was uppermost.[18]

Ware was silent throughout the period in which his poem was the favorite topic of discussion. His mind was neither unobservant nor fallow, however, and April 2, 1876, the editor of the *Daily Monitor*, this time, with an air of pride, made an announcement: "A beautiful little poem from the pen of the 'Philosopher of Paint Creek' is printed in the MONITOR this morning." Again the poem was signed "Ironquill:"

THE REAL
They say
A flower, that blooms I know not whither,
Perhaps in sunnier skies,
Is called the Amaranth. It will not wither
It never dies.

I never saw one.

18. The episode can be followed in the local papers, the *Daily Monitor*, and the *Pioneer*, for the two weeks' period beginning January 31, 1876.

> They say
> A bird of foreign lands, the Condor,
> Never alights,
> But through the air unceasingly doth wander,
> In long aerial flights.
>
> ---
>
> I never saw one.
> They say
> That in Egyptian deserts, massive,
> Half buried in the sands,
> Swept by the hot sirocco, grandly impassive,
> The statue of colossal Memnon stands.
>
> ---
>
> I never saw it.
> They say
> A land faultless, far off, and fairy—
> A summer land, with woods and glens and glades
> Is seen, where palms rise feathery and airy
> And from whose lawns the sunlight never fades.
>
> ---
>
> I never saw it.
> They say
> The stars make melody sonorous
> While whirling on their poles.
> They say through space this planetary chorus
> Magnificently rolls.
>
> ---
>
> I never heard it.
> Now what
> Care I for Amaranth or Condor
> Collossal Memnon, or the Fairy Land,
> Or for the songs of planets as they wander
> Through arcs superlatively grand.
>
> ---
>
> They are not real.
> Hope's idle
> Dreams the Real vainly follows,
> Facts stay as fadeless as the Parthenon
> While Fancies like the summer tinted Swallows
> Flit gaily mid its ruins and are gone.[19]

At the elemental folk level, but in its way as disconcerting as a child's direct reaction, was a letter from one of those people who are no doubt well-meaning, but distressingly literal minded:

---

19. The reading of the poem printed here, except for the correction of a typographical error, is the original version as given in the *Daily Monitor*, April 2, 1876. In the selected poems published later in book form under the title (with variations) *Rhymes of Ironquill* (1885 and later) substantial changes in wording were introduced.

Right here in Southern Kansas, Mr. Ware, in almost any little garden [the Amaranth does grow]. It is unfading and perennial; blooms as well amid January snows as it does in June and July, and when hung up and dried for six months, looks as fresh and beautiful as ever. The Amaranth is a veritable flower, and no creature of imagination.[20]

Of course, it was. Amaranth was a common name applicable to an order and to a genus of plants. Within the genus were many species and in some cases distinctive varieties within a species. The common garden names for those treated in gardens as flowers, are the Red Amaranths, including cockscomb or Crested Amaranth, prince's feather (princess feather) or Jacob's coat, and love-lies-bleeding. Within the genus also were such plants as Pigweed (Green Amaranth) and Tumbleweed (White Amaranth).[21] The dictionaries all agree, however, that the primary literary meaning, chiefly in poetry, was an imaginary flower that was supposed never to fade. The historical dictionaries cite usage in English literature from the early 17th century onward. Thus in Milton's *Paradise Lost* (iii, 353):

> Immortal amarant, a flower which once
> In Paradise, fast by the tree of life,
> Began to bloom; but soon for man's offence
> To Heaven removed, where first it grew.

The title and substance of "The Real" should have made Ware's meaning clear even to the most obtuse. He sought to compare in the sharpest contrast possible, and by varied examples, "The Ideal" and "The Real." And he did it most effectively, emphasized by the off-beat final line in each stanza—in the original printing, set off for added stress by a black line.

Although not so recognized at the time, and no one since has made a serious study of Ware, the publication of "The Real" at this time may be viewed in the perspective here presented, as Ware's rejoinder to the religious debates of the preceding weeks. He was unrepentant. He was agnostic toward both Christianity and Spiritualism—all intangibles that must be accepted on faith. The position of the agnostic must be differentiated, however, from that of the infidel—the agnostic doubted, but he did not deny. It is one thing to render the Scotch verdict "not proven" but quite another to

---

20. Parsons *Eclipse*, April 13, 1876, reprinted in the Fort Scott *Pioneer*, April 27, 1876.
21. Asa Gray, *Manual of the Botany of the Northern United States*. . . . Sixth Edition by Sereno Watson and John M. Coulter (New York, 1889); Harlan P. Kelsey and William A. Dayton, editors, *Standardized Plant Names*, Second Edition (Harrisburg, Pa., 1942); *The Oxford English Dictionary, Being a Reissue . . . of a New English Dictionary on Historical Principles* . . . (Oxford, 1933); *The Century Dictionary: An Encyclopedic Lexicon of the English Language* (New York, First Edition, 1891, Revised, 1913); *Webster's New International Dictionary of the English Language*, Second Edition, Unabridged (Springfield, 1950). The common spelling is Amaranth, but the correct form is Amarant.

declare categorically that a thing is false, or does not even exist. Ware's position—at any rate his ostensible attitude—was that of practical pragmatist—only tangible facts were real and provided a sense of certainty and security. Ware's was a Pragmatism, as was the case of so many other so-called practical-minded Americans of his generation, without a philosophical rationalization. That, however, was already, but unknown to Ware, being supplied by Charles S. Pierce, followed by William James, John Dewey, and others.[22]

The conclusions embodied in "The Real" had not always represented Ware's position. No longer ago than 1872 he had taken the opposite side of identically the same issues and in language and ideology that were in many respects an earlier version of the same poem. At that time he had called it "The Song," arranged in rhymed prose form, and published in the *Daily Monitor*, October 13, 1872. It was signed Ironquill, and was among the first poetic pieces to appear over that pen name. In the *Rhymes of Ironquill*, it was reprinted, arranged in verse form, but scarcely changed in wording, and named "The Bird Song":

THE SONG

In the night air I heard the woodland ringing; I heard it ring with wild and thrilling song. Hidden, the bird whose strange, inspiring singing, seems yet to float in liquid waves along.

Seems yet to float with many a quirk and quaver,—with quirks and quavers and exultant notes, as though the air with sympathetic waver, down through the song the falling starlight floats.

Speaking, I said: O bird, with songs sonorous, O, bird, with songs of such sonorous glee, sing me a note of Joy; and in the chorus—in the same chorus—I will join with thee.

The songs that others sing seem but to sadden; they seem to sadden—those that I have heard. Sing me a song whose gleesome notes will gladden. Sing me a song of joy. Then sang the bird:

"There is a land where blossoming exotic, the amaranths with fadeless colors glow; where notes of birds with melodies chaotic, in tangled songs forever come and go.

"There skies serene and bland will bend above us, and from them blessings like the rain will fall; there those fond friends that have loved shall love us;—in that bright land, those friends shall love us all."

The singer ceased—the melody sonorous, no more through star-lit woodland floats along; and as it ceased my heart refused the chorus—refused to join the chorus of the song.

---

22. James C. Malin, "Notes on the Writing of General Histories of Kansas: Part One, The Setting of the Stage," *Kansas Historical Quarterly*, v. 21 (Autumn, 1954), pp. 192-202; *On the Nature of History* (Lawrence, The Author, 1954), ch. 3, especially p. 77; *The Contriving Brain and the Skillful Hand* (Lawrence, The author, 1955), pp. 348-353.

Talk not, I said, thou bird in branches hidden, Hope's garlands bright, Grief's fingers slowly weave—Grief slowly weaves from blooms that spring unbidden, that spring perennial when the heart doth grieve.

Grief present now proves naught of life eternal; grief proves no future with proud blessings rife—with blessings rife and futures blandly vernal. Facts show no logic in a future life.

And then I said, false is thy song, sonorous; thy song that floats from starlit woodland dim. When we are gone and flowers are blooming o'er us—when man hath gone, there endeth all with him.

Resang the bird: "There skies shall bend above us, and sprinkle blessings like the rains that fall; and those we loved—who loved us not—shall love us, in that bright land, shall love us best of all."

Then came a song-burst of bewildering splendor, that rolled in waves through forest corridors;—up soared the bird, fain did my hopes attend her; and hopes and songs were lost amid the stars.

Now all day long upon my mind intruding, there comes the echo of that last night's song;—Grief claims the wrecks on which my mind is brooding; Hope claims the facts which logic claimed so long.

Who cares, O, bird, for skies that bend above us? Who cares if blessings like the rains shall fall? If only those who loved us not shall love us—in that bright future—love us best of all.

Let logic marshal ranks of facts well stated; it leads them on in brave though vain attacks;—for looking down from bastions crenelated. Hope smiles derision at assaulting facts.

Because the Ware poems have never before been dated, and no one has formerly undertaken to make Ware's philosophy and its background a subject of serious historical study, the relationship of these poems and their significance in terms of relations have been ignored. Although Kansans and some others have visited upon Ware an inordinate amount of highly sentimental admiration and eulogy, their adulation was too superficial for them to feel obliged to search for the structure of his thought or even to assume that it had a structure. For reasons that are not known, Ware himself, purposely or accidentally, contributed to this chaotic situation by the rule of complete irrelevance that seemed to govern the arrangement of the book versions of the *Rhymes*. The unpredictable manner in which contrasting types of poems rubbed elbows with each other gave an impression that the sublime and the ridiculous were never far apart, possibly only the reverse sides of the same thing. Even if, perchance, that or some other deliberately selected principle actually did govern at that time, a study of Ware according to the historical principle is long overdue.

In 1872, when "The Song" was first published, Ware was in the midst of the closing hysteria of the presidential campaign. As a

Greeley Liberal, and editor of the *Daily Monitor,* he was grinding out daily the lowest form of partisan political drivel, such as was considered necessary to win a political campaign. Whether or not "The Song" was written at this time, these were the circumstances under which it was published. Even in that context, Eugene Ware's two selves were involved; the self that was writing daily partisan political trash, which no one would be stupid enough to assume that he believed, and this other self, the poetic, the philosophical, the idealist self, who made his own decision to publish "The Song" at this particular time, even though it might have been written earlier. Indeed, the sublime and the ridiculous were in this case merely the reverse sides of Ware's two selves.

But in 1872 as contrasted with 1876, what was Ware saying? What were his philosophical and theological commitments?—"Hope smiles derision at assaulting facts." Apparently, then Ware was still an orthodox Congregationalist, or near to it, and substantially in accord with his father's conservatism. In "The Real," the terms Ideal and Real had been substituted for Hopes and Facts, but with the Ideal no longer paramount to the Real. Ware had reversed his basic commitments.

And what about Ware's political commitments? In 1872 he was editing a liberal newspaper, though seemingly a conservative in philosophy and theology. In 1875, he published "Text," which appeared in the book version of the *Rhymes* under the title "The Granger's Text." This poem was a practical application of his mother's philosophy: "Smooth it over and let it go": the future, not the past, is important:

THE TEXT [23]

Long the Topeka convention wrangled;
  "Good men for office" got into a balk;
Grange nominations were hopelessly tangled;
  Sargent got up and gave them a talk.
    Said to the delegates quarreling so—
    "Smooth it over and let it go."

Many a time I have thought of the quarrel
  That "good men for office" so often reach,
Many a time I have thought that a moral
  Shone like a lantern in Sargent's speech;
    Look for my text in the line below,
    "Smooth it over and let it go."

---

23. *Daily Monitor,* May 16, 1875, by "The Philosopher of Paint Creek." The version given here is that printed in the *Monitor.* At this time Ware was using two pen names; each for a different kind of rhymes. To be discussed elsewhere.

Eugene Fitch Ware
(1841-1911)
Fort Scott author, lawyer, and legislator, about 1881.

When a fierce editor boiling with fury
    Paints you with hot editorial tar;
Don't start a libel suit, don't hire a jury,
    Don't seek redress from the bench or the Bar
        Lies sometimes vanish, facts always grow;
        "Smooth it over and let it go."

When you consent to be placed on a ticket,
    When you have made up your mind to run,
Leg it your best—the political thicket
    Tears off your clothes, but makes lots of fun,
        If you are minus a vote or so,
        "Smooth it over and let it go."

Efforts and hopes may be lighter or graver
    Either in politics, business, or fame,
Things may go crooked, and friendships may waver,
    Nevertheless, the rule is the same;
        Facts will be facts, when you find it so,
        "Smooth it over and let it go."

In the record of 1875-1876, Ware was considered a political conservative, also a reversal from the position of 1872, but associated with philosophical and theological liberalism. In one or another, all the ferments of the years 1869-1876 had involved the peace of mind of many people in the Fort Scott neighborhood. A number of them have been identified by name in association with the particular ideas to which they were committed. Each fitted into his unique niche in the culture complex of Fort Scott, of Kansas, and of the United States of the 1870's.[24]

But this Fort Scott of 1869-1876, with all its ambitions and inconsistencies, its dreams and disillusionments, was the background of Eugene Ware, and his poem "The Washerwoman's Song," and for that matter, of all his poetry. In the "scientific" language of the day, contemporaries might have said: the product of "the development theory." In a way, the conflict in the community was a mirror of the confusion and uncertainty troubling the minds of many of its citizens confronted with the new science of the middle years of the 19th century.

The McFarland Episode, 1883

A period of quiet followed the flurry of 1876 over "The Washerwoman's Song." Although not forgotten, and reprinted again and again, a revival of interest of some magnitude occurred in 1883 in association with "An Open Letter to Hon. Eugene F. Ware," written

---

24. See the present author's articles dealing with Fort Scott philosophers, *Kansas Historical Quarterly*, v. 24 (1958), pp. 168-197, 314-350.

by N. C. McFarland, commissioner of the General Land Office at Washington, D. C., a lawyer of repute from Kansas. The "Open Letter" was published first in the Topeka *Daily Capital*, November 18, and Ware's reply, November 25, 1883, a poem without a title other than the salutation: "To Hon. N. C. McFarland, Washington, D. C." and introduced by a short note to the editor. A name was not assigned to the poem, apparently, until it appeared in the first edition of *Rhymes of Ironquill*, in 1885, as "Kriterion." [25] Thus far the exact set of circumstances have not been determined which stimulated McFarland to write his letter, nor which explain the remarkable response to the letter and to Ware's reply, along with the original "Washerwoman's Song." The casual but appreciative comment upon the "Song" over the intervening years, 1877 to 1882, was one thing, but the enthusiasm of 1883 was quite another.

When, on November 18, the *Sunday Capital* printed the "Open Letter," it was done without fanfare: "The Washerwoman's Song" was printed at the top of the column, the letter occupying about one and one half columns.[26] McFarland's letter is rather long to print here in its entirety, but these are the most pertinent parts:

DEAR SIR:—I have read again and again with indescribable pleasure and sadness, your "Washerwoman's Song,"—pleasure because it is really beautiful, and voices correctly the joy of Christ's poor ones; sadness because you say you are shut out from a hope, which, though not always so bright and cheerful, is worth more than all else this world affords. You will pardon me for addressing you in this public manner, for I know that many men of intellect and culture occupy positions not dissimilar to your own, and I hope in this way to make some suggestions which will reach both you and them, and not be inappropriate to the subject, whether they shall prove valuable or useless. Reading between the lines, I think I can see a thoughtful interest, a sort of inquiry, a desire to possess a hope like, or at least equal, to the heroine of your song. If this were not so, I could scarcely interest myself sufficiently to write you, for I confess I have but little patience with that class of criticisms that flippantly brushes aside the motives of God, Christ and immortality, as fit only for the contemplation of "women and children." To me these mysteries are the profoundest depths. I have no plummet heavy enough, nor line long enough to reach the bottom. I may push them aside for a time, while other things engross me, but they come unbidden again and again across my path. Is it so with you. . . .

What is God? . . .

I have doubted whether he was "God manifested in the flesh," but I never disbelieved it. . . .

I have written thus far so as to be able to say, that when you write, "I scarce believe a thing" your true position is, that you doubt whether the woman has a real foundation upon which to build her song. And if I am right in this,

---

25. If an earlier use was made of that name between 1883 and 1885, the present writer has not found it.

26. The first line of the sixth stanza read "rub and scrub," instead of the original "rub and rub."

then further to suggest that there is nothing unusual or unreasonable in such doubt. Nay more, when reason, judgment and all other faculties and means for arriving at truth are imperfect, it seems to me that a perfect faith is unattainable, and doubt becomes a necessity; of questions like these and many others, there is no absolute demonstration here and now.

Did it ever occur to you that the woman did not always have that serene faith which you ascribe to her. Do you not know that she often wondered, and wondering, doubted, not, perhaps, whether there is a God, but whether He is merciful, or even just? Do you not know that to her it is an unsolved problem why she was left alone to support four children at one dollar a day, when you could make twenty dollars a day at work less burdensome and exhaustive? If she had called on you, when passing her door, to explain this problem to her understanding, what could you have said? She probably knew that it was as inexplicable to you as to her, and therefore did not ask. There is an answer, but neither you nor I occupy a plane sufficiently exalted to fully comprehend and speak it—"even so, Father, for so it seemeth good in thy sight."

There are two classes of people who may never have doubts; the one who sees through these mysteries at a glance, or think they do; and the other, "who never had a dozen thoughts in all their lives."

The washerwoman sung away most of hers in her beautiful song; and shall we, who cannot sing, linger about Doubting Castle until Old Giant Despair entices us into his gloomy prison house? No. . . .

The *Daily Monitor,* November 20, in Ware's home town wrote proudly:

The open letter addressed to Hon. E. F. Ware by Mr. N. C. McFarland, published this morning, adds new interest to the "Washerwoman's Song," which is considered by many to be Ware's best composition. There can be no higher evidence of the merit of a poem than the fact that it arouses and calls into active being such eloquent and burning thoughts as those contained in Mr. McFarland's letter. . . .

D. W. Wilder's editorial on McFarland's letter stated that the purpose was to give the poet faith in God and to remove his doubts; that the spirit embodied in the letter was as pure as that expressed in the poem. It does not have an "I-am-better-than-thou" tone, and in reference to the purpose it says that perhaps the poet could tell if the letter fulfilled its mission. "Noble letters between two true men would set an example to theological disputants—who always fight and who are not Christ-like." [27]

Another communication on the poem and McFarland's letter was by D. P. Peffley, of Fort Scott, dated November 25, and printed in the *Daily Monitor,* November 28, the day before Thanksgiving. It contained much of the same thoughtfulness and expression, and was nearer to earth:

I have found much to interest me in reading the letter of Mr. McFarland, reprinted in your last issue, discussing Mr. Ware's poem. After the mad whirl

27. Hiawatha *World,* November 22, 1883.

of personal politics, which periodically seems to swallow up everything of such a nature, it is indeed gratifying to those whose sentiments and affections cling to the little circle lighted by the domestic lamp to be allowed a corner in the indispensable and all visiting newspaper. The poem I have read before. I have also seen beauty in it; not the Miltonic beauty of grand imaginative flights, soaring into the loftiest empyrean, where ordinary minds dare not follow; not the giantlike grasp of intellect that seizes something abstract, unreal, and tortures it till it gives out its essence in labored metrical lengths, its beauty lost to untrained intellects in its incomprehensibleness, but the simple beauty of naturalness, of truthfulness. One hears the very "rub" of the washboard in its meter. It requires not the genius of a Gustave Dore to picture to oneself the home it describes, the hopeful sad face of the woman bending over the tub, set perhaps on an upturned chair, the splashed child, the miscellaneous heap of "duds." Alas! the scene too often naturalizes for us.

But the burden of the song: who shall say that the woman realizes its weight? Let us assume that she does, since otherwise our interest must at once fall lifeless. We cannot make an individual case, but must apply this one generally. Mr. McFarland places his stress on the existence of Christian faith. . . . I have long thought, thought seriously, thought honestly, on the same subject. Like him, I have doubted; have questioned; have asked nature; have examined ostensible revelation. But none offer an unchallenged ultimate basis.

Like him, I have never disbelieved entirely, for the same reason that I have offered for not having shared the common faith—lack of sufficient proofs to warrant it. But that immortality is to be inferred from the unsatisfactoriness of this life, I no more believe. For it is not necessarily unsatisfactory. Man makes it so himself. If the average of human life be but a score and a half, man's violations of laws, determinate and known to be inexorable, is the cause of it. In proof of this we need but point to the hoary age and unimpaired powers of some of the famous men of our time, of time but recently past. These men were observant of laws whose penalties they knew to be certain of execution. Does he believe that Bryant went to his grave filled with regrets for the unsatisfactoriness of life? That he went "as the galley slave," and not as one "who wraps the draperies of his couch about him and lies down to pleasant dreams?" That Longfellow yearned for life a second time on earth? Or Franklin, Washington, John Adams? Or further back, Copernicus, the heathen Socrates? The average of life's duration is known to be capable of being raised by proper observance of the common law of hygiene. At the same time it is admitted that we cannot compel universal observance of them [laws]; consequently many of those who find the satisfactoriness of life to consist in the mere fact of existence will continue to be disappointed.

Yet this faith, to those who have it, what a treasure! How it has upheld the desolate heart! How it has bended over the couch of death, cheering the ebbing spirit of life! . . . It has made the tortures of the rack, the stake, of the cross itself become as if they were not. Should we, then, who cannot accept it implicitly, seek, by scoffs and vulgar jeers, as some do, to drive it from those who may have little else? Spirit of compassion, forbid it! Let the untaught washerwoman sing, and believe as she sings, that she has

"a Savior for a friend,
That will keep her to the end."

Among other things, these two letters show how greatly times have changed. People took more time then, in writing such comments and in contemplating poetry in this profound sense. What now seems somewhat wordy and beside the point served as recreation as well as literary art, and when a series of events such as this developed, it was like the serial on the inside of the back page, except that anyone could offer something to the growth of the train of letters. Also, discussions close to the hearts of the people were carried on through the newspapers, often in a literary and informative fashion, taking the place of modern "canned" amusement.

An editorial in the *Sunday Capital*, November 25, 1883, was headed, "The New Poem of Hon. Eugene Ware":

> It will be unnecessary for us to call the attention of our readers to the beautiful poem from Hon. Eugene Ware, of Fort Scott, addressed to Hon. N. C. McFarland in reply to his letter which appeared in the *Capital* last Sunday. The letter of Judge McFarland has been widely copied in the weekly press of Kansas. The poem is rich in pure, deep and reverential feeling, delicate and most beautiful in expression [,] a most appropriate reply to Judge McFarland's thoughtful letter.

In another column of the same page, Ware's contribution was printed with the heading "Hon. Eugene Ware to Hon. N. C. McFarland":

> To the Editor of the Capital:
> Fort Scott, Kan., November 21.—I have just seen in your excellent paper of Sunday an open letter addressed to me by the Hon. N. C. McFarland of Washington, D. C. I assure you that I feel honored that my "Washerwoman's Song" should be noticed by one who to high official position adds a recognized standing as a lawyer and a cultivated gentleman. The kindness of the criticism leads me to venture a reply, which I ask you to publish.

To Hon. N. C. McFarland, Washington, D. C.

> I see the spire,
>   I see the throng,
> I hear the choir,
>   I hear the song;
> I listen to the anthem, while
> It pours its volume down the aisle;
>   I listen to the splendid rhyme
>   That, with a melody sublime,
>   Tells of some far-off, fadeless clime—
> Of man and his finality
> Of hope and Immortality.
>
> Oh, theme of themes!
>   Are men distraught?
> And hopes like dreams
>   To come to naught?

Is all the beautiful and good
Delusive and misunderstood?
    And has a soul no forward reach?
    And do indeed the facts impeach
    The theories the teachers teach?
And is this Immortality
Delusive unreality?

What Hope reveals
    Mind tried to clasp,
But soon it reels
    With broken grasp.
No chain yet forged on anvil's brink
Was stronger than its weakest link;
    And do not arguments maintain
    That many a link along the chain
    Can not resist a reason strain?
And is not Immortality
The child of Ideality?

And yet—at times
    We get advice
That seems like chimes
    From Paradise;
The soul doth sometimes seem to be
In *sunshine* which it cannot see;
    At times the spirit seems to roam
    Beyond the land, above the foam,
    Back to some half-forgotten home.
Perhaps—this immortality
May be indeed reality.[28]

    In reprinting the "Reply," the Junction City *Union*, December 1, 1883, commented: "The letter and the two poems constitute a cheerful oasis in the slush the newspaper man is called upon to deal with." The lack of a name for the poem, besides the term "Reply" was a handicap, but a temporary title was supplied; one of more logical significance by the Emporia *News* in its Holiday edition [December 25], 1883: "It May Be Reality." The Manhattan *Nationalist*, November 23, 1883, put Ware "at the head of Kansas poets," and suggested, "if he would cultivate his talents in this direction, might secure a national fame." [29]

---

28. The wording and arrangement of the lines is that of the poem as published in the *Capital*. The punctuation, however, follows that of the third edition of the *Rhymes of Ironquill* (1892). In that edition, for the first time, changes were introduced including the lines seven, eight, and nine of the third stanza which were revised to read:
    "And are there not along this chain
    Imperfect links that snap in twain
    When caught in logic's tensile strain?"

29. In its issue of November 29, 1883, the Lyndon *Journal*, contrasted McFarland and Sen. John J. Ingalls to the disadvantage of the latter as a sceptic. In his Troy *Kansas Chief*, December 13, 1883, Sol Miller blundered in his reading of the *Journal's* comment, and at-

One of the most remarkable aspects of both the Ware episodes, 1876 and 1883, is the absence of personal hostility toward Ware, or ridicule of his verse or of his ideas. With due regard to the allowances that properly belong to any attempt at generalization, the dictum of "FSM," in 1876, about Western people and religion may again apply—respect for sincere faith even when agnostic toward it.[30]

In Ware's reply to McFarland, which will be referred to henceforth by the later name "Kriterion," what was his position on religious orthodoxy? In "The Washerwoman's Song" Ware had assumed the position of doubt, softened by tolerant compassion. In "The Real" he had stood his ground, but in "Kriterion" he appeared to hedge

> Perhaps—this immortality
> May be indeed reality.

In order to appreciate more accurately and adequately what had happened to Ware's thinking and feeling, it is well to go still farther back into the record. On October 23, 1870, the *Daily Monitor* had printed a poem over the initials "EFW," the first of his poems found there with so explicit an identification. This represented orthodox theological certainty. "The Washerwoman's Song" revealed Ware at the other extreme, a confessed agnostic, but also certain he had found truth. The text of "The Palace," of 1870, which Ware never saw fit to revive or revise for book publication in the *Rhymes of Ironquill*, follows:

THE PALACE

> Father, lay aside your paper—
> See the house that I have builded,
>   With the blocks which uncle gave me
>   Christmas day.
> See! its got a dozen windows,
> On the sides and on the gables,
>   And its made so you can see out every way.
>
> Then its got a little 'zervatory
> Rising from the corner,
>   Where a person stands and looks out at the sky.
> And its roof is very pointed,
> And its made of gilded shingles,
>   And it rises in the middle very high.

---

tributed to it a comparison of Ware and Ingalls; Ware the Christian and Ingalls the sceptic. Miller preferred Ingall's brains to Ware's piety. This is one of the few unkind Kansas reactions to Ware's poetry, and both its error and its animus were evident. If Ware was a candidate for the United States senate, Miller suggested, then, "perhaps there is a necessity for starting a religious boom in his favor."

30. Topeka *Commonwealth*, April 9, 1876.

And its got a lot of porticos
And balconies and arches,
    And great big flights of back steps made of stone;
And inside there are galleries,
And staircases and parlors—
    And that's the kind of house that I will own.

Father, lay aside your paper—
There! Why didn't you look sooner!—
    Its too late now—you should have looked before,
For the wind came through the doorway,
And it tilted up the carpet,
    And it wrecked my little palace on the floor.

That's the way it *always* happens—
When I've got my house finished,
    There is always something sure to happen then;
And there is no use of trying,
For they crumble to the carpet,
    Though I build them over time and time again.

  .   .   .   .

Ah, my curly headed builder,
You have learned the lesson early,
    That there's something always ruining our schemes;
Happiness is but a palace,
Built of hopes and aspirations,
    With its spires and domes and minarets of dreams.

Ah, my little blue-eyed schemer—
Many palaces I'VE builded,
    But the gales and storms would come
        with angry strife;
First the spires and domes and minarets,
And then after that the palace
    Would be wrecked upon the carpet of my life.

You will build them—they will crumble,
And the higher up—the sooner;
    And as often as you build them—o're and o're,
When they're finished, through the doorway
Comes the wind that tilts the carpet,
    And the palace crumbles downward to the floor.

But, my curly headed dreamer—
In the sky there is a palace,
    And its builded there for those who
        love the truth;
And its changeless and uncrumbling,
And the splendor of its beauty,
    Far outrivals all the wildest dreams of youth.

The contrast betwen the texts of "The Palace" and of the "Kriterion" is made the more sharp by the titles supplied for the latter by the Emporia *News*, "It May Be Reality." Ware had reversed himself once, and had gone part way apparently in a return, but had not completed the cycle. Yet, candor must insist upon sticking to the record, although a good case could be made for the view that privately Ware had not abandoned the position of 1876 on "The Washerwoman's Song," and "The Real," but purely as a matter of expediency, had made a concession to what "FSM" had insisted Western People demanded in "fair play" on matters of difference in religion—a sincere respect for a genuine religious character, though not necessarily acceptance of religious form. Unknown is the reason why Ware selected, apparently belatedly, the title "Kriterion," both the idea and the Greek spelling. Yet the public accepted the name without any question about the meaning or about orthography.

THE KRITERION HOAX

All this was written prior to a full realization by the present author of the fact that there was a private view of the "Kriterion" episode quite different from the public view—in fact, a contradiction of both the main facts and the interpretation just given them. In order to reconstruct history as a whole, the private view must now be stated. The "Kriterion" was not a new poem, and it was not written in reply to Judge McFarland. Already it had been published under its proper title, "Kriterion," and over his pen name Ironquill, in the *Daily Monitor*, August 16, 1874, or nearly nine years prior to McFarland's "Open letter." That was long enough before the episode of 1883 that those who may have once known of the earlier printing had long since forgotten. Besides, in 1874, so far as can be discovered, the poem did not attract any attention either at home or abroad. Why should it have created so remarkable a flurry in 1883? Why did Ware misrepresent it; offer it without its title, and as a reply to the open letter? Surely after the remarkable experience with "The Washerwoman's Song" he was aware that he was in the presence of an occasion that might involve portentous responses. Even though unprepared to answer with a new production, and like the preacher who turned his sermon barrel upside down to select off the bottom, he must have weighed the choice with care. Why did he perpetuate the hoax in the book publication of the *Rhymes of Ironquill*, in 1885, and in the many editions thereafter, by printing the McFarland Open Letter as the link between "The Washerwoman's Song" and "Kriterion?"

But more important than this physical manipulation of tangible facts, is the violence which Ware committed upon himself; upon his private intellectual and religious integrity. As pointed out already, if "Kriterion" had been written in response to McFarland, it meant a retreat in thought. In its true chronology, however, it was a way-station along a straight line transition from the orthodoxy of "The Palace," through "Kriterion," to the agnosticism of "The Washerwoman's Song." Already, the suggestion has been made that possibly it was a concession to his public, an act of expediency, without necessarily being a private reversal. That view now becomes more insistent, but for a quite different reason. Henceforth the student of Ware's poetry, and admirers of "The Washerwoman's Song," or of "Kriterion" as individual poems must keep in mind these two views, the private and the public, and their irreconcilability. Viewed as a whole, truth is complex and challenging.

A Chronology of Kansas Political and Military Events, 1859-1865

I. INTRODUCTION

ON January 29, 1861, President James Buchanan signed the bill which made Kansas the 34th state.

For nearly seven years Kansas territory had been strife-torn and bloodied by the struggle over slavery. But statehood did not bring peace. It was the withdrawal of Southern senators which assured the passage of the Kansas bill. Thus joy over the admission of Kansas to the Union was tempered by concern over the departure of the Southern states.

War clouds were threatening when President-elect Abraham Lincoln started from Springfield, Ill., to Washington to take the oath of office. Because of threats of assassination his route in some areas was kept secret. However, he appeared in Philadelphia long enough on Washington's birthday, February 22, 1861, to raise the first flag containing the Kansas star to fly at Independence hall.

Mr. Lincoln's appearance at Philadelphia was reported in the press in part as follows:

FELLOW CITIZENS.—I am invited and called before you to participate in raising above Independence hall the flag of our country, with an additional star upon it. (Cheers.) . . .

I am filled with deep emotion at finding myself standing here, in this place, where were collected together the wisdom, the patriotism, the devotion to principle, from which sprang the institutions under which we live. You have kindly suggested to me that in my hands is the task of restoring peace to the present distracted condition of the country. I can say in return, Sir, that all the political sentiments I entertain have been drawn, so far as I have been able to draw them, from the sentiments which originated and were given to the world from this hall. I have never had a feeling politically that did not spring from the sentiments embodied in the Declaration of Independence. I have often pondered over the dangers which were incurred by the men who assembled here, and framed and adopted that Declaration of Independence. I have pondered over the toils that were endured by the officers and soldiers of the army who achieved that independence. I have often inquired of myself what great principle or idea it was that kept this confederacy so long together. It was not the mere matter of the separation of the colonies from the mother land; but that sentiment in the Declaration of Independence which gave liberty, not alone to the people of this country, but, I hope, to the world for all future time. (Great applause.) It was that which gave promise that in due time the weight would be lifted from the shoulders of all men. This is a sentiment embodied in the Declaration of Independence. Now, my friends, can this country be

(283)

saved upon that basis? If it can, I will consider myself one of the happiest men in the world, if I can help to save it. If it cannot be saved upon that principle, it will be truly awful. But if this country cannot be saved without giving up that principle, I was about to say I would rather be assassinated on this spot than surrender it. (Applause.) Now, in my view of the present aspect of affairs, there need be no bloodshed or war. There is no necessity for it. I am not in favor of such a course, and I may say in advance, that there will be no bloodshed unless it be forced upon the government, and then it will be compelled to act in self-defense. (Applause.)

My friends, this is wholly an unexpected speech, and I did not expect to be called upon to say a word when I came here. I supposed it was merely to do something toward raising the flag. I may, therefore, have said something indiscreet. (Cries of "No, no.") I have said nothing but what I am willing to live by and, if it be the pleasure of Almighty God, die by. . . .

War came, and, though most of the major campaigns were fought in the East, some with Kansas troops participating, the state was still troubled at home. Skirmishes along the eastern and southern borders culminated finally at Mine creek, Linn county. Here, on October 25, 1864, the most important Civil War battle in Kansas was fought, with nearly 25,000 men engaged.

Because of the approaching centennials of Kansas statehood and of the Civil War, the latter to be observed nationally, the following chronology of political and military events covering these stirring years is here submitted. Entries for the most part were taken from D. W. Wilder's *Annals of Kansas.*

II. THE CHRONOLOGY

1859

OCTOBER 4.—The Wyandotte constitution, drawn up in the town of Wyandotte (now Kansas City, Kan.) in July, 1859, was adopted. The popular vote was: For, 10,421; Against, 5,530.

OCTOBER 12.—The Republican "state" convention was held at Topeka.

OCTOBER 16.—Capt. John Brown, with 18 men, took possession of the arsenal at Harper's Ferry, Va. Several were killed and wounded before they were captured by federal troops, under Col. Robert E. Lee, who battered down the doors. John Brown was wounded, and two of his sons were killed.

OCTOBER 22.—Party arrived at site of "Camp on the Pawnee Fork" to begin construction. The name was soon changed to Camp Alert and later to Fort Larned.

OCTOBER 25.—The Democratic convention was held at Lawrence.

NOVEMBER 8.—Marcus Parrott was elected congressional delegate from Kansas. Members of the Kansas territorial legislature also were elected.

NOVEMBER 30.—Abraham Lincoln arrived in Elwood and made a speech.

DECEMBER 1.—Lincoln made a two-hour speech at Troy and a speech of shorter duration at Doniphan.

DECEMBER 2.—John Brown was hanged for treason at Charlestown, Va.

Lincoln traveled from Doniphan to Atchison, where he spoke in the Methodist church.

DECEMBER 3.—Lincoln arrived in Leavenworth. A welcome had been prepared for him and he spoke that night to a large crowd at Stockton hall on the topic of popular sovereignty. He mentioned the execution of John Brown on the previous day saying:

Old John Brown has just been executed for treason against a state. We cannot object, even though he agreed with us in thinking slavery wrong. That cannot excuse violence, bloodshed, and treason. It could avail him nothing that he might think himself right. So, if constitutionally we elect a President, and therefore you undertake to destroy the Union, it will be our duty to deal with you as old John Brown has been dealth with. We shall try to do our duty. We hope and believe that in no section will a majority so act as to render such extreme measures necessary.—Roy P. Basler, *The Collected Works of Abraham Lincoln* (Rutgers University Press, 1953), v. 3, p. 502.

DECEMBER 5.—Lincoln spoke again at Leavenworth and remained there to observe the voting on state officers.

DECEMBER 7.—Lincoln departed for his home in Illinois and Marcus Parrott accompanied him eastward. The Leavenworth *Times* of that date stated: "The River opposite this city has been frozen over since Sunday morning. The ice on an average is six inches thick, and many persons and horses crossed with safety yesterday." It is probable that Lincoln was driven across the ice on his return to St. Joseph.

1860

JANUARY 2.—The Kansas Territorial legislature met at Lecompton. The council consisted of eight Republicans and five Democrats; the house, 23 Republicans and 16 Democrats. The legislature on January 4 voted to adjourn to Lawrence but Governor Medary vetoed the proposal. The legislature passed the adjournment measure over his veto on January 5 and 6.

JANUARY 7.—The legislature moved to Lawrence and remained in session there until January 18, 1860.

JANUARY 18.—Gov. Samuel Medary issued a new proclamation, summoning the legislature to meet at Lecompton on January 19.

JANUARY 19.—The territorial legislature met at Lecompton but again, over the governor's veto, moved to Lawrence where it stayed until adjournment, February 27, 1860.

FEBRUARY 14.—The Wyandotte constitution was presented to the United States senate.

FEBRUARY 15.—Galusha Grow, of Pennsylvania, introduced House Bill No. 23 in the U. S. congress to admit Kansas under the Wyandotte constitution.

FEBRUARY 21.—Sen. William H. Seward, of New York, introduced Senate Bill No. 194, asking for the admission of Kansas.

MARCH 16.—James Montgomery and his followers were prevented by snow from rescuing some of John Brown's men at Charlestown, Va.

MARCH 20.—Raids by Missourians on Bourbon county were reported.

MARCH 27.—The Democratic convention was held at Atchison.

APRIL 3.—The first rider for the Pony Express left St. Joseph for Sacramento, Calif. Until October 26, 1861, the Pony Express was the fastest mode of transmitting messages from St. Joseph to the west coast. For a period of 18 months, until the telegraph took its place, the Pony Express was the vital communication link between the east and west coasts. The Kansas portion of the route ran between Elwood, via Seneca and Marysville, to the area of present Hanover, where it angled northwest into Nebraska.

APRIL 11.—The U. S. house of representatives voted 134 to 73 to admit Kansas under the Wyandotte constitution.

The Republican convention was held at Lawrence to elect delegates to the party's national convention at Chicago, and to select presidential electors.

APRIL 12.—The clerk of the house reported the Kansas admission bill to the senate.

APRIL 13.—The house bill was referred to the senate committee on territories.

MAY 16.—The house bill was reported back from committee without recommendations.

MAY 29.—Camp Alert was renamed Fort Larned.

JUNE 5.—Sen. Edward Wade moved to reconsider the bill, but the motion was defeated 32 to 26.

JUNE 7.—Sen. Robert Hunter, of Virginia, moved to postpone action on the Kansas admission bill. His motion carried 32 to 27.

NOVEMBER 6.—Election of the territorial legislature was held.

NOVEMBER 28.—Governor Medary and Gen. W. S. Harney left Leavenworth for Fort Scott.

DECEMBER 8.—The military expedition sent by the governor of Missouri to the Fort Scott vicinity was encamped near the state line.

DECEMBER 11.—Sen. Jacob Collamer, of Vermont, recalled House Bill No. 23.

DECEMBER 31.—Judge John Pettit of Kansas declared unconstitutional the law abolishing slavery in Kansas.

1861

JANUARY 4.—Fort Leavenworth was placed on short mobilization notice by Gen. Winfield Scott. Every man and horse was to be ready to go to Baltimore at a moment's notice.

JANUARY 7.—The final territorial legislature convened at Lecompton and adjourned to Lawrence where it met until February 2.

JANUARY 10.—The governor's message was presented to the legislature by George Beebe, acting governor, replacing Medary who had resigned.

JANUARY 18.—Sen. James S. Green, of Missouri, proposed an amendment to the Kansas admission bill. This amendment provided that the Platte river region to the north should be added to Kansas, while the Cherokee neutral lands and the Osage lands would be cut off on the south. The measure was defeated, 31 to 23.

JANUARY 19.—Sen. Graham N. Fitch, of Indiana, moved to add sections 4 and 5 to the measure, constituting Kansas a judicial district of the United States, with "like powers and jurisdiction as the district court of the United States for the District of Minnesota." The motion was defeated 27 to 26.

JANUARY 21.—The senators from Mississippi, Alabama, and Florida withdrew; the senators from South Carolina had done likewise in November, 1860. It has been stated that the presence of those members in the senate delayed the passage of the Kansas bill.

Senator Fitch reintroduced his amendment on the judiciary. It was passed 29 to 28.

JANUARY 21.—The senate passed the bill as amended, 36 to 16, and sent it to the house for concurrence.

JANUARY 28.—The house suspended its rules so that it could take up the Kansas admission bill as amended. The senate amendment was concurred in by the house sitting as a committee of the whole, and the Kansas bill was passed, 117 to 42.

JANUARY 29.—Pres. James Buchanan signed the Kansas admission bill and Kansas became a state.

The Leavenworth *Daily Conservative* published an "extra" concerning the passage of the Kansas admission bill.

FEBRUARY 1.—Both houses of the territorial legislature passed a resolution to elect two U. S. senators from the state of Kansas.

FEBRUARY 8.—Marcus Parrott, Kansas delegate to congress, arrived at Lawrence late at night bringing the official notification of the admission of Kansas to Governor-elect Robinson.

FEBRUARY 9.—The first governor of Kansas, Charles Robinson, took the oath of office at Lawrence. The oath was administered by Caleb Pratt, county clerk of Douglas county.

FEBRUARY 20.—James Montgomery wrote to the governor that the southern border of Kansas was in danger of Confederate attack.

FEBRUARY 22.—President-elect Abraham Lincoln, on his way to Washington, paused at Independence hall, Philadelphia, to speak and to raise the flag bearing the Kansas star.

MARCH 5.—An election was held to fill vacancies in the new state legislature.

MARCH 10.—Linn county organized the first militia regiment in the state.

MARCH 26.—The first state legislature convened at Topeka.

APRIL 4.—James H. Lane and Samuel Pomeroy were chosen by the state legislature to be the first U. S. senators from Kansas.

APRIL 12.—Fort Sumter, South Carolina, was fired on by secessionist troops.

APRIL 14.—James H. Lane, senator from Kansas, began enrolling troops in the Frontier Guard. This organization was voluntary and unofficial and was never mustered into the regular army. Its primary mission was to serve as a bodyguard for President Lincoln and it was made up of Kansas men who were in Washington for the inauguration. On the night of April 18 and several nights following, the Frontier Guard bivouacked in the East Room of the White House. The group was disbanded on May 3.

APRIL 17.—Capt. Samuel Walker, of Lawrence, offered Governor Robinson a company of 100 men. A meeting was held in Atchison to form a Union military company but some residents cried "Coercion" and the company was not formed.

APRIL 18.—The steamboat *New Sam Gaty* arrived at Leavenworth from St. Louis with a rebel flag flying. An immense crowd collected on the levee, and the captain was compelled to take down the Confederate ensign.

APRIL 20.—Seven military companies were trained in Douglas county and nine in Leavenworth; one was ordered to Fort Leavenworth for 30-day service.

APRIL 25.—Military companies were being formed in nearly every county.

APRIL 29.—Capt. J. L. Reno, for whom Reno county was later named, was placed in charge of the arsenal at Fort Leavenworth.

MAY 1.—Rebel flags flew in many places in Missouri.

MAY 10.—Capt. Nathaniel Lyon and Col. Francis P. Blair, at the head of 6,000 Union volunteers, surrounded the rebel state guard at St. Louis, and took them prisoners.

MAY 22.—The Republican congressional convention was held at Topeka.

MAY 28.—The First Kansas volunteer infantry regiment began to organize in Leavenworth.

JUNE 1.—Col. William H. Emory and Maj. S. D. Sturgis arrived at Fort Leavenworth from the southwest with United States troops.

JUNE 3.—General Lyon became commander of the Military Department of the West.

The First Kansas infantry regiment was mustered in at Leavenworth.

A rebel flag was captured by Kansans at Iatan, Mo., and was brought to Leavenworth.

JUNE 4.—The state legislature adjourned.

JUNE 10.—Capt. Alfred Sully went from Fort Leavenworth to St. Joseph, with a force of regulars, to organize a home guard.

JUNE 11.—M. F. Conway was elected to Kansas' seat in the U. S. house of representatives.

Capt. William E. Prince and a body of U. S. troops left Fort Leavenworth for Kansas City.

JUNE 13.—Seven companies of the First Kansas left Leavenworth for Kansas City.

JUNE 17.—Governor Robinson called for more troops.

JUNE 20.—The Second Kansas infantry regiment was mustered into service at Kansas City, Mo., for a period of three months.

JUNE 24.—The First Kansas infantry regiment and regular troops, under Maj. Samuel Sturgis, left Kansas City for Springfield, Mo.

JUNE 25.—James Lane published a statement in the Leavenworth *Conservative*: "On the 20th instant I was duly appointed a Brigadier General in the volunteer force of the United States."

JUNE 26.—The Second Kansas infantry regiment left Kansas City for a meeting with Major Sturgis in Missouri.

JULY 4.—Printers in the First and Second Kansas regiments took over the Clinton (Mo.) *Journal* and published a Union issue, remarking that the former editor left in "very indecent haste."

JULY 7.—Kansas troops under Sturgis joined General Lyon at Grand river.

JULY 8.—The Kansas senators, James H. Lane and Samuel C. Pomeroy, drew lots to determine the length of their terms in the U. S. senate.

JULY 12.—Organization of the Fifth Kansas cavalry regiment was started.

JULY 15.—The Third Kansas regiment was organized with James Montgomery as its colonel. The Third and Fourth Kansas regiments were consolidated to form the Tenth Kansas infantry regiment, April 3, 1862.

JULY 24.—The First battery of light artillery was mustered into service. Thomas Bickerton was the captain.

JULY 25.—By a vote at a Union meeting in Leavenworth, business houses were to close early every day to allow all citizens time for military drill.

AUGUST 9.—The rebel John Matthews drove 60 Union families from the Neutral lands.

AUGUST 10.—The Battle of Wilson's creek was fought south of Springfield, Mo. Troops from the First and Second Kansas regiments took an active part.

AUGUST 17.—General Lane began to fortify Camp Lincoln, Bourbon county.

SEPTEMBER 2.—The Battle of Dry Wood. Union men under Cols. James Montgomery, C. R. Jennison, and H. P. Johnson and Capts. Thomas Moonlight, John Ritchie, James M. [?] Williams, and John E. Stewart fought the rebels under Gen. James S. Rains.

SEPTEMBER 7.—Atchison was in danger of invasion by rebels from Missouri. Five companies went to her assistance from Jefferson, Jackson, and Doniphan counties.

SEPTEMBER 8.—The First Kansas infantry regiment was located at Hannibal, Mo.

SEPTEMBER 10.—The Sixth Kansas cavalry was mustered into service at Fort Scott. It had been organized in July.

SEPTEMBER 12.—Humboldt was sacked by rebels.

SEPTEMBER 15.—The Second Kansas infantry regiment arrived in Leavenworth and was given a public reception.

SEPTEMBER 20.—The "John Brown's body" song was first sung in Leavenworth. The song originated with Union soldiers at Fort Warren, Mass.

SEPTEMBER 21.—Col. William R. Judson of the Sixth Kansas regiment returned from the Neutral lands, having routed the Confederate marauders.

SEPTEMBER 23.—Lane took Osceola, Mo., and burned it.

SEPTEMBER 30.—Lane's brigade arrived in Kansas City, joining forces under Sturgis.

OCTOBER.—Organization of the Third Kansas battery was begun.

OCTOBER 11.—Sturgis and Lane left for Springfield, Mo.

OCTOBER 16.—Humboldt was attacked by rebels for the second time and burned.

OCTOBER 24.—Organization of the Ninth Kansas cavalry was begun.

OCTOBER 25.—Gardner, Johnson county, was sacked by Missourians.

OCTOBER 27.—The organization of the Eighth Kansas infantry regiment was completed.

OCTOBER 28.—The Seventh Kansas cavalry regiment was organized at Fort Leavenworth.

OCTOBER 30.—Settlers were driven from Mine creek in Linn county.

OCTOBER 31.—The Second Kansas infantry regiment, a 90-day unit, was honorably discharged.

NOVEMBER 2.—Lane and Sturgis reached Springfield, Mo.

NOVEMBER 5.—Votes for the state legislature and a location for the state capital were cast. Topeka received the majority of the votes, thus making it the permanent capital of Kansas. Lawrence was second in the balloting. Whisky Point, near Fort Riley, received two votes!

NOVEMBER 12.—A new military area, the Department of Kansas, was established with Maj. Gen. David Hunter in charge.

NOVEMBER 15.—The Kansas brigade returned to Fort Scott.

NOVEMBER 27.—The Third Kansas battery was mustered at Leavenworth.

NOVEMBER 30.—Gen. James Denver was ordered to report to Fort Scott.

DECEMBER 11.—Rebels raided Potosi, Linn county.

DECEMBER 14.—Maj. H. H. Williams and his Third Kansas regiment took Papinsville and Butler, Mo.

DECEMBER 20.—The Eighth Kansas infantry was located at Westport, Mo. One hundred contrabands, freed by Colonel Anthony at Independence, arrived at Leavenworth.

DECEMBER 31.—The First Kansas infantry regiment was ordered to Kansas City and Fort Scott.

1862

JANUARY 9.—Capt. John Brown, Jr., arrived at Leavenworth with enough men to fill his company, which was Co. K, Seventh Kansas cavalry. The men in Brown's company were mainly from Ohio.

JANUARY 14.—The state legislature met at Topeka.

JANUARY 15.—Union Indians were defeated in the Indian territory, and were driven to Kansas. They encamped on Fall river.

JANUARY 20.—The Second Kansas cavalry was ordered from Fort Leavenworth to Quindaro (now part of present Kansas City).

JANUARY 21.—The decision of the supreme court, declaring the election of the governor in 1861 illegal, was published. The opinion was handed down by Chief Justice Thomas Ewing, Jr. This decision was considered a defeat for Senator Lane in his attempt to remove Governor Robinson from office.

JANUARY 23.—The Thirteenth Wisconsin volunteer regiment arrived at Fort Leavenworth.

JANUARY 27.—James H. Lane arrived in Leavenworth, supposedly as a major general, to take command of an expedition to the South.

JANUARY 29.—The Ninth Wisconsin volunteer regiment arrived at Fort Leavenworth.

JANUARY 30.—Investigations were begun in the house of representatives against Gov. Charles Robinson, Secretary of State John W. Robinson, and State Auditor George S. Hillyer "for high misdemeanors in office" relating to the sale of state bonds.

FEBRUARY.—The supreme court held that laws passed by the territorial legislature, after Kansas became a state, were valid.

FEBRUARY 14.—The report of the house committee on the negotiation of state bonds was published. It concluded with a resolution to impeach the governor, auditor, and secretary of state.

FEBRUARY 26.—Gen. James Lane wrote the legislature that he would not lead a military expedition but would resign his commission and return to the U. S. senate.

FEBRUARY 28.—The *Daily Inquirer*, a rebel organ, was started in Leavenworth. A meeting was called to mob the newspaper. D. W. Wilder and M. W. Delahay addressed the mob, advocating free speech and the meeting of argument with argument.

The Third Kansas battery was assigned to the Second Kansas cavalry regiment.

MARCH 1.—Three seats in the state senate were declared vacant because the senators had accepted commissions in the volunteer service. They were friends of Governor Robinson and enemies of Senator Lane.

MARCH 6.—The legislature adjourned.

MARCH 7.—The notorious William Quantrill, alias Charley Hart, plundered Aubrey, in Johnson county, and killed at least three citizens.

MARCH 14.—John A. Martin, lieutenant colonel of the Eighth Kansas regiment, was appointed provost marshal at Leavenworth.

MARCH 15.—Kansas soldiers at Fort Riley destroyed the office of the *Kansas Frontier News*, at Junction City, believing it to be a disloyal newspaper.

General Denver was ordered to take command in Kansas. Gen. George W. Deitzler was to join Gen. Samuel R. Curtis in Arkansas.

MARCH 26.—The First Colorado regiment was defeated at Pigeon's Ranch, New Mexico. This regiment was reportedly made up of Kansas men.

MARCH 27.—The Ninth Kansas cavalry was mustered in at Leavenworth.

The Ninth Kansas volunteer regiment was renamed the Second Kansas cavalry.

APRIL 8.—Robert Mitchell and James Blunt were appointed brigadier generals.

MAY 2.—Gen. James Blunt took command of the Department of Kansas.

The First Indian regiment was organized at Le Roy, by Robert Furnas.

MAY 8.—Congress appropriated $100,000 to pay the Lane brigade.

MAY 11.—The Jayhawker, Marshall Cleveland, alias Moore, alias Metz, was killed at the Marias des Cygnes river by men of the Sixth Kansas regiment. He once had been a captain in Jennison's regiment, and stole in the name of liberty.

MAY 24.—Col. William A. Barstow, of the Third Wisconsin, was appointed provost marshal general for the state. Maj. Elias A.

Calkins, of the Third Wisconsin, received the appointment as provost marshal for Leavenworth.

MAY 27-29.—The First, Seventh, and Eighth Kansas regiments, the Second Kansas battery, and the Twelfth and Thirteenth Wisconsin regiments sailed for Corinth, Miss.

MAY 30.—Col. William Weer, of the Tenth Kansas, was given command of an Indian expedition.

JUNE.—The first reoccupation of any part of the Indian territory, now Oklahoma, since May, 1861, was made by Kansas troops, who marched almost to Fort Gibson.

JUNE 2-16.—The Kansas senate met as a court of impeachment. Secretary of State John W. Robinson and Auditor George S. Hillyer were impeached and removed from office, while Gov. Charles Robinson was acquitted.

JUNE 15.—The Leavenworth *Inquirer* was suppressed by General Blunt.

JUNE 18.—D. R. Anthony, lieutenant colonel of the Seventh Kansas, issued the following order: "Any officer or soldier of this command who shall arrest and deliver to his master a fugitive slave, shall be summarily and severely punished, according to the laws relative to such crimes." For issuing this order Colonel Anthony was arrested and deprived of his command in Tennessee.

JUNE 20.—Decision of U. S. Attorney General Edward Bates: "The absence of Governor Robinson from the State did not create the disability contemplated by the Constitution of Kansas, by which the Lieutenant Governor would be authorized to perform the duties of Governor." The need for this decision came about when Governor Robinson and Lieutenant Governor Root appointed different men to the colonelcy of the Seventh Kansas regiment.

JUNE 22.—The organization of the Second Indian regiment began.

JUNE 30.—Bill and Jim Anderson, Quantrill and others, raided into Lyon county, shooting several people and stealing horses.

AUGUST 4.—James Lane opened a recruiting office in Leavenworth for negro and white troops.

AUGUST 8.—General Blunt left Leavenworth to take command of the expedition in the Indian territory.

AUGUST 12.—Preston B. Plumb and Edmund G. Ross were enlisting men for the Eleventh Kansas regiment.

AUGUST 15.—Quantrill issued orders that men going to federal posts to enlist would be shot when captured.

SEPTEMBER.—Organization of the Twelfth and Thirteenth Kansas regiments began.

SEPTEMBER 7.—Quantrill raided Olathe, killing several men, and destroying offices of the *Mirror* and *Herald*.

Governor Robinson issued an order for complete organization of the militia.

SEPTEMBER 10.—Organization of the Second battery began.

SEPTEMBER 14.—Thomas Ewing, Jr., chief justice of Kansas, was mustered as colonel of the Eleventh Kansas cavalry regiment.

John Halderman was appointed major general of the militia of northern Kansas.

SEPTEMBER 15.—The Eleventh Kansas cavalry regiment was mustered at Fort Leavenworth.

SEPTEMBER 16.—Organization of the Third Indian regiment began.

SEPTEMBER 17.—The Republican state convention was held at Topeka.

SEPTEMBER 18.—D. R. Anthony resigned from the Seventh Kansas regiment and returned to Leavenworth.

SEPTEMBER 20.—The Thirteenth Kansas cavalry regiment was mustered at Atchison.

SEPTEMBER 29.—The Union state convention was held at Lawrence.

SEPTEMBER 30.—The Twelfth Kansas infantry regiment was mustered at Paola.

OCTOBER 1.—The Democratic state convention was held at Topeka.

OCTOBER 17.—Quantrill and his gang raided Johnson county, killing three men and burning 13 buildings.

The First Kansas Colored regiment was organized near Fort Lincoln, Bourbon county. It was ordered to Baxter Springs. The Thirteenth regiment was at Fort Scott, the Twelfth on the eastern border and the Eleventh had gone to join Blunt.

NOVEMBER 4.—An election was held for state officers, members of the state legislature and a U. S. representative.

DECEMBER 7.—General Blunt won a victory at Prairie Grove, Ark. He also gained victories at Newtonia, October 4; Old Fort Wayne, October 22; and Cane Hill, November 28. Blunt's forces took Van Buren, December 29.

1863

JANUARY 13.—The state legislature met at Topeka.

The First Colored regiment was mustered at Fort Scott.

JANUARY 17.—Fort Scott was re-established as a permanent military post.

FEBRUARY 10.—The Leavenworth *Daily Inquirer,* a secession paper, ceased to exist. The presses were destroyed, the type thrown out the window and cases burned.

MARCH 3.—The legislature adjourned.

MARCH 13.—Thomas Ewing, Jr., was appointed a brigadier general.

APRIL.—The Fourteenth Kansas cavalry began to organize.

JUNE 1.—Sidney Clarke was appointed provost marshal for Kansas, Nebraska, and Colorado.

JUNE 11.—Col. James Montgomery, of Kansas, with his Colored regiment, left Hilton Head for a raid in Georgia.

JULY 1.—Col. James Williams, with 800 men of the First Kansas Colored regiment and 500 Indians, defeated a force of Texans under the Cherokee Stand Watie at Cabin Creek.

JULY 4.—The surrender of Vicksburg, Miss. Troops of the First Kansas regiment took part in the campaign.

JULY 17.—Blunt gained a victory over Cooper at Honey Springs, south of the Arkansas river in Indian territory.

AUGUST 21.—Quantrill and his guerrillas raided and sacked Lawrence. Approximately 200 buildings were burned and nearly 150 persons were killed.

SEPTEMBER.—The Fifteenth Kansas cavalry regiment was organized to protect border towns from further raids.

SEPTEMBER 8.—A Republican convention was held at Paola. A resolution was passed asking for the removal of Gens. John M. Schofield and Thomas Ewing and the establishment of a new military department.

SEPTEMBER 19.—The Battle of Chickamauga, in Georgia. Members of the Eighth Kansas regiment took an active part.

OCTOBER 6.—General Blunt and a small escort were attacked near Baxter Springs by Quantrill and his Confederate guerrillas. Blunt escaped, but most of his men were killed. Fort Blair was also attacked, but the guerrillas were repelled and several were killed.

Kansas up to this date had furnished the Union 9,613 white troops, 2,262 Indians, and one Colored regiment.

OCTOBER 15.—The Fifteenth Kansas cavalry regiment was mustered at Fort Leavenworth.

OCTOBER 25.—Col. Powell Clayton and the Fifth Kansas regiment took part in the Battle of Pine Bluff, Ark. Negro noncombatants were used to barricade the streets.

NOVEMBER 3.—The general election was held in Kansas. State representatives, district attorneys and a chief justice of the supreme court were elected.

NOVEMBER 25.—The Battle of Chattanooga, Tenn. The Eighth Kansas regiment was instrumental in securing Mission Ridge and Orchard Knob.

DECEMBER 18.—Col. William Phillips defeated a rebel force near Fort Gibson.

1864

JANUARY 1.—Kansas was made a military department with Gen. Samuel Curtis in command.

JANUARY 12.—The Kansas legislature met at Topeka.

FEBRUARY 6.—The Seventh Kansas cavalry regiment was given a reception in Leavenworth.

Eight senators and 19 members of the house protested the forthcoming election of a U. S. senator.

FEBRUARY 9.—Sitting in joint convention, the two houses elected a senator for the term that began March 4, 1865. Gov. Thomas Carney was declared elected but never claimed the office.

FEBRUARY 20.—The Battle of Olustee, Fla. Col. James Montgomery, commanding Colored troops, was in this battle.

FEBRUARY 29.—A reception for the Eighth Kansas infantry regiment was held at Leavenworth.

MARCH 1.—The legislature adjourned.

APRIL 20.—The War Department credited the state with 1,529 Colored troops.

APRIL 21.—The Republican state convention was held at Topeka.

APRIL 30.—A battle at Jenkin's Ferry, Ark. Members of the Second Kansas cavalry participated.

MAY 4.—Kansas had raised 4,500 troops in excess of all calls.

JUNE.—Fort Ellsworth, later known as Fort Harker, was established.

JUNE 1.—Democratic state convention was held at Topeka.

JUNE 17.—The First Kansas infantry regiment was mustered out at Fort Leavenworth, with the exception of two companies of veterans who were mustered at Bovina, Miss., to form the Veteran battalion, First infantry.

JULY 2.—Capt. William Matthews began to raise a Colored battery.

General Curtis was authorized to raise a regiment of "Hundred Days" men. It was to be called the Seventeenth Kansas regiment.

JULY 27.—Confederate Gen. Richard M. Gano attacked an outpost at Fort Smith, Ark., capturing Capt. David F. Medford and 82 of his Sixth Kansas men.

JULY 28.—The Seventeenth Kansas infantry regiment was mustered at Fort Leavenworth.

AUGUST 3.—A state convention of Colored men was held; they asked that the word, "white," be struck from the constitution.

AUGUST 10.—Indians made a serious raid on the Little Blue river near Marysville.

AUGUST 29.—Four companies of the Fifth Kansas, commanded by Maj. Samuel Walker, arrived at Leavenworth.

SEPTEMBER 6.—Fort Zarah was established by General Curtis. He named it for his son, who was killed at the Baxter Springs massacre.

SEPTEMBER 8.—The Republican state convention was held at Topeka.

SEPTEMBER 13.—Republican Union state convention was held at Topeka.

OCTOBER 1.—Confederate Gen. Sterling Price was reported advancing toward Kansas.

OCTOBER 8.—Gov. Thomas Carney called out the state militia, Maj. Gen. George Deitzler commanding.

OCTOBER 10.—General Curtis proclaimed martial law in Kansas.

OCTOBER 14.—General Blunt moved from Olathe to Hickman Mills, Mo. His command was organized into three brigades.

OCTOBER 16.—Blunt moved toward Lexington, Mo., with two brigades.

OCTOBER 19.—Blunt met the Confederate army and was driven back.

OCTOBER 20.—Blunt moved to Independence, Mo. General Moonlight was defeated at the Battle of the Little Blue.

OCTOBER 22.—The Battle of the Big Blue was fought, ending in a Union victory.

Kansas had an estimated 20,000 men under arms.

OCTOBER 23.—The Battle of Westport, with General Price's line extending west nearly to the Shawnee Methodist Mission in Kansas. The rebels were defeated and began to retreat.

OCTOBER 24.—Price's army entered Kansas in Linn county, and camped at Trading Post on the Marais des Cygnes.

OCTOBER 25.—The Battle of Mine Creek. Kansas troops met and routed the Confederate army.

OCTOBER 26.—Generals Curtis and Blunt, along with their brigades, started to follow the retreating Confederates.

OCTOBER 27.—Governor Carney ordered the militia members to return to their homes.

OCTOBER 28.—The Sixteenth Kansas cavalry regiment was mustered at Fort Leavenworth.

The Battle of Newtonia, Mo. Blunt began the fight alone but later was reinforced by Sanborn. The rebels abandoned the field.

OCTOBER 29.—Gen. William S. Rosecrans ordered all troops in his departments to return to their districts; however, Gen. U. S. Grant ordered the pursuit of Price to be resumed.

NOVEMBER 8.—The pursuit of Price was discontinued when Generals Curtis and Blunt reached the Arkansas river.

State and national elections were held. Members of the state legislature, state officers and national congressmen were elected; also several amendments to the state constitution were approved.

1865

JANUARY 10.—The state legislature met at Topeka.

JANUARY 12.—James H. Lane was re-elected U. S. senator.

JANUARY 19.—The legislature adjourned until January 23, to take a railroad excursion to Lawrence and Wyandotte.

FEBRUARY 7.—Gen. G. M. Dodge took command of Fort Leavenworth, succeeding Gen. Samuel R. Curtis.

FEBRUARY 15.—Kansas received a draft call for the first time. Due to an error the state had not been given full credit for her volunteers.

FEBRUARY 20.—The legislature adjourned.

FEBRUARY 21.—The Eleventh Kansas regiment left Fort Riley for Fort Kearny.

FEBRUARY 25.—Gen. Thomas Ewing, Jr., resigned his command and left the army.

MARCH 15.—The draft in Kansas was suspended.

MARCH 18.—Five Kansas regiments left Fort Smith.

APRIL 9.—End of the Civil War.

APRIL 14.—Assassination of President Lincoln, by John Wilkes Booth.

During the four years of the Civil War, Kansas supplied 17 regiments, three batteries, two Negro regiments and a Negro battery. Altogether Kansas is reported to have contributed 18,069 white troops and 2,080 Negroes; an excess of more than 3,000 over all calls. The census of 1860 gave Kansas a white male population between the ages of 18 and 45 as only 27,976 and less than 300 male Negroes.

Mark W. Delahay: Peripatetic Politician
A HISTORICAL CASE STUDY
JOHN G. CLARK

THE Democratic party, in territorial Kansas, was the victim of a deep split engendered by the slavery issue. One faction, composed mainly of Missourians settling in Kansas, supported slavery. A second faction viewed slavery on grounds of expediency and refused to condone the militant tactics of the Proslavery group. As a result of this factionalism Democrats labored under a manifest disadvantage in the contest for political control of Kansas. The Democratic party was early associated in the minds of the electorate with the Proslavery faction, and the possibility of Democratic ascendancy in Kansas became more remote in proportion to the mounting free-state sentiment of the settlers.

Representative of the group opposed to both Abolitionist and Proslavery factions was the politically ubiquitous Mark W. Delahay, a Democrat, and editor of the Leavenworth *Kansas Territorial Register*. Delahay was cognizant of the weak Democratic position in Kansas and threw his support to the formation of the Topeka Free-State government in the spring of 1856, although retaining his position as a Douglas Democrat. The effort at Topeka proved to be a failure but it served the purpose of consolidating the various Free-State groups on a political level. These groups were soon to furnish the nucleus of the Republican party in Kansas. Mark W. Delahay was to be one of the founding fathers of Kansas Republicanism. This study will attempt to trace the reasons and motivation behind Delahay's change in politics. One factor, and probably the decisive one, was Delahay's long association and friendship with Abraham Lincoln.

According to Delahay, his acquaintance with Lincoln began in 1835 in Illinois when both were circuit lawyers.[1] A newspaper man in Kansas, Delahay had gained his experience in the Illinois of the 1840's and had conducted a Democratic paper, the Virginia (Ill.)

JOHN G. CLARK, native of New Jersey, received his B. A. degree from Park College, Parkville, Mo., in 1954. He is currently a graduate student in history and an assistant instructor of Western civilization at the University of Kansas, Lawrence.

1. Mark W. Delahay, *Abraham Lincoln* (New York, Daniel H. Newhall, 1939—a limited edition, reprinted from the Unique Broadside, issued by M. W. Delahay about 1870), p. [2]. Delahay was also a distant relative of Lincoln's, having married the latter's sixth cousin.

(301)

Observer in 1848-1849. About 1840 Delahay was editor of a Whig paper, the Naples (Ill.) *Post*.[2]

Politically, then, Delahay was both Whig and Democrat during this decade. He participated in the Whig nominating convention of 1846 prior to the congressional elections. According to Delahay, his role was crucial. In 1840 the Whig party came to an agreement within the Springfield congressional district that congressmen were to be chosen by rotation. Abraham Lincoln obtained the position guaranteeing nomination in 1846. In that year another Whig leader attempted to supplant Lincoln. This move was defeated by a series of articles composed by Delahay in Whig papers. Delahay was a member of the five-man committee choosing the permanent officers of the convention and thus in a position to exert some influence over the choice of personnel on the nominating and resolutions committees. Both committees were eventually composed of Lincoln's partisans. Furthermore, Lincoln had in January, 1846, expressed doubt as to his receiving the Cass county vote. Delahay was delegate from Cass county and in November, 1845, had been active in Lincoln's interest. Much to Lincoln's surprise, Cass county was delivered for Lincoln,[3] at least partially as a result of Delahay's efforts. According to Delahay ". . . in a letter Mr. Lincoln did me the high honor of ascribing his success to my efforts."[4] Delahay was, perhaps unknowingly, cultivating a future patron for his political wares.

Elections under the Topeka constitution, which Delahay had aided in constructing, were held in January, 1856. Charles Robinson and W. Y. Roberts were elected governor and lieutenant governor; and Delahay was named representative to congress.[5] The Free-State government organized in March, 1856, and elected James H. Lane and Andrew H. Reeder as senators from Kansas.

Territorial comment on Delahay's nomination and election was generally favorable. The Lawrence *Herald of Freedom* accepted Delahay as a Douglas Democrat who would serve to make the ticket popular in "those districts of Kansas where freedom is not regarded as *infinitely* preferable to slavery, but is weighed in the

---

2. Franklin W. Scott, *Newspapers and Periodicals of Illinois 1814-1879* (Collections of the Illinois State Historical Library, v. 6, Springfield, 1910), pp. 258, 345.

3. Donald W. Riddle, *Lincoln Runs for Congress* (Abraham Lincoln Association, Springfield, Ill., Rutgers University Press, New Brunswick, 1948), pp. 154-156.

4. Delahay, *op. cit.*, p. 4.

5. *Herald of Freedom*, Lawrence, December 29, 1855, January 19, 1856. On December 29 the *Herald* cited Robert Klotz and M. F. Conway as his competitors in the Lawrence convention of December, 1855. Delahay ran unopposed in the elections. On the evening of December 22, 1855, Proslavery groups from Missouri invaded Delahay's Leavenworth office, destroyed it, and threw his printing press into the Missouri river.

balance of political expediency, and found to be rather more desirable, if anything, to the peculiar infamy of the South." [6]

Sometime shortly after the Topeka legislature adjourned, Lane and Delahay left Kansas and traveled eastward. A biographer of Lane has indicated that Delahay was present at the Cincinnati Democratic National convention in June, 1856.[7] However, John Speer, contemporary of Lane and Delahay, and biographer of the former, reported a conversation with Delahay stating that Lane and Delahay both campaigned for Fremont in 1856. Allegedly, the Republican party invited Delahay and Lane to New England "for an assault on Democratic Connecticut." [8]

It is certain that Delahay was in Washington, D. C., in July, 1856. In a letter to Governor Robinson and Lane, Delahay reported that Governor Shannon was on his way to Kansas with express instructions from Buchanan to arrest and punish "any and all persons that may take part in the organization of the Independent State Govt. . . ." [9]

Delahay's forebodings were turned into actualities in July. Governor Robinson had been arrested in May, 1856, and then came the dispersion of the Free-State legislature. Armed parties of both Free-State and Proslavery men roamed the territory with occasional meetings and skirmishes. A new governor, John W. Geary, arrived replacing the dismissed Governor Shannon. In October elections were held for representatives to the territorial legislature and on the question of calling a convention to form a state constitution. The Free-State men boycotted the elections and the question was affirmatively answered.

Where was M. W. Delahay during these momentous times? As the *Illinois State Register* put it, "one Mark W. Delahay, sometime general loafer from Kansas, shrieks for freedom at a Republican meeting at Carlinville." [10] Delahay was on the stump in Illinois campaigning for Fremont. One can imagine that Delahay, as a bona fide Kansan, stumping for a party based on anti-slavery principles

---

6. *Ibid.*
7. Wendell H. Stephenson, *The Political Career of General James H. Lane* (Publications of the Kansas State Historical Society, Topeka, v. 3 [1930]), p. 61.
8. John Speer, *Life of Gen. James H. Lane*, "the Liberator of Kansas" (Garden City, Kan., 1897), p. 108.
9. Mark W. Delahay to General Robinson, Colonel Lane and others, Washington, D. C., February 16, 1856.—"Robinson Papers," Mss. division, Kansas State Historical Society, Topeka (hereafter cited as K. S. H. S.). Delahay from the beginning of the Topeka movement had expressed doubt as to its legality, stating that "the power of a Territorial Government ceases only by an act of the body which created it."—*Kansas Territorial Register*, Leavenworth, December 22, 1855.
10. *Illinois State Register*, Springfield, October 18, 1856, quoted in Albert J. Beveridge, *Abraham Lincoln, 1809-1858* (4 vols., Boston and New York, Houghton Mifflin Company, The Riverside Press, Cambridge, 1928), v. 4, p. 56.

and advocating the admission of "Bleeding Kansas" as a free state, made full use of his oratorical powers. The 1,300,000 votes garnered by the Republicans in the nation could not have failed to impress Delahay. Flexibility and willingness to advance with the times were characteristics of Delahay throughout this amorphous period. He was not yet ready to make a final political commitment but when he did it would be the right one.

Lincoln's stature as a Republican leader was on the rise in Illinois and Delahay probably possessed the necessary political astuteness to recognize this trend. In fact, one biographer of Lincoln has asserted that during the entire territorial period Delahay was merely the echo of Lincoln in Kansas. This same authority referred to Delahay as a "dissolute Illinois attorney" who was "among the broken-down politicians, unsuccessful lawyers, and failures in business who . . . went to the new Territories for 'another chance.' " [11] Although Delahay may have been in touch with Lincoln during the earlier territorial period, the former's forthright stand on the Kansas-Nebraska act and its correlative principle, popular sovereignty, seems to invalidate such a conclusion.[12] Delahay perceived that the advocacy of a Democratic position in Kansas was of little value in terms of popular support. However, he remained, at least outwardly, until the presidential campaign of 1856, a faithful exponent of Democracy. In explaining Delahay's position, it seems reasonable to conclude that since Lincoln and the Republican party did not prove themselves nationally until 1856, a sudden switch of politics would have been premature and could have resulted in political suicide.

The year 1857 opened inauspiciously for Free-Staters and Republicans of all shades. In March the supreme court announced the Dred Scott decision which actually destroyed the basic principle upon which the Republican party had organized, that of recognizing congressional authority over slavery in the territories. The Republican *bete noire,* Slavocracy, was stirring aggressively.

In Kansas the Proslavery territorial legislature had issued a call for a June election of delegates to a constitutional convention, which framed, in October, a constitution legalizing slavery. During the same month the Free-State party captured decisive majori-

11. *Ibid,* v. 3, pp. 308, 309.
12. *Kansas Territorial Register,* July 7, 28, August 4, 11, 1855. *See, also,* last issue of *Register,* December 22, 1855, for Delahay's effort to keep any mention of slavery out of the Topeka constitution. *See, also, Daily Kansas Freeman,* Topeka, October 26, 1855, for Delahay's resolution introduced in the Topeka convention supporting the Kansas-Nebraska act.

Mark William Delahay
(1817-1879)

Early Leavenworth publisher and a friend of Abraham Lincoln. Copy of a painting in the collections of the Kansas State Historical Society, Topeka.

ties in both houses of the territorial legislature. The passage of the Lecompton constitution led to the famous, or infamous, Lecompton debates in congress with Douglas combating the Buchanan machine in an effort to defeat the bill admitting Kansas under the Lecompton constitution. Passing in the senate, the bill failed in the house and in April the house approved the Crittenden-Montgomery amendment providing for resubmission of the constitution to a popular vote.[13]

Delahay's reaction to these events is illuminated in a letter to Douglas in April, 1858:

Last night the Steamer brought us the glad news of the defeat of Lecompton in the House (or rather what we regard as equal to a defeat) . . . the people collected on the Hill by the Eldridge House, Drum & fife and a torch light procession with loud calls for me, and the occasion forced me from my *sick room* . . . to speak to the vast crowd. I could not do less than my *duty to you* and *Crittenden* . . . I desire to assure you that all past differences between you and me upon political views, I am disposed as much to regret as I am to forgive; . . . you [I] am at your command whenever I can testify my greatfulness to you.[14]

Then came the compromise English bill and the rejection of the Lecompton constitution in August, 1858, by Kansas voters. Delahay's position, a study in equivocation, is expressed in a letter to Abraham Lincoln in June, 1858. In regard to political parties in Kansas, Delahay stated that:

. . . there are some here who are trying to get up an organization of a Douglas party, but I am oppose[d] to any such folly . . . & again there are others who are trying to inaugurate a Republican party which I also regard as bad policy . . . and to which I am opposed, at least until we become a State; . . . I have today offered to Bet an even Bet of $100 that you will be the next Senator from Ills.[15]

The definitive test of strength between Lincoln and Douglas was yet to come. When it came, Delahay was to be on hand to play an active, if somewhat unethical, role.

As the summer of 1858 commenced, Delahay's field of activities had moved from Kansas back to Illinois. The contest between Douglas and Lincoln for Douglas' seat in the United States senate

---

13. In an extra-legal election on the entire constitution, held in January, 1858, it was rejected 10,226 to 161.

14. Mark W. Delahay to Stephen A. Douglas, Wyandotte, April 7, 1858.—"Stephen A. Douglas Papers," University of Chicago. Copy in the possession of Dr. Robert W. Johannsen, University of Illinois. Delahay had served with Douglas in the Nauvoo expedition against the Illinois Mormons in 1846.

15. Mark W. Delahay to Abraham Lincoln, Leavenworth, June 13, 1858.—"Lincoln Papers," Library of Congress, copy in the possession of Dr. Robert W. Johannsen. *See, also,* Thomas Ewing, Jr., to R. B. Mitchell, December 15, 1858.—"Ewing Papers," K. S. H. S.

had begun, and on May 18, 1858, Lincoln and Delahay, along with other Illinois Republicans, spoke in Edwardsville.[16] This procedure was followed again in Moro, Ill., a short time later.[17]

Stephen A. Douglas was in a precarious position. A letter from Delahay to Lyman Trumbull is illustrative of the type of opposition Douglas faced. Said Delahay:

Last night with Brown, English, and *Lieb* (mail agent),[18] I spent several hours; *Lieb* is drilling the faithful, and I of late, have made a few speeches, sort of Douglass speeches. *Lincoln* and I went out to Edwardsville Tuesday. . . . Lincoln made a fine Republican speech. My speech did not please the Republicans, [but] by Brown and Lincoln, it was understood what I should say beforehand; my policy is to back up Douglass until after the Buckhanan convention nominate their state ticket, then I am for Lincoln.[19]

One authority maintains that Delahay's motive in stumping for Douglas was his bitter hatred for the "little giant."[20] It is doubtful that Delahay hated Douglas. Actually the Republicans found endorsement of Douglas to be a valuable expedient to prevent Buchanan men from harmonizing with the Douglas wing. Delahay had reached that phase in his career where he felt that the correct, politique, and final political allegiance could be consummated with safety. And the allegiance was between Delahay and the man, Lincoln, rather than with the Republican party. In any event, Delahay now concentrated his efforts on securing the election of Lincoln, whom Delahay did not hesitate to advise,[21] and on denouncing Douglas.

Delahay had now achieved orthodoxy. He believed, as other Republicans did, or professed to, that Douglas had planned the entire Lecompton affair "so as to give himself an opportunity to win applause by opposing the abortion." Hence, the Republicans could "make out a plausible case to show that the Buchanan administration had been seeking to destroy the 'little giant'" and that Douglas had used the Lecompton affair to create a new basis for

---

16. Roy P. Basler, ed., *The Collected Works of Abraham Lincoln* (9 vols., The Abraham Lincoln Association, Springfield, Ill., Rutgers University Press, New Brunswick, N. J., 1953), v. 2, p. 447.

17. Beveridge, *op. cit.*, v. 4, p. 195n.

18. George A. Brown, Republican editor of the Alton *Courier;* J. English, a Republican politician in Alton; Lieb, considered to be a Buchanan administration agent working against Douglas.

19. Delahay to Lyman Trumbull, Alton, Ill., May 22, 1858, quoted in Beveridge, *op. cit.*, v. 4, p. 227.

20. Arthur C. Cole, *The Era of the Civil War, 1848-1870* (Illinois Centennial Commission, Springfield, 1919), p. 166.

21. Delahay to Lincoln, Alton, Ill., August 13, 1858, "Lincoln Papers." Delahay advised ". . . misrepresent him [Douglas] and his press . . .," and accused Douglas of infidelity to Illinois Democrats after the elections of 1852 when Illinois did not get a good share of the spoils.

political popularity so as to "groom himself for the presidency."[22] Lincoln had gained national prominence as a result of his struggle with Douglas. Some papers in his home state were already mentioning his name in relation to the presidential elections in 1860. Delahay in January, 1859, wrote Lincoln inviting him to Kansas to speak at a Republican mass convention in Leavenworth. Lincoln's reply was favorable as he planned a trip to Council Bluffs, Iowa, for the summer of that year.[23] Much correspondence passed between Delahay and Lincoln concerning the latter's possible presence in Kansas in May, 1859. The importune Delahay maintained that his presence was necessary for the Republican party which Kansas was to organize in May. He urged that ". . . our Territorial Platform will want your [Lincoln's] aid in devising. . . . success is of first importance. . . . *You* must come. . . ."[24] Lincoln was unable to attend the Osawatomie convention in May but sent a letter of advice to the convention through Delahay and two other Kansans. In it he warned not to lower Republican standards and especially not to surrender the object of Republican organization—"the preventing of the *spread* and *nationalization* of Slavery."[25]

The newly organized Kansas Republican party was put to its first test in June, 1859, during the election of delegates to the Wyandotte constitutional convention. The Republicans captured 35 of the 52 delegates seated. In view of the two-to-one majority the Republicans secured, Delahay's reaction is remarkable. In a letter of ominous tenor to Lincoln, Delahay cried: "We have just barely escaped a defeat in Kansas, by the [Democrats'] use of larger sums of Federal money and by the importation of Irish votes from the River Towns in Mo. . . ." Delahay revealed his intention of running for governor or congress in the fall and continued by asking Lincoln to lend him $100 and to ask mutual Illinois friends to contribute the same.[26]

At this time Delahay and James H. Lane were close associates. They were attempting to publish a newspaper which would be both pro-Delahay and pro-Lane and hence pro-Republican. Delahay considered the newspaper absolutely necessary to forward his

22. Delahay to Lyman Trumbull, November 28, 1857, quoted in Cole, *op. cit.*, p. 174.
23. Lincoln to Delahay, Springfield, February 1, 1859.—Basler, *op. cit.*, v. 3, p. 355.
24. Delahay to Lincoln, Leavenworth, February 8, 1859.—"Lincoln Papers."
25. J. L. Dugger and M. F. Conway; Lincoln to Delahay, Springfield, May 14, 1859; Basler, *op. cit.*, v. 3, 378, 379.
26. Delahay to Lincoln, Chicago, June 15, 1859.—"Lincoln Papers." According to the letter James H. Lane and Delahay had been sent out to solicit funds, ostensibly for the Republican party and the coming campaign.

ambitions.[27] Lane was necessary also as he was an extremely popular figure among the Republicans and Free-Soilers of Kansas.

Delahay was quite optimistic concerning his chances of political success if he could maintain his close association with Lane. Lincoln would also prove useful. In a letter to Lincoln, Delahay stated his ambition for the senate and asked him to "address Genl Lane . . . and say whatever you can in my behalf to him [for] . . . he can I think secure the Election of his Colleague, and he is pledged to me."[28] In November, 1859, Delahay wrote Lincoln evincing his belief that Lincoln was the man for the Republican presidential nomination in 1860, and that Kansas, sure to be a state by then, would go for Lincoln if he would visit and canvass it thoroughly.[29] The very next day Delahay formally invited Lincoln, in behalf of the Republican party, to visit Leavenworth, exhorting him that ". . . This is the most important period of your political life and a compliance with our wishes will be the best thing of all the good ones you have ever done for the Republican Party. . . ."[30]

Delahay was using to advantage whatever influence he possessed to secure the senate seat. Lincoln complied with Delahay's request and visited Kansas late in 1859. He was ably chaperoned by Delahay and spoke at several of the leading settlements.[31] But it is unfair to accuse Delahay, as most authorities are prone to do, of merely using Lincoln to enhance his own prestige.[32] While this is true in part, the fact remains that Delahay felt a certain sense of loyalty to his patron. Lincoln held this trait in high esteem fortunately, for it was the one characteristic which Delahay had to offer.

Delahay, in 1860, continued his efforts to gain a senatorial seat.[33] In February Delahay asked Lincoln to urge his (Delahay's) candidacy upon his friends in Kansas and also requested Lincoln to

---

27. Delahay to Lincoln, Leavenworth, August 7, 1859.—*Ibid.* In it Delahay also repeats his request for $100.
28. Delahay to Lincoln, Leavenworth, September 28, 1859.—*Ibid.*
29. Delahay to Lincoln, Leavenworth, November 14, 1859.—*Ibid.*
30. Delahay to Lincoln, Leavenworth, November 15, 1859.—*Ibid.*
31. For brief accounts of his visit see "Lincoln in Kansas," *Kansas State Historical Collections,* v. 7 (1901-1902), pp. 536, 537, and Fred W. Brinkerhoff, "The Kansas Tour of Lincoln the Candidate," *The Kansas Historical Quarterly,* v. 13 (February, 1945), pp. 294-307.
32. Beveridge, *Abraham Lincoln,* v. 4, p. 342.
33. During this period Delahay was elected chief clerk of the territorial house of representatives. In January, 1860, the Leavenworth *Daily Herald* accused Delahay of tampering with and corrupting the *Journal* of the territorial house. A house committee subsequently vindicated him of these charges.—*House Journal . . . Kansas Territory, Special Session* (Lecompton, 1860), pp. 118, 119, 164, 165.

ask Lyman Trumbull to write in his behalf.[34] Trumbull did write Delahay but was indisposed to interfere in Kansas matters.[35]

The Republican party convention to select candidates for the presidential election of 1860 was rapidly approaching. Delahay schemed to present Kansas for Lincoln in the convention. Lincoln wrote to Delahay in March, 1860, in answer to three letters from Delahay. Lincoln referred to one letter in an extremely suggestive manner:

As to your kind wishes for myself, allow me to say I cannot enter the ring on the money basis—first, because, in the main, it is wrong; . . . but for certain objects, in a political contest, the use of some, is both right, and indispensable. . . . I now distinctly say this: if you shall be appointed a delegate to Chicago, I will furnish one hundred dollars to bear the expenses of the trip.[36]

Lincoln's comment suggested that Delahay had intimated that a sufficient sum of money, placed in capable hands, could secure for Lincoln the Kansas delegation. Delahay's political ethics would not have prevented the presentation to Lincoln of such an offer. But even granting the truth of this supposition, Delahay should not be castigated too hastily for he was playing the game according to rules which he, in no way, invented; and which, at the time, were not subjected to harsh condemnation.

Delahay in the months immediately preceding the Republican convention worked diligently to secure the election of Lincoln delegates from Kansas. He also found time to advise Lincoln that his chances for the nomination were excellent and presented reasons which have proven to be quite accurate.[37] But his efforts were in vain for he failed to deliver Kansas to Lincoln and even to get elected to the Kansas Republican convention at Lawrence in April, 1860. The Kansas convention at Lawrence declared itself for William H. Seward and its delegates were instructed accordingly. Lincoln was supposedly disappointed with Delahay's lack of influence in Kansas.[38] However, Lincoln was probably unconcerned

---

34. Delahay to Lincoln, February 6, 1860.—"Lincoln Papers." See, also, Lincoln to Delahay, March 16, 1860.—Basler, op. cit., v. 4, pp. 31, 32.
35. Lincoln to Trumbull, March 16, 1860.—Basler, op. cit. Trumbull to Delahay, February 11, 1860.—"Delahay Papers," K. S. H. S.
36. Lincoln to Delahay, March 16, 1860.—Basler, op. cit., v. 4, pp. 31, 32.
37. Delahay to Lincoln, Leavenworth, March 26, 1860.—"Lincoln Papers."
38. William Baringer, Lincoln's Rise to Power (Boston, Little, Brown and Company, 1937), p. 175. See Ewing to Lincoln, May 6, 1860, typed copy, "Ewing Papers," K. S. H. S., for an explanation of Delahay's failure. Seward, Ewing stated, had far and away the more zealous and numerous supporters who controlled the presses of Kansas. G. Raymond Gaeddert, The Birth of Kansas (University of Kansas Press, Lawrence, 1940), p. 20, stated that "the Republican people of Kansas were for William H. Seward, who was fighting their battles in the United States Senate."

over Delahay's failure and in a letter to Delahay, noticing that Kansas had chosen Seward, he consoled his friend by saying, "Don't stir them [the elected delegates] up to anger, but come along to the convention, & I will do as I said about expenses." [39]

In May, 1860, Delahay joined the pilgrimage of Republicans to Chicago. According to his own testimony, in letters to Lincoln, he performed important services behind the scenes. Lincoln warned him to "give no offence, and keep cool under all circumstances." [40] During the initial sparring, Delahay reported conscientiously to Lincoln and the tenor of these missives was optimistic; more so than was actually warranted.

What Delahay actually accomplished is in the realm of speculation. His influence was meager. He was not well known in areas other than Illinois and Kansas. He was from a territory with little voice in the affair. And he was not even an elected delegate. It seems probable that Delahay's influence was slight if not nonexistent in securing the nomination for Lincoln.[41]

Lincoln cannot have expected much aid from Delahay. His invitation was probably the result of loyalty to an old friend. But for Delahay a more crucial consideration compelled his presence. Delahay sincerely believed that Lincoln's chances for nomination and election were excellent. This belief translated into an accomplished fact would open wide, and hitherto unknown, political vistas for Delahay. Two alternatives would be available; the senate or a presidential appointment. On May 18, 1860, Lincoln received the Republican nomination and for Delahay half the battle was won.

Delahay was jubilancy personified and immediately wired Lincoln that "I want very much to return to your City [Springfield, Illinois]—But at present I cant say that I will be able to do so. . . . [This] is the happiest day of my Checkquered life." [42] Delahay probably visited Springfield for campaign instructions, and

39. Lincoln to Delahay, April 14, 1860.—Basler, *op. cit.*, v. 4, p. 44.
40. Lincoln to Delahay, Springfield, May 12, 1860.—*Ibid.*, p. 49.
41. William E. Barton, *The Life of Abraham Lincoln* (2 vols., Indianapolis, Bobbs Merrill Co., 1925), v. 1, p. 431, declared that on May 18 Delahay wired Lincoln that his nomination was hopeless and asked if Lincoln would accept the vice-presidential nomination. Lincoln allegedly replied affirmatively. However, no evidence has ever been found to confirm this statement based on personal reminiscences. Furthermore, Delahay wrote Lincoln from Chicago, May 14, 1860, that "all conceed [sic] that you can be easily nominated for *Vice-President*, but we are not *biting* at the Bate [sic]."—David C. Mearns, ed., *The Lincoln Papers* (3 vols., Doubleday and Co., Inc., Garden City, N. Y., 1948), v. 1, pp. 233, 234.
42. Delahay to Lincoln, Chicago, May 18, 1860.—*Ibid*, p. 242.

he and James H. Lane both entered actively in the campaign, especially in the doubtful districts of Indiana and Illinois.[43]

Following the news of Lincoln's election, Delahay enjoyed his reputation as a tried and true friend of the President-elect. Delahay's prestige led many Republicans to apply to him for assistance in getting an appointment to some government post.[44]

Delahay was in Washington for the inauguration and had at least one interview with Lincoln. However, nothing was decided regarding Kansas patronage, for, on March 13, 1861, Lincoln wrote Delahay that "when I saw you . . . this morning, I forgot to ask you about some of the Kansas appointments. . . . If you care much about them, you can write. . . ."[45] Delahay had returned to Kansas to enter into the senatorial campaign. Late in March Delahay answered Lincoln expressing hope that ". . . the appointment of Surveyor General for Kansas . . ." would not be made ". . . until I can see you. . . ."[46]

After the campaign, which saw James H. Lane and Samuel C. Pomeroy elected as the first senators from Kansas, and in which Delahay seemed to concentrate more on advancing Lane's pretensions than his own, both Lane and Delahay journeyed to Washington. There they experienced the first Northern reaction to the bombardment of Fort Sumter. Both were officers of the heroic Frontier Guard which served as the defenders of Lincoln during those first fearful days. Delahay arranged for an interview with the severely harrassed president [47] and within a few days received his appointment as surveyor-general of Kansas. This appointment explains the politically innocuous campaign Delahay conducted for the senate.

Delahay was to receive another appointment in 1863 as Federal District court judge of Kansas,[48] and in 1865, before Lincoln's as-

43. See George W. Deitzler to S. N. Wood, August 18, 1860.—"S. N. Wood Papers," K. S. H. S. Deitzler avers that "if such fellows [Lane and Delahay] . . . are to control matters in any degree, with the new administration, I shall feel but little hope for any good results from the change."
44. William Ward to Delahay, November 8, 1860; Charles Van Lassen to Delahay, November 26, 1860; J. B. McAfee to Delahay, December 7, 1860.—"Delahay Papers," K. S. H. S.
45. Lincoln to Delahay, March 13, 1861.—Basler, op. cit., v. 4, p. 283.
46. Delahay to Lincoln, March 29, 1861.—Ibid.
47. Delahay to J. L. McDowell, Washington [April], 1861.—"McDowell Papers," K. S. H. S.
48. This appointment stimulated a deluge of criticism and opposition, much of which was valid. Lyman Trumbull received numerous letters of protest from Kansans. But there was no trouble over confirmation. See Kansas City (Mo.) Western Journal of Commerce, October 17, 24, 31, 1863, for articles reprinted from the Leavenworth Daily Times, Fort Scott Monitor, and Emporia News, all bitterly attacking the appointment.

sassination, he hoped for a foreign assignment. However, the climax of his career came with his appointment as surveyor-general. This was the goal towards which he had been striving, a federal office, a lifetime sinecure.

Delahay's entire career is a study of the mediocre in politics. In his personal accomplishments he is hardly significant. To be fair, of course, one must mention his position in the Topeka constitutional convention of 1855 and his journalistic efforts. But his tangible, measurable contributions are hardly apparent, verging indeed on the nonexistent.

The question which this investigation raises then is: How did Delahay, possessed of such limited personal and intellectual qualities, progress in politics to a position of some power and responsibility? The obvious answer is Lincoln's use of the patronage at his command. But this is insufficient for it fails to explain why Delahay was so consistently a recipient of Lincoln's favors. In 1858 Delahay made a decision, the result being that he devoted himself unreservedly to Abraham Lincoln. Not many men were willing to commit themselves unequivocally at this early stage. Lincoln could not have failed to recognize this. The combination of Delahay's early commitment and Lincoln's Illinois experiences with Delahay, and perhaps a political debt, created in Lincoln a deep sense of loyalty made manifest when it was within his power to do so.

Delahay's finest, most perfected quality, was political shrewdness. This enabled him, at precisely the proper moment, to tie his fortunes to the career of the right man. Delahay assessed Lincoln's potential with great accuracy and reaped the rewards of this judgment in later years.

Religion in Kansas During the Era of the Civil War

EMORY LINDQUIST

THE settlement and development of a new area, such as Kansas territory, involved the coming of people who brought with them their ideals and institutions. They brought also a pattern of work and worship. The soil was tilled; houses were built; schools and churches were established. Diversity was characteristic of the emigrants who came from various parts of the nation and from many European countries. This diversity was a part of the religious witness on the frontier. There were differences in doctrine, in polity, and in liturgy. People on the Kansas frontier were confronted with the Christian gospel, which had its origin in a distant era. The faith of the people had the rich legacy of the centuries to sustain it. Although frontier conditions produced new challenges, the message and meaning of Christianity was relevant, and believers felt a missionary zeal to transmit it. Religion played a vital role in a time of uncertainty, insecurity, and strife. Individuals and society shared the blessings which came from the promises of the Word of God.

The Kansas frontier attracted people who came for a variety of motives. Adventurers, crusaders for freedom or slavery, restless spirits, seekers after material gain, and ordinary citizens, striving to improve their position, furnished the population of territorial Kansas. The missionary from established areas soon found that the Kansas locale created challenges and problems in the very nature of the population. The sources show that diversity was characteristic. Morever, the observers varied greatly in their evaluation of the people.

An obvious fact was the mixed motives of the emigration to Kansas. The Rev. S. Y. Lum, a Congregationalist, who came to Lawrence in September, 1854, as an agent of the American Home Missionary Society, described the people on two occasions in December, 1854. On December 6 he wrote from Lawrence to the society:

In reference to the character of the emigration as a whole, I hardly know what to think—many there are who come here with a noble purpose. They

DR. EMORY KEMPTON LINDQUIST, Rhodes scholar and former president of Bethany College, is dean of the faculties of the University of Wichita. He is author of *Smoky Valley People: A History of Lindsborg, Kansas* (1953), and numerous magazine articles relating to the history of this region.

(313)

are willing to be martyrs in the cause of Religion & Liberty & yet I am compelled to think that the number of such is small in comparison to those who have some selfish or mercinary end to gain. I must confess that my mind has changed on this subject & I do not think so highly of the aggregate emigration as at first. I find many, perhaps a majority, without any settled moral principles as a basis of action & when once outside the restraints of eastern society, they act out the native depravity of the human heart. . . .[1]

Lum emphasized the mercenary character of the people, but in addition, he was distressed by the open hostility which was shown toward church work. In his first report to the American Home Missionary Society on December 23, 1854, the Kansas situation was graphically described:

The large majority of all who come to the Territory, so far as I have the means of judging, are actuated solely by selfish or mercenary motives. Many such are the open enemies of the dearest doctrines of the Cross, & declare themselves determined to wage war against the introduction of "Orthodox sentiments." In my intercourse with this community, I have been pained to find not a few who have been professors of religion in Eastern Churches, openly avow themselves the enemies of the truths they once espoused, trampling on the Sabbath, & ridiculing sacred things. On the other hand, I find a goodly number of true spirits, who have joyfully sacrificed the comforts of eastern homes, & the communion of eastern Christians, for the rescue & salvation of Kansas & here they maintain a character such as might be expected from such principles. [2]

The pioneer Kansas preacher soon learned that the frontier bred a response of radicalism of various types. The new freedom was often accompanied by a freedom from the restraint of the old order. The decision to leave the old society produced by its very nature a break with tradition. As Lum became better acquainted with the field which he was to serve, he found that the problems increased in number and in intensity. On February 28, 1855, he shared his deep-seated concern with the officials of the American Home Missionary Society as follows:

I find that when I wrote last I had not become fully acquainted with all classes of men I had come in contact with out here & the more of experience [?] I have on this subject, the more I am led to believe that, in many respects, there are few fields of labor more difficult of cultivation than this. All kinds of radical ideas are pretty fully represented here, and I have almost thought, at times, that all this class of persons from the entire Union, are flowing in, in hopes of realizing their wildest schemes. Time after time, they have made

1. Emory Lindquist, ed., "The Letters of the Rev. Samuel Young Lum, Pioneer Kansas Missionary, 1854-1858," *The Kansas Historical Quarterly*, Topeka, v. 25 (Spring, 1959), pp. 45, 46. The original letters to the American Home Missionary Society are in the splendid collection of the Hammond Library, Chicago Theological Seminary, with the exception of a few items. Permission to use these letters has been granted by Harvey Arnold, librarian, of the Hammond Library.
2. Lum to A. H. M. S., December 23, 1854, *ibid.*, pp. 52, 53.

their boast that they would crowd orthodoxy out of Kansas. Yet I trust, in this they will be disappointed; there is no kind of misrepresentation or misstatement, to which they have not already resorted, to shake, if possible, the confidence of the community in those who adhere to the truth. Their influence with candid men is constantly decreasing. I trust that there will be soon large numbers of true men join us who will help to stay the flood of iniquity & infidelity that it threatening.[3]

Lum sensed the impact of the frontier upon the religious life of the people. A spirit of recklessness and abandonment of the principles of the home society created serious problems for the minister. He realized that the evolving pattern might produce victory for forces which would damage the future of Kansas. His concern as well as his hope for the future was expressed in a letter to the American Home Missionary Society in April, 1855:

But there are other dangers that await the comers to this new Territory, than those which grow out of the political agitation. Every month's residence here develops this fact more fully. The circumstances under which mind is thrown in this wild frontier life, for it can be called nothing else as yet, engenders a recklessness, & freedom from restraint, that too often, prove fatal to the principles, as well as the practices of a home society & it is not too much to say, that we have the material, for either the worst, or the best, state of society in our country. There are surely enough influences at work, unless counteracted by the Infinite One through the efforts of His church to overthrow any society.[4]

Lum, however, felt encouraged by recent arrivals to Kansas. In the same letter cited above he described the pattern of his expectation, although it is characterized by eastern provincialism:

The first waves of eastern emigration begin to be felt here, & they bear to us some choice spirits. From present appearances, I think we may hope for a higher state of character in some respects, than that which came last Fall. A greater proportion seem earnest Christians & from the interest, with which they enter into our social gatherings for prayer, they encourage the hope of eminent usefullness in our midst. As the families move in the Sabbath school is rapidly increasing, & the Bible Class receives new accessions & awakens a deeper interest.[5]

The consequences of separation from "the restraints of religious society" were emphasized often by the pioneer missionaries in Kansas. The Rev. F. P. Montfort, a Presbyterian minister, emphasized this factor in his first quarterly report to the Presbyterian board in 1856:

3. Lum to A. H. M. S., February 28, 1855, *ibid.*, p. 57.
4. Lum to A. H. M. S., April, 1855, *ibid.*, p. 59.
5. *Ibid.* Four parties came to Kansas under the auspices of the New England Emigrant Aid Company in September, October, and November, 1854. Six groups arrived in the spring of 1855.—Louise Barry, "The Emigrant Aid Parties of 1854," *The Kansas Historical Quarterly*, v. 12 (May, 1943), pp. 115-155; Louise Barry, "The New England Emigrant Aid Company Parties of 1855," *ibid.*, v. 12 (August, 1943), pp. 227-268.

The people of the territory are from all points of the compass, those who profess, differing not less in their religious sentiments than in their features of countenance, while a vast majority make no profession, and separated from the restraints of religious society show but little respect for the ordinances of religion. Observation has also induced the painful reflection, that of those who have named the name of Christ, many are more interested in political affairs than in Christ's cause and more involved in measures whose tendency is to encourage party jealousies and discord in the Territory, than in the interests of Christ's kingdom, and in the use of those means and instrumentalities which would be subservient to its advancement and prosperity in their midst.[6]

The Rev. M. J. Miller, a minister of the Evangelical Association at Leavenworth wrote in 1858 that the people "are so wild and degraded that they do not desire the gospel. It appears that all the lovers of strife, and wars, and bloodshed, of all states emigrated here to this territory, or else they became so since they are here."[7] Other missionaries recognized the problems associated with the character of the population, but were reluctant to emphasize it in their descriptions of the work in Kansas. Lewis Bodwell, a Congregational minister at Topeka, was generally disposed to overlook these facts, although he implied it in quoting the words of a neighbor missionary who said that "outside of my church & of the others formed here, I do not know of *one* young man who is not addicted to gaming, profanity, intemperance or incestuousness, in some cases to two, three, or *all* of these vices," which was "a sad story & a fearful account."[8]

However, Bodwell was fully sympathetic with Lum's analysis of the problems created by the uncertainty of life on the Kansas frontier in relationship to religious values. He described the situation in these graphic words:

Few facts, in connection with the settlement of this new country, are more sad than the wreck of Christian hopes occasioned by the passage from East to West. Members are found in every community who once stood fair in the church of God, but have here denied their professions, or, what amounts to the same thing, have neglected to reiterate those professions in their new home. With some this is mere neglect—with others it is intentional. Some seem glad of the opportunity, which a change of residence affords, to shake off the restraints of religious professions. . . . Kansas is full of professors of religion from the East, but, instead of shining out of themselves, we need to go round and hunt them out with a torch.[9]

6. Rev. F. P. Montfort, *The Home and Foreign Record of the Presbyterian Church of the United States of America*, Philadelphia, v. 8 (1856), pp. 355, 356. Hereafter referred to as *The Home and Foreign Record*.

7. Rev. M. C. Platz, ed., *Fifty Years in the Kansas Conference, 1864-1914; A Record of the Origin and Development of the Work of the Evangelical Association* (Cleveland, n. d.), p. 19.

8. Russell K. Hickman, "Lewis Bodwell, Frontier Preacher; The Early Years," *The Kansas Historical Quarterly*, v. 12 (August, 1943), p. 291.

9. *The Congregational Record*, Lawrence, v. 1 (April, 1859), pp. 21, 23.

Bodwell in an article in *The Congregational Record,* April, 1860, entitled "Homelessness as a Hindrance to the Gospel" indicated a significant characteristic of the population which had negative influences on church work:

> On this western field, the gospel meets some peculiar obstacles incident to the state of society. Of these hindrances, few are more discouraging than the unsettled character of our population. The western phrase, "I do not live, but only stay," is of almost universal application. The word "home" might be entirely stricken from our vocabulary. . . . It is quite probable that one-half of the present population of Kansas will spend their days here—while, at the same time, there are very few here who have positively made up their minds to make this their home. It is all an experiment.[10]

While there were many declarations of despair from Kansas, other missionaries held different opinions as to the character of the population and the prospects for the church. In the autumn of 1854 an individual identified only as J. G., a Presbyterian colporteur, made an extensive tour of the Kansas territory. He was impressed with the settlers as "enterprising young men, with minds ardent and social, just commencing life for themselves." He believed that "in that confused mass of society too, composed of such heterogeneous elements, all, as it were, severed from their natural associations, and where society is just forming, they are much more open to religious impressions than in old countries where habits and associations are of a stereotype cast."[11] Mrs. Julia Louisa Lovejoy, wife of the Rev. Charles H. Lovejoy, pioneer Methodist missionary, was enthusiastic about the qualities of members of the company who settled in the future Manhattan area in the spring of 1855. She wrote that "our company consists of men of the 'right stamp' mostly from Massachusetts and Rhode Island, including a number of clergymen, and men of liberal education, who have been successfully engaged for years as teachers in our distinguished seminaries of learning in the East, and are henceforth to devote their energies for the benefit of the new territory."[12]

Richard Cordley, the long-time Congregational pastor at Lawrence, recalled later the characteristics of the people with whom

---

10. *Ibid.,* v. 2 (April, 1860), p. 23. Prof. James C. Malin has described the fluidity of population as follows: "Pioneer life was always conspicuously unstable and insecure. Movement was its outstanding characteristic. Of the people present in a given community, according to the census of 1855, for example, very few would probably be there five years later, still fewer in 1865, and 1875. A similar principle could apply to the newcomers of 1860 or 1865, only possibly in less drastic proportions."—James C. Malin, "Notes on the Writing of General Histories . . ." *The Kansas Historical Quarterly,* v. 21 (Spring, 1955), p. 332.

11. *The Home and Foreign Record,* v. 6 (June, 1855), p. 164.

12. Julia Louisa Lovejoy, "Letters From Kanzas," *The Kansas Historical Quarterly,* v. 11 (February, 1942), p. 38.

he associated upon his arrival in Kansas in 1857. He realized that diversity was a real factor as he wrote:

> And these were not the traditional roughs of the frontier. They were people of culture and character who had come to make Kansas a free state. They had come in many cases without any definite idea as to what they were to do or how they were to make a living. They were ready to do anything that offered, their main purpose being to take part in settling the great question of freedom for Kansas. . . . Beside these solid men of solid purpose, the country was full of the curious who came to see what was going on; of adventurers who came to join in the fray; of speculators who came to profit by the occasion.[13]

An unidentified Presbyterian visitor to Kansas in October, 1858, reported to his board of missions that the character of the Kansas people was on a very high level. He cited as an illustration the statement of a reliable friend who had just recently "reckoned up more than one hundred college graduates residing in Lawrence and its immediate vicinity." This unnamed visitor concluded with the question: "Who can estimate the power of such a mass of educated enterprising minds, for good or ill?"[14]

Another observer, the Rev. J. D. Liggett, a Congregationalist at Leavenworth, reported about the quality and attitude of the Kansas people in 1860. He declared in January, 1860, that "I never mingled with a population that embraced so large a proportion of superior and cultivated intellect as is to be found in this city and it is practically infidel and reckless in a moral point of view. Yet the infidelity is more pretended than confirmed I think."[15] Liggett was also impressed with what he saw in 1860 after an extensive trip in the Kansas territory. His enthusiastic appraisal was as follows:

> A trip of some 400 miles through this vast and beautiful territory has very much enlarged my ideas of its size, the number of its inhabitants, and has given me a much more favorable opinion of the character and habits of the settlers. They are as a general thing, an intelligent, sober, and industrious people. Judging from what I had seen in the border and river towns, I had expected to see a good deal of open sin; but in travelling two weeks through the most populous portions of Kansas, I did not see a single drunken man and very few who looked as if they drank at all. In most of the flourishing little towns, of which there are many, intoxicating liquor is a contraband article of trade. I also found the people very willing to hear preaching.[16]

---

13. Rev. Richard Cordley, *Pioneer Days in Kansas* (New York, 1903), pp. 60, 61. A fascinating description of the people in Lawrence during the early territorial era identified as "Easterners" and "Westerners" is found in James C. Malin, "Housing Experiments in the Lawrence Community, 1855," *The Kansas Historical Quarterly*, v. 21 (Summer, 1954), pp. 95-100.
14. *The Home and Foreign Record*, v. 9 (October, 1858), p. 318.
15. Rev. J. D. Liggett to the A. H. M. S., Leavenworth, January 2, 1860.
16. *Ibid.*, July 23, 1860.

Religious life on the Kansas frontier was fashioned by the forces of society and by the character of the people. The latter factor presented the missionaries with a variegated pattern of good and evil. Some observers found that here were men of "the right stamp," and "not the traditional roughs of the frontier." There were "people of culture and character who had come to make Kansas a free state," possessing "superior and cultivated characters." They were described as "intelligent, sober, and industrious people."

There can be little doubt but that many individuals of that type were in Kansas. But other contemporaries portrayed another picture with serious consequences for missionary enterprise. The people were characterized by a "spirit of recklessness and abandonment of the principles of the home society." There were the disastrous effects of "coming outside the restraints of eastern society." Kansas had people who were "full of all kinds of radical ideas." They were "speculators, curious, and adventurers," dominated by "mercenary motives." "The unsettled character of the population" destroyed the stability so necessary for effective congregational life. While there were many professors of religion, it was necessary "to go around and hunt them up with a torch."

Although there might have been problems with the people, at least one individual found that Kansas was an unusual place. While riding one twilight evening across the Kansas prairies in the autumn, Brother Jonas Dodge confessed to the Rev. James Shaw: "I cannot conceive that God ever made Kansas for men to live in. It is altogether too good; he must have made it for the angels, and we are only permitted to sojourn among them for awhile, preparatory to our final dwelling place in heaven." [17]

The frontier provided many great challenges to the pioneer missionary who sought to confront the people in that unsettled and disturbed civilization with the witness of the Gospel. Able and consecrated men devoted themselves unsparingly to their high calling. While they took courage because of their mission, there was full recognition of the facts of frontier life. The Rev. Charles Blood, Manhattan, in a statement to Milton Badger of the American Home Missionary society, in September, 1857, entitled, "Why Kansas is an unpromising field for religious efforts" analyzed the factors as follows:

17. Rev. James Shaw, *Early Reminiscences of Pioneer Life in Kansas* (Atchison, 1886), p. 53.

1. The time and thought of the settlers are so much occupied in preparing to live that it seems impossible to interest their minds in religious matters.

2. The minds of many are full of care and anxiety about their claims. These cares will not be removed until they have paid for their lands and secured a title to them.

3. The unsettled condition of political affairs has operated unfavorably to the promotion of religion.

All these things have operated unfavorably to the moral and religious interests of the people. Intemperance, profanity, sabbath breaking have prevailed to an alarming extent. Still these things are incident to every new country. We hope that soon we shall see an improvement in this respect.[18]

It is understandable that the charge of "worldliness" would be directed against the people on the Kansas frontier. There was no opportunity for the regular regimen of life as was possible in a settled civilization. The contemporary sources portray these factors in an interesting manner. The Rev. J. D. Liggett described from Leavenworth the general situation in January, 1860:

The great and formidable obstacle to the progress of the gospel here is, has been, that people are too much engrossed in worldly affairs to think of religion. I need not remind you of the absorbing character of the politics in Kansas or of the scenes of riot and blood-shed which have demoralized the people. A no less demoralizing cause is the spirit of speculation, which absorbs the hearts of almost every one. Most of those who are here came for the purpose of improving their worldly condition and they manifest by all their conduct, a determination not to be easily divested from that object. When a little good seed is sown, the cares of the world seem to prevent its growth. . . .[19]

Liggett also pointed out in June, 1860, that "the emigration to the gold regions has taken away several of our members, some permanently, and some temporarily. While the stir and excitement of outfitting lasted, a marked effect was produced on the audiences at church, this however lasted only two or three Sabbaths." [20]

Evidence from nonclerical sources is provided by William Stanley Hoole, a young Southerner who lived at Douglas, in November, 1856: "I am astonished to see so little regard paid to the Sabbath, as there is here among people who seem to be enlightened in every other respect. When I went up to Lecompton today, the steam-mill was going just as if it were not Sunday, and all the groceries were open, as on any week-day. But this is pretty much the case all over the Ter.—those who do not work go hunting, or do something else." [21] George H. Hildt found in June, 1857, "Sunday a very dull

---

18. Rev. Charles Blood to the A. H. M. S., Manhattan, September 28, 1857.
19. Rev. J. D. Liggett to the A. H. M. S., Leavenworth, January 2, 1860.
20. Ibid., June 19, 1860.
21. William Stanley Hoole, "A Southerner's Viewpoint of the Kansas Situation, 1856-1857; The Letters of Lieut. Col. A. J. Hoole, C. S A.," The Kansas Historical Quarterly, v. 3 (May, 1934), p. 148.

SOME PIONEER MINISTERS OF KANSAS

Lewis Bodwell
(1827-1894)
Congregationalist
Topeka

Pardee Butler
(1816-1888)
Christian
Atchison county

Richard Cordley
(1829-1904)
Congregationalist
Lawrence

Hugh Dunn Fisher
(1824-1905)
Methodist
Leavenworth

PIONEER MINISTERS OF KANSAS—Continued

Charles H. Lovejoy
(1811-1904)
Methodist
Manhattan

Samuel Young Lum
(1821-1895)
Congregationalist
Lawrence

Peter McVicar
(1829-1903)
Congregationalist
Topeka

Roswell Davenport Parker
(1826-1899)
Congregationalist
Leavenworth and Wyandotte

hot day, a good deal of traveling on the road a great many going to Paoli when the land sales goes off this week." [22]

The situation relative to Sunday observance reached a critical state at Leavenworth in 1861. The ministers began an attack on "Drunkenness, Gambling, Dancing, Profanity, Theater Going, Balls." These evils were denounced in Sunday sermons and in Monday evening discussion groups. The "desecrators" of the Sabbath were determined to have revenge. An attempt was made to prosecute the ministers "for working for hire" on Sunday. Action was taken to put through an "anti-Sunday" law. The slogan was, "Down with the old Massachusetts Blue Laws." The church party, however, won the election. The Rev. H. D. Fisher, who was an active participant in this struggle has described the situation:

I visited the Catholic Bishop, who kindly said: "My people have need of the Sabbath for a day of worship and rest and I will instruct them so to vote. . . . Mr. Stone, the Episcopal Minister, doffed his surplice and gown, Mr. Baldridge put his trousers inside his boots, Brother Pitzer rolled up his trousers and put on a pair of rubbers, while I doffed what little ministerial dignity had hitherto embarrassed me—I have never seen it since—and we pitched in to win. And win we did.[23]

While there were many critics of the lack of Sunday observance, other contemporaries were impressed by the traditional and sober observance of the day. When William P. Tomlinson spent a Sunday at Lawrence in May, 1858, he observed that "the citizens of Lawrence, by their universal observance of the 'day of rest' remind the sojourning traveler that they were the descendants of the stern and rugged Puritans. Not a sign of business was anywhere to be seen. No groups were on the corners of the streets. When the bells ceased ringing their morning chimes, all were gathered in the various houses of prayer." [24] A visitor to Topeka in 1864, David R. Cobb, felt that "the Sabbath here seems more like civilization— the good old Bell chimes forth its notes of peace, of rest, and love." However, he concluded that "the people are not a church going people if I was to judge from those I saw out last Sabbath and today." [25]

---

22. Martha B. Caldwell, ed., "The Diary of George H. Hildt, June to December, 1857, Pioneer of Johnson County," *ibid.*, v. 10 (August, 1941), p. 269.

23. Rev. H. D. Fisher, *The Gun and the Gospel; Early Kansas and Chaplain Fisher* (Chicago and New York, 1897), pp. 156, 157; Rev. Hiram D. Stone, "Memoirs of a Pioneer Missionary and Chaplain in the United States Army," *The Kansas Historical Collections*, Topeka, v. 13 (1913-1914), pp. 343, 344.

24. William P. Tomlinson, *Kansas in Eighteen Fifty-Eight* (New York, 1859), pp. 45, 46.

25. David Glenn Cobb, ed., "Letters of David R. Cobb, 1858-1864," *The Kansas Historical Quarterly*, v. 11 (February, 1942), p. 69.

The ministers generally were cautious in their statements relative to numbers at worship services. It was generally assumed that the church goers were serious in their attendance and undoubtedly this was the true situation for the majority. However, the Rev. Lewis Bodwell, who served the Topeka Congregational church with great devotion, was honestly skeptical at least when he wrote an article for *The Congregational Record* in January, 1860, entitled, "Worship Versus Entertainment":

There is undoubtedly a growing tendency in our communities to underrate worship as such. Our Sabbath assemblies are not regarded distinctly as worshipping assemblies, but as congregations assembled to hear preaching. The services are judged, not by their power to build up christian character, but by their power to entertain. Men go to church for the same reason that they go to a concert. Church services may not be as interesting as a concert would be, but then the Sabbath hours are on their hands. . . . Church service breaks up the monotony, and helps the hours along.[26]

While worldliness and desecration of the Sabbath might be viewed with varying degrees of concern, there was unanimous agreement about the evils of drinking and allied activities. The Rev. Charles Blood felt in 1856 that "in this new territory one of the greatest obstacles to the spread of the gospel is the alarming prevalence of intemperance" although he realized that "temperance has its friends and advocates here."[27] In October, 1856, the committee on temperance at the first session of the initial meeting of the Kansas and Nebraska Conference of the Methodist Episcopal Church in assembly at Lawrence presented the following report which was adopted by the conference:

Viewing the temperance movement as one of the great instrumentalities for the suppression of crime and the promotion of virtue, therefore, Resolved, 1st, that we give king alcohol no quarters within our bounds.

Resolved, 2nd, that we will not patronize nor in any way give our support to the dealers in spirituous liquors.

Resolved, 3rd, that we will preach on the subject of temperance at our various appointments during the year and encourage the formation of a temperance society.[28]

In 1861 the Methodists declared in annual convention that "whereas, Intemperance with all its accumulations of moral and social evils, is still destroying the souls and bodies of many in our State, therefore *Resolved*, That Methodist Preachers should not cease to 'cry

26. *The Congregational Record*, Lawrence, v. 2 (January, 1860), pp. 5, 6.
27. Rev. Charles Blood to the A. H. M. S., Manhattan, March 15, 1856.
28. *Minutes of the First Session of the Kansas & Nebraska Annual Conference of the Methodist Episcopal Church, 1856* (Omaha City, N. T.), p. 7.

aloud and spare not' before all the people." [29] In 1862 in addition to a resolution on alcoholism, the Methodist annual conference resolved, "that it is the duty of Christians to put off all 'filthiness of the flesh' especially that which is involved in the use of Tobacco, and we pledge ourselves to enjoin the same by both precept and example." [30]

Various church groups passed resolutions on the subject of alcohol and drinking. One of the more interesting approaches to this subject was taken under the leadership of the Rev. Peter McVicar at Topeka, who in March, 1861, organized the "Band of Hope." Membership was limited to persons between the ages of five and twenty-one, although older individuals could become honorary members. McVicar reported that 131 people had taken the following pledge as members of the "Band of Hope":

I do Solemly Promise, totally to abstain from the use of all Intoxicating Liquors as a drink, and from the manufacture and sale of them, except for medical, mechanical, and sacramental purposes.

I also promise to abstain totally from the use of Tobacco, in all its forms; also from the use of Profane Language.

I will also use my best endeavors to induce others to sign this pledge.[31]

When the first annual meeting of the Kansas State Temperance Society was held on October 9, 1861, it was resolved "that we look to the churches of our state for earnest cooperation in the work of temperance, and we suggest that self-defense will demand total abstinence from intoxicating drinks as a beverage as one test of membership." A number of clergymen, including the Rev. Peter McVicar of Topeka, were leaders in this society.[32]

The American Home Missionary Society received many reports from the missionaries about the lack of sobriety among certain Kansans. The Rev. Rodney Paine declared from Burlington in January, 1861, that "a more miserable crew of drunkards ought nowhere to be found than have lounged at the grogery and staggered in the streets of Burlington. The restraints of the Gospel have not prevented an increase of this demoralizing influence." [33] The Rev. J. D. Liggett chronicled from Leavenworth in December, 1862, a wide variety of evils as well as one proposed solution:

29. *Minutes of the Annual Conference of the Methodist Episcopal Church, 1861* (Leavenworth), p. 16.
30. *Minutes of the Annual Conference of the Methodist Episcopal Church, 1862,* p. 21.
31. Rev. Peter McVicar to the A. H. M. S., Topeka, March 1, 1861. A one-page circular describing the "Band of Hope" was enclosed with McVicar's letter.
32. Clara Francis, "The Coming of Prohibition to Kansas," *The Kansas Historical Collections,* v. 15 (1919-1922), p. 200.
33. Rev. Rodney Paine to the A. H. M. S., Burlington, January 17, 1861.

We have two theatres of a low order much patronized. Saloons and whiskey shops almost numberless; about 300 prostitutes; whose houses are very prominent and notorious, one of which stands right in front of the Methodist Church, unmolested by Civil authority. A very large proportion of our citizens are young men, away from home and also without the restraints of well-organized and virtuous society and they fall ready victims of the temptations that assail them on all hands. Many of them are intelligent and, have been well-educated under early religious influences, and are respectable as the world goes. They will attend church too as a general thing, but the influences of evil outweighs all good impressions. A free and easy life seems to be the general standard. After much thought, perplexity and prayer as to my duty, I have concluded soon to deliver a series of lectures on sabbath evenings exclusively to young men; and to grapple with these glaring sins in the unrestrained language which such an audience will allow better than a mixed congregation. I can think of no way better than thus to meet such sins with the ungloved hand in open and relentless fight. The ordinary preaching does not seem to meet the exigencies of the case.[34]

While the standard of conduct on the frontier was a factor in the development of the churches, the real facts of hard times and economic distress were also decisive. The financial sources of the settlers were exceedingly limited. There were no old and well-established families who could furnish capital for building and funds for current operations. Moreover, under the best circumstances, a considerable period of time was required before any surplus money was available for either individuals or the community. The missionaries were almost entirely dependent upon the modest grants provided by the home society or upon the sources of income which they could secure by their own labors exclusive of the ministerial appointment.[35]

The nature of the economic problem was made apparent in the report of the committee on necessitous cases at the first session of the Kansas and Nebraska Annual Conference meeting at Lawrence in October, 1856. The committee acknowledged the receipt of $456.20 for "suffering brethren who have labored in Kansas, and who have met with heavy losses and endured very great sufferings and hardships during the late troubles in the territory." Fourteen

---

34. Rev. J. D. Liggett to the A. H. M. S., Leavenworth, December 3, 1862. An interesting description of the theatre and other forms of entertainment in Leavenworth during this period is found in the study by James C. Malin, "Theatre in Kansas, 1858-1868: Background for the Coming of the Lord Dramatic Company to Kansas, 1869," *The Kansas Historical Quarterly*, v. 23 (Spring, 1957), pp. 23-31. The author points out that there were 200 license-paying saloons in Leavenworth in November, 1858.—*Ibid.*, p. 52.

35. Prof. James C. Malin has described these important economic factors in another context: "Kansas could not indefinitely be supported by 'aid' and 'relief' and new capital brought in by immigrants and the general government. Sooner or later Kansas must assume responsibility for paying its own way. How long did Kansas operate on a deficit economy? Certainly until the later 1870's. . . ."—Malin, "Notes on the Writing of General Histories," *loc. cit.*, p. 338.

ministers received amounts from $19.05 to $60.00. It is interesting to observe the feeling of distress on the part of these Kansas Methodists on account of their economic situation as indicated by the resolution at the same meeting that "we sympathize with all our hearts in the enterprise now being prosecuted for the evangelization of Ireland, and but for the peculiar circumstances that now embarrass our condition, would gladly evince our feelings by 'material aid.'"[36] In addition to official action as above, there are many evidences from individual sources as to the economic plight of the missionary. The situation of the Rev. Charles Lovejoy was described in December, 1859, by his wife as follows: "Our Conference year closes the 15th of next March, and we have received this year, as yet, but one dollar and seventy cents from our people, in cash, and only five dollars in every other article, and have no prospect of receiving five dollars more for the year, our people are so poor—we have $100 missionary appropriation. . . ."[37]

The New England Emigrant Aid Company recognized the responsibility of providing financial assistance for the establishment of churches. In the "Circular of the Committee of Clergymen," July 2, 1855, designed "to have all the 'clergymen of New England' made life members of the New England Emigrant Aid Company," Article 2 declared the position of the company as follows:

> The officers of this Company have understood that, to make a free State, they needed, first of all, the Gospel. Every missionary sent there by different boards has received their active assistance. Divine service is regularly maintained in the towns where the company has influence, and, we believe, nowhere else. Every Sabbath school in the Territory has been formed with the assistance of the Company, or its officers. Every church organized has been organized with their cooperation.[38]

The financial support was largely on a personal rather than on a company basis. In 1855 and 1856 money was solicited in New England for building a Congregational church in Lawrence, with Amos A. Lawrence contributing $1,000 personally. In 1855 the Unitarian church was organized in Lawrence under the leadership of Charles Robinson. In 1857 when the Episcopal church was built at Lawrence, the lot was donated by the New England Emigrant Aid Company; Lawrence made a contribution. Dr. Webb's

---

36. *Minutes of the First Session of the Kansas & Nebraska Annual Conference of the Methodist Episcopal Church, 1856* (Omaha City, N. T.), p. 4.
37. "Letters of Julia Louisa Lovejoy," *The Kansas Historical Quarterly*, v. 16 (February, 1948), p. 75.
38. "Letters of New England Clergymen," *The Kansas Historical Collections*, v. 1-2 (1875-1878), p. 194; William Warren Sweet, "Some Religious Aspects of the Kansas Struggle," *Journal of Religion*, Chicago, v. 7 (October, 1927), p. 586.

pamphlet of May, 1857, "Information for Kansas Emigrants," included an appeal for funds to assist various denominations in Lawrence. The company, through S. C. Pomeroy, pledged modest support to the Methodist church at Manhattan.[39]

The precarious economic situation was further accentuated by the great drought of 1860 and the impact of the Civil War. The nature of this combined situation was described by an individual identified only as "E. F." writing from Geneva, Allen county, in December, 1861:

> The famine of last year was a heavy blow to Kansas. Those who look upon this calamity only in the light of the destitution which was experienced have a very inadequate conception of its extent and severity. An instantaneous and entire check of immigration to a new country remote from any market is always a serious pecuniary disaster. But in the case of Kansas, not only has immigration been wholly cut off—thus annihilating the only market on which the people could depend—but many of the settlers becoming discouraged, tempted those who remained to part with what money was left, by offering their effects at half-price in order to procure the means of bearing their expenses to a land of plenty. But the famine with all its effects direct and indirect was a calamity which bears but a feeble comparison to that occasioned by the alarms and demands of the war. . . . Hence the difficulty which churches experience in doing anything in the way of raising money for the support of the gospel here.[40]

The economic situation was a frequent theme of observers in Kansas. The Rev. R. D. Parker at Leavenworth emphasized in August, 1861, that "the interruption of Rail Road Travel and river navigation through Missouri and the uncertainty resting on every enterprise the material prosperity is at a lower ebb than ever." [41] The Rev. Richard Cordley reported from Lawrence in July, 1861, that "'Hard Times' is in everybody's mouth. Business dull and growing duller." [42] A writer in *The Congregational Record,* in an article entitled "The Famine," described the serious consequences of the hard times for churches and church members. He urged his readers to contact friends and organization in the East for funds and especially for seed so that crops could be planted in the new season.[43] The officials of the Plymouth Congregational church in Lawrence described the situation in detail in December, 1861. It was pointed out that the Methodists in Lawrence were raising

---

39. Samuel A. Johnson, *The Battle Cry of Freedom; The New England Emigrant Aid Company in the Kansas Crusade* (Lawrence, 1954), pp. 87, 88, 249.

40. E. F. to the A. H. M. S., Geneva, Allen county, December 2, 1861. A description of conditions in 1860 is found in George W. Glick, "The Drought of 1860," *The Kansas Historical Collections,* v. 9 (1905-1906), pp. 480-485.

41. Rev. R. D. Parker to the A. H. M. S., Wyandotte, August 13, 1861.

42. Rev. Richard Cordley to the A. H. M. S., Lawrence, July 9, 1861.

43. *The Congregational Record,* Lawrence, v. 3 (January, 1861), pp. 10-12.

less than $100 per year for the work of the Gospel. The Presbyterians and Baptists had been unable to support a minister and had abandoned the field. The Unitarian minister was farming and also received support from the American Christian Association; he received nothing from his congregation. The Episcopalian minister had independent sources of income.[44] The Rev. J. D. Liggett at Leavenworth reported in July, 1861, that he had received no funds from his church or from the American Home Missionary Society. He had been boarding himself. "I am entirely out of money and it is a thing that has almost disappeared from this community."[45]

The economic stress was severe throughout Kansas. The churches shared in the consequences. However, at least one observer, the Rev. S. M. Irvin at Highland, in appealing for help to the Presbyterian Home and Foreign Missionary Board placed events in the perspective of a judgment upon the people:

We ask help, seeing that it has pleased God to lay his hand upon us this year, and withhold the crops. We are in affliction and we deserve it. We have sinned greatly in Kansas. Innocent blood has been shed, for which there has been no thought of humiliation or repentance. A rage of mammon and speculation has intoxicated our people, and we need chastisement—and now, while under the stroke, though, in one sense, we do not deserve it, we venture to cry out to our friends whom God has favored with abundance, that they may help us in this our time of need.[46]

While many factors created a pattern which made church work difficult, the most decisive element was the conflict preceding and during the Civil War. The political designs for the future of Kansas produced vast implications for all other aspects of life. Rumors of violence and actual violence destroyed the stability which was necessary for effective community living. Contemporary observers were unanimous at this point.

The Rev. S. Y. Lum at Lawrence expressed many times the deep anxiety occasioned by the conflict. He described the situation in March, 1856, in a letter to Milton Badger of the American Home Missionary Society:

All has for a great part of the time been wild excitement. Our place of worship has been taken for soldiers barracks, & our meetings when we could have any, were held in *little* private rooms, where but very few could be assembled. . . . A few of the brethren & sisters have been drawn nearer to God, & have felt their entire & absolute dependence upon him in every

---
44. Plymouth Congregational church to the A. H. M. S., Lawrence, December 4, 1861.
45. Rev. J. D. Liggett to the A. H. M. S., Leavenworth, July 29, 1861.
46. *The Home and Foreign Record*, v. 11 (1860), p. 363.

trial, but the great majority even of the church have been influenced in a contrary direction. Excitement seemed to dissipate serious reflection, & the mind lost its delight in the worship & service of God.[47]

Lum emphasized his concern four days later in another letter to Badger in which he stated that "those who have not seen, cannot feel as we do, what an awful influence the wild excitements of the past year have had on the morals & virtue of this community. All the efforts of the Missionary are far more than overbalanced by the agencies for evil & the character of the place, as a whole, has been sinking instead of rising.[48]

In December, 1856, Lum again described the consequences of the course of events: "Never in the history of this country, has a Territory been settled in the midst of so many influences calculated to counteract the spread of the truth, & to foster the growth of sin; & unless the tendency of these influences be arrested, we have no reason to expect that they will fail to work out their legitimate results."[49] Lum found also that events conspired to encroach upon the Sabbath as reported in *The Home Missionary:* "It has seemed as though the Sabbath was selected as the day for special excitements; and not infrequently have the members of my congregation and even members of my church, been called from the morning service to go to the rescue of their brethren, attacked by the banditti who surround us."[50] The course of the Civil War further strengthened the trend described by Lum. In October, 1861, *The Congregational Record* carried a leading article entitled "The War and the Sabbath," which drew the conclusion that "among the ill effects of the present war, the desecration of the Sabbath stands prominent."[51]

The spirit of the times was also portrayed by the Rev. F. P. Montfort, a Presbyterian, writing from Highland in October, 1856:

The all-absorbing subject here is the same which engrosses the public mind and the public press in the States; and it is to be feared that the Gospel cannot have a "free course and run and be glorified" among us until this great question which now agitates our citizens shall be settled. When quiet prevails among us, there is no difficulty in securing congregations respectable in size, and attentive; but Christians and infidels alike can, in a moment, and often do give up their interest in the services, to hear reports brought in by

---

47. Rev. S. Y. Lum to the A. H. M. S., Lawrence, March 10, 1856, in *The Kansas Historical Quarterly*, v. 25 (Summer, 1959), p. 172.
48. Lum to A. H. M. S., March 22, 1856, *ibid.*, p. 174.
49. Lum to A. H. M. S., December 24, 1856, *ibid.*, p. 179.
50. Rev. S. Y. Lum in *The Home Missionary*, v. 29 (1856), p. 95, quoted in Colin Brummitt Goodykoontz, *Home Missions on the American Frontier* (Caldwell, Idaho, 1939), p. 297.
51. *The Congregational Record*, Lawrence, v. 3 (October, 1861), pp. 63-65.

the agents of partisans, and the minister must lose half of his hearers and the attention of all. The remainder of God's sacred day is then spent at the hotels and street corners, in canvassing the report, or throughout the community in preparing for war. Under such circumstances the minister feels that but little can be accomplished for Christ and the only encouragement for continuing his labors is the hope of some change for the better in political affairs; and he remains at his post that he may be in readiness to win souls, when men, weary of strife and scenes of blood, shall be ready to reflect on the more serious interests of the soul and eternity.[52]

While there were many disruptions and problems, the Rev. Lewis Bodwell, writing from Topeka, in October, 1856, placed them in a philosophical perspective: "The minister can scarcely do more than keep people reminded of duty, though we must give thanks for the grace which keeps alive and glowing the flame of love in the heart of many Christians. Already I have had the privilege of visiting, praying, eating, sleeping in the unchinked, unplastered cabin of the Christian, where at his bedside, beside his Bible, stood his musket, loaded and primed ready within reach for instant service."[53]

The consequences of the unsettled conditions were not confined to any year. The Rev. S. D. Storrs, writing from Quindaro in February, 1858, described the effect across the years: "The camp, the battlefield & such scenes as have been witnessed at the polls have been anything but favorable to religion. Scarcely a month has passed since the first settlers arrived, after the passage of the 'Nebraska Act,' without something occurring to excite them & not infrequently arouse the worst passions of the heart."[54]

When Kansas was admitted as a state on January 29, 1861, some observers felt that the future for the church would be brighter in Kansas. The Rev. M. J. Miller, a minister of the Evangelical church in Leavenworth, reported that the cannon had been fired when the news arrived of the admission of Kansas into the Union. He wrote: "Thank God for the hard-fought and long-sought-for admission. Kansas now looks for a better state of things, both in the political and moral condition of the country. Many political devils are now being put away. I believe religion will soon prosper more readily than ever before in Kansas."[55] The Rev. Charles Blood wrote from Manhattan about his keen anticipation of the

52. *The Home and Foreign Record,* pp. 355, 356.
53. Rev. Lewis Bodwell to the A. H. M. S., Topeka, October 21, 1856.
54. Rev. S. D. Storrs to the A. H. M. S., Quindaro, February 9, 1858, quoted in Goodykoontz, *op. cit.,* p. 297.
55. Rev. M. J. Miller in the *Evangelical Messenger,* March 7, 1861, quoted in Platz, *op. cit.,* pp. 31, 32.

course of events to the Amercan Home Missionary Society on February 1, 1861. He pointed out that "for more than six years we have been uncertain what would finally be our fate, but now all is certain and fixed so far as relates to freedom. We have a free constitution, and neither Congress nor the president nor all the States combined can interpret to alter the result." [56] The Rev. R. D. Parker at Wyandotte was not so optimistic. On February 6, 1861, he believed that "although public confidence is at the lowest ebb and business at a standstill yet some little courage is given by our admission as a state." [57]

The outbreak of the Civil War intensified the feeling of uncertainty about the future. The Rev. R. D. Parker writing from Wyandotte on May 6, 1861, indicated that there was still peace along the border, "but the fire smoulders that may at any moment 'wheel' us all into ruin." He could see from his home the secessionist flag floating in the breeze at near-by Kansas City. The excitement was intense. He was concerned about how it would all end, "but we pray it may not be until the slave power is crippled and subdued. Such a result would repay even a baptism of blood." [58] The Rev. Richard Cordley shared the same concern as Parker. Writing from Lawrence in July, 1861, he pointed out that his Congregational church was no stronger than it had been two years before. He felt "mortified" to recall that in spite of the auspicious beginnings of Congregationalism in Kansas, there was after seven years not a single self-supporting church in Kansas. "Hard times and the war absorbs all attention." [59]

The Rev. J. D. Liggett described in detail the impact of the war in his letter to Milton Badger from Leavenworth in July, 1861:

Men's minds are wholly engrossed with the war, its news and its prospects. . . . Kansas will take care of herself with the help of the government, but it will convert us all into military men. Much of the old feeling of recklessness, created by the past difficulties has been revived. Our people here will fight,—but the prayers they say when they go at it,—are worthy of the left-handed sort. The wickedness and the malice of the men who have brought these evils upon us and upon themselves, it seems to me, is without a parallel in the history of nations and when and what the end is to be, God only knows.[60]

Liggett went on in this letter to report that only nine members had been added to his church during the past year. At times, as he

---
56. Rev. Charles Blood to the A. H. M. S., Manhattan, February 1, 1861.
57. Rev. R. D. Parker to the A. H. M. S., Wyandotte, February 6, 1861.
58. *Ibid.*, May 6, 1861.
59. Rev. Richard Cordley to the A. H. M. S., Lawrence, July 9, 1861.
60. Rev. J. D. Liggett to the A. H. M. S., Leavenworth, July 29, 1861.

contemplated it, he felt as if he would "almost sink down in despair." However, as he thought about it, he recalled that "Paul may plant and Apollos water but the increase was of God." He was certain that "nothing indeed but a pentecostal effusion can or will move or mould the elements here congregated into materials fit for God's building. He concluded with the prayer "May God pour floods upon this dry ground."[61] However, in August the Rev. R. D. Parker was more encouraged than Liggett when he wrote to Badger from Wyandotte "but notwithstanding the war news seems to absorb every other interest, I am gratified to be able to report a congregation undiminished, a Sabbath School increasing in interest and efficiency, and a system of home evangelization in operation, systematic tract distribution is in progress and we look and pray for the blessings of God."[62]

The year 1861 saw the full impact of the war upon Kansas participants. The Rev. Richard Cordley described the situation in the late summer: "The war absorbs every interest now. Since the battle of Springfield our place has had the aspect of a funeral. The two Kansas regiments were terribly cut up and many of our friends from this place have fallen. The anxious suspense between the news of the battle, and the report of the slain was terrible."[63] The Rev. H. P. Robinson at Grasshopper Falls chronicled also the effects of the war. A large number of the men in his community were now "off to the wars." The course of events had created a situation in which "the present distracted condition of the country has so disarranged society that God, religion, eternity seem almost left out of view. . . . Apathy in regard to religion has taken possession both of the church and community. Many professedly religious people have almost entirely abandoned church going while multitudes of the worldly hardly darken the portals of the sanctuary."[64]

The missionaries and their families were closely identified with

61. *Ibid.*, July 29, 1861. The reference to Paul and Apollos is the scriptural verse found in I Corinthians 3:6.
62. Rev. R. D. Parker to the A. H. M. S., Wyandotte, August 13, 1861.
63. Rev. Richard Cordley to the A. H. M. S., Lawrence, August 26, 1861. The First and Second regiments of Kansas volunteers suffered very heavy casualties in the battle near Springfield, Mo., on August 10, 1861. Maj. John A. Halderman, commanding the First regiment of Kansas volunteers, reported that "with about 800 men we marched upon the field; we left it but with 500.'"—*The War of the Rebellion: Official Records of the Union and Confederate Armies* (Washington, 1881), Ser. I, v. 3, p. 83. The official report listed the following casualties: First Kansas, 77 killed, 187 wounded, 20 missing, for a total of 284; Second Kansas, 5 killed, 59 wounded, 6 missing, for a total of 70.—*Ibid.*, p. 72.
64. Rev. H. P. Robinson to the A. H. M. S., Grasshopper Falls, October 16, 1861. The Rev. Richard Cordley, Lawrence, was not as pessimistic as Robinson. In the letter quoted under date of August 26, 1861, he wrote "considering all things our Sunday congregations have continued good—better than last year at this time."

the people in their churches and communities and with the course of events. The geographic factor was decisive since the greatest hardships were concentrated among the people in the eastern section of the state. The Rev. R. D. Parker at Wyandotte was in the midst of these stirring and tragic events. On November 2, 1863, he gave a graphic description of the general situation and his own intimate role:

> My sixth year of labor as your missionary in Kansas has closed. Like the two preceding years, it has been attended with alarm and danger. Quantrill's bloody band has been prowling like beasts of prey along the Border. We have often seen the fires of Union homes kindled by them. Like my neighbors, I have slept with arms by my side, and beneath my pillows, and have taken my turn in standing guard nights. I have been repeatedly called out to defend the town from threatened attacks, sometimes at the midnight hour. Once the danger signal of the Union League struck upon my church bell, and the terror of the people, especially of the blacks, brought vividly to mind the massacre at Lawrence. Like most of our people, we have kept a few articles of indispensible wearing apparel packed ready for a hasty flight, and in my absence, my sermons, as combustible, and of chief value, have slept out of doors.[65]

The most damaging effect of the Civil War in Kansas was Quantrill's raid on Lawrence on August 21, 1863, when the town was almost completely destroyed and more than 100 people were killed. The ministers were called upon to serve in the deep tragedy of that hour. The Rev. Lewis Bodwell came from Topeka in order to assist his friend the Rev. Richard Cordley, at the burial service of 52 persons whose bodies were placed side by side in a trench.[66] The Rev. Grosevenor C. Morse hastened to Lawrence from Emporia to assist Cordley. In the tragic setting of the time and place he used the 79th Psalm for his Scripture lesson: "O God, the heathen are come into thine inheritance. The dead bodies of thy servants have they given to be meat unto the fowls of heaven, the flesh of thy saints unto the beasts of the earth. Their blood have they shed like water round about Jerusalem and there was none to bury them." [67]

65. Rev. R. D. Parker to the A. H. M. S., Wyandotte, November 2, 1863. Prof. C. B. Goodykoontz's statement that "the remarkable thing about the effect of the Civil War on the home missionary movement is not that it interfered with it, but that it interfered with it to so slight an extent" is not applicable to Kansas.—Goodykoontz, *op. cit.*, p. 303. The geographic position of Kansas, its isolation from the North and East, and the activity of raider bands from Missouri were contributing factors to this situation. The reference to developments in Lawrence is to the tragic raid by Quantrill and his men on August 21, 1863. A full description of the raid is found in Richard Cordley, *A History of Lawrence, Kansas; From the First Settlement to the Close of the Rebellion* (Lawrence, 1895), pp. 187-232.

66. Cordley, *Pioneer Days in Kansas*, p. 220. Cordley lists the names of 126 individuals who were killed in Quantrill's raid.

67. *Ibid.*, p. 221.

When Bodwell visited Cordley at Lawrence on September 4, he witnessed the full implications of the tragedy on all sides. He found Cordley at work in a small attic room from whence he saw the smouldering ruins of Cordley's house, library, and furnishings. Cordley was preparing his first sermon following Quantrill's raid. His library consisted of a pocket Bible and a small Bible concordance, both borrowed items, which Bodwell estimated to be worth $1.60. Cordley had written the subject for his sermon, "The Morning Cometh," across the top of the first page. Then Bodwell continued: "In its light he saw the ruins; across its sunshine drifted the smoke; on its breezes whirled the ashes; but God who had been there in the darkness, had not left at dawn." [68] When Cordley preached to his congregation on the second Sunday following the raid he used as his text a passage from Isaiah 54: "For a small moment have I forsaken thee; but with great mercies will I gather thee. In a little wrath I hid my face from thee for a moment; but with everlasting kindness will I have mercy on thee." [69]

In February, 1864, in a detailed letter to the American Home Missionary Society, Cordley assessed the implications of Quantrill's raid:

Our church here was weakened more than appeared on the surface. . . . Twelve members of the congregation were killed, but more than fifty have left from the same cause. Broken families have left us, and men broken up in their business have left us. . . . I neither carried or owned any arms before, but now I keep a Colt's Navy on my study table and thirty rounds of cartridges in the drawer with my sermon paper.

Still, Lawrence is rapidly recovering and the church is feeling the effect of the general growth. The Sabbath School and congregation are again filling up and things are beginning to assume the former look of prosperity. The town is being rapidly rebuilt. When a few days after the raid, I said, "Lawrence will be rebuilt in two years," many thought me wild. But six months have scarcely passed and as many buildings have been erected or moved into town as Quantrill burned.[70]

68. Rev. Lewis Bodwell, "A Kansas Attic in 1863," *The Kansas Telephone*, Manhattan, v. 1 (April, 1881), p. 1.
69. Cordley, *Pioneer Days in Kansas*, pp. 233, 234. Other ministers and their families suffered great losses from Quantrill's raid. The home and possessions of the Rev. H. D. Fisher were seriously damaged, but Fisher had a miraculous escape due to the imaginative deception of the invaders by his wife.—Fisher, *op. cit.*, pp. 195-210. The raiders burned Jacob Ulrich's house south of Lawrence in the Dunkard settlement and seriously wounded Elder Rothrock.—Elmer LeRoy Craik, *A History of the Church of the Brethren in Kansas* (McPherson, 1922), p. 24.
70. Rev. Richard Cordley to the A. H. M. S., Lawrence, February 29, 1864.

(To Be Concluded in the Winter, 1959, Issue.)

U. S. Army and Air Force Wings Over Kansas—*Concluded*

INDEPENDENCE ARMY AIR FIELD
(1941-1947)

IN January 1941 the Independence Chamber of Commerce under the leadership of C. M. Carman, president, and R. A. McKeen, secretary, resolved to sell the citizens of the Kansas community the idea of a municipal airport. On 26 June 1941, after six months of effective "selling" by Carman, McKeen, and other civic leaders, the city commission decided to ask the voters to approve a $100,000 bond issue for financing work on the airport. The citizens approved by a vote of 1,219 to 173 on 1 August 1941. A short time later the city commission entered into contract with Paulette and White, consulting engineers from Topeka, to survey potential sites for the field. Several locations were considered before any selection was made. The site chosen was in Montgomery county, six miles southwest of Independence.

Early in 1942 the government indicated it was interested in acquiring the site for an Army airfield. During April and May Mayor F. B. Wilhelm of Independence, Pres. J. D. Turner of the Chamber of Commerce, and other civic leaders met with government officials in a series of conferences. Army Engineers made surveys from 8 to 11 April. About six weeks later, on 23 May 1942, the Army officially notified Mayor Wilhelm that it would purchase approximately 1,433 acres.

The contract for planning and supervising the construction of the airfield was awarded to Black and Veatch, architectural engineers from Kansas City, Mo. Work began on 6 June 1942, when Ottinger Brothers of Oklahoma City moved in with a labor crew and began grading operations. Shortly thereafter, work began on the drainage and sewerage systems. During the summer the Missouri Pacific constructed a railroad spur to the site. In August work began on runways and buildings. During the fall of 1942 clearing and grading operations began at four locations that had been selected for auxiliary fields. The four sites were located 8 to 20 miles from the main field. Work progressed satisfactorily throughout the winter despite interruptions caused by heavy rains and sub-zero temperatures. By January of 1943 three concrete runways 5,000 feet in length had been constructed. Electric, gas and water lines also had been completed and sufficient troop housing was available. Most of the buildings were of temporary wartime design—tarpaper over wood, with pot-bellied coal stoves for heating. The major construction work, which cost more than $8,000,000, ended in May 1943.

In the meantime, in June 1942, Lt. Col. (later Col.) Harold L. Mace, commander of the nearby Coffeyville Army Air Field was designated as project officer for the new airfield. He was accompanied by Maj. Temple F. Winburn who acted as the airfield's temporary commander for one month pending arrival of Lt. Col. Richard M. Montgomery (later Major General) to take command. Major Winburn then became Colonel Montgomery's executive officer and was shortly thereafter promoted to Lieutenant Colonel. The base was activated as a Basic Flying School on 12 October 1942, but the personnel to operate the base did not begin arriving until December 1942.

Basic flying training began when 152 cadets arrived for the first class on 26 January 1943. Some of the classes that arrived later had as many as 345 students. The cadets, who had completed primary flying training, received a nine-week course that was divided into flying training and classroom instruction. In the flying training phase, the students practiced landings, made cross-country flights, and flew night navigational missions. During classroom instruction, the students familiarized themselves with aircraft instruments and studied navigation, radio communications, weather, and aircraft recognition.

Basic flying training at Independence continued until January 1945. Nineteen classes, totaling 4,933 students, graduated from the school. The last class completed training on 29 January 1945.

The termination of flying training at Independence resulted in the reassignment of personnel and equipment. Flying personnel were reassigned to airfields in Kansas and Texas during February and March. The BT-13's and BT-14's were moved to airfields in Georgia, Oklahoma, and Missouri. On 15 March Independence Army Air Field was placed on a standby basis. On 11 April 1945, however, the Army announced that the airfield would be used to store World War II aircraft. During the next two months civilian employment on the field jumped from 44 to 505 and military personnel increased from 2 to 272. Aircraft began arriving on 13 April 1945. At first, bomber aircraft (B-17's, B-24's, and B-25's) were prepared for storage and kept at Independence. During October 1945, however, all B-24 and B-17 aircraft were moved to Kingman, Ariz. At the same time P-47's and AT-6's began arriving. During a period of two and a half years the aircraft stored at Independence included 1,542 P-47's, 1,118 AT-6's, 72 B-25's, 401 B-24's, and 260 B-17's.

In the fall of 1947 all aircraft were moved from Independence. Military personnel were transferred effective 11 December 1947. Four days later Independence Army Air Field, which had been listed as surplus, was turned over to the Army's District Engineer, Omaha, Neb. Since then the installation has been operated by the city of Independence as its municipal airport.

LIBERAL ARMY AIR FIELD
(1943-1945)

THE first tangible move to implement the decision to locate a four-engine pilot school on a site selected one mile west of Liberal was the grant of a contract to Murray A. Wilson and Company, engineers, to make a complete survey and layout for the airfield. By 16 January 1943 the survey had been completed. But even before the survey had been officially finished, contracts were let on 9 January, with Peter Kiewit Sons named as prime contractor. Just nine days later construction began on the site.

The new field was situated in western Kansas, 120 miles from Amarillo, Tex., in Sections 1, 6, 25, 30, 31, and 36, Townships 34 and 35 South, and Ranges 33 and 34 West, with a dimension of two miles north and south and two miles east and west. The entire field, some 1,946.7 acres, was purchased by the government. In addition, 3.3 acres on the north extremity of the north-south runway were leased to provide zone clearance space. The field formed part of a flat, low plateau.

Facilities on Liberal Army Air Field were to run to approximately $8,000,000. Three concrete runways were built, each 7,000 feet in length and 150 feet wide, with a gross load capacity of 37,000 pounds. Portable B-2 type runway lights were installed. In addition, a concrete parking apron of some 276,318 square yards was constructed, along with three concrete taxiways 100 feet in width. Training facilities included three school buildings and four Link trainer buildings. Five hangers were built, two of steel and three of wood. Three large warehouses and storage facilities for 591,000 gallons of gasoline were built. Construction coming under the general category of recreation and welfare included a gym-

Boeing B-29 gunners receive operating instructions for the new electric gun turrets at Smoky Hill Army Air Field, Salina.

Free French fliers receive B-26 instruction at the Dodge City Army Air Field.

Upper: Vultee BT-13 taking off from an unidentified air force field in Kansas.
Center: Training planes on ramp, at an unidentified air force field in Kansas.
Lower: Night refueling of Douglas C-54 "Skymaster" at Topeka Army Air Field, October 13, 1945.

Photos on this and preceding page courtesy United States Air Force.

nasium, officers' club, service club, theater, chapel, and three post exchanges. A spur line of the Rock Island railroad was run on to the field from the main line. Housing facilities for 4,934 officers and men and a hospital with a normal bed capacity of 142 were constructed. All buildings were of mobilization type construction.

In addition to the main installation, Gage Auxiliary Field, a former municipal airport, was acquired by lease. This field, some 81 miles from Liberal Army Air Field, comprised 780 acres, providing two hard surfaced runways, each of which was 5,500 feet in length and 150 feet wide.

One officer, Capt. Glen C. Wilson, serving as project officer, was present on the field from the beginning of construction. In April 1943, before completion of construction, additional officers and men of the original cadre reported. Col. Arthur L. Bump arrived on the post on 27 April 1943 and assumed command. Additional personnel arrived during subsequent weeks. In the midst of construction, personnel acquisition moved into an intensified phase during April and May, so that the base was actively manned by the time the first B-24's to be used in training set down on the brand new runways on 20 June. That scheduling was extremely close during those hectic days can be seen in that only ten days later, on 1 July, the members of the first class were introduced to the Liberators. This is the official date of the inauguration of training at Liberal, barely six months after construction began.

Students were predominantly newly-commissioned officers graduated from advanced twin-engine flying schools. The training cycle was nine weeks in length. Half way through the cycle of the first class, another class began the course, so that, afterward, a class graduated every four and a half weeks. By 8 December 1943 Col. R. C. Rockwood, operations and training officer, was able to tell a group of civilian employees that "we are now training approximately one-fourth of the Liberator bomber commanders trained in the continental United States." The pace of training is well illustrated in that it was not until 7 October 1943 that time was found for a formal dedication.

Initially and for a considerable time the commanding officer of the field was in charge of the several squadrons and detachments which performed the various functions requisite to the functioning of the school. The commanding officer was, of course, responsible both for training and for the maintenance of the base services. On 1 May 1944 all the separate units on the field were disbanded except for the 744th AAF Band, the Airways Communications Squadron, and the Base Weather Section. In place of the disbanded organizations the several sections of the 2525th Base Unit were created, distinguished by the nature of the service performed:

Unit Headquarters.
Section "A"—administration and services.
Section "B"—training and operations.
Section "C"—supply and maintenance.
Section "E"—medical.
Section "F"—Negro personnel.
Section "H"—officer students.

In February 1945 these sections were redesignated squadrons, which remained in existence until inactivation of the field.

After victory in Europe the training program of Liberal Army Air Field became somewhat erratic because of the frequent changes of policy in the Training Command. However, with the surrender of the Japanese in August, the mission of the school was definitely over. On 7 September 1945 the commanding officer received official orders for inactivation of the field on or before 30 September. The field was placed at that time on a standby status, which meant maintaining it in such condition as would make possible reactivation within thirty days. Consequently, the field's activities for the greater part of September were largely concerned with the process of inactivation. Considering the magnitude and complexity of the task, the inactivation process proceeded with a minimum of difficulties. Possibly the greatest problem was a scarcity of experienced personnel. On 19 September the officer students slated to complete training at Hondo Army Air Field were ordered to proceed there. All remaining personnel, except officers and enlisted men scheduled to form the standby cadre, were put on movement orders on 29 September. Although the majority of departments were still functioning on 1 October, they were prepared to close down within a few days.

Liberal Army Air Field was fortunate in the relative stability of its commanders. During its entire active period the field had only four commanding officers: Col. Arthur L. Bump from 27 April 1942 to 1 April 1944, Col. Edward H. Underhill from 1 April 1944 to 18 July 1945, Col. Charles Sommers from 18 July 1945 to 18 September 1945, and Col. Ford V. Lauer from 18 September 1945 to 30 September 1945.

Those who had served at Liberal Army Air Field, both military and civilian, might well have been proud of the genuine contribution made by the school to the war effort. During its 27 months of actual training, Liberal Army Air Field graduated 4,468 four-engine airplane commanders. In addition, 1,025 pilots were graduated from the pre-transition course conducted for a period in the middle of 1944. By any standards this was an impressive achievement to come from a place which, as late as the first part of January 1943, was an open prairie.

McCONNELL AIR FORCE BASE
(1942-1957+)

McCONNELL Air Force Base, in Wichita, was known during the first part of its existence as the Wichita Municipal Airport. Although the field was designed originally to serve only municipal needs, it had an Air Force connection almost from the beginning.

On 1 March 1942, the AAF Materiel Center, Midwestern Procurement District (Materiel Command) was established. As soon as construction permitted, the headquarters of the district was established in the administration building of the municipal airport. By the end of 1942, due to the growth and expansion of the organization it occupied practically the entire building save for a few offices occupied by the CAA and airline companies, while some activities of the district were housed at the Boeing Airplane Company Plant No. 1, in Wichita.

The airport, at that time, was located about six miles from the city of Wichita and comprised some 1,337 acres, leased by the government from the city. Although the runways were adequate, other facilities at the airport were meager. There were five runways each 150 feet wide; two were 7,500 feet, one 7,100 feet, one 6,000 feet, and one 4,500 feet in length. All had a wheel load capacity of 60,000 pounds. A parking apron with dimensions of 8,373 by 931 feet, and seven taxi strips were provided. The field could boast of only one hangar and three small warehouses. No facilities were available either for troop housing or troop messing. No fuel storage facilities existed, and all such supplies were handled by commercial contract.

The Midwestern Procurement District was not disturbed at the time of the discontinuance of the Air Materiel Command and the Air Service Command and the creation of the Air Technical Service Command in 1944. However, on 1 August 1945 the Midwestern Procurement District was absorbed by the Western Procurement District, Air Technical Service Command. A few weeks later, on 8 September 1945, Wichita Municipal Airport was transferred from the jurisdiction of Western District, Air Technical Service Command, to that of the Oklahoma City Air Technical Service Command. Personnel formerly assigned to the airport by the ATSC were transferred to the new command. At the same time, the 4156th AAF Base Unit (Air Base) was organized. The new base unit had the mission of servicing, dispatching, and maintaining transient and locally based aircraft. The working personnel were entirely civilian, with a few officers in supervisory capacities.

Slightly over a year later, on 11 October 1946, the 4156th AAF Base Unit was ordered to cease operations by the 30th of the month. Consequently, the remainder of October was spent in closing down operations and transferring property to Tinker Field. On 15 November the field was officially transferred to the Division Engineer, Kansas City, while the 4156th AAF Base Unit was discontinued on the same day. All military personnel were absorbed by Headquarters, Oklahoma Air Materiel Area (the successor of the Oklahoma City Air Technical Service Command).

There followed several years of inactivity, at least insofar as the Air Force was concerned. Then on 5 June 1951 the Air Force activated Wichita Municipal Airport to serve as a training center for combat crews for the B-47 jet bomber, which was being produced at Wichita. To carry on the training the 3520th Combat Crew Training Wing was activated, and an ambitious building program totaling some $22,000,000 was begun. In spite of the difficulty of building an installation and initiating an entirely new program simultaneously, the base developed into a highly specialized training center. Actually, there were two principal parts to the mission of the training center: aircrew training in B-47's and transition training in the same aircraft. A subsequent fluctuation of emphasis from one of those functions to the other reflected the varying demands of the Strategic Air Command. A more inclusive functional title was given the wing in June 1952 when it was redesignated the 3520th Flying Training Wing (M Bomb).

Up to 1 April 1952 the activity at Wichita Municipal Airport was under the jurisdiction of the Flying Training Air Force. On that date it was transferred to the Crew Training Air Force, still remaining, however, in the Air Training Command.

The Air Force was not the sole occupant during this period. In 1952 Wing Headquarters shared the Wichita Municipal Airport Terminal Building with four commercial airlines, Braniff, Central, TWA, and Continental, plus one private flying service: Executive

Airways. These lines were located in the terminal building at the time of government occupation, and were permitted to operate on a temporary basis pending completion of the proposed new municipal airport. By 1952 the Air Force had decided to make a permanent base of the quondam municipal airport. The government took the property by federal court action during the first half of 1952, thus becoming owner and no longer lessee. Reflecting official government ownership, Wichita Municipal Airport was redesignated the Wichita Air Force Base on 15 May 1953.

Some 11 months later, on 12 April 1954, still another redesignation occurred, this time as McConnell Air Force Base. The change was effected to honor the memory of two brothers, former residents of Wichita, Thomas L. and Fred McConnell, Jr. A third brother, still living, is Edwin M. McConnell. The three McConnell brothers had almost identical service careers in the Air Force. From the time they enlisted, won their wings, and served as co-pilots on combat duty in the South Pacific, the McConnell trio stayed together and fought as a team.

Proof of the vigor with which the training center pursued its training function is seen in that the 1,000th B-47 crew graduated at McConnell Air Force Base on 21 April 1955. And at least as late as June 1957, the field was still charged with the same mission.

MARSHALL AIR FORCE BASE
(1912-1950+)

ONE of the oldest military airfields in the United States, Marshall Air Force Base at Fort Riley, made its first appearance in history in November 1912 as the site of the first attempts in the United States to direct artillery fire from an airplane. Among the participants was a young lieutenant, H. H. Arnold, who later became Commanding General of the United States Army Air Forces. Long afterward Arnold recalled the various methods tried for transmitting observations and instructions: a primitive radio, smoke signals, and even colored cards, weighted with iron nuts and dropped through a stovepipe.

The airdrome from which Arnold made his flights was probably the polo field at Fort Riley. How and when the polo field turned into an air base is unknown, but it was used during World War I by both airplanes and balloons. The first regularly constituted air unit at Fort Riley was the 16th Observation Squadron, which was activated there on 7 December 1921. One of its first commanders was Maj. Clarence L. Tinker, who subsequently rose to be commander of Seventh Air Force in World War II and was reported missing in action on a combat mission during the Battle of Midway. Early in 1923 the name of the base was changed from Fort Riley Flying Field to Marshall Field in honor of Brig. Gen. Francis C. Marshall, assistant chief of cavalry, who had been killed in an airplane crash in California on 7 December 1922.

In March 1926 Arnold, then a major, returned as air base commander. He held the post for about two and a half years. When he arrived the only flying unit there was still the 16th Observation Squadron. Considerably below strength, it had about eight officers and four or five De Havilland observation planes (DH-4's) supplemented by eight or ten Curtiss Jennies. Both these planes dated from World War I. A few more modern observation aircraft reached the base, beginning in 1926. The primary responsibility of the fliers at Marshall was to provide demonstrations and participate in training exercises for the Army Cavalry School at Fort Riley. At Arnold's initiative a regular air indoctrination course was set up for the cavalrymen. The 16th Observation Squadron also had to furnish aircraft to work with ground units all over the Seventh Corps Area, which stretched from Arkansas to North Dakota, and for such special assignments as flying President Coolidge's mail from North Platte to Rapid City while he was vacationing in the Black Hills in 1927.

The air base did not change much in size or mission during the 1930's. In March 1931 the 16th Observation Squadron was subdivided into several flights, of which only Flight D was stationed at Marshall. However, it occasionally had company, because from 1930 to 1933 the 35th Division Aviation, National Guard, St. Louis, Mo., was using the field as a training center for its summer encampments. In June 1937 Flight D was absorbed into the 1st Observation Squadron, which fulfilled the traditional responsibilities of flying units at Marshall until 28 December 1941 when it moved to New Orleans for shipment to the Canal Zone.

When the United States entered World War II Marshall possessed two hangars and three unsurfaced landing strips, the biggest strip being 3,700 feet long. These installations were about a mile southeast of Fort Riley proper and three and a half miles from Junction City. During the war the old strips had to be surfaced and lengthened to take increased traffic and heavier, faster planes. Two concrete runways, each 4,500 feet long and 150 feet wide, six taxiways and 5,400 square yards of parking apron were laid down to meet the new needs. However, Marshall remained a relatively small base.

A base detachment activated in January 1941 to operate the field was designated in January 1942 as the 305th Air Base Squadron (Reduced), but in June it was renamed the 305th Base Headquarters and Air Base Squadron (Reduced). It was disbanded in the spring of 1944 and in June the 356th AAF Base Unit was activated to run the base. At the beginning of that year the work of housekeeping and administration was being done by nine officers and 80 enlisted men. Unit and base commander at the end of 1943 was Maj. Victor E. Nelson. He was succeeded on 15 August 1944 by Maj. Herman C. Brigham, who was followed on 13 December by Lt. Col. Jack C. Dale, a veteran fighter pilot with 194 missions to his credit. He left in the spring of 1946. During most of the next two and a half years Col. Eugene H. Snavely commanded the base.

After the departure of the 1st Observation Squadron from Fort Riley, the 6th Observation Squadron (Special) was activated at Fort Sill, Oklahoma, on 7 February 1942 to take its place at the Cavalry School. The squadron moved to Marshall Field on 21 April 1942 with 15 liaison planes. Its commander at that time was Capt. R. S. Wilson, who was followed on 13 June 1943 by Capt. Francis J. Beck. On 28 December 1943 Maj. Dale C. Jones took command and held it until 1 January 1945 when Maj. William Forehand, a fighter pilot back from duty in Europe, replaced him. In June 1943 the squadron was redesignated 6th Reconnaissance Squadron (Special), and on 12 October of that year its name was changed to 2d Composite Squadron (Special).

It well deserved the term "composite" for by that time it had acquired 15 P-39's and five B-25's as well as liaison planes and was flying all sorts of tactical air missions. Besides photographic work, observation, and artillery adjustment, its pilots flew air-ground support demonstrations and simulated strafing, bombing and chemical warfare missions. They "destroyed enemy headquarters" with flour bombs, and sprayed troops with molasses residue in lieu of mustard gas. The commandant of the Cavalry School repeatedly commended the squadron for its "cooperation, enthusiasm and assistance" and wrote "This type of air-ground cooperation . . . is a pleasure to receive." Members of a Colombian military mission said of one air-ground demonstration that it was "worth going to Fort Riley for that alone." Much work was done away from Fort Riley. Teams from Marshall were scheduled to provide the Armored School and the Field Artillery School with six demonstrations apiece in 1944, and they answered many special requests for demonstrations and tests. On 1 August 1945 the airmen at Marshall put on a giant air show in which they displayed to 5,000 Kansan friends and neighbors the tactical skills they had acquired during the war.

Several units besides the 2d Composite Squadron spent some time at Marshall during the war. The 72d Observation Group had its headquarters squadron there briefly in December 1941; the 5th Observation Squadron was there from August 1942 till April 1943; and a Negro unit, the 1018th Guard Squadron trained at Marshall for a short time in 1945. Also, a detachment of the 161st Liaison Squadron with L-5 aircraft visited the base for exercises in November and December 1944. The ground forces at Riley in 1944 had 36 aerial target planes which were serviced by the 356th Base Unit. Marshall was much used as a convenient stop on cross-country flights. Of some 1,400 landings and take-offs at the field in July 1945, 614 were transients. Another and not inconsiderable activity was the flying in and out of distinguished visitors to Fort Riley. Among them were Gens. Ben Lear, Joseph W. Stilwell, and George S. Patton.

On 7 November 1945 the 2d Composite Squadron was inactivated, its place being taken by Detachment "B" of the 69th Reconnaissance Group which inherited some of its personnel and equipment. About the same time the 72d and 167th Liaison Squadrons, equipped with 75 L-5's arrived at the base for training. At the end of the year there were 106 aircraft at Marshall. However, this strength was soon whittled down as the postwar demobilization progressed. Early in 1946 the detachment of the 69th Group was withdrawn and the 72d Squadron was reduced to a two-man cadre, so that by late April only the 167th Squadron remained. On 3 October 1946 it was inactivated and the 163d Liaison Squadron was created to replace it.

Late in 1946 the Cavalry School and the Cavalry Intelligence School at Fort Riley were inactivated and the Ground General School was established there. The principal mission of the 163d Squadron continued to be the giving of air support to the new school as to the old, but it confined its efforts mainly to visual reconnaissance. At first it used only L-5's, but in the spring of 1947 it acquired six helicopters, the novelty of which aroused much interest in subsequent demonstrations. That spring the squadron was also given control of detachments at Biggs Air Force Base, Alamogordo, and Camp Beale. These detachments, with a half-dozen liaison planes, were working with the rocket development center at White

Sands. The Air Force decision in 1948 to eliminate all enlisted pilots by the end of the year caused a drastic shake-up at Marshall. Though they were almost extinct in most flying units, the 163d had had 25 of them and only nine commissioned pilots in 1947.

Undoubtedly the most dramatic episode of the postwar period at Marshall came early in 1949 when the base contributed its facilities, planes, and helicopters to "Operation Haylift," bringing relief to snowbound areas in several Western states. Another memorable event was the emergency landing on 6 August 1948 of a B-29 which had made a record-breaking 5,120-mile non-stop flight from Furstenfeldbruck, Germany, with Capt. Walter E. Abbott as pilot.

On 1 April 1949 the 163d Liaison Squadron was inactivated. Light aviation detachments of the Ground General School and the 10th Infantry Division took over most of its functions. However, in September 1949 Tenth Air Force established an Instrument Training Center at Marshall Air Force Base to provide a refresher course for all its pilots outside the 56th Fighter Wing. The school had eight instructors, commanded by Capt. John J. Davis, and was equipped with ten B-25's which were later replaced by C-45's. In March 1950, after 86 pilots had graduated, the school was moved to Selfridge Air Force Base. The Air Force then withdrew entirely from Marshall and, effective 1 June 1950, the base unit, which on 23 August 1948 had become the 4406th Air Base Squadron, was inactivated.

PRATT ARMY AIR FIELD
(1942-1945)

PRATT Army Air Field was constructed in south central Kansas in Pratt county. The field was located about three miles north of the city of Pratt, a community of about 7,000, and which was the only urban area readily accessible to personnel of the field. The area of the field sloped slightly from west to east, with an elevation varying from 1,969 feet to 1,930 feet.

Construction, begun in 1942, was of the theater of operations type. By the time of the official dedication of the field in May 1943, some 60 barracks had been completed giving accommodations to 2,460 enlisted men. Total authorized construction called for a total of 72 barracks with a capacity of 3,060 enlisted men and eight officers' quarters with a housing capacity of 522.

A few personnel began to arrive well before completion of the field. The first group, a 12-man cadre on detached service, stayed for a time at the Calbeck Hotel in Pratt until facilities at the field had been completed sufficiently for them to move in. In January 1943 the 502d Base Headquarters and Air Base Squadron was activated to function as the administrative and training squadron for the other organizations which would be assigned to the base. On 10 February 1943 Lt. Col. J. F. Nelson assumed command of the field, and by March the installation began to function as a military post with the barest of essentials in housing, messing, and administrative equipment. Construction and personnel manning had progressed so far by May that on the second of the month the field was officially dedicated.

Originally, Pratt Army Air Field had been scheduled to function as one of several bases under the control of the 21st Bombardment Wing. It was the task of this latter organization to process for overseas duty, especially as to equipment, the bombardment wings formed and trained under the Second Air Force. However, to the disappointment of the 21st Wing, which, incidentally, was continually plagued by lack of facilities with which to operate, Pratt never really came under its program. The enormous effort necessary to form and train the B-29 groups diverted Pratt from its original mission with the 21st to one of the several fields dedicated to the special B-29 combat training program.

The function of Pratt Army Air Field, under the administration of the 502d Base Headquarters and Air Base Squadron, was to furnish housekeeping and administrative services to the bombardment groups which made Pratt their temporary station while undergoing combat group training. During 1943 and much of 1944 the newly-formed B-29 bombardment groups conducted their own training at Pratt, with the field and its units serving only in an administrative, housekeeping, and general support capacity. This was true of both the 40th and 497th Bombardment Groups.

As each group went into the latter phases of its training at Pratt, the next group in line to move to Pratt would send its maintenance squadrons ahead in order to acquire experience by assisting in aircraft maintenance for the older group. As a result, when the flight echelon of the new group arrived at Pratt upon departure of the previous group, the maintenance squadrons had acquired sufficient experience to enable them to keep their own group's aircraft in the air.

Early in 1944 a new base unit system was devised throughout the Air Force. At Pratt the 246th Base Unit, OTU (VH), was formed on 1 April 1944. Under the new dispensation the responsibilities of the base were greatly increased, for in addition the base, through the 246th Base Unit, was henceforth to be in charge of the training program of each succeeding B-29 group.[3] For this purpose, a Directorate of Training was authorized.

Such a great increase in function could not, of course, be accomplished immediately. Time was needed in which to acquire personnel sufficiently knowledgeable to supervise the instruction. Consequently, the 497th Bombardment Group trained itself just as the 40th Group had done before it. Indeed, it was not until August 1944, with the advent of the 29th Group, that the 246th Base Unit was able to assume the task of group combat training. Under the same system the 29th Group was succeeded at Pratt by the 346th Group in February 1945, and the latter in turn by the 93d Group in July.

The process of closing down Pratt Army Air Field began in November 1945, while the 93d Group was still in training. The base unit suffered such serious losses of personnel during the month as to render its task of supervising the training of the 93d Group a most difficult one. With the departure of the 93d Group in December, the work of Pratt Army Air Field was done, and there remained only to complete the process of closing down the installation. Col. Reuben Kyle, Jr., as commanding officer, supervised the process. Pratt Army Air Field was officially inactivated on 31 December 1945, with no subsequent period of activation.

Schilling Air Force Base
(Formerly Smoky Hill Air Force Base)
(1942-1958+)

DURING World War II many famous B-29 units were stationed at Smoky Hill Army Air Field, Salina. Both the XX Bomber Command, which handled B-29 operations in the China-Burma-India Theater, and the XXI Bomber Command, which controlled B-29's flying from the Marianas to Japan, were activated at Smoky Hill. Though the XX and XXI Bomber Commands remained at this station for only a brief period of time, Smoky Hill retained the honor of being the birthplace of these two famous units. Also at

---

3. Maj. Robert K. Morgan, who led the first all-American raid over Germany in March, 1943, was assigned at Pratt Army Air Field about this time. Major Morgan was commander of the "Memphis Belle" which became famous as the subject of one of the outstanding documentary motion pictures of World War II.—Pratt *Tailwind*, March 11, April 22, May 6, 1944.

Smoky Hill for a short period was the 58th Bombardment Wing,[4] which operated under the XX Bomber Command in China-Burma-India and later under the XXI Bomber Command in the Marianas. The 73d Bombardment Wing, which served so valiantly in the Marianas under the XXI Bomber Command, was also stationed at Smoky Hill. In addition to the above-mentioned headquarters units, Smoky Hill Army Air Field took care of several B-29 tactical groups. These included the 468th, 499th, and 39th Bombardment Groups.

Though Smoky Hill Air Field was distinguished as a B-29 training station during World War II, the base originally was used as a processing and staging area for heavy bombardment units going to overseas stations. This phase as a processing station lasted from the fall of 1942, when minimum operational facilities first were available, through the first half of 1943. The B-29 units began to arrive in the fall of 1943; and thereafter, until the end of the war in September 1945, Smoky Hill was predominantly a B-29 training base.

The handling of very heavy bombardment units required a base possessing extensive facilities. Two runways at Smoky were 10,000 feet in length, while two other runways were 7,500 feet in length. Twelve taxistrips connected the various runways. The concrete apron measured 4,000 x 600 feet. The size of the base is further indicated by the fact that it comprised approximately 2,600 acres in Smoky Hill and Smolan townships. The area on which buildings were constructed took up 365 acres. The major part of the construction work was completed in 1942, with the working force at one time including 13 civilian contractors with more than 7,000 workers.

Important dates in Smoky Hill's early history include: 5 May 1942, when construction work on the airfield started; 23 December 1942, when the field was officially designated Smoky Hill Army Air Field; 20 November 1943, when the XX Bomber Command was activated at Smoky Hill; and 1 March 1944, when the XXI Bomber Command was activated at Smoky Hill.

After the end of World War II in September 1945, activity at Smoky Hill Army Air Field shifted from wartime to a peacetime

---

4. The First Group of the 58th Bombardment Wing, the first of the B-29 "Superfort" units, was organized at Smoky Hill Army Air Field. The early B-29's delivered to this unit were shipped unfinished, a fact which precipitated the "Salina Blitz" or the "Battle of Kansas," in which Gen. H. H. "Hap" Arnold played a leading role. The result of the blitz was the bombing of Japan by Kansas built B-29's on 15 June 1944.—Wesley Price, "Birth of a Miracle," *Saturday Evening Post*, Philadelphia, August 25, 1945, pp. 11, 52; "The Battle of Kansas," *The Kansas Historical Quarterly*, v. 13, pp. 481-484; Thomas Collison, *The Superfortress Is Born, the Story of the Boeing B-29* (New York, Duell, Sloan & Pearce, 1945), pp. 175-188.

The Collison history gives credit to Brig. Gen. Orval Cook and Maj. Gen. B. E. Meyers, and includes the airfields at Pratt, Great Bend and Walker, in this operation.

basis. In 1946 the base came under the control of the Fifteenth Air Force of Strategic Air Command. From 1946 onward, with the exception of two years (1950-1951) when the field was on a stand-by status, Smoky Hill was a key installation of Strategic Air Command. Two changes of designation occurred in the post World War II period. In 1946 the base became Smoky Hill Air Force Base. And in 1957 the designation was changed to Schilling Air Force Base in honor of Col. David C. Schilling, who was killed in an automobile accident in England in 1956. Colonel Schilling, as a member of the famous 56th Fighter Group, was a leading ace during World War II.[5]

Schilling Air Force Base is now (January 1958) the home of the 40th and 310th Bombardment Wings, both B-47 jet bomber outfits and the 802d Air Division—all assigned to Strategic Air Command. Each wing consists of 45 bombers and 20 large four engine KC-97 aerial tankers aircraft. This base continues as a key one in the defense of our country. Brig. Gen. James C. Wilson commands (1958) the 802d Air Division.

SHERMAN AIR FORCE BASE
(1926-1953+)

FROM its beginning until the Air Force discontinued operations there in 1953, the primary and almost exclusive function of Sherman Air Force Base at Fort Leavenworth was to provide flying facilities for the Command and General Staff School at Fort Leavenworth. Most of its use was for proficiency flights by pilots assigned to the school as students or instructors. In the early 1920's such flying was done at an old polo ground about three miles from Sherman. However, in the spring of 1926 an emergency strip, which had been laid out on the present site in 1923, was converted into a permanent airfield. To run the field an Air Corps detachment was stationed there until 1 July 1937 when the detachment became the Third Staff Squadron.

The base was located on low ground in a bend of the Missouri river one mile northeast of Fort Leavenworth near the Disciplinary Barracks. At first a sod surface was used, but in 1930 construction of three cinder runways was initiated. The largest of these had a

---

5. Col. David C. Schilling was born in Leavenworth and grew up in the Kansas City area. His Air Force career was spectacular. During World War II he shot down 33 German planes. A colonel at 24, he was entitled to wear 40 ribbons by the end of the war. In 1948 he led the first trans-oceanic jet flight from the United States to Germany. In 1950 he made the first non-stop trans-Atlantic single jet engine flight. In 1952 the Air Force Association designated him as the man who had contributed most to U. S. air power the preceding year. He also participated in several speed flights during the early 1950's.—Kansas City (Mo.) *Star*, March 10, 1957.

length of only 2,800 feet in 1937. During the next two years two runways were extended to 4,000 feet, and after the entry of the United States into World War II they were further lengthened to 6,000 feet, a distance sufficient for most types of aircraft used in that war. However, because in wet weather or when the river was high the ground was often too sodden to be satisfactory for use by heavy aircraft, cement aprons were laid down late in 1944 at the ends of the main runways. Intersecting at one end and joined by a short cross-strip, the runways made a pattern like the letter "A." A hangar for the base was built in 1932. Badly damaged in 1934 by a fire which also destroyed several planes, it was repaired and used for the next 20 years. Several temporary buildings, including barracks for enlisted men, were added during World War II.

It appears probable that command of the field was first exercised in 1926 by Capt. Benjamin F. Giles, subsequently commander of the Army Air Forces in the Middle East during the latter part of World War II. The base commander in 1935 was Capt. Harry A. Johnson, who rose to be head of Tenth Air Force before his retirement in 1953. During much of World War II Sherman had the peculiar distinction of being directly under Headquarters, Army Air Forces. However, on 21 January 1944 it was assigned to Third Air Force under which it remained for the duration of the war. The Third Staff Squadron was inactivated on 29 April 1944, its personnel and equipment going to a new organization, the 355th Air Base Unit. Also disbanded at that time and absorbed into the 355th were a medical detachment and the 344th Sub-Depot, which had been in operation at Sherman since its activation on 1 May 1941. About 50 men belonging to an airways communications detachment and a weather detachment remained outside the base unit, though attached to it for rations and quarters. Maj. John F. Buckman, who had commanded the base and the Third Squadron since before February 1944, commanded the base and base unit until 24 September when he was succeeded by Lt. Col. Blair M. Sorenson. Sorenson held the command until 4 September 1945.

Early in the war when bases were scarce Sherman was pressed into service for training purposes. In September and October 1941 two National Guard units, the 124th and 127th Observation Squadrons, were sent there to train. They left in April 1942. Dutch cadets were given primary flight instruction there in 1942 by the 671st School Squadron. Otherwise the mission of the base continued to be to provide facilities for proficiency flying by faculty and students at the Command and General Staff School, for administrative flights, and for transients.

As late as May 1944 Sherman had only 25 planes, most of which were trainers and none models then used in combat. However, an influx of pilots sent to study at Fort Leavenworth after gaining extensive combat experience on tours of duty overseas made it desirable to provide more and better planes for their use. A batch of 15, including some P-40's, arrived in June 1944, and by the end of the war over 60 aircraft, at least ten of which were P-51's, were based at Sherman. Traffic expanded until in July 1945, 868 local and 357 cross-country flights were made from the base.

In recognition of the growing importance of air warfare, Brig. Gen. Robert C. Candee, one-time Commanding General of VIII Air Support Command, was appointed on 5 October 1944 as director of air instruction at the Command and General Staff School. He is believed to have been the first general officer to hold that position. In May 1945 Candee and about 60 other Air Corps officers on the faculty and staff of the school who had been on detached service there were assigned to a specially constituted squadron of the 355th Base Unit.

Over the years Sherman saw a dazzling array of visitors, usually drawn there to transact business or attend ceremonies at Fort Leavenworth. Among them were in 1944 Gen. H. H. Arnold, Commanding General of the Army Air Forces, in 1945 Lt. Gen. Lewis H. Brereton, Commanding General of Third Air Force, and in 1946 the Chief of Staff of the United States Army, General of the Army Dwight D. Eisenhower, and the Deputy Commander of the AAF, Lt. Gen. Ira C. Eaker. Later came Gen. Jacob L. Devers, the commander of the Army Ground Forces, Lt. Gen. Curtis E. LeMay, Commanding General of Strategic Air Command, and Lt. Gen. Elwood R. Quesada, head of Tactical Air Command. Of many foreign dignitaries, the British general, Marshal Sir Bernard L. Montgomery, who attended graduation at Fort Leavenworth in 1953, was the most famous, but probably the most stared at was the only Soviet general ever seen in that area, Maj. Gen. Nicolai V. Slavin, who stopped off in 1944 on his way to the Dumbarton Oaks Conference.

In 1946 Sherman passed from Third Air Force to the newly created Tactical Air Command, under which it remained until the end of 1948 when it was given to Tenth Air Force, a subordinate of Continental Air Command. The name of the installation was changed on 13 January 1948 from Sherman Field to Sherman Air Force Base. The 355th Base Unit was transformed on 23 August 1948 into the 4405th Air Base Squadron, and this in turn was redesignated as the 2223d Air Base Squadron, effective 16 December 1950. Postwar base commanders were Col. Kenneth R. Martin (4 September 1945-25 August 1947), Lt. Col. Elliott H. Reed (26 August 1947-20 July 1948), Lt. Col. O. J. Mosman (21 July 1948-spring 1950), Capt. James B. Murrow, Jr. (spring 1950-14 September 1951), Capt. Wilson B. Swan (15-30 September 1951), Maj. Peter V. Mullen (1 October 1951-13 June 1952), Capt. Laurence J. Rooney (13 June 1952-10 July 1952), and Maj. Witold B. Monkiewicz (11 July 1952-October 1953).

After World War II operations at Sherman sank again to a small scale. By mid-1947 there were only 13 aircraft at the field and later there were even fewer. On 1 July 1950 only four officers and 104 airmen were assigned to the 4405th Air Base Squadron. However, this low manning was possible only because even after the separation of the Air Force from the Army, Fort Leavenworth continued to provide Sherman with almost all necessary quartermaster, ordnance, engineering and finance facilities.

In 1951 the base acquired an additional mission, responsibility for providing minimum flying training for officers at 11 stations, mostly ROTC detachments, in Kansas and neighboring states. Often endangered by floods, Sherman was inundated on 23 April 1952 when one of the dikes protecting it failed. Damage was slight, and the field was back in operation within ten days, but the crisis may have hastened the death of its commander, Major Mullen, who died of a heart attack on 13 June. Command was assumed by Capt. Rooney in addition to his previous duties as operations officer, aircraft maintenance officer, engineering officer, and air installations officer. Only at so extraordinarily small and thinly manned a base as Sherman could one officer have carried even temporarily such a multitude of responsibilities.

During the summer of 1953 Tenth Air Force evaluated Sherman Air Force Base and came to the conclusion that in the interests of economy the base should be discontinued and its training activities be transferred elsewhere. Headquarters USAF approved this measure, and on 25 October the 2223d Air Base Squadron was officially discontinued. Responsibility for final close-out of the base was entrusted to the 2472d AFROTC Detachment at the Olathe Naval Air Station, Olathe.

Strother Army Air Field
(1942-1953)

WHAT began as a joint enterprise of the proximate cities of Winfield and Arkansas City to build a municipal airport evolved, by the force of events, into construction of an Army airfield dedicated to basic flying training. At a joint meeting on 6 February 1941 the two city commissions approved construction of a Class 2 airport comprising some 240 acres with a 100 x 100-foot hangar. Authority to issue bonds had already been granted by the legislature.

During the course of 1941 the government's interest in this site for the establishment of a flying school became known. A site selection board of officers met at Arkansas City, 11 April 1942, and inspected the proposed airport site. In its report three days later, the board approved the proposed site. On the same day of the board meeting, 11 April, the two cities passed a resolution committing the municipalities to obtain approximately 1,400 acres of land to be leased to the government at the rate of one dollar per year, and renewable yearly for 25 years.

Strother Field, named after Capt. Donald R. Strother, who was killed over Java on 13 February 1942,[6] was located midway between Arkansas City and Winfield, in Cowley county on U. S. Highway 77. The entire field comprised some 1,386 acres. In addition, there were four auxiliary fields. Number one, totaling 481 acres, was acquired from seven owners, partly by straight purchase and partly by Decision of Taking of the Federal District Court. Cost of the land was $48,941. Number Two contained 643 acres. It, too, was acquired from seven owners, partly by straight purchase and partly by Decision of Taking. Total cost was $70,409. The 631½ acres of Auxiliary Number Three were acquired from eight owners. Only three acres were purchased; the remainder was acquired on annual lease. Number Five, totaling 656.40 acres, was acquired from eight owners at a total cost of $46,169. A portion was obtained from straight purchase, while a Decision of Taking was necessary to acquire title to the remainder.

Construction at Strother Field, the total cost of which was to approach $9,000,000, began on 16 May 1942. Building operations began on the sites of the auxiliary fields at the same time. At

---

6. Captain Strother was born October 26, 1911, in Winfield. He attended the Winfield schools and Southwestern College, and in 1934 became a cadet in the army air corps. Later he served two years as a civilian air line pilot. In 1938 Strother re-entered the air corps, and at the time of his death commanded a squadron of flying fortresses.—Winfield *Daily Courier*, May 28, 1942; *Official Army Register*, 1942, p. 839.

Strother, four asphalt runways, 5,500, 4,000, and two of 5,840 feet in length and all 150 feet wide, were built. Permanent type runway lights were installed. Connecting these were four taxiways, three of asphalt and one of concrete, two of which were 700 feet in length, another 3,500 feet, and the fourth 1,600 feet. Three were 50 feet wide, one 100 feet.

Storage facilities included three AAF and four Quartermaster buildings. All were of wood frame construction, with cement floors. Two instructional buildings, totaling 15,550 square feet with a total student capacity of 550, were erected. In addition, six Link Trainer buildings were provided, with a total capacity of 34.

Under the general category of recreational and welfare facilities, day rooms, an officers' club and a service club, theater, chapel, post exchange, bowling alley, gymnasium, swimming pool, and library were built. Housing was built to accommodate a total of 4,404 officers and men, while the hospital was designed for a normal bed capacity of 141. Although fuel was readily available locally, a gasoline capacity of 210,216 gallons was provided, and an oil storage capacity of 36,000 gallons.

Col. Joseph F. Carroll arrived in Winfield on 17 September 1942, moved into his office at post headquarters two days later, and took up his duties as project officer. The post was activated on 1 November 1942, construction being still in progress, with Colonel Carroll as commanding officer. Because of his late arrival, Colonel Carroll was not burdened with the greater part of construction as project officer as he himself attests:

I had no predecessor as Commanding Officer of this station, but I wish to pay tribute to the work of Colonel H. W. Dorr, who as the original Project Officer during the early phase of construction, initiated changes in the construction plans to fit the particular requirements of a basic school.

The voracious demand for fighter pilots necessitated a very early inauguration of training on 14 or 15 December 1942 with the arrival of the first class of cadets. At that time, the runways had not been completed and planes were forced to operate from the parking ramp only. A most hazardous situation. Training consisted principally of 70 hours pilot training. Like most new training bases in this period, the greatest initial problem was a scarcity of training aircraft. Training was inaugurated with a ratio of one plane to six students. The 14 months between 1 January 1943 and 1 March 1944 were to bring to Strother Field, including those who arrived in the middle of December 1942 and those who remained after 1 March 1944, 14 classes of students.

The two cities of Winfield and Arkansas City, with populations of 10,000 and 12,000 respectively, and each seven and a half miles from the field, had been from the beginning enthusiastic supporters of the field. The cooperation of these two municipalities continued at the same high level, as Colonel Carroll asseverated:

> My job was made much easier and much more pleasant by the excellent cooperation from the people in the two nearby towns of Winfield and Arkansas City, Kansas. The civic leaders many times took the initiative in formulating plans for projects to improve the morale of the personnel of this station, and to provide things which we were unable to get without their assistance. The townspeople received the military personnel with open arms, and convinced us all that there is such a thing as "Kansas Hospitality."

On 1 June 1944 the basic flying training function at Strother ceased, and the field was taken over by the Second Air Force. With the graduation of Class 44-G on 23 May, Strother Field had accomplished its mission as a basic pilot school of the Central Flying Training Command. This was the 16th class to take basic training at Strother.

On 1 June 1944 Col. Donald E. Meade took command for the Second Air Force. Most of the permanent personnel of the old basic flying school were transferred within the Training Command, and the Second Air Force brought in its own personnel to man the base. The chief problem facing the new command was transition from a basic flying training station to a tactical training station.

For a full year Strother Field functioned as a fighter pilot combat crew training school. With the end of the war in sight, official orders were received on 27 July 1945 providing for the inactivation of the base by 15 August. Consequently, on 30 July a total reduction of force, both military and civilian, was begun. One by one the various units of operation were closed during the first 15 days of August. Flying training ended officially on 8 August, although in fact it had ceased four days before. By 15 August orders had been complied with in full, save for such minor modifications as were authorized by higher headquarters to meet existing needs.

Strother Field was placed on a standby status and assigned to Pratt Army Air Field as an auxiliary field. Colonel Meade, station commander since the Second Air Force took over on 1 June 1944 from the Central Flying Training Command, awaited only the arrival of relieving command from Pratt before his own departure. The Pratt Army Air Field budget and fiscal officer took over the duties of closing the fiscal records of the field. Strother Field served as a satellite for only a few months, for Pratt itself was inactivated in December 1945.

Presumably, no further activity took place at Strother until about July 1948. At that time it assumed a housing function for a reserve composite squadron, Tenth Air Force, Air Defense Command. Sometime during 1949 or the first half of 1950 it ceased to perform even this function. By March 1952 it was housing the 9721st Volunteer Air Reserve Training Squadron. But between November 1953 and September 1954 this activity was removed, and up to March 1958 Strother Field was not used in any Air Force capacity.

WALKER ARMY AIR FIELD
(1942-1946)

WALKER Army Air Field was located in Ellis county, about two and one-half miles northwest of Walker. The main line of the Union Pacific railroad was situated only two miles away, and the field had ready access to U. S. Highway 40. The topography was of such a nature as to permit construction of 10,000-foot runways with minimum grading.

Requisite land was purchased by the government in fee simple from individual owners. Additional areas were leased from the Union Pacific railroad for the location of storage yards. Other auxiliary facilities were acquired as needed. Three gunnery ranges were acquired in Ellis, Ness, and Gove counties, and three bombing ranges in Trego and Graham counties.

In planning the field, the water supply was a particularly difficult problem principally because this site was judged by the state geologist to have the most difficult water situation of any spot in the state. After spending considerable time and money drilling, a fair water supply was located on Little creek about eight miles from the site. In addition, a proven supply was available from the Hays city system about 12 miles distant. A study of comparative costs and results revealed that connection with the Hays city system was the safest and most practical answer. Consequently, a connecting line was run there. The easement for water lines to Hays was purchased by the government subject to expiration six months after termination of the emergency.

Contracts were negotiated on 26 August 1942, and construction got under way on 14 September. Three concrete runways 150 feet in width were paved to a length of 8,000 feet and graded at each end another 1,000 feet so that by adding concrete paving at each end, runways 10,000 feet long would be available. Concrete taxiways 75 feet wide, as well as an apron 300 by 375 feet, were constructed. The cantonment, originally designed for about 1,000 men but later much expanded, was of minimum cost (theater of operations) construction, save for the dispensary and one mess hall which were of mobilization type construction. As an example of subsequent expansion, originally only one hangar was built, but by the time of the field's inactivation five hangars were in use. Completion to the point of limited occupancy was accomplished within 79 days after negotiation of the contracts.

The first military personnel at the base were members of a Quartermaster Corps detachment, which arrived from Smoky Hill Army Air Field, Salina, on 11 November 1942. This advance party was composed of one officer, 2d Lt. Glenn M. Wheeler, and four enlisted men. The first commanding officer of the yet incompleted base was Capt. James E. Altman, who assumed command on 12 December 1942. However, he was quickly replaced by Lt. Col. William A. Cahill on 18 December. The new field acquired its headquarters unit with the activation of the 500th Base Headquarters and Air Base Squadron on 8 February 1943. Real base activity began when the 852d Signal Corps Detachment, the 3d Weather Squadron, the 23d Airways Communications Squadron, the 2064th Ordnance Corps Detachment and a medical detachment were attached to the 500th Base Headquarters and Air Base Squadron for administration, rations, and quarters. Early in 1943 the 502d Bombardment Squadron also arrived, along with a guard squadron, a quartermaster company, and an airdrome squadron. The field was in good enough condition by 4 July 1943 to enable the commanding officer to hold "Open House."

Morale was a problem at Walker Army Air Field, particularly in the early period, principally because there was no town of more than a few thousand people within a radius of 100 miles. Indeed, the nearest large city was Kansas City, 350 miles away. Severely limited in recreational opportunities as the field and the area were, it was nevertheless not until June 1943 that provision was made for construction of a gymnasium, theater, service club, and post exchange.

Intimately connected with the absence of municipalities of any size was a most acute housing problem both for civilian workers and military personnel. Unfortunately, this bad condition was permitted to exacerbate relations between the field and surrounding areas, particularly Hays, during most of 1943. The situation actually deteriorated to the point where vituperative exchanges were printed in the local newspaper during March 1943. However, by the end of the year, with a new commanding officer at the field, relations began to show a marked improvement.

Even though the base and community were plagued with the problem of where to house civilian workers, a chronic shortage of qualified civilians was something successive commanders were forced to live with. Even worse, the shortage did not stop with civilians, for the bane of operations was the paucity of enlisted technicians, especially airplane and engine mechanics, airplane technicians, power plant specialists, electrical specialists, and propeller specialists. This was especially grievous since the field was in large part responsible for all maintenance and repair.

Walker Army Air Field began operations simply as a satellite field of Smoky Hill Army Air Field located at Salina. In this capacity Walker was used merely as a spillover field in the performance of Smoky Hill's mission of processing heavy bombardment crews for overseas shipment. A more important, and more independent mission was given to Walker on 1 February 1943 when the Second Air Force organized the 6th (later replaced by the 7th) Heavy Bombardment Processing Headquarters there. Walker thus became a processing center in its own right. By the middle of 1943 a still further expansion of mission was due at Walker. The field was scheduled to begin training B-29 crews for combat duty, and in about August 1943 the first B-29's were brought in. Walker was to function through the remaining active portion of its career within the training program of the 17th Bombardment Operational Training Wing, which had its headquarters at Sioux City Army Air Base.

As the training program got under way a major problem presented itself in the lack of bombing ranges. Prior to December 1943, Walker had only one bombing range, the result being overcrowding beyond reasonable limits of safety. In an effort to eliminate this dangerous situation arrangements were made with other fields in that area of Kansas whereby planes from Walker could practice bombing on ranges belonging to other fields. But this solution proved unsatisfactory since the bombing schedules of Walker planes often conflicted with those of other fields. A much better solution was found by the acquisition of four tracts of land during December 1943. By the end of January 1944 these ranges were almost ready for use. As was anticipated, not only did the new ranges eliminate a dangerous condition, but it also resulted in accelerating the B-29 training program.

All the units permanently stationed at Walker were reorganized on 25 March 1944 and placed in the 248th AAF Base Unit, which assumed the official designation of the 248th OTU (Operational Training Unit) Training School. The new organization was designed to serve as carrying unit for all permanent party activities, as well as to conduct functions of administration, training, supply, and maintenance.

In April 1944 there was established a Directorate of Training which, it was anticipated, would, when fully manned and equipped, take over and completely train the new bombardment groups which would come thereafter to Walker. This involved preparation of training programs and schedules, the proper coordination of all training activity to ensure fulfillment of Second Air Force requirements with no overlapping or loss of time. As one group would complete operational training and prepare to leave, the leading elements of the next group would arrive and training would begin on the new group. Sometimes overlapping of two groups on the field at the same time caused acute, though temporary, housing problems. Besides training bomb groups for overseas, Air Service Groups, such as the 72d, 75th, and 367th, were also trained for overseas duty.

From very humble beginnings, both the mission and the physical plant of Walker Army Air Field expanded considerably so that by 31 August 1944 a total of 5,936 personnel were stationed at the field. Out of this total 529 officers and 2,742 enlisted men were stationed for training, leaving a permanent party of 235 officers, 1,781 enlisted personnel, and 659 civilians.

With victory over Japan in August 1945, the mission of the 17th Bombardment Operational Training Wing changed and slackened. Salina was the only one of the wing's stations to continue combat crew training. Five other stations were to complete the manning and training of the 449th, 467th, 448th, 44th, and 93d Groups, while three stations, including Walker, were left with no mission at all.

Consequently, Walker was relieved from assignment to the 17th Bombardment Operational Training Wing and reassigned to the Air Technical Service Command, effective 30 September 1945, and further assigned to the Oklahoma City Air Materiel Area. The latter then moved in the 4180th AAF Base Unit to maintain the field on a housekeeping basis. On 31 January 1946 Walker was put on inactive status, and disposition of property became the major activity at the field. The inactive status continued until the War

Department placed the installation in a surplus category in the middle of 1946. A transfer agreement was drawn up on 21 November 1946 between representatives of Oklahoma City Air Materiel Area, Walker Army Air Field, Fifth Army, and the District Engineers, Kansas City. Subsequently, on 19 December 1946, the field was transferred to the District Engineers.

Bypaths of Kansas History

LIFE IN KANSAS

From the *Kansas Weekly Press*, Elwood, November 20, 1858.

A citizen of Kansas thus posts up an eastern correspondent who asked a variety of questions as to the territory and life there:—

"What kind of country do you live in?"

"Mixed and extensive. It is made up principally of land and water."

"What kind of weather?"

"Long spells of weather are frequent. Our sunshine comes off principally during the day time."

"Have you plenty of water and how got?"

"A good deal of water scattered and generally got in pails and whiskey."

"Is it hard?"

"Rather so when you have to go half a mile and wade in mud knee deep to get it."

"What kind of buildings?"

"Allegoric, Ionic, Anti-Baloric, Log and slabs. The buildings are chiefly out of doors and so low between joints that the chimneys all stick out through the roof."

"What kind of society?"

"Good, bad, hateful, indifferent and mixed."

"Any aristocracy?"

"Nary one."

"What do you people do for a living, mostly?"

"Some work, some lay around; one is a shrewd business manager, and several drink whiskey."

"Is it cheap living there?"

"Only fifty cents a glass and water thrown in."

"Any taste for music?"

"Strong. Buzz and buck saws in the daytime, and wolf howling and cat fighting nights."

"Any pianos there?"

"No, but we have several cow bells, and a tin pan in every family."

"Any manufacturers?"

"Every household. All our children are home productions."

"What could a genteel family in moderate circumstances do there for a living?"

"Work, shave notes, fish, hunt, steal, or if hard pinched, buy and sell town property."

A CHAMPION HEN

From the White Cloud *Kansas Chief*, January 27, 1859.

SOME EGG.—Henry Ulsh, of Rush Island, brought into our office, last week, an egg laid by a common hen, which (the egg) measured 5¾ inches in circumference around the centre; and endwise, 7¾ inches in circumference. This was a bigger egg than an elephant could lay! Can anybody lay a bigger one?

Mail Troubles

From *The Big Blue Union*, Marysville, August 15, 1863.

The mail due here from the east a week ago last Friday, by the Overland Coach has never yet turned up. It failed to come Friday morning, but as that was no uncommon occurrence our citizens only made a few wry faces and left the office, expecting it would of course come in a few days.— There were a good many valuable letters and papers in that mail which have been anxiously looked for ever since. Through some scandalous neglect however, it has never arrived. If the coach lost the sack or permitted it to be stolen, they should be made to pay roundly for their carelessness. If the P. M. at Atchison or any along the road are to blame, it should be known and the parties punished.

Since writing the above, the lost mail has arrived. Accompanying it was a letter from the P. M. at Atchison, saying that he put the sack on the coach at the usual time, plainly labeled, and enquiring who is to blame for its return to Atchison unopened.

From the *Union*, April 9, 1864.

The other day the coach carried our mail up to Colorado Territory and back to Atchison before it got to Marysville. Again this week the mail sack was left at Guittard's and lay there until a man came along with a team and hauled it over here. Instead of getting a tri-weekly mail, we get it just as circumstances happen. This is very nice for our post office here through which eight or ten smaller offices are dependent for their mail.

From the *Union*, April 16, 1864.

We have had *one* eastern mail this week. It came with no explanation, and no excuse. We have taken pains to find out who is to blame, and can trace the source of our trouble as far down east as Atchison. The Overland Company is not to blame, neither is Mr. Guittard, who brings it from his place. The coaches bring the sack every time it is furnished them by the Postmaster at Atchison, and Mr. Guittard brings it as soon as it arrives at his place. Either the Postmaster at Atchison fails to put it on board or the sack is not sent down from St. Joseph. How is it? We don't want to be fooled any more this way. Let us know the evil and it shall be remedied. The mail had accumulated at the other end of the route to such an extent that it was sent up in two large sacks, and one of them was an ordinary canvass sack, fastened with a string. This was all the fastening. Think of that. How do you like to have your mail run the gauntlet of inquisitive persons between here and the river, with no protection but an ordinary sack tied with a tow string? [Page 2.]

We stated last week that the mail sack lay at Guittard's until a team came along to bring it to Marysville. It did come in a buggy, but came as quick as it otherwise would. Mr. Mills, a mail contractor was at Guittard's with his buggy when the mail arrived, and as he was on his way to Marysville, he was requested to bring it along, which he did. [Page 3.]

Young in Heart

From the Washington *Republican*, August 22, 1873.

A lady 106 years old passed over the Denver road last week on her way west to take a homestead and grow up with the country.

Kansas History as Published in the Press

In 1866 Mary Smith of Sheffield, Ohio, traveled across the Plains to Colorado territory. Part of the journey was with a wagon train, the remainder by stagecoach. A journal which she kept during the trip has been edited by Dorothy Gardiner and published in *The Westerners Brand Book*, New York, for 1959.

Two articles in the January, 1959, number of *Agricultural History*, Urbana, Ill., are of special interest to Kansans: "From Cattle to Wheat: the Impact of Agricultural Developments on Banking in Early Wichita," by George L. Anderson; and "William Allen White and Dan D. Casement on Government Regulation," by James C. Carey.

Downs as a railroad center was the subject of a series of articles by Doug Brush, beginning in the Downs *News*, January 15, 1959. The town was once the site of railroad shops on the Central branch of the Missouri Pacific railroad.

A history of Rossville's newspapers was published in the *Shawnee County Reporter*, Rossville, January 22, 1959. The first newspaper, *The Kansas Valley Times*, was moved to Rossville by O. LeRoy Sedgwick in 1879, from St. Marys.

In 1854 Alfred Larzelere staked a claim and built a cabin near present Wathena. The following year he brought his family to the new home. A biographical sketch of Larzelere, by Margaret Larzelere Rice, appeared in the *Kansas Chief*, Troy, January 22, 1959.

"Tall Tales in Kansas Newspapers," by Mary Francis White, was the feature of the February, 1959, issue of the *Heritage of Kansas*, Emporia.

Pleasant Ridge school, District No. 59, Marshall county, was organized in 1872, according to a history of the school by Gordon S. Hohn, printed in the Marysville *Advocate*, March 5, 1959.

An article on the early history of the Prairie Range school, Kearny county, by India H. Simmons, was published in the Lakin *Independent*, March 5, 1959. The school was opened in October, 1888, in a dugout.

Early-day experiences of the John Blankenship family are recounted by a daughter, Mrs. Harm Schoen, in the Downs *News* and the Cawker City *Ledger*, February 5, 1959. The family settled in Smith county in 1871.

The battle of Coon creek, fought between U. S. cavalry and the Indians in 1848 near present Kinsley, is reviewed by C. R. Coover in the February 12, 1959, issue of the Kinsley *Mercury*. The attack by the Indians is said to have been led by a squaw.

On February 12, 1959, the Belleville *Telescope* printed Ed Fischer's recollections of an 1888 blizzard in the Republic area. A brief history of the Cuba community appeared in the *Telescope*, February 19.

George W. Coffin is the author of a historical sketch of the Kaw Indians and their reservation in the Council Grove area, published in the Council Grove *Republican*, March 18, 1959. The Kaws were moved to the Council Grove reservation in 1847. Coffin proposes a historical shrine memorializing these Indians and the reservation.

A special 36-page edition was published by the Baldwin *Ledger*, February 19, 1959, in observance of Baker University's centennial year and the *Ledger's* 75th year.

"First Families From Russia Arrived in Catherine Community Years Ago," was the title of a historical article in the Hays *Daily News*, February 22, 1959. The *News* printed "Colonists in Hays and Ellis Enjoyed Bits of Culture With Pioneer Life," March 1.

On February 24, 1959, Orville W. Mosher's column "Museum Notes" in the Emporia *Gazette*, included a biographical sketch of the Rev. Solomon Brown. Brown and his family settled on the Cottonwood river in 1855.

Although chartered in 1889, the Russell State Bank was started 12 years earlier as a private bank by Theodore Ackerman and Charles P. Copeland, it was reported in a sketch of the bank in the Russell *Daily News*, March 4, 1959.

Heinie Schmidt's column "It's Worth Repeating," has continued to appear regularly in the *High Plains Journal*, Dodge City. Included among the stories in recent months were: "Pawnee County Pioneer Farmer [Alvis Bell] Practiced Early Irrigation," April 9, 1959; "Early Day Boom Fails in . . . Hartland," by Mrs. Sarah E. Madison, April 16; "Early Kearny History Story of Violent Weather," by Edgar R. Thorpe, April 23; "1880 Census Shows Dodge City Railroad Town," May 7; "Early Day Kendall," by Mrs. India Harris Simmons, May 14; "Cold Weather Story [1895]," by Andy J. Meyers, May 28; a sketch of the pioneer family of Webb

Snyder, by E. R. Snyder, June 4, 11, 18; "Fourth [of July, 1880] on Chouteau Island," by Francis L. Pierce, July 2, 9; and three articles by Jennie Ross O'Loughlin: "Santa Fe Traffic and Trade," July 23; "Slaughter of Buffalo," July 30; and "Early Day Lakin," August 6.

Some of the history of Nicodemus, Graham county Negro settlement, compiled by Mrs. Clarence Dale and Howard Raynesford, appeared in the *Ellis County Farmer,* Hays, May 28, 1959.

The Wellsville *Globe,* June 4, 1959, published a history of Salem Hall school, in the Wellsville area, by Bernice Holden.

Mrs. Lulu Kassebaum is the author of a history of early Rossville, which began appearing in series in the *Shawnee County Reporter,* Rossville, June 18, 1959.

The history of educational development in Edwards county, compiled by Hubert Fatzer and Mrs. Albert Wilson, was printed in the Kinsley *Mercury,* June 25, 1959.

Will T. Beck is the author of a two-column history of Campbell College in the Holton *Recorder,* July 9, 1959. The college was started in 1882 as Campbell University, a private school. In 1903 the United Brethren Church began operation of the college. Seven years later the school was moved to Kansas City.

Kansas Historical Notes

Programs at recent meetings of the Ottawa County Historical Society included the story of George Washington Carver in Minneapolis, read by A. R. Miller, February 21, 1959; a biographical sketch of the Peter McGee family of Delphos, given by Ray Halberstadt, March 21; and the presentation by Mrs. Ellis Bishop of historical information on Negro families in Minneapolis, April 11.

Edwin J. Walbourn, El Dorado Junior College, was elected president of the Kansas Association of Teachers of History and Social Science at the association's 33d annual meeting in Atchison, March 6 and 7, 1959. W. Stitt Robinson, University of Kansas, was chosen vice-president; C. Robert Haywood, Southwestern College, secretary-treasurer; and Ernest B. Bader, Washburn University, member of the executive council. Peter Beckman, St. Benedict's College, was the retiring president.

Foster Eskelund was named president of the Kearny County Historical Society at the annual meeting in Lakin, March 7, 1959. Mary G. Smith, Lenora B. Tate, and Olivia T. Ramsay were elected vice-presidents; Virginia P. Hicks, recording secretary; Joseph M. Eves, corresponding secretary; Robert O. Coder, treasurer; Margaret O. Hurst, historian; and Vivian P. Thomas, curator. Charles A. Loucks was the retiring president.

The Kauffman Museum at Bethel College, North Newton, was described by E. Lawson May in the Hutchinson *News*, March 22, 1959. The article included biographical notes on Charles J. Kauffman, who collected the relics, stuffed and mounted the birds and animals, and donated the museum.

Township directors were elected at a meeting of the executive committee of the Clark County Historical Society in Ashland, April 13, 1959. They are: Mrs. Cecil Pike, Appleton; Mrs. Gay Hughs, Ashland; Mrs. Lena Smith, Brown (east); Mrs. George Abell, Brown (west); Mrs. Paul Salyer, Center; Roy Shupe, Cimarron; Mrs. Philip Arnold, Edwards; Mrs. Florence Walker, Englewood; Jack Stephens, Lexington; Mrs. Ross Bell, Liberty; Mrs. Kenneth Huck, Sitka; and Mrs. Glenn Dennis, Vesta. Shupe, vice-president of the society, is chairman of the township directors.

Approximately 65 persons listened to a panel discussion on the early history of Pittsburg by a group of students from Lakeside

Junior High School, Pittsburg, at the spring meeting of the Crawford County Historical Society in Pittsburg, April 21, 1959. T. E. Davis is president of the society.

Mrs. E. G. Peterson was re-elected president of the Edwards County Historical Society at a meeting in Kinsley, April 21, 1959. Other officers elected were: M. L. Tatum, first vice-president; Mrs. Iva Herron, second vice-president; Harry Offerle, third vice-president; Mrs. Elsie Jenkins, secretary; Cecil Matthews, treasurer; Myrtle Richardson, historian; Mrs. Mary Cole-Vang, assistant historian; Mrs. Jessie Winchester, custodian; and Mrs. Lloyd Britton, assistant custodian. A fund has been started by the society for building a museum.

An article describing the Fort Riley Museum, by Kent D. Stuart, was printed in the Coffeyville *Daily Journal,* Chanute *Tribune,* Emporia *Gazette,* Pittsburg *Headlight,* and *Southwest Daily Times,* Liberal, April 30, 1959; Manhattan *Mercury,* May 3; and Hutchinson *News,* May 4. The museum is operated by the Fort Riley Historical Society, Lee Rich, president. More than 600 persons have become active members of the society since its start in 1957.

Marshall G. Gardiner described the Fort Leavenworth Museum in an article which appeared in the Leavenworth *Times,* May 5, 1959, and the Ottawa *Herald* and the Kansas City (Mo.) *Times,* May 6. The museum recently moved to new quarters at the fort.

On May 9 and 10, 1959, the Border Queen Museum, Caldwell, held its fourth annual show, featuring a parade and a variety of exhibits. Dr. J. E. Turner is president.

Organization meetings of the Jewell County Historical Society were held in Mankato, May 16 and June 13, 1959. Fred W. Meyer is president of the group. Other officers include: Bradley Judy, vice-president; Mrs. Elton Gillett, secretary; and O. K. Fearing, treasurer. Nyle Miller, secretary of the Kansas State Historical Society, addressed the June 13 gathering.

Dr. Howard C. Clark is chairman of the new Historical Wichita board, appointed in June, 1959, by the Wichita city commission. Other members are: Pat Rowley, Mrs. William I. Robinson, Morris N. Neff, Jr., Larry W. Roberts, Thomas W. Fuller, and Ewing Lawrence. The board will represent the city in the work of preserving and improving points of historical interest in Wichita.

The annual meeting of the Scott County Historical Society was held in Scott City, June 4, 1959. The following trustees were re-elected: W. A. Dobson, Bill Boyer, and Harold Kirk. On June 11 the trustees re-elected Dr. H. Preston Palmer president of the society. John A. Boyer and James W. Wallace were elected vice-presidents; Mrs. C. W. Dickhut was re-elected secretary, and Mrs. Robert Deragowski, treasurer.

Judge Spencer A. Gard was chosen president of the Allen County Historical Society at a meeting of the board of directors in Iola, June 15, 1959. Mary Ruth Carpenter was elected to succeed Judge Gard as secretary. Angelo Scott was the retiring president.

Organization of the Rice County Historical Society was completed at a meeting in Lyons, June 17, 1959, with the approval of a constitution and the election of permanent officers. The officers are: Art Hodgson, president; Mrs. Jo Bundy, vice-president; Paul Jones, secretary; and Ed Kilroy, treasurer.

Bob Bolitho was elected president of the newly organized Harper City Historical Society at a meeting July 25, 1959. Other officers are: Audrey Murray, vice-president; Agnes Nye, secretary; Lenore Murray, treasurer; and Harold Bebermeyer, Tom Hudson, and Lem Laird, directors.

The Fort Scott and Bourbon County Historical Society was reorganized at a meeting July 31, 1959. George Eakle was named president for a two-year term. G. W. Marble was elected vice-president and Mrs. J. R. Prichard, secretary-treasurer. Other members of the executive board are: Mrs. Emma Connolly, Harold Calhoun, Hilton Wogan, Melvin Hurst, John Crain, A. W. Dickerson, Earl Vore, R. H. Waters, Dr. D. E. Torkelson, and Harry Fisher.

Evangeline Louise Mohl is the author of a new 205-page volume consisting of a group of poems entitled *Lyrics of the Night,* and a two-act play, *The Moonlight Sonata.* Early experiences of the author, a native Kansan, are reflected in many of the poems. Pageant Press, Inc., New York, is the publisher.

THE
KANSAS HISTORICAL
QUARTERLY

Winter 1959

Published by
Kansas State Historical Society
Topeka

NYLE H. MILLER KIRKE MECHEM JAMES C. MALIN
Managing Editor *Editor* *Associate Editor*

CONTENTS

PAGE

THE PONY EXPRESS RIDES AGAIN... 369
    With photographs of altered Pony Express stations still standing in Seneca and Marysville, and map of the Kansas portion of the Pony Express route, *frontispiece*.

CRITIQUE OF CARRUTH'S ARTICLES ON FOREIGN SETTLEMENTS IN KANSAS,
                                                    J. Neale Carman, 386

THE FIRST KANSAS LEAD MINES................*Walter H. Schoewe*, 391
    With sketches and photographs of Linn county lead mine area, *between* pp. 400, 401.

EUGENE WARE'S CONCERN ABOUT A WOMAN, A CHILD, AND GOD,
                                                     James C. Malin, 402

RELIGION IN KANSAS DURING THE ERA OF THE CIVIL WAR—
    Concluded .... *Emory Lindquist*, 407

THE CENTENNIAL OF LINCOLN'S VISIT TO KANSAS..................... 438

BYPATHS OF KANSAS HISTORY.. 444

KANSAS HISTORY AS PUBLISHED IN THE PRESS...................... 445

KANSAS HISTORICAL NOTES.. 450

ERRATA, VOLUME XXV 454

INDEX TO VOLUME XXV... 455

The Kansas Historical Quarterly is published four times a year by the Kansas State Historical Society, 120 W. Tenth, Topeka, Kan., and is distributed free to members. Correspondence concerning contributions may be sent to the managing editor at the Historical Society. The Society assumes no responsibility for statements made by contributors.

Second-class postage has been paid at Topeka, Kan.

THE COVER

    A Pony Express rider, from an oil painting in the museum of the Kansas State Historical Society. *Courtesy Mary Huntoon.*

This was the Pony Express station at Seneca. Originally it was a hotel kept by John E. Smith. The building was moved about three blocks from its original location and converted into a private residence.

A Pony Express station also still stands in downtown Marysville. Built of stone, it has undergone considerable remodeling.

For a picture of state-owned Cottonwood station, more familiarly known today as the Hollenberg ranch Pony Express station, see *The Kansas Historical Quarterly,* Summer, 1957 (v. 23), between pp. 144, 145. Hollenberg station is outstanding because it is said to be the only remaining unaltered Pony Express station on the entire route.

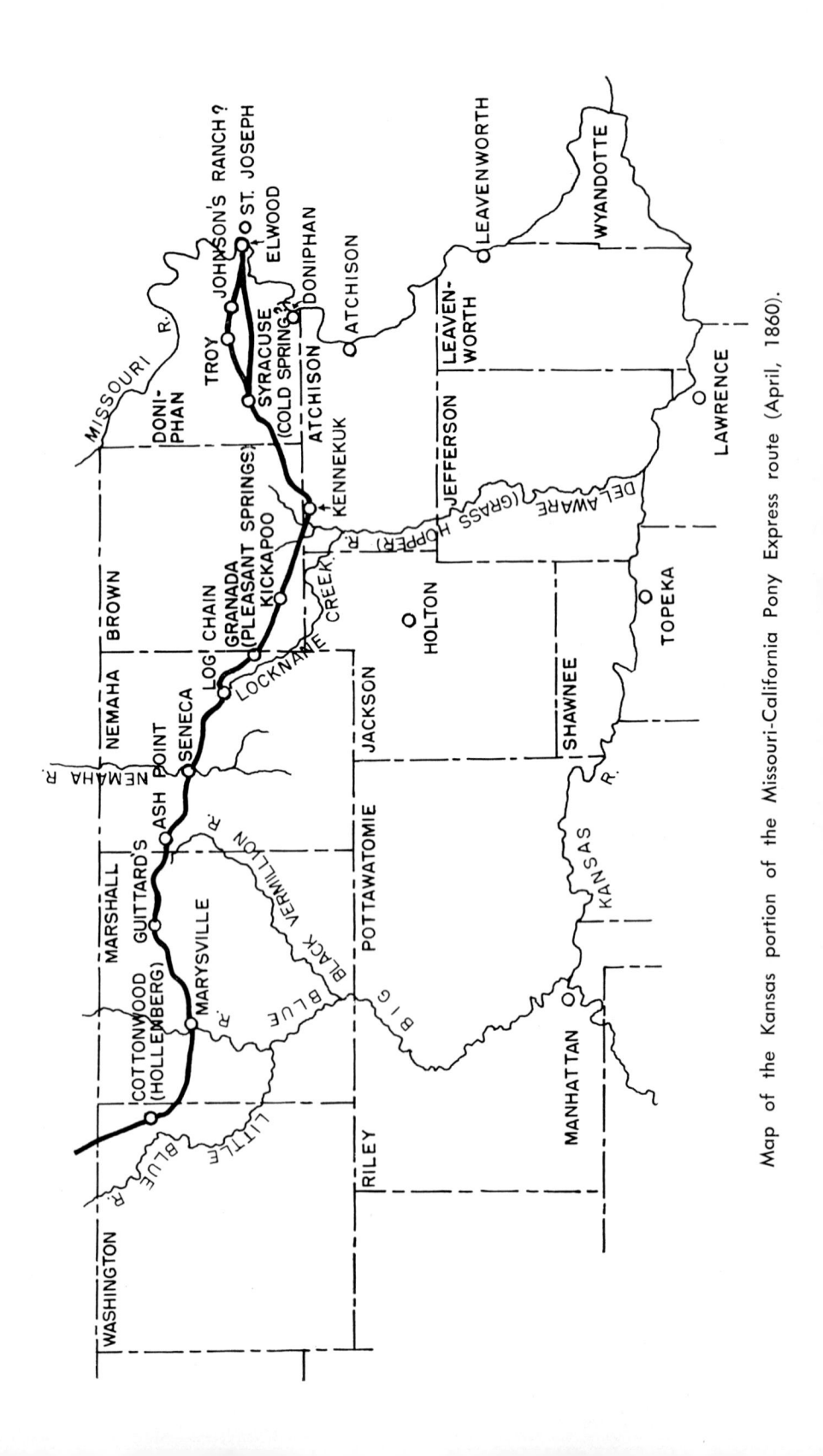

Map of the Kansas portion of the Missouri-California Pony Express route (April, 1860).

THE KANSAS HISTORICAL QUARTERLY

Volume XXV Winter, 1959 Number 4

The Pony Express Rides Again

I. INTRODUCTION

ON April 3, 1860, the Pony Express began operating over a 2,000-mile route connecting the contiguous Eastern states at their western outpost of St. Joseph, Mo., with the ten-year-old Far Western state of California. Averaging less than ten days per run, traveling through the storms and heat of summer, and the snow and cold of winter, with Indian raids and other hazards thrown in, the Express has come to be known as one of the West's most colorful epics.

To commemorate this significant episode in American history plans are being made for reruns of the Pony Express in the year of its 100th anniversary, probably in April or July, 1960. Riders will leave St. Joseph and California simultaneously to begin a series of relays which will carry 1960 mail west and east again in something like the manner it was accomplished a century ago.

The old Pony Express crossed several northeast Kansas counties, generally following a route of the Oregon and California road which headed northwest toward the Platte river in Nebraska, then westward. Riders will be recruited and the 1960 runs will parallel on modern roads as nearly as practicable the original route. The Kansas Centennial Commission and towns and riding clubs along the way will assist in making the reruns a success.

The Pony Express ran for nearly 18 months before the telegraph line was completed making possible the transmission of news across the continent by wire. Inasmuch as a detailed account of the operation of the Pony Express by George A. Root and Russell K. Hickman appeared in *The Kansas Historical Quarterly* in February, 1946 (v. 14, pp. 36-70), its story will not be repeated at this time. However, a map of the Kansas route and a few items concerning the Express published in newspapers of the period are presented here.

II. THE ROUTE OF THE PONY EXPRESS THROUGH KANSAS

Station or Place	Type	Distance (Approximate)	Aggregate Distance (Approximate)
MISSOURI			
St. Joseph	Terminal	0	0
KANSAS			
Elwood	Relay?*	2	2
Johnson's Ranch	Relay?	10	12
Troy	Relay?	2.5	15
Cold Spring (or Syracuse?)	Relay	9	24
Kennekuk	Relay or Home?*	15	39
Kickapoo	Relay?	12	51
Pleasant Springs (Granada)	Passed by?	4	55
Log Chain	Relay	9	64
Seneca	Home	11	75
Ash Point (Laramie Creek?)	Relay?	11	86
Guittard's	Relay	12	98
Marysville	Relay or Home?	14	112
Cottonwood Station (Hollenberg)	Relay	11	123

ELWOOD.—The Elwood *Free Press*, April 21, 1860, said this was the first station and horses were kept here.

JOHNSON'S RANCH.—Places variously known as Thompson's, Cottonwood Springs, Cold Springs, and Johnson's have been listed as points on the Pony Express route between Elwood and Cold Spring. Where these were, or if one and the same, is not known.

TROY.—Apparently there were two routes between Elwood and Cold Spring, one being 20 miles long, the other 24. The latter was through Troy. It is not certain which route was most used. The *Pony Express Courier*, Placerville, Calif., July, 1936 (p. 3, col. 2), said Troy was the first relay station west of St. Joseph. This would make the first run about 15 miles, an average distance.

COLD SPRING.—The aggregate mileage to this station is based on the long route through Troy. Some sources list Cold Spring and Syracuse as separate stations (*see* "Map of the Pony Express Trail" by W. R. Honnell, and Root and Hickman, *KHQ*, v. 13, p. 513). Others list either one or the other or none at all (*see* Raymond W. Settle and Mary Lund Settle, *Saddles and Spurs* (Harrisburg, Pa., 1955), p. 118; Frank A. Root and William E. Connelley, *The Overland Stage to California* (Topeka, 1901), p. 113, and map in end fold). It is

---

* Stations on the Pony Express route were usually nine to fifteen miles apart and were of two kinds. Relay stations were small affairs which housed only a station keeper and a stock tender plus three or four horses. Their purpose was to provide a change of mounts for the riders. Home stations were larger, and usually were also stage stations. Each housed at least two riders, the station keeper, and two to four stock tenders. Spare horses, supplies, and surplus equipment were also kept at the home stations.

The distance between stations was called a "stage." Each rider rode three successive stages on three different horses, and was expected to total at least 33⅓ miles per run. At the home station he turned his mail over to the next rider and rested there until his turn came to make the return trip.

possible Cold Spring and Syracuse were the same station located near the present town of Severance. The location of Syracuse is given as Sec. 36, T. 3 S., R. 19 E.

KENNEKUK.—The Pony Express route met the Fort Leavenworth-Fort Kearny military road at Kennekuk. Its distance from St. Joseph indicates it may have been a home station. The *Pony Express Courier,* June, 1939 (p. 3, col. 3), reported that Kennekuk was the fifth station out of St. Joseph. The location is Sec. 3, T. 5 S., R. 17 E.

KICKAPOO.—This station, on Plum creek, was near a mission school in the Kickapoo Indian reservation. The location was Sec. 14, T. 4 S., R. 15 E.

PLEASANT SPRINGS.—About 1865 the name of this town was changed to Granada. There is some confusion between it and Log Chain station. In 1860 the Granada hotel here, was a station on the Central Overland California & Pike's Peak Express. It was kept by David M. Locknane. It is doubtful that the Pony Express, a sister enterprise of the C. O. C. & P. P. E, officially stopped at Locknane's station since it was only four miles from the Kickapoo station. The location of Pleasant Springs is Sec. 12, T. 4 S., R. 14 E.

LOG CHAIN.—The Pony's next stop was at Log Chain. There is an oft-repeated and varying legend that the creek on which this station was located was once called Log Chain because of the many chains which were broken in attempts to pull wagons across its bed. However, "Log Chain" possibly could be a corruption of "Locknane," the stream's actual name. (On some maps the creek is labeled Locklane and on at least one it is called Muddy creek.) The keeper here was N. H. Rising whose 24 by 40-foot house and 70-foot long barn served as the station. The log cabin house still stands although it has been somewhat altered and is now (1959) covered with shining white clapboard. In 1859 and part of 1860 Rising had kept the Granada hotel in Pleasant Springs, further adding to the confusion surrounding Granada and Log Chain. The location of Log Chain station is Sec. 19, T. 3 S., R. 14 E.

SENECA.—Settle and Settle reported this to have been the first home station on the east end of the Express, 77 miles west of St. Joseph (p. 119). The station was a hotel kept by John E. Smith and the place was noted for its fine food. The old building, now a private residence, still stands in Seneca but it is several blocks down Main street from its location in Pony Express days. The original site, at Fourth and Main, is marked with an inscribed boulder.

ASH POINT.—It is possible that Ash Point, Laramie Creek, and Frogtown stations were the same. It was at Ash Point that "Uncle John" O'Laughlin kept a grocery store and sold whisky to stage passengers. The location was Sec. 8, T. 2 S., R. 11 E.

GUITTARD'S.—This station was kept by the George Guittard family, and is still marked on some maps. Photos of the station and barn are published in Root and Connelley (p. 196). The location is Sec. 4 (probably the N.E. ¼ of the N.E. ¼), T. 2 S., R. 9 E.

MARYSVILLE.—The *Pony Express Courier,* April, 1936 (p. 3, cols. 1, 2), reported Marysville a home station. Settle and Settle (p. 120) said it was a relay station. The original building, considerably altered, is still in use.

COTTONWOOD STATION.—This is the well-known Hollenberg ranch house and was the last Pony Express station in Kansas. It is reported to be the only remaining unaltered Pony Express station. The place is now a state museum. It is located in the S.W. ¼ of the S.W. ¼ of Sec. 2, T. 2 S., R. 5 E., northeast of Hanover.

III. THE STORY OF THE PONY EXPRESS AS PUBLISHED IN 1860-1861 NEWSPAPERS

From the Leavenworth *Daily Times*, January 30, 1860.

From Leavenworth to Sacramento
GREAT EXPRESS ENTERPRISE!
in Ten Days!
Clear the Track and let the Pony Come Through!

In our telegraphic columns a few days ago, there was an item stating that it had been decided by the Government to start an Express from the Missouri river to California, and the time to be ten days; but we were not aware that our fellow-citizen, Wm. H. Russell, Esq., was at the head of the enterprise until we were shown the following dispatch. Its importance can be readily perceived:

WASHINGTON, Jan. 27th, 1860.

To JOHN W. RUSSELL—Have determined to establish a Pony Express to Sacramento, California, commencing the 3rd of April.—Time 10 days.

WM. H. RUSSELL.

That's a short and important dispatch, and the time to travel between here and California is very short also.

The first conclusion almost any one would come to, is, that this is utterly impossible. Even the old mountaineer who has been long months traversing the great Plains between here and California, at first would pronounce the project is entirely impracticable. But when we take into consideration that the men who have undertaken this project know their business, and have carried out other projects of great magnitude, and even excelled their promises, we are prepared to believe that they will carry out to the letter this the greatest enterprise ever undertaken in this western country.

We believe the Express is to be run by Messrs. Jones, Russell & Co., whose Express from here to Pike's Peak has made such extraordinary time since its first inauguration, making almost as good time to and from the Rocky Mountains in the Winter as in the Summer. Their Pike's Peak Express was indeed a great project, but the Pony Express that they will run from the Missouri river to the Sacramento in ten days, will eclipse it.

We have not been informed the route that it is intended to run—in fact, we presume the parties themselves have not fully determined the exact line of travel—but we may be pretty well assured that it will be as straight as possible. We believe the Express will be run for the Government alone, and infer that it will go the shortest and easiest route to Camp Floyd, Utah. Whether it will go by way of the new gold fields or not we can only conjecture. There are three routes from here to the valley of the Great Salt Lake. The usual route is on the South side of the Platte, and through the South Pass; the other route is by way of the new gold mines, and over the Rocky Mountains, by what is called the Cherokee trail. This trail was traveled considerable last Summer, . . . and is represented as being better in Summer, than the old South Pass route, for persons going on horseback; it is said to be a little nearer than the old route.

The distance from here to Denver, the route the Express travels, is 665 miles, and from Denver to Camp Floyd, per Cherokee trail, is estimated at 550 miles, making the distance to Camp Floyd 1,215 miles. From Camp Floyd there is a new route through Skull Valley, which strikes Humboldt river at Gravelly Ford; passes down the Humboldt some distance below Lawson's Meadows, and enters the Sierra Nevada mountains through a pass below Honey Lake Valley, and then goes west to Placerville and Sacramento. The distance from Camp Floyd to Sacramento via Placerville is about 700 miles over this route—making the entire distance from this city to Sacramento, 1,950 miles. We have made some enquiry of persons who are pretty well posted in the distance, and presume they are near correct. If their figures are correct, the Express will have to travel but *eight miles per hour* to get through in ten days.

In connection with this Express to California, we have no doubt but that the Government will start another from Camp Floyd to the Dalles of the Columbia, Ft. Vancouver, Oregon, and Steilacoom on Puget Sound.—These are all important military stations. By a new route discovered by Lieut. Mullen, the distance from Salt Lake to the navigable waters of the Columbia is but 450 miles—so that the trip from the Missouri to the Columbia river, can be made in ab[o]ut nine and one-half days.

That the enterprise will be accomplished we have no doubt. The men who have the matter in charge, are men of means and energy.

Success to the Pony Express!

A jealous note appearing in the *Journal of Commerce,* of Kansas City, Mo., was reprinted and promptly dealt with by the Leavenworth *Daily Times* in its issue of February 4, 1860.

It is said that some of the citizens of Leavenworth have contracted with the government to run a one horse express to California from that city. We should think that such an one would fully meet their demands.—Kansas City Journal.

For the information of that enterprising sheet, we would say that the "citizens of Leavenworth" who "have contracted with the Government to run a one horse Express," are Messrs. Russell, Jones & Co., to whom the Journal is indebted for the only news it publishes from Pike's Peak and Salt Lake, which it copies from THE DAILY TIMES.

It is but just to say that our energetic neighbor of the Journal runs the only Express that goes out from that city; it makes semi-occasional trips to Westport, which is four miles distant, returning same day. As a sample of the extraordinary time made, we refer to the fact that the Journal gave a full account of the burning of the Methodist Mission long before it took place—in fact the Mission stands there yet for aught we know!

We would suggest to our enterprising neighbor that if he would wish to be put in immediate communication with Salt Lake, Santa Fe and Pike's Peak, he must run an Express (a one-horse one is better than none) to this city. We will gladly furnish him the news in advance from our proof-sheets, on the arrival of the Pike's Peak Express every week.

From the Leavenworth *Daily Times,* February 10, 1860.

OVERLAND PONY EXPRESS!
Dispatches from Leavenworth to be Delivered in Sacramento in Eight Days!

By reference to an advertisement in another part of the paper, it will be seen that Jones, Russell & Co. want two hundred grey mares, to put on the Express that is to leave here on the 3d of next April, for Carson Valley, California. It is intended that the trip will be performed in *eight days.* At Carson Valley is the first telegraph station; from there the dispatches will be sent to Sacramento over the California telegraph line.

Short as the time may appear to cross the Rocky Mountains, *the trip will be performed.* The originators of this great enterprise know no such word as fail. To perfect arrangements for so great an undertaking at this season of the year, will require great energy, capital and tact. But those who have undertaken this great feat, are fully equal to the task.

WANTED

TWO HUNDRED GREY MARES, from four to seven years old, not to exceed fifteen hands high, well broke to the saddle, and

Warranted Sound,

With black hoofs, and suitable for running the "Overland Poney Express."
feb 10 lw   JONES, RUSSELL & CO.

From the Leavenworth *Daily Times,* February 22, 1860.

THE PIKE'S PEAK EXPRESS left yesterday morning for Denver. There were two passengers, and a very large freight list. Among the articles, we noticed a lot of saddles and other riggings for the Pony Express. Mr. Van Vleit was the Messenger.

From the Leavenworth *Daily Times,* March 10, 1860.

We are credibly informed that Russell & Co.'s Pike's Peak Express, which has heretofore run between Leavenworth and Denver City, is about to be changed to St. Joseph.—The citizens of St. Jo. subscribed $25,000, which is to be given to the company when the change is perfected. The next Express will probably leave St. Joe instead of Leavenworth, as heretofore.—Kansas City Jour., 7th.

The above rumor was started some days ago. We showed the above extract to the Secretary of the Express Company, and he replied that it was news to him. *There is no truth in the rumor.* They will undoubtedly carry passengers from St. Joe, and perhaps other points, but the head quarters of the establishment will remain at Leavenworth.

There was also a rumor that Messrs. Russell, Majors & Wadell were to remove from this city. This rumor, like the other, *has no foundation,* we are very credibly informed.—Neither of these great firms contemplate leaving Leavenworth. They are fixed institutions—their head-quarters will be at this city.

As the Journal has given currency to the rumor, will it do Leavenworth justice by making the correction?

From the Leavenworth *Daily Times*, April 2, 1860.

THE PONY EXPRESS.

This great western enterprise, the Pony Express to California, starts on Tuesday, or April the 3d. It will run through in ten days, and will carry letters and messages at four dollars each.

The Telegraph on the California side, is finished to Carson Valley. Virtually then, the Pony Express will put the Atlantic States within eight days of San Francisco. For a private enterprise, this is one of the most important yet undertaken in this country.

Unfortunately for Leavenworth, the rumor that the Pony Express would start from St. Joseph proved true. Which accounts for the following sour note in the Leavenworth *Daily Times*, April 5, 1860.

PONY EXPRESS.

Our neighbors of St. Joseph had a jolly time, April 3d, over the starting of the Pony Express. It was to have left at 3, P. M., that day, but an express from New York failed to reach it, as it was delayed. The railroad dispatched a special train to Palmyra—some one hundred and sixty miles distant from St. Joseph—and brought it in in three hours and fifty-one minutes.

All being thus arranged, the Pony Express started at 7¼, P. M., with forty-nine letters, nine telegrams, and newspapers for the California Press. A huge undertaking this! An enterprise great as the country!

From the Elwood *Free Press*, April 7, 1860.

—The Pony Express from St. Joseph to San Francisco left Elwood on Tuesday evening. The following is the time table:

ELWOOD TO		
Marysville,	12	hours.
Fort Kearney,	34	"
Laramie,	80	"
Bridger,	108	"
Salt Lake,	124	"
Camp Floyd,	128	"
Carson City,	188	"
Placerville,	226	"
Sacramento,	232	"
San Francisco,	240	"

The Express carries only telegraphic despatches. It will run weekly from this date.

From the Leavenworth *Daily Times*, April 14, 1860.

ARRIVAL OF THE PONY EXPRESS.

The Pony Express arrived at St. Joseph yesterday, having made the distance from San Francisco in a little less than ten days. The Express carries only telegraph dispatches and letters. The news is unimportant.

From the New York *Daily Tribune,* April 14, 1860.

CALIFORNIA PONY EXPRESS

St. Louis, Friday, April 18 [13], 1860.—The Pony Express that left San Francisco at 4 o'clock on the afternoon of the 3d inst, reached St. Joseph's a few moments after 5 o'clock this afternoon, but while the private dispatches and Associated Press reports were being prepared for transmission, the wire broke down between Kansas City and Leavenworth. It was then too late to repair it to-night, but it will be put in working order the first thing in the morning.

An organized band of horse thieves have seriously interfered with the line all the Spring. They have often cut the line simultaneously in several places and carried off and hid a large quantity of wire, and once they threatened the life of the line repairer.

From the Leavenworth *Daily Times,* April 16, 1860.

THE PONY EXPRESS.

A marvel feat has been accomplished! The Pony Express has galloped across half the continent, and to-day the Pacific is in close neighborhood to the Atlantic. History will record this event as one of the gigantic private enterprises of our day.

The Pony Express left San Francisco on the 3d of March [April], at 4, P. M., and arrived at St. Joseph on the 13th of March [April], at 4, P. M. The difference in time between these points is about three hours. Thus the distance was made in *nine days and twenty-one hours!*

The run from San Francisco to Salt Lake City was made in two days and twenty hours. Had it not been for snow on the mountains, the whole trip could have been made inside of eight days!

Nor is this great triumph to be without fruit. It is the pathway for other and greater ones. Government is laggard. In all that relates to the interests of the West, and the development of the resources of the West, it has been niggard as well as laggard. It can be so no longer. This great success of a private energy will prick the mind of the country to the necessity of Western wants, and compel Government to attend to these wants quickly and well.

We can do but little towards testifying cur respect and admiration of the great action of Messrs Russell, Jones & Majors, but that little should be done in a spirit worthy of the occasion. We should celebrate the triumph—for it is ours, the country's, as well as theirs. We propose, then, a dinner, or a supper, or a testimonial of some kind, that we speak at least the general joy. Will the Mayor of the City, with such other gentlemen as he may associate with him, consider and act upon this suggestion?

From the Elwood *Free Press,* April 21, 1860.

The third Pony started out yesterday. Elwood is the first station on the Express line and the horses are kept here. Another messenger arrived last night—through in eight days.

THE PONY EXPRESS.—This great enterprise has been successful. The first messenger came in ten days, and the trip will be made two days sooner than this after the arrangements have been fully completed. This is the best time ever made. All important intelligence will now be transmitted over the St.

Joseph and San Francisco Pony Express Line. It will leave here every Friday. It goes by way of Kearney, Laramie, Salt Lake City and Placerville.

From the Leavenworth *Daily Times,* April 23, 1860.

ARRIVAL OF THE PONY EXPRESS.

ST. JOSEPH, April 20.

The second messenger of the Central Overland Pony Express, bringing California dates to April 10th, and Carson Valley to the 11th, reached here at 5 o'clock this evening, exactly on time. . . .

From the Elwood *Free Press,* April 28, 1860.

The Pony Express will leave hereafter on Saturday of each week.

From the Leavenworth *Daily Times,* May 8, 1860.

ARRIVAL OF THE PONY EXPRESS.

ST. JOSEPH, May 7.

The Pony Express arrived here last night at half past nine o'clock in nine days and four hours from San Francisco. The last 120 miles on this end were run in eight and one half hours.

SAN FRANCISCO, April 27.—. . . It is estimated that $35,000 in drafts were transmitted eastward by the Pony Express, which may reach their destination twelve days before the steamer having treasure to meet them arrives in New York.

The Pony Express which left St. Joseph on the 13th, arrived at San Francisco in nine days and seventeen hours from the time of starting.

Telegraphic dispatches from Carson Valley to parties interested, not yet published, state that the Indians between Salt Lake and Carson Valley having stolen thirty horses belonging to the Pony Express, a new supply of horses will be sent out speedily from Sacramento, but the incoming Express may be three or four days behind time in consequence of this misfortune. . . .

From the Leavenworth *Daily Times,* May 31, 1860.

ARRIVAL OF THE PONY EXPRESS.

ST. JOSEPH, May 30.

The Pony Express, due on Monday, the 28th, arrived last night at 9 o'clock, but brought no California mail, which is supposed to have been intercepted by Indians.

The only matter brought by the Express is from Salt Lake, at which place it arrived and left on the 24th inst.

All the information we can learn in regard to this failure is the following note on the Salt Lake way-bill, made by the agent at that point:

"Rider just in. The Indians have chased all the men from the stations between Diamond Spring and Carson Valley. The *macheres,* in which the Express matter is carried, is lost. The Indians are reported to have killed two riders on the last trip, and it is supposed that they carried off or destroyed the mail matter belonging to this Express."

The news from Salt Lake is very meagre.

On the 17th, two men, named Myron Brewer and R. Kitt Johnson, were both shot at once, by unknown hands.

The distance from Salt Lake to St. Joseph—1200 miles—was made in five days and seven hours. . . .

From the Leavenworth *Daily Times*, June 5, 1860.

ARRIVAL OF THE PONY EXPRESS!
MISSING MAIL RECOVERED!
Americans Murdered—Fight with 500
Indians—Defeat of Major Ormsby
and His Death—Retreat of the Troops—
Excitement in California.

The Pony Express brings sad news. The dates are from San Francisco May 13th, 3:40 P. M.

Several Americans had been murdered on Carson's river, while asleep, by the Indians. This outrage led to an organization of whites. The volunteers, numbering one hundred and five men, placed themselves under the command of Major Ormsby, and pushed in pursuit of the Indians. The report says:

This force, on the 12th instant, at 4 P. M., came upon the Indians at bend of Truckee river, about sixty-five miles northward towards Pyramid Lake from Virginia City. The Indians were in ambush at a narrow pass thro' which the Ormsby party were proceeding, and numbering, it is supposed, not less than five hundred, all having fire-arms, plenty of ammunition, and one hundred and fifty horses within convenient distance. They opened a fire upon our troops from their safe hiding places, and Major Ormsby ordered a charge, but the Indians continued to skulk, firing occasionally from behind rocks and sage bushes, doing damage without suffering much in return. This condition of things continued two hours, when the ammunition of Ormsby's party gave out. The Indians seeing this, closed upon our men, pouring in volley after volley, killing many on the spot. The balance retreated, scattering in all directions, over hills and among sage bushes. They were pursued twenty-five or thirty miles by the mounted Indians and many detached parties cut off.—The survivors came straggling into Virginia City during the two following days. The exact number of killed is not yet ascertained, but it probably exceeds fifty. Among the slain are Maj. Ormsby, Henry Meredith, a distinguished California lawyer, W. S. Spear, Richard Snowden, Wm. Arrington, Dr. Jader, Charles McLeod, John Fleming, S. Anderson, Andrew Scheald, M. Knezswich, John Gormbo, A. K. Elliot, W. Hawkins, Geo. Jones, Wm. Macintosh, O. McNoughton.

Total known to be killed, 21; wounded, 3. The fate of 43 is unknown. Returned alive, 38. Wagons have been sent out to pick up any wounded that may be found, and also an armed force to protect parties burying the dead, but no account has yet been received from the battle ground.

Great excitement ensued in California.—Money was received, and men volunteered, in every direction to punish the Indians. The State authorities promptly dispatched arms and ammunition to quarters likely to tell against the Indians. The report says further:

General Clarke, commanding the Pacific division, U. S. A., dispatched from San Francisco, on the 14th, 150 United States troops, all the available men in Central California, together with 500 stand of arms and 100,000 rounds of ammunition. He also sent orders to the 100 United States soldiers stationed at Honey Lake, one hundred miles north of Carson Valley, to proceed to the

Pyramid Lake regions and aid in suppressing hostilities. These movements warrant the belief that there are not less than 300 well armed volunteers from California and 260 U. S. soldiers ready for duty on the eastern slope of the mountains, which is an ample force to protect the people as long as unpaid volunteers can afford to remain in the field. At the last accounts the hostile Indians were all to the north of the Pony Express and Salt Lake mail and emigrant route, and the troops will be so posted as to keep that route open. The Indians on the eastern side of the mountains, extending north into Oregon, and westward into the interior of Utah, number probably 2,000, and from their contiguity with Mormons and other unavoidable causes, are all liable to become hostile to Americans, unless permanent means are taken by the government to restrain them. At least 500 U. S. soldiers should be stationed at different exposed points, between the Humboldt and Walker rivers.

From the Leavenworth *Daily Times,* June 23, 1860.

OVERLAND MAIL.
MORE INDIAN TROUBLES.

SPRINGFIELD, MO., June 21.

The Butterfield Overland Mail Coach, with San Francisco dates to the first inst., arrived this evening, bringing the following summary of news:

SAN FRANCISCO, June 1.

The mail departing to-day leaves California in the midst of great excitement on account of the Indian hostilities in Western Utah.—The war is becoming very serious. Within the month just closed the Indians have made attacks on different parties of whites as far South as Walker's river, and Northward as far as Honey Lake. The stations on the Pony Express line, and Salt Lake mail route, are known to have been destroyed, and the stock driven off over a distance of two hundred miles Eastward from Carson Valley. Parties of Indians constantly cross this route, and render it impossible to repair stations and restock the route unless United States troops are provided to protect it, and thus far Gen. Clark has not been able to spare the necessary men from other duties. Under these circumstances, the Pony Express has been discontinued until such time as its trips can be resumed without jeopardizing the interests of its patrons. The main body of Indians are concentrated at Pyramid Lake, where Col. Ormsby's party was recently defeated and over seventy of them killed, as is now ascertained.—They are defiant, and well armed, and number according to information relied on by Col. Jack Hays, from 1,500 to 3,000 warriors.

On the 29th ult., Col. Hays' party, of over six hundred volunteers, and Capt. Stewart, with one hundred and sixty United States troops, started from Carson Valley for the Indian head quarters, at Williams' Station, on Carson River, where the first Indian murders occurred. Col. Hays' party came upon a party of three hundred Indians, attacked and defeated them, killing seven Indians, among them a principal chief. Two of the volunteers were wounded.

Yesterday, the 31st of May, the volunteers marched for Pyramid Lake, and by the 2d inst. they confidently expect to bring on a general battle with the main body of the savages. The most intense anxiety is felt upon the result, for if our men are unsuccessful in striking an overwhelming blow, the most serious Indian war ever known upon this coast will be inevitable. The effect of these disturbances has been to concentrate all the mining population of the Washoe region, now numbering seven or eight thousand men, within a small space in the vicinity of settlements. . . .

A memorial also goes forward to-day praying for a daily overland mail, and Congressional encouragement to the Pony Express. . . .

The Pony Express, with St. Louis dates of May 20th, now five days overdue, has not arrived, and probably has been cut off by Indians.

The outgoing Express of the 18th and 25th of May, passed through Carson Valley on the journey eastward, and it is hoped got safely over the Indian-infested portion of the route. Much apprehension, however, is felt for their safety. They each had about 150 letters. . . .

From the Leavenworth *Daily Times,* July 3, 1860.

OVERLAND MAIL ARRIVED—INDIAN TROUBLES CEASED—OREGON ELECTION.

SPRINGFIELD, MO., July 2.

The Overland Mail Coach, from San Francisco June 11th, and Virsalia June 12th, passed here last night. The following summary has been received:

SAN FRANCISCO, June 11.— . . . Since the Indians fled beyond the reach of Col. Hay's volunteers, all apprehension of further trouble from them in the Washoe mines are over. The regular troops will be stationed near Pyramid Lake, and at other places where they can best protect all the settlements. The company who went through on the Pony Express route expect to obtain a sufficient force from the United States troops, now at Camp Floyd, to keep the route free from danger after it is once cleared, and the stations reestablished. . . .

From the Leavenworth *Daily Times,* July 25, 1860.

THE JOURNEY OF THE PONY.

A correspondent of the St. Louis Republican thus describes the journey of the Pony Express: "Bang goes the signal gun, and away flies the Express pony, with 'news from all nations lumbering at his back.' But whither flies this furious rider on his nimble steed? It is no holiday scamper or gallop that this young Jehu is bent upon. His journey lies two thousand miles across a great continent, and beyond the rivers, plains and mountains that must be passed; a little world of civilization is waiting for the contents of his wallet. He and his successors must hurry on through every danger and difficulty, and bring the Atlantic and Pacific shores within a week of each other. No stop, no stay, no turning aside for rest, shelter or safety, but right forward. By sun light, and moonlight, and starlight, and through the darkness of the midnight storms, he must still fly on, and on toward the distant goal. Now skimming along over the emerald sea, now laboring through the sandy track, now plunging headlong into the swollen flood, now wending his way through the dark canon, or climbing the rock steep, and now picking his way through or around an ambuscade of murderous savages. No danger or difficulty must check his speed or change his route, for the world is waiting for the news he shall fetch and carry. It is a noble enterprise, and as the express hurries down the street and across the river, and I think of the toil and peril of the way, my heart says, 'God speed to the boy and the pony'.["]

THE HERALD's Washington correspondent telegraphs that—

"Majors, Russell & Co., of the Pony Express establishment, received a warrant upon the Territory to-day for $67,000, in consideration of past mail services rendered. The Government is still largely in the debt of this firm for valuable trains of merchandise destroyed on the Plains by the Indians during the Utah rebellion, in consequence of the Government failing to furnish the necessary escort authorized in their contract."

We know nothing of this or any other firm's accounts with the Federal Treasury, and we want to know nothing, save that they are adjusted and paid by the present Administration, not turned over as a legacy to its successor. On every side we see indications that the game of throwing over dues and accounts that should have been previously adjusted, to be dealt with by the next Administration, is systematically pursued. There is the Oregon war debt, which, whatever its amount or validity, ought to have been disposed of long ago, still hanging about Congress and the Treasury, to be carried beyond the 4th of March next, if possible—and this is but a sample. If Majors, Russell & Co. have such a claim as is above asserted, and the Treasury will not or cannot adjust it, why is it not taken to the Court of Claims, and there adjudicated! Why not have *all* outstanding claims so passed upon and promptly settled? If they are left over till next year, they will go into the aggregate expenditures thereof, and be paraded to prove the extravagance of the next Administration. Let each dynasty settle its own bills and make an end of them.—N. Y. Tribune.

From the Leavenworth *Daily Times,* July 26, 1860.

THE PONY EXPRESS

Arrived in St. Joseph July 24th; and, it is thought that regular trips will be made hereafter. . . .

From the Leavenworth *Daily Times,* August 1, 1860.

PONY EXPRESS!
RATES ON LETTERS REDUCED!
ON AND AFTER DATE,
LETTERS WEIGHING 1-4 OUNCE
WILL BE CARRIED THROUGH
For Two Dollars and Fifty Cents.
aug1-tf

From the Leavenworth *Daily Times*, August 25, 1860.

LATEST NEWS FROM CALIFORNIA.
Arrival of the Pony Express.
WAR AMONG THE INDIANS.

ST. JOSEPH, Aug. 24.

San Francisco advices to Aug. 11th, reached this city last night. . . .

The patronage of the Pony Express is greatly increasing, since the trips are made in due time and news received of the safe arrival of all letters sent Eastward. The new buildings being put up on the line of the Express, for three hundred miles East of Carson Valley, in place of the stations recently destroyed by the Indians, are sixty feet square, with stone walls eight feet high, being designed to serve as forts when necessary. . . .

From the Elwood *Free Press,* September 29, 1860.

FAST TIME BY THE PONY EXPRESS—
Wm. H. Russell.

A St. Joe. correspondent of the St. Louis Republican sends an interesting letter to that paper, from which we clip a few paragraphs:

The wonderful rapidity with which the Express riders have to make from station to station, has already caused an occasional display of extraordinary human endurance. Thus, Mr. John Fry, one of the couriers, some time since started from Kennekuk, a station forty-five miles from this place, at 8 o'clock one Saturday night, and reached St. Joseph at midnight. Starting out again from this city on the following morning, he made three stations twenty-five miles apart from one another; and had returned to St. Joseph at 11 P. M. of the same day, thus traveling a distance of not less than one hundred and ninety-five miles in eighteen runing hours, after losing one hour in eating meals, making eight changes of animals, &c. This is certainly fast riding. The individual that accomplished the feat is of a rather youthful appearance and does not at all look like the NAT he must actually be.

The President of the Central Overland Express Company, Mr. William H. Russell, of the well-known firm of Russell, Majors & Waddell, indulges in hardly less rapid locomotion, although in a different way.—He is constantly flying to and from Leavenworth, St. Joseph and Kansas City, St. Louis, Chicago, Washington and New York. He makes from place to place in a rush; drops among his associates and employees like a *deas ex machina;* hurries through with his business and is—seen no more.—I believe he has made the tour from Leavenworth to New York, Washington and back three times within the last five weeks. Mr. Russell has, indeed, the indomitable energy of a true Western man. Risen from a very humble station through his own exertions to a highly influential position, he is a living illustration of Anglo-American activity and enterprise.

From the Leavenworth *Daily Times,* November 5, 1860.

FROM FORT KEARNEY.

FORT KEARNEY, Nov. 3.

The Pony Express, bound West, passed here at 8:35, P. M., on Friday, being a few hours behind time, occasioned by muddy roads.

From the Leavenworth *Daily Times,* November 7, 1860.

FROM FORT KEARNEY.

FORT KEARNEY, Nov. 5.

The Pony Express, bound West, passed this point at six o'clock this evening.

The Pony Express Company have decided to start an extra Pony from this point for California, on Wednesday 7th, carrying election news and private telegrams. It is expected that the Pony will make very quick time. . . .

From the Elwood *Free Press,* November 10, 1860.

FORT KEARNEY, Nov. 7.—An extra of the Pony Express left here for Carson Valley, at 1 P. M. to-day, carrying the election news and a considerable number of private telegrams. The rider and horse were tastefully decorated with ribbons, &c., and departed amid the cheering of a large and enthusiastic gathering. This run is expected to be quicker than any yet made between here and the outer station of the California telegraph lines. The ponies leaving St. Joseph Thursday, the 8th, and Sunday morning, the 11th, are also to make double quick time, calling here for latest telegraphic dates.

From the Leavenworth *Daily Times,* November 20, 1860.

CALIFORNIA CLOSE BETWEEN
LINCOLN AND DOUGLAS.
GREAT UNION SPEECH OF STEVENS.
The South Coming to Her Senses.

FORT KEARNEY, Nov. 18.

The Pony Express from San Francisco the 7th, arrived at half-past nine o'clock last night, bringing California dates, via Fort Churchill, by telegraph, up to ten P. M., on the night of the 8th.

The rider reports a heavy storm between Fort Laramie and Salt Lake. . . .

From the Elwood *Free Press,* November 24, 1860.

GOOD NEWS FROM CALIFORNIA.

The Pony Express brings to us the glad tidings that at least one of the Pacific States is with us on the great question of freedom or slavery. California, which has always been Democratic, always pro-slavery in her tendencies, has at length wheeled into the line of States who are united to prevent the further aggressions of the slave power. Senator Gwin is repudiated at home. His heinous acts will no longer reflect the sentiments of his State. His future is easily read, and his retirement on the accumulations of corrupt years is near at hand.

Oregon will soon, we hope, send across the mountains *her* greeting to the glorious band of kindred free States. She has given us Republican Senators; she will give us Republican electors, and the bright light of freedom shall tint the entire Western Slope of our great Sierras. Thank God! for once the North does as the South has done for years—shows to her enemies a strong, united front. Let South Carolina fret, fume and threat. We are too great to tremble.

From the Leavenworth *Daily Times,* December 1, 1860.

PONY EXPRESS!
CHANGE OF SCHEDULE.

ON and after the first day of December next, the Schedule Time of the Express will be changed and run as follows: Fifteen days between St. Joe and San Francisco; eleven days between Fort Riley and outer telegraph station Utah.

This Schedule will be continued running as new semi-weekly trips during the winter, or until Congress shall provide for a tri-weekly Mail Service, which alone will enable the Company to return to present or a shorter schedule, the present mail service between Julesburg and Placerville being only semi-weekly, which is not sufficient to keep the route open during winter.

WM. RUSSELL, Secretary

decl-dlm

Leavenworth City, K. T., Dec. 1st, 1860

From the Elwood *Free Press*, December 1, 1860.

FROM CALIFORNIA AND OREGON.

FORT KEARNEY, Nov. 28—The Pony Express, which left San Francisco on the evening of the 17th, passed here about one this morning. Reports three feet snow on the South Pass and Rock Ridge. . . .

From the Elwood *Free Press*, January 12, 1861.

FT. KEARNY, Jan. 9—The Pony Express passed about 11 last night.

SAN FRANCISCO, Dec. 26, 3:40 P. M.—The Pony Express, with St. Louis dates, telegraphed to Ft. Kearney on the 10th, arrived at Sacramento on Sunday 23d, where it was detained twenty-four hours waiting for a steamer to take it to San Francisco. There being no Sunday boat. The Pony is delayed at Sacramento from one to two days, whenever it arrives there on Saturday, after two o'clock, P. M. The Express time table ought to be arranged so that the Pony will always arrive at Sacramento between Monday morning and Friday evening.

From the Leavenworth *Daily Times*, February 26, 1861.

LATEST NEWS BY TELEGRAPH.
NEWS BY THE PONY EXPRESS.

SAN FRANCISCO, Feb. 9, 3:40 P. M.

No arrivals or departures since last Pony Express. There are no more failures, and it is believed no more will take place. Shipment of treasury by Monday's steamer, however, is expected to be light.

Notwithstanding the delay of the ponies, the last outgoing Express took over ninety letters, and to-day's Express letters will probably number one hundred and fifty.

Both houses of the Legislature have passed resolutions asking Congress for additional aid to the Pony Express.

From the Leavenworth *Daily Times*, June 11, 1861.

LATEST NEWS BY TELEGRAPH.
PER PONY EXPRESS.

SAN FRANCISCO, May 29.

The overland telegraph expedition left Sacramento on the 27th, for Carson Valley, at which point they are to commence laying wires towards Salt Lake. The expedition embraces 228 head of oxen, 26 wagons, and 50 men.

Pony Express with dates to May 20th, has arrived.

From the Leavenworth *Daily Times*, June 12, 1861.

LATEST NEWS BY TELEGRAPH.
PONY EXPRESS.

FORT KEARNEY, June 11.

The Pony Express passed here at 6 A. M.

SAN FRANCISCO, June 1.—There is no California news of moment. Everybody is waiting with intense anxiety for Eastern news, and as each pony arrives, the announcement of attack on Harper's Ferry, Norfolk, or some other movement toward retaking public property captured by the South, is expected.

From the Leavenworth *Daily Times*, August 29, 1861.

ST. JOSEPH, Aug. 26.—The Pony Express has been abandoned between St. Joseph and a station 110 miles west [Marysville]. Letters will be obliged to go by stage from here to reach the Pony at that starting point.

From *Freedom's Champion*, Atchison, November 2, 1861.

PROGRESS OF THE TELEGRAPH.—It was thought last year, and truly too, that the pony had accomplished wonders when he had given us a communication with the Pacific coast in from six to seven days. But now the Pony has become a thing of the past—his last race is run. Without sound of trumpets, celebrations, or other noisy demonstrations, the slender wire has been stretched from ocean to ocean, and the messages already received from our brethern on the Pacific coast, most conclusively show that the popular heart beats in unison with ours, on the absorbing question of the preservation of the Union. The war has been the all-absorbing topic, so that this great work has been almost entirely lost sight of by the public. . . .

Critique of Carruth's Articles on Foreign Settlements in Kansas

J. NEALE CARMAN

FROM the geographic point of view, the only printed work treating as a whole the problem of the foreigner in Kansas has been the two articles published by William Herbert Carruth in 1892 and 1894.[1] We owe him a debt of gratitude; with no funds at his disposal to aid him in pursuing his investigation he took time from his literary occupations and from scholarly and pedagogic activities, which in those days he necessarily devoted almost exclusively to German, to concern himself with a general matter that could bring him but little immediate recognition. Fortunately he made his study at a time after almost all the rural foreign settlements in Kansas had already been established and before the forces of assimilation had invaded them sufficiently to hide their identity from the casual observers that Carruth had to call on as informants. His articles, if carefully studied, contain much of great value. They are of less interest to the casual reader because they are filled with local names that have no meaning unless detailed maps of the period are consulted at the same time. Carruth provided a map to accompany his articles. It helps a great deal, but as we shall see, not too much confidence can be placed on it.

As inferred above, the articles do not represent a major interest of Carruth's. He merely reported on answers to a questionnaire. He stated his procedures as follows:

As a source of information regarding the origin of the foreign elements of our population when their native speech shall have been forgotten, but when the influence of it will be left in vocabulary and pronunciation, I have thought that a map of the state with the location of all the foreign settlements of even quite small size would be of interest and in time of great value. In the following pages I transmit the results of my inquiries so far as received. It is my intention to make the report complete and to publish the map, when as complete as it can be made, in colors. Unexpected difficulties have delayed the work and prevented its being complete. I depended for my information upon the County Superintendents of the State, a class of unusually intelligent and well-informed men and women. But in not a few cases there seems to have been a suspicion in the mind of my correspondent that I might be a special officer of the state

---

DR. J. NEALE CARMAN, author of several papers on foreign settlements in Kansas, is a professor in the department of romance languages at the University of Kansas, Lawrence.

1. Herbert Carruth, "Foreign Settlements in Kansas," *Kansas University Quarterly*, Lawrence, v. 1 (October, 1892), pp. 71-84; v. 3 (October, 1894), pp. 159-163. A brief exception to the first sentence of this article is: J. Neale Carman, "Babel in Kansas," *Your Government*, v. 6 (1951), No. 7, pp. 1-4.

trying to locate violations of the law requiring district schools to be conducted in English, and hence information regarding schools in foreign tongue was withheld or given but partially. And in some cases my informants were not well posted. A superintendent by the name of Schauermann in a county containing a town called Suabia, tells me that there are no foreigners in his county. In such cases time must be taken to secure a correct result.

Carruth suspected that his informants might deceive him, but apparently did not think of their being involuntarily wrong. He seems to have verified their statements very seldom. The results of such an inquiry could not be expected to be complete; they also exhibit great unevenness of quality. There were scores of omissions that might easily be pardoned, but others are sometimes astounding, not only when the county superintendent reported no foreigners as in Atchison county, but also when he was fully attempting to do so. Here are some glaring cases of omission:

BARTON COUNTY.—The Pawnee Rock Mennonites and the Albert Germans
BROWN COUNTY.—The Norwegian and Welsh settlements
CLAY COUNTY.—The East Border Germans
CLOUD COUNTY.—The Danish settlement, the Germans
CRAWFORD COUNTY.—The Hepler-Brazilton Germans
DICKINSON COUNTY.—The Alida Germans (not reported from Geary county either)
ELLIS COUNTY.—The Ellis Bukovinan Germans
JACKSON COUNTY.—The Germans
LEAVENWORTH COUNTY.—The city and its neighborhood (the text omits; the map shows)
McPHERSON COUNTY.—The New Andover Swedes
MARION COUNTY.—The Lincolnville Germans
MARSHALL COUNTY.—The Axtell Swedes, the Danes
OSAGE COUNTY.—The Vassar Germans
RENO COUNTY.—The Pretty Prairie Mennonites
RICE COUNTY.—The Bushton Germans
RILEY COUNTY.—The Fancy Creek Germans, the Bala Welsh, the Leonardville-Riley Germans
RUSSELL COUNTY.—All but the most important group
SHAWNEE COUNTY.—Topeka itself
WASHINGTON COUNTY.—The Brantford Swedes, the Danes
WYANDOTTE COUNTY.—Slavs (they were already in the packing houses) [2]

In many of these cases the county superintendent probably omitted a report because other foreign elements in the county so impressed him that he momentarily forgot certain important groups. If, for instance, the Ellis Bukovinan Germans had lived in any county

2. The above omissions are "glaring." There are many other omissions. Carruth and his informants might be pardoned for overlooking smaller settlements in western Kansas where the population had not become stabilized, but even in the eastern part of the state there are many. Three counties in which he reports "no foreigners" or as containing only "scattered" individuals may serve as examples:
BOURBON.—The Fort Scott Germans
FRANKLIN.—The Homewood Germans
JOHNSON.—The Lenexa Germans (still others in this county)

but the one in which the Catholic Volgan Germans were centered, an informant could hardly have neglected them.

The omission of the cities of Leavenworth and Topeka must have been occasioned by the county superintendent's understanding that he was to report only on that part of the county where he was himself active. Omissions of certain other urban groups have probably the same explanation. It cannot be applied in Kansas City, however, where the Swedes are reported, but all other groups neglected. It is equally hard to understand how the Riley county superintendent could neglect to report the two most important groups of Germans, while he did name one of lesser size, combining it with the adjacent Czech settlement. Possibly he confused Swede creek and Fancy creek, but he certainly does not have the same excuse for passing over the Leonardville-Riley Germans who were located so near his Manhattan headquarters. The amount of vagueness and inaccuracy was quite in proportion to the number of omissions. Some of it must probably be blamed on Carruth himself. He certainly could have been more accurate about Douglas county where he lived; he did not need to invent Big Springs township. The confusions regarding Russian Germans seem to reflect his own haziness; he apparently thought they all came from the same part of Russia. The Russians of Russell and Rush counties (Catholics, Lutherans, Baptists, Seventh Day Adventists) would have been astonished and indignant if they had known they were being lumped off as Mennonites. Setting up a Greek Catholic Church in Scott county was quite a feat; Carruth's inability to believe that Germans in Russia could be Roman Catholic seems to be at the basis of this error. Similarly, he seemed to feel that everybody in the Austro-Hungarian Empire spoke German by choice. The Moravians of Brown and Shawnee counties would have been hurt to be classified as Ger-lings. The inaccuracies of the informants usually show up in matters of locations, chronology, and statistics. For instance, in Anderson county, the Scipio-Greeley Germans very early had population in townships adjoining as well as in Putnam township; they were there by 1855 instead of 1860. The informants may also confuse the identity of the foreign stocks; in Cloud county, Swedes are identified as Norwegians (the Norwegians were farther north), and in Jewell county, Bohemians, Hollanders, and Norwegians are called Swedes.

In making his map on the basis of the data at hand, Carruth could not help falling into other errors. For instance, in Anderson county, finding that the county superintendent had said that the Scipio-Greeley Germans were in Putnam township, he marked the whole township as occupied by them, whereas they were in the east half only, though, as said above, they were also in adjoining lands to the east and south. When a single settlement occupied parts of more than one county, error was still more likely. The Russell report said there were Russians (called Mennonites by Carruth) in the southwest part of the county. So Carruth marked the two south townships along the west county line as German, left unmarked the most important township next east on the south border and so only casually joined the Milberger Russian Germans to the part of this group in Barton county. He does not distinguish the Hollanders from the Germans, perhaps deliberately because he had used up the colors at his disposal. In any case the Dispatch Dutch appear with the German color in Smith county and the Scandinavian color in Jewell county, so that no one could suspect their unity.

In Greenwood county, the county superintendent reported, "Norwegians, about 200, in the south part of Salem Township." Carruth assigned to them the whole of the township, which was very large, and thus gave a mistaken idea both of the size and of the location of the settlement. In the same county he located correctly "Germans in Shell Rock Township," but he did not realize that the Coffey county superintendent, when he reported "Germans in Liberty" township, was speaking of a portion of the same settlement, and he consequently left a gap in the middle of that settlement. Again, the Washington county report said, "French about midway in Sherman township." Carruth consequently gave the French a full survey township around Linn in territory that is almost solidly German. On the other hand, in Cloud county where the report stated, "Canadian French are scattered over much of the county, with considerable settlements in and around the towns of Concordia, Clyde, St. Joseph and Aurora," Carruth did not guess how much territory was French, and he assigned to the Canadians insufficient space, sometimes wrongly placed. As a final example, the maps make the Danes in Jackson county appear to occupy more territory than those in Lincoln county, because the Lincoln informant specified only one township for Danes, to which Carruth limited them, while the Jackson county superintendent mentioned two townships, and Carruth spread them over most of both although they occupied only a small part of each.

Carruth's articles record the existence of a great many foreign settlements which are otherwise noted only in parish church histories or documents even less widely circulated. As examples, let me cite the Andale-Colwich Germans just west of Wichita, the

Mound Valley Swedes near the Oklahoma line in Labette county, the Cuba Czechs east of Belleville in Republic county, the Cloud county French Canadians to the east of and south of Concordia, the Osage City French and Italians, the Arvonia Welsh in Osage county east of Emporia. This value may exist even when Carruth incorrectly interpreted the data that he had at hand, as occurred in some of the examples already cited.

Another example of value combined with error is the case of the Hungarian Germans of Rawlins county. His article speaks of Hungarians. Though his map shows them with the same color as Bohemians, and his articles do not show that they were German in speech, he has at least recorded their existence. To be sure, the existence of all these groups could be learned in other ways, including inquiry made today; the record of their presence in the 1890's is, however, important. Also, the notes concerning language usage, particularly in schools, are important, for in many instances parish histories are again the only record that we have in this matter. Here is a list of counties having schools in foreign languages as reported by Carruth (schools are German unless otherwise noted):

ANDERSON
BARTON
CHASE
CHEYENNE
CLOUD.—French
DICKINSON.—German and Swedish
ELLIS
ELLSWORTH
FORD
GEARY
HARVEY
LEAVENWORTH
LINCOLN.—German and Danish
LOGAN.—Swedish
McPHERSON.—German and Swedish
MARION
MEADE
MITCHELL
MORRIS.—Swedish
NEMAHA
OSBORNE
PHILLIPS
POTTAWATOMIE.—German and Swedish
RENO
REPUBLIC.—Swedish, Norwegian, Czech
RILEY.—Swedish
SALINE.—Swedish
SEDGWICK
WABAUNSEE
WALLACE
WASHINGTON
WICHITA

As this list shows, in the 1890's there were foreign language schools on all four borders of Kansas and there was a great concentration of counties in central Kansas where such schools existed. Carruth's is the only record of this phenomenon for the state as a whole.

In spite of the omissions and imperfections, Carruth's articles had a very real value. The general picture that they presented was so nearly correct and so valuable that it should have been given more consideration than appears to have been the case.

The First Kansas Lead Mines

WALTER H. SCHOEWE

THE first lead ore mined in Kansas insofar as published records go was in Linn county. The mines were centered around Pleasanton in T. 21 and 22 S., R. 25 E., in the southeastern part of the county. The mines of this area are of special interest because the ore came from strata of Pennsylvanian age rather than from the Mississippian, the lead-bearing rocks of the Tri-State Lead and Zinc District; because most of the lead ore was distributed in a "circle" or "chimney" surrounded by undisturbed strata; and because the genesis of the ore is problematic.

THE ANCIENT DIGGINGS

Ten and more years before Kansas became Kansas territory in 1854, mining for lead had been carried on about two miles southeast of Pleasanton. The evidence was found in a number of diggings or shallow pits surrounded by heaps of debris among which could be found particles of galena and crystals of sphalerite. Who the early miners were and just when the mining was done cannot be determined with absolute certainty. It is definitely known, however, that the mining antedates 1876, the date usually assigned to the commercial mining of the lead and zinc ores of Cherokee county, which is part of the Tri-State Lead and Zinc District, comprising parts of Missouri, Oklahoma, and Kansas and which constitutes one of the most important zinc and lead mining districts in the United States. The occurrence of galena in Cherokee county near Galena and in the vicinity of Baxter Springs at and before 1873 was known to some and anticipated by others.[1] No account, however, is extant indicating mining activity in Cherokee county until about 1876. As far as known, the mining near Pleasanton is the first venture for metals in Kansas. With a fair degree of certainty, it can be ascribed to the late 1830's or early 1840's, for in the spring of 1864, B. F. Mudge visited the site and found oak trees estimated to be at least 25 years old growing on the old mine dumps.[2]

A further clue to the date is found in a letter addressed to the

---

DR. WALTER H. SCHOEWE is head of the division of mineral economics and coal, State Geological Survey of Kansas, and associate professor of geology at the University of Kansas, Lawrence.

1. D. W. Wilder, *Annals of Kansas* (Topeka, 1875), p. 620.
2. B. F. Mudge, *First Annual Report on the Geology of Kansas* (Lawrence, 1866), p. 30.

(391)

editor of the *Observer-Enterprise*, a weekly newspaper published at Pleasanton, by A. R. Wayne, under date of September 20, 1926. According to Wayne, who came to Kansas in 1855 and who searched for lead on Mine creek in Linn county, the excavations were made by the French in the 1840's. Still another clue is to be found in the existence of a small town by the name of Potosi,[3] in the mining area. The writer verified its location at the courthouse at Mound City, the county seat. It was in the S. E. ¼, Sec. 5, T. 22 S., R. 25 E., the same legal description of the old mining site. The date recorded was May, 1844. This 1844 town of Potosi was apparently moved later to another location, a mile or so to the east along Mine creek. The new Potosi consisted of 320 acres and was laid out in 1856 by Proslavery men. The town, which existed until 1869, when Pleasanton was started, consisted of six houses and about 30 inhabitants. This Potosi Town Company was incorporated by a special act, approved February 20, 1857.[4] From the circumstantial evidence presented, it is reasonable to conclude that the diggings southeast of Pleasanton date back at least to the early 1840's.

These mine works have been attributed by some to the Indians, who undoubtedly must have known of the presence of galena in the Pleasanton area; especially since, as stated by Wayne, crystals of galena were plentiful on the surface in the mining area years ago.[5] It is debatable, however, whether the Indians were responsible. Mudge was of the opinion that the pits were not the work of the Indians, for he says "no one, knowing their [Indians'] habits of labor, and ignorance of the reduction of ores, will credit this report. The mining was undoubtedly the work of the early settlers of Missouri."[6] Indirect evidence points to the French, as they were the first white men to enter Linn county.[7] This is indicated by the fact that Pleasanton and the mining area are in Potosi township, and that formerly one, if not two, towns by the name of Potosi existed in and close by the mining center.

The significance of the name Potosi is as follows: In Washington county, Missouri, less than 50 miles southwest of St. Louis is a town by the name of Potosi. Lead and zinc were mined by the French in Washington county as early as 1724 and at Potosi in

3. W. A. Mitchell, *Linn County, Kansas, a History* (Pleasanton, 1928), p. 321.
4. A. T. Andreas and W. G. Cutler, *History of the State of Kansas* (Chicago, 1883), p. 1116.
5. Pleasanton *Observer-Enterprise*, September 23, 1926.
6. B. F. Mudge, "Geology of Kansas," *Fourth Annual Report of the State Board of Agriculture . . . for the Year Ending November 30, 1875* (1875), p. 123.
7. Andreas-Cutler, *op. cit.*, p. 1101.

the same county in 1763.[8] Mining of lead is still carried on in this same general area; it is not only the most important lead mining district in Missouri, producing about 95 percent of all lead mined in that state, but it is foremost in lead production in the United States.[9] It seems logical, therefore, to conclude that at least some of the early settlers of the Pleasanton and lead mining area of Linn county came from the lead-mining district of Potosi and vicinity in Washington county in eastern Missouri. That these early immigrants would apply names reminiscent of their former homes, and also pursue occupations formerly engaged in, is natural and to be expected. Furthermore, old settlers of Linn county described the original metal miners of the county as Frenchmen. It may be concluded, therefore, that these first lead miners were Frenchmen rather than Indians.

THE JUMBO LEAD MINE

The Jumbo lead mine is the present-day representative of the old diggings or pits. It is in the S. E. ¼, Sec. 5, T. 22 S., R. 25 E., about one mile east and one mile south of the southeast corner of Pleasanton (Fig. 1A). At present (1957), the mine is a circular, water-filled pit, 117 feet in diameter and from 50 to 80 feet deep, surrounded on all sides, except on the west, by heaps of debris from 10 to 15 feet high (Fig. 2A). The dump heaps, or mounds, are composed of rocks of various kinds including bituminous limestone (Fort Scott limestone formation), black shale, gray shale, sandstone, and coal. Scattered among the debris one may find today particles of galena and crystals of sphalerite, especially after rains have removed the finer clay and silt particles that ordinarily covered the ore fragments. Some lead ore has been mined, shipped, and sold from the mine. Just when the original shaft of the Jumbo mine was sunk is not known for certain. John Pellegrino reports that the old Jumbo mine was sunk to a depth of 250 feet, but gives no date.[10] Erasmus Haworth states that a shaft was sunk 250 feet in 1873.[11] Whether the two 250-foot shafts are one and the same is not clear. According to Mack Probasco (personal communication), a former owner of the mine, the Jumbo mine was sunk as

---

8. Arthur Winslow, *Lead and Zinc Deposits, Missouri Geological Survey*, v. 6 (1894), pp. 269, 270.

9. E. S. Smith, *The Mineral Industry of Missouri in 1952*, Geological Survey and Water Resources, State of Missouri, Information Circular No. 11 (1955), p. 12.

10. John Pellegrino, *Twenty-fourth Annual Report of the Inspection of Coal Mines and Coal Production, State of Kansas, From January 1, 1916, to December 31, 1916* (1917), p. 240.

11. Erasmus Haworth, W. R. Crane, A. F. Rogers, and others, *Special Report on Lead and Zinc*, University Geological Survey, v. 8 (1904), p. 69.

a double shaft 300 feet deep. This shaft was sunk around 1899 and was operated by two men named Dalton and Morrow, who named their shaft the Jumbo lead mine. The Dalton-Morrow Jumbo mine was either sunk originally to 300 feet or else is the deepened 250-foot shaft sunk in 1873. Good ore is reported to have been found in a drift which extended from the shaft in a northeasterly direction for a distance of 210 feet. An overflow of a near-by stream flooded the mine, resulting in its abandonment; however, not before some lead ore had been hoisted from the mine, shipped, and sold.

The Jumbo mine was next operated by a group of businessmen from Pleasanton, who, finding the venture unprofitable, soon lost interest and ceased mining. In 1924 Mack Probasco, with his brothers Burt and Ted, all drillers from Pleasanton, got possession of the mine and for the next 13 years "played" around, taking out some ore, but not enough to classify the enterprise a commercial success. The ore was hauled by team to a small smelter at Rich Hill, Mo., which was approximately five miles south and 18 miles east of the mine.

According to Probasco, the ore occurred in pockets, and also impregnated all types of rock that surrounded the shaft. When prospecting revealed the presence of the circle, shaft mining was abandoned and was replaced by surface mining. By means of a small drag line the shaft opening was converted into a circular pit from 20 to 25 feet deep and approximately 50 feet in diameter. In 1937 the Probasco brothers leased their Jumbo mine to a company consisting of M. A. Medler and a Dr. Roe of Pittsburg, and Van Cook of Joplin, Mo. The circular pit was deepened for another 50 feet by means of an 80-foot boom drag line. The Pittsburg company operated the mine for about one and one-half years and then ceased its mining activities for more lucrative investments in promoting oil development in Oklahoma. Before ceasing operations, the company drilled a prospect hole down to the Fort Scott limestone formation, which was considered lead bearing. About 1940 (Fig. 2B) the mine was leased to a group of men from Iowa who, after operating for a year and selling about five tons of ore, became involved in financial difficulties which resulted in bringing their activities to an end. Since then no further attempts have been made to work the Jumbo mine.

OTHER PLEASANTON AREA LEAD MINES

In addition to the Jumbo lead mine, other lead mines and prospect shafts and drill holes were sunk or drilled in its vicinity (Fig. 1B). In the spring of 1864 Mudge reported only the presence of the ancient diggings.[12] Between Mudge's visit and the publication of his report in 1866, several small shafts had been sunk, and although some lead was obtained, the enterprise was not profitable. The mining area was also visited by G. C. Swallow and Hawn apparently a year after Mudge's visit, and the conclusion was reached that "whether these mines will prove productive, it is impossible to determine in the present stage of the work."[13] In 1875 Mudge reported that various attempts had been made to mine lead and zinc ores in the Pleasanton area during the preceding 12 years but with little reward.

Between 1873 and 1875, about 30 openings had been made, and approximately 20 tons of ore had been raised near the town of Pleasanton, a few miles from the old Potosi diggings. A new shaft was under construction at the time of Mudge's visit to the Pleasanton area in 1875. Mudge, in company with a Mr. Darlow, one of the proprietors of the mine, descended the new shaft to a depth of 260 feet, where a horizontal drift had just been started. Commenting on this new mine, Mudge stated, "We await the result with much interest."[14]

The discovery of lead and zinc ore in 1899 in the walls of an old shaft, which had been abandoned for years, renewed considerable excitement and interest in prospecting. According to Haworth, mining "companies were organized, grounds leased and subleased, and many prospecting shafts and drill holes begun. Some of the old shafts were opened and examined, and drifts driven out at different levels, with the result that a few thousand pounds of high-grade lead ore and a small amount of zinc ore were obtained."[15] It is at this time that the Jumbo mine may have come into existence. Shafts and drill holes continued to be sunk or drilled for some years. The 1899 to 1904 lead boom resulted in the extraction of about 15 tons of lead ore and a small quantity of zinc ore, all of which was obtained from depths 65 to 85 feet and all of which was shipped to the Kansas City Argentine refinery for smelting.

12. Mudge, *First Annual Report of the Geology of Kansas*, p. 30.
13. G. C. Swallow, *Preliminary Report of the Geological Survey of Kansas* (Lawrence, 1866), pp. 58, 111.
14. Mudge, "Geology of Kansas," *loc. cit.*
15. Erasmus Haworth, *Annual Bulletin on Mineral Resources of Kansas for 1898*, University Geological Survey of Kansas (1899), pp. 23, 24.

Prospecting for the ores continued, if not continuously at least intermittently. In 1916 the Nevada Mining Company sank a prospect shaft one and one-fourth miles east and one and one-fourth miles south of Pleasanton to a depth of 153 feet. This shaft, surrounded by a number of old shafts dating back to 1873, is known only because on May 30, 1916, two men working in the shaft were blown out of it and killed by a gas explosion. The two men, Walter Bray and Edward Riggs, were about 20 feet from the surface with an open carbide lamp, used for illumination, which ignited the escaping natural gas. A second explosion occurred in this same shaft on the following June 23. Two men, W. H. McClintock and E. A. Stockton, were cleaning up the debris caused by the first explosion. No one was fatally injured; McClintock was burned slightly and Stockton seriously. As in the first case, the cause was ignition of escaping natural gas. According to John Pellegrino, assistant commissioner of labor in charge of the Kansas Mine Inspection Department, who investigated the two explosions of the Nevada Mining Company's shaft, there were about ten prospect holes sunk in the vicinity of the Nevada shaft, ranging from 35 to 1,200 feet apart, and to a depth of 35 to 250 feet.[16]

That lead mining was still in progress in the Pleasanton area in 1940 is revealed by the report of State Coal Mine Inspector John Delplace for the year 1940. On July 27, 1940, Charles Jobes and George Dixon were pumping water out of the Linco Lead Company's mine. While sitting at the mouth of the mine, Jobes struck a match to light his cigarette. Escaping gas exploded which killed Jobes and injured Dixon.[17] This mine, according to Delplace, was one-half mile east of Pleasanton.[18] No record of lead mining in the Pleasanton area is extant since 1940.

GEOLOGY OF THE PLEASANTON LEAD MINING AREA

The surface rocks of the Jumbo lead mine and surrounding area are the Nowata shales of the Marmaton group, Pennsylvanian in age (Fig. 1C). Many of the prospect holes and shafts penetrated the Fort Scott limestone formation, which was reached at a depth of approximately 180 feet and which constitutes the base of the Marmaton group. Some of the shafts and drill holes bottomed in what is now classified as the Cabaniss subgroup of the Cherokee

16. Pellegrino, *op cit.*, pp. 239, 240.
17. John Delplace, *Annual Report of the Mine Inspection Division and the Mine Rescue Station, 1940* (1941), p. 66.
18. *Ibid.*, p. 60.

shale[19] at a depth of about 135 feet below the base of the Blackjack creek limestone member, the basal strata of the Fort Scott limestone formation (Fig. 1C). The rocks encountered by the drill or shafts were black to gray shales, gray to reddish sandstones, brown to white limestone, and coal.

Occurrence of the Ores

The discovery of galena in the Pleasanton area was undoubtedly due to the finding of specimens at the surface, presumably by the Indians, who informed the early settlers of their discovery. Wayne stated that in the early days when he searched for lead on Mine creek, and northeast of the Jumbo mine, there was plenty of lead to be picked up on top of the ground about one-fourth of a mile from the mine.[20] Mack Probasco and Roy Cook, two drillers from Pleasanton, who drilled many of the prospect holes in the area, reported to the writer that galena and sphalerite, especially the former, occurred in all the rocks penetrated in drilling from the grass roots down to the bottom of the holes or shafts, which reached depths in some cases from 250 to 315 feet. Specimens at hand containing galena crystals are identified as belonging to the Fort Scott limestone formation, which is reached approximately at 180 feet beneath the surface at the mining site.

According to Swallow the "lead [galena] is found as small crystals in the mass of the shales, or in thin sheets between the laminae of the shales and sandstones."[21] Hawn states that the lead or galena occurs in fissures in sandstone.[22] Haworth, reporting on the occurrence of the Pleasanton lead, states that the "ore occurs in a soft shale, the Pleasanton shales. In most cases it is beautifully crystallized, affording magnificent museum specimens."[23] Further describing the ore, Haworth states that "the galena was of a high grade of purity, was not weathered or oxidized in the least, and produced brilliant surfaces on the crystalline faces, approximating in brilliancy fresh cleavage surfaces."[24] Galena specimens in the writer's possession and reported by Probasco as coming from the Jumbo mine show dull to semidull, well-crystallized galena, some of which also displays striations or slickensides as well as etching or the effects of solution (Fig. 3).

19. W. B. Howe, *Stratigraphy of Pre-Marmaton Desmoinesian (Cherokee) Rocks in Southeastern Kansas*, Kansas Geological Survey, Bulletin 123 (1956), p. 22, pl. 1.
20. Pleasanton *Observer-Enterprise*, September 23, 1926.
21. Swallow, op. cit., p. 58.
22. F. Hawn, "Report of Major F. Hawn, Assistant Geologist," *ibid.*, p. 111.
23. Haworth, *Annual Bulletin on Mineral Resources*, 1898, p. 24.
24. Haworth, et al., *Special Report on Lead and Zinc*, p. 70.

R. L. Snow, a farmer and strip-pit coal mining operator living close to the lead mining center, reported to the writer that the ore occurred in pockets and that some of the galena removed weighed several hundred pounds. Probasco likewise reported the finding of masses of galena weighing from 50 to 60 pounds and some as much as 150 pounds. Many pieces obtained weighed from 5 to 15 pounds. The largest single unit of pure galena seen and measured by the writer, and reported to have been obtained from the Jumbo mine, measured three and one-half by three and one-half by five inches and weighed approximately 16 pounds. Several smaller specimens at hand weigh three pounds and under. All specimens, when broken into, display bright shiny crystals or cleavage faces.

Prospecting revealed the presence of ore, but of greater importance was the discovery that the greatest quantity of ore was found in or restricted to a circular area whose diameter had been enlarged to approximately 120 feet (Fig. 2A). According to Probasco, drilling in the circular area was much easier than outside of it. Not only were the rocks softer but they were also broken, displaced, and occurred as brecciated masses. On the west wall of the circle or chimney, according to Probasco, the shale was very slick, shiny, from five to six feet thick, and its standing in a vertical position indicated movement within the circular area. That some movement did take place is attested by the fact that several specimens of ore and rock in the writer's possession clearly show perfectly flat and smooth planes cutting across limestone and galena alike and bearing striations or slickensides on their surfaces (Fig. 3A). On the reverse sides of the specimens the surfaces are uneven, owing to protruding crystals of galena, slickensides are absent, and effects of solution are evident by the fretwork nature of the limestone (Fig. 3B).

As early as 1865, Swallow associated earth movements with the occurrence of the Pleasanton lead ores, for he states, "There are evidences that the strata have been disturbed, tilted and fractured at this and various other localities between Potosi and Fort Scott. The sandstones and shales have a strong dip to the southeast. They probably form an anticlinal axis on the ridge to the west of the mine, where lead has also been found in the soil." [25] At the time when Swallow made his observations the presence of the circle or chimney-like lead-bearing area was not known or suspected. Swallow's keen observations relate to the local and regional structure of the strata of eastern Kansas extending from the Pleasanton area

---

25. Swallow, *op cit.*, p. 58.

southward through Bourbon county into Crawford county rather than to the local and now-known chimney-like area.

Outcrops of rock in the immediate vicinity of the Jumbo mine are scarce because of the flat topography and hence the attitude of the strata are not readily discernible. Currently, in the vertical west wall of the water-filled pit of the Jumbo mine, just about at the water level, the rock could be seen dipping to the south (Fig. 2C). Whether the actual dip is to the south, southeast, or southwest could not be determined, as there was no way to get to the exposure for close examination. Swallow may have observed the very steeply dipping strata in a small stream bed just north of the northwest corner of Pleasanton (Fig. 1) and at a number of other localities in southern Linn county. Haworth, on the other hand, was aware of the chimney or circle. In discussing the Pleasanton lead mine area, Haworth stated that the exact nature of the disturbance could not be determined and expressed the opinion that since there were no marks found on the surface "it is certain that there was no considerable vertical displacement" and that the regularity in the stratification of the entire surrounding area "precludes the idea of any considerable disturbance." [26]

According to Roy Cook, driller from Pleasanton, several other chimney-like areas containing lead and zinc ore occur in eastern Linn county. Ore, mainly sphalerite, was taken from one of the circles or chimney discovered by Cook in 1945, while stripping coal. The pit, now the site of a pond about 200 feet in diameter and surrounded on the east, south, and west sides by strip-mine spoil banks, is in the N. W. corner Sec. 11, T. 23 S., R. 25 E., about three miles east of Prescott and seven miles southeast of Pleasanton. The coal, Mulberry, just above the Pawnee Limestone is 32 inches thick and 17 feet below the surface.[27] The circle was discovered when stripping for the coal, and revealed the fact that all strata were dipping into a circular area. Based upon prospecting, mining operations were started by excavating the circular area by means of a drag line. The pit was deepened for a total of 30 feet down to the horizon of the Pawnee limestone. Sphalerite with some galena impregnated the rocks, mainly sandstone, from seven feet beneath the surface down to the bottom of the pit. Cook described the rocks removed as being in a shattered state and boulder-like in character.

26. Haworth, et al., *Special Report on Lead and Zinc*, pp. 69, 70.
27. W. H. Schoewe, *Coal Resources of the Marmaton Group in Eastern Kansas*, Kansas Geological Survey, *Bulletin 114* (1955), pl. 2, pp. 49-112.

Origin of the Circles or Chimneys

Several explanations have been given for the origin of the circles or chimneys. Hawn, without discussing any details concerning the disturbed lead-bearing area near Pleasanton, was of the opinion that the circle was of plutonic origin.[28] No evidence of igneous origin is present, however, in the area, and hence the plutonic hypothesis is no longer tenable. The best and perhaps the only explanation of the areas is the one associated with the formation of sinkholes as described by Siebenthal for the Joplin or Tri-State Lead and Zinc District. According to Siebenthal, the circles are the result of the dropping down of the areas owing to solution of the underlying strata in sinkholes developed in the Mississippian rocks. It is now fairly well accepted that the Pennsylvanian strata of the general Ozark region, which includes the Tri-State Lead and Zinc District, were deposited upon the karst or solutional surface developed upon the Mississippian rocks.

In accounting for the ore-bearing circles of the Joplin area, C. E. Siebenthal postulated that the circles were formed before the Pennsylvanian Cherokee shale was eroded from the Joplin region. Continued solution resulted in the formation of new sinks and the collapse of the old sinkhole roofs, thereby causing the overlying Pennsylvanian rocks to drop down. The ensuing displacement resulted in the shattering and general brecciating of the overlying rocks, rendering them accessible to circulating artesian or surface waters and thereby affording favorable sites for the deposition of the metallic ores. Siebenthal was of the opinion that the Linn county circles are analogous in origin to the Tri-State Lead and Zinc District circles and that the Pleasanton circle also reaches to the Mississippian limestones.[29]

That sinkholes in the subsurface in Kansas are not uncommon has been recorded recently by D. F. Merriam and W. R. Atkinson [30] and also by R. F. Walters.[31] The sinkholes in eastern Kansas described by Merriam and Atkinson include strata of Simpson age (Ordovician), especially the St. Peter sandstone, which have been deposited as fill in sinkholes developed on an eroded surface of dolomite and limestone of the Arbuckle group. The sinkholes described by Walters have been developed on the Arbuckle on and along the flanks of the central Kansas uplift in Barton county.

28. Hawn, *op. cit.*
29. C. E. Siebenthal, *Origin of the Zinc and Lead Deposits of the Joplin Region, Missouri, Kansas, and Oklahoma*, U. S. Geological Survey, *Bulletin 606* (1915), pp. 1-283.
30. D. F. Merriam and W. R. Atkinson, "Simpson Filled Sinkholes in Eastern Kansas," Kansas Geological Survey *Bulletin 119* (1956), pt. 2, pp. 61-80.
31. R. F. Walters, "Buried Pre-Cambrian Hills in Northeastern Barton County, Central Kansas," American Association Petroleum Geologists, *Bulletin 30* (1946), pp. 610-710.

FIG. 1.- The Linn County, Kansas Lead Mine Area

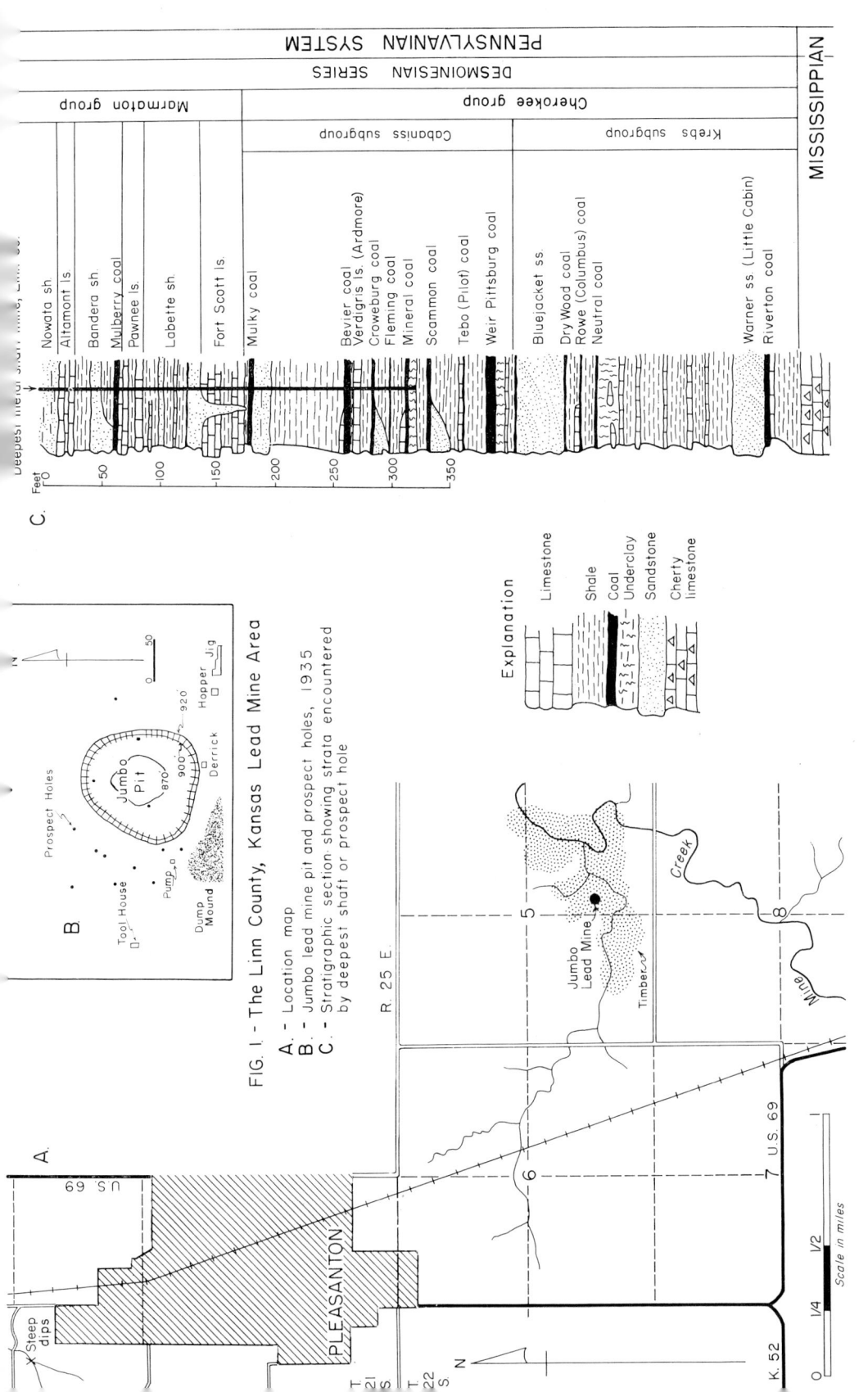

A.- Location map
B.- Jumbo lead mine pit and prospect holes, 1935
C.- Stratigraphic section showing strata encountered by deepest shaft or prospect hole

Figure A, opposite page: Site of first lead mine in Kansas. Circular water-filled Jumbo lead mine, 117 feet diameter, 80 feet deep and 15 to 20 feet below general elevation of surrounding country. View taken in July, 1957.

Figure B: Last of mining equipment, Jumbo lead mine. Water-filled pit visible between machinery and dump heap in background. View taken in November, 1951.

Figure C: West bank of Jumbo lead mine pit showing southward dipping beds.

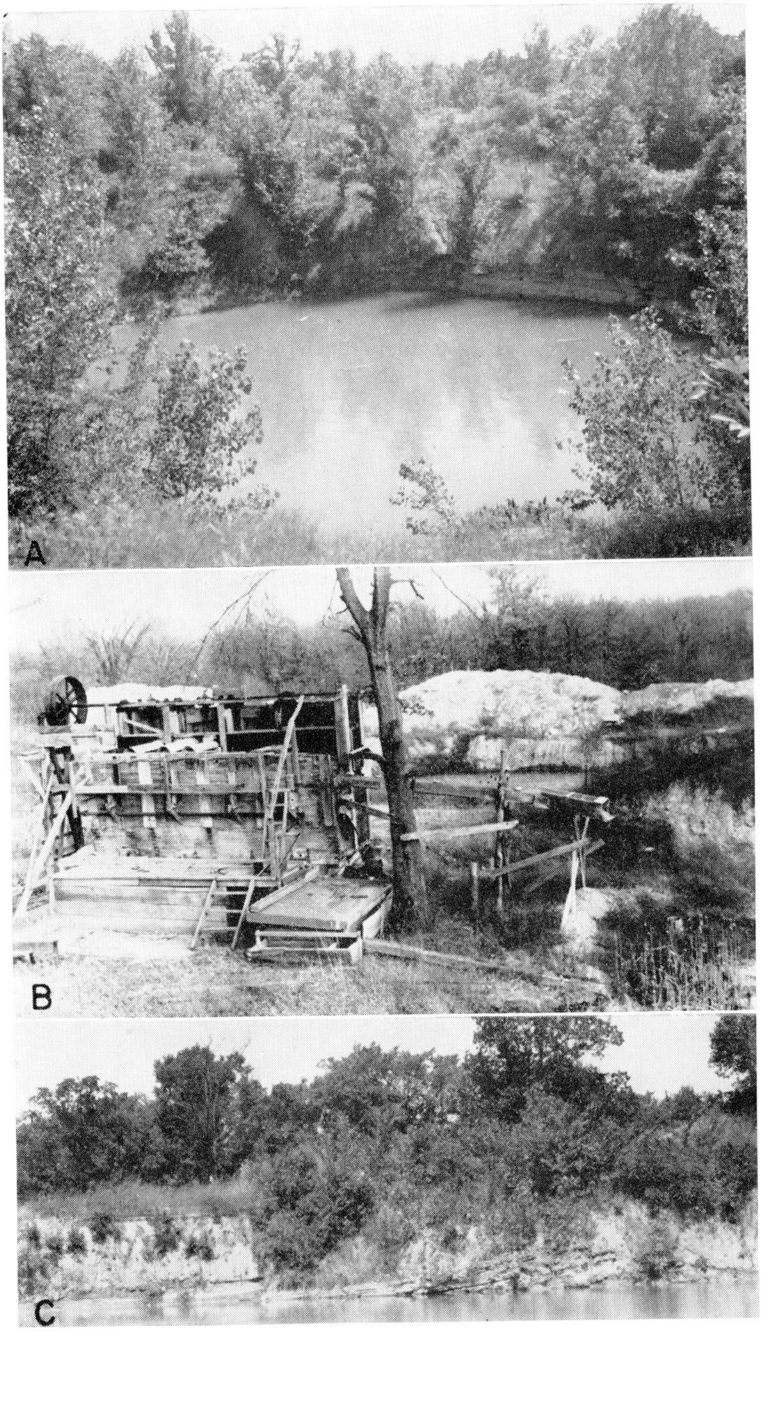
A
B
C

Left: Specimen of galena (lead ore) and limestone from Jumbo lead mine. Note the smooth slickensided surface cutting galena and limestone alike, evidence of faulting or rock movement.
Right: Reverse side of specimen shown in A. Note irregular surface and the effects of solution in the limestone shown by the numerous holes and fretwork.

AGE OF ORE DEPOSITS

The Pleasanton lead ores are unique in that they occur in rocks of Pennsylvanian age (Figs. 1, 6), whereas the ores in southeastern Cherokee county and in the rest of the Tri-State Lead and Zinc District of adjoining Missouri and Oklahoma are obtained from the Boone formation of Mississippian age. The deepest prospect hole for lead, 315 feet, in the Pleasanton area, tested rock to a depth of approximately 135 feet beneath the Fort Scott limestone formation or approximately to the mineral formation in the Cabaniss subgroup of the Cherokee group (Fig. 1C).

On the basis of the sinkhole explanation, metallic ores may reasonably be expected to occur in rocks down to the normal lead and zinc bearing Boone formation of the Tri-State Lead and Zinc District, or an additional 400 to 450 feet below the deepest lead-bearing prospect hole drilled in the area. Since lead and zinc are found in Pennsylvanian rocks involving strata of the Nowata shale formation, Marmaton group, a clue as to the time of ore deposition of the Tri-State Lead and Zinc District is suggested. On the assumption that the Pleasanton and Preston lead and zinc ores in the circles or chimneys of Linn county are related to the ores in the Tri-State Lead and Zinc District, ore deposition in the Tri-State district must be dated at least as post-Nowata in age.

ORIGIN OF THE ORES

The source of the ores and the method of their deposition, whether by ascending artesian waters or by the downward movement of surface or normal ground water, is still a controversial problem. Siebenthal, who has probably made the most exhaustive study of the lead and zinc deposits of the Tri-State Lead and Zinc District, is of the opinion that the source of the ores is Cambrian and Ordovician limestone of the Ozark region and that the ores have reached their present position by ascending artesian waters.[32] Haworth and others, on the other hand, believed that the source of the ores was the Pennsylvanian Cherokee strata and that descending ground water was accountable for the deposition and concentration of the metals in the underlying Mississippian strata.[33] As no new data concerning the occurrence of the Pleasanton ores is available from what was known previously, a discussion of the ore genesis is not germane to the purposes of this historical sketch.

---

32. Siebenthal, *op. cit.*, pp. 41, 42.

33. Haworth, et al., *Special Report on Lead and Zinc*, pp. 117-126; J. H. Wilson, *Lead and Zinc Ore of Southwest Missouri Mines, Authenticated Statistics* (1887), with contributions by F. L. Clere and T. N. Davey, Carthage, Mo., pp. 8-11; E. R. Buckley and H. A. Buehler, *Geology of the Granby Area, Missouri Bureau of Geology and Mines*, 2d ser., v. 4 (1906), pp. 78-110.

Eugene Ware's Concern About a Woman, a Child, and God

JAMES C. MALIN

I. THE WOMAN: THE PROMISE OF A STAR

THE year 1868 was a leap year, so the *Monitor*, January 22, as was more or less the custom, encouraged the girls by compiling a list of the town's most eligible "phat takes." The Wares, father and son, had established themselves in the harness business, apparently in late October or early November of 1867. If no other evidence were available the inclusion of Eugene in the January list of eligible bachelors was testimony that he had already made an impression about town:

E. F. Ware, though lately come among us, stands well in the community. However, he is one that soliloquizes—and has been overheard repeating the following:

> Can it be virgin bashfulness
> That has concealed the tender thought?
> Or fear I might perchance confess
> A love that was not sought?

He would be an easy conquest for some fair one who has what he is devoid of—assurance.

Whether or not this estimate of Ware was altogether accurate may be beside the point. He had made a positive impression, even though, in relations with the fair ones, he lacked assurance. Ware was always a man's man.

After nearly three years, another glimpse of Ware was a matter of record. This was in Ware's own local page of the *Monitor*, October 14, 1870, when as reporter he interviewed a visiting Spiritualist lecturer, a Mrs. C. Fannie Allyn. As Ware told the story, in the seance he made the acquaintance of a Mr. Vinton, formerly of New Hampshire, but then of the spirit world:

He likes a good Yankee joke just as well as we do. . . . [He] poked fun at us in such a rude, bland old way that he just buried himself in our heart. We like a joke even if it is on ourselves . . . and says he, "Mr. Local, you fall in love with every good looking girl you see. You're a *very* susceptible young man, you are; there's a little soft spot in your head on the woman question." We blushed and tried to think of something bright to say but wasn't equal to the emergency, and then the good kind fellow saw how embar-

---

DR. JAMES C. MALIN, associate editor of *The Kansas Historical Quarterly* and author of several books relating to Kansas and the West, is professor of history at the University of Kansas, Lawrence.

rassed we were and he smoothed it all over and gave us compliments that made it all up. . . . But that was a little *too* cruel—that woman joke was. Ain't a "single" man obliged to have a soft spot in his head on the woman question?

During the campaign of 1872 Ware's comments on women were on the acid side. To draw conclusions from that fact, however, would be dangerous. He may have suffered a disappointment, or he may have been indulging in public in a cynicism frequently assumed to mask a quite different feeling toward the opposite sex. When a coroner's verdict on a suicide concluded that it had been caused by a woman, Ware commented: "Some woman is always found to be an accomplice in all such scrapes and we should think they ought to be banished from the community." [1]

But this may have been only one of Ware's peculiar types of humor of exaggeration which sometimes missed the mark. Some weeks later he commented on marriage:

Single lonesomness is being transformed into duplicated cussedness to a vast extent in the counties north and west of us. Every young man ought to have his pie-box packed so as to be able to get out of the country as soon as the epidemic threatens his native health.[2]

The scarcity of young women in Fort Scott apparently overcame such cynicism on the part of unattached young men who slipped out of town as inconspicuously as possible on unannounced business. Ware took notice of such suspicious behavior and published a warning:

Any single young man leaving Fort Scott and going east on a trip who does not file a declaratory statement with the clerk of the District Court, setting forth the nature of his business and the probable length of his absence will be advertised the day after his departure as having gone east to get married.[3]

Some who did not go east, married young school teachers on the spot and brought on a major crisis in Kansas:

The Representative to the Kansas Legislature from Smith county, has been nominated upon a distinct pledge that he will introduce a law making it a felony for a young man to marry . . . a school marm in a county having less than 5,000 population. This is on the grounds of public policy that in the frontier counties it is impossible to educate the young on account of the marriage of the teachers.[4]

Bourbon county had a population in excess of 5,000, so such a law would not have applied in Fort Scott when the following article appeared in the Fort Scott *Border Sentinel,* October 12, 1874:

1. Fort Scott *Daily Monitor,* August 23, 1872.
2. *Ibid.,* October 17, 1872.
3. *Ibid.,* August 9, 1872.
4. *Ibid.,* October 16, 1872.

The Philosopher's Door

On passing along Market street today, we called at the office of the philosopher of paint creek, but found the following on his door:

About three feet of foolscap paper and the same distance of rope, pencil and rubber attached. From the length, of the aforesaid papers, we should suppose the philosopher was on a visit to the Holy Land, or Hungary—*Hun*-gary, we believe is the proper solution. People do not travel with such celerity in those countries as they do in this country of ours. This the philosopher will explain on his return.

The following is a verbatim copy, as appears on the above mentioned paper:

E. F. Ware, present occupant, gone visiting will be back about November 1. Leave orders.

Order I

Come where my love lies dreaming.

Order II

A friend came here on business,
  But found the sanctum closed,
With none to attend to clients,
  Who came here well disposed.

We asked the present occupant,
  When WARE had gone away;
The echo, sent the answer back,
  We went east the other day.

Friend, may pleasure, your companion be,
  While visiting the eastern shore,
But wish you in your sanctum,
  To open the sanctum door.

Two weeks later, the same paper published the following:

Legal Notice

Before Rev. Dr. Buckland, at Rochester, N. Y., in the presence of a large number of witnesses, personally came EUGENE F. WARE, who deposeth and says that he is of lawful age; that he is by occupation a lawyer; that he desires to have and to hold in his peaceful possession, the accomplished JEANETTE P. HUNTINGTON. The evidence on the other side being extremely brief, the prayer of the petitioner was granted; and there being no lawful objection to custody of said JEANETTE P. HUNTINGTON on this 22d day of October, is given to said petitioner.—In testimony thereof, the congratulations of the friends are numerous.

HYMEN & Co., Pl'ffs Attys.

On October 25, the *Daily Monitor* recorded the arrival on the preceding day of E. F. Ware and bride.

The only printed evidence of this period that has been found concerning E. F. Ware's active interest in the welfare of the Fort Scott schools, appeared in the spring of 1873. At that time he was nominated on the Citizens' ticket for treasurer of the school board against the regular Republican ticket, and was defeated. His defeat and his subsequent raid on the faculty of the city schools had no doubt only a casual, not a causal, relationship. Ware's courtship of Nettie Huntington was among those things that for him were strictly private, but to his eldest daughter Abby he wrote reminiscently in 1897: "I promised your mother once if she would marry me I'd get her a star sometime—I haven't been able to get her one yet, and now I'm getting so advanced in years that I can't even catch an airship." [5]

II. A Woman, a Child, and God

Eugene Ware had a concern about God before he met Nettie Huntington. The exact time of their meeting and of their engagement are not now known, but the commitment occurred during the school year 1873-1874. From that time onward he incurred a new obligation to exercise restraint over his expressions about women and about preachers and churches. He had said harsh things on both subjects. Nettie was an orthodox Baptist. The poem "Kriterion" was published August 16, 1874, two months prior to the wedding. In this treatment of the soul and immortality he concluded:

> Perhaps—this Immortality
> May be indeed reality.

The origin of "The Washerwoman's Song" has been the object of legitimate speculation, and much absurd legend. Ware was peculiarly reticent about its origin, and seemed to permit, if he did not encourage the legend, however untenable it obviously was. Possibly, if not probably, he preferred to divert public curiosity away from things most peculiarly private. As already pointed out, "The Washerwoman's Song" was published January 9, 1876. Even if the published stories were substantially true about it being written earlier, being received coldly by his literary friend, Postmaster T. F. Robley, and being laid away until given to a reporter desperate to fill a column on a dull day, there was more than that involved. The first child born to the Wares arrived January 4, or five days prior to the publication of the poem. Thus Abby [Abigail] Ware and "The Washerwoman's Song" were necessarily closely associated. Although the evidence is circumstantial, the washerwoman of the poem appears to have been only a subterfuge to mislead the public and divert attention from the real

---

5. "Eugene F. Ware Papers," Kansas State Historical Society, Topeka.—A typed letter formerly in the possession of Mrs. Justus N. Baird (Amelia Ware).

woman of the poem and attention from the dilemma of Eugene and Nettie. The poem was written during the weeks of tension associated with the first childbirth of their married life:

> Sometimes happening along,
> I had heard the semi-song,
> > And I often used to smile,
> > More in sympathy than guile;
> But I never said a word
> In regard to what I heard,
> > As she sang about her friend
> > Who would keep her to the end.
>
> * * *
>
> It's a song I do not sing,
> For I scarce believe a thing
> > Of the stories that are told
> > Of the miracles of old;
>
> * * *
>
> Human hopes and human creeds
> Have their roots in human needs;
> > And I should not wish to strip
> > From that washerwoman's lip
> Any song that she can sing
> Any hope that songs can bring;
> > For the woman has a friend
> > Who will keep her to the end.

Christmas was just passed, and vividly would the story of Joseph and Mary and the Christ child assume a new and personal meaning. Certainly to Nettie! Then on January 4, 1876, a new soul was born into the world. No longer was the Ware household just Nettie and Eugene. The mother of the child, in prospect now a reality, called for the utmost in sympathetic understanding of her faith. This was no time for cynicism. Even though he could not himself believe on the Christian Miracle, he had been living for months in the intimate presence of a contemporary miracle.

Religion in Kansas During the Era of the Civil War—*Concluded*

EMORY LINDQUIST

THE slavery issue, matters of doctrine, policy relative to missions, and conflicts between frontier groups and parent missionary boards produced wedges of separation in Protestantism in Kansas. Some of these issues reflected national situations; others were due to the Kansas scene. It took years and sometimes decades before the wounds of division were healed.

The Methodists of Kansas were destined to share fully in the split that occurred in 1844 which resulted in the creation of the Methodist Episcopal Church South in 1845. At the General Conference of Methodism in 1844, the Indian Mission Conference was established which included the Kansas territory. This conference voted overwhelmingly to adhere to the Church South. In May, 1854, the Kansas Mission Conference was created at the General Conference of the Methodist Episcopal Church South at its meeting at Columbus, Ga. It was organized by the St. Louis Conference at Springfield on October 24, 1855. Kickapoo was the setting for the first regular session of the Kansas Mission Conference on September 12, 1856.[71] Presiding at the Kickapoo conference was Bishop George Foster Pierce of Georgia. He found that "the Conference met at the appointed hour—every preacher at his place save one or two, whose location in the midst of the depredators compelled them to remain at home, for the protection of their families and their property."[72]

The future of the M. E. Church South was inextricably associated with the development of the controversy over slavery and the future of Kansas as a free or slave state. The feeling became more intense with the passing of the years. In 1860 the Rev. Joab Spencer was informed by his parishioners: "You are regarded as a

---
DR. EMORY KEMPTON LINDQUIST, Rhodes scholar and former president of Bethany College, is dean of the faculties of the University of Wichita. He is author of *Smoky Valley People: A History of Lindsborg, Kansas* (1953), and numerous magazine articles relating to the history of this region.

71. Rev. Joab Spencer, "The Methodist Episcopal Church, South, in Kansas, 1854-1906," *The Kansas Historical Collections*, v. 12 (1911-1912), p. 143; Martha B. Caldwell, ed., *Annals of Shawnee Methodist Mission and Indian Manual Labor School* (Topeka, 1939), p. 98. The arrangements for the division of jurisdiction and property is described in William Warren Sweet, *The Methodist Episcopal Church and the Civil War* (Cincinnati, 1912), pp. 28, 29.

72. George G. Smith, *The Life and Times of George Foster Pierce, D. D., LL. D.* (Sparta, Ga., 1888), p. 288.

'secesh,' and your visits will only bring trouble to those who entertain you. They will be accused of harboring a rebel." Spencer was told that a sermon which he had preached at Marysville over the text Matthew 22:21 had been characterized as a "secesh" sermon. The pressure mounted so that Spencer abandoned temporarily his circuit and went to Missouri. He had also suffered personal losses of clothing and his saddle horse when, according to his account, some soldiers had invaded his property.[73] Other ministers of the Church South had problems of a similar character.[74]

The last session of the Kansas Mission Conference until after the end of the Civil War was held at Atchison, September 5, 1861. The feeling toward the members of the conference increased as the group assembled. Spencer reported that "on account of unusual commotion in the community, we were notified that but two hours would be given us to transact business and leave the city." The meeting was then transferred to Grasshopper schoolhouse 15 miles west of Atchison, where they conducted their business "without molestation though under surveillance." Twenty-three ministers received appointment, but only six were known definitely to have continued work at their assigned places. The nature of the problems confronting the members of the conference is found in the memorial addressed to the General Conference scheduled to meet at New Orleans in May, 1862, which was adopted with one dissenting vote: "Resolved, that the General Conference be and is hereby requested to change the name of our church from 'The Methodist Episcopal Church South' to 'The Episcopal Methodist Church.'" Since the General Conference did not meet, the memorial remains only as an expression of feeling by the Kansas group.[75]

All ministers of the M. E. Church South were forced to quit their ministry in Kansas except Spencer, who continued to serve at Council Grove. Two of the group, the Rev. J. E. Bryan and the Rev. Cyrus R. Rice joined the Methodist Church. Rice became a leader in that group. The Rev. D. C. O'Howell joined the Cumberland Presbyterians, the Rev. J. O. Foresman went to California, and the

73. Spencer, loc. cit., pp. 147, 148.
74. The home of the Rev. L. B. Stateler at Tecumseh was destroyed by an incendiary torch.—Rev. E. J. Stanley, *Life of Rev. L. B. Stateler; A Story of Life on the Old Frontier* (Nashville, 1916), p. 168. Stateler, the Rev. H. B. Burgess, and the Rev. N. H. Watts were the three original judges in the violent election at Tecumseh on March 30, 1855.—*Report of the Special Committee Appointed to Investigate the Troubles in Kansas*, 34th congress, 1st session, report No. 200 (Washington, D. C., 1856), pp. 192-199. Mrs. Sara Robinson found that Burgess was one of those men who "have girded on another sword than that of the spirit."—Mrs. Sara T. D. Robinson, "The Wakarusa War," *The Kansas Historical Collections*, v. 10 (1907-1908), p. 463.
75. Spencer, loc. cit., pp. 152-155; Stanley, op. cit., pp. 160, 161.

Rev. L. B. Stateler to Colorado. Three of the group in addition to Spencer remained in Kansas. They conducted unofficial services and cottage meetings from time to time. The work of the M. E. Church South was resumed in Kansas in 1866.[76]

The members of the ministerium of the M. E. Church South contended that they were never guilty of disloyalty. The Rev. E. J. Stanley described the pattern as follows:

> There was not a man in the ministry of the Methodist Episcopal Church, South, in Kansas that was guilty of a disloyal act or who ever said or did anything inconsistent with his duties as a true citizen or a faithful minister of Jesus Christ, yet because the word "South" happened to be on the name of their Church, or for some other indefinable cause, they were looked upon with suspicion, harassed by squads of armed men who would hoist flags over them while preaching, require them to frame their prayers after a particular fashion, and otherwise disturb their assemblies. In some cases they suffered personal violence for no apparent cause but that of preaching the pure gospel and for keeping clear of political issues.[77]

The Methodist Episcopal Church entered into the work in Kansas in 1848 when the Rev. Abraham Still preached to the Wyandotte Indians. This was in opposition to the agreement of 1844. Other representatives, including the Rev. L. B. Dennis, came to serve in the area. On July 9, 1854, the Rev. William H. Goode in the company of Still and others preached a sermon on the text Matthew 24:14 at Kibbe's cabin at Hickory Point. This was supposedly the first sermon preached under terms of a regular appointment to white settlers in Kansas.[78] On November 26, 1854, Goode discovered when he came to a cabin on the Marais des Cygnes that a man had recently declared himself to be a Methodist preacher "without adding the peculiar *cognomen* assumed to indicate his 'distinct ecclesiastical connection,'" and had secured permission to hold a quarterly meeting there at a date designated a few weeks in advance. This development greatly disturbed Goode who with the co-operation of the man of the family, who had been absent when the other plans were made, assembled some people and held a quarterly meeting. Goode never learned what happened to the Methodist South brother who had preceded him in the area; he had the satisfaction of beating him for the honor of holding the first quarterly meeting.[79] Goode also found that the Rev. Thomas

---

76. Spencer, *loc. cit.*, pp. 152, 153. Rice has presented an interesting portrayal of his activities in Kansas prior to 1860 in Rev. Cyrus B. Rice, "Experiences of a Pioneer Missionary," *The Kansas Historical Collections*, v. 13 (1913-1914), pp. 298-318.

77. Stanley, *op. cit.*, p. 161.

78. William H. Goode, *Outposts of Zion With Limnings of Mission Life* (Cincinnati, 1864), pp. 254, 255; Rev. J. J. Lutz, "The Methodist Missions Among the Indian Tribes of Kansas," *The Kansas Historical Collections*, v. 9 (1905-1906), pp. 219, 230.

79. Goode, *op. cit.*, pp. 313, 314.

Johnson of Shawnee Mission was not responsive when he saw him occasionally in 1854 and 1855 although he had enjoyed his hospitality while in Kansas on a previous occasion. He declared that "I never met an act of recognition from its clerical conductor. And my experience was, so far as I learned, identical in this particular with that of all others who remained firm in their adherence to the Methodist Episcopal Church." [80]

The Methodist Episcopal Church South and the Methodist Episcopal Church each held their first Kansas Conference meeting in 1856. The conference of the Methodist Episcopal Church South met at Kickapoo on September 12 and showed a membership of 13 traveling preachers, 12 local preachers, 672 members including 482 whites, two colored, and 176 Indians. The conference of the Methodist Episcopal Church met at Lawrence October 23-25, and reported 17 preachers and 661 members. When the last conference of the M. E. Church South prior to the end of the Civil War met in 1861 there were 23 preachers and a membership of 1,621, including 1,400 whites, five colored, and 216 Indians. The Methodist Episcopal Church reported that year a membership of 3,020 and a ministerium of 46 preachers. In addition, the German Methodist District joined the conference which added nine more ministers and 316 members.[81]

A sequel to the rivalry between the two Methodist groups was finally settled in 1865 in favor of the M. E. Church South. It was agreed in the Articles of Separation of 1844 that "all the property of the Methodist Episcopal Church in meeting houses, parsonages, colleges, schools, conference funds, cemeteries, and of every kind, within the limits of the Southern organization, shall be forever free from any claim set up on the part of the Methodist Episcopal Church." By a treaty of 1854, three sections of land including the improvements at the Shawnee Mission School were assigned to the missionary society of the M. E. Church South or to persons designated by it. The arrangements were designed to make this land the property of the Rev. Thomas Johnson, who had been identified with the school almost continuously since 1830. A new treaty was proposed in March, 1864, declaring that the contract of March,

---

80. *Ibid.*, pp. 249, 250.
81. Statistics for the M. E. Church South are found in Caldwell, *Annals of the Methodist Shawnee Mission and Indian Manual Labor School*, p. 98; for 1861 in Spencer, *loc. cit.*, p. 152. The information for the Methodist Episcopal Church in 1856 is found in *Minutes of the Annual Conference of the Methodist Episcopal Church, 1856* (New York, 1856), pp. 174, 175; for 1861 in the *Minutes of the Annual Conference of the Methodist Episcopal Church, 1861* (New York, 1861), pp. 41-48.

1855, between the Commissioner of Indian Affairs and the Missionary Society of the Methodist Episcopal Church, null and void on the ground that the M. E. Church South was disloyal. William L. Harris pushed the claim for the Methodist Episcopal Missionary Society. However, after much controversy, J. P. Usher, Secretary of the Interior, approved the claim of the heirs of Thomas Johnson. The patent was delivered to them on May 26, 1865.[82]

The national division among the Baptists in 1845 with the organization of the Southern Baptist Convention also was associated with developments in Kansas. One of the factors in the situation was the formation of the American Indian Mission Association at Cincinnati, Ohio, in October, 1842. The leader in this movement was Isaac McCoy, who had long been identified with events in the future state of Kansas. This movement was enthusiastically supported by Johnston Lykins and Robert Simerwell, well-known Kansas Baptist missionaries. McCoy and his associates felt that the Boston board was not showing enough concern for Indian missions. However, John G. Pratt, Ira D. Blanchard, and Jotham Meeker, other well-known Kansas missionaries, did not favor the new group. The Southern Baptist churches supported the American Indian Mission Association and in 1855 an official relationship was established between the association and the Southern Baptist Convention.

A leader in Baptist circles in Kansas was the Rev. W. Thomas of Delaware City, a missionary in Kansas under the auspices of the Board of Domestic Missions of the Southern Baptist Convention. He was elected temporary chairman at the meeting of the East Kansas Association of Baptists, at Atchison, in October, 1858, the first Baptist Association to be formed in Kansas. He then was elected moderator. Thomas left Kansas before or early in 1859 because of the severity of the climate. The Baptist work was not progressing well in Kansas as indicated in the report of the committee on "Home Destitution" of the East Kansas Association of Baptists in 1858. The political situation had been a factor.

In 1857 the Rev. J. H. Luther found at Kansas City that the conflict over slavery was so great that he decided not to enter the Kansas territory. Southern Baptist work in Kansas was discontinued in 1861. It was not re-established until 1910. In 1867 a treaty conveyed the title to the 320 acres and the Pottawatomie Manual Labor School to the American Baptist Home Mission So-

---

82. This series of events is described in Caldwell, *Annals of the Methodist Shawnee Mission and Indian Manual Labor School*, pp. 79, 84, 113, 114, 117, 118, 120.

ciety rather than to the Board of Domestic Missions of the Southern Baptist Convention.[83]

The division between the Old School and the New School Presbyterians in Kansas was not sharply marked on the issue of slavery. The New School representatives were generally stronger in their antislavery feeling than the Old School on a national basis.[84] The Rev. R. D. Parker wrote in 1860 that "the pro-slavery feeling is kept up by the M. E. Ch. South and the Old School Pres. Ch. It requires no little wisdom to do ones duty and yet avoid strife." [85] The controversy did not attain serious proportions in Kansas.

The Christian Church (Disciples of Christ) in Kansas owed much to Wm. S. Yok of South Carolina, a slave owner and a man of considerable wealth, who was responsible for founding the Christian church at Leavenworth in 1855. Yok was the first elder and minister of the church. He also helped to organize other churches in Kansas. However, the majority of the Disciples were antislavery although they sought a moderate course. The state convention of Disciples at Big Springs in 1860 wanted assurance that Pardee Butler would "preach the Gospel and keep out of politics." However, Butler had friends among both Northern and Southern sympathizers. There was no congregational division in Kansas Christian Churches over the slavery issue. Moreover, there was no national division between North and South over this problem.[86] The Episcopalians and Lutherans, among the major groups, held an antislavery position in Kansas.

The Rev. Thomas Johnson of the M. E. Church South as a slave owner was a rather unusual exception among Protestant missionaries. Included among Johnson's transactions was his purchase of a Negro girl named Harriet from B. M. Lynch for $700 on June 7, 1855, and the acquisition of another Negro girl, Martha, from David Burge for $800 on May 24, 1856.[87] However, when it came to the basic issues associated with the preservation of the Union, Johnson was in direct opposition to the secessionists. On July 4, 1861, when the Union Club held a celebration near Turner in Wyandotte county,

---

83. *Minutes of the First Meeting of the East Kansas Association of Baptists, . . . Atchison, K. T., . . . October 1-3, 1858, . . .* (Atchison, 1858), p. 6; Rev. N. J. Westmorland, "Kansas' First Challenge to Southern Baptists," *The Quarterly Review,* Nashville, v. 15 (third quarter, 1955), pp. 42-55.

84. Goodykoontz, *op. cit.,* pp. 238, 239.

85. Rev. R. D. Parker to the A. H. M. S., Wyandotte, February 9, 1860.

86. Rev. John D. Zimmerman, "Kansas Christian Church History; The Story of a Century," *The Kansas Messenger,* Topeka, v. 57 (January, 1953), pp. 11, 12.

87. Caldwell, *Annals of the Methodist Shawnee Mission and Indian Manual Labor School,* pp. 86, 95.

Johnson made his position clear. He condemned the secession movement as "unjustifiable, and stated in unequivocal terms that he should adhere to the flag of his country, that he had been indirectly for years in official relation with the government, enjoying its protection, and he owed to it fealty, love and support." [88]

Various church conferences and conventions passed resolutions on the subject of slavery. In April, 1857, when the Congregationalists met at Topeka the following resolutions were passed:

Resolved 1. That the system of American Chattel Slavery is a high crime against God and humanity, and, as such, is *prima facie* evidence against the Christian character of those implicated in it.

2. That this Association will in no manner fellowship any other ecclesiastical body which wilfully sustains, directly or indirectly, that system.[89]

In the first meeting of the association following the outbreak of the Civil War, the Congregationalists passed a resolution in which they declared that "in obedience to the injunction of our Divine Master, we, as his disciples, are bound always to take special notice of the 'Signs of the Times,' in order that we may so shape our course as fully to co-operate with Him in carrying forward His providential plans, consummating the subjection of all His enemies and removing every obstacle that hinders the final and speedy triumph of His cause." They continued by expressing their belief that "the President should not only repel aggressions but prosecute the conflict with vigor, and at all hazards, until all government property is regained, and its authority and supremacy fully re-established." [90]

The Baptist convention in 1862 recognized the "chastening hand of God, pledged the people to humble themselves in the midst of the awful disaster, earnestly supplicated the Divine favor and resolved to pray for the 'speedy triumph of freedom.' " [91] The Methodists reiterated their devotion to the Union cause at their annual conference meeting at Leavenworth in March, 1864, when they took the following action: "*Resolved*, that we are immovably devoted to the Union, and are pledged to the maintenance of the authority of the Government of the United States over every inch of its territory; and we will unfalteringly support the Administra-

---
88. *Ibid.*, p. 108.
89. *Minutes of the General Association of Congregational Ministers and Churches in Kansas,* . . . *Topeka, April 25-27, 1857,* p. 6.
90. *The Congregational Record,* Lawrence, v. 3 (July, 1861), pp. 46, 47. The meeting was held at Leavenworth on May 24, 1861.
91. W. A. Elliott, *Historical Address, Kansas Baptist Convention, Fiftieth Anniversary, October 10-13, 1910,* p. [4].

tion in all its measures to put down rebellion and crush out treason, come from what source they may." [92]

Individuals shared in a variety of experiences because of their attitude on slavery. The best known are the two experiences of Rev. Pardee Butler of the Christian church. On August 17, 1855, a demand was made upon Butler at Atchison by a committee under the leadership of Robert S. Kelly, editor of the *Squatter Sovereign*, that he subscribe to a set of resolutions including one "that other emissaries of this Aid Society who are now in our midst tampering with our slaves are warned to leave, else they too will meet the reward which their nefarious designs justly merit—hemp." Butler refused to subscribe to the resolutions. He was then placed on a raft made of two cottonwood logs and set afloat in the river. A flag was placed on it with these words inscribed: "Eastern Emigrant Express. The Rev. Mr. Butler, agent for the underground railroad. The way they are served in Kansas. . . ." [93] On April 30, 1856, Butler was charged with being an active abolitionist and was tarred and feathered at Atchison.[94]

Josiah B. McAfee, a Lutheran minister, arrived at Leavenworth on April 15, 1855. He was soon contacted by a committee which insisted that he preach a sermon on the subject, "slavery is a divine institution and ordained of God." McAfee refused the request and declared that "he would as soon undertake to prove that his satanic majesty was still an angel of light as to prove that slavery was a divine institution." He was notified that he should "leave or hang." The threat was not carried out and McAfee later established a Lutheran church at Leavenworth.[95] Other ministers had problems associated with slavery issues. However, as indicated above, missionaries of the M. E. Church South suffered persecution at the hands of antislavery supporters.[96]

---

92. *Minutes of the Ninth Session of the Kansas Annual Conference of the Methodist Episcopal Church, Leavenworth, March, 1864* (Leavenworth), p. 36. Twelve Kansas ministers of the Methodist Episcopal Church served as chaplains with the Union army.— Sweet, *The Methodist Episcopal Church and the Civil War*, p. 191. Information is not available as to chaplaincy service by Kansas ministers of the M. E. Church South with the Confederate army.—*Ibid.*, p. 222.

93. *Report of the Special Committee Appointed to Investigate the Troubles in Kansas*, pp. 960-963.

94. Rev. Pardee Butler, *Personal Recollections of Pardee Butler* (Cincinnati, 1889), pp. 106-109. Butler recounts the experience as originally printed in a letter to the *Herald of Freedom*, Lawrence, May 6, 1856.

95. Rev. H. A. Ott, *A History of the Evangelical Lutheran Synod of Kansas* (Topeka, 1907), pp. 10, 11.

96. The Rev. John McNamara, an Episcopalian, describes an interesting experience in the Leavenworth area.—[Rev. John McNamara] *Three Years on the Kansas Border* (New York and Auburn, 1856), p. 169ff. The problems of M. E. South missionaries is described *supra*, pp. 407-409.

While the majority sentiment in Kansas was overwhelmingly in favor of the abolition of slavery, there were definite limits to the extent that this articulate group would go in regard to the civil rights of Negroes. This attitude was a matter of genuine concern to many missionaries. The Rev. Lewis Bodwell, Topeka, wrote with great anxiety to Milton Badger of the American Home Missionary Society in March, 1858, asking for Badger's advice and help:

When men around me and among them members of my own church attach their names to documents which in my mind throw away all of vital principle connected with the Kansas struggle & declare themselves *"in favor of a free white state to the exclusion of bound or free blacks,"* I begin to tremble for our cause in Kansas. These signs of selfish ambitions & deep moral corruption already plain & abundant, disgusts me most completely. Who would think of a man with the name & fame which Gov. Charles Robinson has won declaring (as I heard him) in a public meeting at Lawrence "the talk about consistency in a struggle like this is an absurdity." [97]

Bodwell's fears as to the status of the Negro were not unfounded, because when the Wyandotte constitution was adopted on July 29, 1859, "Article V—Suffrage" limited the franchise to "white male" persons.[98] Moreover, when "Article VI—Education" came up for discussion, a militant minority maneuvered strenuously, but unsuccessfully, to exclude Negroes and mulattos from participating in the publicly supported schools.[99] In 1867, when a constitutional amendment was submitted proposing to eliminate the word "white" in the section in suffrage, it was defeated at the polls by a vote of 19,421 to 10,483. The word "white" remained in the Kansas constitution until the 14th amendment was added to the constitution of the United States.[100]

The Civil War brought to Kansas a sizeable number of Negroes, refugees from their former owners, who became known as "contrabands." The missionaries and churches recognized their responsibility to these individuals. The year 1862 witnessed the arrival of a substantial group in various Kansas communities. In March, 1862, the Rev. R. D. Parker reported that his church at Wyandotte was working with the "contrabands" there. Instruction in reading was provided for them in their Sabbath school. He expressed a real

97. Rev. Lewis Bodwell to the A. H. M. S., Topeka, March 18, 1858.
98. *Proceedings and Debates of the Kansas Constitutional Convention* (Wyandot, 1859), p. 582.
99. *Ibid.*, pp. 174-183, 191-195.
100. *Constitution of the State of Kansas and Amendments and Proposed Amendments Submitted* (Topeka, 1953), p. 27; O. E. Learnard, "Organization of the Republican Party," *The Kansas Historical Collections*, v. 6 (1897-1900), p. 313.

interest in them but declared that "this hunted people must leave; for the Kidnapper has already begun his work, and they will not be safe a day after the troops are ordered away." [101]

The Rev. Richard Cordley reported from Lawrence on March 15, 1862, that there were two or three hundred "contrabands" in that community. A Congregational church had been organized among them with eight charter members and others expected to join in the near future. This was the Second Congregational church of Lawrence. Cordley reported that they were "fine specimens of freedom." Only one of the eight charter members had a letter of transfer; the others were admitted on profession. The individual, who had presented a letter of transfer, had one also for his wife but said with tears, "they sold my wife and children down south before I got away." [102] In a letter from Cordley to the American Home Missionary Society on June 17, 1862, was enclosed a clipping from *The Congregational Record* dealing with the "contraband" congregation at Lawrence, which declared that "this is the only Church in Kansas that has a 'value in markets.' The five men are fine looking fellows, and in good times would probably have sold for $1,500 apiece. For piety has commercial value in the slave market. 'The Second Congregational Church in Lawrence,' therefore has a market value of from ten to twelve thousand dollars." [103]

On July 4, 1862, an interdenominational Sabbath school celebration was held at Topeka in which the Congregationalists, Methodists, and Episcopalians participated. The "contrabands" shared in the parade, bringing up the rear of the procession, as they carried the Stars and Stripes, and their motto: "Hail Liberty." The Rev. Peter McVicar was pleased to report that at the picnic following the parade, the "contrabands" had a table by themselves so that they did not need to wait on the white people.[104] The Rev. R. D. Parker at Wyandotte was concerned about the welfare of these Negroes in Kansas and in December, 1863, urged the American Home Missionary Society to do something in their behalf. He was certain that "they are a religious people and will have churches of some kind, but they are at a loss what to do in a free state and surrounded by strange churches." [105]

101. Rev. R. D. Parker to the A. H. M. S., Wyandotte, March 3, 1862.
102. Rev. Richard Cordley to the A. H. M. S., Lawrence, March 15, 1862.
103. *Ibid.*, June 17, 1862. The clipping states that the Second Congregational church at Lawrence was organized on "Sabbath evening," March 16, 1862.—*The Congregational Record*, Lawrence, v. 4 (April, 1862), pp. 47, 48.
104. Rev. Peter McVicar to the A. H. M. S., Topeka, July 28, 1862.
105. Rev. R. D. Parker to the A. H. M. S., Wyandotte, December 11, 1863.

The impact of sectarian influences was also felt in the religious activities of the "contrabands." The Rev. Richard Cordley reported that "they seemed to be of one mind, and no sectarian name was mentioned. They had been members of different churches, but all seemed to go together. . . . Before the year had passed several of their own ministers appeared, and they divided into various ecclesiastical camps. Most of their preachers were very ignorant, some of them not able to read." [106]

The Episcopalians in Kansas reflected national issues within their denomination although the controversy over slavery was not a factor. On December 10, 1856, the Rev. Hiram Stone organized St. Paul's church at Leavenworth. Stone soon found himself in conflict with the Philadelphia association of the church, which was generally identified as a "low church" group. Stone declared that "partisan spirit had developed in the church at large" and it had become "the settled purpose of this society to organize Kansas into a diocese and to supply it with clergy suited to its own stripe of churchmanship." The Philadelphia association sent out several missionaries to Kansas and started parishes in Wyandotte, Lawrence, Topeka, and Atchison.

The mission at Leavenworth founded by Stone was supported by the Domestic committee of the General Board. At a meeting at Wyandotte on August 11, 1859, it was proposed that the group consider the possibility of organizing a diocese. Bishop Kemper was in attendance. The decision was in the affirmative and while Stone opposed the action, it was decided to hold a convention in Topeka on April 11, 1860, to elect a bishop. The opposition party argued that a general convention of the church was to meet at Richmond, Va., two months following the Wyandotte assembly, when a missionary bishop was to be provided for Kansas. Stone characterized the proceedings of organizing the diocese and electing a bishop as "thoroughly partisan in its character besides being irregular, uncanonical, and unnecessary." Stone further pointed out that there were only seven Episcopalian clergy in Kansas at the time and that three of them had never taken demissory letters from the diocese which they had served formerly.[107] The convention at Topeka elected the Rev. Francis M. Whittle of Louisville, Ky., as bishop. However, when it became known that Whittle

106. Cordley, *Pioneer Days in Kansas*, pp. 144, 145.
107. Stone, *loc. cit.*, pp. 320, 321; William Henry Haupt, "History of the American Church, Known in Law as the Protestant Episcopal Church in the State of Kansas," *The Kansas Historical Collections*, v. 16 (1923-1925), p. 358.

was inclined toward the Proslavery position, the laity rejected him by a vote of four to two. Dr. Dyer of New York City was then elected. Dyer declined to serve, and the Rt. Rev. Henry W. Lee, bishop of Iowa, served the Kansas diocese. There were only 147 communicants in Kansas when the Rev. Thomas Hubbard Vail, Muscatine, Iowa, was elected bishop of Kansas in 1864.[108]

The desire to bring the Christian message to Kansas resulted occasionally in duplication of efforts and sometimes in attendant rivalry. In December, 1854, the Rev. S. Y. Lum reported at Lawrence that "there is already a liberal supply of missionaries from the various societies at this point." He identified ministers from the Baptist, United Brethren, Methodist, Christian (Disciples of Christ), and Congregational churches, and one representing the Swedenborgians.[109] The scarcity of facilities provided the background for friction. In October, 1856, the Rev. Lewis Bodwell complained that Constitution Hall, the only adequate building in Topeka, had been usurped by the Methodists morning, afternoon, and evening for their quarterly meeting although that day belonged to the Congregationalists by mutual agreement.[110] Rev. E. W. Whitney, a Congregationalist at Troy, found in February, 1861, that the Methodists interfered with his meetings by getting possession of the courthouse, the only suitable place in the community for public gatherings. He contended that "the course they pursue in Kansas looks very much as if they thought they had a divine right to crowd out every other denomination." However, Whitney rejoiced over the fact that prospects were brighter for the Congregationalists in the future because the individuals who would have control of the courthouse were more sympathetic to them.[111]

The pattern of diversity in Kansas religion was emphasized in a report by the Rev. J. D. Liggett to the American Home Missionary Society in December, 1861, dealing with Leavenworth. Fifteen congregations were reported functioning with various degrees of success. The groups and the estimated attendance were listed as follows: Irish Roman Catholic, 500; German Roman Catholic, 50;

---

108. *Ibid.*, pp. 363, 364, 377. *Journals of the Primary Convention . . . in A. D. 1859 and of the Annual Conventions . . . Following, in A. D. 1860, 1861, 1862, 1863, and 1864 and of the Special Convention in April, 1860,* Protestant Episcopal Church, Kansas Diocese (Lawrence, 1885), pp. 24-26.

109. Rev. S. Y. Lum to the A. H. M. S., Lawrence, December 23, 1854, in *The Kansas Historical Quarterly,* v. 25 (Spring, 1959), p. 53. In January, 1855, G. W. Brown wrote in the *Herald of Freedom* that Lawrence had nearly a dozen lawyers, doctors, and clergymen. He felt that Lawrence needed more of "any class of persons relying upon labor for support. . . ."—Quoted in Malin, "Notes on the Writing of General Histories of Kansas," *loc. cit.,* p. 332.

110. Rev. Lewis Bodwell to the A. H. M. S., Topeka, October 21, 1856.

111. Rev. E. W. Whitney to the A. H. M. S., White Cloud, February, 1861.

Campbellite, 150; German Lutheran, no regular preaching; German Evangelical, 50; Protestant Episcopal, 50; Baptist, no regular preaching; Methodist Episcopal, 200; German Methodist, 50; Old School Presbyterian, no regular preaching; Presbyterian (Westminster), 50; United Presbyterian, 25; Congregational, 150. Liggett estimated the population of Leavenworth at about 10,000.[112] In December of the following year Liggett reported that there had been a split in the Baptist church which had 30 members. The division occurred when a new pastor was to be called. The congregation divided, two men were called, and both came to Leavenworth thus forming two Baptist churches. He concluded his report by stating that "almost all denominations are now struggling for a foothold here, while all are weak." [113]

While there were many occasions for misunderstanding of a general nature, the issue became more specific for the Rev. S. Y. Lum in January, 1857, when he attributed to the Unitarians the greatest responsibility. In writing to Milton Badger of the American Home Missionary Society, he stated that "were no doctrines taught, but those of the truth as it is in Jesus, there would be strong hope then of overcoming these influences but when the truth—as it is called— is so presented as to fall in with all the natural inclinations of the sinful heart, it fortifies the way against that which is distasteful. Thus I find that Unitarianism is more in the way of the progress of the *saving truth* than any or *all other influences combined*." [114]

The contemporary records show no great evidence that the religious scene in Kansas was seriously disrupted in this era by bitter hostility between Roman Catholicism and Protestantism. Ray A. Billington has written that "the desire to save the West from Catholicism" had been an important motive for home mission activity on a national basis. He pointed out that between 1834 and 1856 *The Home Missionary*, official publication of the American Home Missionary Society, was "an outspoken organ of propaganda." The fear generated by the declarations of Samuel F. B. Morse and the Rev. Lyman Beecher did not make a decisive impact upon devel-

112. Rev. J. D. Liggett to the A. H. M. S., Leavenworth, December 2, 1861. The population of Leavenworth in the 1860 census was 7,429.—*Population of the United States in 1860, Eighth Census* (Washington, D. C., 1864), p. 164.
113. Rev. J. D. Liggett to the A. H. M. S., Leavenworth, December 1, 1862.
114. Rev. S. Y. Lum to the A. H. M. S., Lawrence, January 15, 1857, in *The Kansas Historical Quarterly*, v. 25 (Summer, 1959), p. 180. On May 27, 1855, Mrs. Sara Robinson wrote with enthusiasm about the arrival in Lawrence of Mr. Nute, a clergyman sent by the Unitarian Association: "We are glad he has come among us with his genial sympathies, his heart warmth, his earnest ways, his outspoken words for truth, and his abiding love for freedom and the right."—Sara T. L. Robinson, *Kansas; Its Interior and Exterior Life* (Boston, 1857), pp. 59, 60.

opments in Kansas.[115] There were undoubtedly some individuals and groups who were concerned about the expansion of Catholicism in the frontier area. In October, 1858, at the first annual meeting of the East Kansas Association of Baptists, Elder W. Thomas as chairman of the committee to report on "Home Destitution" lamented the prevalence of "Infidelity, Universalism, and Romanism." However, the report also emphasized that "a wide spread destitution of Baptist preaching prevails in Kansas" so that the sectarian concern included Protestants as well as Roman Catholics.[116]

An interesting aspect of Protestantism in Kansas during the era of the Civil War was the controversy, and at times conflict, between the home or parent missionary society or church, and their Kansas representatives. One manifestation of this rivalry occurred within the framework of the American Home Missionary Society. In October, 1858, when the General Association of Congregational Ministers and Churches met at Manhattan, a committee on home evangelization was appointed. The committee should "act as a committee on *missions, church extension* and *colportage*, and should have general oversight of the religious interests of the Territory.[117] This decision was a type of declaration for independent action by the missionaries on the Kansas frontier. It seemed as if this "native" authority would be a threat to the hegemony of the Eastern society. The criticism of the action by Milton Badger and other officials of the society was met by Bodwell in a communication to the society on January 16, 1859, in which he urged the society to send a representative to Kansas. He argued that "we are confident that it would facilitate your labors for the cause among us by giving you a knowledge which you can hardly acquire anywhere but here." He contended that at least six of the brethren, especially the committee on missions, supported his position.[118] Bodwell, as chairman of the committee, urged greater adaptation of missionary methods to frontier conditions in Kansas where there were widely scattered settlements. The Methodist circuit riders were admirably suited to the Kansas scene. The society was committed to a policy of supporting pastors for settled congregations.[119]

The controversy between the society and Bodwell and his group

---

115. Ray A. Billington, "Anti-Catholic Propaganda and the Home Missionary Movement, 1800-1860," *The Mississippi Valley Historical Review*, Lincoln, Neb., and Cedar Rapids, Iowa, v. 22 (December, 1935), pp. 362-373.
116. *Minutes of the First Meeting of the East Kansas Association of Baptists, . . . Atchison, K. T., October 1-3, 1858* (Atchison, 1858), p. 6.
117. *The Congregational Record*, Lawrence, v. 1 (January, 1859), p. 5.
118. Rev. Lewis Bodwell to the A. H. M. S., Topeka, January 16, 1859.
119. Goodykoontz, *op. cit.*, pp. 181, 182. This authoritative study on home missions describes effectively the policies and practices of the American Home Missionary Society.

developed further on the basis of charges that had been reported from Kansas about sectarianism. The Congregationalists and Presbyterians were still associated in the work of the society. A Presbyterian had accused the Bodwell group of sectarian practices. On February 8, 1860, Bodwell declared as to the charges about sectarianism: "Evangelical Kansas is in main the foster child of New England and it is not strange that we should adopt our mother's views." Bodwell was losing patience by this time. He emphasized that Lum, Blood, Jones, Copeland, Adair, Byrd, and he came to Kansas because they chose to do so and not because the society had selected them.[120] On February 28, 1860, Bodwell countered with a charge of sectarianism. He reported soberly to the society that "I need not state at length how sectarian selfishness sought to forestall action; withdrew from co-operation, wouldn't work with Brother B; secured the use of the only capacious Hall (by right *ours* 4 to 1); began a series of meetings which by shouting, screaming, and *dancing!* were under the point of attraction to scores who 'went for fun.' "[121]

Badger and the officials of the American Home Missionary Society were apparently planning to send an agent to Kansas and had provided a description of the qualities which he should possess. This action irritated Cordley who wrote on March 29, 1860, as follows:

> The man *whose pattern you give is not on the ground*. I have *never seen him*, but it would do my eyes good to look on his like. The unanimous opinion of the brethren here is that Bro. Bodwell can do more for *us* and *you* in the present state of things than any other man. . . . He is faithful. We will always be sure that he is doing the best he can. We cannot feel so in regard to Bro. Lum. Then Bro. B. is always willing to receive aid and advice from brethren. . . . He is a worker. He is earnest. Then again he is thoroughly acquainted with the country & the people. It would take two years for a new man to gain the knowledge of the land & the people which Bro. B. possesses to begin with.[122]

This phase of the controversy was settled in favor of the Kansas group in April, 1860, when the society appointed Bodwell to succeed Lum as Kansas agent.[123]

There were occasional conflicts between the American Home

---

120. Rev. Lewis Bodwell to the A. H. M. S., Topeka, February 8, 1860. The New School Presbyterians withdrew from the American Home Missionary Society in 1861. However, the change of name to the Congregational Home Missionary Society was not made until 1893.—Goodykoontz, *op. cit.*, p. 301.
121. Rev. Lewis Bodwell to the A. H. M. S., Topeka, February 28, 1860.
122. Rev. Richard Cordley to the A. H. M. S., Lawrence, March 29, 1860.
123. Rev. Lewis Bodwell to the A. H. M. S., Topeka, April 24, 1860, quoted in Hickman, "Lewis Bodwell, Frontier Preacher; the Early Years," *loc. cit.*, v. 12 (November, 1943), p. 364.

Missionary Society and individuals who allegedly or actually were violating the policy of the society. It was the established policy of the organization to discourage its missionaries from engaging in other activities than those associated directly with their pastoral work. This policy was unrealistic in many situations because of the modest grant from the society and the inability of congregations to render adequate support. In the summer of 1861, the Rev. R. Paine, Burlington, was admonished by Badger that the commission "requires you to be wholly devoted to the preaching of the Gospel and pastoral duties." A portion of Paine's eight page letter is cited as an indication of the varied life of the missionary on the Kansas frontier:

> I begin by saying that I am in the habit of working with my hands. I have gone to the woods alone with four yoke of oxen and taken thence huge logs five miles and a half to the mill. Have often sat upon the load with my heart lifted to God in the ferver of praise and prayer. I have plowed, planted, hoed, choped, split posts, built fence, mowed, pitched hay, drawn grass, and stone and wood and lime and sand. . . . I have as the reward of my labour in part, a very great increase in physical vigour.
>
> Besides, I have a family to support and some debts to pay. . . . I cannot regret that I have planed and laboured in the main as I have. If I had left the word to serve tables: if I had not loved the souls of my people, and had not borne them up in *strong intercession* at the throne of grace: if I had not visited them and not come before them on the Sabbath with the well beaten oil of the sanctuary, then I might be troubled, if my heart was calloused, with the stings of conscience.
>
> Certainly I hope to be able to do more in the vineyard in the future than I ever have done. I look forward with joyful hopes of erelong of obtaining another horse, that I may ride over my field oftener.[124]

At the annual conference of the Methodist Episcopal Church meeting at Atchison in March, 1861, a further demonstration was provided by Bishop Morris as to the status of the frontier church. The Rev. H. D. Fisher, the secretary, presented the nominees for the standing committees. Fisher named the presiding elder and one man from each district as the committee on missions. The Rev. James Shaw, who was present at these deliberations described the scene as follows:

> After he [Fisher] had read his report the Bishop remarked, "It seems to me you have got a new fangled arrangement in your nominations. It is customary to appoint the Presiding Elders alone as the Mission Committee. They

---

124. Rev. R. Paine to the A. H. M. S., Burlington, August 13, 1861. In December, 1861, when the Plymouth Congregational church at Lawrence petitioned the American Home Missionary Society for $300 to support the Rev. Richard Cordley the following statement was made: "He is one of very few ministers in Kansas who devote themselves entirely to the ministry and who have eschewed farming and real estate speculation."— Plymouth Congregational church, Lawrence, to the A. H. M. S., December 1, 1861.

only are competent, from their knowledge of the work, to make a just distribution of the money.

Brother Fisher replied, "This is a Kansas arrangement." But said the Bishop, "Kansas is Methodist soil, and I am here to maintain Methodist usages."

Brother Mahan at once moved to strike out all but the Presiding Elders, which motion prevailed.[125]

There was considerable tension at times between the older conferences and the frontier missionaries. The Rev. William H. Goode who began an important career in Kansas in 1854 has indicated the nature of the tension. He found that generally the men who came to Kansas were "men of the right stamp, volunteers, men of energy, willing to 'endure hardness as good soldiers.'" However, "attempts were made to foist upon us, from the older Conferences, men who were either too indolent or incompetent to labor acceptably where they were; but who, in the judgment of the good brethren, 'would do for the frontier.'" Goode believed that such efforts were generally detected.[126] He, however, had some unpleasant experiences with older conferences. He sought a certain man for an assignment in Kansas, but was told he could not be spared from his present church. Goode identified the nature of the problem by pointing out that "another was kindly offered as 'suitable for our work,' whom, on my declining, they found reason to honor with a location, unsought. Such is the dependent condition of frontier work; and such it must remain, while a mere appendage of other Conferences. Their 'tender mercies are cruel.'"[127]

The Kansas Congregationalists also lamented at times the attitude of Eastern ministers and members. In July, 1859, when a clergyman from West Brookfield, Mass., declined a call to serve the church at Wyandotte, the editor of *The Congregational Record* observed that "our Eastern brethren seem to have a mortal dread of Kansas. We wish something could be done to inspire them with a little more pluck."[128] The attitude of the East toward the West was again a matter of concern in a leading article in *The Congregational Record* for January, 1861, entitled "The West Needs Peculiar Men." The writer argued that Easterners thought that "the West needs peculiar men." He declared that "we need the same peculiarity of which the Apostle speaks; 'A peculiar people, zealous of good works.' We want the same pecularity that is needed in the gospel ministry everywhere, and no more. Any man, who has the

125. Shaw, *op cit.*, pp. 105, 106.
126. Goode, *op. cit.*, p. 323.
127. *Ibid.*, pp. 351, 352.
128. *The Congregational Record*, Lawrence, v. 1 (July, 1859), p. 54.

love of Christ and of souls in his heart can succeed here. . . . Of course, talent and scholarship are an advantage here, as everywhere; but no man who has no other aim than the good of souls, need fear that he is not adapted to the West." [129]

There was considerable personal feeling on the part of the frontier missionary and his family toward the older churches and their members. Mrs. Julia Louisa Lovejoy, the wife of the Rev. Charles Lovejoy, Methodist missionary, was particularly articulate on this point. In great detail she outlined life on the Kansas prairies "for the gratification of the Methodist preachers in New Hampshire, who are disposed to complain of 'hard fare,' in their comfortable parsonages. . . ." After chronicling the hardship, famine, and loneliness she exclaimed: "O, that some of the 'broken fragments' of the well-filled tables, might roll in this direction and feed some of these hungry Missionaries and their families." [130] Mrs. Lovejoy was also a strident combatant in her attack upon a Kansas minister who in an article "Kansas Preachers" in the *Christian Advocate and Journal* had been exceedingly critical in 1858 of the political activities of the missionaries. While denying these charges, she pointed out that the author was generally hostile to and unacquainted with the New England Methodism which the group attacked represented in Kansas.[131]

The Kansas scene also reflected the issues within Protestantism relative to the role of an educated ministry as against the preachers who supposedly were native to the West and possessed a "call" that qualified them to bring the Gospel message. As early as 1847 Horace Bushnell expressed genuine alarm over the degradation of religion and education as a result of emigration. He described the situation: "Still we are rolling on from east to west, plunging into the wilderness, scouring across the great inland deserts and mountains, to plant our habitations on the western ocean. Here again the natural tendency of emigration towards barbarism, or social decline are displayed, in signs that cannot be mistaken." [132]

While Bushnell was lamenting the consequences of emigration, the process was going on with accelerated tempo. A great question confronted Protestantism: Should the Gospel be withheld until a fully trained ministry could provide for the spiritual needs of the

---

129. *Ibid.*, v. 3 (January, 1861), pp. 8-10.
130. "Letters of Julia Louisa Lovejoy, 1856-1864," *loc. cit.*, v. 15 (August, 1947), p. 294.
131. *Ibid.*, p. 383.
132. Horace Bushnell, *Barbarism the First Danger; A Discourse on Home Missions* (New York, 1847), p. 16.

people? The answer was in the negative with some major denominations. A dynamic rationale for this position was found in the strong feelings of some individuals who were represented by the Rev. Peter Cartwright, the distinguished Methodist pioneer missionary. Writing in 1856 he declared that "the great mass of our Western people wanted a preacher that could mount a stump, a block, or old log, or stand in the bed of a wagon and without note or manuscript, quote, expound and apply the word of God to the hearts and consciences of the people."[133] He thought how kind fate had really been when he exclaimed: "Suppose the thousands of early settlers and scores of early Methodist preachers, by some Providential intervention had blundered on a Biblical Institute, or a theological factory, where they dress up little pedantic things they call preachers; suppose ye would have known them from a rams horn? Surely not."[134]

The course of events and the scarcity of ministers did not permit Cartwright's fears to become a reality. There was a wide variety in education among the Kansas missionaries. They ranged from the well-educated Andover Band of Congregationalists, who came directly to Kansas from Andover Theological Seminary, to the rather crude but devoted preacher who felt that he had a direct "call" to preach the Word of God.[135] The educated ministers in Kansas often lamented the activities of the uneducated brethren. The Rev. Richard Knight, an Englishman, described the situation at Hampden, K. T., in August, 1855, as follows: "Our Sabbath meetings are attended by many for a distance of 6 or 8 miles who would otherwise have nothing but the teaching of ignorant men from some of the Western States who have come in as Emigrants and who have already held meetings advancing some of the crudest and strangest notions conceivable. . . ."[136] The Rev. William H. Ward at Oskaloosa found many of the same problems that Knight described. He believed that the lack of religious interest was

---

133. Charles L. Wallis, ed., *Autobiography of Peter Cartwright* (New York and Nashville, 1956), p. 236. Lyman Beecher had argued forcibly for an educated ministry: "The ministry for the West must be a learned and talented ministry. . . . No opinion is more false and fatal than that mediocrity of talent and learning will suffice for the West."—Lyman Beecher, *Plea for the West* (Cincinnati, 1835), p. 25.

134. Wallis, op. cit., p. 316.

135. The Andover Band is described in Charles M. Correll, *A Century of Congregationalism in Kansas, 1854-1954* (Topeka, 1953), pp. 23-28. Carl Becker writing in 1910 showed how knowledge of the Andover Band had degenerated by that time to the point that "some thought it was an iron band, and some a band of Indians."—Carl Becker, "Kansas," in *Essays in American History Dedicated to Frederick Jackson Turner* (New York, 1910), p. 99.

136. Rev. Richard Knight to the A. H. M. S., Hampden, August 1, 1855. William A. Phillips, well-known correspondent for the New York *Tribune*, described Knight, a delegate to the Topeka constitutional convention, as "an Englishman and a clergyman. A man of ability, he was fully conscious of its possession.—William A. Phillips, *The Conquest of Kansas by Missouri and Her Allies* (Boston, 1856), p. 135.

"increased by the fact that there was a year ago this winter a religious excitement under the auspices of the Methodists and most of their converts have relapsed. Their manners here, so noisy and ignorant, quite disgust the more educated part of the community." Ward was requested by the Lyceum of the community to deliver a lecture on geology, "taking the ordinary views in reference to the age of the world." He learned, however, that on "the next Sabbath the Methodist clergyman preached against Geology as a humbug and its defenders as pantheistical, a word which I have no idea he knew the meaning of." [137] The Rev. E. Whitney found at Palermo that "no less than 3 uneducated ministers from Missouri have commenced preaching there. They manifest a great deal of zeal speak very loud." [138]

While there were many occasions for conflicts and tensions among and between groups and denominations there were also situations in which the frontier produced co-operative efforts. In December, 1855, the Rev. Charles Blood and the Congregationalists at Manhattan described co-operative relationships with the Methodists and Baptists in the area, although it was reported with regret that the representatives of the M. E. Church South would not share in these plans.[139] This ecumenical pattern was continued in the Manhattan community. In December, 1856, it was reported that the Baptist, Methodist, and Congregational ministers rotated their services so that the people could have weekly services, but they heard each preacher only once in every three Sundays.[140] On the first Sunday in November, 1856, the Rev. Lewis Bodwell, a Congregationalist, held what was possibly the first communion service at Topeka. Individuals from other denominations participated in this service for administering the sacrament. It appeared that sectarian lines at that occasion were broken down.[141]

In 1860 Bodwell reported an impressive revival in which the Congregationalists, Presbyterians, and Baptists participated.[142] In January, 1861, *The Congregational Record* told its readers that "a powerful revival is in progress in connection with the New School Presbyterian Church at Auburn. . . . The whole community seems stirred for miles around. . . ." [143] There are also evidences

137. Rev. William H. Ward to the A. H. M. S., Oskaloosa, March 19, 1860.
138. Rev. E. Whitney to the A. H. M. S., Elwood, April 3, 1860.
139. Rev. Charles Blood to the A. H. M. S., Manhattan, December 15, 1855.
140. Thomas C. Wells, "*Letters of a Kansas Pioneer,*" *The Kansas Historical Quarterly*, v. 5 (August, 1936), p. 290.
141. Hickman, "Lewis Bodwell, Frontier Preacher; the Early Years," *loc. cit.*, v. 12 (August, 1943), p. 281.
142. *Ibid.*, pp. 294, 295.
143. *The Congregational Record*, Lawrence, v. 3 (January, 1861), p. 17.

of a broad tolerance that went beyond the boundaries of both Protestantism and Christianity. In 1863, when the United Brethren Church at Mound City found it financially impossible to complete its church building, the project was taken over and completed by the Ladies' Enterprise Association. On June 3, 1864, the president and secretary of the association published in the Mound City *Border Sentinel* a communication indicating that the structure was a "Free Meeting House," available not only to all Christian groups but to "spiritualists, infidels, atheists, or any other of the numerous 'ists' or 'isms'! . . ." and that it should be open "for all public meetings and for all innocent amusements." [144]

While there were differences of opinion on matters of doctrine and order of worship among denominations, there was unanimity of belief relative to the right of worship according to the dictates of conscience. Freedom of religion was fully guaranteed in the Topeka, Lecompton, Leavenworth, and Wyandotte constitutions. The section on this phase of the Bill of Rights is similar in intent and spirit in each document. When the Wyandotte constitution was adopted on July 29, 1859, section seven of the 20 sections which constituted the Bill of Rights read as follows:

The right to worship God according to the dictates of conscience shall never be infringed; nor shall any person be compelled to attend or support any form of worship; nor shall any control of, or interference with the rights of conscience be permitted, nor any preference be given by law, to any religious establishment or mode of worship. No religious test or property qualification shall be required for any office of public trust, nor for any vote at any election, nor shall any person be incompetent to testify on account of religious belief.[145]

While the Kansas scene provided many problems which made church work exceedingly difficult, steady, if not spectacular, progress was recorded by the pioneer missionaries and congregations. It soon became apparent that except for times of revival and the special emphasis of camp meetings, the ministers could not measure achievement primarily by numbers in attendance at religious meetings. The fluidity of movement on the frontier, emergency demands upon the people, and the general lack of stability created a pattern quite different from that of an older civilization.

The role of the prayer meeting loomed very large in the life of the church. In July, 1856, Charles B. Lines reported from Wa-

144. "The Letters of Joseph H. Trego, 1857-1864, Linn County Pioneer," *The Kansas Historical Quarterly*, v. 19 (November, 1951), p. 393.
145. *Proceedings and Debates of the Kansas Constitutional Convention* (Wyandotte, 1859), p. 575. There was little debate on this section. The word "man" in the original version was changed to "person" since it was argued that "here is a principle granted to men to worship God according to the dictates of their conscience, while women are left out of the question."—*Ibid.*, p. 287.

baunsee about a regular prayer meeting, which brought 20 persons together in a small tent. He observed that "an expression in one of the prayers, offered by an old settler would have sounded strange in the ears of a New Haven audience. He prayed that God would take care of the interests of our Territory, that He would overturn the existing corrupt government, and especially supply the place of our debased Governor with a better man, and in all this, he spoke right out into the ear of God, what he felt in his soul. . . ."[146] In January, 1857, the Rev. Lewis Bodwell reported from Topeka that a prayer meeting was held every Sunday evening "which is usually largely attended by persons old and young both prosperous & non-prosperous, a goodly number taking a part & making the meeting lively, interesting &, we hope, very profitable."[147]

Another point of strength in the frontier church was the Bible classes. Although the attendance was not generally large, the emphasis in these smaller groups stimulated the life of the congregation and encouraged the pastor. In March, 1860, the Rev. Richard Cordley at Lawrence felt real encouragement because of the activities of five Bible classes in his Congregational church, two for ladies and three for gentlemen. Moreover, a union concert at the church had attracted 300 people.[148] The denominations generally gave great emphasis to the program of Sunday schools. For instance, at the annual meeting of the Kansas Conference of the Methodist Episcopal Church in 1865 the report showed 110 Sunday Schools with 4,372 scholars.[149] *The Congregational Record* carried lengthy articles regularly about children's work and the need for emphasis upon it.

Revivals and camp meetings were typical of the frontier witness of certain Protestant denominations. Camp meetings were held early in the history of Kansas territory. In August, 1855, Mrs. Sara Robinson described the departure of two large carriage loads from the Robinson home in Lawrence for a camp meeting on the Wakarusa. A large number of people participated in the event.

146. Alberta Pantle, "The Connecticut Kansas Colony; Letters of Charles B. Lines to the New Haven *Daily Palladium*," *The Kansas Historical Quarterly*, v. 22 (Summer, 1956), p. 173. Lines wrote a series of interesting letters about the "Beecher Bible and Rifle Colony." These letters were especially interesting to New Haven readers since the colonization movement had its origin in their community. The reference in the prayer to "our debased governor" was to Wilson Shannon who was territorial governor from September 7, 1855, to August 18, 1856.

147. Rev. Lewis Bodwell, first quarterly report to the A. H. M. S., Topeka, January 10, 1857.

148. Rev. Richard Cordley to the A. H. M. S., Lawrence, March 1, 1860.

149. *Minutes of the Tenth Session of the Kansas Annual Conference of the Methodist Episcopal Church . . ., Topeka, March 15, 1865* (Leavenworth), p. 22.

Mrs. Robinson believed that the services would have been impressive if there had not been continual "'Amens,' in shrill as well as deep guttural tones, which the zealous worshippers are sounding in one's ears from all quarters."[150] Mrs. Julia Louisa Lovejoy, the wife of the Rev. Charles Lovejoy, a Methodist minister, described in detail a camp meeting in 1858. She observed that for 30 years she had attended camp meetings in New England, "but seldom have we heard better preaching, or 'seen more religious interest manifested' than at our late meeting. There were about thirty preachers present, and at one time, around the 'sacramental board' on the Sabbath, twenty-six 'heralds of the cross' bowed together as members of one common brotherhood. Ah! sir, you (Mr. Editor, I mean) would not wonder at our emotions, as we stood at that rustic altar, and gazed at the scene!"[151] Mrs. Lovejoy reported that approximately one thousand persons were in attendance at this camp meeting. Her description of the response of these Kansans to the meeting included the following:

We think there is far greater excitability among our Western brethren than New Englanders, who are bred in a clime near the frigid zone. For instance, when the Holy Ghost came down upon our tent's company, and rested upon each "like a tongue of fire," some of the Western brethren and sisters were pressing through the crowd, shaking hands with each other; (as preachers and people almost invariably do when God blesses them) others were prostrate, slapping their hands and shouting in ecstacies, whilst we Yankees could only weep and adore the great mercy of Christ risen and exalted. At another time, when a sister was telling the assembly of the wonderous love of Jesus to the fallen race, one who has been an official member in the West, strided back and forth in front of the altar, shouting every breath, and finally ended this singular exercise by jumping up and down, and shouting till the exhortation concluded. Now we do not mention these matters in a condemnatory spirit by any means, but as being somewhat new to us, having never seen things on this wise in New England. The good effects of this meeting we fully believe will be seen and felt for years to come in Kansas. . . ."[152]

In 1862 Mrs. Lovejoy again reported a great camp meeting at Centropolis in Franklin county. The meeting was scheduled to end after one week, but "such was the wonderful display of the power of God that it commenced again." Mrs. Lovejoy estimated that "from fifty to seventy found peace in believing."[153] While Mrs. Lovejoy reported on large camp meetings, these gatherings were often of more modest proportions. In September, 1861, the

150. Robinson, *Kansas; Its Interior and Exterior Life*, pp. 85, 86.
151. "Letters of Julia Louisa Lovejoy," *loc. cit.*, v. 15 (November, 1947), p. 396.
152. *Ibid.*, pp. 398, 399.
153. *Ibid.*, v. 16 (May, 1948), pp. 185, 186.

Rev. M. J. Miller, Leavenworth, reported on two camp meetings at Holton and Lawrence Mission. Each meeting had four tents, 30 members, five preachers with an average attendance of 100. The meeting at Holton had included a subscription for missions which produced $65.00, a steer, and half a cow.[154]

The Rev. James Shaw, a presiding elder in the Methodist church, stated that in 1861 he was criticized as "a little cold hearted, and formal," and it was "feared that [he] was attempting to 'steady the ark.'" He has described his attempt to promote moderation at a camp meeting when he stated that "the next day I talked with some of them about properly directing our efforts; that while we labored to get our own souls filled with love, joy and fire, we should not hoist the safety valve and let off steam in the open air, but with warm hearts, and burning zeal, we should work for the Master, and devote our renewed energies, lovingly, to bring sinners to the Saviour."[155]

The camp meeting served many purposes on the frontier. Prof. C. B. Goodykoontz has pointed out that "among a people forced to live in more or less isolation these were important social as well as religious gatherings."[156] These occasions afforded opportunities for meeting old friends and making new ones. A sense of group solidarity among Christians was promoted, and this in turn produced real encouragement. In an era before conventions, the camp meeting afforded many of the resources usually associated with such activity. However, the motivation was definitely a religious one; the camp meetings furnished significant support for frontier Christianity.

While there were many obstacles to effective church work in Kansas, they were matched by the enthusiasm and dedication of the pioneer missionary. Adaptation to frontier conditions was essential for survival, but there was no hesitancy in making the adjustments. The ministers from established churches found many great contrasts. Instead of a well-furnished church building, the Kansas scene provided facilities which only by imaginative thought could be transformed into places of worship. In October, 1856, the Rev. Lewis Bodwell described his first service at Topeka: "The place of meeting, Constitution Hall (from which, last July, Col. Sumner, by government order and with U. S. troops, ejected the 'free state legislature'), a rough, unplastered room, board and slab

---

154. Rev. M. J. Miller to *Christliche Botschafter*, September 21, 1861, quoted in Platz, *op. cit.*, p. 36.
155. Shaw, *op. cit.*, p. 119.
156. Goodykoontz, *op. cit.*, p. 32.

seats, a shaky cottonwood table, and an audience of about twenty-five. The Master present to help, his friends to hear and afterward warmhearted greetings and what would I more?"[157] In December, 1857, Bodwell wrote that "we are obliged to preach in the open air, in ball-rooms & bar rooms & kitchens, as we may and where we may. Nor would we by any means neglect such places & opportunities; but you can well understand why we cannot do all our work thus and hope to do it well."[158]

In the winter of 1857 the Rev. Richard Cordley reported from Lawrence that the building of a church was well under way. The project had to be interrupted for lack of funds, but again it was resumed. The windows had no casings, no plaster was upon the walls or ceilings, the only entrance being a board left so that it would swing. Cordley pointed out that "the winter winds used to laugh at these loose boards, and run in through the cracks, and cool the ardor of the congregation. The roof was said to be a good one, but in spite of this the snow would sift through and powder our heads as we worshiped. The seats were rough benches, and along the sides by the wall a row of seats had been made by placing boards on nail kegs and boxes." The room was heated by two big stoves which were unable to accomplish the objective on winter days. When it was especially cold, the congregation huddled around the stoves, and the pulpit was moved to them.[159]

However, there were to be other days when modest, but comfortable houses of worship dotted the Kansas landscape as faithful groups of worshippers came to hear the Gospel message, share in the sacraments, witness happy marriage ceremonies, and say farewell to those near and dear in sad funeral services. The frontier church was a place of consolation and hope in a drab and difficult world. The church was planted, a symbol of growing stability on a fluid frontier.[160]

---

157. Rev. Lewis Bodwell, "Sixty Days Home Missionary Work," *The Kansas Telephone*, Manhattan, v. 2 (August, 1881), p. 1. Bodwell referred to the dispersal of the Topeka legislature by Col. Edwin V. Sumner. It was on that occasion that William A. Phillips is reported to have greeted Sumner with these words: "Colonel, you have robbed Oliver Cromwell of his laurels."—Abby Huntington Ware, "Dispersion of the Territorial Legislature of 1856," *The Kansas Historical Collections*, v. 9 (1905-1906), p. 545.

158. Rev. Lewis Bodwell to the A. H. M. S., Topeka, December 14, 1857.

159. Cordley, *Pioneer Days in Kansas*, pp. 74, 75. It took several years before the Kansas church buildings could meet the specifications as outlined in 1852 on various points including the following: "Pews.—The convenience and comfort, and therefore the real usefulness of a house of worship, are dependent, in no small degree, upon the arrangement of the pews. Much attention is necessary in order to secure, for instance, such a slope for the backs of the pews as will make them consistent with the proper ease of the sitter."—Central committee appointed by the Annual Congregational Convention, October, 1852, *A Book of Plans for Churches and Parsonages* (New York, 1853), p. 25.

160. A fine study of early Kansas churches is found in E. R. Dezurko, "Early Kansas Churches," *Kansas State College Bulletin*, Manhattan, v. 33 (April, 1949). This publication includes reproductions of photographs and prints, floor plans, and other illustrative material. There are striking resemblances between these early churches and the volume, *A Book of Plans for Churches and Parsonages*, referred to in Footnote 159.

The contemporary sources indicate that various denominations were determined to remain on the Kansas frontier even if progress was slow. In 1858 the East Kansas Association of Baptists reported conditions "showing great destitution, but yet great encouragement to put in the sickle and reap an abundant harvest." There was a disposition to hear the Gospel, and in some places there were evident tokens of the awakening and converting power of the Holy Spirit.[161] In 1860 the association reported that at Atchison there was fine progress, with "her number more than doubled"; at Wathena, "a season of spiritual refreshing"; at Troy, "an abundant outpouring of the spirit"; at Mount Pleasant, "an extensive revival of religion"; at Leavenworth, "clouds of discouragement have been dissipated and the clear sunlight of God's presence has been renewed to them."[162] However, the reports were not so favorable during the sessions of the Baptists at Atchison in September, 1863. The church at Atchison was "in need of the reviving influence of God's spirit." The spiritual apathy was a part of the pattern of those times. Wathena reported no special gains but they had "reason to believe that God's spirit had been with them." The Tabernacle church had "nothing especially cheering to report, but rejoice that they are still a branch of the living vine and have communion with their spiritual fountain."[163]

In November, 1862, after five years in Kansas, the Rev. R. D. Parker reported from Wyandotte that "they have been years of some trial and labor; but as I look back upon them I see that they have been filled with blessing." Parker felt that he "should shrink from exchanging my field with any of my classmates in the East, although some of them have attained high positions. My hands and my heart are full of labor and what more can I ask."[164]

The Rev. Richard Cordley described his response to developments in December, 1862, after completing five years in Kansas when he wrote that "there have been many things discouraging, but more to cheer. The country has not developed as rapidly as we expected then. 'War, pestilence, and famine' have reduced the expectations of former years, but on the whole I cannot but feel grateful for the progress we have made." He continued by pointing out that when he arrived in Lawrence, the membership of the First

161. *Minutes of the First Meeting of the East Kansas Association of Baptists, October 1, 1858*, p. 5.
162. *Minutes of the Third Annual Meeting of the East Kansas Association of Baptists, Commencing Aug. 31, 1860*, pp. 4, 5.
163. *Minutes of the Sixth Annual Meeting of the East Kansas Baptist Association, Atchison, September 25, 26, 1863*, p. 5.
164. Rev. R. D. Parker to the A. H. M. S., Wyandotte, November 10, 1862.

Congregational church in Lawrence was 27; in 1862, it was 83. His first service had included 60 persons, now there were five times that many at the services.[165]

A variety of motives fashioned the pattern of missionary activity in Kansas. One dominant motive in the history of American home missions has been described as "the natural desire of the religious men to perpetuate in the West the ideals, traditions, and civilization of the East." [166] This desire is reflected clearly in the Kansas scene. In October, 1854, Thomas H. Webb, secretary of the New England Emigrant Aid Company, described this motive vividly in the context of his recommendation as to the nature of the proposed settlement of Kansas:

> My idea has always been, that it was not well to concentrate our people in one locality. It is desirable that New England principles and New England influences should pervade the whole Territory; this can only be effected by wise foresight and judicious management. Dot Kansas with New England settlements, and no matter how heterogeneous the great living mass which flows into the Territory may be, it will all eventually be moulded into a symmetrical form, and the benefits resulting therefrom will be such that generations yet to come will bless the memory of those thro' whose efforts the boon of freedom, knowledge and pure & undefiled religion were secured for them and their posterity.[167]

When Congregational ministers and delegates assembled at Topeka on April 25, 1857, to promote the activity of the General Association of Congregational Ministers and Churches in Kansas organized in August, 1855, the group declared in their address to other Congregational bodies that "it shall be our aim . . . to transplant the principles and institutions of the Puritans to these fertile plains, and to lay foundations which shall be an honor to us, when in the grave, and a blessing to all coming generations." [168] One way of seeking to transmit the principles of New England was through education. The same conference which affirmed the desire "to transplant the principles and institutions of the Puritans" to Kansas also resolved "that a Committee of five be raised to obtain information in regard to the location of a College, under the patron-

165. Rev. Richard Cordley to the A. H. M. S., Lawrence, December 16, 1862.
166. Billington, *loc. cit.*, p. 362.
167. Dr. Thomas H. Webb to S. C. Pomeroy, October 30, 1854, "Webb Letter Books," quoted in Edgar Langsdorf, "S. C. Pomeroy and the New England Emigrant Aid Company, 1854-1858," *The Kansas Historical Quarterly*, v. 7 (August, 1938), p. 233. The company was instrumental in founding and assisting in founding Lawrence, Osawatomie, Manhattan, Wabaunsee, Hampden (Burlington) and to a lesser extent, Topeka, as well as several smaller communities.—Samuel A. Johnson, "The Emigrant Aid Company in Kansas," *ibid.*, v. 1 (November, 1932), pp. 432-434.
168. *Minutes of the General Association of Congregational Ministers and Churches in Kansas, Topeka, April 25-27, 1857* (Ogden, K. T.), p. 12. A discussion of Congregationalism and Puritanism is found in Correll, *op. cit.*, pp. 55, 56.

age of this body, and, if they deem it expedient, to secure such a location."[169] A committee was appointed and the movement launched which resulted in the establishment of Lincoln College, which furnished the origin for present Washburn University of Topeka, a municipal institution.[170] The Puritan tradition was undoubtedly a valuable point of reference and a strong source of support for the New England Congregationalists who were settling in a wilderness amidst great privation to bring the Christian gospel. While the motivation had deep historic roots, the task of planting a Puritan civilization in the Plains area was a herculean one which was not literally possible, although the vestiges of the attempt have furnished enough evidence in some quarters to create the tradition that the task was in large measure accomplished.

The census of 1860 showed that Kansas had a population of 107,206 and that only 4,208 were born in the New England states. The neighboring state of Missouri, with its earlier origin and longer history, had 8,013 natives of New England in the same census.[171] While many residents of Kansas territory were from Ohio, Indiana, and Illinois, a sizeable number of whom had antecedents in New England, the sheer force of numbers as well as frontier conditions made the odds too heavy for the achievement of the objective as declared by the General Association of Congregational Ministers and Churches.[172] During the period 1854 to 1865, 51 Congregational ministers came to serve in Kansas, 36 arriving before the end of 1860. The number in the ministerium of the Congregational church in Kansas was 30 in 1865. Forty-one congregations were established between 1854 and 1865.[173] While this number represents a substantial effort at missionary enterprise, it was scarcely adequate for the achievement of establishing New England Congregationalism in the large expanse of Kansas territory. However,

169. *Minutes of the General Association of Congregational Ministers and Churches in Kansas, Topeka, April 25-27, 1857*, p. 6.

170. These interesting developments are portrayed in Russell K. Hickman, "Lincoln College, Forerunner of Washburn Municipal University," *The Kansas Historical Quarterly*, v. 18 (February, 1950), pp. 20-54; (May, 1950), pp. 164-204.

171. *Population in the United States in 1860, Eighth Census* (Washington, D. C., 1864), p. 166, 301.

172. Samuel A. Johnson states that while it is difficult to know how many people came to Kansas under the auspices of the Emigrant Aid Company, he believes that it was less than 2,000 and a third of them may have returned home. The parties were small and infrequent after June, 1855. He contends that "one must agree with those who have published independent studies of the subject that, numerically speaking, the emigrant aid movement was at best a minor factor in the peopling of Kansas."—Johnson, "The Emigrant Aid Company," *loc. cit.*, pp. 431, 432.

173. Correll, *op. cit.*, pp. 185-202. The statistics for 1865 are found in *The Congregational Record*, Lawrence, v. 7 (June, 1865), appendix following p. 18. A comprehensive description of early Congregationalism in Kansas is found in the article by the Rev. Richard Cordley, "Congregationalism in Kansas," *The Congregational Quarterly*, Boston, v. 18 (new series, v. 8), July, 1876, pp. 367-386.

the idealism of these individuals should not be discounted; their influence was greater than the numbers indicate.[174]

The Congregationalists were not unique among Kansas Protestant groups in recognizing the role of education in promoting the Christian witness and in improving the cultural level of the people. When the delegates to the first Kansas and Nebraska Annual Conference of the Methodist Episcopal Church met in Lawrence on October 23, 1856, the committee on education presented a report which resulted in action to take steps to secure "such lands for sites of seminaries or universities, and their building and endowment by legislative action and otherwise." On February 9, 1859, the Kansas territorial legislature granted a charter for Baker University, which has had a continuous history since its founding.[175] The Methodists in 1858 received a charter for Bluemont Central College, Manhattan, the forerunner of Kansas State University.[176] On December 19, 1857, the Presbyterians organized Highland University at Highland, which has a continuous history in present Highland College. Faith in the venture was expressed in the resolution that "a thorough and Christian education is second only to a preached gospel in the world's redemption. . . ."[177] In October, 1858, the East Kansas Association of Baptists resolved "that we cheerfully unite with our Brethren in the Territory in building up a College, in some central locality." Roger Williams University, which became Ottawa University and has a continuous history to the present day, received its charter on February 27, 1860.[178]

When the Primary Convention of the Protestant Episcopalian churches met at Wyandotte August 11-12, 1859, it was observed that "our brethren of other denominations, in Kansas, are fully awake to the state of things, and have already taken advantage of it in a manner creditable to themselves and worthy of imitation."

---

174. The late Carl Becker in his famous essay on Kansas written in 1910 stated that "ideas, sometimes, as well as the star of empire, move westward, and so it happens that Kansas is more Puritan than New England today."—Becker, op. cit., p. 87.

175. *Minutes of the First Session of the Kansas & Nebraska Annual Conference of the Methodist Episcopal Church, Lawrence, K. T., October 23-25, A. D., 1856* (Omaha City, N. T., 1856), p. 6; *Private Laws of the Territory of Kansas, . . . 1858* (Lecompton, 1858), pp. 71-74. The background factors in the founding and development of Baker University are presented in Homer Kingsley Ebright, *The History of Baker University* (Baldwin, 1951).

176. J. T. Willard, "Bluemont Central College, the Forerunner of Kansas State College," *The Kansas Historical Quarterly*, v. 13 (May, 1945), p. 329. An interesting description of the founding of the college is presented in detail by Dr. Willard.—*Ibid.*, pp. 323-357.

177. *The Home and Foreign Record*, v. 9 (March, 1858), p. 74.

178. *Minutes of the First Meeting of the East Kansas Association of Baptists, 1858*, p. 5; *Private Laws of the Territory of Kansas, 1860*, pp. 446-449. The background of these events and later developments are portrayed in B. Smith Haworth, *Ottawa University: Its History and Spirit* (Ottawa, 1957).

The convention endorsed the plans to erect a female seminary at Tecumseh.[179] The Big Springs convention of the Disciples of Christ considered "the propriety of establishing a literary institution for the Christian brotherhood in Kansas." It was resolved to take "initiatory steps" to found a university. Western Christian University was established at Ottumwa, Kan., in the Spring, 1863.[180]

In the four years of Kansas territorial history between 1857 and 1860, 35 acts were passed by the legislature to authorize colleges, universities, and educational associations.[181]

While many motives stimulated missionary activity, the responsibility of Christianizing Kansas territory was the decisive consideration for committed ministers who left the comforts and security of established communities and congregations to suffer the privations of frontier life. It would be unrealistic and inaccurate to minimize this aspect of the situation. In July, 1855, the Rev. Timothy Hill, a well-known Presbyterian minister, declared that "if Christians neglect that Territory, the emissaries of Satan will not; and amidst all the tumult, Oh! that the authoritative voice of God's Law may be heard, commanding men to love one another, and to remember that He will soon call them to give account to Him for their conduct." [182] In August, 1858, the Rev. M. J. Miller identified the role of the church by declaring that "Kansas needs not only a free constitution to liberate her slaves but a free gospel to liberate her sinners." [183] This imperative was taken seriously by many men. Kansas was a great mission field and in the course of events, political factors and the human emotions associated with slavery made the sense of mission increasingly articulate.

A minister's wife, Mrs. Charles Lovejoy, expressed multiple motives in a letter in 1858. She contended that "no temptation would induce Mr. L. to leave Kansas, for this is the spot for him, in preference to all others. Now is a chance for preachers with families to secure to themselves homes in the finest country that lies beneath the sun." After recounting a series of great hardship and deep tragedy, including the fact that "we have seen our heart's idol laid

---

179. *Journals of the Primary Convention of the Diocese of Kansas in A. D. 1859 and of the Annual Conventions Following in A. D. 1860, 1861, 1862, 1863, and 1864 and of the Special Convention in April, 1860*, Protestant Episcopal Church, Kansas Diocese (Lawrence, 1885), pp. 8, 9.

180. Zimmerman, *loc. cit.*, p. 23.

181. *Private Laws of the Territory of Kansas*, 1857, 1858, 1859, 1860.

182. Letter of the Rev. Timothy Hill, July, 1855, in John B. Hill, "Timothy Hill and Western Presbyterianism; A Review of the Life and Letters of a Superintendent of Missions," p. 242. This interesting manuscript is in the Presbyterian Historical Library, Philadelphia, and a copy is in the Kansas State Historical Society library. Hill wished to go to Kansas but his Missouri Presbytery voted against it.

183. Rev. M. J. Miller in the *Evangelical Messenger*, quoted in Platz, *op. cit.*, p. 18.

in her cold, damp grave in Kansas," Mrs. Lovejoy concluded by declaring that "we are glad we came to Kansas, to labor for truth, and justice, and we shall triumph." [184] This was a sincere expression that could be multiplied by many "soldiers of the cross" on the Kansas frontier.

In October, 1856, Bishop George F. Pierce came to Kickapoo to preside at the first assembly of the Kansas Mission Conference of the Methodist Episcopal Church South. His experiences had deepened his appreciation of the frontier preacher and enabled him to recognize the type of individual who should seek to serve there. He asked the important question, "Who will go to Kansas?" and answered it as follows: "We want no steel-clad warriors, but men with 'tongues of fire.' We want no land-hunters, but strangers and pilgrims, who declare plainly that they seek a country, even a heavenly." He declared that the church would seek to provide the necessities of life, but "other expenses may be charged to Him who pledges 'everlasting life' in the world to come." The bishop was certain that "it is a little nearer to heaven from the field of self-denying labor than from the home of self-indulgent rest. And sure I am, the prairie grass will weave sweeter memorials over your lonely grave, than all the monuments art can fashion, or affection buy. In the city cemetery or the country churchyard, human friends may come to weep, but above the tombs of the pioneer preacher, the angels of God will encamp." [185]

184. "Letters of Julia Louisa Lovejoy, 1856-1864," *loc. cit.*, v. 15 (August, 1947), p. 819.
185. George F. Pierce, *Incidents of Western Travel* (Nashville, 1857), p. 182; Smith, *op. cit.*, p. 291.

The Centennial of Lincoln's Visit to Kansas

I. INTRODUCTION

THE visit of Abraham Lincoln to northeast Kansas 100 years ago was re-enacted December 5, 1959, as a preliminary to the celebration of the state centennial in 1961. Although Lincoln spent seven days (November 30-December 7) on his Kansas speaking tour of 1859, the 1959 re-enactment was accomplished in several hours by motor car.

Commemoration of the Lincoln tour, under the sponsorship of the Kansas Centennial Commission and the State Historical Society, was proposed by Fred W. Brinkerhoff, editor of the Pittsburg *Headlight* and *Sun,* a director of the commission and former president of the Society. Rolla Clymer, editor of the El Dorado *Times,* also a director of the commission and former president of the Society, was cast in the role of the Illinois statesman. Marshall Gardiner of Leavenworth, Al Bennett of Atchison, and C. C. Calnan of Troy, assisted by other citizens and officials, planned the programs and parades along the way.

The caravan traveled from St. Joseph, Mo., through Elwood to Troy, Atchison, and Leavenworth. Stops for speeches were made at the latter three cities—from steps of the courthouses in Troy and Atchison, and from a platform in a downtown street at Leavenworth, near the site of old Stockton hall where Lincoln gave two of his speeches. The weather was cold in 1959, but not as cold as when Lincoln huddled under a buffalo robe in an open buggy 100 years earlier. This buggy, used by Lincoln on part of his Kansas journey, is now the property of the Fort Leavenworth museum and was transported on a truck-drawn trailer. The 1959 Lincoln made entrances into some of the towns in this authentic but now horseless carriage.

Clymer's talks included words and phrases of the Lincoln speeches as reported in contemporary newspapers and in Roy P. Basler's *Collected Works of Abraham Lincoln* (Rutgers University Press, 1953). With these, Clymer reconstructed the political scene of 1859 and gave the essence of what Lincoln, who the next year was to announce himself a candidate and to win the Presidency, may have said in several long speeches in these Kansas cities.

II. Rolla Clymer's 1959 Presentation of Lincoln's Speeches in Kansas

TROY

This is the first time I have set foot on Kansas soil, and I am glad to be here.

It is possible that you people of Kansas have local questions with regard to Railroads, Land Grants and internal improvements—which are matters of deeper interest to you than the questions arising out of national politics. Of these I know nothing, and can say nothing.

You have, however, just adopted a state constitution and it is probable that, under that Constitution, you will soon cease your territorial existence and come forward to take your place in the brotherhood of states, and act your part as a member of the confederation.

Kansas will be free, but the same questions aroused here in regard to freedom or slavery will arise with regard to other territories—and Kansas will have to take a stand in deciding them.

People often ask: "Why make such a fuss about a few Negroes?" I answer the question by asking, what will you do to dispose of this question? The slaves constitute one-seventh of our entire population. Wherever there is an element of this magnitude in government, it will be talked about.

The general feeling in regard to slavery has changed entirely since the early days of the Republic. You may examine the debates under the Confederation, in the convention that framed the constitution, and in the first session of Congress—and you will not find a single man saying Slavery is a good thing. They all believed it was an evil.

They made the Northwest Territory—the only territory then belonging to the government—forever Free. They prohibited the African slave trade. Having thus prevented its extension and cut off the supply, the Fathers of the Republic believed that Slavery must soon disappear.

There are only three clauses in the Constitution which refer to Slavery, and in neither of them is the word Slave or Slavery mentioned. The word is not used in the clause prohibiting the African slave trade; it is not used in the clause which makes Slaves a basis of representation; it is not used in the clause requiring the return of fugitive Slaves.

And yet in all the debates in the Convention the question was discussed and Slaves and Slavery talked about. Now why was this word kept out of this instrument and so carefully kept that a European, be he ever so intelligent, if not familiar with our institutions, might read the Constitution over and over again and never learn that Slavery existed in the United States?

The reason is this: The Framers of the Organic Law believed that the Constitution would outlast Slavery, and they did not want a word there to tell future generations that Slavery had ever been legalized in America.

Tomorrow John Brown will be hanged for treason in Virginia. We are forced to believe that the attack of Brown on Harpers Ferry was wrong for two reasons: It was a violation of law; and it was, as all such attacks must be, futile as far as any effect it might have on the extinction of a great evil.

We have provided a means for the expression of our belief in regard to slavery—and that is through the ballot box—the peaceful method provided by the Constitution. John Brown has shown great courage, rare unselfishness, as even Governor Wise testifies. But no man, North or South, can approve of violence or crime.

And now I thank you, and extend the wish that all of you go to your own state election on Tuesday and vote as becomes the Free Men of Kansas.

ATCHISON

You are, as yet, the people of a territory, but you probably soon will be the people of a state of the union.

Then you will be in possession of new privileges—and new duties will be upon you. You will have to bear a part in all that appertains to the administration of the national government.

That government, from the beginning, has had, has now, and must continue to have a policy in relation to domestic slavery. It cannot, if it would, be without a policy upon that subject.

And that policy must, of necessity, take one of two directions. It must deal with the institution as being wrong, or not being wrong.

The nationality of Freedom is as old as the government itself. In all states where slavery did not exist by municipal law, or was not made a distinctive feature of the articles of cession, Freedom was established.

The Fathers opposed interfering with slavery where it existed, or allowing it to encompass the national domain. That is alike my doctrine, and the doctrine of the Republican party.

We hear much today about the doctrine of Popular Sovereignty. If you carry out that doctrine to its full meaning, it would renew the African slave trade.

Who can show that one people have a better right to carry slaves to where they never have been, than another people to buy slaves wherever they please, even in Africa?

The advocates of Popular Sovereignty by their efforts to brutalize the Negro in the public mind—denying him any share in the Declaration of Independence, and comparing him to the crocodile—are beyond what avowed pro-slavery men ever do. These people do as much, or more, as the pro-slavery men toward making the institution national and perpetual.

Many of these Popular Sovereignty advocates say they are "as much opposed to slavery as anyone," but they never seem to find any time or place to oppose it.

In their view, it must not be opposed to politics, because that is agitation; nor in the pulpit, because that is religion; nor in the Free States because it is not there; nor in the slave states because it is there.

These gentleman are never offended by hearing slavery supported in any of these places. Still, they are "as much opposed to slavery as anybody." One would suppose that it would exactly suit them if the people of the slave states themselves would adopt emancipation.

But when Frank Blair tried this last year in Missouri, and was beaten, everyone of them threw up his hat and shouted, "Hurrah for Democracy."

Your territory has had a marked history. No territory has ever had such a history. There has been strife and bloodshed here. Both parties have been guilty of outrages.

Whatever the relative guilt of the parties, one fact is certain—that there has been loss of life, destruction of property and material interests have been retarded.

Can anyone say this has been desirable?

There is a peaceful way of settling these questions—the way adopted by government until a recent period. The bloody code has grown out of the new policy in regard to the government of territories.

We have a means provided for the expression of our belief in regard to slavery—through the ballot box—as the peaceful method provided by the constitution.

You who object to Republicans say you are for the Union, and you greatly fear the success of the Republicans would destroy the Union. Why?

Do the Republicans declare against the Union? Nothing like it. Your own statement is that if the Black Republicans elect a president, you won't stand it. You will break up the Union.

That will be your act, not ours. To justify it, you must show that our policy gives you just cause for such desperate action. Can you do that?

When you attempt it, you will find that our policy is exactly the policy of the men who made the Union. Nothing more and nothing less.

While you elect a president, we submit—neither breaking nor attempting to break up the Union. If we shall constitutionally elect a president, it will be our duty to see that you submit.

Old John Brown has just been executed for treason against a state. We cannot object, even though he agreed with us in thinking slavery wrong. That cannot excuse violence, bloodshed and treason. It could avail him nothing that he might think himself right.

So, if we constitutionally elect a President, and therefore you undertake to destroy the Union, it will be our duty to deal with you as John Brown has been dealt with.

We shall try to do our duty.

We hope and believe that in no section will a majority so act as to render such extreme measures necessary.

Ladies and gentlemen, I appeal to you all—opponents as well as friends—to think soberly and maturely on all these questions, and never fail to cast your vote.

LEAVENWORTH

You are, as yet, the people of a territory, but you probably will soon be the people of a state of the Union. Then you will be in possession of new privileges, and new duties will be upon you.

You will have to bear a part in all that pertains to the administration of the National government. That government, from the beginning, has had, has now, and must continue to have a policy in relation to domestic slavery.

It cannot, if it would, be without a policy on that subject. And that policy must, of necessity, take one of two directions. It must deal with the institution as being wrong, or not being wrong.

The early action of the general government upon the question—in relation to the foreign slave trade, the basis of federal representation, the prohibition of slavery in the federal territories, and the Fugitives slave clause in the Constitution, was based upon the idea of slavery being wrong. The government tolerated slavery so far, and only so far, as the necessity of its actual presence required.

The policy of the Kansas-Nebraska act, about which so much has been said, was based on the opposite idea—that is, the idea that slavery is not wrong.

You, the people of Kansas, furnish the example of the first application of this new policy. At the end of about five years, after having almost continual struggles, fire and bloodshed, over this very question, and after having framed several state constitutions, you have at last secured a Free-State constitution, under which you will probably be admitted into the Union.

At the end of all this difficulty, you have attained what we in the old Northwest territory attained without any difficulty at all. Compare, or rather contrast, the actual working of the new policy with that of the old, and say whether, after all, the old way—the way adopted by Washington and his compeers—was not the better way.

This new policy has proved false to all its promises—namely, to end slavery agitation, and to afford greater control of their affairs to the people of the territories.

You have already had, I think, five governors, and yet, although their doings in their respective days, were of some little interest to you, it is doubtful whether you now even remember the names of half of them.

They are all gone (all but the last) leaving without a trace upon your soil, or having done a single act which can, in the least degree, help or hurt you— in all the indefinite future before you. This is the size of the governor question.

Now, how is it with the slavery question? If your first settlers had so far decided in favor of slavery, as to have got 5,000 slaves planted on your soil, you could, by no moral possibility, have adopted a Free-State constitution.

Their owners would be influential men whose property it would be impossible to destroy. If you freed the slaves, you would not know what to do with them. You would not wish to keep them as underlings, and could not elevate them to social and political equality.

You could not send them away. Neither the slave states nor the free states would let you send them there. All of the rest of your property would not pay for sending them to Liberia. You could more easily have disposed of not five, but five hundred governors.

Which is the greater—this or the governor question? Which could more safely be entrusted to the first few people to settle a territory?

The Fathers did not seek to interfere with slavery where it existed, but to prevent its extension. This is the policy of the Republican party of today.

We must not disturb slavery in the states where it exists, because the Constitution and the peace of the country both forbid us. But we must, by a national policy, prevent the spread of slavery into the new states, or free states, because the Constitution does not forbid us, and the general welfare does require the prevention.

We must prevent these things being done either by Congress or the courts. The people—the people—are the rightful masters of both Congress and the courts—not to overthrow the Constitution, but to overthrow the men who pervert it.

Senator Douglas has assured us of a great line, a line ordained of God—a line on one side of which slave labor alone could be employed, and on the other only free labor could be utilized.

It may be that the Missouri river was the line suggested by Douglas. If the line was ordained of God, it ought to be plain and palpable—though I have never been able to put my finger on it.

The attempt to identify the Republican party with the John Brown business is simply an electioneering dodge. I have yet to find the first Republican who endorsed Brown's proposed insurrection. If there was one, I would invite him to step out of the ranks and correct his politics.

It is imperative that the races be kept distinct. Because I do not wish to hold a Negro woman as a slave, it does not follow that I want her for a wife. Such flimsy diatribes, as the political arguments over "amalgamation," have been perpetrated by the Democracy to divert the public mind from the real issue—the extension or nonextension of slavery—its localization or nationalization.

The aims and principles of the Republican party harmonize with the teachings of those by whom the Government was founded, and their predominance is essential to the proper development of the country, to its progress and glory, to the salvation of the Union and the perpetuity of Free Institutions.

Bypaths of Kansas History

An Early Day Beatnik

From *The Kansas News*, Emporia, January 8, 1859.

Cool.—A gentleman entered our office a few days since, and stated that he would like to subscribe for the paper for *forty days*, provided we would change the day of publication and "prent his'n on Monday," and also provided he could pay his subscription in instalments of ten cents at a time, as he did not wish to risk a large amount of cash in our hands. We thought that "rather cool."

P. S. Since writing the above, we found out that the individual alluded to, wanted to pay his subscription in frozen pumpkins.

"Home, Sweet Home"

From the Topeka *Tribune*, quoted in the Emporia *News*, August 20, 1859.

Mr. Ingham, of Topeka, and several others returned from a trip to the Gold Mines on Saturday evening last. Mr. Ingham brought a few specimens of the metal back, but is of [the] opinion that the mines will not pay as well as staying at home with one's wife, when the sweets and comforts of home are necessary to the enjoyment of married men, and we dare say, the returned husband will be duly appreciated by an anxious and affectionate wife.

Too Much Freedom With Religion

From *The Weekly Free Press*, Atchison, February 15, 1868.

A man was expelled from the Methodist church at Junction City the other day for having obtained admission on forged papers.

Frozen Rivers

From the Wyandott *Herald*, February 29, 1872.

On the 5th day of November the Kansas river froze over at this point [present Kansas City], and on the 22d of the same month the Missouri was closed. Both rivers remained in this condition until Friday last, the 23d day of February. The former river remaining closed for the period of 110 days, and the latter for the period of 93 days; being a much longer period of time for the Ice King to hold his sway than ever before since the settlement of the country by the whites.

Exit the Buffalo

From the *Wabaunsee County News*, Alma, November 20, 1872.

South of the Arkansas river 2,000 men are engaged in shooting buffalo for their hides alone.

Kansas History as Published in the Press

"Kansas City's Hannibal Bridge: Western Town-booming and Eastern Capital," by Charles N. Glabb, comprised the March, 1959, number of *The Trail Guide*, Independence, Mo., published by the Kansas City posse of the Westerners.

Elizabeth Barnes' column, "Historic Johnson County," has continued to appear regularly in the *Johnson County Herald*, Overland Park. Among subjects covered during the past year were: "Corinth Community—the Church," March 5, 1959; "Corinth Community—the Cemetery," March 12; baseball in the Kansas City area, March 19, 26; "Santa Fe Trade Based in N. E. Johnson County," April 2, 16, 23, 30, May 7; "Corinth Community School," May 14; biographical sketch of Thomas C. Porter family, July 2; and "Story of Oxford and New Santa Fe [Mo.]," August 6, 13, 20.

Dr. B. E. Ebel, Redlands, Calif., a native of Hillsboro, is author of a series of articles on the history of Hillsboro, beginning in the Hillsboro *Star-Journal*, March 5, 1959. Founded in 1879 by John G. Hill, the town was first called Hill City.

Histories of the Greeley Evangelical United Brethren church were published in the Garnett *Review*, March 9, and *Anderson Countian*, April 2, 1959. Organization of the church was completed in June, 1859, and a building erected the following year.

Among historical articles appearing in the Hays *Daily News* in recent months were: "Lawlessness at Ellis 63 Years Ago Led to All-Feminine City Government," by Kittie Dale, March 22, 1959; "Early Tests for Gold and Oil in [Ellis] County Brought Excitement and Disappointment," March 29; "Legend of Old Mulvey Hall at Ellis Grows Five Years After Last Dance," by Kittie Dale, May 10; "Yocemento Once Held Great Promise but Idea of Founders [Cement Plant] Born Too Soon," May 24; "Two Ellis Old Timers [Howard C. Raynesford and August Schutte] Map and Mark Butterfield Overland Despatch Trail," May 31; "Hays City Fourth of July Celebration 81 Years Ago Enlivened by Soldiers," July 3; "Bat Masterson Favored City Over Prairie in Later Years," September 6; "Harper's Magazine Files Yield Account of Old Fort Hays' Trials With Indians," November 1.

McPherson county's first courthouse, built around 1870, was the subject of an article in the Lindsborg *News-Record*, March 30,

1959. On June 15 the *News-Record* printed a history of the Holmberg-Johnson Blacksmith and Wagon Shop of Lindsborg. The shop was built in 1874.

"The Pony Express, Heroic Effort—Tragic End," by Raymond W. Settle, appeared in the April, 1959, issue of the *Utah Historical Quarterly*, Salt Lake City.

In observance of the 50th anniversary of the dedication of the present building of the Council Grove Methodist church, the Council Grove *Republican* published a brief history of the church, April 1, 1959. The congregation's history goes back to 1855 when the Methodist Church, South, organized a church in Council Grove.

On April 1, 1959, the El Dorado *Times*, published a page-length sketch of the Rogler family of Chase county. The article was written by Austin Showman and first published in the *Weekly Star Farmer*, Kansas City, Mo., August 10, 1955. Charles W. Rogler settled on a tract of land near present Matfield Green in 1859. The tract, now several thousand acres, is presently owned and operated by Henry and Wayne Rogler, son and grandson of Charles. The *Times*, May 30, printed a letter written by Mrs. Pearl B. Harsh, giving a sketch of her father, Henry Brandley, who came to Kansas with Charles Rogler, and likewise, was a Chase county pioneer.

Among articles of a historical nature in the Colby *Press-Tribune* in recent months were: a Thomas county history, by Ernest Snell, April 16, 20, 1959; history of Colby and the Cooper Hotel, Colby, May 21; and an article on the Colby Christian church, August 3.

Histories of the First Baptist church of Oswego appeared in the Oswego *Democrat*, April 24 and May 1, 1959. The church was organized April 28, 1869.

Mary Liz Montgomery's column, "Incidentally . . .," in the Junction City *Weekly Union*, April 30, 1959, included a history of the Lyon creek community south of Junction City. The first settlers in the area arrived in 1856. The Lyona Methodist church was organized April 10, 1859. A sketch of the church appeared in the Abilene *Reflector-Chronicle*, April 16.

"Cowboys Had Own Paper," by Mary Einsel, a history of *The Kansas Cowboy*, Dodge City, was printed in the Hutchinson *News*, May 3, 1959. Don Kendall reviewed central Kansas history and noted towns celebrating anniversaries in an article published in the *News*, May 31.

Ninety-year-old Mrs. H. W. Todd, Independence, was the subject of a biographical sketch by Wilma Schweitzer in the Independence *Daily Reporter*, May 3, 1959. On May 10 the *Reporter* published an article, by Ed Guilinger, on Mount Hope Cemetery, of Independence, and its sexton, C. R. Hibbens. A short sketch, by Guilinger, of the old Wilson county courthouse, built in 1886, was printed May 31. An article by Lily B. Rozar on the Dalton gang appeared in the November 22 issue.

Included in the May 13, 1959, issue of the Concordia *Blade-Empire* was a three-page history of the Sisters of St. Joseph in Concordia. The Sisters arrived in Concordia and established a school in 1884.

One hundred years ago, through the efforts of Lt. J. E. B. Stuart of Fort Riley, the Episcopal Church of the Covenant in Junction City was built, according to a history of the church by Kent Stuart in the Pittsburg *Sun*, May 21, and the Junction City *Weekly Union*, May 28, 1959.

The *Southwest Daily Times*, Liberal, published a history of the city's library in the issue of May 23, 1959. The library was started in 1903 with the establishment of a reading room. The present building, commenced in 1953, was recently completed with the addition of two new wings.

Early history of the military post of Fort Scott was briefly sketched in the Fort Scott *Tribune*, May 30, 1959. A section devoted to the history of the Fort Scott area was published in the *Tribune*, September 4. Of particular interest were articles and pictures of the Fort Blair blockhouse, built in 1862-1863, which has been restored and was rededicated September 7.

A history of the Grandview Methodist church, near Arkansas City, was printed in the Arkansas City *Daily Traveler*, June 3, 1959. The original church building was dedicated June 13, 1909.

A history of Earlton, Neosho county, by Emma Barnes Frazier, was printed in the Thayer *News* and the St. Paul *Journal*, June 4, 1959.

On June 6, 1959, the Clay Center *Dispatch* began publication of the diary of Thomas J. Ingham in series form. The diary describes Ingham's journey from Pennsylvania to Clay county in 1859.

The German Evangelical Lutheran Zion church of Junction City was organized June 9, 1884, according to a history of the church, now called the Zion United Church of Christ, in the Junction City *Weekly Union,* June 11, 1959.

On June 11, 1959, the Mullinville *News* began publication of a series of articles on the history of Mullinville by Mrs. Marilla Alford Blau. The town was started in 1884 by Alfred A. Mullin.

A history of the Americus United Presbyterian church appeared in the Emporia *Gazette,* June 18, and in the Emporia *Weekly Gazette,* July 2, 1959. The congregation was organized March 15, 1859, by the Rev. J. N. Smith.

"A Half Century at Hicks Chapel Church," a history of the Hicks Chapel Methodist church, Cowley county, by Mrs. Dwight Mosier, was published in three parts in the Cedar Vale *Messenger,* June 18, 25, and July 2, 1959.

The Hanover *News,* June 19, 1959, printed a history of the Horseshoe Farmers Band of near Hanover. The band was organized in 1909 with 15 members.

The Iola *Register,* June 25, 1959, printed a history of the Carlyle Presbyterian church in observance of the church's 100th anniversary. A Sunday School was started in 1858 and on June 27, 1859, the church was organized.

In 1889 the Burns German Methodist church, now known as the Ebenezer church, southwest of Burns, was organized. A three-column history of the church was published in the Burns *News,* July 3, 1959.

The Topeka *Capital-Journal,* July 5, 1959, printed an article by Lucille T. Kohler on Mrs. L. D. Whittemore, who "has been called the mother of art at Washburn and in Topeka." Mrs. Whittemore's presentation of "Living Pictures," representing the works of the masters with living persons, in 1913 and 1915, was a feature of the article.

"Early Days in Bucklin . . .," a series by Mrs. F. A. Gresham, began appearing in the Bucklin *Banner,* July 9, 1959. Bucklin's beginning was in 1887 when all the buildings from Colcord and Corbitt were moved to a location on the railroad.

The Attica *Independent* published a 32-page souvenir edition July 9, 1959, in observance of Attica's 75th anniversary. The town's history and anniversary celebration were featured.

"Pioneer Days in Scott County, Kansas" is the title of a history by Mrs. E. W. Vaughn, published serially in the *News Chronicle,*

Scott City, beginning July 9, 1959. Mrs. Vaughn's parents, the N. H. Baileys, homesteaded in Scott county in 1885.

A 24-page jubilee edition was published by *The Clark County Clipper,* Ashland, August 6, 1959, in observance of the 75th anniversaries of Ashland and the *Clipper.*

August 12, 1959, marked the 50th anniversary of the St. Stanislaus parish at Ingalls. A history of the parish appeared in the *Jacksonian,* Cimarron, August 6, 1959. As early as the 1880's priests occasionally visited the area. Mass was offered in the homes until completion of the building in 1909.

Articles by Russ Hyatt in recent issues of the Wichita *Beacon* included: "Historic West Kansas Timepiece Restored to Mark Time at Newton," and "Pioneer Effort to Build Town Recalled in Story of Lake City," August 9, 1959, and "Bohemians on Border [Sumner and Harper Counties] Overlooked by Historians," August 23.

On the occasion of the completion of its 96th year, the *Enterprise-Chronicle,* Burlingame, September 3, 1959, printed a review of the years since its beginning. The newspaper was founded by Marshall M. Murdock as the *Osage County Chronicle.*

"Cigar Factories and Four Papers on Marysville Scene in 1902-03," by Gordon S. Hohn, appeared in the Marysville *Advocate,* September 3, 1959. A history of the Bigelow Methodist church, by Mrs. Chas. Walls, was printed in the *Advocate,* September 10. The church, established in 1887, will soon be a victim of the Tuttle Creek dam reservoir.

On September 3, 1959, the Junction City *Union* published an article by Mrs. Wilber M. Brucker, which included a historical sketch of Fort Riley.

Caney's early history as recalled by Ollie Smith, its senior native citizen, was printed in the Caney *Chronicle,* September 24, 1959. The town celebrated its 90th anniversary in 1959.

Clearwater was incorporated in 1884 but the history of the area goes back to the 1860's, according to a column-length history of the town in the Clearwater *News,* October 1, 1959.

Some of the early history of Fort Larned was reviewed in the *Tiller and Toiler,* Larned, October 22, 1959. The fort was established 100 years ago by Maj. Henry W. Wessells.

Kansas Historical Notes

An Old Abilene Town Company has been formed to construct a replica of early Abilene. Work is well under way with a number of buildings completed. Henry B. Jameson is president of the organization. William A. Guilfoyle is first vice-president; Dorothy Bath, secretary; Charles Stapf, treasurer; and Charles Cruse, Holly Callahan, H. W. Keel, Dale Snider, and Dr. Tracy Conklin, honorary vice-presidents.

Officers of the Finney County Historical Society, elected April 14, 1959, are: C. H. Cleaver, president; A. M. Fleming, first vice-president; Damon Cobb, second vice-president; Claudine Lindner, secretary; and Mrs. Cecil Wristen, treasurer.

Hillsboro observed its 75th anniversary with a celebration June 7-10, 1959. Featured event of the program was a historical pageant entitled "Glimpses of Our Heritage."

"Pageant of the Prairie," was the feature of Coldwater's diamond jubilee celebration, August 29-September 2, 1959. Other events included a parade, union religious service, and chuck-wagon breakfast.

Re-elected as officers of the Chase County Historical Society at the society's annual meeting in Cottonwood Falls, September 5, 1959, were: Charles O. Gaines, president; Paul B. Wood, vice-president; George Dawson, treasurer; and Mrs. Ruth Conner, historian. Whitt Laughridge is the newly elected secretary. The executive committee consists of Mrs. Conner, Mrs. Ida Vinson, Mrs. Helen Austin, Beatrice Hays, Hugh K. Campbell, and R. Z. Blackburn.

L. W. Hubbell was re-elected president of the Hodgeman County Historical Society at a meeting September 10, 1959, in Jetmore. Bert Brumfield was elected vice-president; Nina Lupfer, secretary; and Mrs. Muriel Eichman, treasurer. Directors chosen were: Margaret Raser, Lula Jones, Lida Benge, and J. W. Lang.

On September 13, 1959, the Fort Wallace Memorial Association placed a marker at the site of the massacre of the John German family by Cheyenne Indians in September, 1874, near present Russell Springs. At a meeting in Wallace, November 5, members of the association discussed plans for increased activity in the preservation of western Kansas history, including a new museum to be located near Wallace. E. M. Beougher, Grinnell, is president of the association.

Harold O. Taylor is the new president of the Crawford County Historical Society, elected at the society's annual meeting, in Pittsburg, September 29, 1959. Other officers include: Robert O. Karr, vice-president; Mrs. Ethel Atkinson, secretary; and Mrs. J. W. Black, treasurer. T. E. Davis, Belle Provorse, Vivian Walker, and Mrs. Hugh Friel were named directors. Fred W. Brinkerhoff, Pittsburg publisher, was the principal speaker.

Officers of the Lane County Historical Society, elected at a meeting in Dighton, October 12, 1959, are: Bill Pike, president; Mrs. Roy Hagans, vice-president; Mrs. Joe Hanna, secretary; Mrs. Dale Jewett, treasurer; and Roy Hagans, Mrs. J. E. Mowery, and Walter Herndon, members of the board. Herndon was the retiring president.

New directors of the Allen County Historical Society, elected at the annual meeting, October 13, 1959, in Iola, are: J. Glenn Dickerson, Mrs. Ruth Crowl, and Lillian Johnson. Directors re-elected were: Col. R. L. Thompson, Spencer Gard, Angelo Scott, Mary Ruth Carpenter, and Mary Hankins. Judge Gard is president of the society.

B. H. Oesterreich, Woodbine, was re-elected president, and Mrs. Viola Ehrsam, Enterprise, first vice-president, of the Dickinson County Historical Society at a meeting in the Lyona Methodist church, October 22, 1959. Elmer Sellin, Abilene, was named secretary.

Robert Hanson was elected president of the Cloud County Historical Society at the annual meeting, October 26, 1959, in Concordia. Ernest W. Powell was chosen vice-president; Mrs. Raymond A. Hanson, recording secretary; Mrs. Sid Knapp, membership secretary; Ernest F. Swanson, treasurer; and Dr. Leo Haughey, Robert B. Wilson, Leo Paulsen, George Palmer, and Mrs. Wilfred Trembley, directors. Martin Van De Mark was the retiring president.

The Thomas County Historical Society was organized at a meeting in Colby, November 12, 1959. Carl G. Eddy was elected president of the new society. Other officers are: W. D. Ferguson, vice-president; Jessie Dimmitt, secretary; Bertha Louis, treasurer; and Harry Eicher, Lulu Hutchinson, and Esther Sewell, directors. Ed Beougher, Grinnell, was the principal speaker.

Election of officers was held by the Ottawa County Historical Society in Minneapolis, November 14, 1959. Ray Halberstadt was elected president; A. R. Miller, vice-president; Mrs. Ray Halberstadt, secretary; Mrs. Fred Jagger, treasurer; Mrs. Zella Heald, reporter; and Louis Ballou, Rolla Geisen, and Paul Wilkins, directors.

Abraham Lincoln's Kansas tour of 1859 was re-enacted December 5, 1959, with Rolla Clymer, El Dorado publisher, playing the part of Lincoln. For further information on the 1959 tour and the text of Clymer's talks, *see* pp. 438-443.

For significant accomplishment in the field of preservation, the Chase County Historical Society was presented a citation by the Jackson County (Missouri) Historical Society at the annual dinner of the Jackson county society in Kansas City, Mo., December 8, 1959. The award was presented to the Chase county society for its work in restoring the Chase county courthouse.

Recently elected officers of the Leavenworth County Historical Society are: James E. Fussell, president; Helen Yoakum, first vice-president; Hans Frienmuth, second vice-president; Mrs. Gorman Hunt, secretary; and Col. Ralph B. Stewart, treasurer. Directors of the society are: D. R. Anthony, III, E. Bert Collard, Sr., Ella V. Carroll, Mrs. Carl Behrle, Mrs. Minnie Mae Maier, Julius Waldstein, and A. W. Johnson.

American Airlines has recently published a 47-page booklet entitled *History Below the Jet Trails*, for distribution to passengers traveling between St. Louis and Los Angeles. Written by the Rev. John Francis Bannon, S. J., the booklet tells of those who traveled the route in an earlier day—Indians, soldiers, pioneers, prospectors, traders—and something of the history of the land in the shadow of the jet planes.

A 44-page pamphlet presenting the story of the early life of Fort Hays and Hays City was published in May, 1959, by the Old Fort Hays Historical Association, Inc. Fort Hays, established October 11, 1865, was first called Fort Fletcher.

Travel Memories From America, by Carl Johan Nyvall, originally published in 1876, has been translated and edited by E. Gustav Johnson, and published in a 126-page volume by the Covenant Press, Chicago, in 1959. Nyvall, a Swedish evangelist, visited America in 1875-1876, spending part of the time with his former countrymen in Kansas.

Roy S. Bloss is the author of a 159-page volume entitled *Pony Express—the Great Gamble,* recently published by Howell-North Press, Berkeley, Calif.

They Seek a Country is the title of a 222-page work by David V. Wiebe, printed by the Mennonite Brethren Publishing House, Hillsboro, in 1959. It is the story of the Mennonite migrations and their pioneer settlements, especially those in Kansas.

The Fighting Parson, a 284-page biography of Col. John M. Chivington, by Reginald S. Craig, was published by the Westernlore Press, Los Angeles, in 1959. Chivington is best known for his part in the Sand Creek massacre against the Cheyenne Indians in 1864.

Dale L. Morgan edited, and Fred A. Rosenstock of the Old West Publishing Co., recently published *The Overland Diary of James A. Pritchard From Kentucky to California in 1849.* The 221-page volume also includes a biography of Pritchard by Hugh Pritchard Williamson.

Great Train Robberies of the West, a 310-page work by Eugene B. Block, was published by Coward-McCann, Inc., New York, in 1959.

Errata, Volume XXV

Page 11, lines 19 and 20, A. J. Isaacs should be A. J. Isacks.
Page 113, line 7, Mr. and Mrs. R. L. Kingman should be Mr. and Mrs. R. H. Kingman.

Index to Volume XXV

A

Abbott, Capt. Walter E. 345
Abell, Mrs. George, Clark co. 366
Abilene. See Old Abilene Town Company (1959).
Abilene *Reflector-Chronicle*: article in, noted 446
Ackerman, Theodore, Russell: banker.. 364
Adams, Rev. Charles J.: at Wichita... 91*n*
Agricultural History, Urbana, Ill.: articles in, noted 363
Airplanes: article "U. S. Army and Air Force Wings Over Kansas" 129- 157
334- 360
—at Army airfields in Kansas, World War II (photographs) ...... *facing* 337
—B-17's, B-24's, and B-29's, at Forbes, noted 142, 144
—B-24's, at Liberal 337
—B-25, notes on 139- 141
—B-26, notes on 137, 140
—B-29, groups trained at Pratt... 346, 347
— —personnel trained at Great Bend 150- 153
— —photograph of Super Fortresses .... *facing* 128
— —units at Smoky Hill, history of 347, 348
—B-47, jet bomber crews trained at Wichita 340
—Douglas C-54 (photograph). *facing* 337
—helicopters at Marshall Air Force Base 345
—training planes (photograph), *facing* 337
—Vultee BT-13 (photograph)... *facing* 337
—World War I types, note on 342
Aitchison, Robert T., Wichita, 117, 121, 123
Allen, Frank: donor 116
Allen, Otis, Shawnee co. 127
Allen County Historical Society: 1959 meeting, notes on 368, 451
Allyn, Mrs. C. Fannie: at Fort Scott.. 402
Alma *Signal-Enterprise*: articles in, noted 252
Altman, Capt. James E.: at Walker Field 357
Amaranth: discussed 269
American Airlines: booklet published by, noted 452
American Baptist Home Mission Society, 411
American Bible Society: S. Y. Lum an agent for 40
American Home Missionary Society, New York. 110, 323, 415, 416, 418- 420
—Kansas efforts 1854-1858 (the Rev. S. Y. Lum's letters).... 39-67, 172- 196
—notes on 40, 41*n*
—Rev. S. Y. Lum a missionary for.. 39, 40
American Indian Mission Association: formed, 1842 411
American Missionary Association: in Kansas, 1857 187
—note on 187*n*
Americus: United Presbyterian church history, noted 448
Anderson, Bill and Jim: raids, 1862, noted 294
Anderson, George L., Lawrence 123
—article by, noted 363
Anderson, John Byars: buyer of K. P. stock 13

Anderson, S., of California: killed, 1860 378
Anderson Countian, Garnett: articles in, noted 126, 445
Andover Band of Congregationalists... 425
Ansdell, Fred, Jamestown 255
Anthony, Daniel R., Leavenworth..... 123
—Civil War activities, noted, 292, 294, 295
Anthony, Daniel R., III, Leavenworth.. 452
Anthony *Republican*: article in, noted, 254
Archaeological surveys: in 1958, notes on 112
Arkansas City: population loss, 1893-94, noted 31
—role in Cherokee strip opening, notes on 20, 22-25, 27- 31
Arkansas City *Daily Traveler*: article in, noted 447
Armstrong, Silas (Wyandotte Indian).. 5
Arnold, Gen. H. H. ("Hap")........ 351
—at Fort Riley 341, 342
—part in "Salina Blitz" noted 348*n*
—recollections, noted 341
Arnold, Mrs. Philip, Clark co. 366
Arrington, William, of California: killed, 1860 378
Arthur, Mrs. Elizabeth Barr 252
Ash Point, Nemaha co.: Pony Express stop 371
Ashland, Riley co.: comment on, 1857, 188
Atchison, David Rice: town named for, 185
Atchison: S. Y. Lum's comments on... 185
—tables of distances to the gold mines (1859) from ...... *facing* 160 and 161
—telegraph office in, 1859 36
Atchison, Topeka & Santa Fe railroad: donor 112
Atherton, John G., Lyon co. 255
Atkinson, Mrs. Ethel, Crawford co. ... 451
Atkinson, W. R. 400
Attica: 75th anniversary, noted 448
Attica *Independent*: souvenir edition, 1959, noted 448
Atwood *Citizen-Patriot*: article in, noted 254
Aubrey, Johnson co.: raid, 1862, noted, 293
Augusta Historical Society: 1959 officers, listed 127
Austin, Mrs. Helen, Chase co. 450

B

Bader, Ernest B., Topeka 366
Badger, Rev. Milton, New York 40
—S. Y. Lum's letters to (1855-58) ..44-47, 172-177, 180- 196
Bailey, N. H., Scott co.: pioneer of 1885 449
Bailey, Roy F., Salina 123
Baker, Wallace, Protection: donor.... 112
Baker University, Baldwin: founding, noted 435
Baldridge, Rev. B. L.: at Leavenworth, 1861 321
Baldwin, Mrs. Nellie, Osborne: donor. 114
Baldwin, Prof. S. S.: lecturer on spiritualism 267
Baldwin: historical marker for, noted. 106
Baldwin *Ledger*: special edition, 1959, noted 374
Ballhagen, Lloyd: article by, noted .. 253

(455)

456 GENERAL INDEX

Ballinger, Mrs. Ethel, Ozawkie: donor, 112
Ballou, Don D., Kansas City: donor.. 114
Ballou, Louis, Ottawa co. 452
"Band of Hope": note on 323
Bands. *See* Horseshoe Farmers Band.
Bannon, Rev. John Francis, S. J.: booklet by, noted 452
Baptist Church: 1862 resolution, noted, 413
—split in, 1845, notes on 411
Baptists, East Kansas Association of.. 435
—formation of, 1858 . . . . 411, 420
—report, 1858, noted 432
Baptists, Southern: in Kansas, notes on, 411
Barker, Mrs. C. T., Liberal: donor. . . 111
Barlow, Capt. Robert V.: Air Medal winner 140
Barnes, Mrs. Charles, El Dorado: killed, 1893 27
Barnes, Elizabeth, Johnson co.: column by, noted 252, 445
Barnes, Mrs. Lela: treasurer, Historical Society 117, 119, 120
Barnes *Chief*: article in, noted 252
Barr, Frank, Wichita 122, 124
Barstow, Col. William A., of Wisconsin, 293
Bartlett, Alison Barbour 5, 13
Barton County Bank, Great Bend: data on, given Historical Society 109
Basye, Ruby: article by, noted 126
Bates, Edward: U. S. attorney general, 294
Bates, Mrs. Norma Comer: donor 116
Bath, Dorothy, Abilene 450
Battle Canyon, battle of, 1878: article on, noted 253
Baugher, Charles A., Ellis 123
Baughman, Robert W., Liberal 123
Baxter Springs massacre, 1863: noted, 296
Beaton, Jack, Wyandotte 10
Beatty, Mrs. Marion, Topeka 128
Bebermeyer, Harold, Harper 368
Beck, Capt. Francis J.: at Marshall Field 343
Beck, Will T., Holton 104, 119-123
—article on Campbell College by, noted 365
Beckman, Rev. Peter, Atchison 366
Beebe, George: acting ter. governor . . 287
Beecher, Henry Ward: W. S. White's comments on lectures of 200
Beeler, Ness co.: historical marker for G. W. Carver at, noted 106
Beezley, George F., Girard 123
Behrle, Mrs. Carl, Leavenworth co. 452
Bell, Alvis, Pawnee co.: article on, noted 364
Bell, Mrs. Olive, Topeka: donor 112
Bell, Mrs. Ross, Clark co. 366
Belleville *Telescope*: articles in, noted, 364
Belmont, Doniphan co. 110
Beloit *Daily Call* 256
Benge, Lida, Hodgeman co. 450
Bennett, Al, Atchison 438
Benoit, Theresa and Armond: article by, noted 254
Benson, E. A., Kansas City: donor. . . . 111
Benson, J. Leland, Topeka: donor 114
Bentley, Roderick, Shields: donor 112
Beougher, Edward M., Grinnell 123, 450, 451
Berger, William E., Emporia 121
Berglund, Mr. and Mrs. V. E. 117
Berryman, Jerome, II (grandson of Rev. Jerome C.) 117
Berryman, Jerome C., Ashland 120, 122, 124
Bethel College, North Newton: Kauffman Museum article, noted 366
Bickerton, Thomas: a captain, 1861 . . 290
Big Blue, battle of the, 1864: noted . . 298
Big Blue river: 1854 settlement on, noted 45

Big Springs: comment on, 1857 187
Bigelow, Marshall co.: Methodist church history, noted 449
Bill, Edward E., Garden City: donor . . 111
"Bird Song, The": poem by E. F. Ware 270, 271
Bishop, Mrs. Ellis, Ottawa co. 366
Bittmann, Mrs. R. R. 130
Black, Mrs. J. W., Crawford co. 451
Blackburn, Forrest R.: newspaper division head, Historical Society 117
Blackburn, R. Z., Chase co. 450
Blair, Col. Francis P. 289
Blake, Mrs. Henry, Sr., Topeka: donor 111, 112, 114
Blanchard, Rev. Ira D. 411
Blankenship, John, Smith co.: family experiences, noted 363
Blau, Mrs. Marilla Alford: articles by, noted 448
Block, Eugene B.: book by, noted . . . 453
Blood, Rev. Charles 426
—quoted 319, 320, 322, 329, 330
—work in Kansas, 1854-58, notes on . . 43
                                   45, 53, 188
Bloss, Roy S.: book by, noted 453
Blue, Alexander 161, 162
Blue, Charles 161, 162
Blue, Daniel: and brothers, story of 161, 162
Blue, Mrs. James V., Topeka 128
Bluejacket, Charles: Edna Williams a relative of 117
Bluemont Central College, Manhattan . 435
Blunt, Gen. James G. . . . 293-296, 298, 299
Bodwell, Rev. Lewis, Topeka 187, 332
          333, 418, 420, 421, 426, 428
—involved in controversy, 1859-60 . . . . 420, 421
—photograph . . . . *facing* 320
—quoted 316, 322, 329, 415, 430, 431
Boeing Airplane Company 339
Bohemians in Kansas: article on, noted 449
Bolitho, Bob, Harper 368
Bonner, Thomas Neville: book *The Kansas Doctor* by, note on 256
Books: list of additions to the Society's library, 1957-58 229-250
Booth, John Wilkes 300
Border Queen Museum, Caldwell: 1959 show, noted 367
Border Queen Museum Association: 1958 meeting, note on 127
Border troubles: 1854-58, S. Y. Lum's comments on 48-51, 58, 59, 64-67
               172-178, 184, 192, 193
—1860. *See under* Bourbon co.
Bourbon county: border troubles, 1860, notes on 286, 287
Bowers, Mrs. Eugene L., Topeka: donor 112
Bowlby family: manuscript of, microfilmed 110
Bowlus, Thomas H., Iola 123
Bowman, Bishop Thomas 198
Boyd, Mrs. Frank W., Mankato 128
—donor 111
Boyd, Mrs. McDill, Phillipsburg 128
Boyer, Bill, Scott co. 368
Boyer, John A., Scott co. 368
Bradshaw, Alfred B., Turon: reminiscences, noted 108
Bradstreet, Mrs. Myrtle: article by, noted 253
Bramick, Mrs. Floyd: donor 116
Brandley, Henry, Chase co.: biographical sketch, noted 446
Branson, Jacob: rescue, noted 66n
Brant, Maj. Gen. G. C.: letter, quoted 137, 138

General Index

Bray, Walter: killed in mine, 1916... 396
Brereton, Lt. Gen. Lewis H.......... 351
Brewer, Myron: death, noted........ 377
Brey, Mrs. Claude, Ozawkie: donor.. 112
Brigham, Maj. Herman C.: at Marshall Field 343
Brigham, Mrs. Lalla Maloy: death, noted 104
—note on........................ 104
Brinkerhoff, Fred W., Pittsburg 121-123, 451
—commemoration of Lincoln's Kansas visit proposed by 438
Brinkley, Dr. John R.: F. W. Schruben's thesis on, noted........... 108
Britton, Mrs. Lloyd, Edwards co..... 367
Brock, Roland F., Goodland: biographical data 121, 122
—death, noted................... 104
—memorial to............... 121, 122
—note on....................... 104
Brodrick, Lynn R.: death, noted.... 104
—note on....................... 104
Broughton, Clay co.: article on, noted, 254
—earlier names of, noted.......... 254
Brown, Mrs. D. J., Rochester, N. Y.: donor 112
Brown, Mrs. Dale, Delphos: donor... 114
Brown, Mrs. E. B., Denison......... 110
Brown, John: Lincoln's remarks on execution of, quoted............ 285
—Montgomery's attempt to rescue followers of, noted................ 286
—note on Harper's Ferry insurrection, 284
—song "John Brown's body," note on, 291
Brown, John, Jr.: a captain in 7th Kan. cav...................... 292
Brown, Rev. John S., Lawrence: family letters, given to Historical Society.. 109
Brown, Mrs. Paul G., Riley co...... 127
Brown, R. G., Finney co........... 255
Brown, Rev. Solomon, Lyon co.: biographical sketch, noted........... 364
Brownback, Mr. and Mrs. J. L....... 117
Brownville, Neb.: telegraph line in, 1860 38
Brucker, Mrs. Wilber M.: article by, noted 449
Brumfield, Bert, Hodgeman co....... 450
Brush, Doug, Downs: articles by, noted 363
Bryan, Rev. J. E.: note on 408
Buchanan, Pres. James............. 288
Buck, Myrtle, Lyon co............. 255
Bucklin, Ford co.: series of articles on, noted 448
Bucklin *Banner*: articles in, noted.... 448
Buckman, Maj. John F.: in Kansas .. 350
Buckmaster, Mrs. Maurene, Topeka: donor 114
Buffalo: article on slaughter of, noted, 365
—item on killing of, 1872.......... 444
Bulkley, Roy, Topeka.............. 128
Bump, Col. Arthur L.: at Liberal, 337, 338
Bundy, Mrs. Jo, Rice co............ 368
Burchfiel, Rev. J. R.: in Harper co... 255
Burge, David: slave owner......... 412
Burlington: comment on, 1857....... 191
—drunkenness in, 1861, note on..... 323
Burns, Marion co.: German Methodist church history, noted............. 448
Burns *News*: article in, noted....... 448
Bushnell, Horace.................. 424
Butcher, Mrs. Maclure, Neodesha: donor 112
Butcher, Dr. Thomas P., Emporia.... 255
Butler, Rev. Pardee........... 185, 412
—outrages on, 1855, 1856, noted.... 414
—photograph .... *facing* 320

Butler, Mo........................ 292
Butler County Historical Society: officers, 1959, listed................ 128
Butterfield Overland Despatch: mapping and marking of route of, noted, 445
Butterfield Overland Mail........... 379
Byington, W. C., Winchester: donor.. 112
"Bypaths of Kansas History" 125, 251, 361, 362, 444

C

Cabin Creek, I. T., battle of, 1863: noted 296
Cahill, Lt. Col. William A.: at Walker Field 357
Caldwell: population loss, 1893-94... 31
—role in Cherokee strip opening, notes on 20, 22, 23, 25-27, 29, 31
Cale, Cowley co. 20, 31
Calhoun, Harold, Bourbon co........ 368
Calkins, Maj. Elias A., of Wisconsin 293, 294
Callahan, Holly, Abilene 450
Calnan, C. C., Troy................ 438
Camp Lincoln, Bourbon co.......... 290
Camp Supply: land reserved for, 1893, noted 21
Campbell, Hugh K., Chase co........ 450
Campbell, Mrs. Minnie, Topeka: donor, 112
Campbell College: article on, noted... 365
Campbellites: in Ashland, 1857, noted, 188
Candee, Brig. Gen. Robert C.: in Kansas 351
Caney, Montgomery co.: history, noted, 449
Caney *Chronicle*: article in, noted.... 449
Cannibalism: story of Blue brothers, 1859 .... 161, 162
Cannon, E. C., Phillipsburg: donor... 112
Capper, Arthur, estate of: donor..... 112
Carey, James C., Manhattan........ 127
—article by, noted 363
Carlyle, Allen co.: Presbyterian church history, noted 448
Carman, C. M., Independence....... 334
Carman, J. Neale: "Critique of Carruth's Articles on Foreign Settlements in Kansas," article by 386- 390
—note on....................... 386n
Carney, Thomas: elected senator..... 297
—governor 298, 299
Carpenter, Mary Ruth, Allen co., 368, 451
Carroll, Ella V., Leavenworth co..... 452
Carroll, Col. Joseph F.: at Strother Field 354, 355
—quoted 355
Carruth, Gorton V., Pleasantville, N. Y., donor 114
Carruth, William Herbert: J. N. Carman's critique on foreign settlements, articles of 386- 390
Carson Valley, Calif.: Indian troubles in 377- 380
Carter, Mrs. J. O., Garden City...... 128
Cartwright, Rev. Peter............. 425
Carver, George Washington: historical marker for, noted................ 106
—in Ottawa co., paper on, noted..... 366
Casement, Dan D.: and Wm. A. White on govt. regulation, article on, noted, 363
Catharine, Ellis co.: article on, noted.. 364
Cawker City *Ledger*: article in, noted, 363
Cedar Vale *Messenger*: articles in, noted 254, 448
Centennial Commission. See Kansas (state) Centennial Commission.
Central Overland California & Pike's Peak Express............. 371, 382

458 GENERAL INDEX

Central Pacific railroad......... 2, 9
Centropolis, Franklin co.: Christian
  church history, noted............ 253
—notes on, 1857............. 189, 190
Cessna, Mr. and Mrs. Eldon W., El
  Segundo, Calif.: donors......... 112
Chadborn, G. L., Kansas City: donor, 115
Chaffee, Mrs. Harry, Topeka........ 128
Chambers, Lloyd, Clearwater....... 123
Chandler, C. J., Wichita........... 123
Chanute, *Tribune:* article in, noted... 253
Chapman, Berlin B., Stillwater, Okla.:
  donor 111
Charlson, Sam C.,
  Manhattan 110, 122, 124, 127
Chase, Mrs. Eugene: donor......... 116
Chase County Historical Society:
  award for courthouse restoration,
  noted 452
—1959 meeting, note on............ 450
Chattanooga, Tenn., battle of, 1863:
  noted 297
Cheney *Sentinel:* 1894-1940, microfilmed 111
Cherokee county: St. Peter Lutheran
  church history, noted............ 252
Cherokee Indians: interest in 1893
  "run" noted...................... 23
Cherokee strip: campers awaiting opening of, 1893 (photograph) ..*facing* 17
—preparation for the "run," 1893
  (photograph) ....*facing* 16
—role of southern Kansas towns in
  opening of (Jean C. Lough's
  article) 17- 31
—tragedies of the opening, noted, 26, 27
—verse of song the "boomers" sang.. 26
Cherokee Town Site Trust Company.. 28
Cheyenne Indians: battle, 1878, with
  U. S. troops, article on, noted... 253
—thesis on Little Wolf's northern band
  of, noted........................ 108
Chicago, Rock Island & Pacific railroad: train in Cherokee strip
  "robbed" 1893, noted............. 24
Chicago Theological Seminary....... 110
Chickamauga, Ga., battle of, 1863:
  noted 296
Chilocco Indian Industrial School.... 21
Chinese: treatment of, 1880's, noted.. 103
Chivington, John M.: R. S. Craig's
  book on, noted................... 453
Chouteau, Fred (grandson of Cyprian), 117
Chouteau's Island: article on Fourth
  of July, 1880, on, noted......... 365
Chrisman, Mrs. Charles F., Jackson
  Heights, N. Y.: donor............ 112
Christian, Clark, Clyde............ 255
Christian Church (Disciples of Christ):
  in territorial Kansas, note on... 412
—Western Christian University of,
  noted 254
Christmas: at Marysville, 1858,
  article on, noted................ 254
"Chronology of Kansas Political and
  Military Events, 1859-1865, A", 283- 300
Civil War: and Kansas events,
  chronology of 287- 300
—effect on religion in Kansas
  discussed 329-333, 407- 417
—Kansas' contribution, note on..... 300
—nurses, book on, noted............ 256
Clark, Dr. Howard C., Wichita...... 367
Clark, John G.: "Mark W. Delahay:
  Peripatetic Politician," article
  by 301- 312
—note on 301*n*
Clark, Dr. Orville R., Topeka: donor.. 112
Clark, Ralph, Wyandotte co......... 128
Clark County Clipper, The, Ashland:
  jubilee edition, 1959, noted..... 449

Clark County Historical Society:
  1959 meeting, note on............ 366
Clarke, Gen. — —: in command,
  Pacific division, 1860........... 378
Clarke, Adna G., Jr., Honolulu:
  donor 112, 114
Clarke, Philo H.: telegrapher....... 32
Clarke, Sidney: provost marshal..... 296
Clarkson, Mrs. Martina, Harper:
  donor 112
Clay Center *Dispatch:* articles in,
  noted 252, 254
—Ingham diary in, noted........... 447
Clayton, Powell: Civil War colonel... 297
Clearwater, Sedgwick co.: history,
  noted 449
Clearwater News: article in, noted.... 449
Cleaver, C. H., Finney co.......... 450
Cleveland, Pres. Grover............ 20
Cleveland, Marshall: note on....... 293
Cloud County Historical Society: 1959
  meetings, notes on...........255, 451
Clowry, Robert C., Leavenworth:
  telegraph office supt............36, 38
Clymer, Rolla A.,
  El Dorado 121, 123, 128
—role of Lincoln played by.....438, 452
Coal: strip-mined in Linn co.,
  noted 399
Cobb, Damon, Finney co........255, 450
Cobb, David R.: quoted............ 321
Cobb, Mrs. George C., Rutland, Vt.:
  donor 109
Cochran, Elizabeth, Pittsburg 123
Coder, Robert O., Kearny co........ 366
Coe, Rev. David B., New York...... 40
—S. Y. Lum's letters to, 1855....54- 65
Coffeyville Army Air Field:
  history 130- 134
Coffin, George W.: article by, noted.. 364
Coker, Jessy Mae: donor.......*facing* 16
Colby, Thomas co.: Christian church
  history, noted................... 446
—Cooper Hotel history, noted...... 446
—plat, 1887, of, given Historical
  Society 115
Colby *Press-Tribune:* articles in,
  noted 446
Cold Spring, Doniphan co.: Pony
  Express station 370, 371
Coldwater: diamond jubilee, 1959,
  note on 450
Coleman, Franklin: killer of Dow,
  notes on 66
Collamer, Sen. Jacob, of Vermont.... 287
Collard, E. Bert, Sr.,
  Leavenworth co. 452
College of Emporia................ 114
Collinson, Mrs. W. B., Topeka:
  donor 112
Colonial Dames 117
—National Society of, donor....... 108
—Wichita Town Committee of,
  donor 108
Coltrane, V. A.: donor............. 116
Concordia *Blade-Empire:* articles in,
  noted 126, 447
Concordia *Kansan:* article in, noted.. 126
Cone, Mrs. Harold, Topeka......... 255
Congregational Church: early Kansas
  churches, notes on............39, 40
—in Kansas, 1854-65, note on...... 434
—missionary papers microfilmed 110
—S. Y. Lum's letters
  (1854-58) on 40-67, 172- 196
—stand on slavery................. 413
Congregational Ministers and Churches,
  General Association of: 1958
  meeting, note on 420
—note on, 1857 ....433, 434
Conklin, Dr. Tracy, Abilene........ 450
Connecticut Kansas Colony......... 187

GENERAL INDEX 459

Conner, Mrs. Ruth, Chase co. 450
Connolly, Mrs. Emma, Bourbon co. ... 368
Conway, Martin F.: congressman.... 289
Cook, Brig. Gen. Orval.............348n
Cook, Roy, Pleasanton 397
Cook, Van, Joplin, Mo............. 394
Coon creek, battle of, 1848: article on, noted 364
Cooper, Capt. J. M.: at Dodge City.. 136
Coover, C. R., Kinsley: article by, noted 364
Copeland, Charles P., Russell: banker 364
Corbett, Boston: biographical data, noted 126
—marker at homestead site, noted.... 126
Cordley, Rev. Richard, Lawrence ... 332, 416, 417, 428, 431
—illness, 1857, noted............. 193
—losses in Quantrill raid, noted.... 333
—photograph ....facing 320
—quoted 317, 318, 326, 330, 331, 432
Corporation farming in Kansas: Emy K. Miller's thesis on, noted........ 108
Correll, Charles M., Manhattan......104, 114, 119-122, 124
Correll, Mrs. Charles M., Manhattan.. 127
Cost of living: in 1854-'55, notes on 47, 63
—in 1857, notes on 194
Cotton, Corlett J., Lawrence 123
Cottonwood station, Washington co.: Pony Express stop 371, 372
Council Grove: Methodist church history, noted 446
—Rose of Lima Catholic church history, noted 253
Council Grove *Republican*: articles in, noted 253, 364, 446
Courtney, Mrs. Gerald J., Topeka: donor 112
Courtright, Alfaretta: article by, noted, 254
Cowboy newspaper (Dodge City): article on, noted 446
Cowley county: Grandview Methodist church history, noted 447
—Hicks Chapel Methodist church history, noted 448
Craig, Reginald S.: book on J. M. Chivington by, noted 453
Crain, John, Bourbon co............ 368
Crane, Dr. Franklin Loomis: papers of given Historical Society 110
—portrait, given Historical Society... 112
Crane, Mrs. Franklin Loomis: portrait, given Historical Society 112
Crase, Mrs. Frank, Finney co. 255
Crawford, Berry, Topeka: donor 112
Crawford, Mrs. Roy, Topeka: donor 108, 112
Crawford, Samuel J.: governor 14
Crawford County Historical Society: 1959 meetings, notes on, 366, 367, 451
Creighton, Edward, St. Joseph, Mo.: surveyor 37
Cron, F. H., El Dorado 123
Crosby, Mrs. Warren M., Jr., Topeka: donor 112
Crowl, Mrs. Ruth, Allen co. 451
Cruise, John D., Wyandotte: quoted on Hallett murder 10
Cruse, Charles, Abilene 450
Cuba, Republic co.: article on, noted, 364
Curtis, Gen. Samuel R. 293, 297- 299
Czechs in Kansas: notes on 388, 390

D

Daily Inquirer, Leavenworth: notes on 293, 294, 296
Daisy, Annette: colony organizer, 1893 24
Dale, Mrs. Clarence: cocompiler Nicodemus history................. 365
Dale, Lt. Col. Jack C.: at Marshall Field 343
Dale, Kittie: articles by, noted...... 445
Dalton and Morrow: Linn co. lead mine operators.................. 394
Dalton gang: and Starr gang, in Cherokee strip 24, 25
—article on, noted................ 447
Damar, Rooks co.: article on, noted.. 254
Dana, Charles A.: letters by, given Historical Society.............. 109
Danes in Kansas: notes on, 387, 389, 390
Dannett, Sylvia, G. L.: book by, noted, 256
Danville, Harper co.: Immaculate Conception Catholic church history, noted 254
Darlow, — —, Linn co.: co-owner of lead mine.................. 395
Darnell, Charles, Wamego: and wife, donors 111, 112
Darwinism 199
Daughters of American Colonists..... 117
—Elizabeth Knapp chapter, Manhattan: donor................. 108
—Kansas Society: donor........... 108
Daughters of 1812................ 117
Daughters of the American Revolution, 117
—Kansas Society: donor........... 108
Davies, Anne Jones (Mrs. John), Osage co.: diary data given Historical Society 110
Davies, John, Osage co.: note on..... 110
Davies, Priscilla, Denver, Colo.: donor, 110
Davis, Mrs. Edwin W., Topeka: donor, 112
Davis, Rev. I. F.: at Wichita 91n, 92
Davis, Capt. John J.: at Marshall Air Force Base................. 345
Davis, T. E., Crawford co...... 367, 451
Davis, W. W., Lawrence...... 122, 124
Davison, Mrs. Flora E., Kansas City, Mo.: donor.................. 112
Dawson, George, Chase co......... 450
Dawson, John S., Topeka.. 104, 121, 123
Day, Mrs. Lyndon, Topeka: donor .. 112
Dayhoff, Mrs. Jessie Adee, Ottawa co., 127
DeBolt, Capt. R. E................ 135
Deitzler, George W........... 293, 298
Delahay, Mark W................ 293
—in Kansas ter. politics, J. G. Clark's article on 301- 312
—painting of (reproduction) ..facing 304
Delaware, Leavenworth co.: note on, 1857 184
Delaware, The (locomotive)........ 7
Delaware Indians: telegraph line impeded by..................... 34
DeLew, Rev. Dr. L.: at Wichita.... 91n
Delker, Esther, Chapman: donor..... 112
Delplace, John................... 396
Democratic party: in territorial Kansas, comment on................ 301
—state convention, 1859, noted...... 284
— —1860, noted................ 286
— —1862, noted................ 295
— —1864, noted................ 297
Denious, Jess C.: efforts for army air field, noted.................. 135

460 GENERAL INDEX

Denious, Jess C., Jr., Dodge
 City 114, 122, 124
Dennis, Mrs. Glenn, Clark co........ 366
Dennis, Rev. L. B.................. 409
Denver, Gen, James........... 291, 293
Deragowski, Mrs. Robert, Scott co.... 368
Devers, Gen. Jacob L................ 351
Dickerson, A. W., Bourbon co..... 368
Dickerson, J. Glenn, Allen co....... 451
Dickhut, Mrs. C. W., Scott co...... 368
Dickinson County Historical Museum,
 Abilene 114
Dickinson County Historical Society:
 1959 meeting, note on 451
Dighton *Herald:* article in, noted... 253
Dimmitt, Jessie, Thomas co......... 451
Disciples of Christ. *See* Christian
 Church.
Dittman, Lt. Col. Henry: at Hering-
 ton 155, 157
Dixon, George: injured in mine acci-
 dent 396
Dixon, Leo B., Hanston............. 110
Dobbin, Dr. B. M.: pamphlet by,
 noted 256
Dobson, Mrs. Harry, Wichita: donor, 109
Dobson, W. A., Scott co............ 368
Docking, George, Lawrence......... 123
—and wife: at Society's annual meet-
 ing 121
Doctor, The Kansas: book by T. N.
 Bonner, note on 256
Dodderidge, Russell: donor......... 116
Dodge, Gen. Grenville M.: at Fort
 Leavenworth 299
Dodge, Jonas: quoted.............. 319
Dodge City: in 1880, article on, noted, 364
Dodge City Army Air Field:
 history 135- 138
Dodge City *Daily Globe:* articles in,
 noted 252
Dolbee, Cora: papers of, given His-
 torical Society.................... 109
Donalson, Israel B.: U. S. marshal, 176n
Dongle, Vern, and sons, Soldier: don-
 ors 112
Doniphan: comment on, 1857....... 185
Dorr, Col. H. W.: at Strother Field.. 354
Douglas, Stephen A.: M. W. Dela-
 hay's backing of, discussed........ 306
—political activities, 1858, comment
 on 305, 306
Dow, Charles W.: killing of, note on, 66
Downs: as a railroad center, articles on,
 noted 363
Downs *News:* articles in, noted..... 363
Drake, Samuel: agent for C. M.
 Stebbins 33
Dry Wood, battle of, 1861: noted... 290
Dunn, Mrs. Chester, Oxford 128
Dunn, Lt. Col. Frank E.: at Coffey-
 ville 133
Duran, Lupe, Teseque Pueblo, N. M.:
 donor 112
Durant, Thomas C.: vice-pres., U. P.
 railroad 12, 15
Dwight Library: donor 116

E

Eaker, Lt. Gen. Ira C. 351
Eakle, George, Bourbon co. 368
Earhart, Arrold R., Topeka: donor... 112
Earlton, Neosho co.: history, noted.. 447
Eastham, Mrs. Lavilla, McPherson:
 donor 111
Ebel, Dr. B. E., Redlands, Calif: arti-
 cles by, noted 445
Ebright, Homer K., Baldwin 123
Eckdall, Mrs. Ella Funston, Emporia:
 donor 111

Eckdall, Frank F., Emporia 123
Eddy, Carl G., Thomas co.......... 451
Eddy, Elizabeth Ann Berryman, To-
 peka: papers, microfilmed 110
Edmunds, Sarah Emma: Civil War
 spy 256
Edson, Rev. E. H.: at
 Wichita 91n, 204- 207
Edwards, Mabel, Emporia 255
Edwards, Mary and A. Blanche, Abi-
 lene: donors 111
Edwards county: article on develop-
 ment of education in, noted 365
Edwards County Historical Society:
 1959 meeting, note on 367
Egan, Col. John W.: at Dodge City.. 147
Ehrsam, Mrs. Viola, Enterprise 451
Eicher, Harry, Thomas co.......... 451
Eichman, Mrs. Muriel, Hodgeman co., 450
Eighth Kansas infantry: notes
 on 291, 292, 294, 296, 297
Einsel, Mary: article by, noted...... 446
Eisenhower, Gen. Dwight D........ 351
Eisenhower Museum, Abilene....... 114
El Dorado *Times:* article in, noted.... 446
Election: Nov., 1854, comment on... 50
—Mar., 1855, comment on 58
—June, 1859, note on............. 307
—1862, noted.................... 295
Eleventh Kansas regiment: notes
 on 294, 295, 299
Elliot, A. K., of California: killed,
 1860 378
Ellis, Bob, Topeka: donor.......... 114
Ellis, Mulvey Hall, article on, noted, 445
—women in city govt., 1896, article
 on, noted 445
Ellis county: pioneer life article, noted, 364
Ellis County Farmer, Hays: articles
 in, noted 126, 365
Elwood: Pony Express station at.... 370
Emory, Col. William H.: at Fort
 Leavenworth 289
Emporia: comment on, 1857....191, 192
Emporia *Gazette:* articles in,
 noted 126, 364, 448
—old press of, given Lyon Co. Hist.
 Society 255
Emporia *Weekly Gazette:* article in,
 noted 448
Engle, Mrs. C. H., Topeka: donor... 114
Enterprise-Chronicle, Burlingame: his-
 tory, noted 449
Eskelund, Foster, Kearny co........ 366
Eudora: centennial booklet, noted.... 108
Eureka: New York Emigration co.
 site, 1854 45
Eustace, Dr. E. W., Lebanon: donor.. 112
Euwer, Elmer E., Goodland........ 123
Evans, Mrs. Merle, Finney co....... 255
Eves, Joseph M., Kearny co........ 366
Ewing, Thomas, Jr..... 292, 295, 296, 299

F

Fager, Emory, Overbrook 128
Fager, Maurice E., Topeka 112
Fairfax Field, Kansas City:
 history 138- 141
Fairport, Russell co.: history, noted.. 254
Fallin, Mrs. J. P., Wichita 128
Fant, William, Finney co. 255
Farley, Alan W., Kansas City ...123, 128
—cocompiler imprints list 106
—donor 111, 114
—note on 1n
—president, Historical Society... 104, 117
                                120, 121, 123
—"Samuel Hallett and the Union Pacific Railway Company in Kansas,"
 article by........................1- 16

General Index

Farman, D. S., Manhattan: donor.... 112
Farrell, F. D., Manhattan 121, 123
Fatzer, Hubert, Edwards co. 365
Fearing, O. K., Jewell co. 367
Ferguson, Mrs. Earl, Valley Falls: donor 112
Ferguson, W. D., Thomas co. 451
Ferris, Col. Carlisle I.: at Coffeyville 131, 133
Field, R. E., Wichita: *Leader* editor.. 90
Fifteenth Kansas cavalry: notes on 296, 297
Fifth Kansas cavalry: notes on 290, 297, 298
Filinger, George A., Riley co. 127
Filley, Giles F., St. Louis, Mo.: merchant.................. 11, 13
Finney County Historical Society: 1959 meeting, note on 255
—officers, 1959-60, listed 450
First Colorado regiment: defeat, 1862, noted 293
First Indian regiment: note on 293
First Kansas battery: mustered 290
First Kansas Colored regiment: notes on 295, 296
First Kansas infantry: losses, 1861, noted 331n
—notes on, 289, 290, 292, 294, 296, 297
"First Kansas Lead Mines, The": article by W. H. Schoewe 391- 401
Fischer, Ed.: recollections, noted.... 364
Fisher, Harry, Bourbon co. 368
Fisher, Rev. Hugh Dunn 422, 423
—escape in Quantrill raid, noted .. 333n
—photograph .... *facing* 320
—quoted 321
Fitch, Sen. Graham N., of Indiana... 287
Fleming, A. M., Finney co. 450
Fleming, John, of California: killed, 1860 378
Floods in Kansas: data on, given Historical Society 110
Flora, Snowden Dwight, Topeka: donor 110
Folklore of Kansas: P. J. Wyatt's thesis on, noted 108
Forbes, Maj. Daniel H., Jr.: Air Force base named for 144
—note on 144n
Forbes Air Force Base: history... 142- 145
Ford, Evelyn, Topeka 128
Forehand, Maj. William: at Marshall Field 343
Foreign settlements in Kansas: article on Bohemians, noted 449
—J. N. Carman's critique on Carruth's articles of the 1890's......... 386- 390
Foresman, Rev. J. O. 408
Fort Blair: article on, noted 447
—attacked, 1863 296
Fort Harker: establishment, noted... 297
Fort Hays: articles on, noted.... 126, 445
—pamphlet history, noted 452
Fort Hays Museum: article on, noted.. 126
Fort Kearny, South Pass and Honey Lake wagon road, 1857-59: data on, microfilmed 110
Fort Leavenworth: telegraph service, 1859, at 35
Fort Leavenworth Museum: article on, noted 367
—Lincoln buggy in, noted 438
Fort Riley: article on, noted 449
—mention of, 1857 188
—photographs, given Historical Society 114
—*see, also,* Marshall Air Force Base.
Fort Riley Historical Society........ 367
Fort Riley Museum: article on, noted, 367

Fort Scott (military post): early history, article on, noted 447
—re-established, 1863............. 296
Fort Scott and Bourbon County Historical Society: reorganization, note on 368
Fort Scott Foundry................ 261
Fort Scott *Monitor*: E. F. Ware's "The Washerwoman's Song" published in 258
Fort Scott *Tribune*: articles in, noted 447
Fort Wallace Memorial Association: German family massacre site marked by 450
Fort Zarah: establishment, noted..... 298
Foster, Ivy: donor................. 116
Fourteenth Kansas cavalry: notes on.. 296
Fourth Kansas regiment: note on.... 290
Fourth of July: at Salina, 1860, noted, 169
—in 1880, on Chouteau's Island, noted, 365
Fox, Mrs. Philip, Evanston, Ill.: donor 111, 112
Franklin county: Salem Hall school history, noted.................. 365
Frazier, Emma Barnes: article by, noted 447
Fredonia: courthouse, article on, noted, 447
Free-State prisoners, 1856: S. Y. Lum's comments on 177
Fremont, John C.: connections with U. P., E. D., noted............3, 8
—explorations, 1840's, noted 160
French Canadians: in Rooks co., noted, 254
French in Kansas: lead miners in Linn co. area, in 1840's, note on....... 392
—notes on....................389, 390
Friel, Mrs. Hugh, Crawford co....... 451
Frienmuth, Hans, Leavenworth co.... 452
"Frogtown," Nemaha co............. 371
Frontier and pioneer life. *See* Pioneer life.
Frontier Guard: Delahay an officer in, 311
—notes on 288
Fry, Maj. William J.: at Fairfax Field, 139
Fry(e), John: Pony Express rider.... 382
Fuller, Thomas W., Wichita 367
Funk, John M., Wyandotte: mayor... 10
Funston, Barbara, Mill Valley, Calif.: donor 112, 116
Funston, Frederick: relics of, given Historical Society 116
Furnas, Robert: head of First Indian regt. 293
Fussell, James E., Leavenworth co.... 452

G

Gaffney, Henry, Jr., Irvington, N. J.: donor 111
Gaines, Charles O., Chase co........ 450
Galena (lead ore): in the Pleasanton area, data on................397, 398
—specimen (photograph)...... *facing* 401
Galloway, Mrs. Wilber, Shawnee co... 127
Game: in 1873, note on 251
Gano, Richard M.: Confederate general, 298
Gard, Spencer A., Iola..... 123, 368, 451
Garden City Army Air Field: history......................... 145- 149
Garden City Municipal Airport: used by Army, 1943................. 147
Gardiner, Dorothy: editor........... 363
Gardner, Marshall G., Leavenworth... 438
—article by, noted................ 367
Gardner, Alexander: photographs (at Wyandotte) by, reproduced... *frontispiece* and *facing* iv

462　GENERAL INDEX

Gardner, Johnson co.: centennial booklet, noted ... 108
—sacked, 1861 ... 291
Garnett *Review:* article in, noted ... 445
"Gateways to the Promised Land": Jean C. Lough's article ... 32-38
Gauch, Mrs. Fred W., Kansas City: donor ... 112
Geary, John W.: territorial governor ... 303
Geary, Mrs. Meta Howard, Wichita: donor ... 111, 112
Geary county: Lyon creek community article, noted ... 446
Geisen, Rolla, Ottawa co. ... 452
Geneva, Allen co.: economic situation, 1861 ... 326
Geology: of the Pleasanton lead mining area ... 396-401
George Eastman House, Rochester, N. Y. ... 114
German family: massacre site marked, 1959, note on ... 450
German Methodists: note on, 1861 ... 410
Germans in Kansas: notes on settlements of ... 387-390
Gibler, Rev. ——: at Wichita ... 209
Gibler, Paul, Claflin ... 114
Gibson, Mrs. Roy, Chanute ... 128
Giles, Capt. Benjamin F.: in Kansas ... 350
Gillespie, Alexander: "strip" claim lost by ... 28
Gillespie, Amy, Finney co. ... 255
Gillett, Mrs. Elton, Jewell co. ... 367
Gilpin, Mrs. Edna Piazzek, Phoenix, Ariz.: donor ... 111, 112
Gilson, Mrs. F. L., Emporia ... 255
Glabb, Charles N.: article by, noted ... 445
Glandon, Mrs. Clyde, Wyandotte co. ... 128
Gold rush (1859-60): routes used by gold seekers discussed ... 158-171
—tables of distances from Atchison to the mines ... facing 160, 161
—use of the Smoky Hill route, C. W. Gower's article on ... 158-171
Goode, Rev. William H. ... 409, 423
Goodhue, Mr. and Mrs. R. A., San Gabriel, Calif. ... 110
Goodykoontz, C. B. ... 430
Gormbo, John, of California: killed, 1860 ... 378
Governor's office, Topeka: donor ... 112
Gower, Calvin W.: note on ... 158n
—"The Pike's Peak Gold Rush and the Smoky Hill Route, 1859-1860," article by ... 158-171
Graham, James S.: letter, 1858, noted, 159n
Granada, Nemaha co.: note on ... 371
Grant, Emma, Cedar Vale: biographical sketch, noted ... 254
Grant, Gen. U. S. ... 299
Grasshopper Falls: mentioned, 1857 ... 189
Great Bend: Trinity Lutheran church histories, noted ... 126
Great Bend Army Air Field: history ... 149-153
—photographs ... between 144, 145
Great Bend *Herald-Press:* article in, noted ... 126
Great Bend *Tribune:* article in, noted ... 126
Greathouse, J. E., Finney co. ... 255
Greeley: Evangelical U. B. church histories, noted ... 445
Green, Henry T.: 1860 expedition of ... 169-171
—note on ... 169
Green, Sen. James S., of Missouri ... 287
Gresham, Mrs. F. A., Bucklin: articles by, noted ... 448
Griffing, Ward C., Riley co. ... 127
Grimsley, Ben, Garden City ... 145
Grinnell, Harold C., Cedar Point: donor ... 112

Guide books: of 1859, noted ... 159
Guilfoyle, William A., Abilene ... 450
Guilinger, Ed: articles by, noted ... 447
Guittard, George, Marshall co. ... 362, 371
Guittard's: Pony Express station ... 371
Gunn, Otis Berthoude: surveyor ... 3
Guthrie, Okla.: food shortages, 1893, noted ... 22
—Negro colony, 1893, noted ... 24

H

Hagans, Mrs. Asa, Melvern: donor ... 112
Hagans, Mrs. Roy, Lane co. ... 451
Haines, Joe D., Riley co. ... 127
Haines, Stella B., Augusta ... 127
Haise family, Russell: donors ... 111
Halberstadt, Ray, Ottawa co. ... 366, 451
Halberstadt, Mrs. Ray, Ottawa co. ... 452
Hale, Harold L., Topeka: donor ... 113
Hale, John K., Wyandotte ... 13
Hall, Dale W., Topeka: donor ... 113
Hall, Fred, Topeka ... 123
Hall, Standish, Wichita ... 122, 124
Hallett, Ann Eliza (Mrs. Samuel), 12, 13, 15, 16
Hallett, John L. ... 12
Hallett, Samuel: and the U. P. railroad in Kansas, A. W. Farley's article on ... 1-16
—killed by Talcott ... 10, 11
—note on family of ... 12
—photograph ... facing 1
Hallett, Thomas ... 12
Hamilton, R. L., Beloit ... 123
Hampden, Coffey co.: note on ... 191
Handy, Brig. Gen. Roger M. ... 156
Hankins, Mary, Allen co. ... 451
Hanna, Rev. J. T.: at Wichita ... 91
Hanna, Mrs. Joe, Lane co. ... 451
Hannibal & St. Joseph railroad ... 2, 5
—telegraph line on right-of-way of ... 37
Hanover *News:* article in, noted ... 448
Hanson, Harry E., Wyandotte co. ... 128
Hanson, Mrs. Raymond A., Jamestown ... 255, 451
Hanson, Robert H., Jamestown ... 255, 451
Hanst, Maj. Charles E.: at Fairfax Field ... 139
Harding, Mrs. R. C., Wamego: donor, 113
Hardy, Mr. and Mrs. Harry A. ... 117
Harlan, James, of Iowa ... 13-15
Harney, Gen. William S. ... 287
Harper, Mrs. Jesse C., Ashland ... 123
Harper, Rev. W. F.: at Wichita, 91n, 96
Harper *Advocate:* article in, noted ... 254
Harper City Historical Society: organized ... 368
Harper county: Burchfiel Methodist church history, noted ... 254
Harris, William L. ... 411
Harrison, H. C., Brandon, Vt.: papers of, given Historical Society ... 109
Harsen, Rev. J. P.: at Wichita ... 91n, 93, 197, 198, 208
Harsh, Mrs. Pearl B.: letter by, noted, 446
Hartland, Kearny co.: article on, noted ... 364
Harvey, Mrs. A. M., Topeka ... 123
Harvin, Lt. Col. Charles B.: at Coffeyville ... 133
Haskins, Joe (part Sioux Indian) ... 98
Haucke, Frank, Council Grove ... 104
Haucke, Mrs. Frank, Council Grove: donor ... 119-123, 113
Haughey, Dr. Leo, Concordia ... 255, 451
Haven, Grace, Council Grove: donor, 113
Haven, Reno co.: Congregational church histories, noted ... 253
Haven *Journal:* article in, noted ... 253

GENERAL INDEX 463

Hawkins, W., of California: killed, 1860 378
Hawley, Lorene Anderson (Mrs. George): cocompiler imprints list, 106
Hawn, Frederick 395, 400
Haworth, Erasmus 393, 399, 401
Hays, Beatrice, Chase co. ...., 450
Hays, Col. Jack: in California, 1860, 379
Hays: Catholic church history, noted, 126
—Fourth of July, 1878, article on, noted 445
—pamphlet history, noted 452
Hays *Daily News:* articles in, noted 254, 364, 445
Haywood, C. Robert, Winfield 366
Heald, Mrs. Zella, Ottawa co. 452
Heflin, Mrs. Ralph W., Pearland, Tex.: donor 111, 113, 114
Hegler, Ben F., Wichita 122, 124
Heilmann, Charles E., Butler co. 128
Heizer, Chester, Caldwell: donor 113
Hemphill, Harry, Paola: donor 115
Hereford, Mrs. Bessie, Topeka: donor, 113
Herington: St. Paul Lutheran church history, noted 253
Herington *Advertiser-Times:* articles in, noted 126, 253
Herington Army Air Field: history 153- 157
Heritage of Kansas, Emporia, article in, noted 363
Herndon, Walter, Lane co. 451
Herneison, Wayne, Wamego: donor .. 112
Herron, Mrs. Iva, Edwards co. 367
Hewitt, Rev. J. D.: at Wichita 91n, 93, 211, 213
—quoted 93
Hibbens, C. R., Independence: article on, noted 447
Hickman, Russell K.: article by, noted, 369
Hicks, Virginia P., Kearny co. 366
High Plains Journal, Dodge City: articles in, noted 364, 365
Highland University, Highland 435
Hildt, George H.: quoted 320, 321
Hill, John G., Marion co.: Hillsboro founder 445
Hill, Rev. Timothy: quoted, 1855 ... 436
Hill City, Marion co.: note on 445
Hillsboro, Marion co.: Dr. B. E. Ebel's history, noted 445
—75th anniversary, noted 450
Hillsboro *Star-Journal:* articles in, noted 445
Hillyer, George S.: impeached, 1862 .... 292, 294
Hinman, Ralph S., Jr.: article by, noted 252
—editorial (1958), noted, and quoted, 252
Historical markers: erected, 1959, noted 106, 450
Historical Society, Organizing a Local: C. M. Silvestro's booklet, noted 256
History: political and military, 1859-1865, a chronology 283- 300
Hodgeman County Historical Society: 1959 meeting, note on 450
Hodges, Frank, Olathe 123
Hodgson, Art, Rice co. 368
Hodgson, Rev. T. S.: at Wichita 91n
Hohn, Gordon S., Marshall co.: articles by, noted 363, 449
Holden, Bernice: article by, noted ... 365
Hollenberg ranch house: a Pony Express station 371, 372
Holmberg-Johnson Blacksmith and Wagon Shop, Lindsborg: article on, noted 446
Holmstrom, John, Riley co. 127
Holton *Recorder:* article in, noted ... 365
Home Missionary, The: comment on .. 419
Hood, Dr. Leroy, Garden City 255

Hoole, William Stanley: quoted 320
Hope *Dispatch:* note on press used by, 255
Horgas, Lt. Col. Maurice: at Herington 157
Hornsby, Brig. Gen. A.: letter, quoted, 148
Horses: use in Cherokee strip opening, notes on 22, 23, 25- 27
Horseshoe Farmers Band, Washington co.: history, noted 448
Hough, Lela, Topeka 128
Houghton, Alan B.: booklet by, noted, 256
How, John, St. Louis, Mo.: merchant 11, 13
Howard County Ledger, Longton: 1871 issue given Historical Society 114
Howard *Courier-Citizen:* article in, noted 254
Hoyt, Mrs. Hobart, Lyons 128
Hubbell, L. W., Hodgeman co. 450
Huck, Mrs. Kenneth, Clark co. 366
Hudson, Florence, Augusta 127
Hudson, Tom, Harper 368
Huffman, Mrs. Frank, Topeka 128
Hughs, Mrs. Gay, Ashland 366
Humboldt, Allen co.: burned, 1861 .. 291
Humboldt *Union:* article in, noted .. 253
Hunnewell, Sumner co.: cowtown in early 1890's 19
—role in Cherokee strip opening, noted 19, 22, 23, 25, 31
Hunt, Mrs. Gorman, Leavenworth co., 452
Hunter, Maj. Gen. David: Head, Dept. of Kansas 291
Hunter, Sen. Robert, of Virginia 286
Huntington, Jeanette P., Rochester, N. Y. 404
Huntoon, Mary, Topeka ...... *facing* 368
Hurst, Margaret O., Kearny co. 366
Hurst, Melvin, Bourbon co. 368
Hurt, Wesley R., Vermillion, S. D.: donor 113
Hutchinson, Rev. G. W.: at Centropolis, 253
Hutchinson, Lulu, Thomas co. 451
Hutchinson *News:* articles in, noted, 253, 366, 446
Huxman, Walter A., Topeka: donor .. 111
Hyatt, Russ, Wichita: articles by, noted 449
Hyattville: mentioned, 1857 191

I

Iatan, Mo.: rebel flag captured at 289
Illinois State Historical Library: donor, 114
Illinois State Register, Springfield, Ill. .. 303
Independence: Mount Hope Cemetery, article on, noted 447
Independence Army Air Field 129
—history 334- 336
Independence *Daily Reporter:* articles in, noted 253, 447
Indian battle, 1878. See *under* Battle Canyon.
Indian territory: Kansas troops in, 1862 294
Indian troubles: A. B. Houghton's booklet on Mitchell co. raid, noted .. 256
—in California, 1860 .... 377- 380
—raid of 1878, article on, noted 254
Indianola: reference to, 1857 189
Indians, loyal: refugees in Kansas, 1862 292
Ingalls, Ann Downs, Shokan, N. Y. ... 109
Ingalls, John James: three letters by, given Historical Society 109
Ingalls: St. Stanislaus parish history, noted 449
Ingham, ——, Topeka 444
Ingham, Thomas J., Clay co.: diary (1859) noted 447
Iola *Register:* article in, noted 448
Iowa Point: reference to, 1857 186

464 GENERAL INDEX

Ironquill. See Ware, Eugene Fitch.
"Ironquill's 'The Washerwoman's Song' ": article by J. C. Malin, 257- 282
Isacks, Andrew Jackson............ 11
Italians in Kansas: noted.......... 390

J

Jacks, John W., of Missouri: Perry, Okla. newspaper planned by...... 21
Jackson County (Mo.) Historical Society: award to Chase co. society, noted.......................... 452
Jacksonian, Cimarron: article in, noted............................ 449
Jacobs, Mrs. Minnie, Council Grove: donor....................113, 116
Jader, Dr. ——, of California: killed, 1860............................ 378
Jaeger, E. W., Hope: donor........ 112
Jagger, Mrs. Fred, Ottawa co....... 452
Jameson, Henry B., Abilene........ 450
Jameson, Tom: burned to death, 1893, 27
Jamieson, W. F.: "spiritualist"..... 267
Jarboe, A. M., Topeka: donor...... 113
Jenista, Harry, Caldwell........... 127
Jenkins, Mrs. Elsie, Edwards co..... 367
Jenkins' Ferry, Ark., battle of, 1864: noted............................ 297
Jennings, J. B., St. Joseph, Mo.: telegraph interests, noted............ 37
Jennison, Charles R................ 290
Jent, J. S., Cedar Vale............. 254
Jewell County Historical Society: organization, noted................ 367
Jewett, Mrs. Dale, Lane Co........ 451
Jobes, Charles: killed in mine accident, 396
Johnson, A. W., Leavenworth co.... 452
Johnson, Pres. Andrew..........13, 14
Johnson, Mrs. Bea, Kansas City..... 128
Johnson, Hampton P.: Civil War colonel............................ 290
Johnson, Capt. Harry A.: in Kansas.. 350
Johnson, Lillian, Allen co........... 451
Johnson, Oscar, McPherson co.: manager of colony bound for Cherokee strip............................. 24
Johnson, R. Kitt: death, noted..... 377
Johnson, Ruby: article by, noted... 252
Johnson, Rev. Thomas........409, 410
—quoted on loyalty to Union....... 413
—slave owner..................... 412
Johnson, Mrs. Virginia A., Gardner: donor........................... 113
Johnson county: Corinth community history, noted................... 445
—Linwood church and cemetery history, noted................... 252
—Quantrill raids in, 1862, noted... 295
Johnson County Herald, Overland Park: articles in, noted...........252, 445
—history, noted................... 252
—1942-1956 file microfilmed....... 111
Johnston, William Crane, Jr.: thesis by, noted........................... 158n
Jones, Mrs. Carl, Topeka: donor.... 113
Jones, Maj. Dale C.: at Marshall Field, 343
Jones, Mr. and Mrs. Elwood........ 117
Jones, George, of California: killed by Indians, 1860.................... 378
Jones, Horace, Lyons............122, 124
Jones, Lucina, Emporia............ 255
Jones, Lula, Hodgeman co.......... 450
Jones, Paul, Rice co............... 368
Jones, Samuel J.: arrest of Branson, noted........................... 66n
Jones, Taylor, Finney co........... 255
Jones, Russell & Co., Leavenworth: comment on enterprises of....372- 374
Jordan, Dean L., Sr., Abilene: donor.. 113
Judson, Col. William R.: head Sixth Kansas regt...................... 291

Judy, Bradley, Jewell co............ 367
Jumbo lead mine, Linn co.: account of...........................393, 394
Junction City: 1862 raid on newspaper, noted....................... 293
—Episcopal Church of the Covenant, article on, noted................. 447
—German Evangelical Lutheran Zion church history, noted........447, 448
—Zion United Church of Christ, article on, noted..................... 448
Junction City Union: article in, noted, 449
Junction City Weekly Union: articles in, noted....................... 447

K

Kambach, Mrs. Frank, Shawnee co... 255
Kampschroeder, Mrs. Jean Norris, Garden City 122, 124
Kansapolis: reference to, 1857..... 189
Kansas (ter.) Legislature: 1860, notes on 285, 286
—1861, notes on 287, 288
Kansas (state): capital, located at Topeka, 1861 291
—Centennial commission 438
— —1958 work of, noted 106
—Legislature, 1862, notes on...292, 293
— —1863, notes on 296
— —1864, notes on 297
— —1865, notes on 299
—Militia, reorganized, 1862........ 295
—Printing Plant, Topeka: donor ... 113
Kansas: books, list of additions to the Society's library, 1957-58 ...229- 235
—congressional steps leading to admission as state, listed 287, 288
—early pictures of, notes on 114
—hard times in, 1861 ....326, 327
—post card views of, given Historical Society 114
Kansas Association of Teachers of History and Social Science: 1959 meeting, note on 366
Kansas brigade 291
Kansas Central Railroad Company... 2
Kansas Chief, Troy: article in, noted.. 363
Kansas City: Fairfax Field history 138- 141
Kansas City, Mo.: first telegraph, 1858 ....34, 35
—Hannibal bridge, article on, noted, 445
Kansas City Labor Bulletin: 1940-1957 file microfilmed 111
Kansas Cowboy, The, Dodge City: article on, noted 446
Kansas Free Fair, 1958: Historical Society display, note on 112
Kansas Frontier News, Junction City: office destroyed, 1862 293
"Kansas Historical Notes" ..127, 128, 255 256, 366-368, 450- 453
"Kansas History as Published in the Press", 126, 252-254, 363-365, 445- 449
Kansas Imprints, 1854-1876: a supplement, note on 106
Kansas Indians: G. W. Coffin's article on, noted 364
Kansas Pacific railroad [including the U. P., Eastern Division, which became the K. P. Railway Co.]: construction, 1863-64, data on 6, 7
—1864 excursion, noted 7
—history, 1862-1865.............1- 16
—"Samuel Hallett and the Union Pacific Railway Company in Kansas," article by Alan W. Farley 1- 16
—three photographs at Wyandotte, 1867 ....facing iv and *frontispiece*

GENERAL INDEX

Kansas river: frozen over at Wyandotte for 110 days, 1872 444
—Wyandotte bridge construction, 1867 (photograph) .... *frontispiece*
Kansas State Historical Society: annual meeting, 1958, proceedings.... 121- 123
—appropriations and budget requests, 105
—archives division report, 1957-58 .... 106, 107
—display at Kansas Free Fair, note on, 112
—executive committee report ... 1958, 119
—First Capitol report, 1957-58..... 116
—Funston Home report, 1957-58.... 116
—*Kansas Historical Quarterly, The*, note on 105
—Kaw Mission report, 1957-58..... 116
—library, additions to, 1957-58.. 229- 250
——report, 1957-58.......... 107- 109
—manuscript division report, 1957-58, 111
—*mirror*, note on, 1958 106
—museum report, 1957-58.... 111- 113
—newspaper and census divisions report, 1957-58 .... 113, 114
—nominating committee report, 1957-58 120
—photographs and maps report, 1957-58 .... 114, 115
—presidential address, 1958...... 1- 16
—publications and special projects report, 1957-58 .... 105, 106
—research subjects, 1957-58........ 115
—secretary's report, 1957-58.... 104- 117
—Shawnee Mission report, 1957-58.. 117
—treasurer's report, 1957-58.... 117- 119
Kansas State Temperance Society: 1861 meeting, noted 323
Kansas Valley Times, The: first Rossville paper 363
Karr, Robert O., Crawford co........ 451
Kassebaum, Mrs. Lulu, Rossville: articles by, noted 365
Kaul, Robert H., Wamego...... 122, 124
Kaw River Telegraph Co.: incorporated, 1855 33
Kearny county: a history of, planned, 127
—early-day storms article, noted.... 364
—Prairie Range school history, noted.. 363
Kearny County Historical Society: county historical project, noted..... 127
—1959 meeting, note on 366
Keel, H. W., Abilene 450
Keller, Erwin, Topeka.......... 127
—and wife, donors.......... 112
Kelley, Robert S., Atchison: editor... 185*n*
Kellogg, Royal S.: letter by, noted.... 254
Kelly, Rev. Barney: at Wichita 91*n*, 93, 95
Kelly, Father Gregory: at Danville.... 254
Kelly, Rev. John: at Wichita 209-211, 221
Kemper, Bishop Jackson.......... 417
Kendall, Don: article by, noted...... 446
Kendall, Hamilton co.: article on, noted 364
Kennekuk, Atchison co.: Pony Express station 371
Kenny, Mrs. B. Gage, Lincoln: donor.. 113
Kibbe, ——, Hickory Point.......... 409
Kickapoo, Brown co.: Pony Express station 371
Kickapoo, Leavenworth co.: M. E. Church South conference of 1856 at 407, 410, 437
Kilroy, Ed, Rice co........... 368
Kingman, Robert H., Topeka......... 127
—and wife: donors.......... 113
Kingman, W. A., Springfield, Mo.: donor 113
Kingman: 75th anniversary, noted.... 127
Kinley, C. L., Augusta: donor........ 113

Kinsley Mercury: articles in, noted 364, 365
—1899-1956 file microfilmed.......... 111
Kiowa: population loss, 1893-94.... 31
—role in Cherokee strip opening, noted, 20
22, 31
Kirby, Rev. John: at Wichita.... 91- 93
Kirk, Harold, Scott co........... 368
Knapp, Dallas W., Coffeyville........ 123
Knapp, Mrs. Sidney, Concordia.. 255, 451
Knezswich, M., of California: killed, 1860 378
Knight, Rev. Richard: Hampden colonist 191, 425
Knox, Mrs. C. B., Manhattan......... 127
Koch, William E., Manhattan.... 123, 127
Kotterman, Mrs. Eugene.......... 123
"Kriterion": poem by E. F. Ware, 277, 278
——notes on 274, 277- 282
Kyle, Col. Reuben, Jr.: at Pratt...... 347

L

Laird, Lem, Harper.......... 368
Lake City, Barber(?) co.: article on, noted 449
Lakin, Kearny co.: article on, noted.. 365
Lakin *Independent:* article in, noted... 363
Landes, H. R., Topeka: donor... 111, 115
Landon, Alfred M.: papers of, given Historical Society 109
Landrith, Mrs. O. H., Enid, Okla.: donor 111
Lane, James H.......... 294, 302
—a general 289- 292
—a Lincoln supporter, 1860.......... 311
—campaigner for Fremont, 1856.... 303
—interest in Doniphan, noted.......... 185
—Kansas route of U. P. influenced by 7, 12
—M. W. Delahay an associate of.... 303
307, 308, 311
—military commission resigned 292
—U. S. senator 288, 290, 299, 311
Lane, Vincent J........... 7
Lane County Historical Society: 1959 meeting, note on.......... 451
Lane's brigade 291, 293
Lang, J. W., Hodgeman co.......... 450
Langsdorf, Edgar: asst. secretary, Historical Society 104, 117
Laramie creek, Nemaha co.......... 371
Large, Mrs. Lucy M., Lecompton: donor 113
Larimer, William, Jr., Denver, Colo... 160
Larson, Oscar: donor.......... 116
Larzelere, Alfred, Doniphan co.: article on, noted 363
Lauer, Col. Ford V.: at Liberal...... 338
Laughridge, White, Chase co......... 450
Lauterbach, August W., Colby.. 122, 124
—donor 115
Lawrence, Ewing, Wichita.......... 367
Lawrence: Congregational church of 1857, described 431
—descriptive notes, 1854..... 41, 46, 52
——1855 .... 63, 64
—1854-1858, S. Y. Lum's letters from 40-67, 172- 196
—Emigrant Aid Co. sawmill, 1854, notes on 48
—hard times in, 1861.......... 326, 327
—Plymouth Congregational Church, first service, noted 39
——S. Y. Lum's reports (1854-58) on .... 40-67, 172-196 *passim*
—photographs of, given Historical Society 114
—"Pioneer Boarding House" of 1854, note on 42

30—961

466   GENERAL INDEX

Lawrence: public school history articles, noted 252, 253
—Quantrill raid 296
—recovery from Quantrill raid, note on 333
—Second Congregational church, note on 416
—Unitarian church, S. Y. Lum's comments on 1855-57... 61, 173, 180, 182
—Western Bakery daybook pages (1861) given Historical Society.... 109
Lawrence, sack of, 1856: S. Y. Lum's comment on 176
Lawrence citizens: petition to Hallett & Co., 1863, noted............... 7
Lawrence *Journal-World:* articles in, noted 253
Leach, Mrs. Richard W., Evanston, Ill.: donor 114
Lead mines in Kansas: Linn county's Jumbo mine (photographs) ..... *between* 400, 401
—maps and diagram of Linn co. area .... *facing* 400
—W. H. Schoewe's article on the early mines 391- 401
Lead ore: specimen (photograph) .... *facing* 401
Leahy, David D., Wichita: his story of Ware's "The Washerwoman's Song" 266
Lear, Gen. Ben 344
Learned, Edward: interest in U. P., E. D., noted 14, 15
Leavenworth: boom period, 1860's, noted 4
—churches, 1861, statistics of... 418, 419
—comment on, 1854 45
—1859-60 support for Smoky Hill route by 159, 162- 171
—general situation in, 1860, discussed 320
— —1862, discussed 324
—loss of U. P., E. D. line by, notes on 4, 5
—rebel newspaper, 1862, notes on 293, 294, 296
—religious needs, 1857, noted...... 184
—telegraph in, 1859 35
Leavenworth, Sisters of Charity of: history, noted 256
Leavenworth & Pike's Peak Express: comment on 372, 373
Leavenworth County Historical Society: officers, 1959-60, listed 452
Leavenworth *Daily Inquirer:* notes on 293, 294, 296
Leavenworth, Pawnee and Western Railroad Company: history...... 2, 3
                                                              8- 10
Lecompton: religious needs, 1857, noted 183, 186, 187
Lecompton constitution: M. W. Delahay quoted on defeat of 305
Lecompton constitution movement: C. W. Trow's thesis on, noted 108
Lee, Rt. Rev. Henry W., of Iowa 418
Lee, Col. Robert E. 284
Lees, Raymond, Wyandotte co. 128
LeMay, Maj. Gen. Curtis E. 156, 351
LeRoy: comment on, 1857 191
Leuenberger, Fritz, Jr., Topeka: donor, 109
Liberal: library history, noted 447
Liberal Army Air Field: history, 336- 339
Liberal League, Wichita 200, 204
Liggett, Rev. J. D., Leavenworth, 418, 419
—quoted 318, 320, 323, 324
                            327, 330, 331
Lillard, Thomas M., Topeka 104
                             119-122, 124
Lilleston, W. F., Wichita 123

Lincoln, Abraham: assassination noted 300
—at Philadelphia, Feb. 22, 1861, 283, 288
—his ties to M. W. Delahay discussed, 312
—Kansas "speeches" of 439- 443
—M. W. Delahay a friend and promoter of 301- 312
—photograph (clean-shaven, ca., 1859) .... *facing* 256
—speech, Feb. 22, 1861, quoted, 283, 284
—visit to Kansas, chronology of 285
— —notes on ...... *facing* 257 and 438
— —observance of centennial of 438
— —sponsored by Delahay 307, 308
— —tour of 1859 re-enacted, note on, 452
Lincoln College, Topeka 434
Lindner, Mrs. Claudine, Finney co. 255, 450
Lindquist, Emory Kempton, Wichita 122, 124
—"The Letters of the Rev. Samuel Young Lum, Pioneer Kansas Missionary, 1854-1858," edited by 39-67, 172- 190
—notes on 39n, 172n, 313n, 407n
—"Religion in Kansas During the Era of the Civil War," article by, 313- 333
                                        407- 437
Lindsborg: Holmberg-Johnson shop, article on, noted 446
Lindsborg *News-Record:* articles in, noted 445, 446
Lines, Charles B., Wabaunsee 427
Lingenfelser, Rev. Angelus, Atchison, 123
Linn county: first state militia regt. raised in 288
—history of lead mining in 391- 399
—Jumbo lead mine (photographs) ..... *between* 400, 401
—lead mine area maps, and diagram .... *facing* 400
—Mine creek settlers driven out, 1861, 291
Liquor problem: in Lawrence, 1855, notes on 65
Litchfield, Lewis L.: death, 1855, noted 56
Little Blue, battle of the, 1864: noted, 298
Locknane, David M., Nemaha co. .. 371
Locknane creek, Nemaha co. 371
Log Chain station: on Pony Express route 371
Long, Richard M., Wichita: president, Historical Society 120, 121, 123
Lorenson, Jacob, Saginaw, Mich.: suicide attempt, noted 30
Lose, Harry F., Topeka 123
Loucks, C. A., Kearny co. 127
Lough, Mrs. Jean C.: "Gateway to the Promised Land," article by 17- 31
—note on 17n
Loughmiller, Mrs. Laura, Topeka: donor 111, 113
Louis, Bertha, Thomas co. 451
Love, Leon: pseudonym of T. M. Nichol............... 260, 262, 263
Lovejoy, Rev. Charles H.: photograph .... *facing* 321
Lovejoy, Julia Louisa (Mrs. Chas. H.): comment on................... 424
—quoted 317, 325, 429, 436, 437
Lovewell, Mrs. P. A., Topeka: donor.. 113
Lucifer, the Light-Bearer, Chicago, Ill.: 1897-1907 file microfilmed........ 111
Lum, Caroline Keep (Mrs. S. Y.) 39, 63, 195
Lum, Rev. Samuel Young........ 418, 419
—and wife, to Kansas, 1854 ...... 39, 40
—biographical sketch 39, 40
—death of child of, 1855 .... 60, 63
—letters, 1854-1858 (edited by E. K. Lindquist) 39-67, 172- 196

General Index

Lum, Rev. Samuel Young,
  photograph .... *facing,* 321
  —quoted 313-315, 327, 328
Lungren, Maurice C.: thesis by, noted, 108
Lupfer, Nina, Hodgeman co.. 450
Luther, Rev. J. H. 411
Lykins, Rev. Johnston 411
Lynch, B. M.: slave owner 412
Lyon, Capt. Nathaniel: 1861 activities 289, 290
Lyon county: guerrilla raids in, 1862, noted 294
—O. W. Mosher's column on history of, noted 126
Lyon County Historical Society 126
—1959 meeting, notes on 255
Lyon creek community, Dickinson co.: article on, noted 446
Lyona, Dickinson co. 451
—Methodist church history, noted.... 446

M

McAfee, Rev. Josiah B.: slavery stand noted 414
McArthur, Mrs. Vernon E., Hutchinson, 123
—donor 113
McBee, John: and family, history of, noted 254
McBratney, Robert 185n
McCain, James A., Manhattan 123
McCall, Florence, Salina: donor 113
McCallum, Gen. Daniel Craig[?].... 14
McClintock, W. H.: injured in mine blast 396
McConnell, Thomas L., Fred, Jr., and Edwin M.: air base at Wichita named for 341
McConnell Air Force Base: history 339- 341
McCoy, Rev. Isaac 411
McDowell, George 12
McDowell, James H.: L. P. & W. president 3
McDowell, William C.: L. P. & W. president 8, 9
Mace, Col. Harold L.: at Coffeyville 335
McFarland, Helen M., Topeka 123
McGee, Peter, Delphos: biographical sketch, noted 366
McGill, Mrs. Charles, Paola: donor.. 114
McGinley, Joseph P. 130
McGrew, Mrs. William E., Kansas City, 123
McInerney, Dr. William, Abilene: donor 112
Macintosh, William, of California: killed by Indians, 1860 378
McKeen, R. A., Independence 334
McKeever, Dr. Duncan C., Houston, Tex.: donor 113, 114
McLeod, Charles, of California: killed, 1860 378
McNoughton, O., of California: killed by Indians, 1860 378
McPherson: first courthouse, articles on, noted 445, 446
McVicar, Rev. Peter 416
—"Band of Hope" organizer 323
—photograph .... *facing* 321
Madison, Mrs. Sarah E.: article by, noted 364
Mahoney, Elmo, Dorrance 114
Maier, Mrs. Minnie Mae, Leavenworth co. 452
Majors, Alexander: steamboat named for 6
Majors, Russell & Co.: Pony Express firm 381

Malin, James C., Lawrence 121, 123
—"Eugene Ware's Concern About a Woman, a Child, and God," article by 402- 406
—"Ironquill's 'The Washerwoman's Song,'" article by 257- 282
—notes on 257n, 402n
—"William Sutton White, Swedenborgian Publicist," article by (parts two and three) 68-103, 197- 228
Malone, James, Gem 123
Manhattan: in 1857, mentioned..... 188
Manhattan Town Association: records (1855-1877) microfilmed 110
Manlove, ——, Fort Scott: editor.... 265
Manshardt, Mrs. F. M., Topeka: donor 113
Maple Hill, Wabaunsee co.: articles on history of, noted 252
Mapleton: in 1857, mentioned 191
Maranville, Lea, Ness City..... 122, 124
Marble, G. W., Bourbon co. 368
Mariadahl, Pottawatomie co.: Lutheran church history, note on 252
Marion county: Ebenezer church history, noted 448
Marion *Record:* 1875-1900 file microfilmed 111
Marquart Music Co., Topeka: donor.. 113
Marshall, Brig. Gen. Francis C.: air base named for 342
—death, noted 342
Marshall, Francis J., Marysville..... 254
Marshall Air Force Base: history, 341- 345
Marshall county: Pleasant Ridge school, Dist. No. 59, history, noted....... 363
Martin, Donald F. (grandson of George W.) 122
Martin, John A.: provost marshal at Leavenworth 293
Martin, Col. Kenneth R.: in Kansas... 352
Marysville: in 1902-03, article on, noted 449
—mail service, 1860's, items on..... 362
—Pony Express station 371
— —photograph *frontispiece,* Winter issue.
Marysville *Advocate:* articles in, noted, 254
363, 449
Masons, A. F. & A.: Shawnee lodge history, noted 252
Masterson, Bat: article on, noted..... 445
Mather, William D.: thesis on Cheyennes by, noted 108
Matson, Simon E.: articles by, noted.. 126
Matthews, Cecil, Edwards co. 367
Matthews, John: rebel activities, noted, 290
Matthews, William: captain, 1864 ... 298
Maus, Pearl, Topeka: donor 111
Mayhew, Mrs. Patricia Solander, Wichita 123
Meade, Col. Donald E.: at Strother Field 355
Meade, E. R.: attorney for E. Learned, 14
Meade, Lakin, Topeka: donor 113
Means, Hugh, Lawrence 122, 124
Mechem, Kirke, Lindsborg.. 117, 121, 123
Medary, Samuel: governor...... 286, 287
Medbury, Col. ——: surveyor...... 3
Medford, David F.: and troops, captured, 1864 298
Medill, Mrs. Harold, Independence.... 128
Medler, M. A., Pittsburg 394
Meeker, Rev. Jotham 411
Meier, Adolphus, St. Louis, Mo.: merchant 11, 13
Mendez, Roy, Topeka: donor........ 113
Menninger, Mrs. Grace, Topeka 255
—donor 113

GENERAL INDEX

Menninger, Karl, Topeka............ 123
Mennonites: D. V. Wiebe's story of, noted.................. 453
—notes on settlements of............ 387
Mercer, Rev. L. P., Chicago........ 85
Meredith, Henry, of California: death, noted.................. 378
Merriam, D. F.................... 400
Messick, B. F., Topeka: donor..113, 114
Methodist Episcopal Church: devotion to Union cause noted........413, 414
—early days in Kansas, notes on..407- 411
—Kansas conference, 1856, notes on........................410, 435
——1865, note on................. 428
—split in the church, 1844, noted.... 407
Methodist Episcopal Church South: created, 1845.................. 407
—effect of Civil War on Kansas ministers of...................407- 409
—Kansas Mission Conference, 1856, notes on............407, 410, 437
——1861, note on................. 408
—return to Kansas 1866, noted..... 409
Meyer, Fred W., Jewell co......... 367
Meyer, Henry A., Evansville, Ind.: donor....................... 111
Meyers, Andy J.: story by, noted.... 364
Meyers, Maj. Gen. B. E............348n
Miami county: 1958 ownership map of, given Historical Society....... 115
Military events: and politics, 1859-1865, a chronology of........283- 300
Militia. See Kansas (state) Militia.
Miller, A. R., Ottawa co........... 452
—paper by, noted................. 366
Miller, Emy K.: thesis by, microfilmed..................... 108
Miller, Mrs. Esther Pennock, Topeka: donor....................... 113
Miller, Mr. and Mrs. Henry W., Delavan: donors.................. 113
Miller, Karl, Dodge City.......... 123
Miller, Rev. M. J., Leavenworth..430, 436
—quoted....................316, 329
Miller, Nyle H.: secretary, Historical Society...................117, 127
—talks by, noted.........127, 255, 367
Miller, Solomon: comment on E. F. Ware.....................278n, 279n
Mills, Robert, Baltimore, Md.: note on, 1
—quoted on need for overland railroad, 1
Mine Creek, battle of, 1864: notes on........................284, 299
Mining of metals: first in Kansas, noted....................... 391
Minneapolis: Negro families in, paper on, noted.................... 366
Missouri and Western Telegraph Company......................... 38
Missouri river: frozen over at Wyandotte for 93 days, 1872......... 444
—map, 1878-81, noted............. 115
Mitchell, Robert: a brigadier general......................... 293
Mitchell county: Indian raids, booklet by A. B. Houghton on, noted..... 256
Mohl, Evangeline Louise: book by, note on...................... 368
Moneka: notes on, 1857............ 190
Monkiewicz, Maj. Witold B.: in Kansas....................... 352
Montfort, Rev. F. P.: quoted, 1856...............315, 316, 328, 329
Montgomery, Marshal Sir Bernard L... 351
Montgomery, James................ 288
—attempt to rescue John Brown's men, noted....................... 296
—Civil War activities, noted....... 296
—head of Third Kansas regt........ 290

Montgomery, John D., Junction City....................116, 122, 124
Montgomery, Mary Liz, Junction City: column by, noted.............. 446
Montgomery, Maj. Gen. Richard: plaque honoring, note on......... 129
Montgomery, Maj. Gen. Richard M...................129, 130
—in Kansas, note on.............. 129
Montgomery county: name origin... 129
Moonlight, Thomas: Civil War soldier, 290
—defeated at battle of Little Blue... 298
Moore, Bessie, Auburn............. 127
Moore, Mrs. Myrtle, Harper co.: article by, noted.................. 254
Moore, Russell, Wichita........... 123
Moore family, Ellis co.: article on, noted....................... 126
Morgan, Dale L.: editor J. A. Pritchard diary, noted.................. 453
Morgan, Maj. Robert K.: note on..........................347n
Mormonism: W. S. White's comments on........................98- 101
Morris, Warren, Lyon co........... 255
Morse, Rev. Grosvenor C........... 332
—at Emporia, 1857...........192- 194
Mosher, Orville W., Emporia....... 255
—column by, noted............126, 364
Mosier, Mrs. Dwight, Cowley co.: article by, noted................. 448
Mosman, Lt. Col. O. J.: in Kansas, 352
Motz, Frank, Hays: death, noted.... 104
—note on....................104, 105
Motz, Mrs. Frank, Hays........... 114
Mound City: Ladies' Enterprise Association..................... 427
—United Brethren Church, note on... 427
Mowery, Mrs. J. E., Lane co....... 451
Mudge, Benjamin F., Manhattan...............391, 392, 395
Mueller, Harrie S., Wichita........ 123
Mullen, Maj. Peter V.: death, noted, 352
—in Kansas..................... 352
Mullendore, Carl, Howard: donor.... 113
Mullin, Alfred A., Kiowa co.: town founded by................... 448
Mullinville: historical articles on, noted....................... 448
Mullinville News: articles in, noted, 448
Murdock, Marshall M.: Burlingame paper founded by............... 449
—comment on.................... 90
Murphy, Franklin D., Lawrence.... 123
Murray, Audrey, Harper........... 368
Murray, Lenore, Harper........... 368
Murrow, Capt. James B., Jr.: in Kansas....................... 352
Myers, C. W., & Co., Topeka: ledgers (1903-08) given Historical Society, 109
Myers, Mrs. Lillian (McBee): article by, noted.................... 254

N

Naples (Ill.) Post................ 302
Napper, Mrs. Laura (Knight): article by, noted.................... 254
Native Sons and Daughters of Kansas: 1959 meeting, notes on......... 128
Natoma, Osborne co.: Presbyterian church history, noted........... 253
Natoma-Luray Independent: article in, noted....................... 253
Nebraska City, Neb.: telegraph line, 1860........................ 38
Neff, Morris N., Jr., Wichita....... 367
Negroes: refugees in Kansas, 1862, notes on...................415- 417
—state convention, 1864, noted..... 298
—to Cherokee strip, 1893, noted.... 24

GENERAL INDEX 469

Nellans, Mrs. Pearl, Portland, Ore.: donor 113
Nelson, Lt. Col. J. F.: at Pratt..... 346
Nelson, Maj. Victor E.: at Marshall Field.......................... 343
Nemaha Courier, Seneca: issues of 1863-65 given Historical Society... 114
Neosho City: mention of, 1857.... 191
Nevada Mining Company........... 396
New Church, Missouri-Kansas association of................... 84
New England Emigrant Aid Company: aid to religion in Kansas, noted 325, 326
New Santa Fe, Mo.: articles on, noted, 445
New York Emigration Company.. 45, 49
New York State Historical Society: donor 114
News-Chronicle, Scott City: articles in, noted................ 253, 448, 449
Newspapers, Kansas weekly: thesis on editorials in, noted............ 108
Newton: historic clock, article on, noted 449
Newtonia, Mo., battle of, 1864: noted, 299
Niccum, Norman, Tecumseh: donor.. 114
Nichol, Thomas M., Fort Scott: his poems discussed 260-264, 267
—notes on............ 261, 262, 267
—"The Washerwoman's Friend," poem by 260, 261
Nickell, Maj. Gen. Joe............. 116
Nicodemus, Graham co.: article on, noted 365
Ninth Kansas cavalry: organized.... 291
—notes on 293
Ninth Wisconsin regiment: at Fort Leavenworth 292
Norwegians in Kansas: noted....387- 390
Noyes, Rev. Daniel P., New York... 40
—S. Y. Lum's letter to, 1857....194, 195
Nute, Rev. Ephraim: to Lawrence, 1855........................... 61
—Unitarian efforts, noted........... 182
Nye, Agnes, Harper................ 368
Nyvall, Carl Johan: book by, note on, 452

O

Oberg, Maj. Alfred: at Fairfax Field.. 140
Obrecht, R. C., Shawnee co.......... 127
Occidental Telegraph Co.: incorporated, 1855..................... 33
O'Donnell, Brig. Gen. Emmett...... 156
Oesterreich, B. H., Woodbine....... 451
Offerle, Harry, Edwards co......... 367
Ogden: reference to, 1857.......... 188
Ohio City: note on, 1857.......... 190
O'Howell, Rev. D. C............... 408
Oklahoma. See Cherokee strip.
Oklahoma City Air Technical Service Command 148, 340
Olathe: Quantrill raid, 1862, noted.. 295
Olathe Naval Air Station...... 141, 352
O'Laughlin, "Uncle John," Nemaha co. 371
Old Abilene Town Company: note on 450
Old Fort Hays Historical Association, Inc.: pamphlet published by, noted, 452
Oldfield, Col. Charles B.: at Dodge City 137
O'Loughlin, Jennie Ross: articles by, noted 365
Olson, Col. Jergan B.: at Dodge City 147, 148
Omaha, Neb.: telegraph line in, 1860, 38
Omer, Maj. George, Jr., Fort Riley: donor 114
Once A Week, Lawrence: 1883 issue given Historical Society.......... 114

Orlando, Okla.: role in Cherokee strip opening, notes on........... 23, 28
Ormsby, Maj. — —: and men, ambushed 1860 .... 378, 379
Osage City *Free Press:* 1875-1916 file microfilmed 111
Osage County Chronicle, Burlingame.. 449
Osawatomie: in early 1855, comment on 56
Osborne, Mrs. Elizabeth, Newton, Mo.: burned, 1893 27
Osborne: views of (1890's), given Historical Society 114
Osborne County Farmer, Osborne: article in, noted 253
Osceola, Mo.: burned, 1861........ 291
Oskaloosa *Independent:* 1870-1900 file microfilmed 111
Oswego, Labette co.: First Baptist church history, noted........... 446
Oswego Democrat: article in, noted... 446
Ottawa county: views of, given Historical Society 114
Ottawa County Historical Society: donor 111
—1958 meeting, note on........... 127
—1959 meetings, notes on.. 366, 451, 452
Ottawa Herald: article in, noted.... 253
Ottawa University: chartered, 1860... 435
Ottumwa: Western Christian University at, 1863 436
Overland journey: of Mary Smith, to Colo. ter., 1866, noted........... 363
Overland Stage Company: mail service, 1860's, items on................ 362
Owen, Arthur K., Topeka....... 122, 124
Owen, Mrs. E. M., Lawrence.... 122, 124
Owen, Jennie Small, Topeka: donor.. 111
Owen, Lyle, Tulsa, Okla.: donor..... 111
Owens, Mrs. Claude, Finney co...... 255
Oxford, Johnson co.: articles on, noted, 445

P

Pacific railroad of Missouri.......... 2
Page, Euphemia, Topeka........... 127
Paige, — — (lecturer): at Wichita 198, 199
Paine, Rev. Rodney, Burlington: quoted 323, 422
Painter, Maj. Harold: at Herington 153- 155
"Palace, The": poem by E. F. Ware 279, 280
Palmer, George, Miltonvale......... 451
Palmer, Mrs. George, Miltonvale..... 255
Palmer, Dr. H. Preston, Scott co..... 368
Palmer, William J.: secretary-treasurer, U. P., E. D..................... 15
Pantle, Alberta: compiler "Recent Additions to the Library"......... 229
—librarian, Historical Society... 117- 250
Papinsville, Mo. 292
Paris, Linn co.: mention of, 1857.... 191
Parker, Rev. Roswell Davenport.... 193
.... 415, 416
—photograph .... *facing* 321
—quoted 326, 330-332, 432
Parker, Mrs. Thomas T., Phoenix, Ariz.: donor 109
Parrott, Marcus: delegate to congress 284, 288
—with Lincoln, 1859.............. 285
Parsons, Rev. J. U.: at Ogden....... 188
Patton, Gen. George S............. 344
Paulsen, Leo, Jamestown 255, 451
Payne, David L.: Oklahoma "boomer" 18
Payne, Mrs. L. F., Manhattan ...122, 124
Payne, Rev. Rodney: at Burlington.. 191

Peabody, Rev. Adams: at Wichita... 83
Peffley, D. P., Fort Scott: quoted on
 N. C. McFarland letter 275, 276
Pellegrino, John 393, 396
Pendleton, Capt. Robert P.: flights by,
 noted 140
People of Kansas: character of early
 settlers discussed............313- 322
Perkins, Col. Nicholas T.: at Coffey-
 ville 133, 134
Perrings, Mrs. Myra, Topeka: donor, 113
Perry, John D., St. Louis: banker, 8, 11
—president of U. P., E. D. ..8, 11- 15
Perry, Okla.: expected (1893) to be
 "the" Cherokee strip city 21
—note on creation of, 1893 28
Peterson, Mrs. E. G., Edwards co... 367
Pettit, John: chief justice, K. T..... 287
Phelps, A. O. (lecturer): at
 Wichita 201, 204
—S. W. White's comments on
 lectures of 201- 204
Phillips, William A.: Civil War
 colonel 297
Philosophers of Kansas: J. C. Malin's
 article (parts two and three) on
 W. S. White........68-103, 197- 228
Pickett, Mrs. A. G., Topeka: donor... 113
Pierce, Francis L.: article by, noted, 365
Pierce, Bishop George Foster, of
 Georgia 407, 437
Pike, Bill, Lane co. 451
Pike, Mrs. Cecil, Clark co. 366
Pike, Lt. Col. Glenn M.: at Great
 Bend 150
Pike's Peak gold rush: and the Smoky
 Hill route, 1859-1860, C. W. Gow-
 er's article on..............158- 171
Pine Bluff, Ark., battle of, 1863:
 noted 297
Pioneer life: 1854-1858, S. Y. Lum's
 letters 40-67 passim and 172-196 passim
Pittsburg Sun: article in, noted..... 447
Pitzer, Rev. A. W.: at Leavenworth, 321
Platte area: addition to Kansas pro-
 posed 287
Platte route to the gold mines....158, 163
—table of distances from Atchison,
 1859 ....facing 160
Pleasant Hill: 1855 plat of, given Historical Society 114
Pleasant Springs, Nemaha co.: Pony
 Express stop 371
Plows: T. M. Nichol's "Kansas Clip-
 per" inventions, note on 261
Plumb, Preston B.: Civil War
 activities 294
Politics: and military events, 1859-
 1865, a chronology of.......283- 300
—in territorial Kansas, M. W. Delahay's
 role 301- 312
Pomeroy, Samuel Clarke........62, 326
—aid to S. Y. Lum, noted........40, 41
—an Atchison promoter 185
—U. S. senator............288, 290, 311
Ponca Town Company 28
Pony Express: data on Kansas
 stations 370- 372
—Indian troubles 377- 380
—items from 1860 newspapers
 on 372- 385
—map of Kansas portion of
 route ....facing 369
—Marysville station (photograph)
 frontispiece, Winter issue.
—note on 286
—note on planned 1960 rerun of..... 369
—R. S. Bloss' book on, noted........ 453
—R. W. Settle's article on, noted.... 446
—Seneca station (photograph)
 frontispiece, Winter issue.

Pony Express: table of distances on
 Kansas route 370
—time table 375
Pony Express rider: reproduction of a
 painting ....facing 368
"Pony Express Rides Again"......369- 385
Poole, Elder ——: at Wichita...... 213
Porter, Mrs. George W., Topeka: estate
 of, donor 113
Porter, Thomas C.: and family, article
 on, noted 445
Post, Rev. J. C.: at Wichita........ 91n
Postal service: in the 1860's, items on, 362
Potosi, Linn co.: notes on.......... 392
—raided, 1861 292
Potosi Town Company: incorporation,
 noted 392
Pottawatomie Manual Labor School.. 411
Powell, Ernest W., Cloud co........ 451
Prairie City: "college" at, 1857...... 189
—note on, 1857 189
Pratt, Caleb, Douglas co............ 288
Pratt, Rev. John G................. 411
Pratt Army Air Field: history....345- 347
—mosaic map of.............facing 144
—photographs ....between 144, 145
 and facing 145
Presbyterian Church: slavery issue in
 Kansas, noted 412
—See, also, United Presbyterian Church
 of N. A.
Price raid, 1864: notes on......298, 299
Prichard, Mrs. J. R., Bourbon co..... 368
Pritchard, James A.: overland diary
 (1849) of, noted................ 453
Probasco, Burt, Pleasanton 394
Probasco, Mack, Pleasanton 393, 394
 397, 398
Probasco, Ted, Pleasanton.......... 394
Protestant Episcopal Church: 1859
 convention in Kansas, note on..... 435
—in Kansas territory, notes on....... 417
Provorse, Belle, Crawford co........ 451
Pugh, James K., Lane co.: and family,
 article on, noted 253

Q

Quantrill raid(s): in 1862, noted 293- 295
—in Johnson co.................293, 295
—on Baxter Springs................ 296
—on Lawrence, notes on........332, 333
Queendale, Wabaunsee co.......... 187
Quesada, Lt. Gen. Elwood R........ 351
Quindaro: Hallett's murderer a resident of 11
—notes on, 1857..........181, 184, 185
—telegraph office in, 1858.......... 35

R

Railroads: locomotive (Kansas Pacific)
 of 1860's (photograph)......facing iv
Rains, Gen. James S............... 290
Ralston, Mrs. Ralph, Augusta...... 127
Ramsay, Olivia T., Kearny co...... 366
Ramsey, Ray B., Topeka: donor..... 113
Randall, Wayne, Osage City........ 128
Rankin, Charles C., Lawrence...... 123
Raser, Margaret, Hodgeman co..... 450
Raupp, Mrs. Mabel Moore: article by,
 noted 126
Ray, Earl, Riley co................. 127
Raynesford, Howard C., Ellis... 123, 445
—cocompiler Nicodemus history.... 365
"Real, The": poem by E. F. Ware, 267, 268
Ream, Cora E., Kansas City, Mo.: es-
 tate of, donor.................... 113
Redpath, James: editor...........185n
Reed, Clyde M., Jr., Parsons........ 123

General Index 471

Reed, Lt. Col. Elliott H.: in Kansas.................................. 352
Reeder, Andrew H................. 302
Reid, Capt. Theodore C.: at Great Bend............................... 149
"Religion in Kansas During the Era of the Civil War," article by E. K. Lindquist..........313-333, 407- 437
Reno, Capt. J. L.: at Fort Leavenworth............................... 289
Republic county: 1888 blizzard, article on, noted....................... 364
Republican party: convention in Kansas, 1859, noted............... 284
——1860, noted.................... 286
—organized in Kansas, 1859........ 307
—state convention, 1862, noted..... 295
——1864, noted..............297, 298
Republican Union party: state convention, 1864, noted................ 298
Reser, Mrs. C. H., Hamilton....122, 124
—donor 113
Reveal, Clarence: donor........... 116
Rhoads, R. H.: KIDC employee.... 145
Rice, Rev. Cyrus R.: note on...... 408
Rice, Margaret Larzelere: article by, noted............................... 363
Rice County Historical Society: organization, note on................ 368
Rich, Lee: president Fort Riley Historical Society.................... 367
Richards, Charles R., Detroit, Mich.: donor 113
Richards, Walter M., Emporia....122, 124
Richardson, Elmo, Lawrence: donor.. 111
Richardson, Myrtle, Edwards co..... 367
Richardson, Ned, Topeka: donor.... 113
Richie, Helen: WASP, and flying record noted......................... 139
Richmond, Robert W.: state archivist, 117
Riegle, Wilford, Emporia...121, 122, 124
Riggs, Edward: killed in mine, 1916.. 396
Riley county: pioneer roads and trails map given Historical Society by... 115
Riley County Historical Society..... 114
—officers, 1959, listed.............. 127
Ripley, John, Topeka............. 255
—donor 113
—talk by, noted 121
Rising, N. H., Nemaha co.: note on.. 371
Ritchie, John: Civil War soldier.... 290
Robbins, Richard W., Pratt......122, 124
Roberts, Larry W., Wichita......... 367
Roberts, William Y................. 302
Robinson, Charles 302
—first state governor............... 288
—investigated, 1862 ....292, 294
—prisoner, 1856 ....177n, 303
—Unitarian church leader 325
Robinson, Rev. H. P.: at Grasshopper Falls 331
Robinson, John W.: impeached, 1862 ....292, 294
Robinson, Mrs. Sara T. D........177, 428
Robinson, W. Stitt, Lawrence....... 366
Robinson, Mrs. William I., Wichita... 367
Robley, T. F., Fort Scott........... 405
Rockwood, Col. R. C.: at Liberal.... 337
Rodkey, Clyde K., Manhattan....... 123
Roe, Dr. ——, Pittsburg........... 394
Rogers, Mrs. —— (evangelist): at Wichita, 1882 210
Rogler, Charles W., Chase co.: pioneer of 1859 446
Rogler, Henry, Chase co............ 446
Rogler, Wayne, Matfield Green...123, 446
Rogler family, Chase co.: article on, noted............................... 446
Rooks County Record, Stockton: article in, noted 254
Rooney, Capt. Laurence J.: in Kansas, 352

Root, Lt. Col. Charles B.: at Dodge City 137
Root, Mrs. Eliza Abbott: clothing of, given Historical Society........... 112
Root, George A.: article by, noted.... 369
Rosa, Joseph G., Ruislip, Middlesex, England: donor 111
Rosecrans, Gen. William S.......... 299
Rosecrans Field, St. Joseph, Mo...... 139
Rosenstock, Fred A.: publisher...... 453
Ross, Edmund G.................... 294
Ross, Steele & Company, Montreal, Canada 4, 9
Rossville: Mrs. L. Kassebaum's history of, noted 365
—newspaper history, noted......... 363
Rothrock, Elder ——: wounded, 1863 .... 333n
Rowley, Pat, Wichita.............. 367
Rozar, Lily B.: articles by, noted, 253, 447
Rupp, Mrs. Jane C., Lincolnville..122, 124
Ruppenthal, J. C., Russell........114, 123
Ruppenthal, Mrs. J. C., Russell: donor, 113
Russell, Green. *See* Russell, William Green.
Russell, Joe (grandson of Rev. Jerome C. Berryman)..................... 117
Russell, John W., Leavenworth...... 372
Russell, Robert (grandson of Rev. Jerome C. Berryman)............. 117
Russell, William Green: 1860 Smoky Hill expedition of............165- 167
Russell, William H., Leavenworth: note on 382
—Pony Express started by.......... 372
Russell county: historical data, noted.. 254
—photographs of, given Historical Society 114
Russell, Majors & Waddell: backers of telegraph line 33
Russell Daily News: article in, noted.. 364
Russell Record: articles in, noted.... 254
Russell State Bank: article on, noted.. 254
Russian-Germans in Kansas: note on.. 388
Rust, Mrs. Lucile, Manhattan....... 128
Ruttledge, Leslie: donor 116

S

St. Benedict's College, Atchison..... 114
St. Francis: S. E. Matson's articles on, noted............................. 126
St. Francis Herald: articles in, noted.. 126
St. John, John P.: at Wichita, 1880.. 93
St. Joseph, Mo.: gold rush travel from, noted...........................158, 167
—starting point of Pony Express..374, 375
—telegraph lines in, 1859........... 37
St. Paul Journal: article in, noted.... 447
Salina: centennial booklet, noted.... 108
—Fourth of July, 1860, noted...... 169
Salyer, Mrs. Paul, Clark co......... 366
Sanborn, Gen. John B.............. 299
Santa Fe trade: articles on, noted, 365, 445
Santa Fe trail: article on, noted..... 126
—Dodge City *Daily Globe* section on, noted 252
—route to the gold mines..158, 159, 163
Sargent, U. F., Fort Scott: editor, 262- 264
Savonburg, Allen co.: Evan. Mission Covenant church history, noted... 253
Scandinavians: colony in Cherokee strip planned by.................. 24
Scheald, Andrew, of California: killed, 1860................................ 378
Schenck, Leland, Topeka.......... 255
Schilling, Col. David C.: air base named for......................... 349
—biographical note.............. 349n
Schilling Air Force Base: history, 347- 349

472   GENERAL INDEX

Schmidt, Heinie, Dodge City: column by, noted 364
Schoen, Mrs. Harm: article by, noted, 363
Schoewe, Walter H. "The First Kansas Lead Mines," article by 391- 401
—note on 391n
Schofield, Gen. John M. 296
Schruben, Francis W.: thesis by, microfilmed 108
Schutte, August, Ellis co. 445
Schwegler, Mrs. R. A., Lawrence: donor 113
Schweitzer, Wilma: article by, noted.. 447
Science and technology: W. S. White's philosophy in regard to 214- 221
Scipio, Anderson co.: St. Boniface Catholic church history, noted..... 126
Scott, Angelo, Iola, 121, 122, 124, 368, 451
Scott, Harvey D., of Indiana........ 14
Scott, Gen. Winfield................ 287
Scott county: Battle Canyon site a county park 253
—1878 Indian battle, article on, noted, 253
—Mrs. E. W. Vaughn's history of pioneer days in, noted........... 448, 449
Scott County Historical Society..... 253
—1959 meeting, note on........... 368
Scudder, "Capt."——: agent for C. M. Stebbins 33
Sears Roebuck & Co., Topeka: donors, 113
Second Indian regiment: organized.. 294
Second Kansas battery: organized.... 295
Second Kansas regiment: notes on 289-293, 297, 331n
Sedalia, Mo.: railroad terminal, 1861, 2
Sedgwick, O. LeRoy, Rossville: editor, 363
Sellin, Elmer, Abilene 451
Seneca, Nemaha co.: marker for Pony Express, noted................... 371
—Pony Express station at.......... 371
——photograph *frontispiece*, Winter issue.
Senne, Rev. Martin: at Herington... 253
Settle, Raymond W.: Pony Express article by, noted................. 446
Seventeenth Kansas regiment: notes on 298
Seventh Kansas cavalry: notes on 291, 292, 294, 297
Seward, William H.: Kansas Republicans for, 1860.................. 309
Sewell, Esther, Thomas co........... 451
Shahan, Mrs. Paul, Marion.......... 114
Shannon, Wilson: territorial governor, 303
Shaw, Rev. James 319, 422, 430
Shaw, Joseph C., Topeka............ 123
Shawnee County Historical Society: 1958 meeting, note on........... 127
—1959 meeting, note on........... 255
Shawnee County Reporter, Rossville: articles in, noted 363, 365
Shawnee Methodist Mission: article on, noted 253
Shawnee Mission Indian Historical Society 117
Shawnee State Savings Bank: history, noted 252
Shelton, Rev. T. J.: at Wichita 91n
—note on 91n
Shemwell, Ocie: donor 116
Shepherd, Rev. Paul: in Kansas 1856-57 187
Sherman Air Force Base: history, 349- 352
Shoemaker, Robert M.: his company employed to build Kansas Pacific... 15
Showman, Austin: article by, noted.. 446
Shriver, Mrs. Esther, Augusta....... 127
Shupe, Roy, Clark co. 366
Siebenthal, C. E. 400

Silvestro, Clement M.: booklet by, noted 256
Simerwell, Rev. Robert 411
Simmons, Mrs. India Harris: articles by, noted 363, 364
Simons, Dolph, Lawrence 123
Simpson, Lt. Col. James H. 14
Sioux Indians: religious beliefs, noted, 98
Sisters of Charity of Leavenworth: history, noted 256
Sisters of St. Joseph: in Concordia, article on, noted 447
Sixteenth Kansas cavalry 299
Sixth Kansas cavalry: notes on...290, 293
Sixth Kansas infantry 298
Slagg, Mrs. C. M., Manhattan 123
Slavery issue: among Kansas church denominations discussed, 407-437 *passim*
Slavin, Maj. Gen. Nicolai V. 351
Slavs in Kansas: noted 387
Sloan, E. R., Topeka........ 120, 122, 124
Smelley, Col. James M.: at Coffeyville 134
Smelser, Mary M., Lawrence....122, 124
Smith, Hoke 23
Smith, Rev. J. N.: at Emporia, 1859, 448
Smith, John E., Seneca: hotelkeeper, 371
Smith, Mrs. Lena, Clark co. 366
Smith, Lena M., Princeton, Ind.: donor 114
Smith, Louis R., Shawnee co. 127
Smith, Mary, New York: donor..108, 114
Smith, Mary, Sheffield, Ohio: overland journey, 1866, noted 363
Smith, Mary Alice, Abilene: donor.. 113
Smith, Mary G., Kearny co. 366
Smith, Ollie, Caney: recollections, noted 449
Smith County Historical Society: 1959 meeting, note on 255
Smith County Pioneer, Smith Center, 114
Smoky Hill Air Force Base: history, 347- 350
—photographs .... *facing* 128 between 144, 145, *facing* 145, and *facing* 336.
Smoky Hill expedition: of Green Russell, 1860 .... 165- 167
—of H. T. Green, 1860 .... 169- 171
Smoky Hill route (1859-1860): and the Pike's Peak gold rush, C. W. Gower's article on........... 158- 181
—table of distances......... *facing* 161
Smoot, Russell & Company: backers of telegraph line 33
Snavely, Col. Eugene H.: at Marshall Field 343
Snell, Ernest, Thomas co.: article by, noted 446
Snider, Dale, Abilene............... 450
Snowden, Richard, of California: killed, 1860 378
Snyder, E. R.: article by, noted.... 365
Snyder, Mr. and Mrs. W. V., Berryton: donors 113
Snyder, Webb: and family, article on, noted 364, 365
Socolofsky, Homer, Manhattan....114, 127
—bibliography edited by, noted..... 108
Sohl, Stanley, Topeka: donor....... 113
—museum director, Historical Society 104, 117
Soley, ——: death, 1859, noted.... 162
Somers, John G., Newton........... 123
Sommers, Col. Charles: at Liberal... 338
Song: "John Brown's Body," note on.. 291
"Song, The": poem by E. F. Ware 270, 271
Sorenson, Lt. Col. Blair M.: in Kansas, 350

General Index 473

Souders, Floyd, Cheney.........114, 128
Southern Baptist Convention......... 411
Southern Baptist Convention, Board of
 Domestic Missions of the......... 412
Southern Baptists: in Kansas, notes on, 411
Southern Kansan, Lawrence: 1886
 issue given Historical Society...... 114
Southwest Daily Times, The, Liberal:
 articles in, noted.............126, 447
Sparks, Rev. R. H.: at Wichita..... 91n
Spear, W. S., of California: killed,
 1860 378
Speer, Mr. and Mrs. Albert, Topeka:
 donors 113
Spencer, Herbert: his philosophical
 ideas, and works discussed......81- 83
Spencer, Rev. Joab: 1860 troubles of,
 noted 407, 408
Spillman, C. H., St. Joseph, Mo.: telegraph office of, noted............ 37
Splitlog, Matthias (Wyandotte Indian), 5
Stanley, Rev. E. J.: quoted......... 409
Stanley, Mrs. William E., Wichita:
 donor 111, 113
Stapf, Charles, Abilene............ 450
Starr gang. See Dalton-Starr gang.
Stateler, Rev. L. B................. 409
Stead, Lt. Col. Charles B.: at
 Herington 155
Steamboat(s): Alexander Majors.... 6
—Emilie 7
—New Sam Gaty, rebel flag on,
 lowered 288
Stebbins, Charles M.: account of his
 telegraph line 32- 38
Stephens, Jack, Clark co........... 366
Stewart, Capt. ——: in California,
 1860 379
Stewart, Donald, Independence 123
Stewart, Mrs. James G., Topeka..122, 124
Stewart, John E.: Civil War soldier... 290
Stewart, Col. Ralph B., Leavenworth.. 452
Stile, Doyle, Caldwell.............. 127
Still, Rev. Abraham 409
Stilwell, Gen. Joseph W............ 344
Stockton, E. A.: injured in mine blast, 396
Stone, Arthur, Finney co...........255
Stone, Clifford W., Butler co........ 128
Stone, Rev. Hiram..............321, 417
Stone, James C., Leavenworth: U. P.,
 E. D. stock sold by............8, 11
Storrs, Rev. Sylvester D.: at Quindaro....................193, 329
Straley, Mrs. Fred, Topeka: donor.. 113
Stratton, Mrs. Clif, Topeka: donor... 108
Stringfellow, Dr. John H........... 185
Strother, Capt. Donald R.: air field
 named for 353
—biographical note................353n
Strother Army Air Field: history 353- 356
Stuart, Lt. J. E. B.: Junction City
 church efforts, noted............. 447
Stuart, Kent D.: articles by
 noted 367, 447
Sturgis, Maj. Samuel D.: activities,
 1861, noted 289- 291
Stutzman, Mrs. Claude R., Kansas City, 128
Sully, Capt. Alfred: 1861 activities,
 noted 289
Sunder, John E.: note on.......... 32n
—"Telegraph Beginnings in Kansas,"
 article by.....................32- 38
Swallow, G. C............395, 397, 398
Swan, Capt. Wilson B. in Kansas.. 352
Swanson, Ernest F., Cloud co.....255, 451
Swanzey, Mrs. E. E., Abilene: donor, 111
Swedenborg, Emanuel: biographical
 sketch 68, 69
Swedenborg Foundation: gift to Wichita Library Assn., noted......... 84

Swedenborg theology: summary of, 69- 81
Swedes in Kansas: C. J. Nyvall's book,
 note on 452
—notes on...............387, 388, 390
Sweet, Annie B., Topeka........... 127
—donor 113
Syracuse, Doniphan co.: Pony Express
 station 370, 371

T

Tabor, Milton, Topeka.............. 127
Talcott, Orlando: murderer of Samuel
 Hallett.........................10, 11
Tall tales: article on, noted......... 363
Tate, Lenora B., Kearny co......... 366
Tatum, M. L., Edwards co.......... 367
Taylor, Harold O., Crawford co..... 451
Taylor, James E., Sharon
 Springs 120, 122, 124
Tecumseh: comment on, 1854...... 49
——1857 187
"Telegraph Beginnings in Kansas": article by John E. Sunder......32- 38
Telegraph in Kansas: history (J. E.
 Sunder's article).............32- 38
Telegraph office: at Wyandotte, 1863, 6
Temperance: early steps in Kansas, 322, 323
—Methodist action in early Kansas, 322, 323
Templar, George, Arkansas City..... 123
Templeton, Etta, Topeka: donor.... 114
Tenth Kansas infantry: note on..... 290
"Text, The": poem by E. F. Ware, 272, 273
Thayer News: article in, noted..... 447
Third Indian regiment: organized... 295
Third Kansas battery: notes on..291, 293
Third Kansas regiment...........290, 292
Thirteenth Kansas regiment........ 295
Thirteenth Wisconsin regiment...292, 294
Thomas, Ailine, Merriam: donor... 111
Thomas, E. A., Topeka..........120, 123
Thomas, Vivian P., Kearny co...... 366
Thomas, Rev. W., Delaware City..411, 420
Thomas county: historical article,
 noted 446
Thomas County Historical Society:
 organization, note on............. 451
Thompson, Frederick, Jr., Caldwell.... 127
Thompson, Col. R. L., Allen co...... 143
Thomson, Capt. Dorr, Hutchinson:
 donor 113
Thorpe, Edgar R.: article by, noted.. 364
Throckmorton, Mrs. J. R., Hays:
 donor 111
Tibbets, Col. Paul W., Jr........... 142
Tiller and Toiler, Larned: article in,
 noted 449
Tillotson, Mrs. J. C., Norton........ 128
Tindell, Mrs. Elsa M., Burlingame:
 donor 113
Tinker, Maj. Clarence L.: at Fort
 Riley, 1920's 341
—note on.....................341, 342
Tinkham, C. C., Topeka............ 114
Titus, Henry T.: S. Y. Lum's comment
 on 178
Todd, Mrs. H. W., Independence:
 biographical sketch, noted........ 447
Tomlinson, William P.: at Lawrence,
 1858 321
Topeka: comment on, 1857......... 187
—Constitution Hall described...430, 431
—Free Congregational Church, 1856,
 noted 39, 61n
—photographs, given Historical Society, 114
—S. Y. Lum's notes on, 1854....44, 48
 53, 54
—Sabbath school celebration, 1862,
 note on 416
—state capital located at, 1861...... 291
—theater programs, gift of, noted.... 108

31—961

General Index

Topeka *Capital-Journal:* article in, noted 448
Topeka *Commonwealth:* 1869-1888 file microfilmed 111
Topeka constitution: elected officials, noted 302
Topeka *State Journal:* 1943-1946 and 1949-1957 files microfilmed 111
Topeka Town Association 110
Torkelson, Dr. D. E., Bourbon co..... 368
Townsley, Will, Great Bend......... 123
Trace, Mrs. Carl F., Topeka: donor 110, 114
Tracy, John F., Atchison: telegraph office of, noted.................. 36
Trading Post, Linn co.: Price's army at, 1864 299
Trail Guide, The, Independence, Mo.: article in, noted................. 445
Train robberies: E. B. Block's book on, noted 453
Trans-World Airlines: Kansas City shops, noted 141
Trautwine, John Hannibal: diary (1873) given Historical Society.... 109
Trembley, Mrs. Wilfred, Cloud co..... 451
Trow, Clifford Wayne: thesis by, noted 108
Trowbridge, Harry M., Wyandotte co... 128
Trowbridge, Mrs. Harry M., Wyandotte co. 123, 128
Trower, Mr. and Mrs. Chester, Topeka: donor 113
Troy: Pony Express station at....... 370
Trueblood, Alva Curtis: letters, and diary (1860's) microfilmed 110
Truman, Harry S.: flight to Washington, Nov., 1944, noted.......... 140
Trumbull, Lyman 306, 309
Turner, J. D., Independence......... 334
Turner, Dr. J. E. Caldwell......127, 367
Turner, Mrs. W. V., and sons, Las Vegas, Nev.: donors.............. 111
Tweedman, Neil L.: donor........... 116
Twelfth Kansas regiment: notes on... 295
Twelfth Wisconsin regiment......... 294
Twentieth Kansas regiment: pictures of, given Historical Society........... 114

U

Ulrich, Jacob, Douglas co.: house burned, 1863 ....333n
Ulsh, Henry, Doniphan co. 361
Underhill, Col. Edward H.: at Liberal, 338
Union Pacific railroad: created 2
Union Pacific Railway Co., Eastern Division. See Kansas Pacific railroad.
Unitarian Church: reference to 192
United Domestic Missionary Society of New York: note on 40n
United Presbyterian Church of N. A.: Synod of the Plains history (by Dr. B. M. Dobbin), noted 256
United States: Air Force, Kansas air fields and bases, article on 129- 157
and 334-360 *passim*
— — —Fairfax (Kansas City) history. 138- 141
— — —Forbes (Topeka) history, 142- 145
— — —McConnell (Wichita) history.................339- 341
— — —Marshall (Fort Riley) history.................341- 345
— — —Schilling (Salina) history.................347- 349
— — —Sherman (Fort Leavenworth) history.................349- 352

United States: Army Air Forces, Kansas air fields, article on...129- 157
article on 129- 157
and 334-360 *passim*
— — —Coffeyville, history......130- 134
— — —Dodge City, history 135- 138
— — —photograph of Free French fliers at............*facing* 336
— — —Garden City, history....145- 149
— — —Great Bend, history....149- 153
— — —photographs, *between* 144, 145
— — —Herington, history.......153- 157
— — —Independence, history....334- 336
— — —Liberal, history..........336- 339
— — —Pratt, history 345- 347
— — —mosaic map of ....*facing* 144
— — —photographs *between* 144, 145 and *facing* 145
— — —Smoky Hill (Salina), history............150, 347- 349
— — —photographs .....*facing* 128 *between* 144, 145, *facing* 145, and *facing* 336.
— — —Strother (Cowley co.), history.....................353- 356
— — —Walker (Ellis co.), history 356- 360
—District Court for Kansas: M. W. Delahay appointed judge, 1863 ... 311
—Surveyor General for Kansas: M. W. Delahay appointed as, 1861 311
"U. S. Army and Air Force Wings Over Kansas": article on......129- 157
334- 360
Unruh, Mrs. R. T., Kinsley 128
Usher, John P.: his Union Pacific interests, noted 13, 14
—secretary of the interior..4, 8, 13, 411
Utah Historical Quarterly, Salt Lake City: article in, noted 446

V

Vail, Rev. A. L.: at Wichita, 91n, 93, 199
Vail, Bishop Thomas Hubbard 206, 207, 418
Valentine, L. F., Clay Center: article by, noted.................... 254
Valley Falls: Rev. O. L. Woodford at, 1857......................... 183n
Van De Mark, Martin V. B., Concordia 122, 124, 255, 451
Vang, Mrs. Mary Cole, Edwards co... 367
Van Vleit, — —: Pony Express messenger 374
Vaughn, Mrs. E. W., Scott co.: articles by, noted..............448, 449
Veitch, Isaac M.: telegraph interest, noted 33
Vinson, Mrs. Ida, Chase co.......... 450
Vin Zant, Mrs. Larry E., Wichita.... 128
Virginia (Ill.) *Observer*........301, 302
Voigts, Herman J., Mission: reminiscences, noted..................... 252
von der Heiden, Mrs. W. H., Newton 123
Vore, Earl, Bourbon co.............. 368
Wabaunsee: First Church of Christ (Congregational), notes on.....39, 187

W

WAC's: at Herington............... 155
Wade, Sen. Edward................. 286
Wagner, W. H.: travel notes of 1859, microfilmed 110
Wahwasseck, Jim, Topeka: donor... 113
Wakarusa War (1855): S. Y. Lum's account 66, 67

GENERAL INDEX 475

Walbourn, Edwin J., El Dorado..... 366
Walddy, Louis, Americus: donor.... 113
Waldstein, Julius, Leavenworth co.... 452
Walker, Mrs. Florence, Clark co..... 366
Walker, Mrs. Ida M., Norton....... 123
Walker, Samuel, Lawrence.......... 288
—major, Fifth Kansas regt.......... 298
Walker, Vivian, Crawford co........ 451
Walker Army Air Field (Ellis co.):
 history......................356- 360
Wallace, James W., Scott co........ 368
Wallbridge, Caroline K., Topeka:
 donor............................ 110
Walls, Mrs. Charles, Bigelow: article
 by, noted....................... 449
Walters, R. F..................... 400
Ward, Mrs. Duane McQueen, Peabody:
 donor............................ 112
Ward, Rev. William H.: at Oskaloosa
 ....425, 426
Ware, Abigail (dau. of E. F.)....... 405
Ware, Amelia (dau. of E. F.)......405n
Ware, Eugene Fitch: comment on,
 1867............................. 402
—his comments on women...... 402, 403
—his concern about a woman, a child
 and God (J. C. Malin's article
 on)........................402- 406
—his philosophy discussed..... 269- 282
—"Kriterion," poem by.........277, 278
——notes on............. 274, 277- 282
—marriage, noted................. 404
—"The Palace," poem by......279, 280
—photograph ....facing 272
—"The Real," poem by........267, 268
—discussed................... 268- 270
—reply to N. C. McFarland's
 letter......................277, 278
—"The Song," poem by........270, 271
—"The Text," poem by........272, 273
—"The Washerwoman's Song," poem
 by..........................257, 258
——J. C. Malin's article on.... 257- 282
——J. C. Malin's conclusions on, 405, 406
Ware, Jeanette P. (Mrs. E. F.): marriage, noted..................... 404
Wark, George H., Caney........122, 124
Wark, Rev. Homer: diaries, given Historical Society.................. 109
Wark, Mrs. Homer, Topeka: donor.. 109
Warneke, John Adam and Barbara: article on descendants of, noted...... 126
Washabaugh, Mrs. Lillie, Natoma.... 128
Washburn University, Topeka: donor, 113
"Washerwoman's Friend, The": poem
 by T. M. Nichol.............260, 361
"Washerwoman's Song, The": poem by
 E. F. Ware..................257, 258
WASP's: at Dodge City........137, 148
—at Fairfax Field................ 139
Waters, R. H., Bourbon co.......... 368
Watie, Stand: force of, defeated, 1863, 296
Watson, Mrs. Charles H., Evanston,
 Ill.: donor...................... 111
Watson, Maj. Harry E.: at Fairfax
 Field............................ 139
Wayne, A. R.: pioneer of 1855...... 392
Webb, Thomas H.: quoted, 1854.... 433
"Webb Scrapbooks": remounting,
 noted............................ 107
Weekly Star Farmer, Kansas City, Mo.:
 article in, noted................. 446
Weer, Col. William................ 294
Weidman, Mr. and Mrs. J. D., Topeka:
 donors........................... 113
Wells, William, of Brown and Graham
 cos.............................. 251
Wellsville Globe: article in, noted... 365
Welsh in Kansas: notes on..... 387, 390
Wendell, Walter W., Topeka: donor.. 113

Wendling, George E.: at Wichita, 198, 199
Werner, Morris, Manhattan: donor.... 115
Wessells, Maj. Henry W.: Fort Larned
 founder.......................... 449
Western Christian University, Ottumwa, 436
Western Union: C. M. Stebbins' telegraph lines controlled by....32, 37, 38
Westerners, Kansas City Posse of the.. 123
Westerners Brand Book, The, New
 York............................ 363
Westport, Mo., battle of, 1864: noted, 299
Wheeler, 2d Lt. Glenn M.: at Walker
 Field............................ 357
Whig party 302
Whisky Point, Geary co............ 291
White, Mr. and Mrs. Ben E., Bonner
 Springs: donor.................. 113
White, Mary Francis: article by, noted, 363
White, William Allen: and Dan Casement on govt. regulation, article on,
 noted............................ 363
White, William Sutton: comment on.. 90
—J. C. Malin's article on (parts two
 and three)..........68-103, 197- 228
White Cloud: reference to, 1857.... 186
Whitfield, John W.: delegate to congress............................. 50
Whitney, Rev. E. W.: in Doniphan
 co.........................418, 426
Whittemore, Mrs. L. D., Topeka: article on, noted................... 448
Whittle, Rev. Francis M., Louisville,
 Ky.............................. 417
Wichita: Historical Wichita board,
 note on.......................... 367
—impact of agricultural developments
 on banking in, article on, noted.... 363
—Methodist church, lecture series,
 1879-81, notes on............198, 199
——revival, 1877, noted.......... 207
—"New Church" history (in J. C.
 Malin's article on W. S. White).... 83
                                    84, 89
—W. S. White's criticisms of ministers,
 1870's-1880's, notes on 89- 97
Wichita Air Force Base: renamed McConnell Air Force Base.......... 341
Wichita Beacon: articles in,
 noted.......................252, 449
—Wm. S. White's editorship of,
 notes on .... 84, 89-103 passim
Wichita Eagle: 1953-1957 file microfilmed............................ 111
Wichita Library Association: note on.. 227
Wichita Municipal Airport: Air Force
 connection, notes on..........339- 341
Wichita Secular Union 200
Widder, Mrs. George, Kansas City.... 128
Wiebe, David V.: Mennonite history
 by, noted........................ 453
Wigginton, Joy, Butler co.......... 128
Wilder, Daniel W.................. 293
—quoted on N. C. McFarland letter.. 275
Wiley, R. D., Melvern: donor...... 113
Wilhelm, F. B., Independence: mayor, 334
Wilkins, Paul, Ottawa co.......... 452
Will Rogers Army Air Field, Oklahoma
 City, Okla....................... 134
Willbrandt, Mary, Washington: donor, 113
Willes, S. L., Lawrence.......... 171n
William Allen White Foundation..... 255
Williams, Charles A., Bentley...122, 124
Williams, Edna: relative of Charles
 Bluejacket....................... 117
Williams, Frances R.: article by, noted, 254
Williams, Maj. H. H.: head Third
 Kansas regt..................... 292
Williams, James M.: Civil War
 colonel.....................290, 296
Williamson, Hugh Pritchard 453

476   General Index

Wilmeth, Roscoe: archaeological survey, 1958, noted 112
Wilson, Mrs. Albert, Edwards co...... 365
Wilson, Mrs. Alice Gordon, Topeka: donor 108, 111, 113, 114
Wilson, Bruce, Riley co............ 127
Wilson, Capt. Glen C.: at Liberal..... 337
Wilson, Brig. Gen. James C.: at Schilling Air Force Base.......... 349
Wilson, Capt. R. S.: at Marshall Field, 343
Wilson, Robert B., Concordia....255, 451
Wilson county: courthouse article, noted 447
Wilson's creek, battle of, 1861: noted, 290
Winburn, Lt. Col. Temple F.: at Independence 335
Winchester, Mrs. Jessie, Edwards co., 367
Wind: and the "short grass voice".... 251
"Wings Over Kansas, U. S. Army and Air Force": article on, 129-157, 334- 360
Wise, Louis A., Lawrence........... 109
Wogan, Hilton, Bourbon co.......... 368
Woman's Kansas Day Club: 1959 meeting, notes on 128
Women: Annette Daisy's "colony," 1893, noted 24
Women's Air Force Service Pilots. See WASP's.
Womer, Parley Paul: ms. of, given Historical Society 110
Womer, Mrs. Parley Paul: donor..... 110
Wood, Paul B., Chase co............ 450
Wood, Samuel Newitt: a Branson rescuer, noted 66n
Woodford, Rev. O. L.: to Kansas, 1857 .... 183, 185, 189
Woodring, Harry H., Topeka........ 123
Woodson county: map, ca. 1910, given Historical Society 115
Woodward, Mrs. Louise S., Eskridge: donor 112
Wristen, Mrs. Cecil, Finney co....... 450

Wyandotte: comment on, 1857...... 185
—1869 lithograph copy, given Historical Society 115
—Garno House 10
—McAlpin's Hall 7, 8
—telegraph office, 1858 35
— —1863, noted 6
—Union Pacific, E. D., construction, 1863, notes on................. 6
— —offices moved to 5
— —photographs (by Gardner, 1867) *facing* iv, and *frontispiece*.
Wyandotte, The (locomotive): note on 6, 7
Wyandotte constitution: notes on, 284, 286
Wyandotte County Historical Society: 1959 meeting, note on........... 128
Wyatt, P. J.: Kansas folklore thesis by, noted 108

Y

Yingling, Dean, Topeka 128
Yoakum, Helen, Leavenworth co..... 452
Yocemento, Ellis co.: article on, noted, 445
Yok, Elder William S., of South Carolina 412
Young, Walker, Caldwell 127

Z

Zartman, Lt. Col. Paul A.: at Coffeyville 134
Zeidler, Mr. and Mrs. William J., Topeka: donors 113
Zeitler, Mr. and Mrs. Blodwen Williams, Ft. Madison, Iowa: donors 111, 114
Zeller, Hazel, Wyandotte co......... 128
Ziebolz, Mr. and Mrs. J. I., Ness City.. 114
Zimmerman, Mrs. J. F., Valley Falls: donor 113

PRINTED IN
THE STATE PRINTING PLANT
TOPEKA, KANSAS
1960

28-961

OLATHE PUBLIC LIBRARY
OLATHE, KANSAS 66061